Principles and Practice of
AMERICAN
POLITICS

Principles and Practice of
AMERICAN POLITICS
CLASSIC AND CONTEMPORARY READINGS

Second Edition

edited by

Samuel Kernell
University of California, San Diego

Steven S. Smith
Washington University, St. Louis

CQ PRESS

A Division of Congressional Quarterly Inc.
Washington, D.C.

CQ Press
1255 22nd Street, N.W., Suite 400
Washington, D.C. 20037

Phone, 202-729-1900
Toll-free, 1-866-4CQ-PRESS (1-866-427-7737)

www.cqpress.com

Cover design: Michael Pottman

Cover: Photo of George W. Bush (top left) by Reuters. Photo of town meeting (lower center) by Associated Press.

Printed and bound in the United States of America

07   06   05   04   03   5   4   3   2   1

LIBRARY OF CONGRESS CATALOGING-IN-PUBLICATION DATA

Principles and practice of American politics : classic and contemporary readings / edited by Samuel Kernell, Steven S. Smith.—2nd ed.
        p. cm.
Includes bibliographical references and index.
    ISBN 1-56802-793-1 (alk. paper)
    1. United States—Politics and government. 2. Political culture—United States. I. Kernell, Samuel, 1945–   II. Smith, Steven S., 1953–   III. Title.
    JK21.P76 2004
    320.973—dc21

                                          2003013996

CONTENTS

Federal appeals court judge Martha Craig Daughtrey reviews the history of the Equal Rights Amendment and recent advances in women's rights and considers whether the ERA is still needed.

Chapter 5. Civil Liberties   168

Gerald Rosenberg examines the political and legal environment surrounding abortion policy, still a source of conflict thirty years after *Roe v. Wade.*

Michael Scardaville and Robert Levy discuss the trade-off between civil liberties and national security measures taken in the wake of 9/11 and come to opposite conclusions about the long-term effects.

In this landmark case on the protection of Fifth Amendment rights, the Supreme Court outlines procedures to be followed by police officers and prosecutors.

In this controversial decision, the Supreme Court considers whether the Constitution protects a woman's right to terminate her pregnancy against the objections of the state.

Chapter 6. Congress   222

Richard Fenno introduces the differences between the House and the Senate that originate in the Constitution and explores the implications of these differences for governing and campaigning.

In an excerpt from his classic work, David Mayhew argues that legislators' efforts to gain reelection produce predictable behavior while in office.

Steven Smith describes the major changes in congressional politics in recent decades.

Scott Althaus examines the levels of news consumption in post–9/11 America and notes that television, rather than newspapers, has become the primary source for news.

PREFACE

ASSEMBLING THIS SET of readings for students of American politics has been a pleasure and a challenge. The pleasure has come in discovering so many articles that illuminate American politics. The challenge has come in finding far more than can be contained in a single volume. Consequently, despite its heft, *Principles and Practice* represents a small sampling of the literature.

The selection of articles has been guided by our shared perspective on politics. Political actors pursue goals informed by self-interest. This perspective does not require one to abandon all hope that politics can result in public policy that serves the common interests of the public today and for future generations. It says simply that to understand politics we need to understand what the different political actors want and how this leads them to engage in various strategies to achieve their goals. For government actors these goals will largely reflect the offices they serve in, the constituents they represent, and their constitutional and other legal obligations and opportunities. Other major actors—the public, the news media, and activists in political parties and interest groups—are similarly motivated by self-interest. They do not occupy offices of government, and so their behavior is regulated by a different constellation of opportunities and limitations. Each chapter's readings introduce the interests, rules, and strategic contexts of political action in a major forum of national politics.

Since 9/11 America has been at war. War changes the strategic environment of American politics. It recasts the public agenda, raising the salience of some issues while putting others on the back burner. It changes the way ordinary citizens think about leaders and policies and, therefore, affects the preferences people express in public opinion polls and in the voting booth. And, as a consequence, it gives some actors—most notably, the president—greater opportunity to shape public policy than it does others. Given the extraordinary events since 9/11, we have in this second edition included selections that assess the impact of war on the business of politics and governance.

We have chosen the readings to serve two audiences. Many instructors will employ *Principles and Practice* as a supplement to an introductory American politics textbook. For others, this book may constitute the core reading material for the course. For the former, we looked to readings that will animate the institutional processes described in the text. For the latter, we have sought readings that do not assume more than an elementary knowledge of America's government and politics.

Some of the selections are classics that all instructors will recognize; others address contemporary political developments or proposals for reform and may be unfamiliar. Each article adds emphasis and depth to textbook coverage and illustrates an important theme; most introduce an important writer on American politics. We hope students' understanding of American politics is enriched by them all.

We have taken care to include as much of each original source as possible. In the interest of making them appropriate for use in the classroom, we have edited some of the pieces. Ellipses indicate where material has been excised, and brackets enclose editorial interpolations. Other changes are explained in the source note for the reading.

We wish to thank the editorial staff of CQ Press for its expertise, energy, and patience in helping us bring this project to completion. Brenda Carter, James Headley, and Charisse Kiino provided essential encouragement and guidance throughout the effort. Jarelle Stein and Joan Gossett provided superb editorial assistance, and Niall O'Donnell demonstrated persistence in gaining permission to reprint the selections. Several anonymous reviewers and the following political scientists provided very helpful comments on our first edition and plans for this edition: Holly Brasher, Duke University; Andrea Campbell, University of Illinois, Urbana-Champaign; Jack Citrin, University of California, Berkeley; Gerald Gamm, University of Rochester; Eric Lawrence, George Washington University; Myron Levine, Albion College; Brad Lockerbie, University of Georgia; Forrest Maltzman, George Washington University; Kimberly Maslin-Wicks, Hendrix College; Steven Pfeffer, University of California, Santa Barbara; Donald Raber, Furman University; and Paige Schneider, University of the South.

Samuel Kernell
Steven S. Smith

Chapter 1

Designing Institutions

1-1

from *The Logic of Collective Action*

Mancur Olson Jr.

With the publication of The Logic of Collective Action *in 1965, Mancur Olson introduced the fundamental dilemma of collective action to all who study politics. When members of a group agree to work together to achieve a collective goal, each member as an individual faces powerful disincentives, Olson showed, that can frustrate the efforts of the group as a whole. For example, when each can foresee that his or her relatively small contribution to a collective enterprise will not affect its overall success, many will fail to contribute—a phenomenon known as free riding—and leave to everyone else the burden of supplying the collective good. As a consequence, collective enterprises based on cooperation, and supported by the entire collectivity, nevertheless often fail.*

IT IS OFTEN taken for granted, at least where economic objectives are involved, that groups of individuals with common interests usually attempt to further those common interests. Groups of individuals with common interests are expected to act on behalf of their common interests much as single individuals are often expected to act on behalf of their personal interests. This opinion about

Source: Mancur Olson Jr., *The Logic of Collective Action: Public Goods and the Theory of Groups* (Cambridge: Harvard University Press, 1971), 1–19.

group behavior is frequently found not only in popular discussions but also in scholarly writings. Many economists of diverse methodological and ideological traditions have implicitly or explicitly accepted it. This view has, for example, been important in many theories of labor unions, in Marxian theories of class action, in concepts of "countervailing power," and in various discussions of economic institutions. It has, in addition, occupied a prominent place in political science, at least in the United States, where the study of pressure groups has been dominated by a celebrated "group theory" based on the idea that groups will act when necessary to further their common or group goals. Finally, it has played a significant role in many well-known sociological studies.

The view that groups act to serve their interests presumably is based upon the assumption that the individuals in groups act out of self-interest. If the individuals in a group altruistically disregarded their personal welfare, it would not be very likely that collectively they would seek some selfish common or group objective. Such altruism is, however, considered exceptional, and self-interested behavior is usually thought to be the rule, at least when economic issues are at stake; no one is surprised when individual businessmen seek higher profits, when individual workers seek higher wages, or when individual consumers seek lower prices. The idea that groups tend to act in support of their group interests is supposed to follow logically from this widely accepted premise of rational, self-interested behavior. In other words, if the members of some group have a common interest or objective, and if they would all be better off if that objective were achieved, it has been thought to follow logically that the individuals in that group would, if they were rational and self-interested, act to achieve that objective.

But it is *not* in fact true that the idea that groups will act in their self-interest follows logically from the premise of rational and self-interested behavior. It does *not* follow, because all of the individuals in a group would gain if they achieved their group objective, that they would act to achieve that objective, even if they were all rational and self-interested. Indeed, unless the number of individuals in a group is quite small, or unless there is coercion or some other special device to make individuals act in their common interest, *rational, self-interested individuals will not act to achieve their common or group interests.* In other words, even if all of the individuals in a large group are rational and self-interested, and would gain if, as a group, they acted to achieve their common interest or objective, they will still not voluntarily act to achieve that common or group interest. The notion that groups of individuals will act to achieve their common or group interests, far from being a logical implication of the assumption that the individuals in a group will rationally further their individual interests, is in fact inconsistent with that assumption. . . .

A Theory of Groups and Organizations

The Purpose of Organization

Since most (though by no means all) of the action taken by or on behalf of groups of individuals is taken through organizations, it will be helpful to consider organizations in a general or theoretical way.[1] The logical place to begin any systematic study of organizations is with their purpose. But there are all types and shapes and sizes of organizations, even of economic organizations, and there is then some question whether there is any single purpose that would be characteristic of organizations generally. One purpose that is nonetheless characteristic of most organizations, and surely of practically all organizations with an important economic aspect, is the furtherance of the interests of their members. That would seem obvious, at least from the economist's perspective. To be sure, some organizations may out of ignorance fail to further their members' interests, and others may be enticed into serving only the ends of the leadership.[2] But organizations often perish if they do nothing to further the interests of their members, and this factor must severely limit the number of organizations that fail to serve their members.

The idea that organizations or associations exist to further the interests of their members is hardly novel, nor peculiar to economics; it goes back at least to Aristotle, who wrote, "Men journey together with a view to particular advantage, and by way of providing some particular thing needed for the purposes of life, and similarly the political association seems to have come together originally, and to continue in existence, for the sake of the *general* advantages it brings."[3] More recently Professor Leon Festinger, a social psychologist, pointed out that "the attraction of group membership is not so much in sheer belonging, but rather in attaining something by means of this membership."[4] The late Harold Laski, a political scientist, took it for granted that "associations exist to fulfill purposes which a group of men have in common."[5]

The kinds of organizations that are the focus of this study are *expected* to further the interests of their members.[6] Labor unions are expected to strive for higher wages and better working conditions for their members; farm organizations are expected to strive for favorable legislation for their members; cartels are expected to strive for higher prices for participating firms; the corporation is expected to further the interests of its stockholders;[7] and the state is expected to further the common interests of its citizens (though in this nationalistic age the state often has interests and ambitions apart from those of its citizens).

Notice that the interests that all of these diverse types of organizations are expected to further are for the most part *common* interests: the union members'

common interest in higher wages, the farmers' common interest in favorable legislation, the cartel members' common interest in higher prices, the stockholders'
common interest in higher dividends and stock prices, the citizens' common
interest in good government. It is not an accident that the diverse types of organizations listed are all supposed to work primarily for the *common* interests of
their members. Purely personal or individual interests can be advanced, and usually advanced most efficiently, by individual, unorganized action. There is obviously no purpose in having an organization when individual, unorganized action
can serve the interests of the individual as well as or better than an organization;
there would, for example, be no point in forming an organization simply to play
solitaire. But when a number of individuals have a common or collective interest—when they share a single purpose or objective—individual, unorganized
action (as we shall soon see) will either not be able to advance that common
interest at all, or will not be able to advance that interest adequately. Organizations can therefore perform a function when there are common or group interests, and though organizations often also serve purely personal, individual interests, their characteristic and primary function is to advance the common
interests of groups of individuals.

The assumption that organizations typically exist to further the common
interests of groups of people is implicit in most of the literature about organizations, and two of the writers already cited make this assumption explicit: Harold
Laski emphasized that organizations exist to achieve purposes or interests which
"a group of men have in common," and Aristotle apparently had a similar notion
in mind when he argued that political associations are created and maintained
because of the "general advantages" they bring. . . . As Arthur Bentley, the
founder of the "group theory" of modern political science, put it, "there is no
group without its interest."[8] The social psychologist Raymond Cattell was
equally explicit, and stated that "every group has its interest."[9] This is also the
way the word "group" will be used here.

Just as those who belong to an organization or a group can be presumed to
have a common interest,[10] so they obviously also have purely individual interests,
different from those of the others in the organization or group. All of the members of a labor union, for example, have a common interest in higher wages, but
at the same time each worker has a unique interest in his personal income, which
depends not only on the rate of wages but also on the length of time that he
works.

Public Goods and Large Groups

The combination of individual interests and common interests in an organization suggests an analogy with a competitive market. The firms in a perfectly

competitive industry, for example, have a common interest in a higher price for the industry's product. Since a uniform price must prevail in such a market, a firm cannot expect a higher price for itself unless all of the other firms in the industry also have this higher price. But a firm in a competitive market also has an interest in selling as much as it can, until the cost of producing another unit exceeds the price of that unit. In this there is no common interest; each firm's interest is directly opposed to that of every other firm, for the more other firms sell, the lower the price and income for any given firm. In short, while all firms have a common interest in a higher price, they have antagonistic interests where output is concerned. . . .

For these reasons it is now generally understood that if the firms in an industry are maximizing profits, the profits for the industry as a whole will be less than they might otherwise be.[11] And almost everyone would agree that this theoretical conclusion fits the facts for markets characterized by pure competition. The important point is that this is true because, though all the firms have a common interest in a higher price for the industry's product, it is in the interest of each firm that the other firms pay the cost—in terms of the necessary reduction in output—needed to obtain a higher price.

About the only thing that keeps prices from falling in accordance with the process just described in perfectly competitive markets is outside intervention. Government price supports, tariffs, cartel agreements, and the like may keep the firms in a competitive market from acting contrary to their interests. Such aid or intervention is quite common. It is then important to ask how it comes about. How does a competitive industry obtain government assistance in maintaining the price of its product?

Consider a hypothetical, competitive industry, and suppose that most of the producers in that industry desire a tariff, a price-support program, or some other government intervention to increase the price for their product. To obtain any such assistance from the government, the producers in this industry will presumably have to organize a lobbying organization; they will have to become an active pressure group.[12] This lobbying organization may have to conduct a considerable campaign. If significant resistance is encountered, a great amount of money will be required.[13] Public relations experts will be needed to influence the newspapers, and some advertising may be necessary. Professional organizers will probably be needed to organize "spontaneous grass roots" meetings among the distressed producers in the industry, and to get those in the industry to write letters to their congressmen.[14] The campaign for the government assistance will take the time of some of the producers in the industry, as well as their money.

There is a striking parallel between the problem the perfectly competitive industry faces as it strives to obtain government assistance, and the problem it faces in the marketplace when the firms increase output and bring about a fall in price. *Just as it was not rational for a particular producer to restrict his output in order that there might be a higher price for the product of his industry, so it would not be rational for him to sacrifice his time and money to support a lobbying organization to obtain government assistance for the industry. In neither case would it be in the interest of the individual producer to assume any of the costs himself.* A lobbying organization, or indeed a labor union or any other organization, working in the interest of a large group of firms or workers in some industry, would get no assistance from the rational, self-interested individuals in that industry. This would be true even if everyone in the industry were absolutely convinced that the proposed program was in their interest (though in fact some might think otherwise and make the organization's task yet more difficult).

Although the lobbying organization is only one example of the logical analogy between the organization and the market, it is of some practical importance. There are many powerful and well-financed lobbies with mass support in existence now, but these lobbying organizations do not get that support because of their legislative achievements. . . .

Some critics may argue that the rational person will, indeed, support a large organization, like a lobbying organization, that works in his interest, because he knows that if he does not, others will not do so either, and then the organization will fail, and he will be without the benefit that the organization could have provided. This argument shows the need for the analogy with the perfectly competitive market. For it would be quite as reasonable to argue that prices will never fall below the levels a monopoly would have charged in a perfectly competitive market, because if one firm increased its output, other firms would also, and the price would fall; but each firm could foresee this, so it would not start a chain of price-destroying increases in output. In fact, it does not work out this way in a competitive market; nor in a large organization. When the number of firms involved is large, no one will notice the effect on price if one firm increases its output, and so no one will change his plans because of it. Similarly, in a large organization, the loss of one dues payer will not noticeably increase the burden for any other one dues payer, and so a rational person would not believe that if he were to withdraw from an organization he would drive others to do so.

The foregoing argument must at the least have some relevance to economic organizations that are mainly means through which individuals attempt to obtain the same things they obtain through their activities in the market. Labor unions, for example, are organizations through which workers strive to get the same things they get with their individual efforts in the market—higher wages, better working conditions, and the like. It would be strange indeed if the workers did not confront some of the same problems in the union that they meet in the market, since their efforts in both places have some of the same purposes.

However similar the purposes may be, critics may object that attitudes in organizations are not at all like those in markets. In organizations, an emotional or ideological element is often also involved. Does this make the argument offered here practically irrelevant?

A most important type of organization—the national state—will serve to test this objection. Patriotism is probably the strongest non-economic motive for organizational allegiance in modern times. This age is sometimes called the age of nationalism. Many nations draw additional strength and unity from some powerful ideology, such as democracy or communism, as well as from a common religion, language, or cultural inheritance. The state not only has many such powerful sources of support; it also is very important economically. Almost any government is economically beneficial to its citizens, in that the law and order it provides is a prerequisite of all civilized economic activity. But despite the force of patriotism, the appeal of the national ideology, the bond of a common culture, and the indispensability of the system of law and order, no major state in modern history has been able to support itself through voluntary dues or contributions. Philanthropic contributions are not even a significant source of revenue for most countries. Taxes, *compulsory* payments by definition, are needed. Indeed, as the old saying indicates, their necessity is as certain as death itself.

If the state, with all of the emotional resources at its command, cannot finance its most basic and vital activities without resort to compulsion, it would seem that large private organizations might also have difficulty in getting the individuals in the groups whose interests they attempt to advance to make the necessary contributions voluntarily.[15]

The reason the state cannot survive on voluntary dues or payments, but must rely on taxation, is that the most fundamental services a nation-state provides are, in one important respect, like the higher price in a competitive market: they must be available to everyone if they are available to anyone. The basic and most elementary goods or services provided by government, like defense and police protection, and the system of law and order generally, are such that they go to everyone or practically everyone in the nation. It would obviously not be feasible, if indeed it were possible, to deny the protection provided by the military services, the police, and the courts to those who did not voluntarily pay their share of the costs of government, and taxation is accordingly necessary. The common or collective benefits provided by governments are usually called "public goods" by economists, and the concept of public goods is one of the oldest and most important ideas in the study of public finance. A common, collective, or public good is here defined as any good such that, if any person X_i in a group $X_1, \ldots, X_i, \ldots, X_n$ consumes it, it cannot feasibly be withheld from the others in that group.[16] In other words, those who do not purchase or pay for any of the public or collective good cannot be excluded or kept from sharing in the consumption of the good, as they can where noncollective goods are concerned.

Students of public finance have, however, neglected the fact that *the achievement of any common goal or the satisfaction of any common interest means that a public or collective good has been provided for that group.*[17] The very fact that a goal or purpose is *common* to a group means that no one in the group is excluded from the benefit or satisfaction brought about by its achievement. As the opening paragraphs of this chapter indicated, almost all groups and organizations have the purpose of serving the common interests of their members. As R. M. MacIver puts it, "Persons . . . have common interests in the degree to which they participate in a cause . . . which indivisibly embraces them all."[18] It is of the essence of an organization that it provides an inseparable, generalized benefit. It follows that the provision of public or collective goods is the fundamental function of organizations generally. A state is first of all an organization that provides public goods for its members, the citizens; and other types of organizations similarly provide collective goods for their members.

And just as a state cannot support itself by voluntary contributions, or by selling its basic services on the market, neither can other large organizations support themselves without providing some sanction, or some attraction distinct from the public good itself, that will lead individuals to help bear the burdens of maintaining the organization. The individual member of the typical large organization is in a position analogous to that of the firm in a perfectly competitive market, or the taxpayer in the state: his own efforts will not have a noticeable effect on the situation of his organization, and he can enjoy any improvements brought about by others whether or not he has worked in support of his organization.

There is no suggestion here that states or other organizations provide *only* public or collective goods. Governments often provide noncollective goods like electric power, for example, and they usually sell such goods on the market much as private firms would do. Moreover . . . large organizations that are not able to make membership compulsory *must also* provide some noncollective goods in order to give potential members an incentive to join. Still, collective goods are the characteristic organizational goods, for ordinary noncollective goods can always be provided by individual action, and only where common purposes or collective goods are concerned is organization or group action ever indispensable.[19]

NOTES

1. Economists have for the most part neglected to develop theories of organizations, but there are a few works from an economic point of view on the subject. See, for example, three papers by Jacob Marschak, "Elements for a Theory of Teams," *Management Science*, I (January 1955), 127–137, "Towards an Economic Theory of Organization and Information," in *Decision*

Processes, ed. R. M. Thrall, C. H. Combs, and R. L. Davis (New York: John Wiley, 1954), pp. 187–220, and "Efficient and Viable Organization Forms," in *Modern Organization Theory,* ed. Mason Haire (New York: John Wiley, 1959), pp. 307–320; two papers by R. Radner, "Application of Linear Programming to Team Decision Problems," *Management Science,* V (January 1959), 143–150, and "Team Decision Problems," *Annals of Mathematical Statistics,* XXXIII (September 1962), 857–881; C. B. McGuire, "Some Team Models of a Sales Organization," *Management Science,* VII (January 1961), 101–130; Oskar Morgenstern, *Prolegomena to a Theory of Organization* (Santa Monica, Calif.: RAND Research Memorandum 734, 1951); James G. March and Herbert A. Simon, *Organizations* (New York: John Wiley, 1958); Kenneth Boulding, *The Organizational Revolution* (New York: Harper, 1953).

2. Max Weber called attention to the case where an organization continues to exist for some time after it has become meaningless because some official is making a living out of it. See his *Theory of Social and Economic Organization,* trans. Talcott Parsons and A. M. Henderson (New York: Oxford University Press, 1947), p. 318.

3. *Ethics* viii.9.1160a.

4. Leon Festinger, "Group Attraction and Membership," in *Group Dynamics,* ed. Dorwin Cartwright and Alvin Zander (Evanston, Ill.: Row, Peterson, 1953), p. 93.

5. *A Grammar of Politics,* 4th ed. (London: George Allen & Unwin, 1939), p. 67.

6. Philanthropic and religious organizations are not necessarily expected to serve only the interests of their members; such organizations have other purposes that are considered more important, however much their members "need" to belong, or are improved or helped by belonging. But the complexity of such organizations need not be debated at length here, because this study will focus on organizations with a significant economic aspect. The emphasis here will have something in common with what Max Weber called the "associative group"; he called a group associative if "the orientation of social action with it rests on a rationally motivated agreement." Weber contrasted his "associative group" with the "communal group" which was centered on personal affection, erotic relationships, etc., like the family. (See Weber, pp. 136–139, and Grace Coyle, *Social Process in Organized Groups,* New York: Richard Smith, Inc., 1930, pp. 7–9.) The logic of the theory developed here can be extended to cover communal, religious, and philanthropic organizations, but the theory is not particularly useful in studying such groups. See Olson, pp. 61n17, 159–162.

7. That is, its members. This study does not follow the terminological usage of those organization theorists who describe employees as "members" of the organization for which they work. Here it is more convenient to follow the language of everyday usage instead, and to distinguish the members of, say, a union from the employees of that union. Similarly, the members of the union will be considered employees of the corporation for which they work.

8. Arthur Bentley, *The Process of Government* (Evanston, Ill.: Principia Press, 1949), p. 211. David B. Truman takes a similar approach; see his *The Governmental Process* (New York: Alfred A. Knopf, 1958), pp. 33–35. See also Sidney Verba, *Small Groups and Political Behavior* (Princeton, N.J.: Princeton University Press, 1961), pp. 12–13.

9. Raymond Cattell, "Concepts and Methods in the Measurement of Group Syntality," in *Small Groups,* ed. A. Paul Hare, Edgard F. Borgatta, and Robert F. Bales (New York: Alfred A. Knopf, 1955), p. 115.

10. Any organization or group will of course usually be divided into subgroups or factions that are opposed to one another. This fact does not weaken the assumption made here that

organizations exist to serve the common interests of members, for the assumption does not imply that intragroup conflict is neglected. The opposing groups within an organization ordinarily have some interest in common (if not, why would they maintain the organization?), and the members of any subgroup or faction also have a separate common interest of their own. They will indeed often have a common purpose in defeating some other subgroup or faction. The approach used here does not neglect the conflict within groups and organizations, then, because it considers each organization as a unit only to the extent that it does in fact attempt to serve a common interest, and considers the various subgroups as the relevant units with common interests to analyze the factional strife.

11. For a fuller discussion of this question see Mancur Olson, Jr., and David McFarland, "The Restoration of Pure Monopoly and the Concept of the Industry," *Quarterly Journal of Economics,* LXXVI (November 1962), 613–631.

12. Robert Michels contends in his classic study that "democracy is inconceivable without organization," and that "the principle of organization is an absolutely essential condition for the political struggle of the masses." See his *Political Parties,* trans. Eden and Cedar Paul (New York: Dover Publications, 1959), pp. 21–22. See also Robert A. Brady, *Business as a System of Power* (New York: Columbia University Press, 1943), p. 193.

13. Alexander Heard, *The Costs of Democracy* (Chapel Hill: University of North Carolina Press, 1960), especially note 1, pp. 95–96. For example, in 1947 the National Association of Manufacturers spent over $4.6 million, and over a somewhat longer period the American Medical Association spent as much on a campaign against compulsory health insurance.

14. "If the full truth were ever known . . . lobbying, in all its ramifications, would prove to be a billion dollar industry." U.S. Congress, House, Select Committee on Lobbying Activities, *Report,* 81st Cong., 2nd Sess. (1950), as quoted in the *Congressional Quarterly Almanac,* 81st Cong., 2nd Sess., VI, 764–765.

15. Sociologists as well as economists have observed that ideological motives alone are not sufficient to bring forth the continuing effort of large masses of people. Max Weber provides a notable example:

> All economic activity in a market economy is undertaken and carried through by individuals for their own ideal or material interests. This is naturally just as true when economic activity is oriented to the patterns of order of corporate groups. . . .
>
> Even if an economic system were organized on a socialistic basis, there would be no fundamental difference in this respect. . . . The structure of interests and the relevant situation might change; there would be other means of pursuing interests, but this fundamental factor would remain just as relevant as before. It is of course true that economic action which is oriented on purely ideological grounds to the interest of others does exist. But it is even more certain that the mass of men do not act this way, and it is an induction from experience that they cannot do so and never will. . . .
>
> In a market economy the interest in the maximization of income is necessarily the driving force of all economic activity. (Weber, pp. 319–320)

Talcott Parsons and Neil Smelser go even further in postulating that "performance" throughout society is proportional to the "rewards" and "sanctions" involved. See their *Economy and Society* (Glencoe, Ill.: Free Press, 1954), pp. 50–69.

16. This simple definition focuses upon two points that are important in the present context. The first point is that most collective goods can only be defined with respect to some spe-

cific group. One collective good goes to one group of people, another collective good to another group; one may benefit the whole world, another only two specific people. Moreover, some goods are collective goods to those in one group and at the same time private goods to those in another, because some individuals can be kept from consuming them and others can't. Take for example the parade that is a collective good to all those who live in tall buildings overlooking the parade route, but which appears to be a private good to those who can see it only by buying tickets for a seat in the stands along the way. The second point is that once the relevant group has been defined, the definition used here, like Musgrave's, distinguishes collective good in terms of infeasibility of excluding potential consumers of the good. This approach is used because collective goods produced by organizations of all kinds seem to be such that exclusion is normally not feasible. To be sure, for some collective goods it is physically possible to practice exclusion. But, as Head has shown, it is not necessary that exclusion be technically impossible; it is only necessary that it be infeasible or uneconomic. Head has also shown most clearly that nonexcludability is only one of two basic elements in the traditional understanding of public goods. The other, he points out, is "jointness of supply." A good has "jointness" if making it available to one individual means that it can be easily or freely supplied to others as well. The polar case of jointness would be Samuelson's pure public good, which is a good such that additional consumption of it by one individual does not diminish the amount available to others. By the definition used here, jointness is not a necessary attribute of a public good. As later parts of this chapter will show, at least one type of collective good considered here exhibits no jointness whatever, and few if any would have the degree of jointness needed to qualify as pure public goods. Nonetheless, most of the collective goods to be studied here do display a large measure of jointness. On the definition and importance of public goods, see John G. Head, "Public Goods and Public Policy," *Public Finance,* vol. XVII, no. 3 (1962), 197–219; Richard Musgrave, *The Theory of Public Finance* (New York: McGraw-Hill, 1959); Paul A. Samuelson, "The Pure Theory of Public Expenditure," "Diagrammatic Exposition of A Theory of Public Expenditure," and "Aspects of Public Expenditure Theories," in *Review of Economics and Statistics,* XXXVI (November 1954), 387–390, XXXVII (November 1955), 350–356, and XL (November 1958), 332–338. For somewhat different opinions about the usefulness of the concept of public goods, see Julius Margolis, "A Comment on the Pure Theory of Public Expenditure," *Review of Economics and Statistics,* XXXVII (November 1955), 347–349, and Gerhard Colm, "Theory of Public Expenditures," *Annals of the American Academy of Political and Social Science,* CLXXXIII (January 1936), 1–11.

17. There is no necessity that a public good to one group in a society is necessarily in the interest of the society as a whole. Just as a tariff could be a public good to the industry that sought it, so the removal of the tariff could be a public good to those who consumed the industry's product. This is equally true when the public-good concept is applied only to governments; for a military expenditure, or a tariff, or an immigration restriction that is a public good to one country could be a "public bad" to another country, and harmful to world society as a whole.

18. R. M. MacIver in *Encyclopaedia of the Social Sciences,* VII (New York: Macmillan, 1932), 147.

19. It does not, however, follow that organized or coordinated group action is *always* necessary to obtain a collective goal.

1-2

The Tragedy of the Commons

Garrett Hardin

In this seminal article, Garrett Hardin identifies another class of collective action problems, the "tragedy of the commons." The concept—a "tragedy" because of the inevitability with which public goods, or the "commons," will be exploited—is generally applied to study cases in which natural resources are being misused. Unlike the problems we have already encountered, which concern the production of public goods, the tragedy of the commons affects their conservation. Because public goods are freely available, members of the community will be tempted to overly consume them—to overfish, to overuse national parks, to pollute public water or air—even as they realize their behavior and that of their neighbors is destroying the goods. Hardin discusses social arrangements that can substitute for the commons, or public ownership of scarce resources, and argues that the tragedy of the commons is becoming a more pressing concern as the population increases. As with the problem of free riding described by Mancur Olson, government authority offers one solution extricating participants from their bind.

AT THE END of a thoughtful article on the future of nuclear war, Wiesner and York concluded that: "Both sides in the arms race are . . . confronted by the dilemma of steadily increasing military power and steadily decreasing national security. *It is our considered professional judgment that this dilemma has no technical solution. If the great powers continue to look for solutions in the area of science and technology only, the result will be to worsen the situation.*"[1]

I would like to focus your attention not on the subject of the article (national security in a nuclear world) but on the kind of conclusion they reached, namely that there is no technical solution to the problem. An implicit and almost universal assumption of discussions published in professional and semipopular scientific journals is that the problem under discussion has a technical solution. A technical solution may be defined as one that requires a change only in the techniques of the natural sciences, demanding little or nothing in the way of change in human values or ideas of morality.

Source: Garrett Hardin, "The Tragedy of the Commons," *Science*, December 3, 1968, 1243–1248.

In our day (though not in earlier times) technical solutions are always welcome. . . . [Yet of the] class of human problems which can be called "no technical solution problems" . . . [i]t is easy to show that [it] is not a null class. Recall the game of tick-tack-toe. Consider the problem, "How can I win the game of tick-tack-toe?" It is well known that I cannot, if I assume (in keeping with the conventions of game theory) that my opponent understands the game perfectly. Put another way, there is no "technical solution" to the problem. I can win only by giving a radical meaning to the word "win." I can hit my opponent over the head; or I can drug him; or I can falsify the records. Every way in which I "win" involves, in some sense, an abandonment of the game, as we intuitively understand it. (I can also, of course, openly abandon the game—refuse to play it. This is what most adults do.)

The class of "No technical solution problems" has members. My thesis is that the "population problem," as conventionally conceived, is a member of this class. How it is conventionally conceived needs some comment. It is fair to say that most people who anguish over the population problem are trying to find a way to avoid the evils of overpopulation without relinquishing any of the privileges they now enjoy. They think that farming the seas or developing new strains of wheat will solve the problem—technologically. I try to show here that the solution they seek cannot be found. The population problem cannot be solved in a technical way, any more than can the problem of winning the game of tick-tack-toe.

What Shall We Maximize?

Population, as Malthus said, naturally tends to grow "geometrically," or, as we would now say, exponentially. In a finite world this means that the per capita share of the world's goods must steadily decrease. Is ours a finite world?

A fair defense can be put forward for the view that the world is infinite; or that we do not know that it is not. But, in terms of the practical problems that we must face in the next few generations with the foreseeable technology, it is clear that we will greatly increase human misery if we do not, during the immediate future, assume that the world available to the terrestrial human population is finite. "Space" is no escape.[2]

A finite world can support only a finite population; therefore, population growth must eventually equal zero. . . . When this condition is met, what will be the situation of mankind? Specifically, can [Jeremy] Bentham's goal of "the greatest good for the greatest number" be realized? . . .

The . . . reason [why not] springs directly from biological facts. To live, any organism must have a source of energy (for example, food). This energy is utilized for two purposes: mere maintenance and work. For man, maintenance of life requires about 1600 kilocalories a day ("maintenance calories"). Anything that he does over and above merely staying alive will be defined as work, and is supported by "work calories" which he takes in. Work calories are used not only for what we call work in common speech; they are also required for all forms of enjoyment, from swimming and automobile racing to playing music and writing poetry. If our goal is to maximize population it is obvious what we must do: We must make the work calories per person approach as close to zero as possible. No gourmet meals, no vacations, no sports, no music, no literature, no art. . . . I think that everyone will grant, without argument or proof, that maximizing population does not maximize goods. Bentham's goal is impossible. . . .

The optimum population is, then, less than the maximum. The difficulty of defining the optimum is enormous; so far as I know, no one has seriously tackled this problem. Reaching an acceptable and stable solution will surely require more than one generation of hard analytical work—and much persuasion. . . .

We can make little progress in working toward optimum population size until we explicitly exorcize the spirit of Adam Smith in the field of practical demography. In economic affairs, *The Wealth of Nations* (1776) popularized the "invisible hand," the idea that an individual who "intends only his own gain," is, as it were, "led by an invisible hand to promote . . . the public interest."[3] Adam Smith did not assert that this was invariably true, and perhaps neither did any of his followers. But he contributed to a dominant tendency of thought that has ever since interfered with positive action based on rational analysis, namely, the tendency to assume that decisions reached individually will, in fact, be the best decisions for an entire society. If this assumption is correct it justifies the continuance of our present policy of laissez-faire in reproduction. If it is correct we can assume that men will control their individual fecundity so as to produce the optimum population. If the assumption is not correct, we need to reexamine our individual freedoms to see which ones are defensible.

Tragedy of Freedom in a Commons

The rebuttal to the invisible hand in population control is to be found in a scenario first sketched in a little-known pamphlet in 1833 by a mathematical amateur named William Forster Lloyd (1794–1852).[4] We may well call it "the tragedy of the commons," using the word "tragedy" as the philosopher Whitehead used it: "The essence of dramatic tragedy is not unhappiness. It resides in the solemnity of the remorseless working of things."[5] He then goes on to say, "This inevitableness of destiny can only be illustrated in terms of human life by incidents which in fact involve unhappiness. For it is only by them that the futility of escape can be made evident in the drama."

The tragedy of the commons develops in this way. Picture a pasture open to all. It is to be expected that each herdsman will try to keep as many cattle as possible on the commons. Such an arrangement may work reasonably satisfactorily for centuries because tribal wars, poaching, and disease keep the numbers of both man and beast well below the carrying capacity of the land. Finally, however, comes the day of reckoning, that is, the day when the long-desired goal of social stability becomes a reality. At this point, the inherent logic of the commons remorselessly generates tragedy.

As a rational being, each herdsman seeks to maximize his gain. Explicitly or implicitly, more or less consciously, he asks, "What is the utility *to me* of adding one more animal to my herd?" This utility has one negative and one positive component.

1. The positive component is a function of the increment of one animal. Since the herdsman receives all the proceeds from the sale of the additional animal, the positive utility is nearly +1.

2. The negative component is a function of the additional overgrazing created by one more animal. Since, however, the effects of overgrazing are shared by all the herdsmen, the negative utility for any particular decision-making herdsman is only a fraction of –1.

Adding together the component partial utilities, the rational herdsman concludes that the only sensible course for him to pursue is to add another animal to his herd. And another. . . . But this is the conclusion reached by each and every rational herdsman sharing a commons. Therein is the tragedy. Each man is locked into a system that compels him to increase his herd without limit—in a world that is limited. Ruin is the destination toward which all men rush, each pursuing his own best interest in a society that believes in the freedom of the commons. Freedom in a commons brings ruin to all.

Some would say that this is a platitude. Would that it were! In a sense, it was learned thousands of years ago, but natural selection favors the forces of psychological denial.[6] The individual benefits as an individual from his ability to deny the truth even though society as a whole, of which he is a part, suffers. Education can counteract the natural tendency to do the wrong thing, but the inexorable succession of generations requires that the basis for this knowledge be constantly refreshed.

A simple incident that occurred a few years ago in Leominster, Massachusetts, shows how perishable the knowledge is. During the Christmas shopping season the parking meters downtown were covered with plastic bags that bore tags reading: "Do not open until after Christmas. Free parking courtesy of the mayor and city council." In other words, facing the prospect of an increased demand for already scarce space, the city fathers reinstituted the system of the commons. (Cynically, we suspect that they gained more votes than they lost by this retrogressive act.)

In an approximate way, the logic of the commons has been understood for a long time, perhaps since the discovery of agriculture or the invention of private property in real estate. But it is understood mostly only in special cases which are not sufficiently generalized. Even at this late date, cattlemen leasing national land on the western ranges demonstrate no more than an ambivalent understanding, in constantly pressuring federal authorities to increase the head count to the point where overgrazing produces erosion and weed-dominance. Likewise, the oceans of the world continue to suffer from the survival of the philosophy of the commons. Maritime nations still respond automatically to the shibboleth of the "freedom of the seas." Professing to believe in the "inexhaustible resources of the oceans," they bring species after species of fish and whales closer to extinction.[7]

The National Parks present another instance of the working out of the tragedy of the commons. At present, they are open to all, without limit. The parks themselves are limited in extent—there is only one Yosemite Valley—whereas population seems to grow without limit. The values that visitors seek in the parks are steadily eroded. Plainly, we must soon cease to treat the parks as commons or they will be of no value to anyone.

What shall we do? We have several options. We might sell them off as private property. We might keep them as public property, but allocate the right to enter them. The allocation might be on the basis of wealth, by the use of an auction system. It might be on the basis of merit, as defined by some agreed-upon standards. It might be by lottery. Or it might be on a first-come, first-served basis, administered to long queues. These, I think, are all the reasonable possibilities. They are all objectionable. But we must choose—or acquiesce in the destruction of the commons that we call our National Parks.

Pollution

In a reverse way, the tragedy of the commons reappears in problems of pollution. Here it is not a question of taking something out of the commons, but of putting something in—sewage, or chemical, radioactive, and heat wastes into water; noxious and dangerous fumes into the air; and distracting and unpleasant advertising signs into the line of sight. The calculations of utility are much the same as before. The rational man finds that his share of the cost of the wastes he discharges into the commons is less than the cost of purifying his wastes before releasing them. Since this is true for everyone, we are locked into a system of "fouling our own nest," so long as we behave only as independent, rational, free-enterprisers.

The tragedy of the commons as a food basket is averted by private property, or something formally like it. But the air and waters surrounding us cannot readily be fenced, and so the tragedy of the commons as a cesspool must be prevented by different means, by coercive laws or taxing devices that make it cheaper for the polluter to treat his pollutants than to discharge them untreated. We have not progressed as far with the solution of this problem as we have with the first. Indeed, our particular concept of private property, which deters us from exhausting the positive resources of the earth, favors pollution. The owner of a factory on the bank of a stream—whose property extends to the middle of the stream—often has difficulty seeing why it is not his natural right to muddy the waters flowing past his door. The law, always behind the times, requires elaborate stitching and fitting to adapt it to this newly perceived aspect of the commons.

The pollution problem is a consequence of population. It did not much matter how a lonely American frontiersman disposed of his waste. "Flowing water purifies itself every 10 miles," my grandfather used to say, and the myth was near enough to the truth when he was a boy, for there were not too many people. But as population became denser, the natural chemical and biological recycling processes became overloaded, calling for a redefinition of property rights.

How to Legislate Temperance?

Analysis of the pollution problem as a function of population density uncovers a not generally recognized principle of morality, namely: *the morality of an act is a function of the state of the system at the time it is performed.*[8] Using the commons as a cesspool does not harm the general public under frontier conditions, because there is no public; the same behavior in a metropolis is unbearable. A hundred and fifty years ago a plainsman could kill an American bison, cut out only the tongue for his dinner, and discard the rest of the animal. He was not in any important sense being wasteful. Today, with only a few thousand bison left, we would be appalled at such behavior.

In passing, it is worth noting that the morality of an act cannot be determined from a photograph. One does not know whether a man killing an elephant or setting fire to the grassland is harming others until one knows the total system in which his act appears. "One picture is worth a thousand words," said an ancient Chinese; but it may take 10,000 words to validate it. It is as tempting to ecologists as it is to reformers in general to try to persuade others by way of the photographic shortcut. But the essence of an argument cannot be photographed: it must be presented rationally—in words.

That morality is system-sensitive escaped the attention of most codifiers of ethics in the past. "Thou shalt not . . ." is the form of traditional ethical directives which make no allowance for particular circumstances. The laws of our society follow the pattern of ancient ethics, and therefore are poorly suited to governing a complex, crowded, changeable world. Our epicyclic solution is to augment statutory law with administrative law. Since it is practically impossible to spell out all the conditions under which it is safe to burn trash in the back yard or to run an automobile without smog-control, by law we delegate the details to bureaus. The result is administrative law, which is rightly feared for an ancient reason—*Quis custodiet ipsos custodes?*—"Who shall watch the watchers themselves?" John Adams said that we must have "a government of laws and not men." Bureau administrators, trying to evaluate the morality of acts in the total system, are singularly liable to corruption, producing a government by men, not laws.

Prohibition is easy to legislate (though not necessarily to enforce); but how do we legislate temperance? Experience indicates that it can be accomplished best through the mediation of administrative law. We limit possibilities unnecessarily if we suppose that the sentiment of *Quis custodiet* denies us the use of administrative law. We should rather retain the phrase as a perpetual reminder of fearful dangers we cannot avoid. The great challenge facing us now is to invent the corrective feedbacks that are needed to keep custodians honest. We must find ways to legitimate the needed authority of both the custodians and the corrective feedbacks.

Freedom to Breed Is Intolerable

The tragedy of the commons is involved in population problems in another way. In a world governed solely by the principle of "dog eat dog"—if indeed there ever was such a world—how many children a family had would not be a matter of public concern. Parents who bred too exuberantly would leave fewer descendants, not more, because they would be unable to care adequately for their children. David Lack and others have found that such a negative feedback demonstrably controls the fecundity of birds.[9] But men are not birds, and have not acted like them for millenniums, at least.

If each human family were dependent only on its own resources; *if* the children of improvident parents starved to death; *if,* thus, overbreeding brought its own "punishment" to the germ line—*then* there would be no public interest in controlling the breeding of families. But our society is deeply committed to the welfare state,[10] and hence is confronted with another aspect of the tragedy of the commons.

In a welfare state, how shall we deal with the family, the religion, the race, or the class (or indeed any distinguishable and cohesive group) that adopts over-breeding as a policy to secure its own aggrandizement?[11] To couple the concept of freedom to breed with the belief that everyone born has an equal right to the commons is to lock the world into a tragic course of action.

Unfortunately this is just the course of action that is being pursued by the United Nations. In late 1967, some 30 nations agreed to the following: "The Universal Declaration of Human Rights describes the family as the natural and fundamental unit of society. It follows that any choice and decision with regard to the size of the family must irrevocably rest with the family itself, and cannot be made by anyone else." [12] It is painful to have to deny categorically the validity of this right; denying it, one feels as uncomfortable as a resident of Salem, Massachusetts, who denied the reality of witches in the 17th century. At the present time, in liberal quarters, something like a taboo acts to inhibit criticism of the United Nations. There is a feeling that the United Nations is "our last and best hope," that we shouldn't find fault with it; we shouldn't play into the hands of the archconservatives. However, let us not forget what Robert Louis Stevenson said: "The truth that is suppressed by friends is the readiest weapon of the enemy." If we love the truth we must openly deny the validity of the Universal Declaration of Human Rights, even though it is promoted by the United Nations. We should also join with Kingsley Davis in attempting to get Planned Parenthood–World Population to see the error of its ways in embracing the same tragic ideal.[13] . . .

. . . The argument has here been stated in the context of the population problem, but it applies equally well to any instance in which society appeals to an individual exploiting a commons to restrain himself for the general good—by means of his conscience. To make such an appeal is to set up a selective system that works toward the elimination of conscience from the race.

Pathogenic Effects of Conscience

It is a mistake to think that we can control the breeding of mankind in the long run by an appeal to conscience. . . . If we ask a man who is exploiting a commons to desist "in the name of conscience," what are we saying to him? What does he hear?—not only at the moment but also in the wee small hours of the night when, half asleep, he remembers not merely the words we used but also the nonverbal communication cues we gave him unawares? Sooner or later, con-sciously or subconsciously, he senses that he has received two communications, and that they are contradictory: (i) (intended communication) "If you don't do as we ask, we will openly condemn you for not acting like a responsible citizen"; (ii) (the unintended communication) "If you *do* behave as we ask, we will secretly condemn you for a simpleton who can be shamed into standing aside while the rest of us exploit the commons." . . .

To conjure up a conscience in others is tempting to anyone who wishes to extend his control beyond the legal limits. Leaders at the highest level succumb to this temptation. Has any President during the past generation failed to call on labor unions to moderate voluntarily their demands for higher wages, or to steel companies to honor voluntary guidelines on prices? I can recall none. The rhetoric used on such occasions is designed to produce feelings of guilt in noncooperators.

For centuries it was assumed without proof that guilt was a valuable, perhaps even an indispensable, ingredient of the civilized life. Now, in this post-Freudian world, we doubt it.

Paul Goodman speaks from the modern point of view when he says: "No good has ever come from feeling guilty, neither intelligence, policy, nor compassion. The guilty do not pay attention to the object but only to themselves, and not even to their own interests, which might make sense, but to their anxieties."[14]

One does not have to be a professional psychiatrist to see the consequences of anxiety. We in the Western world are just emerging from a dreadful two-centuries-long Dark Ages of Eros that was sustained partly by prohibition laws, but perhaps more effectively by the anxiety-generating mechanisms of educa-tion. Alex Comfort has told the story well in *The Anxiety Makers;* it is not a pretty one.[15]

Since proof is difficult, we may even concede that the results of anxiety may sometimes, from certain points of view, be desirable. The larger question we should ask is whether, as a matter of policy, we should ever encourage the use of a technique the tendency (if not the intention) of which is psychologically path-ogenic. We hear much talk these days of responsible parenthood; the coupled words are incorporated into the titles of some organizations devoted to birth control. Some people have proposed massive propaganda campaigns to instill responsibility into the nation's (or the world's) breeders. But what is the mean-ing of the word responsibility in this context? Is it not merely a synonym for the word conscience? When we use the word responsibility in the absence of sub-stantial sanctions are we not trying to browbeat a free man in a commons into acting against his own interest? Responsibility is a verbal counterfeit for a sub-stantial *quid pro quo.* It is an attempt to get something for nothing.

If the word responsibility is to be used at all, I suggest that it be in the sense Charles Frankel uses it.[16] "Responsibility," says this philosopher, "is the product of definite social arrangements." Notice that Frankel calls for social arrangements—not propaganda.

Mutual Coercion, Mutually Agreed Upon

The social arrangements that produce responsibility are arrangements that create coercion, of some sort. Consider bank-robbing. The man who takes money from a bank acts as if the bank were a commons. How do we prevent such action? Certainly not by trying to control his behavior solely by a verbal appeal to his sense of responsibility. Rather than rely on propaganda we follow Frankel's lead and insist that a bank is not a commons; we seek the definite social arrangements that will keep it from becoming a commons. That we thereby infringe on the freedom of would-be robbers we neither deny nor regret.

The morality of bank-robbing is particularly easy to understand because we accept complete prohibition of this activity. We are willing to say "Thou shalt not rob banks," without providing for exceptions. But temperance also can be created by coercion. Taxing is a good coercive device. To keep downtown shoppers temperate in their use of parking space we introduce parking meters for short periods, and traffic fines for longer ones. We need not actually forbid a citizen to park as long as he wants to; we need merely make it increasingly expensive for him to do so. Not prohibition, but carefully biased options are what we offer him. A Madison Avenue man might call this persuasion; I prefer the greater candor of the word coercion.

Coercion is a dirty word to most liberals now, but it need not forever be so. As with the four-letter words, its dirtiness can be cleansed away by exposure to the light, by saying it over and over without apology or embarrassment. To many, the word coercion implies arbitrary decisions of distant and irresponsible bureaucrats; but this is not a necessary part of its meaning. The only kind of coercion I recommend is mutual coercion, mutually agreed upon by the majority of the people affected.

To say that we mutually agree to coercion is not to say that we are required to enjoy it, or even to pretend we enjoy it. Who enjoys taxes? We all grumble about them. But we accept compulsory taxes because we recognize that voluntary taxes would favor the conscienceless. We institute and (grumblingly) support taxes and other coercive devices to escape the horror of the commons.

An alternative to the commons need not be perfectly just to be preferable. With real estate and other material goods, the alternative we have chosen is the institution of private property coupled with legal inheritance. Is this system perfectly just? As a genetically trained biologist I deny that it is. It seems to me that, if there are to be differences in individual inheritance, legal possession should be perfectly correlated with biological inheritance—that those who are biologically more fit to be the custodians of property and power should legally inherit more. But genetic recombination continually makes a mockery of the doctrine of "like father, like son" implicit in our laws of legal inheritance. An idiot can inherit millions, and a trust fund can keep his estate intact. We must admit that our legal system of private property plus inheritance is unjust—but we put up with it because we are not convinced, at the moment, that anyone has invented a better system. The alternative of the commons is too horrifying to contemplate. Injustice is preferable to total ruin.

It is one of the peculiarities of the warfare between reform and the status quo that it is thoughtlessly governed by a double standard. Whenever a reform measure is proposed it is often defeated when its opponents triumphantly discover a flaw in it. As Kingsley Davis has pointed out,[17] worshippers of the status quo sometimes imply that no reform is possible without unanimous agreement, an implication contrary to historical fact. As nearly as I can make out, automatic rejection of proposed reforms is based on one of two unconscious assumptions: (i) that the status quo is perfect; or (ii) that the choice we face is between reform and no action; if the proposed reform is imperfect, we presumably should take no action at all, while we wait for a perfect proposal.

But we can never do nothing. That which we have done for thousands of years is also action. It also produces evils. Once we are aware that the status quo is action, we can then compare its discoverable advantages and disadvantages with the predicted advantages and disadvantages of the proposed reform, discounting as best we can for our lack of experience. On the basis of such a comparison, we can make a rational decision which will not involve the unworkable assumption that only perfect systems are tolerable.

Recognition of Necessity

Perhaps the simplest summary of this analysis of man's population problems is this: the commons, if justifiable at all, is justifiable only under conditions of low-population density. As the human population has increased, the commons has had to be abandoned in one aspect after another.

First we abandoned the commons in food gathering, enclosing farm land and restricting pastures and hunting and fishing areas. These restrictions are still not complete throughout the world.

Somewhat later we saw that the commons as a place for waste disposal would also have to be abandoned. Restrictions on the disposal of domestic sewage are widely accepted in the Western world; we are still struggling to close the commons to pollution by automobiles, factories, insecticide sprayers, fertilizing operations, and atomic energy installations.

In a still more embryonic state is our recognition of the evils of the commons in matters of pleasure. There is almost no restriction on the propagation of sound waves in the public medium. The shopping public is assaulted with mindless music, without its consent. Our government is paying out billions of dollars to create supersonic transport which will disturb 50,000 people for every one person who is whisked from coast to coast 3 hours faster. Advertisers muddy the airwaves of radio and television and pollute the view of travelers. We are a long way from outlawing the commons in matters of pleasure. Is this because our Puritan inheritance makes us view pleasure as something of a sin, and pain (that is, the pollution of advertising) as the sign of virtue?

Every new enclosure of the commons involves the infringement of somebody's personal liberty. Infringements made in the distant past are accepted because no contemporary complains of a loss. It is the newly proposed infringements that we vigorously oppose; cries of "rights" and "freedom" fill the air. But what does "freedom" mean? When men mutually agreed to pass laws against robbing, mankind became more free, not less so. Individuals locked into the logic of the commons are free only to bring on universal ruin; once they see the necessity of mutual coercion, they become free to pursue other goals. I believe it was Hegel who said, "Freedom is the recognition of necessity."

The most important aspect of necessity that we must now recognize, is the necessity of abandoning the commons in breeding. No technical solution can rescue us from the misery of overpopulation. Freedom to breed will bring ruin to all. At the moment, to avoid hard decisions many of us are tempted to propagandize for conscience and responsible parenthood. The temptation must be resisted, because an appeal to independently acting consciences selects for the disappearance of all conscience in the long run, and an increase in anxiety in the short.

The only way we can preserve and nurture other and more precious freedoms is by relinquishing the freedom to breed, and that very soon. "Freedom is the recognition of necessity"—and it is the role of education to reveal to all the necessity of abandoning the freedom to breed. Only so, can we put an end to this aspect of the tragedy of the commons.

NOTES

1. J. B. Wiesner and H. F. York, *Sci. Amer.* 211 (No. 4), 27 (1964).
2. G. Hardin, *J. Hered.* 50, 68 (1959); S. von Hoernor, *Science* 137, 18 (1962).

3. A. Smith, *The Wealth of Nations* (Modern Library, New York, 1937), p. 423.

4. W. F. Lloyd, *Two Lectures on the Checks to Population* (Oxford Univ. Press, Oxford, England, 1833), reprinted (in part) in *Population, Evolution, and Birth Control*, G. Hardin, Ed. (Freeman, San Francisco, 1964), p. 37.

5. A. N. Whitehead, *Science and the Modern World* (Mentor, New York, 1948), p. 17.

6. G. Hardin, Ed. *Population, Evolution and Birth Control* (Freeman, San Francisco, 1964), p. 56.

7. S. McVay, *Sci. Amer.* 216 (No. 8), 13 (1966).

8. J. Fletcher, *Situation Ethics* (Westminster, Philadelphia, 1966).

9. D. Lack, *The Natural Regulation of Animal Numbers* (Clarendon Press, Oxford, 1954).

10. H. Girvetz, *From Wealth to Welfare* (Stanford Univ. Press, Stanford, Calif., 1950).

11. G. Hardin, *Perspec. Biol. Med.* 6, 366 (1963).

12. U. Thant, *Int. Planned Parenthood News*, No. 168 (February 1968), p. 3.

13. K. Davis, *Science* 158, 730 (1967).

14. P. Goodman, *New York Rev. Books* 10(8), 22 (23 May 1968).

15. A. Comfort, *The Anxiety Makers* (Nelson, London, 1967).

16. C. Frankel, *The Case for Modern Man* (Harper, New York, 1955), p. 203.

17. J. D. Roslansky, *Genetics and the Future of Man* (Appleton-Century-Crofts, New York, 1966), p. 177.

Arkansas Rice Farmers Run Dry, and U.S. Remedy Sets Off Debate

Douglas Jehl

This news article reports a classic instance of a potential "tragedy of the commons" as described in the previous selection. The farmers in the region continue to extract water from the shrinking aquifer as if no problem lies ahead, though all know and worry that their current course will eventually prove disastrous. Yet unless the farmers find some means to collectively solve the problem, each one, acting rationally, will continue to irrigate inefficiently and deplete the aquifer.

ULM, ARK., NOV. 5—Rice farmers like John Kerksieck are on the brink of draining one of Arkansas' biggest aquifers dry.

That alone is troublesome, in a state that gets almost 50 inches of rain a year. But even more confounding—since these Southern farmers will not be the last to find themselves in such a pickle—is the question of what to do about it.

Most of the farmers want the government to send them replacement water from the White River. The Army Corps of Engineers and the state support a plan to spend more than $200 million in federal money on the project, or about $300,000 a farmer. It is time, they say, for the government to do in other states what has long been done in the West—provide irrigation water to farmers who have no other resort.

But others are concerned about the precedent such a project would set. If the government rewards farmers who use up their water here, they say, what is to stop others from doing the same?

The debate touches on issues of water rights and responsibilities, and spills over into farm policy, because one issue is whether taxpayers should have to spend more to help grow rice, which is already heavily subsidized. It also involves wrangling about whether the corps, which has been limited to navigation and flood control, has any business wading into irrigation.

Source: Douglas Jehl, "Arkansas Rice Farmers Run Dry, and U.S. Remedy Sets Off Debate," *New York Times,* November 11, 2002, sec. A.

One interest group, Taxpayers for Common Sense, contends the plan is a boondoggle of the first order.

Farmers here in Arkansas' Grand Prairie, one of the country's richest rice-growing areas, see it differently. "We really don't have a water problem," said Mr. Kerksieck, 42, in hunting garb in anticipation of the duck season, which rivals rice farming as the Grand Prairie's main preoccupation. Like many here, he traces his lineage to the farmers who arrived in the early 1900's, starting a century of pumping from the aquifer at rates that could not be sustained.

"There's plenty of water in the river," Mr. Kerksieck said. "They've just got to let us divert it."

Another farmer, Lynn Sickel, 51, said: "I'm a conservative person. But if this is what it's going to take for highly productive farmland to continue to provide food nationally and internationally, well, that's the taxpayer's burden."

David Carruth, a local lawyer who had led opposition to the plan, posed the question a different way. "Why shouldn't we say to these farmers in the Grand Prairie: 'You've known since 1940 that you had a problem with your aquifer, and you went ahead and overpumped it anyway,'" he said. "'Why should we go ahead and grant you another resource?'"

Neither Congress nor the Bush administration has made a final decision about the plan, with total cost estimated at $319 million, with the federal government paying 65 percent. But nearly all sides agree that time for a decision is running short. Water levels in the shallow aquifer, known as the Alluvial, are declining at rates so fast that by 2015 there will not be enough left underground to sustain the area's 1,000 farms, which cover about 250,000 acres and represent about 5 percent of the country's rice production.

The economic impact of such a collapse could surpass $46 million a year, the corps has estimated.

The Grand Prairie is not the only area in trouble because of declining groundwater. Underground water accounts for 22 percent of American water use, and in many areas, including much of the Great Plains, coastal Florida and North Carolina and parts of the Mississippi Delta, it is being depleted. Even in eastern Arkansas, whose aquifers are fed by the Mississippi River, overuse has prompted state officials to designate a second area as critical because of scarce groundwater.

But the Grand Prairie area is the first whose aquifer problems have prompted the Corps of Engineers to propose stepping in, a move that many see as an important test case as water shortages, even in the East, have become common.

"One could take the position that, hey, the farmers are the ones who created this mess, so why don't we just let their wells go dry and let everybody go broke, and then the problem will fix itself," G. Alan Perkins, a Little Rock lawyer and an authority on water law, said. "But the critical problem is that right now, we're facing an imminent aquifer failure."

Like many states, Arkansas has essentially never limited the amount of water that farmers can pump from their land. In the last 50 years in the Grand Prairie, farmers have relied increasingly on irrigation, over and above ample rains, to increase the yields of their crops. The farmers have increased by nearly tenfold the amount of water pumped from the Alluvial Aquifer, even as its level was declining by more than a foot a year, the state Soil and Water Commission said.

"By allowing limitless access to such a resource, we encourage overexploitation," said Robert Glennon, a law professor at the University of Arizona and the author of *Water Follies*, a new book on groundwater depletion.

Even now, under the critical area designation, state law permits limits on pumping only if an alternative source of water is made available to the current users at equal or lower cost. Arkansas hopes that alternative can be the White River, but it says it cannot carry out the project without significant federal help.

"We see groundwater depletion in Arkansas being a major problem, and one that involves the national interest, and really the only federal agency with the expertise and ability to deal with it is the corps," Earl T. Smith, chief of the Arkansas commission's water resources management division, said.

Under the corps' current plan, about 2 percent of water from the White River would be diverted for farm use, a project that would include pumping stations, canals and reservoirs. The plan, which the corps said would save the aquifer by reducing pumping to sustainable levels, has passed an environmental review, but faces opposition from outdoor and environmental groups like the Arkansas Wildlife Federation. The groups contend that lower river flows could alter the habitats of certain fish and migratory birds, including ducks, and thus hurt fishing and hunting.

Congress has allocated $45 million for the project, and farmers and the State of Arkansas have spent an additional $11 million. The Bush administration has not included the plan in its budgets. Although withholding a final decision, the Office of Management and Budget has limited how the corps can spend money already allocated for the plan, restricting it to conservation purposes.

Mr. Carruth, the critic of the plan, said a better approach would be to retire some farmland and to spend federal money on technology to enable farmers to use water more efficiently. That approach, he says, eases overpumping of the aquifer without the costly river diversion.

"Why should we subsidize a pump that will sell subsidized water to grow a subsidized crop?" he asked, noting that federal price guarantees mean that rice farmers receive $3.10 a bushel for their crop, more than twice the current $1.40 market price.

An analysis by the corps said that without White River water, there was no way to save enough underground water to continue irrigation at anything but a tiny fraction of current levels.

The farmers say the goal of maintaining a domestic food and fiber industry, and avoiding further reliance on foreign suppliers, is well worth the federal cost, even if it means guaranteeing water and crop payments for their rice.

"There is a long and established history of the federal government being involved in water resources development and protection," John C. Edwards, the executive director of the White River Irrigation District, which represents the 1,000 Grand Prairie farmers, said. "There has been a federal interest in irrigation in 17 Western states. Now that water problems are coming to the East, we can learn from the past to make this a better project for the future."

1-4

The Prosperous Community

SOCIAL CAPITAL AND PUBLIC LIFE

Robert D. Putnam

*The solutions to all of the problems presented in this chapter require partici-
pants to cooperate—to pay their taxes, to refrain from overfishing, to fix their
polluting vehicles, and the like—even as each participant recognizes that he
or she would be rewarded by failing to cooperate. This situation not only
endangers a community's ability to achieve its collective goals but also engen-
ders mutual suspicion and hostility among community members. In the article that follows, Robert Putnam argues persuasively that successful cooperation breeds success in the future. If we trust our neighbors to follow through
on their commitments, then we are more likely to do the same.*

> Your corn is ripe today; mine will be so tomorrow. 'Tis profitable for us
> both, that I should labour with you today, and that you should aid me
> tomorrow. I have no kindness for you, and know you have as little for me.
> I will not, therefore, take any pains upon your account; and should I
> labour with you upon my own account, in expectation of a return, I
> know I should be disappointed, and that I should in vain depend upon
> your gratitude. Here then I leave you to labour alone; You treat me in the
> same manner. The seasons change; and both of us lose our harvests for
> want of mutual confidence and security.
>
> —DAVID HUME

THE PREDICAMENT of the farmers in Hume's parable is all too familiar in communities and nations around the world:

- Parents in communities everywhere want better educational opportunities
  for their children, but collaborative efforts to improve public schools falter.
- Residents of American ghettos share an interest in safer streets, but collective action to control crime fails.
- Poor farmers in the Third World need more effective irrigation and marketing schemes, but cooperation to these ends proves fragile.

Source: Robert D. Putnam, "The Prosperous Community: Social Capital and Public Life," *The American
Prospect*, March 21, 1993.

- Global warming threatens livelihoods from Manhattan to Mauritius, but joint action to forestall this shared risk founders.

Failure to cooperate for mutual benefit does not necessarily signal ignorance or irrationality or even malevolence, as philosophers since Hobbes have underscored. Hume's farmers were not dumb, or crazy, or evil; they were trapped. Social scientists have lately analyzed this fundamental predicament in a variety of guises: the tragedy of the commons; the logic of collective action; public goods; the prisoners' dilemma. In all these situations, as in Hume's rustic anecdote, everyone would be better off if everyone could cooperate. In the absence of coordination and credible mutual commitment, however, everyone defects, ruefully but rationally, confirming one another's melancholy expectations.

How can such dilemmas of collective action be overcome, short of creating some Hobbesian Leviathan? Social scientists in several disciplines have recently suggested a novel diagnosis of this problem, a diagnosis resting on the concept of *social capital*. By analogy with notions of physical capital and human capital— tools and training that enhance individual productivity—"social capital" refers to features of social organization, such as networks, norms, and trust, that facilitate coordination and cooperation for mutual benefit. Social capital enhances the benefits of investment in physical and human capital.

Working together is easier in a community blessed with a substantial stock of social capital. This insight turns out to have powerful practical implications for many issues on the American national agenda—for how we might overcome the poverty and violence of South Central Los Angeles, or revitalize industry in the Rust Belt, or nurture the fledgling democracies of the former Soviet empire and the erstwhile Third World. . . .

How does social capital undergird good government and economic progress? First, networks of civic engagement foster sturdy norms of generalized reciprocity: I'll do this for you now, in the expectation that down the road you or someone else will return the favor. "Social capital is akin to what Tom Wolfe called the 'favor bank' in his novel *The Bonfire of the Vanities*," notes economist Robert Frank. A society that relies on generalized reciprocity is more efficient than a distrustful society, for the same reason that money is more efficient than barter. Trust lubricates social life.

Networks of civic engagement also facilitate coordination and communication and amplify information about the trustworthiness of other individuals. Students of prisoners' dilemmas and related games report that cooperation is most easily sustained through repeat play. When economic and political dealing is embedded in dense networks of social interaction, incentives for opportunism and malfeasance are reduced. This is why the diamond trade, with its extreme possibilities for fraud, is concentrated within close-knit ethnic enclaves. Dense social ties facilitate gossip and other valuable ways of cultivating reputation—an essential foundation for trust in a complex society.

Finally, networks of civic engagement embody past success at collaboration, which can serve as a cultural template for future collaboration. The civic traditions of north-central Italy provide a historical repertoire of forms of cooperation that, having proved their worth in the past, are available to citizens for addressing new problems of collective action.

Sociologist James Coleman concludes, "Like other forms of capital, social capital is productive, making possible the achievement of certain ends that would not be attainable in its absence. . . . In a farming community . . . where one farmer got his hay baled by another and where farm tools are extensively borrowed and lent, the social capital allows each farmer to get his work done with less physical capital in the form of tools and equipment." Social capital, in short, enables Hume's farmers to surmount their dilemma of collective action.

Stocks of social capital, such as trust, norms, and networks, tend to be self-reinforcing and cumulative. Successful collaboration in one endeavor builds connections and trust—social assets that facilitate future collaboration in other, unrelated tasks. As with conventional capital, those who have social capital tend to accumulate more—them as has, gets. Social capital is what the social philosopher Albert O. Hirschman calls a "moral resource," that is, a resource whose supply increases rather than decreases through use and which (unlike physical capital) becomes depleted if *not* used.

Unlike conventional capital, social capital is a "public good," that is, it is not the private property of those who benefit from it. Like other public goods, from clean air to safe streets, social capital tends to be underprovided by private agents. This means that social capital must often be a by-product of other social activities. Social capital typically consists in ties, norms, and trust transferable from one social setting to another. . . .

Social Capital and Economic Development

Social capital is coming to be seen as a vital ingredient in economic development around the world. Scores of studies of rural development have shown that a vigorous network of indigenous grassroots associations can be as essential to growth as physical investment, appropriate technology, or (that nostrum of neoclassical economists) "getting prices right." Political scientist Elinor Ostrom has explored why some cooperative efforts to manage common pool resources, like grazing grounds and water supplies, succeed, while others fail. Existing stocks of social capital are an important part of the story. Conversely, government interventions that neglect or undermine this social infrastructure can go seriously awry.

Studies of the rapidly growing economies of East Asia almost always emphasize the importance of dense social networks, so that these economies are sometimes said to represent a new brand of "network capitalism." These networks, often based on the extended family or on close-knit ethnic communities like the overseas Chinese, foster trust, lower transaction costs, and speed information and innovation. Social capital can be transmuted, so to speak, into financial capital: In novelist Amy Tan's *Joy Luck Club,* a group of mah-jong–playing friends evolves into a joint investment association. China's extraordinary economic growth over the last decade has depended less on formal institutions than on *guanxi* (personal connections) to underpin contracts and to channel savings and investment. . . .

Bill Clinton's proposals for job-training schemes and industrial extension agencies invite attention to social capital. The objective should not be merely an assembly-line injection of booster shots of technical expertise and work-related skills into individual firms and workers. Rather, such programs could provide a matchless opportunity to create productive new linkages among community groups, schools, employers, and workers, without creating costly new bureaucracies. Why not experiment with modest subsidies for training programs that bring together firms, educational institutions, and community associations in innovative local partnerships? The latent effects of such programs on social capital accumulation could prove even more powerful than the direct effects on technical productivity.

Conversely, when considering the effects of economic reconversion on communities, we must weigh the risks of destroying social capital. Precisely because social capital is a public good, the costs of closing factories and destroying communities go beyond the personal trauma borne by individuals. Worse yet, some government programs themselves, such as urban renewal and public housing projects, have heedlessly ravaged existing social networks. The fact that these collective costs are not well measured by our current accounting schemes does not mean that they are not real. Shred enough of the social fabric and we all pay.

Social Capital and America's Ills

Fifty-one deaths and 1 billion dollars in property damage in Los Angeles . . . put urban decay back on the American agenda. Yet if the ills are clear, the prescription is not. Even those most sympathetic to the plight of America's ghettos are not persuaded that simply reviving the social programs dismantled in the last decade or so will solve the problems. The erosion of social capital is an essential and under-appreciated part of the diagnosis.

Although most poor Americans do not reside in the inner city, there is something qualitatively different about the social and economic isolation experienced by the chronically poor blacks and Latinos who do. Joblessness, inadequate education, and poor health clearly truncate the opportunities of ghetto residents. Yet so do profound deficiencies in social capital.

Part of the problem facing blacks and Latinos in the inner city is that they lack "connections" in the most literal sense. Job-seekers in the ghetto have little access, for example, to conventional job referral networks. Labor economists Anne Case and Lawrence Katz have shown that, regardless of race, inner-city youth living in neighborhoods blessed with high levels of civic engagement are more likely to finish school, have a job, and avoid drugs and crime, controlling for the individual characteristics of the youth. That is, of two identical youths, the one unfortunate enough to live in a neighborhood whose social capital has eroded is more likely to end up hooked, booked, or dead. Several researchers seem to have found similar neighborhood effects on the incidence of teen pregnancy, among both blacks and whites, again controlling for personal characteristics. Where you live and whom you know—the social capital you can draw on—helps to define who you are and thus to determine your fate.

Racial and class inequalities in access to social capital, if properly measured, may be as great as inequalities in financial and human capital, and no less portentous. Economist Glenn Loury has used the term "social capital" to capture the fundamental fact that racial segregation, coupled with socially inherited differences in community networks and norms, means that individually targeted "equal opportunity" policies may not eliminate racial inequality, even in the long run. Research suggests that the life chances of today's generation depend not only on their parents' social resources, but also on the social resources of their parents' ethnic group. Even workplace integration and upward mobility by successful members of minority groups cannot overcome these persistent effects of inequalities in social capital. William Julius Wilson has described in tragic detail how the exodus of middle-class and working-class families from the ghetto has eroded the social capital available to those left behind. The settlement houses that nurtured sewing clubs and civic activism a century ago, embodying community as much as charity, are now mostly derelict.

It would be a dreadful mistake, of course, to overlook the repositories of social capital within America's minority communities. . . . Historically, the black church has been the most bounteous treasure-house of social capital for African Americans. The church provided the organizational infrastructure for political mobilization in the civil rights movement. Recent work on American political participation by political scientist Sidney Verba and his colleagues shows that the church is a uniquely powerful resource for political engagement among blacks— an arena in which to learn about public affairs and hone political skills and make connections.

In tackling the ills of America's cities, investments in physical capital, financial capital, human capital, and social capital are complementary, not competing alternatives. Investments in jobs and education, for example, will be more effective if they are coupled with reinvigoration of community associations.

Some churches provide job banks and serve as informal credit bureaus, for example, using their reputational capital to vouch for members who may be ex-convicts, former drug addicts, or high school dropouts. In such cases the church does not merely provide referral networks. More fundamentally, wary employers and financial institutions bank on the church's ability to identify parishioners whose formal credentials understate their reliability. At the same time, because these parishioners value their standing in the church, and because the church has put its own reputation on the line, they have an additional incentive to perform. Like conventional capital for conventional borrowers, social capital serves as a kind of collateral for men and women who are excluded from ordinary credit or labor markets. In effect, the participants pledge their social connections, leveraging social capital to improve the efficiency with which markets operate.

The importance of social capital for America's domestic agenda is not limited to minority communities. Take public education, for instance. The success of private schools is attributable, according to James Coleman's massive research, not so much to what happens in the classroom nor to the endowments of individual students, but rather to the greater engagement of parents and community members in private school activities. Educational reformers like child psychologist James Comer seek to improve schooling not merely by "treating" individual children but by deliberately involving parents and others in the educational process. Educational policymakers need to move beyond debates about curriculum and governance to consider the effects of social capital. Indeed, most commonly discussed proposals for "choice" are deeply flawed by their profoundly individualist conception of education. If states and localities are to experiment with voucher systems for education or child care, why not encourage vouchers to be spent in ways that strengthen community organization, not weaken it? Once we recognize the importance of social capital, we ought to be able to design programs that creatively combine individual choice with collective engagement.

Many people today are concerned about revitalizing American democracy. Although discussion of political reform in the United States focuses nowadays on such procedural issues as term limits and campaign financing, some of the ills that afflict the American polity reflect deeper, largely unnoticed social changes.

"Some people say that you usually can trust people. Others say that you must be wary in relations with people. Which is your view?" Responses to this question, posed repeatedly in national surveys for several decades, suggest that social trust in the United States has declined for more than a quarter century. By contrast, American politics benefited from plentiful stocks of social capital in earlier times. Recent historical work on the Progressive Era, for example, has uncovered evidence of the powerful role played by nominally non-political associations (such as women's literary societies) precisely because they provided a dense social network. Is our current predicament the result of a long-term erosion of social capital, such as community engagement and social trust?

Economist Juliet Schorr's discovery of "the unexpected decline of leisure" in America suggests that our generation is less engaged with one another outside the marketplace and thus less prepared to cooperate for shared goals. Mobile, two-career (or one-parent) families often must use the market for child care and other services formerly provided through family and neighborhood networks. Even if market-based services, considered individually, are of high quality, this deeper social trend is eroding social capital. There are more empty seats at the PTA and in church pews these days. While celebrating the productive, liberating effects of fuller equality in the workplace, we must replace the social capital that this movement has depleted.

Our political parties, once intimately coupled to the capillaries of community life, have become evanescent confections of pollsters and media consultants and independent political entrepreneurs—the very antithesis of social capital. We have too easily accepted a conception of democracy in which public policy is not the outcome of a collective deliberation about the public interest, but rather a residue of campaign strategy. The social capital approach, focusing on the indirect effects of civic norms and networks, is a much-needed corrective to an exclusive emphasis on the formal institutions of government as an explanation for our collective discontents. If we are to make our political system more responsive, especially to those who lack connections at the top, we must nourish grass-roots organization.

Classic liberal social policy is designed to enhance the opportunities of *individuals*, but if social capital is important, this emphasis is partially misplaced. Instead we must focus on community development, allowing space for religious organizations and choral societies and Little Leagues that may seem to have little to do with politics or economics. Government policies, whatever their intended effects, should be vetted for their indirect effects on social capital. If, as some suspect, social capital is fostered more by home ownership than by public or private tenancy, then we should design housing policy accordingly. Similarly, as Theda Skocpol has suggested, the direct benefits of national service programs might be dwarfed by the indirect benefits that could flow from the creation of social networks that cross class and racial lines. In any comprehensive strategy for improving the plight of America's communities, rebuilding social capital is as important as investing in human and physical capital. . . .

Wise policy can encourage social capital formation, and social capital itself enhances the effectiveness of government action. From agricultural extension services in the last century to tax exemptions for community organizations in this one, American government has often promoted investments in social capital, and it must renew that effort now. A new administration that is, at long last, more willing to use public power and the public purse for public purpose should not overlook the importance of social connectedness as a vital backdrop for effective policy.

Students of social capital have only begun to address some of the most important questions that this approach to public affairs suggests. What are the actual trends in different forms of civic engagement? Why do communities differ in their stocks of social capital? What *kinds* of civic engagement seem most likely to foster economic growth or community effectiveness? Must specific types of social capital be matched to different public problems? Most important of all, how is social capital created and destroyed? What strategies for building (or rebuilding) social capital are most promising? How can we balance the twin strategies of exploiting existing social capital and creating it afresh? The suggestions scattered throughout this essay are intended to challenge others to even more practical methods of encouraging new social capital formation and leveraging what we have already.

We also need to ask about the negative effects of social capital, for like human and physical capital, social capital can be put to bad purposes. Liberals have often sought to destroy some forms of social capital (from medieval guilds to neighborhood schools) in the name of individual opportunity. We have not always reckoned with the indirect social costs of our policies, but we were often right to be worried about the power of private associations. Social inequalities may be embedded in social capital. Norms and networks that serve some groups may obstruct others, particularly if the norms are discriminatory or the networks socially segregated. Recognizing the importance of social capital in sustaining community life does not exempt us from the need to worry about how that community is defined—who is inside and thus benefits from social capital, and who is outside and does not. Some forms of social capital can impair individual liberties, as critics of communitarianism warn. Many of the Founders' fears about the "mischiefs of faction" apply to social capital. Before toting up the balance sheet for social capital in its various forms, we need to weigh costs as well as benefits. This challenge still awaits.

Progress on the urgent issues facing our country and our world requires ideas that bridge outdated ideological divides. Both liberals and conservatives agree on the importance of social empowerment, as E. J. Dionne recently noted ("The Quest for Community (Again)," *TAP*, Summer 1992). The social capital approach provides a deeper conceptual underpinning for this nominal convergence. Real progress requires not facile verbal agreement, but hard thought and ideas with high fiber content. The social capital approach promises to uncover new ways of combining private social infrastructure with public policies that work, and, in turn, of using wise public policies to revitalize America's stocks of social capital.

Will 9/11 and the War on Terror Revitalize American Civic Democracy?

Theda Skocpol

During the early days after the 9/11 attack, Americans rallied to each other's aid and support in a way that appears to belie the decay of trust and civic spirit described in the previous essay. Displays of empathy as well as sympathy for victims impressed even the most cynical members of the citizenry. Though these displays were heartening, Skocpol observes that, unlike during other national crises, the American public actually had few opportunities to contribute. Private associations that once channeled volunteer activities and displays of patriotism have atrophied. Nor does the panoply of federal programs—spawned in some instances by failures of voluntary cooperation during times of crisis—encourage or provide opportunities for most citizens to contribute. Consequently, after 9/11 civic attitudes changed significantly, but without obvious avenues for action, civic behavior did not.

OBSERVERS OF AMERICAN LIFE have seen a silver lining in the dark clouds that billowed from the Twin Towers and the Pentagon on September 11, 2001. Along with the horror wrought by the terrorist attacks came an outpouring of solidarity and patriotism—a sudden change of heart for many Americans who, prior to that fateful day, had seemed to be drifting inexorably toward individualism, self-absorption, and cynical disinterest in public affairs. As Stanley Greenberg (2001) aptly puts it, suddenly the "we" mattered more than the "me." People reached out to family members, neighbors, and friends, while proudly declaring their membership in the American national community.

Seventy percent of Americans reportedly gave time or money to charities attempting to help the victims of 9/11 (Independent Sector 2001). Anonymous commuter suburbs in New Jersey suddenly organized to provide constant care for dozens of families who lost loved ones.[1] In the days and weeks after 9/11, more than four-fifths of Americans displayed the U.S. flag on homes, cars and trucks, and clothing.[2] And Americans declared renewed trust in the federal gov-

Source: Theda Skocpol, "Will 9/11 and the War on Terror Revitalize American Civic Democracy?" *Political Science* (September 2002): 537–540.

ernment to "do the right thing." In April 2000, only 29% said they felt such trust "always" or "most of the time," but 64% expressed such faith in a poll taken shortly after 9/11.[3]

In important respects, popular reactions to 9/11 and the subsequent fight against terrorists in Afghanistan resemble what happened in previous U.S. wars. Despite grievous episodes of repression and exclusion, U.S. wars have promoted civic vitality. In a nation whose citizens are famous for their proclivity to organize and join voluntary endeavors, outbreaks of martial conflict have sparked voluntarist upsurges that repeatedly carried over into postwar eras.

The American revolutionary struggle against Great Britain was waged and won by committees of correspondence and volunteer militias—and the era during and after the revolution brought the first great explosion of voluntary group formation in the new nation (Brown 1974). The Civil War of 1861 to 1865 was fought and supported by volunteers (with the military draft responsible for at most 15% of the men who fought). In turn, the Union victory unleashed fresh rounds of civic organizing by men and women who modeled peacetime association building on war mobilizations. At national and local levels alike, the foundations of modern American civic life were laid as the Civil War generation matured between the 1860s and the 1910s (for details and references, see Skocpol 2003, ch. 2). Thereafter, U.S. involvements in World Wars I and II brought new partnerships between government agencies and federated voluntary associations. From the Red Cross and the YMCA to trade unions and business and professional groups, from the General Federation of Women's Clubs and the PTA to dozens of fraternal groups, voluntary associations contributed vitally to World War mobilizations—and, in the process, gained new infusions of duespaying members (Skocpol et al. 2002).

Understandably, the dramatic shifts registered in post-9/11 surveys have encouraged observers to speculate that America's current wartime crisis may again spur civic revitalization (cf. Galston 2001; Putnam 2002).[4] But deeper consideration of the conditions that allowed past wars to contribute to civic engagement suggests why today's conflict might turn out differently. In the Civil War and World Wars I and II, new attitudes coincided with government efforts to mobilize the citizenry for war, and preexisting membership associations channeled popular participation. But so far in this new crisis, official efforts to mobilize citizens have been sporadic and weak, while existing civic organizations provide few channels for group involvement.

Political scientists need not rely on attitude surveys alone to assess possibilities for civic renewal in America's new war on terror. Historical comparisons bring into sharper relief the full set of attitudinal and institutional factors that influence the civic impact of war.

Attitudes Shift at the Outbreak of War

For long-past wars, we do not have national surveys comparable to the opinion polls that enable us to track attitudinal changes today. Qualitative evidence nevertheless reveals that outpourings of patriotic and community sentiment accompanied the onset of conflict in April 1861, April 1917, and December 1941. Newspapers, organizational declarations, community demonstrations, and personal memoirs all provide relevant evidence. When wars break out—and especially when the nation is attacked—millions of Americans become aware of their shared national identity and are willing to work together on local and national responses to the crisis.

Government Authorities May—or May Not—Call for Mass Mobilization

If popular attitudes invariably shift with the outbreak of war, the willingness of government authorities to orchestrate voluntary citizen participation varies considerably, depending on the nature of the conflict and the capacities of government. Modern wars require major domestic as well as military commitments, but government bureaucracies only sometimes possess the capacities and resources to act directly.

When the U.S. federal government suddenly found itself challenged by a massive secessionist movement in 1861, for example, President Abraham Lincoln desperately needed organized volunteer contributions. At that point, U.S. standing armies consisted of a mere 16,000 men, mostly deployed in the West, and led by a small corps of aging professional officers, many of whom "went South" to fight for the Confederacy. In the North and South alike—but especially in the North—the Civil War was fought by an outpouring of military volunteers assembled by local community leaders, combined into state-level units, and knit together to form the Union Army. To support the troops and organize relief efforts at home, women and older men created similar volunteer federations— the forerunner of what would later become the American Red Cross.

Federal bureaucracies were more developed by the outbreak of World War I than in the 1860s. Nevertheless, executive agencies had little capacity to reach directly into local communities and individual homes, so they turned to the national and state leaders of voluntary federations for the organizational networks they needed to run drives to conserve foodstuffs and sell Liberty Bonds, campaigns for relief and military recruitment, and campaigns to maximize economic production. . . .

By the time the United States fought World War II, government capacities were sufficiently developed that authorities did not need voluntary groups as badly as in 1917. Yet it was clear from the start that this conflict would be massive, lengthy, and costly. Remembering how World War I was fought, U.S. officials saw advantages in getting masses of Americans directly involved. Conservation and fund-raising drives were rerun in much the same way as in 1917–19, with women's groups, fraternal groups, the Red Cross, the Knights of Columbus, the YMCA, and hundreds of professional, business, and ethnic associations called upon to mobilize their members to contribute to the war effort. Again, memberships in voluntary associations surged forward into the postwar era.

In the post-9/11 war against terrorism, U.S. authorities have not been so eager to engage in mass mobilization. Obviously, this is a different kind of conflict, waged by a relatively small number of highly trained professional military personnel backed by a few newly mobilized National Guard units. . . . What is more, in 2001 and early 2002, heightened homeland security measures and efforts to cope with the anthrax scare seemed to call for professionals, not citizen volunteers. . . .

Given all of this, in the months following 9/11, federal officials such as Director of Homeland Security Tom Ridge stressed managerial coordination and professional expertise. With limited U.S. military quotas filled, volunteers were turned away. To be sure, President George W. Bush sporadically called on Americans to volunteer in their communities. But his appeals seemed largely symbolic, not connected to vital wartime activities, even as Bush administration officials visibly puzzled over what to do with volunteers.[5] President Bush did not launch any big new civic effort, such as mandatory national service for young Americans.[6] Instead, for weeks after 9/11, his most prominent appeals were commercial rather than civic. The Travel Industry Association of America estimated that two-thirds of Americans saw the President starring in a television advertisement calling for people to express "courage" by taking more trips. And the president repeatedly asked people to go shopping to stimulate the economy. If enduring images of World Wars I and II featured posters of Uncle Sam encouraging citizens to do their duty, perhaps we need a revised version poster to capture the main presidential message in 2001!

Civic Organizations Channel Participation

In historic wars, citizens were eager to volunteer and the federal government engaged in mass mobilization. Yet the nature of existing voluntary associations at the time of the Civil War and the World Wars also contributed to wartime mobilizations and helped to sustain gains in civic connectedness.

From the early 1800s until the 1960s, membership-based voluntary associations were at the center of American public life (for further evidence and citations, see Skocpol 2003, chapters 1–3). Leaders established civic reputations by helping to organize fellow citizens into membership groups. Clubs, lodges, and posts were as ubiquitous as churches and schools—and most local membership groups were linked together into state and national federations. When national crises struck, therefore, leaders knew how to mobilize fellow citizens, and there were well-worn institutional channels through which people could work together and pool resources.

After the 1960s, however, U.S. civic life was radically reorganized (Skocpol 1999; Skocpol 2003, chapters 4–5). In the wake of the Civil Rights and feminist movements, traditional chapter-based membership federations, most of which had been racially and gender segregated, failed to attract many younger members. The war in Vietnam, ultimately unpopular and militarily unsuccessful, rendered traditional patriotic associations less appealing to many Americans. Challenged by movements and defections from below, traditional voluntary associations were also bypassed in national politics by professionally managed advocacy associations, which proliferated in the 1970s and 1980s. Professionally run citizen-advocacy groups often had no individual members at all, or else recruited monetary contributions through the mail (Berry 1977, 1999). At the state and local levels, meanwhile, nonprofit social agencies proliferated. Like advocacy groups, these are professionally managed civic organizations that raise money from donors, government agencies, or mailing-list adherents, rather than from members who attend meetings and pay regular dues.

Well before the crisis of 9/11, therefore, professionally managed associations and institutions had become central to American civic life. Churches remain vital centers of membership activity in many U.S. communities, but other kinds of membership associations have dwindled or disappeared. When a national crisis happens nowadays, there are fewer well-established channels through which people can volunteer together—and fewer ways to link face-to-face activities in local communities to state and national projects. Throughout much of American history in war and peace, voluntary membership federations teamed up with local, state, and national public officials to pursue important public projects (Skocpol 2003, ch. 3). But today, partnerships between civic organizations and government are primarily a matter of collaborations among professionals.

Against this background, we can better understand why, following 9/11, Americans suddenly displayed new attitudes of social solidarity and trust in government, while barely changing their patterns of civic participation. I prepared Figure 1 using data gathered by Robert D. Putnam in a nationally representative panel survey conducted months before and, again, months after 9/11. As the

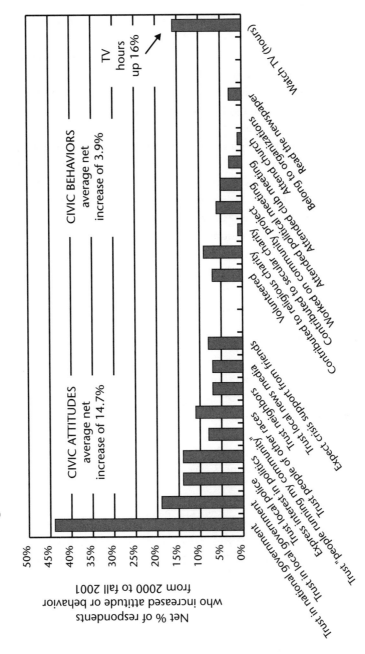

Figure 1. Net Gains in Civic Attitudes and Civic Behaviors, 2000—Fall 2001

figure shows, net gains in civic attitudes were much greater than net gains in civic behavior. Not surprisingly, given the spectacular nature of the terrorist attacks, the one sort of activity that exhibited a big net upward jump after 9/11 was mass TV viewing.

Wartime crises may immediately evoke attitudes of civic solidarity, but some combination of government mobilization and available organizational channels is needed to enable people to act together. If this hypothesis is true, we should see less of a gap between attitudinal and behavioral change among Americans *already engaged* with membership associations prior to 9/11—and we should see positive responses when government offers new opportunities to participate. There is some evidence on both scores. According to a report from the Pew Research Center (2001), a large majority of Americans perceived religion to be more important after 9/11, yet religious *behaviors* changed very little, *except* among people who were already regular churchgoers. Moreover, after President Bush backed modest expansions in national service programs and appealed to Americans to join, applications to AmeriCorps and related programs shot up.

Institutional shifts also help us to understand imbalances in U.S. charity following 9/11. Prior to the 1960s, charitable giving was typically channeled through chapter-based federations, which took advantage of wartime sensibilities to raise resources both for the immediate crisis and for long-run organizational and community needs. Federations with thousands of local chapters could also move funds around to meet a variety of needs. Yet U.S. charities today are highly professionalized operations, very dependent on media-driven messages to attract money from contributors who expect their money to go exactly where the advertisements promise. . . . [I]n the months after 9/11, charities that routinely help the poor in communities across the United States were starved for necessary resources.[7] Food banks and other local agencies were out of the media limelight as their regular donors gave to 9/11 causes.

An Urge to Act—but How?

The American "public feels urge to act—but how?" asked an insightful article appearing in the *Christian Science Monitor* not long after the terrorist attacks of 9/11 (McLaughlin 2001). "What Americans are being called upon to do—live normal lives—hardly seems heroic. Unlike during World War II, citizens aren't needed to roll bandages for GIs or collect scrap metal to make airplanes." My analysis of the roots of war-encouraged spurts in civic engagement suggests that, indeed, Americans since 9/11 may be willing to do more than they have been asked to do by government, and more than they have been allowed to do, given the structure of existing civic organizations.

If they persist, post-9/11 attitude shifts toward patriotism, trust, and community responsibility may contribute to electoral trends and changes in individual behavior, especially among young people just coming of age. There is, however, little evidence that 9/11 and its martial aftermath led to any immediate upsurge in collective voluntary activities at all comparable to the upsurges associated with historic wars. This twenty-first-century conflict has different requirements, and Americans today live in a very different governmental and civic universe than their forebears—a changed public world in which political authorities and nonprofit organizations rely on professional management and media messages rather than on organized popular participation. . . . Absent organizational innovations and new public policies, the reinvigorated sense of the American "we" that was born of the travails of 9/11 may well gradually dissipate, leaving only ripples on the managerial routines of contemporary U.S. civic life.

NOTES

1. Andrew Jacobs, "Town Sheds Its Anonymity to Comfort the Bereaved," *New York Times*, 14 October 2001, Sec. B.

2. William Risser and Sam Ward, "USA Today Snapshots: Stars and Stripes Flying High," *USA Today*, 19 October 2001, Sec. A.

3. Dana Milbank and Richard Morin, "Poll: Americans' Trust in Government Grows," *Washington Post*, www.washingtonpost.com/wp-dyn/articles/A42864-2001Sep28.html (June 28, 2002).

4. See also E. J. Dionne Jr., "Our New Spirit of Community," *Boston Globe*, 26 December 2001, Sec. A.

5. Alison Mitchell, "Asking for Volunteers, Government Tries to Determine What They Will Do," *New York Times*, 10 November 2001, Sec. B.

6. Albert R. Hunt, "Waiting for the Call," *Wall Street Journal*, 30 March 2002, Sec. A.

7. Winnie Hu, "Outpouring for Sept. 11 Groups Means Less for Food Banks," *New York Times*, 21 November 2001, Sec. B.

REFERENCES

Berry, Jeffrey M. 1977. *Lobbying for the People: The Political Behavior of Public Interest Groups.* Princeton, N.J.: Princeton University Press.

———. 1999. *The New Liberalism: The Rising Power of Citizen Groups.* Washington, D.C.: Brookings Institution Press.

Brown, Richard D. 1974. "The Emergence of Urban Society in Rural Massachusetts, 1760–1820." *Journal of American History* 61(1):29–51.

Galston, William A. 2001. "Can Patriotism Be Turned into Civic Engagement?" *Chronicle of Higher Education*, November 16, B16.

Greenberg, Stanley B. 2001. "'We'—Not 'Me': Public Opinion and the Return of Government." *The American Prospect*, December 17, 25–27.

Independent Sector. 2001. "A Survey of Charitable Giving After September 11, 2001." October 23, 1–10. www.independentsector.org.

McLaughlin, Abraham. 2001. "Public Feels Urge to Act—but How?" *Christian Science Monitor,* October 16, 1, 11.

Pew Research Center. 2001. "Post September 11 Attitudes: Religion More Prominent; Muslim-Americans More Accepted." Online report from the Pew Research Center for The People and The Press. www.people-press.org.

Putnam, Robert. 2002. "Bowling Together: The United State of America." *The American Prospect,* February 11, 20–22.

Skocpol, Theda. 1999. "Advocates without Members: The Recent Transformation of American Civic Life." In *Civic Engagement in American Democracy,* ed. Theda Skocpol and Morris P.Fiorina. New York and Washington, DC: Russell Sage Foundation and Brookings Institution Press.

———. 2003. *Diminished Democracy: From Membership to Management in American Civic Life.* Rothbaum Lecture Series. Norman: University of Oklahoma Press.

Skocpol, Theda, et al. 2002. "Patriotic Partnerships: Why Great Wars Nourished American Civic Voluntarism." In *Shaped by War and Trade: International Influences on American Political Development,* ed. Ira Katznelson and Martin Shefter. Princeton, N.J.: Princeton University Press.

Sontag, Deborah. 2001. "Who Brought Bernadine Healy Down?" *New York Times Magazine,* December 23, 32–40, 52–55.

Chapter 2

The Constitutional Framework

2-1

The Founding Fathers: A Reform Caucus in Action

John P. Roche

Textbook consideration of the Constitution's Framers reverentially casts them as political philosophers conveying to future generations timeless laws of proper civic relations. Students of the era delve into arguments of The Federalist and other source materials to detect the intellectual roots of the Framers in the political theories of Locke, Montesquieu, Hume, and even Machiavelli. In this essay Roche reminds us that we should not forget that these were politicians charged with proposing a reform that had to win the endorsement of at least nine states before it became more than the collective ruminations of thirty-nine delegates. The Framers were certainly conversant with the leading political thought of their era—so conversant, indeed, that they exhibited great versatility in invoking these theorists in behalf of whatever scheme they were endorsing. Roche makes a persuasive case that the Constitution reflects the at times brilliant but always pragmatic choices of Framers ever mindful of the preferences of their constituents. Consequently, the Constitution was, in Roche's assessment, a "patch-work sewn together under the pressure of both time and events."

Source: John P. Roche, "The Founding Fathers: A Reform Caucus in Action," *American Political Science Review* 55, no. 4 (December 1961): 799–816. Some notes appearing in the original have been deleted.

OVER THE LAST century and a half, the work of the Constitutional Convention and the motives of the Founding Fathers have . . . undergone miraculous metamorphoses: at one time acclaimed as liberals and bold social engineers, today they appear in the guise of sound Burkean conservatives, men who in our time would subscribe to *Fortune*. . . . The implicit assumption is that if James Madison were among us, he would be President of the Ford Foundation, while Alexander Hamilton would chair the Committee for Economic Development.

The "Fathers" have thus been admitted to our best circles; the revolutionary ferocity which confiscated all Tory property in reach and populated New Brunswick with outlaws has been converted by . . . American historians into a benign dedication to "consensus" and "prescriptive rights." The Daughters of the American Revolution have . . . at last found ancestors worthy of their descendants. It is not my purpose here to argue that the "Fathers" were, in fact, radical revolutionaries; that proposition has been brilliantly demonstrated by Robert R. Palmer in his *Age of the Democratic Revolution*. My concern is with the further position that not only were they revolutionaries, but also they were democrats. Indeed, . . . they were first and foremost superb democratic politicians. I suspect that in a contemporary setting, James Madison would be Speaker of the House of Representatives and Hamilton would be the *eminence grise* dominating . . . the Executive Office of the President. They were, with their colleagues, *political men*—not metaphysicians, disembodied conservatives or Agents of History— and as recent research into the nature of American polities in the 1780s confirms,[1] they were committed (perhaps willy-nilly) to working within the democratic framework, within a universe of public approval. Charles Beard *and* the filiopietists to the contrary notwithstanding, the Philadelphia Convention was not a College of Cardinals or a council of Platonic guardians working within a manipulative, predemocratic framework; it was a *nationalist* reform caucus which had to operate with great delicacy and skill in a political cosmos full of enemies to achieve the one definitive goal—popular approbation.

Perhaps the time has come, to borrow Walton Hamilton's fine phrase, to raise the Framers from immortality to mortality, to give them credit for their magnificent demonstration of the art of democratic politics. The point must be reemphasized; they *made* history and did it within the limits of consensus. There was nothing inevitable about the future in 1787. . . . What they did was to hammer out a pragmatic compromise which would both bolster the "National interest" and be acceptable to the people. What inspiration they got came from their collective experience as professional politicians in a democratic society. As John Dickinson put it to his fellow delegates on August 13, "Experience must be our guide. Reason may mislead us."

In this context, let us examine the problems they confronted and the solutions they evolved. The Convention has been described picturesquely as a counter-revolutionary junta and the Constitution as a *coup d'etat*,[2] but this has been accomplished by withdrawing the whole history of the movement for constitutional reform from its true context. No doubt the goals of the constitutional elite were "subversive" to the existing political order, but it is overlooked that their subversion could only have succeeded if the people of the United States endorsed it by regularized procedures. Indubitably they were "plotting" to establish a much stronger central government than existed under the Articles, but only in the sense in which one could argue equally well that John F. Kennedy was, from 1956 to 1960, "plotting" to become President. In short, on the fundamental *procedural* level, the Constitutionalists had to work according to the prevailing rules of the game. Whether they liked it or not is a topic for spiritualists—and is irrelevant: one may be quite certain that had Washington agreed to play the De Gaulle (as the Cincinnati once urged), Hamilton would willingly have held his horse, but such fertile speculation in no way alters the actual context in which events took place.

I

When the Constitutionalists went forth to subvert the Confederation, they utilized the mechanisms of political legitimacy. And the roadblocks which confronted them were formidable. At the same time, they were endowed with certain potent political assets. The history of the United States from 1786 to 1790 was largely one of a masterful employment of political expertise by the Constitutionalists as against bumbling, erratic behavior by the opponents of reform. Effectively, the Constitutionalists had to induce the states, by democratic techniques of coercion, to emasculate themselves. To be specific, if New York had refused to join the new Union, the project was doomed; yet before New York was safely in, the reluctant state legislature had *sua sponte* to take the following steps: (1) agree to send delegates to the Philadelphia Convention; (2) provide maintenance for these delegates (these were distinct stages: New Hampshire was early in naming delegates, but did not provide for their maintenance until July); (3) set up the special *ad hoc* convention to decide on ratification; and (4) concede to the decision of the *ad hoc* convention that New York should participate. New York admittedly was a tricky state, with a strong interest in a *status quo* which permitted her to exploit New Jersey and Connecticut, but the same legal hurdles existed in every state. And at the risk of becoming boring, it must be reiterated that the *only* weapon in the Constitutionalist arsenal was an effective mobilization of public opinion.

The group which undertook this struggle was an interesting amalgam of a few dedicated nationalists with the self-interested spokesmen of various parochial bailiwicks. The Georgians, for example, wanted a strong central authority to provide military protection for their huge, underpopulated state against the Creek Confederacy; Jerseymen and Connecticuters wanted to escape from economic bondage to New York; the Virginians hoped to establish a system which would give that great state its rightful place in the councils of the republic. The dominant figures in the politics of these states therefore cooperated in the call for the Convention. In other states, the thrust towards national reform was taken up by opposition groups who added the "national interest" to their weapons system; in Pennsylvania, for instance, the group fighting to revise the Constitution of 1776 came out four-square behind the Constitutionalists, and in New York, Hamilton and the Schuyler *ambiance* took the same tack against George Clinton. There was, of course, a large element of personality in the affair: there is reason to suspect that Patrick Henry's opposition to the Convention and the Constitution was founded on his conviction that Jefferson was behind both, and a close study of local politics elsewhere would surely reveal that others supported the Constitution for the simple (and politically quite sufficient) reason that the "wrong" people were against it.

To say this is not to suggest that the Constitution rested on a foundation of impure or base motives. It is rather to argue that in politics there are no immaculate conceptions, and that in the drive for a stronger general government, motives of all sorts played a part. Few men in the history of mankind have espoused a view of the "common good" or "public interest" that militated against their private status; even Plato with all his reverence for disembodied reason managed to put philosophers on top of the pile. Thus it is not surprising that a number of diversified private interests joined to push the nationalist public interest; what would have been surprising was the absence of such a pragmatic united front. And the fact remains that, however motivated, these men did demonstrate a willingness to compromise their parochial interests in behalf of an ideal which took shape before their eyes and under their ministrations.

. . . [W]hat distinguished the leaders of the Constitutionalist caucus from their enemies was a "Continental" approach to political, economic and military issues. To the extent that they shared an institutional base of operations, it was the Continental Congress (thirty-nine of the delegates to the Federal Convention had served in Congress), and this was hardly a locale which inspired respect for the state governments. . . . [M]embership in the Congress under the Articles of Confederation worked to establish a continental frame of reference, that a Congressman from Pennsylvania and one from South Carolina would share a universe of discourse which provided them with a conceptual common denominator *vis à vis* their respective state legislatures. This was particularly true with respect to external affairs: the average state legislator was probably about as concerned with foreign policy then as he is today, but Congressmen were constantly forced to take the broad view of American prestige, were compelled to listen to the reports of Secretary John Jay and to the dispatches and pleas from their frustrated envoys in Britain, France and Spain. From considerations such as these, a "Continental" ideology developed which seems to have demanded a revision of our domestic institutions primarily on the ground that only by invigorating our general government could we assume our rightful place in the international arena. Indeed, an argument with great force—particularly since Washington was its incarnation—urged that our very survival in the Hobbesian jungle of world politics depended upon a reordering and strengthening of our national sovereignty.[3]

Note that I am not endorsing the "Critical Period" thesis; on the contrary, Merrill Jensen seems to me quite sound in his view that for most Americans, engaged as they were in self-sustaining agriculture, the "Critical Period" was not particularly critical.[4] In fact, the great achievement of the Constitutionalists was their ultimate success in convincing the elected representatives of a majority of the white male population that change was imperative. A small group of political leaders with a Continental vision and essentially a consciousness of the United States' *international* impotence provided the matrix of the movement. To their standard other leaders rallied with their own parallel ambitions. Their great assets were (1) the presence in their caucus of the one authentic American "father figure," George Washington, whose prestige was enormous;[5] (2) the energy and talent of their leadership (in which one must include the towering intellectuals of the time, John Adams and Thomas Jefferson, despite their absence abroad), and their communications "network," which was far superior to anything on the opposition side;[6] (3) the preemptive skill which made "their" issue The Issue and kept the locally oriented opposition permanently on the defensive; and (4) the subjective consideration that these men were spokesmen of a new and compelling credo: *American* nationalism, that ill-defined but nonetheless potent sense of collective purpose that emerged from the American Revolution.

Despite great institutional handicaps, the Constitutionalists managed in the mid-1780s to mount an offensive which gained momentum as years went by. Their greatest problem was lethargy, and paradoxically, the number of barriers in their path may have proved an advantage in the long run. Beginning with the initial battle to get the Constitutional Convention called and delegates appointed, they could never relax, never let up the pressure. In practical terms, this meant that the local "organizations" created by the Constitutionalists were perpetually in movement building up their cadres for the next fight. (The word organization has to be used with great caution: a political organization in the United States—as in contemporary England—generally consisted of a magnate and his following, or a coalition of magnates. This did not necessarily mean that it was "undemocratic" or "aristocratic," in the Aristotelian sense of the word: while a few magnates such as the Livingstons could draft their followings, most exercised their leadership without coercion on the basis of popular endorsement. The absence of organized opposition did not imply the impossibility of competition any more than low public participation in elections necessarily indicated an undemocratic suffrage.)

The Constitutionalists got the jump on the "opposition" (a collective noun: oppositions would be more correct) at the outset with the demand for a Convention. Their opponents were caught in an old political trap: they were not being asked to approve any specific program of reform, but only to endorse a meeting to discuss and recommend needed reforms. If they took a hard line at the first stage, they were put in the position of glorifying the *status quo* and of denying the need for *any* changes. Moreover, the Constitutionalists could go to the people with a persuasive argument for "fair play"—"How can you condemn reform before you know precisely what is involved?" Since the state legislatures obviously would have the final say on any proposals that might emerge from the Convention, the Constitutionalists were merely reasonable men asking for a chance. Besides, since they did not make any concrete proposals at that stage, they were in a position to capitalize on every sort of generalized discontent with the Confederation.

Perhaps because of their poor intelligence system, perhaps because of over-confidence generated by the failure of all previous efforts to alter the Articles,[7] the opposition awoke too late to the dangers that confronted them in 1787. Not only did the Constitutionalists manage to get every state but Rhode Island (where politics was enlivened by a party system reminiscent of the "Blues" and the "Greens" in the Byzantine Empire)[8] to appoint delegates to Philadelphia, but when the results were in, it appeared that they dominated the delegations. Given the apathy of the opposition, this was a natural phenomenon: in an ideologically non-polarized political atmosphere those who get appointed to a special committee are likely to be the men who supported the movement for its creation. Even George Clinton, who seems to have been the first opposition leader to awake to the possibility of trouble, could not prevent the New York legislature from appointing Alexander Hamilton—though he did have the foresight to send two of his henchmen to dominate the delegation. Incidentally, much has been made of the fact that the delegates to Philadelphia were not elected by the people; some have adduced this fact as evidence of the "undemocratic" character of the gathering. But put in the context of the time, this argument is wholly specious: the central government under the Articles was considered a creature of the component states and in all the states but Rhode Island, Connecticut and New Hampshire, members of the national Congress were chosen by the state legislatures.

This was not a consequence of elitism or fear of the mob; it was a logical extension of states'-rights doctrine to guarantee that the national institution did not end-run the state legislatures and make direct contact with the people.[9]

II

With delegations safely named, the focus shifted to Philadelphia. While waiting for a quorum to assemble, James Madison got busy and drafted the so-called Randolph or Virginia Plan with the aid of the Virginia delegation. This was a political master-stroke. Its consequence was that once business got underway, the framework of discussion was established on Madison's terms. There was no interminable argument over agenda; instead the delegates took the Virginia Resolutions—"just for purposes of discussion"—as their point of departure. And along with Madison's proposals, many of which were buried in the course of the summer, went his major premise: a new start on a Constitution rather than piecemeal amendment. This was not necessarily revolutionary—a little exegesis could demonstrate that a new Constitution might be formulated as "amendments" to the Articles of Confederation—but Madison's proposal that this "lump sum" amendment go into effect after approval by nine states (the Articles required unanimous state approval for any amendment) was thoroughly subversive.[10]

Standard treatments of the Convention divide the delegates into "nationalists" and "states'-righters" with various improvised shadings ("moderate nationalists," etc.), but these are *a posteriori* categories which obfuscate more than they clarify. What is striking to one who analyzes the Convention as a case-study in democratic politics is the lack of clear-cut ideological divisions in the Convention. Indeed, I submit that the evidence—Madison's *Notes,* the correspondence of the delegates, and debates on ratification—indicates that this was a remarkably homogeneous body on the ideological level. Yates and Lansing, Clinton's two chaperones for Hamilton, left in disgust on July 10. (Is there anything more tedious than sitting through endless disputes on matters one deems fundamentally misconceived? It takes an iron will to spend a hot summer as an ideological *agent provocateur.*) Luther Martin, Maryland's bibulous narcissist, left on September 4 in a huff when he discovered that others did not share his self-esteem; others went home for personal reasons. But the hard core of delegates accepted a grinding regimen throughout the attrition of a Philadelphia summer precisely because they shared the Constitutionalist goal.

Basic differences of opinion emerged, of course, but these were not ideological; they were *structural.* If the so-called "states'-rights" group had not accepted the fundamental purposes of the Convention, they could simply have pulled out and by doing so have aborted the whole enterprise. Instead of bolting, they returned day after day to argue and to compromise. An interesting symbol of this basic homogeneity was the initial agreement on secrecy: these professional politicians did not want to become prisoners of publicity; they wanted to retain that freedom of maneuver which is only possible when men are not forced to take public stands in the preliminary stages of negotiation.[11] There was no legal means of binding the tongues of the delegates: at any stage in the game a delegate with basic principled objections to the emerging project could have taken the stump (as Luther Martin did after his exit) and denounced the convention to the skies. Yet Madison did not even inform Thomas Jefferson in Paris of the course of the deliberations[12] and available correspondence indicates that the delegates generally observed the injunction. Secrecy is certainly uncharacteristic of any assembly marked by strong ideological polarization. This was noted at the time: the *New York Daily Advertiser,* August 14, 1787, commented that the "... profound secrecy hitherto observed by the Convention [we consider] a happy omen, as it demonstrates that the spirit of party on any great and essential point cannot have arisen to any height."[13]

Commentators on the Constitution who have read *The Federalist* in lieu of reading the actual debates have credited the Fathers with the invention of a sublime concept called "Federalism." Unfortunately *The Federalist* is probative evidence for only one proposition: that Hamilton and Madison were inspired propagandists with a genius for retrospective symmetry. Federalism, as the theory is generally defined, was an improvisation which was later promoted into a political theory. Experts on "federalism" should take to heart the advice of David Hume, who warned in his *Of the Rise and Progress of the Arts and Sciences* that "... there is no subject in which we must proceed with more caution than in [history], lest we assign causes which never existed and reduce what is merely contingent to stable and universal principles." In any event, the final balance in the Constitution between the states and the nation must have come as a great disappointment to Madison, while Hamilton's unitary views are too well known to need elucidation.

It is indeed astonishing how those who have glibly designated James Madison the "father" of Federalism have overlooked the solid body of fact which indicates that he shared Hamilton's quest for a unitary central government. To be specific, they have avoided examining the clear import of the Madison-Virginia Plan,[14] and have disregarded Madison's dogged inch-by-inch retreat from the bastions of centralization. The Virginia Plan envisioned a unitary national government effectively freed from and dominant over the states. The lower house of the national legislature was to be elected directly by the people of the states with membership proportional to population. The upper house was to be selected by the lower and the two chambers would elect the executive and choose the judges: The national government would be thus cut completely loose from the states.[15]

The structure of the general government was freed from state control in a truly radical fashion, but the scope of the authority of the national sovereign as Madison initially formulated it was breathtaking. . . . The national legislature was to be empowered to disallow the acts of state legislatures, and the central government was vested, in addition to the powers of the nation under the Articles of Confederation, with plenary authority wherever ". . . the separate States are incompetent or in which the harmony of the United States may be interrupted by the exercise of individual legislation."[16] Finally, just to lock the door against state intrusion, the national Congress was to be given the power to use military force on recalcitrant states.[17] This was Madison's "model" of an ideal national government, though it later received little publicity in *The Federalist*.

The interesting thing was the reaction of the Convention to this militant program for a strong autonomous central government. Some delegates were startled, some obviously leery of so comprehensive a project of reform,[18] but nobody set off any fireworks and nobody walked out. Moreover, in the two weeks that followed, the Virginia Plan received substantial endorsement *en principe*; the initial temper of the gathering can be deduced from the approval "without debate or dissent," on May 31, of the Sixth Resolution which granted Congress the authority to disallow state legislation ". . . contravening *in its opinion* the Articles of Union." Indeed, an amendment was included to bar states from contravening national treaties.[19]

The Virginia Plan may therefore be considered, in ideological terms, as the delegates' Utopia, but as the discussions continued and became more specific, many of those present began to have second thoughts. After all, they were not residents of Utopia or guardians in Plato's Republic who could simply impose a philosophical ideal on subordinate strata of the population. They were practical politicians in a democratic society, and no matter what their private dreams might be, they had to take home an acceptable package and defend it—and their own political futures—against predictable attack. On June 14 the breaking point between dream and reality took place. Apparently realizing that under the Virginia Plan, Massachusetts, Virginia and Pennsylvania could virtually dominate the national government—and probably appreciating that to sell this program to "the folks back home" would be impossible—the delegates from the small states dug in their heels and demanded time for a consideration of alternatives. One gets a graphic sense of the inner politics from John Dickinson's reproach to Madison: "You see the consequences of pushing things too far. Some of the members from the small States wish for two branches in the General Legislature and are friends to a good National Government; but we would sooner submit to a foreign power than . . . be deprived of an equality of suffrage in both branches of the Legislature, and thereby be thrown under the domination of the large States."[20]

The bare outline of the *Journal* entry for Tuesday, June 14, is suggestive to anyone with extensive experience in deliberative bodies. "It was moved by Mr. Patterson [*sic,* Paterson's name was one of those consistently misspelled by Madison and everybody else] seconded by Mr. Randolph that the further consideration of the report from the Committee of the whole House [endorsing the Virginia Plan] be postponed til tomorrow. and before the question for postponement was taken. It was moved by Mr. Randolph seconded by Mr. Patterson that the House adjourn."[21] The House adjourned by obvious prearrangement of the two principals: since the preceding Saturday when Brearley and Paterson of New Jersey had announced their fundamental discontent with the representational features of the Virginia Plan, the informal pressure had certainly been building up to slow down the streamroller. Doubtless there were extended arguments at the Indian Queen between Madison and Paterson, the latter insisting that events were moving rapidly towards a probably disastrous conclusion, towards a political suicide pact. Now the process of accommodation was put into action smoothly—and wisely, given the character and strength of the doubters. Madison had the votes, but this was one of those situations where the enforcement of mechanical majoritarianism could easily have destroyed the objectives of the majority: the Constitutionalists were in quest of a qualitative as well as a quantitative consensus. This was hardly from deference to local Quaker custom; it was a political imperative if they were to attain ratification.

III

According to the standard script, at this point the "states'-rights" group intervened in force behind the New Jersey Plan, which has been characteristically portrayed as a reversion to the *status quo* under the Articles of Confederation with but minor modifications. A careful examination of the evidence indicates that only in a marginal sense is this an accurate description. It is true that the New Jersey Plan put the states back into the institutional picture, but one could argue that to do so was a recognition of political reality rather than an affirmation of states'-rights. A serious case can be made that the advocates of the New Jersey Plan, far from being ideological addicts of states'-rights, intended to substitute for the Virginia Plan a system which would both retain strong national power and have a chance of adoption in the states. The leading spokesman for the project asserted quite clearly that his views were based more on counsels of expediency than on principle; said Paterson on June 16: "I came here not to speak my own sentiments, but the sentiments of those who sent me. Our object is not such a Governmt. as may be best in itself, but such a one as our Constituents have authorized us to prepare, and as they will approve." . . . In his preliminary speech on June 9, Paterson had stated . . . to the public mind we must accommodate ourselves,"[22] and in his notes for this and his later effort as well, the emphasis is the same. The *structure* of government under the Articles should be retained:

> 2. Because it accords with the Sentiments of the People
>
> [Proof:] 1. Coma. [Commissions from state legislatures defining the jurisdiction of the delegates]
>
> > 2. News-papers—Political Barometer. Jersey never would have sent Delegates under the first [Virginia] Plan—
>
> Not here to sport Opinions of my own. Wt. [What] can be done. A little practicable Virtue preferrable to Theory.[23]

This was a defense of political acumen, not of states'-rights. In fact, Paterson's notes of his speech can easily be construed as an argument for attaining the substantive objectives of the Virginia Plan by a sound political route, *i.e.,* pouring the new wine in the old bottles. With a shrewd eye, Paterson queried:

> Will the Operation and Force of the [central] Govt. depend upon the mode of Representn.—No—it will depend upon the Quantum of Power lodged in the leg. ex. and judy. Departments—Give [the existing] Congress the same Powers that you intend to give the two Branches, [under the Virginia Plan] and I apprehend they will act with as much Propriety and more Energy . . .[24]

In other words, the advocates of the New Jersey Plan concentrated their fire on what they held to be the *political liabilities* of the Virginia Plan—which were matters of institutional structure—rather than on the proposed scope of national authority. Indeed, the Supremacy Clause of the Constitution first saw the light of day in Paterson's Sixth Resolution; the New Jersey Plan contemplated the use of military force to secure compliance with national law; and finally Paterson made clear his view that under either the Virginia or the New Jersey systems, the general government would ". . . act on individuals and not on states."[25] From the states'-rights viewpoint, this was heresy: the fundament of that doctrine was the proposition that any central government had as its constituents the states, not the people, and could only reach the people through the agency of the state government.

Paterson then reopened the agenda of the Convention, but he did so within a distinctly nationalist framework. Paterson's position was one of favoring a strong central government in principle, but opposing one which in fact *put the big states in the saddle.* (The Virginia Plan, for all its abstract merits, did very well by Virginia.) As evidence for this speculation, there is a curious and intriguing proposal among Paterson's preliminary drafts of the New Jersey Plan:

> Whereas it is necessary in Order to form the People of the U. S. of America in to a Nation, that the States should be consolidated, by which means all the Citizens thereof will become equally intitled to and will equally participate in the same Privileges and Rights . . . it is therefore resolved, that all the Lands contained within the Limits of each state individually, and of the U. S. generally be considered as constituting one Body or Mass, and be divided into thirteen or more integral parts.
>
> Resolved, That such Divisions or integral Parts shall be styled Districts.[26]

This makes it sound as though Paterson was prepared to accept a strong unified central government along the lines of the Virginia Plan if the existing states were eliminated. He may have gotten the idea from his New Jersey colleague Judge David Brearley, who on June 9 had commented that the only remedy to the dilemma over representation was ". . . that a map of the U. S. be spread out, that all the existing boundaries be erased, and that a new partition of the whole be made into 13 equal parts."[27] According to Yates, Brearley added at this point ". . . then a government on the present [Virginia Plan] system will be just."[28]

This proposition was never pushed—it was patently unrealistic—but one can appreciate its purpose: it would have separated the men from the boys in the large-state delegations. How attached would the Virginians have been to their reform principles if Virginia were to disappear as a component geographical unit (the largest) for representational purposes? Up to this point, the Virginians had been in the happy position of supporting high ideals with that inner confidence born of knowledge that the "public interest" they endorsed would nourish their private interest. Worse, they had shown little willingness to compromise. Now the delegates from the small states announced that they were unprepared to be offered up as sacrificial victims to a "national interest" which reflected Virginia's parochial ambition. Caustic Charles Pinckney was not far off when he remarked sardonically that " . . . the whole [conflict] comes to this": "Give N. Jersey an equal vote, and she will dismiss her scruples, and concur in the Natil. system."[29] What he rather unfairly did not add was that the Jersey delegates were not free agents who could adhere to their private convictions; they had to take back, sponsor and risk their reputations on the reforms approved by the Convention— and in New Jersey, not in Virginia.

Paterson spoke on Saturday, and one can surmise that over the weekend there was a good deal of consultation, argument, and caucusing among the delegates. One member at least prepared a full length address: on Monday Alexander Hamilton, previously mute, rose and delivered a six-hour oration.[30] It was a remarkably apolitical speech; the gist of his position was that *both* the Virginia and New Jersey Plans were inadequately centralist, and he detailed a reform program which was reminiscent of the Protectorate under the Cromwellian *Instrument of Government* of 1653. It has been suggested that Hamilton did this in the best political tradition to emphasize the moderate character of the Virginia Plan,[31] to give the cautious delegates something *really* to worry about; but this interpretation seems somehow too clever. Particularly since the sentiments Hamilton expressed happened to be completely consistent with those he privately—and sometimes publicly—expressed throughout his life. He wanted, to take a striking phrase from a letter to George Washington, a "strong well mounted government";[32] in essence, the Hamilton Plan contemplated an elected life monarch, virtually free of public control, on the Hobbesian ground that only in this fashion could strength and stability be achieved. The other alternatives, he argued, would put policy-making at the mercy of the passions of the mob; only if the sovereign was beyond the reach of selfish influence would it be possible to have government in the interests of the whole community.[33]

From all accounts, this was a masterful and compelling speech, but (aside from furnishing John Lansing and Luther Martin with ammunition for later use against the Constitution) it made little impact. Hamilton was simply transmitting on a different wave-length from the rest of the delegates; the latter adjourned after his great effort, admired his rhetoric, and then returned to business.[34] It was rather as if they had taken a day off to attend the opera. Hamilton, never a particularly patient man or much of a negotiator, stayed for another ten days and then left, in considerable disgust, for New York.[35] Although he came back to Philadelphia sporadically and attended the last two weeks of the Convention, Hamilton played no part in the laborious task of hammering out the Constitution. His day came later when he led the New York Constitutionalists into the savage imbroglio over ratification—an arena in which his unmatched talent for dirty political infighting may well have won the day. For instance, in the New York Ratifying Convention, Lansing threw back into Hamilton's teeth the sentiments the latter had expressed in his June 18 oration in the Convention. However, having since retreated to the fine defensive positions immortalized in *The Federalist,* the Colonel flatly denied that he had ever been an enemy of the states, or had believed that conflict between states and nation was inexorable! As Madison's authoritative *Notes* did not appear until 1840, and there had been no press coverage, there was no way to verify his assertions, so in the words of the reporter, ". . . a warm personal altercation between [Lansing and Hamilton] engrossed the remainder of the day [June 28, 1788]."[36]

IV

On Tuesday morning, June 19, the vacation was over. James Madison led off with a long, carefully reasoned speech analyzing the New Jersey Plan which, while intellectually vigorous in its criticisms, was quite conciliatory in mood. "The great difficulty," he observed, "lies in the affair of Representation; and if this could be adjusted, all others would be surmountable."[37] (As events were to demonstrate, this diagnosis was correct.) When he finished, a vote was taken on whether to continue with the Virginia Plan as the nucleus for a new constitution: seven states voted "Yes"; New York, New Jersey, and Delaware voted "No"; and Maryland, whose position often depended on which delegates happened to be on the floor, divided. Paterson, it seems, lost decisively; yet in a fundamental sense he and his allies had achieved their purpose: from that day onward, it could never be forgotten that the state governments loomed ominously in the background and that no verbal incantations could exorcise their power. Moreover, nobody bolted the convention: Paterson and his colleagues took their defeat in stride and set to work to modify the Virginia Plan, particularly with respect to its provisions on representation in the national legislature. Indeed, they won an immediate rhetorical bonus; when Oliver Ellsworth of Connecticut rose to move that the word "national" be expunged from the Third Virginia Resolution ("Resolved that a *national* Government ought to be established consisting of a *supreme* Legislative, Executive and Judiciary"[38]), Randolph agreed and the motion passed unanimously.[39] The process of compromise had begun.

For the next two weeks, the delegates circled around the problem of legislative representation. The Connecticut delegation appears to have evolved a possible compromise quite early in the debates, but the Virginians and particularly Madison (unaware that he would later be acclaimed as the prophet of "federalism") fought obdurately against providing for equal representation of states in the second chamber. There was a good deal of acrimony and at one point Benjamin Franklin—of all people—proposed the institution of a daily prayer; practical politicians in the gathering, however, were meditating more on the merits of a good committee than on the utility of Divine intervention. On July 2, the ice began to break when through a number of fortuitous events[40]—and one that seems deliberate[41]—the majority against equality of representation was converted into a dead tie. The Convention had reached the stage where it was "ripe" for a solution (presumably all the therapeutic speeches had been made), and the South Carolinians proposed a committee. Madison and James Wilson wanted none of it, but with only Pennsylvania dissenting, the body voted to establish a working party on the problem of representation.

The members of this committee, one from each state, were elected by the delegates—and a very interesting committee it was. Despite the fact that the Virginia Plan had held majority support up to that date, neither Madison nor Randolph was selected (Mason was the Virginian) and Baldwin of Georgia, whose shift in position had resulted in the tie, was chosen. From the composition, it was clear that this was not to be a "fighting" committee: the emphasis in membership was on what might be described as "second-level political entrepreneurs." On the basis of the discussions up to that time, only Luther Martin of Maryland could be described as a "bitter-ender." Admittedly, some divination enters into this sort of analysis, but one does get a sense of the mood of the delegates from these choices—including the interesting selection of Benjamin Franklin, despite his age and intellectual wobbliness, over the brilliant and incisive Wilson or the sharp, polemical Gouverneur Morris, to represent Pennsylvania. His passion for conciliation was more valuable at this juncture than Wilson's logical genius, or Morris' acerbic wit.

There is a common rumor that the Framers divided their time between philosophical discussions of government and reading the classics in political theory. Perhaps this is as good a time as any to note that their concerns were highly practical, that they spent little time canvassing abstractions. A number of them had some acquaintance with the history of political theory (probably gained from reading John Adams' monumental compilation *A Defense of the Constitutions of Government*,[42] the first volume of which appeared in 1786), and it was a poor rhetorician indeed who could not cite Locke, Montesquieu, or Harrington *in support* of a desired goal. Yet up to this point in the deliberations, no one had expounded a defense of states'-rights or the "separation of powers" on anything resembling a theoretical basis. It should be reiterated that the Madison model had no room either for the states or for the "separation of powers": effectively *all* governmental power was vested in the national legislature. The merits of Montesquieu did not turn up until *The Federalist;* and although a perverse argument could be made that Madison's ideal was truly in the tradition of John Locke's *Second Treatise of Government*,[43] the Locke whom the American rebels treated as an honorary president was a pluralistic defender of vested rights,[44] not of parliamentary supremacy.

It would be tedious to continue a blow-by-blow analysis of the work of the delegates; the critical fight was over representation of the states and once the Connecticut Compromise was adopted on July 17, the Convention was over the hump. Madison, James Wilson, and Gouverneur Morris of New York (who was there representing Pennsylvania!) fought the compromise all the way in a last-ditch effort to get a unitary state with parliamentary supremacy. But their allies deserted them and they demonstrated after their defeat the essentially opportunist character of their objections—using "opportunist" here in a non-pejorative sense, to indicate a willingness to swallow their objections and get on with the business. Moreover, once the compromise had carried (by five states to four, with one state divided), its advocates threw themselves vigorously into the job of strengthening the general government's substantive powers—as might have been predicted, indeed, from Paterson's early statements. It nourishes an increased respect for Madison's devotion to the art of politics, to realize that this dogged fighter could sit down six months later and prepare essays for *The Federalist* in contradiction to his basic convictions about the true course the Convention should have taken.

V

Two tricky issues will serve to illustrate the later process of accommodation. The first was the institutional position of the Executive. Madison argued for an executive chosen by the National Legislature and on May 29 this had been adopted with a provision that after his seven-year term was concluded, the chief magistrate should not be eligible for reelection. In late July this was reopened and for a week the matter was argued from several different points of view. A good deal of desultory speech-making ensued, but the gist of the problem was the opposition from two sources to election by the legislature. One group felt that the states should have a hand in the process; another small but influential circle urged direct election by the people. There were a number of proposals: election by the people, election by state governors, by electors chosen by state legislatures, by the National Legislature (James Wilson, perhaps ironically, proposed at one point that an Electoral College be chosen by lot from the National Legislature!), and there was some resemblance to three-dimensional chess in the dispute because of the presence of two other variables, length of tenure and reeligibility. Finally, after opening, reopening, and re-reopening the debate, the thorny problem was consigned to a committee for resolution.

The Brearley Committee on Postponed Matters was a superb aggregation of talent and its compromise on the Executive was a masterpiece of political improvisation. (The Electoral College, its creation, however, had little in its favor as an *institution*—as the delegates well appreciated.) The point of departure for all discussion about the presidency in the Convention was that in immediate terms, the problem was non-existent; in other words, everybody present knew that under any system devised, George Washington would be President. Thus they were dealing in the future tense and to a body of working politicians the merits of the Brearley proposal were obvious: everybody got a piece of cake. (Or to put it more academically, each viewpoint could leave the Convention and argue to its constituents that it had *really* won the day.) First, the state legislatures had the right to determine the mode of selection of the electors; second, the small states received a bonus in the Electoral College in the form of a guaranteed minimum of three votes while the big states got acceptance of the principle of proportional power; third, if the state legislatures agreed (as six did in the first presidential election), the people could be involved directly in the choice of electors; and finally, if no candidate received a majority in the College, the right of decision passed to the National Legislature with each state exercising equal strength. (In the Brearley recommendation, the election went to the Senate, but a motion from the floor substituted the House; this was accepted on the ground that the Senate already had enough authority over the executive in its treaty and appointment powers.)

This compromise was almost too good to be true, and the Framers snapped it up with little debate or controversy. No one seemed to think well of the College as an *institution;* indeed, what evidence there is suggests that there was an assumption that once Washington had finished his tenure as President, the electors would cease to produce majorities and the chief executive would usually be chosen in the House. George Mason observed casually that the selection would be made in the House nineteen times in twenty and no one seriously disputed this point. The vital aspect of the Electoral College was that it got the Convention over the hurdle and protected everybody's interests. The future was left to cope with the problem of what to do with this Rube Goldberg mechanism.

In short, the Framers did not in their wisdom endow the United States with a College of Cardinals—the Electoral College was neither an exercise in applied Platonism nor an experiment in indirect government based on elitist distrust of the masses. It was merely a jerry-rigged improvisation which has subsequently been endowed with a high theoretical content. When an elector from Oklahoma in 1960 refused to cast his vote for Nixon (naming Byrd and Goldwater instead) on the ground that the Founding Fathers intended him to exercise his great independent wisdom, he was indulging in historical fantasy. If one were to indulge in counter-fantasy, he would be tempted to suggest that the Fathers would be startled to find the College still in operation—and perhaps even dismayed at their descendants' lack of judgment or inventiveness.[45]

The second issue on which some substantial practical bargaining took place was slavery. The morality of slavery was, by design, not at issue;[46] but in its other concrete aspects, slavery colored the arguments over taxation, commerce, and representation. The "Three-Fifths Compromise," that three-fifths of the slaves would be counted both for representation and for purposes of direct taxation (which was drawn from the past—it was a formula of Madison's utilized by Congress in 1783 to establish the basis of state contributions to the Confederation treasury) had allayed some Northern fears about Southern overrepresentation (no one then foresaw the trivial role that direct taxation would play in later federal financial policy), but doubts still remained. The Southerners, on the other hand, were afraid that Congressional control over commerce would lead to the exclusion of slaves or to their excessive taxation as imports. Moreover, the

Southerners were disturbed over "navigation acts," *i.e.,* tariffs, or special legislation providing, for example, that exports be carried only in American ships; as a
section depending upon exports, they wanted protection from the potential
voracity of their commercial brethren of the Eastern states. To achieve this end,
Mason and others urged that the Constitution include a proviso that navigation
and commercial laws should require a two-thirds vote in Congress.

These problems came to a head in late August and, as usual, were handed to
a committee in the hope that, in Gouverneur Morris' words, ". . . these things
may form a bargain among the Northern and Southern states."[47] The Committee reported its measures of reconciliation on August 25, and on August 29 the
package was wrapped up and delivered. What occurred can best be described in
George Mason's dour version (he anticipated Calhoun in his conviction that permitting navigation acts to pass by majority vote would put the South in economic bondage to the North—it was mainly on this ground that he refused to
sign the Constitution):

> The Constitution as agreed to till a fortnight before the Convention rose was
> such a one as he would have set his hand and heart to. . . . [Until that time]
> The 3 New England States were constantly with us in all questions . . . so that
> it was these three States with the 5 Southern ones against Pennsylvania, Jer-
> sey and Delaware. With respect to the importation of slaves, [decision-
> making] was left to Congress. This disturbed the two Southernmost States
> who knew that Congress would immediately suppress the importation of
> slaves. Those two States therefore struck up a bargain with the three New
> England States. If they would join to admit slaves for some years, the two
> Southern-most States would join in changing the clause which required the
> 2/3 of the Legislature in any vote [on navigation acts). It was done.[48]

On the floor of the Convention there was a virtual love-feast on this happy
occasion. Charles Pinckney of South Carolina attempted to overturn the committee's decision, when the compromise was reported to the Convention, by
insisting that the South needed protection from the imperialism of the Northern
states. But his Southern colleagues were not prepared to rock the boat and General C. C. Pinckney arose to spread oil on the suddenly ruffled waters; he admitted that:

> It was in the true interest of the S[outhern] States to have no regulation of
> commerce; but considering the loss brought on the commerce of the Eastern
> States by the Revolution, their liberal conduct towards the views of South
> Carolina [on the regulation of the slave trade] and the interests the weak
> Southn. States had in being united with the strong Eastern states, he thought
> it proper that no fetters should be imposed on the power of making com-
> mercial regulations; *and that his constituents, though prejudiced against the East-
> ern States, would be reconciled to this liberality.* He had himself prejudices agst

the Eastern States before he came here, but would acknowledge that he had found them as liberal and candid as any men whatever. (Italics added)[49]

Pierce Butler took the same tack, essentially arguing that he was not too happy about the possible consequences, but that a deal was a deal.[50] Many Southern leaders were later—in the wake of the "Tariff of Abominations"—to rue this day of reconciliation; Calhoun's *Disquisition on Government* was little more than an extension of the argument in the Convention against permitting a congressional Majority to enact navigation acts.[51]

VI

Drawing on their vast collective political experience, utilizing every weapon in the politician's arsenal, looking constantly over their shoulders at their constituents, the delegates put together a Constitution. It was a makeshift affair; some sticky issues (for example, the qualification of voters) they ducked entirely; others they mastered with that ancient instrument of political sagacity, studied ambiguity (for example, citizenship), and some they just overlooked. In this last category, I suspect, fell the matter of the power of the federal courts to determine the constitutionality of acts of Congress. When the judicial article was formulated (Article III of the Constitution), deliberations were still in the stage where the legislature was endowed with broad power under the Randolph formulation, authority which by its own terms was scarcely amenable to judicial review. In essence, courts could hardly determine when ". . . the separate States are incompetent or . . . the harmony of the United States may be interrupted"; the National Legislature, as critics pointed out, was free to define its own jurisdiction. Later the definition of legislative authority was changed into the form we know, a series of stipulated powers, *but the delegates never seriously reexamined the jurisdiction of the judiciary under this new limited formulation.*[52] All arguments on the intention of the Framers in this matter are thus deductive and *a posteriori*, though some obviously make more sense than others.

The Framers were busy and distinguished men, anxious to get back to their families, their positions, and their constituents, not members of the French Academy devoting a lifetime to a dictionary. They were trying to do an important job, and do it in such a fashion that their handiwork would be acceptable to very diverse constituencies. No one was rhapsodic about the final document, but it was a beginning, a move in the right direction, and one they had reason to believe the people would endorse. In addition, since they had modified the impossible amendment provisions of the Articles (the requirement of unanimity which could always be frustrated by "Rogues Island") to one demanding approval by only three-quarters of the states, they seemed confident that gaps in the fabric which experience would reveal could be rewoven without undue difficulty.

So with a neat phrase introduced by Benjamin Franklin (but devised by Gouverneur Morris)[53] which made their decision sound unanimous, and an inspired benediction by the Old Doctor urging doubters to doubt their own infallibility, the Constitution was accepted and signed. Curiously, Edmund Randolph, who had played so vital a role throughout, refused to sign, as did his fellow Virginian George Mason and Elbridge Gerry of Massachusetts. Randolph's behavior was eccentric, to say the least—his excuses for refusing his signature have a factitious ring even at this late date; the best explanation seems to be that he was afraid that the Constitution would prove to be a liability in Virginia politics, where Patrick Henry was burning up the countryside with impassioned denunciations. Presumably, Randolph wanted to check the temper of the populace before he risked his reputation, and perhaps his job, in a fight with both Henry and Richard Henry Lee.[54] Events lend some justification to this speculation: after much temporizing and use of the conditional subjunctive tense, Randolph endorsed ratification in Virginia and ended up getting the best of both worlds.

Madison, despite his reservations about the Constitution, was the campaign manager in ratification. His first task was to get the Congress in New York to light its own funeral pyre by approving the "amendments" to the Articles and sending them on to the state legislatures. Above all, momentum had to be maintained. The anti-Constitutionalists, now thoroughly alarmed and no novices in politics, realized that their best tactic was attrition rather than direct opposition. Thus they settled on a position expressing qualified approval but calling for a second Convention to remedy various defects (the one with the most demagogic appeal was the lack of a Bill of Rights). Madison knew that to accede to this demand would be equivalent to losing the battle, nor would he agree to conditional approval (despite wavering even by Hamilton). This was an all-or-nothing proposition: national salvation or national impotence with no intermediate positions possible. Unable to get congressional approval, he settled for second best: a unanimous resolution of Congress transmitting the Constitution to the states for whatever action they saw fit to take. The opponents then moved from New York and the Congress, where they had attempted to attach amendments and conditions, to the states for the final battle.

At first the campaign for ratification went beautifully: within eight months after the delegates set their names to the document, eight states had ratified. Only in Massachusetts had the result been close (187–168). Theoretically, a ratification by one more state convention would set the new government in motion, but in fact until Virginia and New York acceded to the new Union, the latter was a fiction. New Hampshire was the next to ratify; Rhode Island was involved in its characteristic political convulsions (the Legislature there sent the Constitution out to the towns for decision by popular vote and it got lost among a series of local issues); North Carolina's convention did not meet until July and then postponed a final decision. This is hardly the place for an extensive analysis of the conventions of New York and Virginia. Suffice it to say that the Constitutionalists clearly outmaneuvered their opponents, forced them into impossible political positions, and won both states narrowly. The Virginia Convention could serve as a classic study in effective floor management: Patrick Henry had to be contained, and a reading of the debates discloses a standard two-stage technique. Henry would give a four- or five-hour speech denouncing some section of the Constitution on every conceivable ground (the federal district, he averred at one point, would become a haven for convicts escaping from state authority!);[55] when Henry subsided, "Mr. Lee of Westmoreland" would rise and literally poleaxe him with sardonic invective (when Henry complained about the militia power, "Lighthorse Harry" really punched below the belt: observing that while the former Governor had been sitting in Richmond during the Revolution, *he* had been out in the trenches with the troops and thus felt better qualified to discuss military affairs).[56] Then the gentlemanly Constitutionalists (Madison, Pendleton and Marshall) would pick up the matters at issue and examine them in the light of reason.

Indeed, modern Americans who tend to think of James Madison as a rather desiccated character should spend some time with this transcript. Probably Madison put on his most spectacular demonstration of nimble rhetoric in what might be called "The Battle of the Absent Authorities." Patrick Henry in the course of one of his harangues alleged that Jefferson was known to be opposed to Virginia's approving the Constitution. This was clever: Henry hated Jefferson, but was prepared to use any weapon that came to hand. Madison's riposte was superb: First, he said that with all due respect to the great reputation of Jefferson, he was not in the country and therefore could not formulate an adequate judgment; second, no one should utilize the reputation of an outsider—the Virginia Convention was there to think for itself; third, if there were to be recourse to outsiders, the opinions of George Washington should certainly be taken into consideration; and finally, he knew from privileged personal communications from Jefferson that in fact the latter *strongly favored* the Constitution.[57] To devise an assault route into this rhetorical fortress was literally impossible.

VII

The fight was over; all that remained now was to establish the new frame of government in the spirit of its framers. And who were better qualified for this task than the Framers themselves? Thus victory for the Constitution meant simultaneous victory for the Constitutionalists; the anti-Constitutionalists either capitulated or vanished into limbo—soon Patrick Henry would be offered a seat on the Supreme Court[58] and Luther Martin would be known as the Federalist "bull-dog."[59] And irony of ironies, Alexander Hamilton and James Madison would shortly accumulate a reputation as the formulators of what is often alleged to be our political theory, the concept of "federalism." Also, on the other side of the ledger, the arguments would soon appear over what the Framers "really meant"; while these disputes have assumed the proportions of a big scholarly business in the last century, they began almost before the ink on the Constitution was dry. One of the best early ones featured Hamilton versus Madison on the scope of presidential power, and other Framers characteristically assumed positions in this and other disputes on the basis of their political convictions.

Probably our greatest difficulty is that we know so much more about what the Framers *should have meant* than they themselves did. We are intimately acquainted with the problems that their Constitution should have been designed to master; in short, we have read the mystery story backwards. If we are to get the right "feel" for their time and their circumstances, we must in Maitland's phrase, ". . . think ourselves back into a twilight." Obviously, no one can pretend completely to escape from the solipsistic web of his own environment, but if the effort is made, it is possible to appreciate the past roughly on its own terms. The first step in this process is to abandon the academic premise that because we can ask a question, there must be an answer.

Thus we can ask what the Framers meant when they gave Congress the power to regulate interstate and foreign commerce, and we emerge, reluctantly perhaps, with the reply that . . . they may not have known what they meant, that there may not have been any semantic consensus. The Convention was not a seminar in analytic philosophy or linguistic analysis. Commerce was *commerce*— and if different interpretations of the word arose, later generations could worry about the problem of definition. The delegates were in a hurry to get a new government established; when definitional arguments arose, they characteristically took refuge in ambiguity. If different men voted for the same proposition for varying reasons, that was politics (and still is); if later generations were unsettled by this lack of precision, that would be their problem.

There was a good deal of definitional pluralism with respect to the problems the delegates did discuss, but when we move to the question of extrapolated intentions, we enter the realm of spiritualism. When men in our time, for instance, launch into elaborate talmudic exegesis to demonstrate that federal aid to parochial schools is (or is not) in accord with the intentions of the men who established the Republic and endorsed the Bill of Rights, they are engaging in historical Extra-Sensory Perception. (If one were to join this E. S. P. contingent for a minute, he might suggest that the hard-boiled politicians who wrote the Constitution and Bill of Rights would chuckle scornfully at such an invocation of authority: obviously a politician would chart his course on the intentions of the living, not of the dead, and count the number of Catholics in his constituency.)

The Constitution, then, was not an apotheosis of "constitutionalism," a triumph of architectonic genius; it was a patch-work sewn together under the pressure of both time and events by a group of extremely talented democratic politicians. They refused to attempt the establishment of a strong, centralized sovereignty on the principle of legislative supremacy for the excellent reason that the people would not accept it. They risked their political fortunes by opposing the established doctrines of state sovereignty because they were convinced that the existing system was leading to national impotence and probably foreign domination. For two years, they worked to get a convention established. For over three months, in what must have seemed to the faithful participants an endless process of give-and-take, they reasoned, cajoled, threatened, and bargained amongst themselves. The result was a Constitution which the people, in fact, by democratic processes, did accept, and a new and far better national government was established.

Beginning with the inspired propaganda of Hamilton, Madison and Jay, the ideological build-up got under way. *The Federalist* had little impact on the ratification of the Constitution, except perhaps in New York, but this volume had enormous influence on the image of the Constitution in the minds of future generations, particularly on historians and political scientists who have an innate fondness for theoretical symmetry. Yet, while the shades of Locke and Montesquieu *may* have been hovering in the background, and the delegates *may* have been unconscious instruments of a transcendent *telos*, the careful observer of the day-to-day work of the Convention finds no over-arching principles. The "separation of powers" to him seems to be a by-product of suspicion, and "federalism" he views as a *pis aller*, as the farthest point the delegates felt they could go in the destruction of state power without themselves inviting repudiation.

To conclude, the Constitution was neither a victory for abstract theory nor a great practical success. Well over half a million men had to die on the battlefields of the Civil War before certain constitutional principles could be defined—a baleful consideration which is somehow overlooked in our customary tributes to the farsighted genius of the Framers and to the supposed American talent for "constitutionalism." The Constitution was, however, a vivid demonstration of effective democratic political action, and of the forging of a national elite which literally persuaded its countrymen to hoist themselves by their own boot straps. American pro-consuls would be wise not to translate the Constitution into Japanese, or Swahili, or treat it as a work of semi-Divine origin; but when students of comparative politics examine the process of nation-building in countries newly freed from colonial rule, they may find the American experience instructive as a classic example of the potentialities of a democratic elite.

NOTES

1. The view that the right to vote in the states was severely circumscribed by property qualifications has been thoroughly discredited in recent years. See Chilton Williamson, *American Suffrage from Property to Democracy, 1760–1860* (Princeton, 1960). The contemporary position is that John Dickinson actually knew what he was talking about when he argued that there would be little opposition to vesting the right of suffrage in freeholders since "The great mass of our Citizens is composed at this time of freeholders, and will be pleased with it." Max Farrand, *Records of the Federal Convention*, Vol. 2, p. 202 (New Haven, 1911). (Henceforth cited as *Farrand.*)

2. The classic statement of the *coup d'etat* theory is, of course, Charles A. Beard, *An Economic Interpretation of the Constitution of the United States* (New York, 1913). . . .

3. "[T]he situation of the general government, if it can be called a government, is shaken to its foundation, and liable to be overturned by every blast. In a word, it is at an end; and, unless a remedy is soon applied, anarchy and confusion will inevitably ensue." Washington to Jefferson, May 30, 1787, *Farrand*, III, 31. See also Irving Brant, *James Madison, The Nationalist* (New York, 1948), ch. 25.

4. Merrill Jensen, *The New Nation* (New York, 1950). Interestingly enough, Prof. Jensen virtually ignores international relations in his laudatory treatment of the government under the Articles of Confederation.

5. The story of James Madison's cultivation of Washington is told by Brant, *op. cit.*, pp. 394–97.

6. The "message center" being the Congress; nineteen members of Congress were simultaneously delegates to the Convention. One gets a sense of this coordination of effort from Broadus Mitchell, *Alexander Hamilton, Youth to Maturity* (New York, 1957), ch. 22.

7. The Annapolis Convention, called for the previous year, turned into a shambles: only five states sent commissioners, only three states were legally represented, and the instructions to delegates named varied quite widely from state to state. Clinton and others of his persuasion may have thought this disaster would put an end to the drive for reform. See Mitchell, *op. cit.*, pp. 362–67; Brant, *op. cit.*, pp. 375–87.

8. See Hamilton M. Bishop, *Why Rhode Island Opposed the Federal Constitution* (Providence, 1950) for a careful analysis of the labyrinthine political course of Rhode Island. For background see David S. Lovejoy, *Rhode Island Politics and the American Revolution* (Providence, 1958).

9. The terms "radical" and "conservative" have been bandied about a good deal in connection with the Constitution. This usage is nonsense if it is employed to distinguish between two economic "classes"—*e.g.,* radical debtors versus conservative creditors, radical farmers versus conservative capitalists, etc.—because there was no polarization along this line of division; the same types of people turned up on both sides. And many were hard to place in these terms: does one treat Robert Morris as a debtor or a creditor? or James Wilson? See Robert E Brown,

Charles Beard and the Constitution (Princeton, 1956), passim. The one line of division that holds up is between those deeply attached to states'-rights and those who felt that the Confederation was bankrupt. Thus, curiously, some of the most narrow-minded, parochial spokesmen of the time have earned the designation "radical" while those most willing to experiment and alter the *status quo* have been dubbed "conservative"! See Cecelia Kenyon, "Men of Little Faith," *William and Mary Quarterly*, Vol. 12, p. 3 (1955).

10. Yet, there was little objection to this crucial modification from any quarter—there almost seems to have been a gentlemen's agreement that Rhode Island's *liberum veto* had to be destroyed.

11. See Mason's letter to his son, May 27, 1787, in which he endorsed secrecy as "a proper precaution to prevent mistakes and misrepresentation until the business shall have been completed, when the whole may have a very different complexion from that in which the several crude and indigested parts might in their first shape appear if submitted to the public eye." *Farrand*, III, 28.

12. See Madison to Jefferson, June 6, 1787, *Farrand*, III, 35.

13. Cited in Charles Warren, *The Making of the Constitution* (Boston, 1928), p. 138.

14. "I hold it for a fundamental point, that an individual independence of the states is utterly irreconcilable with the idea of an aggregate sovereignty," Madison to Randolph, cited in Brant, *op. cit.*, p. 416.

15. The Randolph Plan was presented on May 29, see *Farrand*, I, 18–23; the state legislatures retained only the power to *nominate* candidates for the upper chamber. Madison's view of the appropriate position of the states emerged even more strikingly in Yates' record of his speech on June 29: "Some contend that states are sovereign when in fact they are only political societies. There is a gradation of power in all societies, from the lowest corporation to the highest sovereign. The states never possessed the essential rights of sovereignty. . . . The states, at present, are only great corporations, having the power of making by-laws, and these are effectual only if they are not contradictory to the general confederation. The states ought to be placed under the control of the general government—at least as much so as they formerly were under the king and British parliament." *Farrand*, I, 471. Forty-six years later, after Yates' "Notes" had been published, Madison tried to explain this statement away as a misinterpretation: he did not flatly deny the authenticity of Yates' record, but attempted a defense that was half justification and half evasion. Madison to W. C. Rives, Oct. 21, 1833. *Farrand*, III, 521–24.

16. Resolution 6.

17. *Ibid.*

18. See the discussions on May 30 and 31. "Mr. Charles Pinkney wished to know of Mr. Randolph whether he meant to abolish the State Governts. altogether . . . Mr. Butler said he had not made up his mind on the subject and was open to the light which discussion might throw on it . . . Genl. Pinkney expressed a doubt . . . Mr. Gerry seemed to entertain the same doubt." *Farrand*, I, 33–34. There were no denunciations—though it should perhaps be added that Luther Martin had not yet arrived.

19. *Farrand*, I, 54. (Italics added.)

20. *Ibid.*, p. 242. Delaware's delegates had been instructed by their general assembly to maintain in any new system the voting equality of the states. *Farrand*, III, 574.

21. *Ibid.*, p. 240.

22. *Ibid.*, p. 178.

23. *Ibid.*, p. 274.

24. *Ibid.*, pp. 275–76.

25. "But it is said that this national government is to act on individuals and not on states; and cannot a federal government be so framed as to operate in the same way? It surely may." *Ibid.*, pp. 182–83; also *ibid.* at p. 276.

26. *Farrand*, III, 613.

27. *Farrand*, I, 177.

28. *Ibid.*, p. 182.

29. *Ibid.*, p. 255.

30. J. C. Hamilton, cited *ibid.*, p. 293.

31. See, *e.g.*, Mitchell, *op. cit.*, p. 381.

32. Hamilton to Washington, July 3, 1787, *Farrand*, III, 53.

33. A reconstruction of the Hamilton Plan is found in *Farrand*, III, 617–30.

34. Said William Samuel Johnson on June 21: "A gentleman from New-York, with boldness and decision, proposed a system totally different from both [Virginia and New Jersey]; and though he has been praised by every body, he has been supported by none." *Farrand*, I, 363.

35. See his letter to Washington cited *supra* note 43.

36. *Farrand*, III, 338.

37. *Farrand*, I, 321.

38. This formulation was voted into the Randolph Plan on May 30, 1787, by a vote of six states to none, with one divided. *Farrand*, I, 30.

39. *Farrand*, I, 335–36. In agreeing, Randolph stipulated his disagreement with Ellsworth's rationale, but said he did not object to merely changing an "expression." Those who subject the Constitution to minute semantic analysis might do well to keep this instance in mind; if Randolph could so concede the deletion of "national," one may wonder if any word changes can be given much weight.

40. According to Luther Martin, he was alone on the floor and cast Maryland's vote for equality of representation. Shortly thereafter, Jenifer came on the floor and "Mr. King, from Massachusetts, valuing himself on Mr. Jenifer to divide the State of Maryland on this question . . . requested of the President that the question might be put again; however, the motion was too extraordinary in its nature to meet with success." Cited from "The Genuine Information, . . ." *Farrand*, III, 188.

41. Namely Baldwin's vote *for* equality of representation which divided Georgia—with Few absent and Pierce in New York fighting a duel, Houston voted against equality and Baldwin shifted to tie the state. Baldwin was originally from Connecticut and attended and tutored at Yale, facts which have led to much speculation about the pressures the Connecticut delegation may have brought on him to save the day (Georgia was the last state to vote) and open the way to compromise. To employ a good Russian phrase, it was certainly not an accident that Baldwin voted the way he did. See *Warren*, p. 262.

42. For various contemporary comments, see *Warren*, pp. 814–18. On Adams' technique, see Zoltan Haraszti, "The Composition of Adams' *Defense*," in *John Adams and the Prophets of Progress* (Cambridge, 1952), ch. 9. In this connection it is interesting to check the Convention discussions for references to the authority of Locke, Montesquieu and Harrington, the theorists who have been assigned various degrees of paternal responsibility. There are no explicit references to James Harrington; one to John Locke (Luther Martin cited him on the state of

nature, *Farrand*, I, 437); and seven to Montesquieu, only one of which related to the "separation of powers" (Madison in an odd speech, which he explained in a footnote was given to help a friend rather than advance his own views, cited Montesquieu on the separation of the executive and legislative branches, *Farrand*, II, 34). This, of course, does not prove that Locke and Co. were without influence; it shifts the burden of proof, however, to those who assert ideological causality. See Benjamin F. Wright, "The Origins of the Separation of Powers in America," *Economica*, Vol. 13 (1933), p. 184.

43. I share Willmoore Kendall's interpretation of Locke as a supporter of parliamentary supremacy and majoritarianism; see Kendall, *John Locke and the Doctrine of Majority Rule* (Urbana, 1941). Kendall's general position has recently received strong support in the definitive edition and commentary of Peter Laslett, *Locke's Two Treatises of Government* (Cambridge, 1960).

44. The American Locke is best delineated in Carl Becker, *The Declaration of Independence* (New York, 1948).

45. See John P. Roche, "The Electoral College: A Note on American Political Mythology," *Dissent* (Spring, 1961), pp. 197–99. The relevant debates took place July 19–26, 1787, *Farrand*, II, 50–128, and September 5–6, 1787, *ibid.*, pp. 505–31.

46. See the discussion on August 22, 1787, *Farrand*, II, 366–75; King seems to have expressed the sense of the Convention when he said, "the subject should be considered in a political light only." *Ibid.* at 373.

47. *Farrand*, II, 374. Randolph echoed his sentiment in different words.

48. Mason to Jefferson, cited in *Warren*, p. 584.

49. August 29, 1787, *Farrand*, II, 449–50.

50. *Ibid.*, p. 451. The plainest statement of the matter was put by the three North Carolina delegates (Blount, Spaight and Williamson) in their report to Governor Caswell, September 18, 1787. After noting that "no exertions have been wanting on our part to guard and promote the particular interest of North Carolina," they went on to explain the basis of the negotiations in cold-blooded fashion: "While we were taking so much care to guard ourselves against being over reached and to form rules of Taxation that might operate in our favour, it is not to be supposed that our Northern Brethren were Inattentive to their particular Interest. A navigation Act or the power to regulate Commerce in the Hands of the National Government . . . is what the Southern States have given in Exchange for the advantages we Mentioned." They concluded by explaining that while the Constitution did deal with other matters besides taxes—"there are other Considerations of great Magnitude involved in the system"— they would not take up valuable time with boring details! *Farrand*, III, 83–84.

51. See John C. Calhoun, *A Disquisition on Government* (New York, 1943), pp. 21–25, 38. Calhoun differed from Mason, and others in the Convention who urged the two-thirds requirement, by advocating a functional or interest veto rather than some sort of special majority, *i.e.*, he abandoned the search for quantitative checks in favor of a qualitative solution.

52. The Committee on Detail altered the general grant of legislative power envisioned by the Virginia Plan into a series of specific grants; these were examined closely between August 16 and August 23. One day only was devoted to the Judicial Article, August 27, and since no one raised the question of judicial review of *Federal* statutes, no light was cast on the matter. A number of random comments on the power of the judiciary were scattered throughout the discussions, but there was another variable which deprives them of much probative value: the

proposed Council of Revision which would have joined the Executive with the judges in *legislative* review. Madison and Wilson, for example, favored this technique—which had nothing in common with what we think of as judicial review except that judges were involved in the task.

53. Or so Madison stated, *Farrand*, II, 643. Wilson too may have contributed; he was close to Franklin and delivered the frail old gentleman's speeches for him.

54. See a very interesting letter, from an unknown source in Philadelphia, to Jefferson, October 11, 1787: "Randolph wishes it well, & it is thought would have signed it, but he wanted to be on a footing with a popular rival." *Farrand*, III, 104. Madison, writing Jefferson a full account on October 24, 1787, put the matter more delicately—he was working hard on Randolph to win him for ratification: "[Randolph] was not inveterate in his opposition, and grounded his refusal to subscribe pretty much on his unwillingness to commit himself, so as not to be at liberty to be governed by further lights on the subject." *Ibid.*, p. 135.

55. See *Elliot's Debates on the Federal Constitution* (Washington, 1836), Vol. 3, pp. 436–38.

56. This should be quoted to give the full flavor: "Without vanity, I may say I have had different experience of [militia] service from that of [Henry]. It was my fortune to be a soldier of my country. . . . I saw what the honorable gentleman did not see—our men fighting. . . ." *Ibid.*, p. 178,

57. *Ibid.*, p. 329.

58. Washington offered him the Chief Justiceship in 1796, but he declined; Charles Warren, *The Supreme Court in United States History* (Boston, 1947), Vol. 1, p. 139.

59. He was a zealous prosecutor of seditions in the period 1798–1800; with Justice Samuel Chase, like himself an alleged "radical" at the time of the Constitutional Convention, Martin hunted down Jeffersonian heretics. See James M. Smith, *Freedom's Fetters* (Ithaca, 1956), pp. 342–43.

2-2

Federalist No. 10

James Madison
November 22, 1787

When one reads this tightly reasoned, highly conceptual essay, it is easy to forget that it was published in a New York newspaper with the purpose of persuading that state's ratification convention to endorse the Constitution. Although after ratification this essay went unnoticed for more than a century, today, it stands atop virtually every scholar's ranking of The Federalist *papers. Written in November 1787, it was James Madison's first contribution to the ratification debate, and it develops a rationale for a large, diverse republic that he had employed several times at the Convention. His allies admired the inventive way it rebutted opponents' arguments that only small republics were safe. The modern reader can appreciate how it resonates with the nation's diversity of interests in the twenty-first century. And everyone, then and now, can admire the solid logic employed by this smart man, who begins with a few unobjectionable assumptions and derives from them the counterintuitive conclusion that the surest way to avoid the tyranny of faction is to design a political system in which factions are numerous and none can dominate. This essay repays careful reading.*

AMONG THE NUMEROUS advantages promised by a well-constructed Union, none deserves to be more accurately developed than its tendency to break and control the violence of faction. The friend of popular governments never finds himself so much alarmed for their character and fate, as when he contemplates their propensity to this dangerous vice. He will not fail, therefore, to set a due value on any plan which, without violating the principles to which he is attached, provides a proper cure for it. The instability, injustice, and confusion introduced into the public councils, have, in truth, been the mortal diseases under which popular governments have everywhere perished; as they continue to be the favorite and fruitful topics from which the adversaries to liberty derive their most specious declamations. The valuable improvements made by the American constitutions on the popular models, both ancient and modern, cannot certainly be too much admired; but it would be an unwarrantable partiality, to contend that they have as effectually obviated the danger on this side, as was wished and expected.

Complaints are everywhere heard from our most considerate and virtuous citizens, equally the friends of public and private faith, and of public and personal liberty, that our governments are too unstable, that the public good is disregarded in the conflicts of rival parties, and that measures are too often decided, not according to the rules of justice and the rights of the minor party, but by the superior force of an interested and overbearing majority. However anxiously we may wish that these complaints had no foundation, the evidence, of known facts will not permit us to deny that they are in some degree true. It will be found, indeed, on a candid review of our situation, that some of the distresses under which we labor have been erroneously charged on the operation of our governments; but it will be found, at the same time, that other causes will not alone account for many of our heaviest misfortunes; and, particularly, for that prevailing and increasing distrust of public engagements, and alarm for private rights, which are echoed from one end of the continent to the other. These must be chiefly, if not wholly, effects of the unsteadiness and injustice with which a factious spirit has tainted our public administrations.

By a faction, I understand a number of citizens, whether amounting to a majority or a minority of the whole, who are united and actuated by some common impulse of passion, or of interest, adversed to the rights of other citizens, or to the permanent and aggregate interests of the community.

There are two methods of curing the mischiefs of faction: the one, by removing its causes; the other, by controlling its effects. There are again two methods of removing the causes of faction: the one, by destroying the liberty which is essential to its existence; the other, by giving to every citizen the same opinions, the same passions, and the same interests.

It could never be more truly said than of the first remedy, that it was worse than the disease. Liberty is to faction what air is to fire, an aliment without which it instantly expires. But it could not be less folly to abolish liberty, which is essential to political life, because it nourishes faction, than it would be to wish the annihilation of air, which is essential to animal life, because it imparts to fire its destructive agency.

The second expedient is as impracticable as the first would be unwise. As long as the reason of man continues fallible, and he is at liberty to exercise it, different opinions will be formed. As long as the connection subsists between his reason and his self-love, his opinions and his passions will have a reciprocal influence on each other; and the former will be objects to which the latter will attach themselves. The diversity in the faculties of men, from which the rights of property originate, is not less an insuperable obstacle to a uniformity of interests. The protection of these faculties is the first object of government. From the protection of different and unequal faculties of acquiring property, the possession of different degrees and kinds of property immediately results; and from the influence of these on the sentiments and views of the respective proprietors, ensues a division of the society into different interests and parties.

The latent causes of faction are thus sown in the nature of man; and we see them everywhere brought into different degrees of activity, according to the different circumstances of civil society. A zeal for different opinions concerning religion, concerning government, and many other points, as well of speculation as of practice; an attachment to different leaders ambitiously contending for preeminence and power; or to persons of other descriptions whose fortunes have been interesting to the human passions, have, in turn, divided mankind into parties, inflamed them with mutual animosity, and rendered them much more disposed to vex and oppress each other than to co-operate for their common good. So strong is this propensity of mankind to fall into mutual animosities, that where no substantial occasion presents itself, the most frivolous and fanciful distinctions have been sufficient to kindle their unfriendly passions and excite their most violent conflicts. But the most common and durable source of factions has been the various and unequal distribution of property. Those who hold and those who are without property have ever formed distinct interests in society. Those who are creditors, and those who are debtors, fall under a like discrimination. A landed interest, a manufacturing interest, a mercantile interest, a moneyed interest, with many lesser interests, grow up of necessity in civilized nations, and divide them into different classes, actuated by different sentiments and views. The regulation of these various and interfering interests forms the principal task of modern legislation, and involves the spirit of party and faction in the necessary and ordinary operations of the government.

No man is allowed to be a judge in his own cause, because his interest would certainly bias his judgment, and, not improbably, corrupt his integrity. With equal, nay with greater reason, a body of men are unfit to be both judges and parties at the same time; yet what are many of the most important acts of legislation, but so many judicial determinations, not indeed concerning the rights of single persons, but concerning the rights of large bodies of citizens? And what are the different classes of legislators but advocates and parties to the causes which they determine? Is a law proposed concerning private debts? It is a question to which the creditors are parties on one side and the debtors on the other. Justice ought to hold the balance between them. Yet the parties are, and must be, themselves the judges; and the most numerous party, or, in other words, the most powerful faction must be expected to prevail. Shall domestic manufactures be encouraged, and in what degree, by restrictions on foreign manufactures? are questions which would be differently decided by the landed and the manufacturing classes, and probably by neither with a sole regard to justice and the public good. The apportionment of taxes on the various descriptions of property is an act which seems to require the most exact impartiality; yet there is, perhaps, no legislative act in which greater opportunity and temptation are given to a predominant party to trample on the rules of justice. Every shilling with which they overburden the inferior number, is a shilling saved to their own pockets.

It is in vain to say that enlightened statesmen will be able to adjust these clashing interests, and render them all subservient to the public good. Enlightened statesmen will not always be at the helm. Nor, in many cases, can such an adjustment be made at all without taking into view indirect and remote considerations, which will rarely prevail over the immediate interest which one party may find in disregarding the rights of another or the good of the whole. The inference to which we are brought is, that the causes of faction cannot be removed, and that relief is only to be sought in the means of controlling its effects.

If a faction consists of less than a majority, relief is supplied by the republican principle, which enables the majority to defeat its sinister views by regular vote. It may clog the administration, it may convulse the society; but it will be unable to execute and mask its violence under the forms of the Constitution. When a majority is included in a faction, the form of popular government, on the other hand, enables it to sacrifice to its ruling passion or interest both the public good and the rights of other citizens. To secure the public good and private rights against the danger of such a faction, and at the same time to preserve the spirit and the form of popular government, is then the great object to which our inquiries are directed. Let me add that it is the great desideratum by which this form of government can be rescued from the opprobrium under which it has so long labored, and be recommended to the esteem and adoption of mankind.

By what means is this object attainable? Evidently by one of two only. Either the existence of the same passion or interest in a majority at the same time must be prevented, or the majority, having such coexistent passion or interest, must be rendered, by their number and local situation, unable to concert and carry into effect schemes of oppression. If the impulse and the opportunity be suffered to coincide, we well know that neither moral nor religious motives can be relied on as an adequate control. They are not found to be such on the injustice and violence of individuals, and lose their efficacy in proportion to the number combined together, that is, in proportion as their efficacy becomes needful.

From this view of the subject it may be concluded that a pure democracy, by which I mean a society consisting of a small number of citizens, who assemble and administer the government in person, can admit of no cure for the mischiefs of faction. A common passion or interest will, in almost every case, be felt by a majority of the whole; a communication and concert result from the form of government itself; and there is nothing to check the inducements to sacrifice the weaker party or an obnoxious individual. Hence it is that such democracies have ever been spectacles of turbulence and contention; have ever been found incompatible with personal security or the rights of property; and have in general been as short in their lives as they have been violent in their deaths. Theoretic politicians, who have patronized this species of government, have erroneously supposed that by reducing mankind to a perfect equality in their political rights, they would, at the same time, be perfectly equalized and assimilated in their possessions, their opinions, and their passions.

A republic, by which I mean a government in which the scheme of representation takes place, opens a different prospect, and promises the cure for which we are seeking. Let us examine the points in which it varies from pure democracy, and we shall comprehend both the nature of the cure and the efficacy which it must derive from the Union.

The two great points of difference between a democracy and a republic are: first, the delegation of the government, in the latter, to a small number of citizens elected by the rest; secondly, the greater number of citizens, and greater sphere of country, over which the latter may be extended. The effect of the first difference is, on the one hand, to refine and enlarge the public views, by passing them through the medium of a chosen body of citizens, whose wisdom may best discern the true interest of their country, and whose patriotism and love of justice will be least likely to sacrifice it to temporary or partial considerations. Under such a regulation, it may well happen that the public voice, pronounced by the representatives of the people, will be more consonant to the public good than if pronounced by the people themselves, convened for the purpose. On the other hand, the effect may be inverted. Men of factious tempers, of local prejudices, or of sinister designs, may, by intrigue, by corruption, or by other means, first obtain the suffrages, and then betray the interests, of the people. The question resulting is, whether small or extensive republics are more favorable to the election of proper guardians of the public weal; and it is clearly decided in favor of the latter by two obvious considerations.

In the first place, it is to be remarked that, however small the republic may be, the representatives must be raised to a certain number, in order to guard against the cabals of a few; and that, however large it may be, they must be limited to a certain number, in order to guard against the confusion of a multitude. Hence, the number of representatives in the two cases not being in proportion to that of the two constituents, and being proportionally greater in the small republic, it follows that, if the proportion of fit characters be not less in the large than in the small republic, the former will present a greater option, and consequently a greater probability of a fit choice.

In the next place, as each representative will be chosen by a greater number of citizens in the large than in the small republic, it will be more difficult for unworthy candidates to practice with success the vicious arts by which elections are too often carried; and the suffrages of the people being more free, will be more likely to centre in men who possess the most attractive merit and the most diffusive and established characters.

It must be confessed that in this, as in most other cases, there is a mean, on both sides of which inconveniences will be found to lie. By enlarging too much the number of electors, you render the representatives too little acquainted with all their local circumstances and lesser interests; as by reducing it too much, you render him unduly attached to these, and too little fit to comprehend and pursue great and national objects. The federal Constitution forms a happy combination in this respect; the great and aggregate interests being referred to the national, the local and particular to the State legislatures.

The other point of difference is, the greater number of citizens and extent of territory which may be brought within the compass of republican than of democratic government; and it is this circumstance principally which renders factious combinations less to be dreaded in the former than in the latter. The smaller the society, the fewer probably will be the distinct parties and interests composing it; the fewer the distinct parties and interests, the more frequently will a majority be found of the same party; and the smaller the number of individuals composing a majority, and the smaller the compass within which they are placed, the more easily will they concert and execute their plans of oppression. Extend the sphere, and you take in a greater variety of parties and interests; you make it less probable that a majority of the whole will have a common motive to invade the rights of other citizens; or if such a common motive exists, it will be more difficult for all who feel it to discover their own strength, and to act in unison with each other. Besides other impediments, it may be remarked that, where there is a consciousness of unjust or dishonorable purposes, communication is always checked by distrust in proportion to the number whose concurrence is necessary.

Hence, it clearly appears, that the same advantage which a republic has over a democracy, in controlling the effects of faction, is enjoyed by a large over a small republic,—is enjoyed by the Union over the States composing it. Does the advantage consist in the substitution of representatives whose enlightened views and virtuous sentiments render them superior to local prejudices and schemes of injustice? It will not be denied that the representation of the Union will be most likely to possess these requisite endowments. Does it consist in the greater security afforded by a greater variety of parties, against the event of any one party being able to outnumber and oppress the rest? In an equal degree does the increased variety of parties comprised within the Union, increase this security. Does it, in fine, consist in the greater obstacles opposed to the concert and accomplishment of the secret wishes of an unjust and interested majority? Here, again, the extent of the Union gives it the most palpable advantage.

The influence of factious leaders may kindle a flame within their particular States, but will be unable to spread a general conflagration through the other States. A religious sect may degenerate into a political faction in a part of the Confederacy; but the variety of sects dispersed over the entire face of it must secure the national councils against any danger from that source. A rage for paper money, for an abolition of debts, for an equal division of property, or for any other improper or wicked project, will be less apt to pervade the whole body of the Union than a particular member of it; in the same proportion as such a malady is more likely to taint a particular county or district, than an entire State.

In the extent and proper structure of the Union, therefore, we behold a republican remedy for the diseases most incident to republican government. And according to the degree of pleasure and pride we feel in being republicans, ought to be our zeal in cherishing the spirit and supporting the character of Federalists.

2-3

Federalist No. 51

James Madison
February 8, 1788.

Where Federalist No. 10 finds solution to tyranny in the way society is orga-
nized, No. 51 turns its attention to the Constitution. In a representative
democracy citizens must delegate authority to their representatives. But what
is to prevent these ambitious politicians from feathering their own nests or
usurping power altogether at their constituencies' expense? The solution,
according to James Madison, is to be found in "pitting ambition against ambi-
tion," just as the solution in No. 10 lay in pitting interest against interest. In
this essay, Madison explains how the Constitution's system of checks and bal-
ances will accomplish this goal.

TO WHAT EXPEDIENT, then, shall we finally resort, for maintaining in practice the
necessary partition of power among the several departments, as laid down in the
Constitution? The only answer that can be given is, that as all these exterior provisions are found to be inadequate, the defect must be supplied, by so contriving
the interior structure of the government as that its several constituent parts may,
by their mutual relations, be the means of keeping each other in their proper
places. Without presuming to undertake a full development of this important
idea, I will hazard a few general observations, which may perhaps place it in a
clearer light, and enable us to form a more correct judgment of the principles
and structure of the government planned by the convention.

In order to lay a due foundation for that separate and distinct exercise of the
different powers of government, which to a certain extent is admitted on all
hands to be essential to the preservation of liberty, it is evident that each department should have a will of its own; and consequently should be so constituted
that the members of each should have as little agency as possible in the appointment of the members of the others. Were this principle rigorously adhered to, it
would require that all the appointments for the supreme executive, legislative,
and judiciary magistracies should be drawn from the same fountain of authority,
the people, through channels having no communication whatever with one
another. Perhaps such a plan of constructing the several departments would be
less difficult in practice than it may in contemplation appear. Some difficulties,

however, and some additional expense would attend the execution of it. Some deviations, therefore, from the principle must be admitted. In the constitution of the judiciary department in particular, it might be inexpedient to insist rigorously on the principle: first, because peculiar qualifications being essential in the members, the primary consideration ought to be to select that mode of choice which best secures these qualifications; secondly, because the permanent tenure by which the appointments are held in that department, must soon destroy all sense of dependence on the authority conferring them.

It is equally evident, that the members of each department should be as little dependent as possible on those of the others, for the emoluments annexed to their offices. Were the executive magistrate, or the judges, not independent of the legislature in this particular, their independence in every other would be merely nominal.

But the great security against a gradual concentration of the several powers in the same department, consists in giving to those who administer each department the necessary constitutional means and personal motives to resist encroachments of the others. The provision for defense must in this, as in all other cases, be made commensurate to the danger of attack. Ambition must be made to counteract ambition. The interest of the man must be connected with the constitutional rights of the place. It may be a reflection on human nature, that such devices should be necessary to control the abuses of government. But what is government itself, but the greatest of all reflections on human nature? If men were angels, no government would be necessary. If angels were to govern men, neither external nor internal controls on government would be necessary. In framing a government which is to be administered by men over men, the great difficulty lies in this: you must first enable the government to control the governed; and in the next place oblige it to control itself. A dependence on the people is, no doubt, the primary control on the government; but experience has taught mankind the necessity of auxiliary precautions.

This policy of supplying, by opposite and rival interests, the defect of better motives, might be traced through the whole system of human affairs, private as well as public. We see it particularly displayed in all the subordinate distributions of power, where the constant aim is to divide and arrange the several offices in such a manner as that each may be a check on the other; that the private interest of every individual may be a sentinel over the public rights. These inventions of prudence cannot be less requisite in the distribution of the supreme powers of the State.

But it is not possible to give to each department an equal power of self-defense. In republican government, the legislative authority necessarily predominates. The remedy for this inconveniency is to divide the legislature into different branches; and to render them, by different modes of election and different principles of action, as little connected with each other as the nature of their common functions and their common dependence on the society will admit. It may even be necessary to guard against dangerous encroachments by still further precautions. As the weight of the legislative authority requires that it should be thus divided, the weakness of the executive may require, on the other hand, that it should be fortified. An absolute negative on the legislature appears, at first view, to be the natural defense with which the executive magistrate should be armed. But perhaps it would be neither altogether safe nor alone sufficient. On ordinary occasions it might not be exerted with the requisite firmness, and on extraordinary occasions it might be perfidiously abused. May not this defect of an absolute negative be supplied by some qualified connection between this weaker department and the weaker branch of the stronger department, by which the latter may be led to support the constitutional rights of the former, without being too much detached from the rights of its own department? . . .

Showdown: The Election of 1800

James MacGregor Burns

Constitutions are contracts. For each officeholder, they identify a network of rights and obligations. And they specify the terms that entitle a given politician to occupy an office. Like all contracts, constitutions can be broken if one "party" reneges on its obligations when it finds its interest better served by doing so. Therefore one of the most critical tests of a constitution arises the first time those who control the government must surrender power to their opponents. In this sense, the election of 1800 was a critical event, a kind of behavioral ratification of the U.S. Constitution. The following excerpt from James MacGregor Burns's broader investigation into the Constitution's early development conveys the palpable tension felt by all participants to the first serious challenge to the governing Federalist political party. When to the surprise of nearly everyone the Republicans won control of the presidency and both houses of Congress, a true constitutional crisis was at hand. Federalist politicians worried that if the "radical" Republicans were allowed to assume control, they would import the French Revolution to America. Republican politicians worried that the Federalists would try some subterfuge to change the outcome of the election or simply refuse to surrender power. Many people feared that "ballots would give way to bullets." That the Federalists, despite their deep concerns, surrendered control of government, just as the Constitution prescribed, reinforced future generations' confidence that the Constitution was a contract opposing politicians would live by.

ON THE EVE of the last year of the century, American leaders were intent more on political prospects than moral. The looming national elections were tending to focus their minds. The decisive figure in this election would be Thomas Jefferson. But Jefferson hardly appeared decisive at the time. His political course during the late 1790s had mirrored the political uncertainties and party gropings of those years. Tentatively he looked for some kind of North-South combination.

"If a prospect could be once opened upon us of the penetration of truth into the eastern States; if the people there, who are unquestionably republicans, could discover that they have been duped into the support of measures calculated to

Source: James MacGregor Burns, *The Vineyard of Liberty* (New York: Vintage Books, 1983), 144–155.

sap the very foundations of republicanism, we might still hope for salvation," Jefferson had written Aaron Burr some weeks after Adams' inauguration in 1797. ". . . But will that region ever awake to the true state of things? Can the middle, Southern and Western States hold on till they awake?" He asked Burr for a "comfortable solution" to these "painful questions."

Immensely flattered, Burr requested an early meeting with the Vice-President in Philadelphia. Jefferson now became more active as party leader, working closely with Madison in Virginia and with Gallatin in the House of Representatives. Following the election setbacks to Republicans in 1798, he redoubled his efforts especially as a party propagandist. He asked every man to "lay his purpose & his pen" to the cause; coaxed local Republican leaders into writing pamphlets and letters to editors; stressed the issues of peace, liberty, and states' rights; turned his office into a kind of clearinghouse for Republican propaganda. "The engine is the press," he told Madison.

Hundreds of other men too were busy with politics, but like Jefferson earlier, in an atmosphere of uncertainty and suspense. Intellectual leaders—clergymen, editors, and others—were still preaching against the whole idea of an open, clear-cut party and election battle. Party formations were still primitive in many areas. Even fiercer than the conflict between Federalists and Republicans was the feuding between factions within the parties—especially between the Adams following and the Hamilton "cabal." Certain high Federalists were hinting at the need for armed repression of the opposition, particularly in the event of war, and Jefferson and Madison were openly pushing the Kentucky and Virginia resolutions—a strategy of nullification and even secession still in flat contradiction to the idea of two-party opposition and rotation in power. All these factors enhanced the most pressing question of all—could the American republic, could any republic, survive a decisive challenge by the "outs" to the "ins"? Or would ballots give way to bullets?

Not intellectual theorizing but heated issues, fierce political ambitions, and the practical need to win a scheduled national election compelled the political testing of 1800.

In Philadelphia, John Adams contemplated the coming test with apprehension and anger. Political and personal affairs had gone badly for him since the euphoria of '98. Abigail was ill a good part of the time, and his beloved son Charles, a bankrupt and an alcoholic, was dying in New York. As proud, captious, sensitive, and sermonizing as ever, he hated much of the day-to-day business of the presidency, and he longed to take sanctuary in Quincy; but he desperately wanted to win in 1800, to confound his enemies, to complete his work. He tried to lend some direction and unity to the Federalists, but he was handicapped by his concept of leadership as a solitary search for the morally correct course, regardless of day-to-day pressures from factions and interests. He sensed, probably correctly, that his party should take a more centrist course to win in 1800. But his own moderate positions on foreign and domestic policy left him isolated between high Federalists and moderate Republicans.

The Fries "rebellion" epitomized his difficulty. A direct federal tax on land and houses, enacted by Congress in 1798, touched off the next winter an uprising by several hundred Pennsylvanians—and especially by the women, who poured scalding water on assessors who came to measure their windows. John Fries, a traveling auctioneer, led a band of men to Bethlehem, where they forced the release of others jailed for resisting the tax. The President promptly labeled the act treasonable and ordered Fries and his band arrested. Unlucky enough to be tried before Justice Samuel Chase, the auctioneer was convicted of treason and, amid great hubbub, sentenced to die. Later the President, without consulting his Cabinet, pardoned Fries—only to arouse the fury of high Federalists. Not the least of these was Alexander Hamilton, who, his biographer says, would have preferred to load the gibbets of Pennsylvania with Friesians and viewed the pardon as one more example of Adams' petulant indecisiveness.

By the spring of 1800 Adams' wrath against the Hamiltonians in his Cabinet—especially Pickering and McHenry—was about to burst out of control. Politically the President faced a dilemma: he wished to lead the Federalists toward the center of the political spectrum, in order to head off any Republican effort to preempt the same ground, but he feared to alienate the high Federalists and disrupt his party when unity was desperately needed. His uncertainty and frustration only exacerbated his anger. One day, as he was talking with McHenry about routine matters, his anger boiled over. He accused the frightened McHenry to his face of being subservient to Hamilton—a man, he went on, who was the "greatest intriguant in the world—a man devoid of every moral principle—a bastard and as much a foreigner as Gallatin." Adams accepted McHenry's resignation on the spot. A few days later he demanded that Pickering quit. When the Secretary of State refused, Adams summarily sacked him. Oddly, he did not fire Secretary of the Treasury Wolcott, who was Hamilton's main conduit to the high Federalists in Adams' administration.

Thomas Jefferson, watching these events from his vice-presidential perch, had the advantage of being close to the government, if not inside it, with little of the burden of power and none of the responsibility. By early 1800 he was emerging clearly as the national leader of the Republicans. Gone were the doubts and vacillations of earlier days. He was eager to take on the "feds," as he called them, to vanquish their whole philosophy and practice of government, to establish his party and himself in control of Congress and the presidency. He consciously assumed leadership of his party. Unable to campaign across the country—

stumping was contrary to both his own nature and the custom of the day—he cast political lines into key areas through letters and friends.

His meeting with Burr paid off handsomely. The dapper little New Yorker set to work uniting New York Republicans against the divided Federalists. Then he organized his lieutenants tightly on a ward-by-ward basis; had the voters' names card-indexed, along with their political background, attitudes, and need for transportation on election day; set up committees for house-to-house canvassing for funds; pressed more affluent Republicans for bigger donations; organized rallies; converted Tammany into a campaign organization; debated Hamilton publicly; and spent ten hours straight at the polls on the last day of the three-day state election. He won a resounding victory in the election of state assemblymen—and got full credit for it from Republican leaders in Philadelphia.

The New York victory buoyed Jefferson's hopes. He recognized the critical role of the central states, and how they hung together. "If the *city* election of N York is in favor of the Republican ticket, the issue will be republican," he had instructed Madison; "if the federal ticket for the city of N York prevails, the probabilities will be in favor of a federal issue, because it would then require a republican vote both from Jersey and Pennsylva to preponderate against New York, on which we could not count with any confidence." What Jefferson called the "Political arithmetic" looked so good after the New York victory that he shrugged off the Federalist "lies" about him. He would not try to answer them, "for while I should be engaged with one, they would publich twenty new ones." He had confidence in the voters' common sense. "Thirty years of public life have enabled most of those who read newspapers to judge of one for themselves."

Doubtless Jefferson was too optimistic. The Federalists in 1800 were still a formidable party. While they were losing some of the vigorous younger men to the Republicans, they were still the party of Washington and Adams and Jay and Pinckney and Hamilton, and the vehicle of a younger generation represented by men like John Marshall and Fisher Ames. The Federalists had never been a purely mercantile or urban party; their strength lay also in rural areas and along the rivers and other avenues of commerce into the hinterland, such as the Connecticut Valley. Adams as President had immense national prestige, if not always popularity, and his "move toward the middle" broadened the party's appeal. Stung by losses in New York, the Federalists rallied their forces in other states. In New Jersey, where women were not expressly barred from voting, they "marched their wives, daughters, and other qualified 'females' to the polls," in one historian's words, and won the state's seven electoral votes.

Not only was the parties' popular support crucial, but also the manner in which that support was translated into presidential electoral votes. The selection of presidential electors was not designed for accurate translation. For one thing, state legislatures set selection of electors on a statewide basis or on a district basis, or took on the task themselves, according to a guess by the party dominating the legislature as to which system would help that party's candidate. More and more legislatures moved to choose electors themselves, rather than by popular vote. Electors were supposed to exercise some independent judgment. But more important in 1800, the electoral system was still so novel as to be open to flagrant rigging, such as changing the method of choosing electors. Broaching to John Jay such a scheme for New York, Hamilton said that "in times like these in which we live, it will not do to be over-scrupulous." It was permissible to take such a step to "prevent an atheist in religion, and a fanatic in politics, from getting possession of the helm of state." Jay was not impressed.

And so the presidential campaign proceeded, in its noisy, slightly manipulated, but nonviolent way. During the summer candidates for state legislatures toured the districts and talked to crowds where they could find them—"even at a horse race—a cock fight—or a Methodist quarterly meeting." ...

... By fall the presidential race was reaching a climax. Slander on both sides was uncontained—and the politicos of the day were masters at it. Adams was called a would-be dictator and a "monocrat" who would make the country a monarchy and his children successors to the throne. Even Adams could smile at a story that he had sent a United States frigate to England to procure mistresses for himself. The Federalists gave even better than they got. Jefferson was an infidel, a "howling" atheist, an "intellectual voluptuary" who would "destroy religion, introduce immorality, and loosen all the bonds of society" at home. The Jacobin leader was the real debauchee, Federalists whispered, having sired mulatto children at Monticello. Somehow the voters groped their way through the invective to a sense of the genuine issues. They faced a real choice. Jefferson was still silent as a candidate, but he had repeatedly made clear his stands for a frugal government, a small Navy and Army, states' rights, the Bill of Rights liberties, a small diplomatic establishment. The Federalists had made their positions clear through legislation they had passed, or tried to pass. The election would be a showdown between men, platforms, and ideologies.

Slowly the returns came in as electors met and voted in their states. The Federalists had a moment of euphoria as Adams picked up some unexpected support. By late November the two parties were running neck and neck. For a time Federalist hopes were pinned on South Carolina, on whether Charles Cotesworth Pinckney, Adams' running mate, could deliver that state's eight electoral votes. But Pinckney could not even deliver all the Pinckneys, least of all Charles Pinckney, leader of the Republican branch of the family, who through generous offers of jobs under a Republican administration, managed to persuade enough members of the state legislature to choose a pro-Jefferson slate of electors.

By late December the total vote was in. It was Jefferson over Adams, 73 to 65. But it was also Burr over Pinckney, 73 to 64, with one of Pinckney's votes diverted to John Jay.

The Republicans had won, but Jefferson had not been elected. Burr had an equal constitutional claim to the presidency. Something new and extraordinary had happened in American politics: the parties had disciplined their ranks enough to produce the same total (73) for the two Republican running mates and an almost equal tally (65 to 64) for the two Federalists. In order to prevent votes from being thrown away, each party caucus had pledged equal support to both candidates on the ticket. To do this was to run the risk that, under the Constitution, a presidential tie vote would go to the House of Representatives for decision. Both parties knowingly ran that risk. But the politics of the lower chamber would be quite different from the politics of the electoral groups meeting separately in the state capitols. The presidential race would now be focused in the nation's capitol; it would take place in a lame-duck, Federalist-dominated House of Representatives; and each state delegation in the House, whether large or small, would have a single vote.

The remarkable result was that the Federalists had lost the presidency, but in the Congress they had the power to throw the election to either Jefferson or Burr, or possibly stall indefinitely. What would they do with this exquisite consolation prize? Most of the congressional Federalists feared Jefferson the ideologue more than they hated Burr the opportunist. "They consider Burr as actuated by ordinary ambition, Jefferson by that & the pride of the Jacobinic philosophy," high Federalist George Cabot wrote Hamilton. "The former may be satisfied by power & property, the latter must see the roots of our Society pulled up & a new course of cultivation substituted." If Burr was ambitious, slippery, and even venal, well, perhaps the Federalists could make use of such qualities; "they loved Burr for his vices," John Miller has noted. Other Federalists disagreed. No matter how much they hated Jefferson, they were not going to put into the presidency a man they considered a knave and a blackguard.

The competing forces were so counterpoised that the House of Representatives went through thirty-five ballotings, all resulting in a vote of eight states for Jefferson, six for Burr, and two divided. The stalemate lasted as long as the representatives stuck to their convictions, or biases; it ended when three men—Jefferson, Burr, and Hamilton—acted out of character. Jefferson, no longer the relaxed and diffident philosopher, responded to the looming crisis with anger, but also with decisiveness and determination. He began to act like the President-elect as soon as the unofficial returns were in; thus he wrote Robert R. Livingston to ask him to serve as Secretary of the Navy—the New Yorker declined—and incidentally to discuss the bones of a mammoth that had been found near New

York. He wrote Burr, congratulating him on the election results but implying ever so delicately that Jefferson expected him to serve as Vice-President. He wrote Burr again to warn that the "enemy" would try to "sow tares between us," and branding as a forgery a letter purportedly by Jefferson that criticized Burr. At the same time Jefferson subtly let out word that, while he would not make deals—he knew that Burr could outdeal him—he could be counted on to act moderately as President, to be "liberal and accommodating."

Hamilton had no time for subtleties. His clear hierarchy of animosities—he resented Adams, hated Jefferson, and despised Burr—helped him to decide early that if the choice lay between Jefferson and Burr, he would thwart the latter. While Jefferson was only a "contemptible hypocrite," crafty, unscrupulous, and dishonest, Hamilton told his Federalist friends, Burr was a "most unfit and dangerous man," a Jacobin who would overthrow the fiscal system, a rogue who would "employ the rogues of all parties to overrule the good men of all parties," and above all a Catiline who would take over the government as Napoleon had just done in France. Hamilton had little influence with the Federalist "highflyers" (as Jefferson called them) in Congress, but his principled view that his party must not bargain with the likes of Aaron Burr carried weight with national Federalist leaders such as John Jay.

Burr played a waiting game. He assured Jefferson and his friends so convincingly that he would not deal with the enemy and balk the real will of the people that Jefferson confided to his daughter: "The Federalists were confident, at first, they could debauch Col. B from his good faith by offering him their vote to be President," but his "conduct has been honorable and decisive, and greatly embarrasses them." Burr's behavior was curious all the way through. He evidently did spurn a deal with the Federalists, but he did not take the honorable course of simply withdrawing; he never made perfectly clear that he would not serve as President if elected; he apparently allowed some of his friends to put out feelers on his behalf, and his best strategy in any event would have been inaction, since the Federalist bloc in Congress was cemented to his cause as a result of their hatred and fear of Jefferson. Still, the long-drawn-out constitutional crisis afforded Burr countless opportunities to undercut Jefferson and perhaps to win the presidency—but he remained in Albany, attending to his law practice.

Twelve weeks passed as Jefferson remained resolute, Hamilton busy, Burr inactive, and the election stalemated. There is no record of all that happened in the last confused, crisis-ridden days; in particular we know little of the role of less visible but influential politicians. John Marshall evidently angled for his own selection as President should the deadlock persist. But this much seems clear: during the final weeks the nation veered toward disunion and civil war, as Republicans threatened to bring in state militias from Pennsylvania and Virginia if the

Federalists further thwarted the "popular will." The crisis revealed not merely two parties in combat but four party factions: Jeffersonians, Burrites, high Federalists mainly centered in Congress, and a group of moderate Federalists led on this occasion by Hamilton and nurtured in the nationalist, moderate leadership of George Washington.

As March 4, 1801, approached and tension mounted two developments staved off a constitutional and perhaps military debacle. Jefferson, all the while asserting that he would not "receive the government" on capitulation, that he would not go into it "with my hands tied," told a Federalist intermediary that the public credit would be safe, the Navy increased, and lesser federal jobholders left in their places. And ingenious mediators worked out an artifice that enabled Jefferson to be elected President without a single Federalist voting for him. A number of Federalists cast blank ballots, and a single congressman from Vermont now cast his state's vote for Jefferson. That congressman was "Spitting Matt" Lyon.

The crisis was over—Thomas Jefferson was elected President of the United States. Much would be made in later years of this unprecedented example of a peaceful shift from one party to another, of the avoidance of violence and bloodshed, of the example Americans had set for other constitutional republics. But it had been a close-run thing. If Jefferson had not been firm in his ambition, Hamilton not principled in his hatred, Burr not inactive; if moderates in both parties had not been in control, or if fewer politicians had respected the Constitution, the American republic probably would have lived a briefer life than many republics before and since. Perhaps most decisive in the whole episode was the willingness of state and local leaders, Federalist and Republican, to wait for the crisis to be resolved rather than break into local magazines, gather arms, and march on the Capitol. Once again "followers" had acted as leaders.

The suspense of the election quickly changed into excitement over the coming of a new President, a new party, a new government, a new program. Later Jefferson would argue that the "Revolution of 1800 was as real a revolution in the principles of our government as that of 1776 was in its form." ...

Chapter 3

Federalism

3-1

Federalism as an Ideal Political Order and an Objective for Constitutional Reform

James M. Buchanan

In this essay Nobel laureate economist James M. Buchanan makes a case for federalism. Buchanan, a market-oriented economist, arrives at a solution to the threat of concentrated power nearly opposite to that proposed by Madison. Whereas Madison thought that the nation would be safe from such a threat if power were reposed in an inherently factious and weak national majority, Buchanan prefers a more decentralized approach. He would give states greater authority and let market mechanisms regulate them—as in the residence decisions of a mobile citizenry, the subject of the excerpt below.

MY AIM HERE is to discuss federalism, as a central element in an inclusive political order, in two, quite different, but ultimately related, conceptual perspectives. First, I examine federalism as an ideal type, as a stylized component of a constitutional structure of governance that might be put in place ab initio, as emergent from agreement among citizens of a particular community before that community, as such, has experienced its own history. Second, the discussion shifts dramatically toward reality, and the critical importance of defining the historically

Source: James Buchanan, "Federalism as an Ideal Political Order and an Objective for Constitutional Reform," *Publius: The Journal of Federalism* 25 (spring 1995): 19–27.

determined status quo is recognized as a necessary first step toward reform that may be guided by some appreciation of the federalist ideal.

Ideal Theory

Federalism as an Analogue to the Market

An elementary understanding and appreciation of political federalism is facilitated by a comparable understanding and appreciation of the political function of an economy organized on market principles. Quite apart from its ability to produce and distribute a highly valued bundle of "goods," relative to alternative regimes, a market economy serves a critically important political role. To the extent that allocative and distributive choices can be relegated to the workings of markets, the necessity for any politicization of such choices is eliminated.

But why should the politicization of choices be of normative concern? Under the standard assumptions that dominated analysis before the public choice revolution, politics is modeled as the activity of a benevolently despotic and monolithic authority that seeks always and everywhere to promote "the public interest," which is presumed to exist independently of revealed evaluations and which is amenable to discovery or revelation. If this romantic image of politics is discarded and replaced by the empirical reality of politics, any increase in the relative size of the politicized sector of an economy must carry with it an increase in the potential for exploitation.[1] The well-being of citizens becomes vulnerable to the activities of politics, as described in the behavior of other citizens as members of majoritarian coalitions, as elected politicians, and as appointed bureaucrats.

This argument must be supplemented by an understanding of why and how the market, as the alternative to political process, does not also expose the citizen-participant to comparable exploitation. The categorical difference between market and political interaction lies in the continuing presence of an effective exit option in market relationships and in its absence in politics. To the extent that the individual participant in market exchange has available effective alternatives that may be chosen at relatively low cost, any exchange is necessarily voluntary. In its stylized form, the market involves no coercion, no extraction of value from any participant without consent. In dramatic contrast, politics is inherently coercive, independently of the effective decision rules that may be operative.

The potential for the exercise of individual liberty is directly related to the relative size of the market sector in an economy. A market organization does not, however, emerge spontaneously from some imagined state of nature. A market economy must, in one sense, be "laid on" through the design, construction, and implementation of a political-legal framework (i.e., an inclusive constitution) that protects property and enforces voluntary contracts. As Adam Smith emphasized, the market works well only if these parameters, these "laws and institutions," are in place.[2]

Enforceable constitutional restrictions may constrain the domain of politics to some extent, but these restrictions may not offer sufficient protection against the exploitation of citizens through the agencies of governance. That is to say, even if the market economy is allowed to carry out its allocational-distributional role over a significant relative share of the political economy, the remaining domain of actions open to politicization may leave the citizen, both in person and property, vulnerable to the expropriation of value that necessarily accompanies political coercion.

How might the potential for exploitation be reduced or minimized? How might the political sector, in itself, be constitutionally designed so as to offer the citizen more protection?

The principle of federalism emerges directly from the market analogy. . . . Under a federalized political structure, persons, singly and/or in groups, would be guaranteed the liberties of trade, investment, and migration across the inclusive area of the economy. Analogously to the market, persons retain an exit option; at relatively low cost, at least some persons can shift among the separate political jurisdictions. Again analogously to the market, the separate . . . state governments would be forced to compete, one with another, in their offers of publicly provided services. The federalized structure, through the forces of interstate competition, effectively limits the power of the separate political units to extract surplus value from the citizenry.

Principles of Competitive Federalism

The operating principles of a genuinely competitive federalism can be summarized readily.[3] As noted, the central or federal government would be constitutionally restricted in its domain of action, severely so. Within its assigned sphere, however, the central government would be strong, sufficiently so to allow it to enforce economic freedom or openness over the whole of the territory. The separate states would be prevented, by federal authority, from placing barriers on the free flow of resources and goods across their borders.

The constitutional limits on the domain of the central or federal government would not be self-enforcing, and competition could not be made operative in a manner precisely comparable to that which might restrict economic exploitation by the separate states. If the federal (central) government, for any reason, should move beyond its constitutionally dictated mandate of authority, what protection might be granted—to citizens individually or to the separate states—against the extension of federal power?

The exit option is again suggested, although this option necessarily takes on a different form. The separate states, individually or in groups, must be constitutionally empowered to secede from the federalized political structure, that is, to form new units of political authority outside of and beyond the reach of the existing federal government. Secession, or the threat thereof, represents the only means through which the ultimate powers of the central government might be held in check. Absent the secession prospect, the federal government may, by overstepping its constitutionally assigned limits, extract surplus value from the citizenry almost at will, because there would exist no effective means of escape.[4]

With an operative secession threat on the part of the separate states, the federal or central government could be held roughly to its assigned constitutional limits, while the separate states could be left to compete among themselves in their capacities to meet the demands of citizens for collectively provided services. . . .

We should predict, of course, that the separate states of a federal system would be compelled by the forces of competition to offer tolerably "efficient" mixes of publicly provided goods and services, and, to the extent that citizens in the different states exhibit roughly similar preferences, the actual budgetary mixes would not be predicted to diverge significantly, one from the other. However, the point to be emphasized here (and which seems to have been missed in so much of the discussion about the potential European federalism) is that any such standardization or regularization as might occur, would itself be an emergent property of competitive federalism rather than a property that might be imposed either by constitutional mandate or by central government authority.

The Path Dependency of Constitutional Reform

From Here to There: A Schemata

The essential principle for meaningful discourse about constitutional-institutional reform (or, indeed, about any change) is the recognition that reform involves movement from some "here" toward some "there." The evaluative comparison of alternative sets of rules and alternative regimes of political order, as discussed above in the first section, aims exclusively at defining the "there," the idealized objective toward which any change must be turned. But the direction for effective reform also requires a definition of the "here." Any reform, constitutional or otherwise, commences from some "here and now," some status quo that is the existential reality. History matters, and the historical experience of a political community is beyond any prospect of change; the constitutional-institutional record can neither be ignored nor rewritten. The question for reform is, then: "How do we get there from here?"

These prefatory remarks are necessary before any consideration of federalism in discussion of practical reform. The abstracted ideal—a strong but severely limited central authority with the capacity and the will to enforce free trade over the inclusive territory, along with several separate "states," each one of which stands in a competitive relationship with all other such units—of this ideal federal order may be well-defined and agreed upon as an objective for change. However, until and unless the "here," the starting point, is identified, not even the direction of change can be known.

A simple illustration may be helpful. Suppose that you and I agree that we want to be in Washington, D.C. But, suppose that you are in New York and I am in Atlanta. We must proceed in different directions if we expect to get to the shared or common objective.

Constitutional reform aimed toward an effective competitive federalism may reduce or expand the authority of the central government relative to that of the separate state governments. . . . If the status quo is described as a centralized and unitary political authority, reform must embody devolution, a shift of genuine political power from the center to the separate states. On the other hand, if the status quo is described by a set of autonomous political units that may perhaps be geographically contiguous but which act potentially in independence one from another, reform must involve a centralization of authority, a shift of genuine power to the central government from the separate states.

Figure 1 offers an illustrative schemata. Consider a well-defined territory that may be organized politically at any point along the abstracted unidimensional spectrum that measures the extent to which political authority is centralized. At the extreme left of this spectrum, the territory is divided among several fully autonomous political units, each one of which possesses total "sovereignty," and among which any interaction, either by individuals or by political units, must be subjected to specific contractual negotiation and agreement. At the extreme right of this spectrum, the whole of the territory is organized as an inclusive political community, with this authority centralized in a single governmental unit. Individuals and groups may interact, but any such interaction must take place within the uniform limits laid down by the monolithic authority.

An effective federal structure may be located somewhere near the middle of the spectrum, between the regime of fully autonomous localized units on the one hand and the regime of fully centralized authority on the other. This simple illustration makes it easy to see that constitutional reform that is aimed toward the competitive federal structure must be characterized by some increase in centralization, if the starting point is on the left, and by some decrease in centralization, if the starting point is on the right.

The illustration prompts efforts to locate differing regimes at differing places in their own separate histories on the unidimensional scalar. In 1787, James

Figure 1. A Constitutional Reform Schemata

Madison, who had observed the several former British colonies that had won their independence and organized themselves as a confederation, located the status quo somewhere to the left of the middle of the spectrum, and he sought to secure an effective federalism by establishing a stronger central authority, to which some additional powers should be granted. Reform involved a reduction in the political autonomy of the separate units. In the early post–World War II decades, the leaders of Europe, who had observed the terrible nationalistic wars, located their status quo analogously to Madison. They sought reform in the direction of a federalized structure—reform that necessarily involved some establishment of central authority, with some granting of power independently of that historically claimed by the separate nation-states.

By comparison and contrast, consider the United States in 1995, the history of which is surely described as an overshooting of Madison's dreams for the ideal political order. Over the course of two centuries, and especially after the demise of any secession option, as resultant from the great Civil War of the 1860s, the U.S. political order came to be increasingly centralized. The status quo in 1995 lies clearly to the right of the spectrum, and any reform toward a federalist ideal must involve some devolution of central government authority and some increase in the effective independent power of the several states. . . .

Constitutional reform in many countries, as well as the United States, would presumably involve devolution of authority from the central government to the separate states.

Constitutional Strategy and the Federalist Ideal

The simple construction of Figure 1 is also helpful in suggesting that it may be difficult to achieve the ideal constitutional structure described as competitive federalism. Whether motivated by direct economic interest, by some failure to understand basic economic and political theory, or by fundamental conservative instincts, specific political coalitions will emerge to oppose any shift from the status quo toward a federal structure, no matter what the starting point. If, for example, the status quo is described by a regime of fully autonomous units (the nation-states of Europe after World War II), political groups within each of these units will object to any sacrifice of national sovereignty that might be required by a shift toward federalism. . . .

Similar comments may be made about the debates mounted from the opposing direction. If a unitary centralized authority describes the status quo ante, its supporters may attempt to and may succeed in conveying the potential for damage through constitutional collapse into a regime of autonomous units, vulnerable to economic and political warfare. The middle way offered by devolution to a competitive federalism may, in this case, find few adherents.[5] . . .

As the construction in Figure 1 also suggests, however, the fact that the federalist structure is, indeed, "in the middle," at least in the highly stylized sense discussed here, may carry prospects for evolutionary emergence in the conflicts between centralizing and decentralizing pressures. Contrary to the poetic pessimism of William Butler Yeats, the "centre" may hold, if once attained, not because of any intensity of conviction, but rather due to the location of the balance of forces.[6]

Federalism and Increasing Economic Interdependence

In the preceding discussion, I have presumed that the economic benefits of a large economic nexus, defined both in territory and membership, extend at least to and beyond the limits of the political community that may be constitutionally organized anywhere along the spectrum in Figure 1, from a regime of fully autonomous political units to one of centralized political authority. Recall that Adam Smith emphasized that economic prosperity and growth find their origins in the division (specialization) of labor and that this division, in turn, depends on the extent of the market. Smith placed no limits on the scope for applying this principle. But we know that the economic world of 1995 is dramatically different from that of 1775. Technological development has facilitated a continuing transformation of local to regional to national to international interactions among economic units. Consistently with Smith's insights, economic growth has been more rapid where and when political intrusions have not emerged to prevent entrepreneurs from seizing the advantages offered by the developing technology.

Before the technological revolution in information processing and communication, however, a revolution that has occurred in this half-century, politically motivated efforts to "improve" on the workings of market processes seemed almost a part of institutional reality. In this setting, it seemed to remain of critical economic importance to restrict the intrusiveness of politics, quite apart from the complementary effects on individual liberties. Political federalism, to the extent that its central features were at all descriptive of constitutional history, did serve to facilitate economic growth.

The modern technological revolution in information processing and communications may have transformed, at least to some degree, the setting within which politically motivated obstructions may impact on market forces. This technology may, in itself, have made it more difficult for politicians and governments, at any and all levels, to check or to limit the ubiquitous pressures of economic interdependence.[7] When values can be transferred worldwide at the speed of light and when events everywhere are instantly visible on CNN, there are elements of competitive federalism in play, almost regardless of the particular constitutional regimes in existence.

Finally, the relationship between federalism, as an organizing principle for political structure, and the freedom of trade across political boundaries must be noted. An inclusive political territory, say, the United States or Western Europe, necessarily places limits on its own ability to interfere politically with its own internal market structure to the extent that this structure is, itself, opened up to the free workings of international trade, including the movement of capital. On the other hand, to the extent that the internal market is protected against the forces of international competition, other means, including federalism, become more essential to preserve liberty and to guarantee economic growth.

Conclusion

The United States offers an illustrative example. The United States prospered mightily in the nineteenth century, despite the wall of protectionism that sheltered its internal markets. It did so because political authority, generally, was held in check by a constitutional structure that did contain basic elements of competitive federalism. By comparison, the United States, in this last decade of the twentieth century, is more open to international market forces, but its own constitutional structure has come to be transformed into one approaching a centralized unitary authority.

Devolution toward a competitive federal structure becomes less necessary to the extent that markets are open to external opportunities. However, until and unless effective constitutional guarantees against political measures to choke off external trading relationships are put in place, the more permanent constitutional reform aimed at restoring political authority to the separate states offers a firmer basis for future economic growth along with individual liberty. . . .

NOTES

1. James M. Buchanan, "Politics without Romance: A Sketch of Positive Public Choice Theory and Its Normative Implications," Inaugural Lecture, Institute for Advanced Studies, Vienna, Austria, *IHS Journal, Zeitschrift des Instituts für Höhere Studien* 3 (1979): B1–B11.

2. Adam Smith, *The Wealth of Nations* (1776; Modern Library ed.; New York: Random House, 1937).

3. See Geoffrey Brennan and James M. Buchanan, *The Power to Tax: Analytical Foundations of a Fiscal Constitution* (New York: Cambridge University Press, 1980), pp. 168–186, for more comprehensive treatment.

4. For formal analysis of secession, see James M. Buchanan and Roger Faith, "Secession and the Limits of Taxation: Towards a Theory of Internal Exit," *American Economic Review* 5 (December 1987): 1023–1031; for a more general discussion, see Allen Buchanan, *Secession: The Morality of Political Divorce from Fort Sumter to Lithuania and Quebec* (Boulder, Colo.: Westview, 1991).

5. The theory of agenda-setting in public choice offers analogies. If the agenda can be manipulated in such fashion that the alternatives for choice effectively "bracket" the ideally preferred position, voters are confronted with the selection of one or the other of the extreme alternatives, both of which may be dominated by the preferred option. See Thomas Romer and Howard Rosenthal, "Political Resource Allocation, Controlled Agendas, and the Status Quo," *Public Choice* 33 (Winter 1978): 27–43.

6. William Butler Yeats, "The Second Coming," *The Collected Works of W. B. Yeats*, vol. 1, *The Poems*, Ed. Richard J. Finneran (New York: Macmillan, 1989), p. 187.

7. Richard McKenzie and Dwight Lee, *Quicksilver Capital: How the Rapid Movement of Wealth Has Changed the World* (New York: Free Press, 1991).

Federalism: Battles on the Front Lines of Public Policy

Donald F. Kettl

Where "separation of powers" refers to the division of authority across the institutions of the national government (as discussed in The Federalist No. *51 in chapter 2), "federalism" refers to the vertical division of authority and responsibility between Washington and the states. Other countries, such as Germany, Canada, and India, are similarly federal, but all have their own form of federalism, reflecting the specific details of each nation's history and political development. Although the U.S. Constitution defines the basic division of authority between the national government and the states, their respective roles have changed dramatically over the past two centuries. As national transportation and mass communications systems and an integrated national economy emerged in the second half of the twentieth century, political forces began moving issues up the federalism ladder to Washington for resolution. The state of federalism at any moment reflects the demands on, and resources available to, each level of government. The following essay updates the current trends in federalism as a function of this continuing political process.*

AMERICA'S FOUNDERS never intended to create the bold innovation we call American federalism. They were supremely practical men (women were not invited to Philadelphia to help frame the new nation) with a supremely practical problem. Northern states did not trust southern states. Farmers did not trust merchants. Most of all, larger states did not trust smaller states and vice versa. The fledgling nation's army had won independence from Great Britain, but the notables gathered in Philadelphia in 1787 needed to find some glue to hold the new country together. If they had failed, the individual states would have been too small to endure—and would surely have proven easy pickings for European nations eager to expand.

It is not surprising, therefore, that the nation's founders relied on a supremely pragmatic strategy for solving the practical problem of how to balance power

Source: This piece is an original essay commissioned for this volume. Some of the material in this reading first appeared in the author's "Potomac Chronicle" column, which is featured every other month in *Governing* magazine, a publication for state and local governments.

among the states. They made the national[1] government supreme but passed the Tenth Amendment to remind everyone that the states retained any power not explicitly given the national government. Except for forbidding the states from interfering with commerce between them, the Constitution allowed the states to govern themselves.

The system of federalism the Founders created had few rules and fewer fixed boundaries. As federalism has developed over the centuries, however, two important facts about the system have become clear. First, federalism's very strength comes from its enormous flexibility—its ability to adapt to new problems and political cross pressures. Second, it creates alternative venues for political action. Interests that fight and lose at the state level have been able to find clever ways of taking their battles to the national government. Losers at the national level have been able to refight their wars in the states.

Throughout American history, we have frequently looked on federalism as a rather sterile scheme for determining who is in charge of what in our governmental system. But that misses most of what makes federalism important and exciting. It makes far more sense to view federalism as an ever-evolving, flexible system for creating arenas for political action. Americans have long celebrated their basic document of government as a "living Constitution." No part of it has lived more—indeed, changed more—than that involving the relationship between the national and the state governments, and the relationships among the states. This can be seen clearly by considering three different arenas offering variations on the federalism theme: political, fiscal, and administrative.

Political Federalism

In the 1990s South Carolina business owners launched the *Tropic Sea* as a casino boat for "cruises to nowhere." However, it soon became a cruise to a very important somewhere by raising the question, Just how far can—and should—federal power intrude on the prerogatives of the states?

This balance-of-power question is as old as the American republic and in fact predates the Constitution. When the colonies declared their independence from King George III, they formed a loose confederation. It proved barely strong enough to win the war and not nearly strong enough to help govern the new nation. Problems with the country's Articles of Confederation led the nation's leaders to gather in Philadelphia to draft a new constitution. At the core of their debate was the question of how much power to give the national government and how much to reserve to the states. The Founders followed a time-honored tradition in resolving such tough issues—they sidestepped it. The Constitution itself is silent on the issue, and the Tenth Amendment simply reinforces the obvious: The national government has only the powers that the Constitution gives it. By leaving the details vague, the authors of the Constitution avoided a wrenching political battle. They also ensured that generations of Americans after them would refight the same battles—most often with legal stratagems in the nation's courts, but sometimes, as in the Civil War, with blood.

A Cruise to Somewhere?

The *Tropic Sea* sailed into an ongoing struggle in South Carolina politics. While developers loved gambling ships such as the *Tropic Sea*, which lured tourists to the state, several legislators and local officials did not and had been actively campaigning against the ships. As a result, when the *Tropic Sea* asked permission to dock at Charleston's State Ports Authority (SPA) Pier, the SPA said no. The boat ended up at anchor in the harbor while its owners sought help from the Federal Maritime Commission (FMC). The FMC sided with the boat owners but was overturned by a federal appeals court. The case eventually ended up in the U.S. Supreme Court.

South Carolina argued that, as a state government, it wasn't subject to the FMC's jurisdiction, and in a bitter 5–4 decision at the end of its 2002 term, the Supreme Court agreed. Writing for the majority, Justice Clarence Thomas looked past the usual foundation of political struggles over state power, the Tenth Amendment, and instead built his argument on the little-noticed Eleventh Amendment, ratified in 1798, which holds that the judicial power of the United State does not extend to the states. This amendment supported the notion of "dual federalism"—separate spheres of federal and state action. In the succeeding decades, the dual federalism argument, however, gradually eroded, especially after 1868, under the weight of the "equal protection" clause of the Fourteenth Amendment. That amendment asserts that all citizens have the right to equal treatment under the law. In establishing a national standard, the Fourteenth Amendment gave the courts power to enforce national policy over state objections. That pushed away the "dual federalism" concept and helped shift the balance of power to the national government. After William Rehnquist became chief justice in 1986, however, dual federalism resurfaced and surged ahead again.

In ruling for South Carolina, Justice Thomas admitted that there was little textual evidence to support his position. Rather, he said, dual federalism was "embedded in our constitutional structure." The concept helped uphold the "dignity" of the states as dual sovereigns. That, he said, was the core of the decision.[2]

Asserting the "dignity" of the states is a new constitutional standard. The Eleventh Amendment explicitly applies to federal courts, not federal administrators, such as employees of the FMC. Conservatives, of course, had long criticized liberals for making law from the bench. In this case, however, it was the conservatives on the Court who crafted a new principle, which they used to push back the scope of the national government's power.

Federalism Means War

The Supreme Court under Rehnquist has gradually chipped away at national power and has aggressively worked to strengthen the role of the states. The major federalism decisions have all been by votes of 5–4, built on the conservative bloc of Rehnquist, Thomas, Anthony Kennedy, Sandra Day O'Connor, and Antonin Scalia. The disputes, on the Court as well as off, have become increasingly intense. As *New York Times* reporter Linda Greenhouse put it, "These days, federalism means war."[3]

The battles have become so sharp that a candidate's views on federalism seem certain to be critical in selecting new appointments to the Supreme Court. Any future justice's views on federalism will determine whether the Court remains on its pro–dual federalism course. Staying that course, however, raises two very difficult questions.

First, just how far is the Court prepared to go in pursuing dual federalism? In the past, it has ruled that workers cannot sue states for discrimination under federal age and disability standards. It has also protected states from suits by people claiming unfair competition from state activities in the marketplace, such as photocopying by state universities. Thus bit by bit the Court has extended state power at the expense of the national government's jurisdiction.

At some point, however, the pursuit of state "dignity" will collide with national standards for equal protection. At some point, state protection against national labor standards will crash into national protection of civil rights and civil liberties. It might come in debates over family leave or prescription drugs, in voting rights or in transportation of nuclear waste. But a collision is certain. From the Fourteenth Amendment, there is a long tradition of asserting national power over the states. From the Rehnquist court, there is a new legal argument for reasserting state power.

Neither argument is an absolute. In some issues (such as civil rights), there is a strong case for national preeminence. In other issues (such as the states' own systems of law), there is a strong case for state preeminence. However, still other issues (such as gambling boats) rest squarely in the middle. The nation then has to determine how best to balance competing policy goals and constitutional principles. Sometimes those battles are fought out in the legislative and executive branches, but most often they are contested in the courts.

Since the dawn of Roosevelt's New Deal in the 1930s, national power grew at the expense of the states. Now, with an uncommon purpose, the conservatives on the Court are pushing that line back. The Rehnquist court can continue the campaign to reassert the power of the states, but clearly at some point it will have to hold national interests paramount. What is less clear is where and how the Court will draw that line.

The second question raised by the Court's pro–dual federalism course is even tougher: How far can the Court advance state-centered federalism without running headlong into the new campaign for homeland security, which demands a strong national role? It is one thing for the Court to pursue the principles of state sovereignty and dignity. But beefing up homeland security inevitably means strengthening federal power. There is a vital national interest in ensuring that state and local governments protect critical infrastructure, such as water systems and harbors. The nation needs not only a strong intelligence apparatus but also a powerful emergency response system.

Federalism and the Living Constitution

It may be that relatively few Americans care about whether a gambling boat can dock at a South Carolina port. But the basic issue—where to draw the line between national and state power, and who ought to draw it—is an issue that all Americans care about, even if they usually spend little time thinking about it in those terms. It has been the stuff of bloody battles and endless debate. As political scientist Howard Gillman told the *New York Times*, federalism has become "the biggest and deepest disagreement about the nature of our constitutional system."[4] The equal protection and homeland security issues will only intensify that disagreement as we wade deeper into the real meaning of the states' "dignity."

These issues are scarcely ones that the Founders could have anticipated when they wrote the Constitution and the Bill of Rights. Few present-day Americans, after all, had heard the phrase "homeland security" before September 11, 2001. The genius of the Founders was that they recognized the importance of federalism, that they put broad boundaries around it but did not try to resolve it for all time, and that they created a mechanism for Americans in subsequent generations to adjust the balance, subtly and continually.

It was no easy matter to recognize the key questions out of thousands that engaged the members of the Constitutional Convention in Philadelphia. It was even tougher to resolve the battles just enough to win the Constitution's adoption without pushing so hard as to deepen the divisions. And it was quite remarkable to do so in a way that has allowed us to reshape the balance in our time.

Fiscal Federalism

These grand debates are what most Americans think of when they think of "federalism." They are the stuff of high school civics classes and the enduring classics of American history. For national, state, and local policy makers, however, the soft underbelly of federalism is, much more often, the question of who pays for what.

This has not always been the case. But in the 1950s, as the nation—and the national government—became much more ambitious about domestic policy, fiscal federalism became increasingly important. During this period, citizens and national policy makers wanted the country to undertake new, large-scale projects, such as building a national network of highways and tearing down decaying slums. State and local governments could not, or would not, move ahead on such matters. Often they simply did not have the funds to do so; sometimes local political forces opposed the policies. Even without these impediments, state and local governments almost always lacked the ability to coordinate the creation of such complex systems as effective high-speed highways with other jurisdictions. (Who would want to drive on a modern four-lane road only to hit a two-lane gravel path at the state line?) Therefore citizens and national policy makers pressed to empower the national government to undertake these projects.

National Goals through Intergovernmental Grants

The national government tackled the problem of getting local and state governments to do what it wanted done by offering them grants. If local governments lacked the resources to tear down dilapidated housing, the national government could create an "urban renewal" program and provide the money, thus avoiding the constitutional problem that would have come with national coercion. The national government did not *make* local governments accept the money or tear down the slums. But few local officials could resist a national program that helped them do what they, too—or at least many of their constituents—wanted done.

The same was true at the state level. In the 1950s Americans were buying cars in record numbers, but they found the roads increasingly clogged. Long-distance driving often proved a special chore because road systems did not connect well and the quality of the roads fell far below the performance ability of the cars driving on them. During the Eisenhower administration, the national government decided to tackle that problem by creating a new program—the interstate highway system—and inducing states to join it by funding 90 percent of the construction cost. With motorists demanding better roads, the offer was too good to refuse. Since this was occurring amid the hottest moments of the cold war, President Dwight D. Eisenhower reinforced the idea of a national interest by arguing that the system served both transportation and defense goals—it would allow troops to move quickly to wherever they might be needed. (Wags have since joked that the system could best serve the national defense by luring Russian tanks onto the Washington Beltway and challenging them to cope with the traffic and find the right exit.)[5]

The strategy continued to be utilized through the 1960s. When Lyndon B. Johnson announced his War on Poverty, he decided to fight it primarily through national grants to state and local governments. He created the Model Cities program, which provided aid to local communities trying to uproot poverty and rebuild urban neighborhoods, and established other programs to provide better housing for poor Americans. He founded Medicaid, which provided grants to state governments so that they, in turn, could provide health care to the poor. More grants followed to support job training, criminal justice, public health, and a host of other national goals.

It was a clever strategy in a number of ways. For one it sidestepped constitutional limitations on national interference in state and local issues: the national government did not force state and local governments to join the programs, it simply made them financially irresistible. No state or local official wanted to have to explain to constituents why they left cheap money on the table, especially when their neighbors were benefiting from the programs.

This approach sidestepped another tough constitutional problem as well: the national government's dealing directly with local governments. Through long-standing constitutional interpretation and practice, local governments are considered creatures of the states, not the national government. The states created the national government, so constitutionally the national government must deal with the states. Hence the states alone have the power to control what local governments can—and cannot—do. Before Johnson's program, local governments struggled to deal with increasing problems of poverty, substandard housing, and other human needs. They often found themselves without power or adequate money to attack the problems. Few state governments themselves had adequate resources to address these serious issues, and in many states, political forces prevented the creation of new programs that might have helped.

Many analysts concluded that the only solution was to create a direct link between the national and local governments—a link that bypassed the states. But given both constitutional limits and political conflicts, how could such a link be established? Federal grants to local governments proved the answer. Across the nation, state governments gave permission for local governments to receive

Figure 1. Federal Aid to State and Local Governments

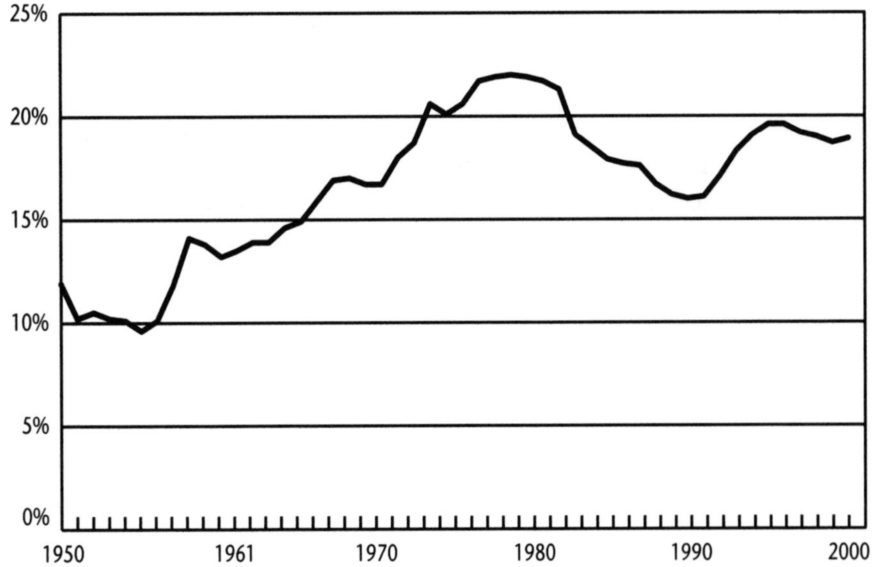

Source: Council of Economic Advisers, *Economic Report of the President* (Washington: Government Printing Office, 2002), Table B-86, at http://w3.access.gpo.gov/usbudget/fy2003/sheets/b86.xls.

the money. If the national government agreed to take on the problems and keep state officials out of the process, the programs seemed an attractive proposition to state and local officials alike.

From the 1950s through the 1970s, these intergovernmental aid programs became increasingly popular and important. They not only grew in size but also became ever more vital elements of state and local government revenue. In 1938 federal aid had amounted to just 8.7 percent of state and local revenue. As Figure 1 shows, while the number grew to almost 12 percent in 1950, it surged to 22 percent in 1978—accounting for more than one out of every five dollars raised by state and local governments.

As the national government used its funds to support state and local governments and to induce them to do things they might not have done otherwise, federal aid became not only an increasingly important part of the policy system but also something on which those governments became ever more dependent. When the national government began tightening its fiscal belt in the late 1970s, state and local governments felt the effects keenly. By 1990 federal aid had dropped to just 16 percent of state and local revenue, a level not seen since before the launch of Johnson's Great Society. Few federal programs, however, were abolished. Rather, the national government simply cut back support—leaving state and local governments to deal with ongoing commitments and, in many cases, powerful supporters who fought hard to keep the programs alive. In the federal highway program, federal support mostly provided aid for construction, not maintenance. As highways aged, state governments found themselves with huge bills for repairing crumbling bridges and old roadbeds.

When recession hit in 2002, state and local governments looked expectantly to Washington for some hope—and help.

No News Was Bad News

The nation's governors, in particular, were hoping for good news when President George W. Bush began 2003 by announcing his plans for a $670 billion tax cut. They hoped the speech would contain at least some help for their ailing budgets. However, except for a modest proposal on unemployment insurance, they found themselves left out in the January cold.

With their budgets in the biggest crisis since World War II, governors had been lobbying hard for national help. They hoped for a short-term resuscitation of revenue sharing, which had ended in 1982. Failing that, they pressed for at least tinkering with the formula for reimbursing Medicaid spending, the fastest growing program in many state budgets and one, as noted earlier, originally launched through the incentive of national grants. Changes in the Medicaid formulas, they hoped, would ease their budget worries.

Ignoring most of the states' pleas, Bush instead advanced a bold stroke to restructure the national tax system. The administration did suggest some changes to the Medicaid program, but they would have reduced aid (or increased costs) for the poor, and the proposal immediately incited opposition from groups struggling to protect the program. The states were left on their own with a $90 billion budget hole, which threatened to soak up all—and more—of the short-term economic stimulus Bush was proposing. The net effect promised to be an economic wash surrounded by political conflict.

Who is at fault here? The feds for failing to extend a helping hand when the states needed it most? Or the states for digging themselves into the hole and whining when Bush refused to help them out? As with most questions of fault, the answer is, both.

If Bush truly had been interested in jump-starting the economy, pumping money through the states would quickly have done just that. But the president was concerned more with long-term revision of the tax code than with short-term economic stimulus, especially through the states. As for the states, their fault lies in having hitched their spending to the booming economy of the 1990s. They forgot "Stein's Law," derived by the late Herbert Stein, once chairman of the president's Council of Economic Advisers: "Things that can't go on forever—won't."[6] When the economy collapsed, the states found themselves hooked on spending increases they could not support.

Exploding Health Care Costs

In the 1990s national aid to state and local governments had actually resumed its upward swing (see Figure 2). But it was not because the national government had decided to resume its generosity to state and local governments. Rather, it was because national aid for payments to individuals—mostly Medicaid—suddenly accelerated, as the benefits became more generous and health care costs began to grow rapidly. Grants for all other purposes had leveled off or shrunk, but national aid for health care had swung quickly upward—as had state governments' own spending for their matching share of the costs.

As the new century began, health care costs, particularly for Medicaid, exploded at precisely the same moment that state revenues collapsed. Spending for doctor visits, hospital care, and especially prescription drugs swelled at the highest rate in a decade, growing to 30 percent of state spending. Medicaid alone rose 13.2 percent in 2002, compared with just a 1.3 percent increase for all state spending. The explosion of national health care costs could not have come at a worse time for state governments. They have swamped the states' efforts to control the rest of their budgets and have aggravated their financial hemorrhage. The big monster in the states' budgetary basement has become health care: treating the uninsured, providing long-term care for the elderly, and buying prescription drugs. With the baby boomers nearing retirement age, the budgetary problem promises to get worse.

The Bush tax cut plan will further aggravate the states' bleeding. The national tax exemption on their debt has long kept down state and local borrowing costs. If corporate capital gains also become tax exempt, the advantage of investing in state bonds will decrease, and that will drive up the states' borrowing costs. And because, under the guise of tax simplification, most states have tied their income taxes to the national code, the Bush plan has created a second drain on state revenues. Eliminating national taxes on capital gains will also eliminate *state* taxes on those gains and further drain state revenues.

These forces—state spending pegged to unsustainable revenue growth, the sudden increase in health care costs, and the risk of further revenue erosion from

Figure 2. Federal Grants to State and Local Governments

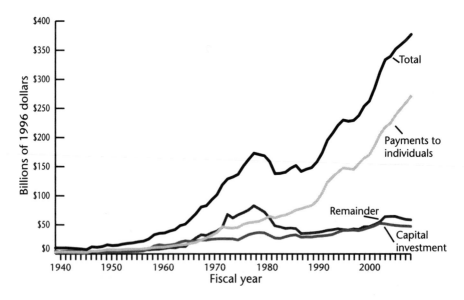

Note: Total outlays include off-budget outlays; however, all grant outlays are from on-budget accounts. Grants that are both payments for individuals and capital investment are shown under capital investment. Figures for FY2003 and after are estimates.
Source: U.S. Office of Management and Budget, *Budget of the United States Government: Fiscal Year 2004— Historical Tables* (Washington: Government Printing Office, 2003), Table 12.1.

the Bush plan—threaten a profound crisis for state policy makers. Aggravating it is the projection by most economists that economic growth is not expected to proceed fast enough to bail out the states any time soon. It's little wonder that, in some states, Democrats were quietly rooting for Republican governors to make the hard budgetary decisions, and vice versa. If the states are the laboratories of democracy, the lurching of budgetary Frankensteins could litter broken test tubes across the floor. This is a long way from the salad days of national-state relations in the 1960s and early 1970s. The feds then saw state and local problems as their own. Democrats and Republicans joined together to provide national funds to leverage state and local action. The partnership might have been paternalistic, but it shaped policy for decades. When budget cuts hit in the late 1970s and early 1980s, national-state ties became increasingly frayed. They further unraveled with the Bush administration's 2002 loosening of air pollution regulations, which complicated the job many states faced in meeting pollution standards, and again with the administration's capital gains tax plan.

The states can—indeed, they have to—deal with some of these problems by putting their spending back into balance with a realistic view of their revenues. They need to update their revenue systems. But they cannot solve their fundamental fiscal problems without a new partnership between the states and the feds. And that will be hard to realize as long as the two groups move in such different orbits that the fundamental problems they share never come together.

Administrative Federalism

A close corollary of the rise of fiscal federalism has been the growing importance of state and local governments as administrative agents of national programs. As close observers of Washington politics know, the national government has increased its spending without increasing (in fact, while decreasing) the number of bureaucrats. The reason it has been able to do so? The national government has leveraged the activity of state and local governments as agents to do much of its work. As is the case in fiscal federalism, the states usually have discretion about whether to enlist as national agents, but the construction of the programs typically leaves them little choice. Consider, for example, the case of environmental policy. Under national environmental laws, state governments have substantial responsibility for issuing permits and monitoring emissions.

The Environmental Protection Agency (EPA) relies heavily on state governments for much of the frontline work. In the process, however, some states have used this role to set their own policies, which often have been far broader than those of the EPA. In a peculiar up-from-the-bottom style of federalism, that has meant that some states have, in practice, set policy for the entire nation.

Policymaking for the Nation—in Sacramento

Top officials in the capital have been increasingly consumed by war about the air, and there is a good chance that the EPA administrator will not be setting much environmental policy a decade from now. Recent agency administrators, both Republican and Democratic, have been pinned down in a fierce guerrilla battle between some congressional members who are trying to lighten the regulatory burden of environmental rules and others who are trying to toughen pollution standards and reduce global warming. The administrator's job increasingly has been to chart the EPA's course through the political crossfire. As the mêlée has raged in Washington, the policy initiative has shifted to the states—and to foreign governments.

Californians, of course, have as much at stake as anyone in the campaign to clean the air. Pollution problems in the Los Angeles basin are legendary. Medical research has shown that kids growing up in the area suffer a 10 to 15 percent decrease in lung function and suffer more from asthma and respiratory infections than their counterparts elsewhere in the country. Autopsies of 152 young people who died suddenly from crime or health problems revealed that all of them had inflamed airways and 27 percent had severe lung damage.

It is little wonder that California has been so aggressive in campaigning to reduce air pollution. The state has set tougher standards than required by federal regulations, and in the past twenty-five years the results have been remarkable. The number of health advisories for high levels of ozone shrank from 166 in 1976 to just 15 in 2001.

In July 2002 California took another tough step. The legislature passed a bill requiring all cars sold in California after 2009 to meet tough standards for greenhouse gases, the carbon-based emissions scientists believe promote global warming. In signing the bill, Governor Gray Davis chided the national government for "failing to ratify the Kyoto treaty on global warming." They "missed their opportunity to do the right thing," Davis said. "So it is left to California, the nation's most populous state and the world's fifth largest economy, to take the lead." California was proud to "join the long-standing and successful effort of European nations against global warming."[7]

With its legislation, California rendered President Bush's March 2001 decision to withdraw the United States from the Kyoto treaty moot, at least for carbon dioxide pollution from cars. Carmakers had waged a fierce battle against the California bill, but in the end they could not beat the forces of environmentalists and citizens worried about public health. They found themselves trooping off to Sacramento to haggle over the details of the new regulations.

No automaker can afford to ignore California and its huge market as was clear from the state's earlier decision to mandate cleaner gas and catalytic converters. When California mandated catalytic converters to scrub auto exhaust, it soon became impossible to buy cars in Wisconsin or Texas that did not contain the device as well. As California goes, at least in air pollution, so goes the nation.

For California regulators, the aggressive antipollution campaign has not been a one-way street. The new California law requires regulators to reduce not only smog but also greenhouse gases, such as carbon dioxide. New-generation diesel engines are more fuel efficient than many gasoline-powered engines. That means less fuel and fewer carbon dioxide emissions. And that, in turn, has brought California regulators into close negotiations with automakers about encouraging production of diesel-powered cars.

For those who have long seen diesels as blue-smoke belching behemoths, the idea that diesel power might be a pollution-reducing strategy may seem preposterous. It may seem even more unlikely that government would be encouraging a shift to diesel engines or that the conversations would happen with government regulators hammering out deals with automakers to do so. Above all, it may seem incredible that the government doing so would be at the state level. But that is exactly what is happening in California.

All this, in turn, has led to budding ties between state regulators and the European Union (EU). European nations have been working as hard and as long on global warming as anyone. The EU's aggressive efforts to reduce greenhouse gases have led to new diesel technologies. So California regulators find themselves steering in the same direction as their counterparts abroad. Put together this means that American policy for auto emissions is subtly shifting course, driven by activities at the state and international levels.

State governments have long prided themselves on being the nation's policy laboratories, and healthy competition among them might produce new breakthroughs. But there is also a profound risk that the nation could find its policy strategies increasingly evolving through accidental bits and bumps, without a national debate about what is truly in the national interest. The trend is already briskly underway. General Electric chief executive Jeffrey Immelt has said that 99 percent of all new regulations the company faces are, over time, coming not from the national government but from the European Union.[8] The states are vigorously developing new pollution standards. Meanwhile, as Washington policy makers focus on the interest-group battles that constantly consume them, they risk fighting more and more about less and less.

Conclusion

If James Madison strolled down to Washington from his Virginia estate at Montpelier today, would he recognize the system of federalism he helped to craft? He would undoubtedly be stunned at the very idea of using federalism to work out problems of ship-based gambling, health care for the poor, or global warming. However, on a few moments' reflection—and perhaps after a bit of conversation to get up to speed on the stunning policy predicaments of the twenty-first century—he would see in these puzzles an echo of the same issues he and his colleagues wrestled with in Philadelphia.

The glue holding together America's special—and peculiar—democratic system comes from a unique blending of federal, state, and local responsibilities.

Early Americans faced a fundamental, dramatic choice: to assign those responsibilities clearly to different levels of government, and then write rules for governments to coordinate their inevitable differences; or to allow governments to share responsibilities, and then to allow them to negotiate their differences through a political process. The latter is the cornerstone of American federalism.

Thus federalism is a much-revered constitutional principle, rooted deeply in the American tradition, which draws its life from political bargaining. It is tempting to read the Constitution, think of the stirring rhetoric of the Founders, and celebrate federalism as a set of rules. In reality, federalism is a set of political action arenas. It is far less an institution than a living organism, one that breathes, grows, shrinks, and changes in response to the forces pressing upon it.

Federalism has helped Americans survive the pressures that led to the Civil War, and it has often made possible programs and policies that might not otherwise have existed. It would be hard to imagine, for example, that the national government itself would have taken on the job of building the massive interstate highway system. Only through federalism did this crucial system come into being, because federalism introduced the possibility of a political, fiscal, and administrative partnership that made possible a program no one government alone could have produced. By the same means, federalism has transformed American cities (for better or worse) through urban renewal, launched a war on poverty, helped clean the environment, and produced a health care program for the nation's poor.

Of course, this partnership has not always been a happy or peaceful one. Governors are never convinced that the national government provides enough money, and national policy makers constantly find it difficult to corral fifty different states—and tens of thousands of local governments—into a coherent policy system. But in the end, the system's constant flexibility has not only made it possible to work out accommodations for the tough issues but also created arenas in which Americans, with many different points of view, can continue to contest and struggle over the future of the nation's public policy.

NOTES

1. Throughout this chapter, I will use *national* to refer to what most people call the *federal* government. To use *federal* in discussing *federalism* often causes endless confusion, so I am resorting to the less-common usage to maintain clarity. Readers who find that in itself confusing can simply replace *federal* for *national* wherever it appears!

2. *Federal Maritime Commission v. South Carolina Ports Authority,* No. 01–46. See Linda Greenhouse, "Justices Expand States' Immunity in Federalism Case," *New York Times,* May 29, 2002, sec. A.

3. Linda Greenhouse, "The Nation: 5-to-4, Now and Forever; At the Court, Dissent over States' Rights Is Now War," *New York Times,* June 9, 2002, sec. 4.

4. Ibid.

5. For a map of the system, see http://www.fhwa.dot.gov/hep10/nhs.

6. Interview with the author.

7. Gray Davis, "California Takes on Air Pollution," *Washington Post,* July 22, 2002, sec. A.

8. Brandon Mitchener, "Increasingly, Rules of Global Economy Are Set in Brussels," *Wall Street Journal,* April 23, 2002, sec. A.

3-3

Clean-Air Battlefield

Matthew L. Wald

Which policies should the national government assume responsibility for and which should be left to the states? This is an age-old question that has been repeatedly asked and variously answered since the founding of the American republic. A number of principles have been offered to guide the location of such responsibilities. A paramount one is that those who benefit from a policy should assume responsibility for providing it. Everyone benefits from national defense, for example; by this criterion national defense is a quintessential responsibility of the federal government. Ignoring who benefits in assigning responsibility to a particular level of government runs the risk of encouraging free riding and other inefficiencies. Of course, in the real world economic reasoning yields to politics, which is not always rational. The following news article reports just such an instance. Here the federal Environmental Protection Agency (EPA) holds states responsible for air pollution within their borders even when it originates in another state and drifts in with the wind.

WASHINGTON, Nov. 30—The Bush administration's move to relax air pollution standards on old industrial plants has quickly attracted more powerful opposition than decisions to drill for oil and gas in fragile areas or log trees in the wilderness.

The reason is the unusual way the 1977 Clean Air Act assigns blame.

Other pollution laws blame the polluter. The Clean Air Act does that too, but it also blames the pollutee: if the air is dirty, states are supposed to clean it, and if they do not they can lose highway money. Even private development can be halted.

The difference is obvious to the states. "If you had somebody dump hazardous waste on your lawn, it wouldn't be interpreted as your fault," said Kenneth A. Colburn, formerly New Hampshire's chief air pollution official and now the executive director of Northeast States for Coordinated Air Use Management, a group of officials in state environmental departments. The Environmental Protection Agency has created an instant, well-organized, well-equipped opposition;

Source: Matthew L. Wald, "Clean-Air Battlefield," *New York Times,* December 1, 2002, sec. 1.

the eight states in the group (the six New England states plus New York and New Jersey), joined by Maryland, are suing.

The states are concerned for another reason. The standards they must meet are about to get stricter.

For years, smog levels have been measured in hourly averages. In a three-year period, areas that record four hours in which pollution was over the limit (125 parts per million of ozone) are "in nonattainment." Such areas get nasty letters from the E.P.A., urging states to set new rules on pollution sources.

But in about 18 months, the standard will be 80 parts per million measured over an eight-hour period, which the agency says is more in line with damage to human health. Air pollution experts predict that the shift will increase the number of places in nonattainment. A new standard on very small soot particles will take effect soon; most of the Eastern seaboard from Richmond, Va., to Nashua, N.H., will violate the new rules, as will much of the industrial Southeast and Gulf coasts and large parts of California.

The states must bring their violating areas into compliance under a little-recognized system called delegation. In air pollution and in other areas of regulation, the federal government sets the rules and delegates a state agency to carry them out. The idea is this: Air blows across state lines, thus a state's actions affect its neighbors. So all states should be held to a minimum standard, but they should have choices among programs, from inspecting car exhaust to controls on power plants.

Faced with getting their jurisdictions to comply, the states complain that the relaxation of standards announced on Nov. 22, affecting old plants that seek to modernize, gives them fewer tools. State officials say it is more like moving first base farther from home plate and making the bat smaller.

The Environmental Protection Agency sees it differently. Officials there say the new rules will give the old factories more flexibility and result in some reductions.

"We're going to get more reductions under the rules," said Jeffrey R. Holmstead, the agency's assistant administrator for air and radiation.

Mr. Holmstead pointed out that the National Governors Association and a multistate organization of air officials had called for changing the rules on old factories. The states, he said, are unhappy because they wanted to give the industries some flexibility but require steady reductions in emissions, an offer he said few factories would take.

State and local officials disagree, but they privately acknowledge that they might not face sanctions for missing the goals. The rule changes will take about a quarter of all pollution emissions off the table, some experts maintain. But even in the Clinton administration, the E.P.A. seldom sought sanctions, and state officials say the Bush administration may be even less eager.

One former state environmental commissioner, who spoke on condition of anonymity, said that there was value in the threat of "the big, bad E.P.A." coming after the state, because such a threat could help persuade the governor to take unpopular steps to reduce emissions.

Mr. Holmstead said the threat of sanctions gave state officials "a lot more urgency when they go to their governors or legislatures."

Chapter 4

Civil Rights

———◦◦———

4-1

Minority Rights in Direct Democracy

Zoltan L. Hajnal and Elisabeth R. Gerber

No cleavages in American society appear to display James Madison's factional competition thesis (see Federalist No. 10, chapter 2) so well as do those between whites and blacks and recently the Latino and Asian American populations. For the past half-century civil rights issues have been at the forefront of national policy and from time to time have pitted the preferences of white and black citizens against one another. School busing and affirmative action in employment and education are two instances. In the past decade the civil rights issues have broadened dramatically to include issues of language and citizenship special to the nation's growing Hispanic population. Yet the research reported here suggests that the pattern of conflict and cooperation is considerably more complex than the simple image of white versus black. Comparing the opinions of California's Asian American, black, Latino, and white voters on referenda issues, this study reports that majorities of each group generally agree on policy. As a result, African Americans, Asian Americans, and to a lesser degree Latinos generally find themselves on the winning side of most referenda elections. The exceptions can be important, however, in that they typically concern votes on civil rights policies—such as affirmative action and immigrant access to state services.

DO MINORITIES REALLY have a say in democracy, or are they subject to the whims and wishes of the majority? The fate of minorities and of minority rights in the face of majority rule is one of the most critical issues with which democracies must contend. America is no exception. From the Founders on, critics have been concerned about the fate of minorities in our democracy. James Madison feared that with direct majority rule policy would be "too often decided, not according to the rule of justice and the rights of the minor party but by the superior force of an interested and overbearing majority" (Hamilton, Madison, and Jay 1961, 77). More recently civil rights activists have argued that America's white majority is using the country's democratic system to trample over the rights of African Americans, Latinos, Asian Americans, and other minorities (Guinier 1994).

Nowhere is this question of minority rights more central than in the arena of direct democracy, where voters get to decide policy directly, with few of the checks and balances found in other democratic arenas. Direct democracy, by its very nature, gives a slim majority of the voters (that is, 50 percent plus one) the ability to pass laws that a large minority strongly opposes. In the context of American racial politics, the fear is that a white majority will use the initiative ballot to usurp the rights of racial and ethnic minorities. Recently, the passage of statewide ballot propositions ending affirmative action, eliminating bilingual education programs, and cutting services to illegal immigrants has led many political observers to suggest that this fear has become reality (Schrag 1998; Maharidge 1996; Tolbert and Hero 1996). As Derek Bell puts it, the initiative should be seen as "democracy's barrier to racial equality" (Bell 1978, 1).

This concern about minority interests and direct democracy is not an idle one. More and more important policy decisions are being made through direct legislation. Nationwide, the number of initiatives has increased dramatically in recent years (I&R Institute 2000). In the past decade alone the twenty-four states with direct democracy voted on 317 different measures, 159 of which were passed. Over the same period, municipalities across the country voted on thousands of measures, most aimed at significantly altering the distribution of public resources. As Peter Schrag has noted, "The initiative . . . has not just been integrated into the regular governmental-political system, but has begun to replace it" (1998, 2).

Yet are racial and ethnic minorities really losing out in direct democracy? To what extent does the white majority dominate outcomes at the expense of Asian Americans, blacks, and Latinos? In this essay, we answer these questions by looking systematically at voting across the whole array of issues addressed through direct democracy to see if there is a systematic bias in outcomes against any particular racial or ethnic group. Specifically, we address the debate over direct democracy and minority rights by analyzing who has won and who has lost and how often they have won and lost in direct democracy in California over the past thirty years.

Our analysis of these votes indicates that, in fact, there is little overall antiminority bias in the system of direct democracy. Voters from every group we examined won more regularly than they lost, and no one group fared much better than other groups across the range of issues addressed in direct democracy. Even on issues that members of racial and ethnic minority groups care the most about, majorities of these groups voted for the winning side of the initiative most of the time. Yet we do see two significant and potentially disturbing trends. First, when direct legislation was explicitly focused on racial and ethnic minorities, nonwhites tended to do the worst. Second, we found important differences in the fates of members of different minority groups. More than any other group, Latinos wound up on the losing side of direct democracy. We speculate that this anti-Latino bias is a result of the perceived economic and political threat that a large and growing Latino population poses.

Beyond this focus on who wins and loses, this study also examines underlying patterns in the vote. Why is it that minorities fare relatively well in a purely majoritarian system? We find that the success of racial and ethnic minority groups is a function of two factors: no one racial or ethnic group is particularly united, and on most issues whites and nonwhites tend to agree more than they disagree.

Measuring Winners and Losers

There are different methods one could consider for measuring winners and losers in direct democracy. One might want to directly measure the economic, social, and psychological effects of a given initiative on a particular minority group. For example, if the median household income of Asian Americans goes up as a result of the passage of a particular initiative, then Asian Americans should be considered winners. Yet in practice, it is extremely difficult, if not impossible, to make these kinds of inferences. What effect, for example, did Proposition 13, California's famous tax limitation initiative, have on the Asian American community? Making that determination is complicated by the fact that initiatives are not passed in a static environment. Many factors, such as national economic conditions, could also affect Asian American income. Moreover, we might be concerned about the effects of this particular initiative on the educational achievement or the quality of life of a particular group, factors even more difficult to calculate. In addition, Asian Americans are an extremely diverse group. Japanese families who have been in California for generations often live in very different circumstances than newly arrived, poor Filipino families. Policies that benefit one segment of the Asian American community in one location may have negative consequences for another segment of the community in another location. This increases the difficulty of determining winners and losers in any straightforward way.

We can, however, examine individual voting behavior. Does a particular individual from a particular group support or oppose a given initiative? With the vote, we have a measure of an individual's preference on an initiative. We can compare the individual vote with the actual outcome to determine who has voted for the winning side. Did an individual vote in favor of an initiative that ultimately failed? If so, his or her preferences were not met, and he or she clearly lost that vote. If the individual voted against an initiative that failed, however, his or her preferences were met, and he or she can be considered a winner. The starting point for this analysis is a simple calculation of whether a given voter voted with the side that won on a particular initiative.

Concerns with Using the Vote

By focusing on voting patterns in initiative ballot elections, we can accurately assess how well racial and ethnic minority voters have fared across a wide array of issues. However, this focus on the vote is not without some costs and concerns. First, by focusing on voters we exclude nonvoters, whose preferences could differ from those of voters. Fortunately, the vast majority of research on this subject suggests that nonvoters do not have substantially different preferences than voters (Verba, Schlozman, and Brady 1995; Wolfinger and Rosenstone 1980).[1] Another concern is that voters may not know what is really in their own best interests when they vote.[2] While this is undoubtedly true for some voters, evidence suggests that most are able to use informational shortcuts such as endorsements to regularly determine the side of the vote that best fulfills their interests (Lupia 1994; Bowler and Donovan 1998). A third concern is that certain voters, especially minority voters, may not be given a meaningful choice. The issues that actually make it to the statewide ballot may be totally unrelated to the issues certain groups care about.[3] However, this does not appear to be the case in California. Both the variety of groups that have sponsored initiatives on statewide ballots and the wide array of issues that have been put on the ballot suggest that access to the initiative process is not limited to the wealthiest segments of the state (Gerber 1999; Donovan et al. 1998).[4] Thus the vote in direct democracy appears to meaningfully measure the interests of different racial and ethnic groups.

Data

To evaluate tyranny of the majority, we analyze data from the direct democracy in California. We choose to focus on California not only because the quality of the data far surpasses that available in other states but also because California has been viewed as being at the forefront of the backlash against a growing racial and ethnic minority population (Maharidge 1996; Schrag 1998). As Dale Maharidge has claimed, "California is leading the nation in the revolt" against minorities (1996, 7). Thus if the initiative process lends itself to tyranny of the majority, evidence of such tyranny can probably be found in California. In addition, since initiatives first on the ballot in California tend to spread throughout the rest of the country and its racial makeup today mirrors the projected makeup of the whole country by midcentury, California is likely to be a harbinger of things to come elsewhere.[5] Yet we should clearly state that the results of our research cannot be taken as representative of other states at this point in time.

The primary data for this study are ... seventeen *Los Angeles Times* exit polls taken during primary and general elections between 1978 and 2000. The *Times* exit polls queried people about their votes on fifty-one different propositions. Though the exit polls tended to ask respondents about the more controversial or high-profile initiatives on the ballot, they also measured voting behavior on one legislative constitutional amendment and four bonds.

Each survey contains a representative sample of California's voters (average N of 4,145 in each poll, for a total of 195,019 proposition votes by respondents in the data set) and generally includes a large enough sample of African American, Latino, and Asian American voters to allow for analysis of each group. The demographic characteristics of each racial and ethnic group in each poll closely match the demographic characteristics of the total population of each group in the state. Thus by using this data set we include both a large number of minority respondents and a wide array of questions in our study.

Furthermore, the exit poll data are very accurate, correctly reflecting the winning side in fifty of the fifty-one votes. The actual vote and the estimated vote based on the exit poll data differ by an average of 2.6 percentage points (standard deviation 2.3). We have further tested the accuracy of our data by comparing the statewide Asian American, black, Latino, and white votes on each proposition with estimates from Voter News Service / CBS exit polls as well as with estimates derived from analysis of actual precinct-level returns.[6] In both cases, the estimates and the patterns of minority success and failure correspond closely to the *Los Angeles Times* data.[7]

One limitation of the *Los Angeles Times* exit polls is that racial and ethnic groups are not broken down by country of origin. This is less of a problem in the case of Latinos, since the vast majority of Latinos in California are Mexican Americans. However, it is a severe restriction for our analyses of Asian Americans. California's Asian American population is fairly evenly divided among Chinese, Filipino, Korean, Japanese, and Vietnamese Americans (Nakanishi 1998). Moreover, existing research suggests that the views and politics of these different

Asian American subgroups often differ significantly (Tam 1995). Thus we are limited in our ability to generalize about tyranny of the majority against specific Asian American subgroups.

Methodology

Because we are interested in how well racial and ethnic minorities fared as well as in how groups with different class, regional, or political backgrounds fared, we have included in our statistical analysis measures of race and ethnicity, age, income, gender, education, region, political ideology, and party identification. To help predict which types of voters were the most likely to vote for the winning side, we have employed a statistical procedure, logit regressions, that allows us to calculate the likelihood that a voter from a particular group will end up on the winning side while controlling for an array of potentially relevant racial, regional, political, and class factors.[8] However, we might also want to know how each group fared without controlling for other factors. In this case, measuring how well a group is doing simply means adding up how many times voters from a particular group voted for the winning side and comparing that with the same data for other groups. In almost every case, these percentages closely follow the results from the regression analyses.

Outcomes across Direct Democracy

Are whites able to control the outcome of direct democracy at the expense of racial and ethnic minorities? At least theoretically that possibility exists. Although racial and ethnic minorities now compose roughly half of California's population, the state's voters are largely white. Whites currently make up 68 percent of the voters in the state (Baldassare 2000). Latinos are well behind, with only 19 percent of the electorate, and blacks and Asian Americans follow with 6 and 7 percent respectively. In theory, the large white majority means that whites could determine the outcome of every proposition on the ballot. Even if every member of all three nonwhite groups voted in the same direction on a given issue, the majoritarian logic of direct democracy suggests that nonwhites could all wind up losers.

In table 1, we provide our first analysis of the fate of racial and ethnic minorities under direct democracy in California. The numbers in Table 1 show the probability that voters from different demographic groups vote for the winning side across the fifty-one initiatives in the *Los Angeles Times* data set. Thus, for example, a value of .619 for whites indicates that the average white voter is likely to end up on the winning side of the vote 62 percent of the time.

Table 1. Probability of Being on the Winning Side of
Direct Democracy by Demographic Group

Voter	Probability of Winning
Asian American	.599
Black	.596
Latino	.593[a]
White	.619
Income—high	.620
Income—low	.605
Education—bachelor's	.598[a]
Education—no high school	.607
Age—under 30	.615
Age—over 65	.613
Gender—female	.629
Gender—male	.619
Region—Bay area	.620
Region—Los Angeles	.618
Region—Other Southern California	.633[a]
Ideology—conservative	.632
Ideology—liberal	.606
Partisanship—Democrat	.613
Partisanship—Republican	.624

[a] significantly different from mean voter $p < .05$

The general conclusion from Table 1 is that there are no really big winners or losers in California's direct democracy system. Every group we consider wins just about as often as every other group. In no case does being in a particular racial, demographic, or political group greatly increase or decrease the probability that a respondent will be on the winning side of the vote. In fact, for only two groups (Latinos and voters with a bachelor's degree) is the outcome significantly different from that of the median voter ($p < .05$). Moreover, voters from every group we examine have well over a 50 percent chance of voting with the majority side.

Of the personal features of the voter that do at least play some role, race and ethnicity are clearly among the most important. Nonwhite voters are among the least successful voters in direct democracy. While Asian Americans, blacks, and Latinos all have between a 59 and 60 percent chance of being on the winning side of a given vote, whites have about a 62 percent chance. There is only one other group to have less than a 60 percent chance of being on the winning side (college-educated voters). Still it is also clear that even race and ethnicity make little difference in the outcomes across the whole range of propositions. White voters are, after all, only about 2 percentage points more successful than nonwhite voters. The fact that well over half of Asian Americans, blacks, and Latinos were able to have their preferences met contradicts the notion that the initiative is only "marginally respectful of minority rights and interests" (Schrag 1998, 21).

Initiatives Relevant to Minorities

This initial analysis is important to gauge the extent that direct legislation, as an institution, systematically biases policy against the rights and interests of minorities. It shows that most of the time, members of minority groups are not harmed by direct democracy in the sense of systematically losing important policy battles. However, examining all types of initiatives on the ballot in California may cast too wide a net. It is possible that by examining all types of propositions on the ballot in California, we may have biased our results against finding any important effects on minorities. If there are many measures in our data set only marginally important to racial and ethnic groups, then we may mask the impact of those measures that do matter to these groups. In other words, our estimates may place too much weight on relatively unimportant issues and not enough on important ones. Therefore we now restrict our analysis to those propositions that are, by various accounts, important to racial and ethnic minorities. Specifically, we focus on three subsets of initiatives: 1) propositions on issues that minority voters say are the most important to them, 2) propositions where racial and ethnic minorities have a clear preference (vote cohesively), and 3) propositions that directly target or focus on racial and ethnic minorities.

The Issues Minorities Think Are Most Important

We first examine propositions on issues that minorities consider most important. Over the past three years, a series of statewide polls have repeatedly asked Californians the following open-ended question: "What do you think is the *most* important public policy issue facing California today?" Although the order differs for African Americans, Latinos, and Asian Americans, the five issues that each group consistently ranks as most important are education, crime, economy/jobs, immigration, and poverty.[9]

To assess how well minority voters fare on these issues, we identified all of the propositions in our data set that directly addressed at least one of these areas. Our approach once again involves identifying which factors helped to explain whether a voter was on the winning or the losing side of a proposition vote. The first column of Table 2 presents the probabilities that voters from different racial

Table 2. Probability of Being on the Winning Side of Direct Democracy by Demographic Group. Propositions That Matter to Latinos, Blacks, and Asian Americans

| | On Most Important Issues | When Minorities Have a Clear Preference | | | Minority Targeted Propositions |
		Asians Vote Cohesively	Blacks Vote Cohesively	Latinos Vote Cohesively	
Asian	.587	.631	.618	.613	.556[a]
Black	.586	.563[a]	.613	.633	.644[a]
Latino	.518[a]	.631	.639	.601[a]	.395[a]
White	.592	.630	.617	.627	.705

[a] significantly different from white voter, p < .05.

and ethnic groups wind up on the winning side of the vote, based on the fifteen propositions that addressed issues minorities see as important.

On the set of issues that minorities themselves say are important, the majority of voters from all three minority groups are on the winning side most of the time. For blacks and Asian Americans, the difference in the probability of winning, relative to whites, is less than one percent. The probability that a Latino voter prevails on a proposition in one of these five issue areas is 52 percent, which is seven percent less than the probability of winning for white voters. Thus while Latinos are less likely to prevail on important issues than the other racial and ethnic groups, these results suggest that most Latino voters nevertheless wind up on the winning side. In short, the data do not support the notion that minority voters regularly lose out on the issues they care most about.

When Minorities Have a Clear Preference

A second way to identify propositions important to minorities is to single out those measures where a large majority of Asian Americans, blacks, and Latinos voted in the same direction. Presumably, if the vast majority of black voters disapprove of a particular initiative, then it matters to the black community as a whole whether that proposition passes.[10] By voting cohesively, minorities are in essence indicating a clear preference on an issue.[11]

Although somewhat arbitrary, we define cohesiveness as those measures with over 60 percent support or over 60 percent opposition from minority group members.[12] Columns 2–4 of table 2 present the predicted probability that members of each racial and ethnic group wind up winners for each set of measures.

How does cohesive voting on the part of each racial and ethnic group change the outcomes of direct democracy? The results in Table 2 show that when racial and ethnic minorities vote cohesively, they at least marginally improve their odds of being on the winning side of the vote. For Asian Americans (column 2) and African Americans (column 3), cohesive voting means that each group is not significantly more likely than white voters to be on the losing side of the proposition vote. For Latinos (column 4), cohesive voting has less of an impact. On propositions where Latinos vote cohesively, they are significantly less likely than whites to find themselves on the winning side. However, this effect is quite small. The probability of voting for the winning side for Latinos is only 3 percent less than for whites. Overall then, it is clear that minorities are not systematically losing out on the initiatives where they have a clear preference and vote cohesively. Latinos fare marginally worse than blacks and Asian Americans when they vote cohesively, but all racial and ethnic groups win more often than they lose.

Initiatives that Directly Target Minority Rights

Finally, we consider the small subset of propositions that directly target members of minority groups. Much of the contemporary concern about how direct democracy affects racial and ethnic minorities seems to stem from this small number of initiatives explicitly focusing on them. It is on these issues that critics claim the "demagogic potential of the initiative" (Schrag 1998, 226) has been reached. They see the success of propositions that cut affirmative action (Proposition 209) or that require public servants to report suspected illegal immigrants (Proposition 187) as signs of a white population that feels threatened and is eager to use direct democracy to lash out at minorities (Tolbert and Hero 1996; Maharidge 1996).

To test this claim, we performed a content analysis of every California statewide proposition in the past three decades to identify all of the "minority targeted" propositions. Of the 128 initiatives and referendums since 1970, we singled out 8 that directly targeted racial and ethnic groups. However, because neither the *Los Angels Times* exit poll nor the California Poll asked questions about 2 of these measures, we have complete data on only 6. These 6 initiatives deal with several policy issues especially sensitive to minorities: eliminating attempts to integrate schools through school busing (Proposition 21 in 1972), mandating English-only ballots (Proposition 38 in 1984), proclaiming English as the official language of the state (Proposition 63 in 1986), eliminating services for illegal immigrants (Proposition 187 in 1994), ending affirmative action (Proposition 209 in 1996), and ending bilingual education (Proposition 227 in 1998).

Are minorities losing out on these highly controversial initiatives? The answer is more complicated than many critics have claimed. On the one hand, the evidence confirms some of the criticisms of direct democracy. Whites are much more likely to vote for the winning side than are racial and ethnic minorities. The probability that a white voter ends up on the winning side of the vote is 71 percent on minority-targeted propositions, which suggests that whites are indeed dominating these initiative contests. And in each case, members of minority groups are clearly less likely than whites to prevail.

However, the results also highlight some important differences between Asian Americans, blacks, and Latinos. African American or Asian American voters are, in fact, more likely than not to be on the winning side of these propositions (64 and 56 percent respectively). So for these two groups, we conclude that direct democracy should not be seen as a major barrier to achieving their political goals, even on issues that directly seek to limit some of their rights.

Latinos are a different story altogether. On these minority-targeted initiatives, Latinos consistently lose out.[13] In fact, Latino voters have only a 40 percent chance of being on the winning side. Given that several of these initiatives were on subjects of fundamental importance to the Latino community, this result shows that Latinos, indeed, have much to worry about when issues that target their rights are decided via direct democracy.

These results seem to indicate that the prime target of white antiminority policy is the newly emerging immigrant minorities. As a small, stable population, blacks in California may be perceived as posing less of an economic, political, or social threat to the white population. Thus there is little reason to single them out in statewide initiatives. In contrast, as a large, visible, and increasingly powerful population, Latinos may be perceived as posing a much greater threat. Some policy advocates may feel the need to target Latinos and to try to enact policies that curb their growing political, economic, and social influence. Asian Americans, as a growing but significantly smaller and often less politically visible population, fall somewhere in between the other two groups.

Why Don't Whites Dominate? Underlying Patterns in the Vote

The relative success of nonwhite voters in direct democracy in California leads us to an interesting and important question: Why are white voters not dominating the outcomes of direct democracy at the expense of nonwhite voters? After all, whites make up the clear majority of voters in all of the direct legislation elections we examined. Even if 100 percent of all Asian American, black, and Latino voters voted in the same direction on a given issue, they could still end up losers.

Nevertheless, white control of the outcomes in California and other states is far from automatic. In particular, two conditions are necessary for tyranny of the white majority to exist. First, the interests of white and nonwhite voters must be opposed. If most voters agree on what is good policy, regardless of their race or

Table 3. Divisions in Proposition Voting

	Average Difference in the Yes Vote
White-Asian	8.9
White-Black	12.2
White-Latino	9.8
Black-Asian	12.1
Black-Latino	7.1
Latino-Asian	9.7
Democrat-Republican	21.1
Liberal-Conservative	26.5
Men-Women	4.6
No High School-College Education	9.5
Low-High Income	6.4

ethnicity, then clearly there can be no tyranny of the white majority. Second, each racial and ethnic minority group must, to a certain extent, vote as a unified bloc. If a particular minority group is divided, then it is unclear whether that group lost or won, regardless of the outcome. Moreover, if whites, as the majority, are not unified, then they cannot determine the outcome of the vote, and minorities will have a significant say in determining who wins and who loses.

In California over the time period we examined, neither of these conditions was met regularly. First, it seems that white voters are much more apt to agree with nonwhite voters than they are to disagree with them. Table 3 shows the average difference in the percentage voting "yes" of various racial, demographic, and political groups across the fifty-one initiatives in the *Los Angeles Times* exit polls. Larger numbers indicate greater divisions between the two groups.

As the table indicates, differences between white and nonwhite voters do exist. The white vote differs from the black vote by an average of 12 percentage points. The white-Latino divide and the white–Asian American divide are a little smaller, averaging about 10 and 9 percentage points respectively. None of these numbers suggests a huge divide. For example, if 70 percent of white voters favored an initiative, then one might see 60 percent Latino, 61 percent Asian American, and 58 percent black support for the same initiative.

Interestingly, divisions among the three nonwhite groups are roughly similar to the divide between whites and nonwhites. The average black–Asian American divide is 12 points. For Latinos and Asian Americans, it is nearly 10 points. Blacks and Latinos tend to vote more similarly (a difference of 7 points) than any other racial and ethnic groups.

One way to gauge the magnitude of these numbers is to compare them with divisions among other important demographic and political groups. Racial and ethnic divisions are, in fact, dwarfed by divisions between the political groups that we examined. The liberal-conservative divide (27 percent) and the Democrat-Republican divide (21 percent) are roughly twice as large as the divide between white and nonwhite voters. Table 3 also reveals that race and ethnicity divide voters just slightly more than education. The divide between whites and nonwhites is, however, more than twice as large as the gender gap.

Put another way, initiatives popular among whites also tend to be popular among Asian Americans, blacks, and Latinos. The aggregate white "yes" vote, across propositions, is highly correlated with the Asian American, black, and Latino "yes" vote. The white vote is most closely correlated with the Asian American vote (r = .67, p < .01), but whites also regularly agreed with Latinos (r = .52, p < .01) and African Americans (r = .49, p < .01). In short, regardless of race or ethnicity, people seem to want many of the same things.[14]

The second reason why whites don't dominate proposition voting is a lack of unity among voters of every race and ethnicity. The white community is anything but monolithic, and voting patterns in direct legislation elections reflect this. On the average proposition, only 61 percent of white voters voted in the same direction. That means that in the typical case, 39 percent of the white electorate disagree with the "white" position. Even on the minority-targeted initiatives where one might suspect whites to have a clear agenda, there is still considerable disagreement. Averaging across the six minority-targeted initiatives, only 63 percent of white voters wound up on the same side of the vote.

By this measure, whites vote cohesively about as often as other racial and ethnic groups, though considerably less often than political groups. Table 4 presents the level of cohesiveness for several important voting groups in California. Among racial and ethnic groups, whites and Asian Americans are slightly less cohesive than other groups. Given the diverse backgrounds of Asian Americans in California, it is probably not surprising that just over 60 percent of Asian American voters support their group's preferred position in the average case. Blacks and Latinos tend to vote in a slightly more unified fashion. On average, almost 63 percent of Latino voters support the majority Latino position. Blacks are close behind with 62 percent voting for the same side.[15]

Other major demographics groups in the state are as cohesive as whites. Men and women, high- and low-income voters, older and younger voters, and those with a little or a great deal of education all vote at about the same level of unity as whites. In fact, there are almost no notable differences among these groups.

Of all the groups we examined, only politically defined groups tend to vote together regularly. Republicans, conservatives, and liberals were the three most

Table 4. Voting Cohesiveness

Group	Average Percentage Voting for the Same Side
All Respondents	61.2
Asians	60.1
Blacks	62.4
Latinos	62.6
Whites	61.1
Democrats	62.9
Republicans	66.7
Conservatives	66.5
Liberals	65.0
Age 18–29	60.8
Age 65+	61.7
No high school degree	61.2
College degree	59.9
Low income	60.8
Medium income	60.4
High income	61.2

unified groups. In each case, 65 to 66 percent of the members of the group supported the group's preferred position on average. Democrats were not far behind, with an average of 63 percent supporting the group's preferred position.

These findings suggest that the conditions that would create white majority control of the initiative process do not exist in California. At present, whites could choose to regularly target and defeat nonwhites, but this has not happened. Asian Americans, blacks, and Latinos have been able to achieve relative success via direct democracy not because the system prevents whites from dominating the nonwhite voting minority but because there exists widespread agreement on policy that cuts across racial and ethnic boundaries. For most issues, white and nonwhite voters tend to agree on the kinds of policies they prefer and those they dislike. This is an important factor that should not be overlooked in discussions of race, ethnicity, and direct democracy.

What Do Racial and Ethnic Minorities Think of Direct Democracy?

Our analysis of direct legislation elections in California suggests that racial and ethnic minorities win more often than they lose. This finding generally persists

Table 5. Support for Direct Democracy across Racial and Ethnic
Groups (in percentages)

	Are Ballot Propositions a Good Thing?			
	Asian Americans	Blacks	Latinos	Whites
1979	80	60	83	87
1982	78	69	83	85
1997	77	57	73	73

Source: Field Institute, California Polls 7904, 8206, 9004.

even when we look at issue areas minorities care most about. Since minority voters are faring reasonably well in direct legislation elections, this should be reflected in the views minority voters hold toward direct democracy. Thus we expect nonwhite voters to have generally favorable impressions of direct democracy in California over this time period.

Since 1979 the California Poll has periodically asked voters about their support for direct democracy. In Table 5 we present data on patterns in support for direct democracy from these polls. The results are clear: widespread support for ballot propositions exists. Asked whether they thought "statewide ballot proposition elections are a good thing for California, a bad thing, or don't make much difference," majorities of every racial and ethnic group felt that ballot proposition elections are a good thing for the state. Least positive on this question are African Americans. However, even among black respondents in 1997, 57 percent felt that ballot elections were a good thing, compared with only 9 percent who thought they were a bad thing. Support for direct democracy has clearly waned in California over time, but it is still something that most minority (and white) voters support.

Conclusion

This analysis has important implications for how we understand the impact of direct democracy on minorities and minority rights. The data presented here reveal a system that occasionally tramples minority preferences but at the same time generally gives minorities a voice and more often than not leads to policies most minorities favor. Nonwhite voters fare poorly when initiatives are directly linked to race and ethnicity. On affirmative action, illegal immigration, bilingual education, and other minority-focused issues, racial and ethnic minorities are much more apt than whites to vote for the losing side.

Of all the demographic and political groups we examined, Latinos fare the worst. Blacks and Asian Americans vote for the losing side of initiative elections slightly more than white voters, but Latinos are far and away the most likely to lose out, especially on minority-focused initiatives. Indeed, the majority of Latino voters vote for the losing side on minority-focused initiatives. If this pattern continues or is amplified, relations between Latinos and other racial and ethnic groups could sour.

At the same time, the outcomes of direct democracy usually follow the preferences of Latinos, Asian Americans, and African Americans. Systemwide, we find little evidence of a major bias against any group. When we focus on the whole array of initiatives addressed through direct democracy in the past twenty years, every racial, ethnic, and demographic group we examine winds up on the winning side of the vote about as often as every other group. Moreover, every group wins regularly. Latinos, who are the least successful racial or ethnic group, still vote for the winning side over 50 percent of the time. Even when we look at issue arenas that Latinos, African Americans, and Asian Americans say they care most about, the groups do reasonably well in most initiative elections.

Perhaps the most important set of findings concerns patterns underlying the vote. African Americans, Asian Americans, and Latinos often wind up on the winning side of direct democracy not because they outvote the white majority but because they usually agree with the majority of whites. The system we study in this report is not one defined by racial and ethnic divisions. Rather, whites and nonwhites are much more apt to agree than to disagree over matters of policy. And just as important, our analysis of the vote in direct democracy indicates that no racial or ethnic group is particularly unified. Each racial and ethnic group is fairly divided over which initiatives to support and which to oppose.

Thus we conclude that Madison's concerns about an interested and overbearing majority trampling the rights of minorities have not been realized in the arena of direct democracy. Nevertheless, the potential for a majority to use direct democracy to usurp the rights of minorities still exists. If the fairly widespread agreement across racial and ethnic groups and the fairly large divisions within each racial and ethnic group were to change, outcomes might also change, and the relative success of minority voters could be a thing of the past. The well-being of minorities in direct democracy is not assured but instead rests on a continued pattern of accord across groups.

NOTES

1. Our own analysis of a series of statewide surveys conducted by the Public Policy Institute of California between 1998 and 2000 suggests that nonvoters tend to be slightly more

liberal than voters on a number of subjects that emerge in direct democracy in California, but these differences tend to be fairly small.

2. Critics of the initiative process claim that voters often have very little knowledge about particular initiatives and are confused or manipulated by expensive media campaigns (California Commission on Campaign Finance 1992). Moreover, initiatives can be extremely complicated and have unintended consequences.

3. Control over the initiative agenda by whites, the wealthy, or others could restrict the issues that arise and limit the options that voters have (Broder 2000; Garrett 1999).

4. In focusing on the outcome of the vote and the question of who wins and who loses, we also overlook other important elements of the initiative process, such as its indirect effects on the behavior of the state legislature and the issues of nonimplementation (Gerber and Hug 2000; Gerber et al. 2000).

5. Almost immediately after Proposition 13 passed in California, thirty-seven other states reduced property taxes, twenty-eight cut income taxes, and thirteen restricted sales tax collections (Magleby 1994). In the eight months after California's Proposition 209 sought to end affirmative action in California, twenty states moved on bills or resolutions to limit affirmative action, with fifteen of them copying California's Proposition 209 word for word (Maharidge 1996).

6. To derive statewide estimates of the vote by race and ethnicity from the actual vote total at the precinct level, we employed ecological inference (King 1997), combining the vote and census data on racial demographics for each precinct. Ecological inference employs a complex statistical procedure to derive estimates of a particular group's behavior in a particular precinct based on the actual outcome for that precinct as a whole and patterns of behavior across the thousands of precincts in the state.

7. As a final check on the data, we analyzed statewide surveys conducted by the Field Institute between 1970 and 1998. This Field Institute California Poll series has the advantage of covering a longer time span and asking about voter preferences on a much larger set of propositions (131), but it is limited by a significantly smaller sample size and the fact that it is a pre-election poll rather than an exit poll. We repeated all of the analyses with the California Poll data and have found that in almost all cases both data sets produce equivalent results.

8. We pooled the individual respondents' votes from every *Los Angeles Times* exit poll for the initiative elections relevant to a particular set of analyses. We used the King, Tomz, and Wittenberg simulation procedure to convert the logit coefficients to expected probabilities (King, Tomz, and Wittenberg, 2000), which we report in the text.

9. Answers are based on the mean from ten statewide surveys conducted between May 1998 and September 2000 by the Public Policy Institute of California. Answers were coded into one of thirty categories. Racial issues were ranked seventh most important by Latinos but only fifteenth and seventeenth most important by blacks and Asian Americans, respectively.

10. There may also be cases where a group voted unanimously on something of minor importance. Content analysis suggests that the issues we included in this estimation are of importance to minority voters.

11. Overall, each group was cohesive on a similar number of initiatives—twenty-four for Asian Americans, thirty for blacks, thirty-two for Latinos, and twenty-nine for whites. Though some overlap exists, each racial and ethnic group voted cohesively on a distinct set of initiatives, yielding different analyses for each one. Blacks tend to be more cohesive on initiatives

that focused on business or commerce, housing, and the environment. Surprisingly, blacks tended not to be cohesive on minority-targeted or taxation propositions. Latinos were more cohesive on minority-targeted and environmental initiatives and least cohesive on taxation propositions. Asian Americans tended to vote cohesively on propositions dealing with health and the environment while being more divided over business or commerce, criminal justice, and language issues.

12. As a test of robustness, supplemental analyses that employed higher thresholds of cohesiveness produced very similar results.

13. The other losers on minority-targeted initiatives are liberals and Democrats. The probability that self-identified liberals and Democrats are on the winning side of the vote is 30 percent and 51 percent, respectively.

14. This finding conforms well with research on public attitudes in California, which suggests that differences of opinion between racial and ethnic groups are not that pronounced on most public policy issues (Hajnal and Baldassare 2001).

15. Interestingly, minorities were also not all that unified on minority-targeted propositions. Seventy percent of Latinos voted on the same side on average on these propositions, but only 60 percent of African Americans did so and for Asian Americans unity fell to 56 percent.

BIBLIOGRAPHY

Baldassare, Mark. 2000. *California in the New Millennium: The Changing Social and Political Landscape.* San Francisco: Public Policy Institute of California.

Bell, Derrick. 1978. "The Referendum: Democracy's Barrier To Racial Equality." *Washington Law Review* 54 (March): 1–29.

Bowler, Shaun, and Todd Donovan. 1998. *Demanding Choices: Opinion Voting and Democrat Democracies.* Ann Arbor: University of Michigan Press.

Broder, David. 2000. *Democracy Derailed: The Initiative Campaigns and the Power of Money.* New York: Harcourt.

California Commission on Campaign Finance. 1992. "Democracy by Initiative: Shaping California's Fourth Branch of Government." Los Angeles: Center for Responsive Politics.

Donovan, Todd, Shaun Bowler, David McCuan, and Ken Fernandez. 1998. "Contending Players and Strategies: Opposition Advantages in Initiative Campaigns." In *Citizens as Legislators: Direct Democracy in the United States.* Edited by S. Bowler, T. Donovan, and C. Tolbert. Columbus: Ohio State University.

Garrett, Elizabeth. 1999. "Money, Agenda Setting, and Direct Democracy." *Texas Law Review* 77 (November): 1845–1890.

Gerber, Elisabeth R. 1999. *The Populist Paradox: Interest Group Influence and the Promise of Direct Legislation.* Princeton: Princeton University Press.

Gerber, Elisabeth R., and Simon Hug. 2000. "Minority Rights and Direct Legislation: Theory, Methods, and Evidence." Working paper, University of California, San Diego.

Gerber, Elisabeth R., Arthur Lupia, Mathew D. McCubbins, and D. Roderick Kiewiet. 2000. *Stealing the Initiative: How State Government Responds to Direct Democracy.* Upper Saddle River, N.J.: Prentice Hall.

Guinier, Lani. 1994. *The Tyranny of the Majority: Fundamental Fairness in Representative Democracy.* New York: Free Press.

Hajnal, Zoltan L., and Mark Baldassare. 2001. *Finding Common Ground: Racial and Ethnic Attitudes in California*. San Francisco: Public Policy Institute of California.

Hamilton, Alexander, James Madison, and John Jay. 1961. *The Federalist Papers*. Edited by Clinton Rossiter. New York: Mentor.

I&R Institute. 2000. Historical Database. www.iandrinstitute.org.

King, Gary. 1997. *A Solution to the Ecological Inference Problem*. Princeton: Princeton University Press.

King, Gary, Michael Tomz, and Jason Wittenberg. 2000. "Making the Most of Statistical Analyses: Improving Interpretation and Presentation." *American Journal of Political Science* 44 (April): 341–355.

Lupia, Arthur. 1994. "Shortcuts Versus Encyclopedias: Information and Voting Behavior in California Insurance Reform Elections." *American Political Science Review* 88 (March): 63–76.

Magleby, David B. 1994. "Direct Legislation in the American States." In *Referendums around the World*. Edited by David Butler and Austin Ranney. London: Macmillan.

Maharidge, Dale. 1996. *The Coming White Minority: California's Eruptions and America's Future*. New York: Times Books.

Nakanishi, Don. 1998. "When Numbers Do Not Add Up: Asian Pacific Americans and California Politics." In *Racial And Ethnic Politics in California*. Edited by Michael B. Preston, Bruce E. Cain, and Sandra Bass. Berkeley: Institute of Governmental Studies Press.

Reyes, Belinda, ed. 2001. *A Portrait of Race and Ethnicity in California: The Social and Economic Well-Being of Racial and Ethnic Groups*. San Francisco: Public Policy Institute of California.

Schrag, Peter. 1998. *Paradise Lost: California's Experience, America's Future*. New York: New Press.

Tam, Wendy K. 1995. "Asians—A Monolithic Voting Bloc?" *Political Behavior* 17 (March): 223–249.

Tolbert, Caroline J., and Rodney E. Hero. 1996. "Race/Ethnicity and Direct Democracy: An Analysis of California's Illegal Immigration Initiative." *Journal of Politics* 58 (August): 806–818

Verba, Sidney, Kay Lehman Schlozman, and Henry E. Brady. 1995. *Voice and Equality: Civic Voluntarism in American Politics*. Cambridge: Harvard University Press.

Wolfinger, Raymond E., and Steven J. Rosenstone. 1980. *Who Votes?* New Haven: Yale University Press.

4-2

American Diversity and the 2000 Census

Nathan Glazer

Since the earliest days of the republic, race has proved a difficult issue for each generation of politicians to resolve. While the problem began with slavery, it did not, of course, end with the institution's eradication during the Civil War. Throughout the nineteenth and twentieth centuries, the core issues of "white over black" never receded far from the surface of America's politics. As the country has entered the twenty-first century there have been signs of change in the racial picture, change that has been occurring for some time but has suddenly become manifest. For one, Hispanics have now eclipsed African Americans as the nation's largest racial minority. In this essay, Nathan Glazer ponders a couple of fundamental, yet easily overlooked, issues of race for this next century. They concern how the government defines race and, more important, how in our increasingly multiracial and at the same time assimilated society we define ourselves.

THE 2000 CENSUS, on which the Census Bureau started issuing reports in March and April of 2001, reflected, in its structure and its results, the two enduring themes of American racial and ethnic diversity, present since the origins of American society in the English colonies of the Atlantic coast: first, the continued presence of what appears to be an almost permanent lower caste composed of the black race; and second, the ongoing process of immigration of races and peoples from all quarters of the globe, who seem, within a few generations, to merge into a common American people.

To make two such large generalizations is admittedly a bold move. Undoubtedly, as further data from the census is released, we will have evidence of the continuing progress of American blacks in education, occupational diversity, and income. We will have grounds for arguing that the effects of integration into a common people can be seen, at long last, among American blacks. And when it comes to the new waves of immigration of the past few decades, some will question whether the process of assimilation and incorporation, which has swallowed

Source: Nathan Glazer, "American Diversity and the 2000 Census," *Public Interest* 144 (summer 2001): 3–18.

up so many groups and races and religions into a common American people, will continue to work its effects on the new groups now gathered together under the terms "Hispanic" and "Asian." Yet I believe it can be argued that this large distinction in the processes of assimilation and integration that has persisted during the three- or four-century history of American diversity—the distinction between blacks and others—still shows itself, and still poses some of the most difficult questions for American society.

The First Census

The distinction makes itself evident in the very history and structure of the census, and in the character of the data that it first presents to the public today. In the first census of 1790, required for purposes of apportionment [seats in the House of Representatives] by the U.S. Constitution adopted in 1787, the separation between blacks and whites was already made. Indeed, that separation was itself foreshadowed by the Constitution, which, in a famous compromise, decreed that "Representatives . . . shall be apportioned among the several states . . . according to their respective numbers, which shall be determined by adding to the whole number of free persons . . . three-fifths of all other persons." Those "other persons" were slaves. The "three-fifths" was a compromise between excluding all slaves for purposes of apportionment (which would have reduced the weight of the Southern slave states in the union) or counting them simply as persons (which would have given the slave states too great weight).

The census could have fulfilled the requirements of the Constitution by counting only slaves. But what was to be done with free blacks? There were, even then, free blacks, but their civil status was sharply below that of whites. It was apparently decided that they could not be simply numbered among the "free persons" referred to in the Constitution but had to be clearly distinguished from whites. So the first census went beyond the Constitution: It counted "free white males and females" as one category, "slaves" as another, but then added a category of "all other free persons." The count of "other persons"—slaves—and "all other free persons"—free blacks—produced the total number of blacks. Thus from the beginning, white could be differentiated from black. That has remained the most enduring distinction in the U.S. census.

In that first census, following the apportionment provision of the Constitution, "Indians not taxed" were also excluded. Over time, this simple scheme has been extended to cover other races and ethnic groups as they entered the new nation through immigration, to a degree which is possibly unique among national censuses, and which we will explore below. But the census begins crucially with the distinction between white and black. As Clara Rodriguez writes in her book *Changing Race:*

> Between the drafting of the Constitution of 1787 and the taking of the first census in 1790, the term white became an explicit part of [the free population]. . . . Theoretically, those in political charge could have chosen another definition for the [free population]. . . . They could have chosen "free English-speaking males over sixteen" or "free males of Christian descent" or "of European descent." But they chose color. Having named the central category "white" gave a centrality and power to color that has continued throughout the history of the census.

But of course this reflected the centrality of the black-white distinction in American society and the American mind. Rodriguez goes on to note that on occasion in the pre-Civil War censuses "aliens and foreigners not naturalized," separately numbered, are combined in one table with native whites and citizens in a table of "total white." "In the 1850 census, the category 'free whites' is changed to simply 'whites,' which suggests by this time it was evident that all the people in this category were free."

The Color Line

Color—race—has since been elaborated to a remarkable degree in the U.S. census. The most striking aspect of the American census of 2000—as of the few before—is that the short form, which goes to all American households, consists mostly of questions on race and "Hispanicity." Two large questions ask for the respondent's race, and whether the respondent is of "Spanish/Hispanic" origin, and both go into considerable detail in trying to determine just what race, and just what kind of "Hispanic," the respondent is. The race question lists many possibilities to choose from, including, to begin with, "white" and "black," and going on to "Indian (Amer.)," with an additional request to list the name of the tribe, "Eskimo," or "Aleut." And then under the general heading "Asian or Pacific Islander (API)," it lists as separate choices Chinese, Filipino, Hawaiian, Korean, Vietnamese, Japanese, Asian Indian, Samoan, Guamanian, "Other API," and finally "Other race (print name)." In the 2000 census, it was possible for the first time for the respondent to check more than one race. This change was made after an extended discussion in the 1990s about how to account for those with parents of different race, who wanted to check off both, or perhaps more than two.

The question on whether one is Spanish/Hispanic also goes on to list a range of possibilities: "Mexican, Mexican-Am. [for "American"], or Chicano" (to account for the fact that Mexican Americans choose different terms to describe themselves), "Puerto Rican," "Cuban," and "other Spanish/Hispanic," with again the request to write in one group. In the 1990 census, a host of examples—"Argentinean, Colombian, Dominican, Nicaraguan, Salvadoran, Spaniard, and so on," was offered.

The observant and conscientious citizen may note that many other matters of interest to the census and the polity—whether one is of foreign birth or not, a citizen or not, and one's education, occupation, income, housing status, etc.—are all relegated to the long form, which goes to a large sample of citizens. And he may also ask why the census pays such great and meticulous attention to race and ethnicity (or rather one kind of ethnicity, that of Spanish-Hispanic background).

Many answers, going back to the first census of 1790, and before that, to the Constitution that prescribed a regular decennial census, and before that, to the first arrival of black slaves in the English colonies in the early seventeenth century, are available to explain why the first statistics the census makes available today, along with the raw number of the population in each state and locality, are those describing race and ethnicity. But there is also an immediate and proximate answer of much more recent currency: Congress requires that ethnic and racial statistics be available within a year of the census for the purpose of redrawing the boundaries of congressional districts, and the other electoral districts for state legislative assemblies, and for city and county elected officials.

Ethnic and racial statistics have become so significant for redistricting because of the Civil Rights Act of 1964, the Voting Rights Acts of 1965, and the latter's amendments of 1970, 1975, and 1982. . . . The right enshrined in the Voting Rights statute, to the free exercise of the vote, has been extended through litigation and administrative and judicial rule-making to cover rights to the drawing of congressional and other district boundaries in such a way as to protect or enhance the ability of minority groups, blacks in particular, but others too, to elect representatives of their own group. If blacks are to be protected from discrimination . . . then detailed statistics of how a race is distributed are necessary.

That is why the first statistics that come out of the census are those that make it possible to redraw district lines immediately on the basis of the new census, and for various groups to challenge the new district lines if they are aggrieved. . . . For those with the responsibility of drawing up the new districts—the state legislatures primarily—the central concern is generally the maximization of the number of representatives of the party in power in the state legislature. A second concern is to maintain for the incumbents of the favored party district boundaries that secure their return. But overlaying these historic political reasons for drawing district lines, which courts accept in some measure as legitimate, is a new imperative, the protection of minority groups.

The Four "Official" Minorities

"Portrait of a Nation" is the title of a major story on the first results of the census in the *New York Times,* and it is accompanied by elaborate colored maps. The colors provide information on the distribution of the minority population—blacks, Hispanics, Asians, American Indians.

To explain how these have become the American minorities—to the exclusion of many other possible minorities—and why their numbers and distribution are in every newspaper report considered the most important information to look for in the census, would require a precis of American history. It is hardly necessary to explain why blacks are the first of the minority groups. They have been a significant presence in the United States and its predecessor colonies from the beginning. Our greatest national trauma—the Civil War—was directly occasioned by the problem of black slavery, and the most significant amendments to the Constitution became part of that quasi-sacred document in order to deal with the consequences of black slavery.

American Indians were there even before the beginning but were considered outside the society and polity unless they individually entered into non-Indian-American society, as many have, through intermarriage and assimilation. Their status has changed over time, from outside the polity as semi-sovereign foreign nations, to subjects almost without rights, to a population confined on reservations, to one that now increasingly becomes part of the society. Indeed, today, to be able to claim an American-Indian heritage is a plus for one's social status. This is too complex a history to be reviewed here. There is good reason to maintain a separate count of Indians, though there are great complexities in doing so.

"Hispanics," too, were there from before the beginning, if we take into account the Spaniards and Creoles moving up from Mexico who had already established colonial settlements in northern Mexico—what is now the Southwest of the United States—before the first English colonists had established permanent settlements on the Atlantic coast. Of course, they were not "Hispanics" then. Two hundred and fifty years later, this mixed population became part of the United States as a result of the annexation of the northern part of Mexico after the Mexican-American war. But it contained then a small population of Mexicans and Indians, and interestingly enough, despite the sense of racial difference felt by the Anglo-Americans, and despite the prejudice against Mexicans, they were not differentiated in the census as a separate group until 1930. Until then, one presumes, they were "white." In that year, Clara Rodriguez notes, a census publication, responding to the increase in immigration from Mexico as a result of the revolutionary wars and troubles of the 1920s, reported that "persons of Mexican birth or parentage who were not definitely reported as white or Indian were designated

Mexican" and included in "other races." In 1940, this policy was changed, and Mexicans became white again. By 1950, added to the growing number of Mexicans in the Southwest, as a result of immigration in the previous decades, was a large number of Puerto Ricans in New York City, migrants from the island of Puerto Rico, which had been annexed after the Spanish-American war of 1898. In that census year, the two were combined in the census—along with smaller numbers of other groups—into a "Spanish-surnamed" group.

In the wake of Castro's victory in Cuba, a third large group of Latin Americans emigrated to the United States. Whether or not one could make a single meaningful category out of Mexicans, Puerto Ricans, and Cubans, separated as they are by culture, history, and to some extent by racial characteristics, they were so combined, with a host of other Spanish-speaking groups, into a "Hispanic" category in the census of 1970. The creation of the category was a response to political pressure from Mexican Americans. It now includes large numbers of Nicaraguans, Guatemalans, Salvadorans, Dominicans, Colombians, Ecuadorians, and others fleeing the political and economic troubles of their homelands.

Racial and ethnic groups are conventionally described today as "constructed," but it is worth noting that this "construction" is not simply the result of white determinations—it is also the result of group insistence, at least to some degree. As Peter Skerry tells us in his book *Counting on the Census:*

> The finalized questionnaires for the 1970 census were already at the printers when a Mexican American member of the U.S. Interagency Committee on Mexican American affairs demanded that a specific Hispanic-origin question be included. . . . Over the opposition of Census Bureau officials, who argued against inclusion of an untested question so late in the process, [President] Nixon ordered the secretary of commerce and the census director to add the question.

And so "Hispanics" were born. The pressure to maintain the category, with all its subdistinctions, persists. The distinguished demographer Stanley Lieberson has written about a well-intentioned intervention at a conference preparatory to the 1990 census:

> I naively suggested that there was no reason to have an Hispanic question separate from the ethnic ancestry question [an ancestry question has been part of the long form since 1980] since the former . . . could be classified as a subpart of the latter. Several participants from prominent Hispanic organizations were furious at such a proposal. They were furious, by the way, not at me (just a naive academic), rather it was in the form of a warning to census personnel of the consequences that would follow were this proposal to be taken seriously.

The last of the four minorities distinguished in the census is the "Asian," a creation—or construction—that has as complex a history as that of the Hispanic. Chinese and Japanese individuals were undoubtedly present in the United States before they were first listed as "races" in 1870—by then there was a substantial population of Chinese in California, and they were already the subject of racist legislation. In 1930, "Filipino," "Hindu" [sic], and "Korean" were added as separate races, and it became the pattern to add a new "race" for each Asian immigrant group as it became numerous. Eventually, we have the complex category of "Asian and Pacific Islander" (API), with all its listed subgroups.

As in the case of the Mexicans, the initial discrimination that made each of these a separate group was undoubtedly racist and reflected a sense of white superiority. The Asian groups were all subjected to discriminatory legislation. One could be naturalized as a citizen only if one were "white" (or, after the Civil War, black). All sorts of restrictions, from land ownership to the pursuit of certain professions or occupations, were imposed on them by various states because they were noncitizens. But Asian immigrants were denied because of race the right of becoming citizens. These groups were indeed nonwhite, but their separate classification was more than a matter of keeping neat statistics. An identity was being selected for a group felt to be inferior. This identity may well have been the one the members of the group would have chosen, but it was not they who decided they should be numbered aside from the dominant whites. . . .

A Melting Pot?

These then are the four "official" minorities, though no law names these and only these as minorities. But what has happened then to all those others once considered "minorities," ethnic groups that were in the first quarter of the twentieth century in the eye of public attention because of the recency of their immigration, their lower social and economic status, and the concern that they could not be assimilated? Immigration was largely cut off by law in the 1920s because of these concerns. The United States has been a country of immigration since its origins, and by some measures the immigration of the first two decades of the twentieth century was much greater than the immigration of the last three decades, which has swelled the numbers of the new minorities. Had one picked up a book on American minorities and race relations in the 1950s, Jews might have been presented as the typical minority: Much of the social theory and social psychology on minority status was formulated with the position of Jews in mind. Jews were a major element in the mass immigration that preceded the present one, from the 1880s to the 1920s. Other major components of this immigration were Italians, Poles, Hungarians, Czechs, Slovaks, Slovenes, Croats, Serbs, Greeks, Armenians, Lebanese, Syrians, and many other peoples of Eastern and Southern Europe and the Near East. Are they no longer included in the story of American minorities?

One can go further back and ask, what has happened to the Irish, the Germans, the Swedes, Norwegians, and Danes, and the host of immigrants who came earlier and were also once sharply distinguished as separate groups, different from the founding group, the English? Does not the story of American diversity include all these too? How has the palette become restricted to the four minorities that play so large a role in the current census?

The simple answer is that integration and assimilation reduce over time the differences that distinguish one group from another, or from the original settler group, what Tocqueville called the "Anglo-Americans." We have no good term for this group. WASP ("White Anglo-Saxon Protestant") has been used in recent decades, ironically or derisively, for the founding element and their descendants. But aside from the necessity to distinguish such a group historically, no term is currently really necessary: Immigrants merge in two or three generations into a common American people, and ethnic distinctions become less and less meaningful. Ethnicity becomes symbolic, a matter of choice, to be noted on the basis of name or some other signifier on occasion, of little matter for most of one's life.

At one time, the census distinguished the foreign-born by place of birth, and the foreign-born parents of the native-born by place of birth, permitting us to track ethnic groups (somewhat uncertainly, owing to the lack of fit between ethnicity and national boundaries) for two generations. The rest of the population was classed as natives of native parentage, not further distinguishable, at least in the census, on the basis of their ethnicity. In 1980, the question on birthplace of parents was dropped, to the distress of sociologists and students of ethnicity. A new question on "ancestry" was added, which, in theory, would permit us to connect people to ethnic groups in the third generation and beyond. But the amount of mixture among groups, through marriage, is today such that the answers to the ancestry question, if one is not an immigrant or the child of an immigrant with a clear sense of ancestry, are not helpful in distinguishing an ethnic group much beyond the second generation. The answers then become so variable, so dependent on cues from the census itself—such as the examples the census form gives to the respondent regarding what is intended by the term "ancestry," which is by no means clear to many people—as to be hardly meaningful. It is a question that permits some 40 million Americans, seven times the population of Ireland, to declare that they are of "Irish" ancestry.

There are indeed differences of some significance based on ethnicity among the native white population, and sometimes these become evident—when home countries are involved in conflict, for example—or even paramount. This is particularly evident for Jews, who are marked not only as a religion (but the census rigorously refrains from asking any question or accepting any response on religion) but also by ethnicity (but to the census, Jews are not an ethnic group but a religion). The exceptional history that resulted in the killing of most of the Jews of Europe, and the creation of a regularly imperiled State of Israel, ties Jews to their past and to their co-religionists abroad much more than other ethnic groups. They are not to be found in any census count—they are not a "race" and not even, for the census, an "ancestry," even though that answer would make sense for most Jews.

Sociologists and political scientists can plumb for differences among the native white population, and they will find not insignificant differences in income, occupation, political orientation, and so on. Jews, for example, are exceptional among "whites" for their regular overwhelming support for Democrats. Indeed, the differences among native whites, ethnically distinguished, may be greater than those among the official minority groups or between any of them and the native white population. Yet from the point of view of public opinion and official notice, these differences are not significant. The ethnic groups of the great immigrations of the nineteenth and early twentieth century have sunk below the horizon of official attention. They have merged into the "white" population, become integrated and assimilated, and only emerge as a special interest on occasion, stimulated by a conflict or crisis involving the home country.

"Whiteness Theory"

Recently, this somewhat benign view of American history, one in which immigrant groups steadily assimilate to, and become part of, the common American people, has been challenged by historians who argue that this was a strictly limited process, available only to whites, and, further, that many of those who were eventually included as full Americans had to overcome a presumption that they were not "really" white. In other words, race is crucial, both at its beginning and, by implication, throughout American history, for full inclusion. To take one powerful and clear statement of this position:

> The saga of European immigration has long been held up as proof of the openness of American society, the benign and absorptive powers of American capitalism, and the robust health of American democracy. "Ethnic inclusion," "ethnic mobility," and "ethnic assimilation" on the European model set the standard upon which "America," as an ideal, is presumed to work; they provide the normative experience against which others are measured. But this pretty story suddenly fades once one recognizes how crucial Europeans'

racial status as "free white persons" was to their gaining entrance in the first place; how profoundly dependent their racial inclusion was upon the racial exclusion of others; how racially accented the native resistance was even to their inclusion for something over half a century. [Matthew Frye Jacobsen, in *Whiteness of a Different Color.*] The implication of this point of view is that the present minorities as commonly understood exist not only because of the recency of their immigration but primarily because of color: They are not white. Their ability to become full and equal participants in American society is thereby limited because of America's racist character.

But I believe these "whiteness theorists" are wrong. The racist character of the past is clear, and a degree of racism in the present is also evident, despite radical changes in public opinion and major changes in law and legal enforcement. But there has been a striking and irreversible change between the 1920s—when immigration from Eastern and Southern Europe was sharply reduced and immigration from Asia was banned entirely—and the postwar decades and, in particular, the period since the 1960s. Public institutions and significant private institutions today may only take account of race for the purpose of benefiting minorities.

The whiteness theorists may have a story to tell about the past, but it is one that has limited bearing on the present. The new immigrant groups are for the most part distinguished by race or quasi-racial characteristics from the population of European white origin. Yet it seems likely they progress pretty much at the same rate, affected by the same factors—their education and skills, their occupations, the areas of the country in which they settle, and the like—as the European immigrants of the past.

They merge into the common population at the same rate too. We will soon have analyses of marriages between persons of different race and ethnicity, to the extent the census makes possible, but we already know that the number and percentage of intermarriages between persons from the minorities and the majority has grown greatly in recent decades. One analysis of the 1990 census, reported by David T. Canon in his *Race, Redistricting and Representation,* shows that "for married people between the ages of twenty-five and thirty-four, 70 percent of Asian women and 39 percent of Hispanic women have white [sic] husbands." But only 2 percent of black women in the same age group were married to white men. The theme of black difference contrasted with the intermixture and merger of other groups is clearly sounded in these and other statistics.

The End of "Race"?

The first studies conducted by independent analysts of the 2000 census statistics brought up sharply the degree to which blacks are still distinguished from other minorities or subgroups in the United States by residential segregation. "Analysis of Census Finds Segregation Along With Diversity," reads one headline. "Segregation" in this analysis is measured by the diversity of census tracts, as experienced by the "average" person of a given group or race. The average white person lives in a tract that is 80 percent white, down from 85 percent in 1990; the average black person lives in a tract that is 51 percent black, down from 56 percent in 1990; the average Hispanic is less "segregated" by this measure—his tract is 45 percent Hispanic, and increased from 43 percent in 1990. But one may explain this degree of segregation and its rise since 1990 by the huge increase, based on immigration, much of it illegal, of the Hispanic population. The average Asian lives in a tract that is not particularly Asian—18 percent, as against 15 percent in 1990. This rise reflects to some degree the 50 percent increase of the Asian population, mostly through immigration, in the decade.

Local reporting focused on the relative proportions of the minority groups in each community, and also on the degree of segregation. Integration proceeds, but slowly. There are black census tracts in Boston with almost no whites and white tracts with almost no blacks. We calculate these figures every census, as if watching a fever report. The overall picture is that the segregation of blacks is great, the segregation of Hispanic groups, despite the recency of their immigration and their foreign tongue, is rather less, and little segregation is noted among Asians.

The big news of the census was that "Hispanics" had for the first time surpassed blacks in number, but that was only the case if one excluded from the black population those individuals who had chosen the race "black" along with another race. Hispanics rose to 35.3 million, a 61 percent increase in 10 years; blacks rose by about 16 percent to 34.7 million, or 36.4 million if one added those who chose more than one race. Blacks are 12.3 percent of the population, about the same percentage they have maintained for the past century. The increase in Hispanics was much greater than expected: It was generally agreed that one reason for this increase was a larger number of illegal immigrants than had been previously calculated, 9 million according to one demographer instead of 7, perhaps as much as 11 million according to another demographer.

Making the comparison between the two largest minorities was complicated by the fact that respondents could choose more than one race for the first time, and 7 million did so. Analysis of these mixed-race choices, even reporting on them, is not easy. A reporter writes: "Five percent of blacks, 6 percent of Hispanics, 14 percent of Asians and 2.5 percent of whites identified themselves as multi-racial." But why are these multi-race choosers labeled "black" or "Asian"? Is the "one drop" rule once used by the southern states operating here? If someone chooses "American Indian" and another race, do we include that person in the count of American Indians? If we do, that would increase the number of American Indians by more than 50 percent. The Office of Management and Budget oversees the race and ethnic statistics compiled by federal agencies, and it has determined that for their purposes (affirmative-action monitoring and the like) all multi-race choosers who chose white and a minority race are to be counted as being part of the minority, a decision that has pleased minority advocates. But does it reflect how these individuals see themselves?

The mixed-race choices complicate the issue of choosing a base on which to measure the progress of, or possible discrimination against, minorities, an important step in affirmative action programs. That is the reason some minority leaders opposed allowing the mixed-race option. If the base becomes smaller, the degree of discrimination that one may claim in noting how many members of the group have attained this or that position is reduced.

Now that the option exists, it is clear many are eager to choose two or even more races. Among blacks there seems to be less willingness to choose two races than among Asians and American Indians—perhaps because it may be seen as something like race betrayal. But it is noteworthy that younger persons more often choose two races than older ones. If one creates a combined black group by putting together blacks with those who choose black as one of the races they tick off, 2.3 percent of this combined group 50 years of age or older turn out to be multi-race choosers, but 8.1 percent of those 17 and younger choose more than one race. But those who choose the option of black-white are still quite few—fewer in number than those who choose white-other ("other" in the racial category means Hispanic), or white-Asian, or white-American Indian.

When the statistics of intermarriage are analyzed, one can be sure there will be a considerable rise in white-black marriages since 1990, even if the percentage of such intermarriages is considerably less than white-Asian or Hispanic-non-Hispanic marriages. Blacks are still more segregated, more separated, in residence than other minority groups. They are more sharply defined in their consciousness as separate: History has made them so. But even among blacks, one sees the process of assimilation and integration, as measured by choice of race and by intermarriage, at work. By the census of 2010 or 2020, these processes will be further advanced. Indeed, one may perhaps look forward to a time when our complex system of racial and ethnic counting is made so confusing by the number of possible choices, singular and multiple, that the whole scheme is abandoned. Many Americans hope so.

4-3

Women and the Constitution

WHERE WE ARE AT THE END OF THE CENTURY

Martha Craig Daughtrey

Many aspects of women's rights have followed precedents and laws initially established to protect racial minorities. For instance, Title IX, the federal law requiring equal campus opportunity for women, was an addition to legislation directed toward opening facilities to black student athletes. (Ironically, Title IX was added by the bill's opponents, who were thereby hoping to kill it.) There have been, however, two distinct pieces of legislation that targeted women's rights. Both were constitutional amendments; the first was the Nineteenth Amendment ratified in 1920, which guaranteed women the right to vote. The second was the Equal Rights Amendment, which barely failed to secure ratification from the required two-thirds of the states. In this essay a federal appeals court judge reviews the recent history of women's rights and weighs the need for the Equal Rights Amendment.

[In 1999] the *ABA Journal* published a cover story on the renewed efforts to amend the U.S. Constitution to prohibit discrimination on the basis of gender.[1] As it turns out, the Equal Rights Amendment (ERA) which, if ratified, would have become the twenty-seventh amendment to the Federal Constitution—but which "died" for lack of ratification by three additional states in 1982—was reintroduced in the 106th Congress in 1999. The prospect of a renewed effort to pass the ERA in Congress and to mount ratification campaigns in the fifty state legislatures raises a number of questions that I would like to explore with you this evening.

Setting aside the issue of symbolic desirability for the moment, the most obvious question, of course, is whether such an undertaking is even necessary at this point in our constitutional history. The answer depends on an understanding of where we are as the century and the millennium turn, and that, I believe, can only be measured in terms of how far we have come, how far we still have to go,

Source: Martha Craig Daughtrey, "Women and the Constitution: Where We Are at the End of the Century," in *The Unpredictable Constitution,* by Norman Dorsen (NYU Press: 2002), 238–308. Some notes appearing in the original have been deleted.

152

and what would be the quickest and, not incidentally, the safest route to take to reach the goal of gender equality. . . .

I. The Equal Rights Amendment as History

. . . In its original form and even in its current stage of development, the U.S. Constitution speaks only in the male gender. Moreover, as Walter Dellinger has pointed out,

> [T]hroughout the process of drafting the Constitution, every draft of every provision used the pronoun "he." It is a commonplace observation that "he" is used in the Constitution in its generic sense as encompassing both genders. This is, of course, technically true. But [one] draft provision casts a very different light on the Constitution's use of the pronoun "he." For this provision, adopted unanimously for the next-to-last draft of the Constitution, uses the phrase "he or she." Although the pronouns drop out altogether from the final wording of this provision of the Constitution, it is nonetheless extraordinary to find the Convention unanimously adopting a draft provision using the phrase "he or she." At the conclusion of the compromise over navigation and slavery Mr. Butler moved to insert the following clause: "If any person bound to service or labor in any of the U[nited] States shall escape into another State, he or she shall not be discharged from such service or labor . . . but shall be delivered up to the person justly claiming their service or labor." Throughout the Constitution and all its drafts, "he" is used to refer to President, Vice-President, Senator; "she" appears but once in the evolving drafts of the Constitution, and "she" can be one, and only one thing: a fugitive slave.[2]

The leaders of the nineteenth-century women's rights movement had hoped, of course, that the Fourteenth Amendment's Equal Protection Clause would enfranchise women as well as former male slaves and provide a basis for establishing America's women as first-class citizens in every respect. Given that the word "male," although it nowhere appears in the substantive clause of the Amendment, is used three times in the second section,[3] there was little basis for optimism. Indeed, when Susan B. Anthony was arrested for voting in the 1872 presidential election, she was prohibited by the court from testifying on her own behalf because she was a woman.[4] Equally outrageous is the fact that the trial judge directed a verdict of guilty, giving the jury no option but to convict[5]—a course of conduct, to my knowledge, otherwise unknown to American criminal procedure. (The judge did give Anthony a chance to speak before pronouncing sentence, and—as you might imagine—she said a mouthful.)[6]

It would be another half century before universal suffrage was finally achieved. During that period, Anthony, her stalwart compatriot Elizabeth Cady

Stanton, and their followers, having failed repeatedly in their efforts to secure enfranchisement by means of the Federal Constitution, attacked the problem on a state-by-state basis. They had some success in the new western states such as Wyoming and Utah,[7] and with local elections here and there around the country, but the piecemeal approach was costly and largely ineffective. As Carrie Chapman Catt, Anthony's protégée, later described it:

> To get the word male . . . out of the constitution cost the women of the country [more than seventy] years of pauseless campaign. . . . During that time they were forced to conduct fifty-six campaigns of referenda to male voters; 480 campaigns to get Legislatures to submit suffrage amendments to voters; 47 campaigns to get State constitutional conventions to write woman suffrage into State constitutions; 277 campaigns to get State party conventions to include woman suffrage planks; 30 campaigns to get presidential party conventions to adopt woman suffrage planks in party platforms, and 19 campaigns with 19 successive Congresses. Millions of dollars were raised, mainly in small sums, and expended with economic care. Hundreds of women gave the accumulated possibilities of an entire lifetime, thousands gave years of their lives, hundreds of thousands gave constant interest and such aid as they could. It was a continuous, seemingly endless, chain of activity. Young suffragists who helped forge the last links of that chain were not born when it began. Old suffragists who forged the first links were dead when it ended.[8]

Included among those who did not live to see the fulfillment of the suffrage movement was Susan B. Anthony herself, affectionately known as "Aunt Susan." She died at age eighty-six in 1906, fourteen years before the Nineteenth Amendment,[9] the "Susan B. Anthony Amendment," was finally ratified in 1920.[10]

Three years later, in 1923, the original Equal Rights Amendment was first introduced into Congress. The initial language, changed in 1943, provided: "Men and women shall have equal rights throughout the United States and every place subject to its jurisdiction." It had been drafted by the radical suffragist Alice Paul, whose National Woman's Party had split from the ranks of mainstream suffragism, led by Anthony and later by Catt.[11] It was Alice Paul and her sisters-in-arms who chained themselves to the White House gates and were force-fed in prison when their protests took the form of hunger strikes. Once the Nineteenth Amendment took effect in 1920, Paul's followers continued to agitate for the expansion of women's rights, convinced that the vote would not be sufficient to bring about equality between the sexes. The old-line suffragists formed the League of Women Voters, convinced to the contrary that they could rally newly enfranchised women to vote in the reforms they deemed necessary to protect women and children in postwar America.[12] It was an early indication of the dichotomy between the philosophies of "equality feminism" and "difference feminism," which persists to this day.[13]

Some form of the Equal Rights Amendment was introduced in nearly every succeeding session of Congress, but it garnered little serious attention until 1970, a half century after passage of the Suffrage Amendment. That year a renewed effort, influenced by political agitation from the outside, pressed by the Citizen's Council on the Status of Women, and managed on the inside by sponsors Representative Martha Griffiths and Senators Birch Bayh and Marlow Cook, led to hearings that included testimony urging ratification by several prominent constitutional scholars, including New York University's own Norman Dorsen. Sponsors finally achieved passage on March 22, 1972, principally because politically antagonistic factions within the women's movement were able to coalesce, joined finally by various labor leaders, liberal religious groups, the National Federation of Republican Women—even the League of Women Voters.[14]

Following passage by wide margins in both the House and the Senate, the ERA met with initial success, as states vied to see which could be the first to ratify. Despite the early momentum, however, the amendment fell three states short of ratification at the end of the seven-year ratification period specified in the resolution that accompanied the proposed amendment. Congress then extended the period three years, until June 30, 1982. When no new states had ratified by that date, the amendment famously died,[15] and activists turned their attention to conceivable alternate ways to achieve gender equality—efforts that were already under way across the land.

The alternatives were basically two: piecemeal legislation and extension of the Equal Protection Clause of the Fourteenth Amendment. Viewed from the perspective of the 1970s, neither looked particularly attractive. Until 1971, the year before passage of the ERA, the Fourteenth Amendment had never been invoked successfully in a case involving gender discrimination. Moreover, the prospect of overhauling thousands of individual state and federal laws to protect against the many forms of discrimination existing at that point in the country's history was also daunting. As women's rights activist Florynce Kennedy repeatedly described the challenge, it amounted to winning the Civil War one plantation at a time. Nevertheless, men and women committed to the notion of equality rallied to the challenge and commenced a process of major law reform that continues to this day.

II. Extension of the Equal Protection Clause

It was in the arena of constitutional litigation, however, that the most dramatic changes first occurred, and the success of that litigation can be largely attributed to the ACLU's newly formed Women's Rights Project and to its founder and indomitable director, Ruth Bader Ginsburg. Her first case in pursuit of gender equity, mounted while she was still a law professor at Rutgers, involved a New Jersey law under which schoolteachers who became pregnant lost their jobs. There followed a string of Supreme Court cases in which Ginsburg was either the prime mover or the force behind the litigation. Of the six cases she argued before the Court during this period, she was successful in five.

The first of these was the ground-breaking case of *Reed v. Reed*,[16] in which Ginsburg represented an Idaho mother who applied, unsuccessfully, to become the executor of her son's estate. So did her ex-husband, and state law provided that as between persons equally qualified to administer estates, males were to be preferred to females. In representing Sally Reed, Ginsburg had a long-term goal to get the Supreme Court to abandon the rational basis test that had always been utilized in sex discrimination cases. Instead, Ginsburg campaigned for a strict scrutiny test, the standard that the Court had begun to formulate and apply to race-based classifications in the late 1940s and that had been applied to race discrimination uniformly since the Court abandoned the "separate but equal" doctrine in 1954. It was undoubtedly clear to her, as it must have been to Thurgood Marshall two decades earlier, that the barriers would not all fall at once, like the walls of Jericho. That proved to be the case with *Reed*, in which the Court declined to apply the higher standard but did reverse the state court's ruling and held that "a difference in the sex of competing applicants for letters of administration bears [no] rational relationship to a state objective that is sought to be advanced by the operation of [the Idaho statute]."[17]

Despite the fact that she had fallen short in convincing the Court to treat gender as a suspect classification, Ginsburg had scored a significant victory—the first successful equal protection challenge on the basis of gender. As Judge Stephanie K. Seymour so vividly put it: "With the *Reed* decision the genie was out of the bottle, the toothpaste was out of the tube. . . . '[R]ights, once set loose, are very difficult to contain; rights consciousness—on and off the Court—is a powerful engine of legal mobilization and change.'"[18]

Indeed, it was. Two years later, in 1973, Ginsburg was back before the Court in the case of *Frontiero v. Richardson*[19] and again urged the Court to apply strict scrutiny to statutes that provided that wives of servicemen were automatically considered dependents for purposes of obtaining increased quarters allowances and medical benefits, but that husbands of servicewomen were not considered covered dependents unless their wives provided more than one-half of their support.[20] This round, four members of the Court bought Ginsburg's argument in a strong plurality opinion by Justice Brennan, finding that the statute could not withstand strict scrutiny on the asserted ground of administrative convenience.[21] Justice Stewart, however, was the "swing vote" in the case and was unwilling to go beyond the holding in *Reed*, as were three other justices who concurred separately in the judgment.[22] And, although the Court periodically notes that application of the strict scrutiny standard in gender discrimination cases is still an open question, this split would turn out to be as close to the outright adoption of gender as a suspect classification as the Court would come.

The next case in the series, *Kahn v. Shevin*,[23] represented a setback for Ginsburg. Just a year after her near total victory in *Frontiero,* the Court held, in an opinion authored by Justice Douglas (who had been in the plurality in the prior case), that a Florida statute giving widows but not widowers a five-hundred-dollar exemption from property taxes did not violate equal protection. In the six-to-three decision, the majority held that the challenged statute was designed to further the "state policy of cushioning the financial impact of spousal loss upon the [gender] for which that loss impose[d] a disproportionately heavy burden." Thus, the Court concluded, the distinction in the law rested on "some ground of difference having a fair and substantial relation to the object of the legislation," in its view a justifiable variation of the rational basis standard applied in *Reed.*

Undaunted, Ginsburg returned to the Supreme Court during its next term, again representing a male client, as she would in so many of the cases she litigated in the 1970s. *Weinberger v. Wiesenfeld*[24] involved another widower, this time one who wanted to raise his infant son himself after his wife had died in childbirth. He applied for and was denied survivor benefits under the Social Security Act because it was strictly a mother's benefit.[25] Perhaps because of the outcome in *Kahn,* Ginsburg changed her strategy in *Wiesenfeld,* arguing not for strict scrutiny but for a "heightened scrutiny" falling somewhere between rational basis analysis and strict scrutiny analysis. Although she won the case for her client, Ginsburg did not succeed in convincing the Court to adopt the intermediate standard that she had presented. Instead, the Court invalidated the provision, which allowed survivors' benefits automatically for widows, but not for widowers on the basis of their wives' covered employment. The Court noted that the "gender-based distinction made by [the statute] is indistinguishable from that invalidated in *Frontiero*" and that it operated "to deprive women of protection for their families which men receive as a result of their employment." Writing for the Court, Justice Brennan did give lip service to the ruling in *Kahn* regarding the weight to be given a "reasonably designed" state policy, but he went on to make clear that "the mere recitation of a benign, compensatory purpose is not an automatic shield which protects against any inquiry into the actual purposes underlying a statutory scheme;[26] a pronouncement that signaled a retreat from *Kahn* and presaged the Court's subsequent departure from rational basis analysis in the gender discrimination setting.

The breakthrough came in 1976, in a case in which Ginsburg filed an amicus brief but did not argue: *Craig v. Boren.*[27] The substance of the case was certainly not weighty. The equal protection challenge concerned an Oklahoma statute that permitted young women to buy "near-beer" at age eighteen, but restricted men to age twenty-one. Once again, Ginsburg argued in her brief for heightened rather than strict scrutiny, and this time she succeeded where she had failed before. Justice Brennan, writing for a majority of six, interpreted prior holdings of the Court to require that "classifications by gender must serve important governmental objectives and must be substantially related to the achievement of those objectives." The new standard prevails, at least ostensibly, as I shall later note, to this day.

Ginsburg's final victory before the Supreme Court as a lawyer was not in an equal protection case but one decided under the Sixth Amendment's provision guaranteeing the right to an impartial jury. *Duren v. Missouri,*[28] announced in 1979—less than two years before her appointment to the Court of Appeals for the D.C. Circuit—invalidated a Missouri jury selection statute that permitted women to opt out of jury service based on nothing other than their gender. As Ginsburg left the world of lawyering for the rarefied atmosphere of the judiciary, where she would continue to have an impact on the development of equal protection doctrine, her legacy as an advocate for women's rights stood unequaled. As Lynn Hecht Schafran noted at the time of Ginsburg's elevation to the Supreme Court, "I can't imagine how anyone could get from where we were in 1970 to . . . contemporary theories [of gender equality] if Ruth had not done her equal protection work. People forget how things were."[29] . . .

III. The Way Things Were

. . . In the fall of 1972 I was lucky enough to attend a conference entitled "Symposium on the Law School Curriculum and the Legal Rights of Women," which turned out to be a truly seminal meeting held at New York University School of Law. . . . It was a pretty heady time: The ERA was gaining steam around the country, and the halls of the academy were filled with talk about strategies for the great transition period following ratification. Looking at the casebooks' tables of contents gives a remarkable snapshot of how much there was to be done. The following recitation hits only some highlights.

Materials on the development of equal protection were key, of course, with explorations of the well-known constitutional trio *Bradwell v. Illinois,*[30] *Goesaert v. Cleary,*[31] and *Hoyt v. Florida,*[32] and the recent appearance on the scene of *Reed* and *Frontiero.* But the casebooks also concentrated on employment law, where adequate enforcement of Title VII and the Equal Pay Act had yet to develop. Job restrictions abounded, some the result of the so-called "protective labor laws" still in existence around the country that generally had the effect of barring women from holding higher paid positions. The existence of segregated "help wanted" notices also perpetuated the problem. Discrimination abounded in pension plans, insurance benefits, what was at the time called workman's compensation, in the Social Security statutes, and, most significantly, in the determination of what constituted a "bona fide occupational qualification," which was the usual defense raised in employment discrimination cases in the 1970s and one that all too often succeeded on the basis of flimsy excuses rather than actual job functions. The fact that some women could and did become pregnant raised barriers for all women workers. "Sexual harassment" as a form of discrimination had not yet been recognized.

In the area of family law, distinctions based on gender and the inequality that resulted were systemic and far-reaching. The casebooks covered the effects of the doctrine of "feme covert"[33] in all its many manifestations, including its effect on grounds for divorce in the virtually universal fault-based system of the era, on a married woman's domicile, her name, her credit rating, the doctrine of interspousal immunity, loss of consortium, the ability of a wife to contract freely, inheritance laws, property settlement, and the right of support following dissolution of the marriage. Inequities abounded not only in property law, but even in community property law. For example, in 1972 when the ERA was passed, and as late as 1980, the Louisiana community property statute, ostensibly giving married women joint ownership of marital property, included this provision: "The husband is the head and master of the partnership or community of gains; he administers its effects, disposes of the revenues which they produce, and may alienate them by an onerous title, without the consent and permission of his wife."[34]

In education, Title IX, which has played such a crucial role in literally leveling the playing field for women, had yet to exert its influence. In 1971, the Supreme Court declined to invalidate a South Carolina scheme that barred men from a women's college that was part of the state university system.[35] Thinking ahead to *Mississippi University for Women v. Hogan*,[36] authored by Justice O'Connor, and *United States v. Virginia*,[37] the VMI decision written by Justice Ginsburg, it is easy to substantiate the claim that having women on the appellate bench makes a difference in the development of constitutional law. Actually, one of my favorite discrimination cases came out of the Sixth Circuit and involved a state university, this one in Eastern Kentucky.[38] During the academic year 1971–72, the school had a curfew that applied only to its women students—known in those days as "coeds"—and that required them to be in their dorms by 10:30 P.M. Monday through Thursday, 1:00 A.M. Friday and Saturday, and midnight Sunday. One of the students, Ruth Robinson, sued, claiming a violation of equal protection. The court responded as follows:

The State's basic justification for the classification system is that of safety. It asserts that women are more likely to be criminally attacked later at night and are physically less capable of defending themselves than men. It concludes that the safety of women will be protected by having them in their dormitories at certain hours of the night. The goal of safety is a legitimate concern of the Board of Regents and this court cannot say that the regulations in question are not rationally related to the effectuation of this reasonable goal.

The appellant claims that the safety justification is undermined by the shifting curfew for different nights of the week asserting that the streets are no safer at 12:30 A.M. on Saturday than they are at 12:30 A.M. on Wednesday. We hold, however, that the State could properly take into consideration the fact that on weekend nights many coeds have dates and ought to be permitted to stay out later than on weekday nights. A classification having some reasonable basis does not offend the equal protection merely because it is not drawn with mathematical nicety.[39]

Robinson was an easy case to teach. Invariably, someone in the class would raise her hand and suggest that if safety were truly the concern, and if the court was correct in its implication that men were the threat to the women students' safety, then perhaps the men on campus should be subject to curfew and the "coeds" should be allowed to go wherever and whenever they pleased.

Gender restrictions were likewise legally sanctioned in public accommodations, in the military, in criminal law—especially in the area of sentencing—and in many other areas of American life. According to one review of the Davidson, Ginsburg, Kay casebook, "[t]he text contains an insuperable exposition of the fact that our legal system simply has not shown basic fairness to men or women qua persons, and, indeed, that there has been and continues to be a sex-divided legal system on many fronts."[40] For those men and women who were not born until the mid-seventies, these early sex discrimination casebooks would be a revelation. To the rest of us, they are a fascinating reminder of how far we have come in the quarter century since debate about the ERA was last abroad in the land. But I cannot leave the discussion without a few words about the subject I have always found the most intriguing: jury service for women. . . .

V. Is a Twenty-First-Century Equal Rights Amendment Necessary?

In its 1982 opinion in *Hogan,* the Supreme Court held that a state-supported university's policy of limiting enrollment in its School of Nursing to females, and thereby denying admission to otherwise qualified males, violated equal protection.[41] The Court split five-to-four in the case, and the deciding vote was cast by the author of the opinion, newly appointed Justice Sandra Day O'Connor. She noted that the party seeking to uphold a statute that classifies on the basis of gender has the burden of "showing at least that the classification serves 'important governmental objectives and that the discriminatory means employed,' are 'substantially related to the achievement of those objectives,'" the routine middle ground standard of review in sex discrimination cases. However, O'Connor provided, too, that the burden also requires the establishment of an "exceedingly persuasive justification" for the gender-based classification. This language went unremarked by the dissenters, who were much more interested in a lengthy exposition on the history and virtues of single-sex higher education. But the language was picked up and emphasized by Justice Ginsburg in *United States v. Virginia*,[42] the VMI admissions case decided fourteen years after *Mississippi University for Women*:

> To summarize the Court's current directions for cases of official classification based on gender: Focusing on the differential treatment or denial of opportunity for which relief is sought, the reviewing court must determine whether the proffered justification is "exceedingly persuasive." The burden of justification is demanding and it rests entirely on the State. . . . The justification must be genuine, not hypothesized or invented post hoc in response to litigation. And it must not rely on overbroad generalizations about the different talents, capacities, or preferences of males and females.[43]

In formulating these "directions," had Justice Ginsburg ratcheted up the already "heightened scrutiny" another notch or two? The Chief Justice certainly thought so. Concurring in the judgment and thus producing a seven-to-one decision, with Scalia dissenting and Thomas, whose son was a VMI student, not sitting, Rehnquist pointed to the "exceedingly persuasive justification" language of the Court's opinion and noted that "[i]t is unfortunate that the Court thereby introduces an element of uncertainty respecting the appropriate test."[44]

Justice Ginsburg was most certainly not oblivious to what she had accomplished in the VMI opinion. According to a *New York Times* report:

> [She] recounted in a 1997 speech to the [Washington, D.C.] Women's Bar Association . . . that a year earlier, as she announced her opinion declaring unconstitutional the all-male admissions policy at the Virginia Military Institute, she looked across the bench at Justice O'Connor and thought of the legacy they were building together.

Justice Ginsburg's opinion in the Virginia case cited one of Justice O'Connor's earliest majority opinions for the Court, a 1982 decision called *Mississippi University for Women v. Hogan* that declared unconstitutional the exclusion of male students from a state-supported nursing school. Justice O'Connor, warning against using "archaic and stereotypic notions" about the roles of men and women, herself cited in that opinion some of the Supreme Court cases that Ruth

Ginsburg, who was not to join the Court for another eleven years, had argued and won as a noted women's rights advocate during the 1970s.

Addressing the women's bar group, Justice Ginsburg noted that the vote in Justice O'Connor's 1982 opinion was 5 to 4, while the vote to strike down men-only admissions in Virginia fourteen years later was 7 to 1.

"What occurred in the intervening years in the Court, as elsewhere in society?" Justice Ginsburg asked. The answer, she continued, lay in a line from Shakespeare that Justice O'Connor had recently spoken in the character of Isabel, Queen of France, in a local production of *Henry V*: "Haply a woman's voice may do some good."[45]

Did the VMI decision move us to the point that an equal rights amendment might have? Ginsburg herself apparently thinks so. She has been quoted as saying, in an address to the University of Virginia School of Law shortly after the VMI decision was announced, "There is no practical difference between what has evolved and the ERA."[46]

The advocates of a renewed effort at ratification of the ERA contend not only that women deserve a place in the Federal Constitution, but that amendment of the Constitution is required in order to ensure that we are not forced to retreat on any of the fronts on which progress for women's rights has been so long in coming and so laboriously achieved. They argue that by retaining the language of the failed amendment, the legislative history will remain intact. Moreover, much of the opposition to ratification in the 1970s surely will have dissipated. As the *ABA Journal* reporter points out in an article in the summer of 1999:

> When Congress sent the equal rights amendment to the states for ratification in 1972, ERA opponents warned of dire consequences: co-ed bathrooms, women drafted into the military, the repeal of spousal support laws.
>
> The ERA failed, but the consequences happened anyway. Unisex bathrooms are in college dorms around the country. Women are joining the armed forces—by choice. And modern alimony laws look at sex-neutral factors, such as need and contribution, when determining who should receive support.[47]

The Equal Rights Amendment has the dubious distinction of being one of only six amendments submitted by Congress to the states that have failed at ratification. They were originally among the over five thousand bills proposing amendments to the Federal Constitution introduced in Congress since 1789.[48] Currently, for example, there are a handful of proposed amendments, in addition to the ERA, that are under debate in Congress, in the press, and in the academy. They include a "Ten Commandments" amendment passed by the House of Representatives on June 17, 1999.[49] Its first section provides that "[t]he power to display the Ten Commandments on or within property owned or administered by the several States or political subdivisions thereof is hereby declared to be among the powers reserved to the States respectively." A second section purports to protect "[t]he expression of religious faith by individual persons on or within property owned or administered by the several States." Similarly, the House has passed the so-called "flag burning amendment," giving Congress the power to "prohibit the physical desecration of the flag of the United States." And there are perennial attempts to amend the Constitution to permit prayer in the schools and to ban abortion. It seems to me that there is a legitimate question whether a renewed Equal Rights Amendment would be in very good company if it, too, were to be passed by the House of Representatives, as its House sponsor, Representative Carolyn Maloney (D-N.Y.) proposes.

Perhaps the ERA, resubmitted to the states, would draw little opposition and would be ratified without controversy, as a quasi-dead letter. However, while the "foxhole issue" and the "potty issue" seem to have disappeared from the scene, we can imagine that the forces opposed to gay rights will see the amendment as a threat and vocally and vociferously rejoin the fight against ratification. They would do well to note that in the seven states that have an equal rights amendment in their state constitutions,[50] as well as in the thirteen other states with some provision guaranteeing equality as a matter of constitutional right,[51] society continues to progress without the social, legal, and cultural upheavals that the Stop ERA adherents predicted a quarter century ago.[52]

In conclusion, it is altogether fitting to honor Ruth Bader Ginsburg for her many accomplishments, and for the gumption and the dedication she continues to evidence by pulling on her black robe and showing up for the opening of Court this past Monday, less than three weeks after undergoing major cancer surgery. But while Ruth Ginsburg was busy litigating and deciding equal protection cases, many others in this country were busy in the political arena, fighting the good fight for gender equity on many fronts, committed to bringing about a better world through law reform in the name of constitutional rights and responsibilities. In tribute to them, . . . I am going to take the liberty of quoting one of the many influential women activists of the 1970s, Jill Ruckelshaus, a cofounder of the National Women's Political Caucus. In 1977, she spoke words that have stayed with me over two decades. She said:

> We are in for a very, very long haul. . . . I am asking for everything you have to give. We will never give up. . . . You will lose your youth, your sleep, your arches, your patience, your sense of humor . . . and occasionally . . . the understanding and support of the people that you love very much. In return, I have nothing to offer you but . . . your pride in being a woman, all your dreams you've ever had for your daughters, and nieces, and granddaughters, your future and the certain knowledge that at the end of your days you will be able to look back and say that once in your life you gave everything you had for justice.[53]

NOTES

1. See Debra Baker, "The Fight Ain't Over," A.B.A. J., Aug. 1999, at 52.

2. Walter E. Dellinger III, "1787: The Constitution and 'The Curse of Heaven,'" 29 Wm. & Mary L. Rev. 145, 153 (1987) (footnote omitted).

3. See U.S. Const. amend. XIV, § 2.

4. See Sandra Day O'Connor, "Speech on 75th Anniversary of Women's Right to Vote," 27 U. West L.A. L. Rev. 7, 11 (1996).

5. See *United States v. Anthony*, 24 F. Cas. 829, 832 (C.C.N.D.N.Y. 1873) (No. 14,459).

6. See Barbara Allen Babcock et al., *Sex Discrimination and the Law* 9–10 (1975) (relating Anthony's impassioned speech given despite obvious hostility from bench).

7. See Eleanor Flexner & Ellen Fitzpatrick, *Century of Struggle: The Women's Rights Movement in the United States* 149–56, 167–70 (1996).

8. Carrie Chapman Catt & Nettle Rogers Shuler, *Woman Suffrage and Politics* 107–8 (1923).

9. The Amendment provides:

> The right of citizens of the United States to vote shall not be denied or abridged by the United States or by any State on account of sex.
>
> Congress shall have the power to enforce this article by appropriate legislation.

U.S. Const. amend. XIX.

10. Anthony's last and perhaps most famous public utterance, "Failure is impossible!" came at the conclusion of her remarks at a suffrage rally in Washington, D.C., three days before her death. See Lynn Sherr, *Failure Is Impossible* 324 (1995).

11. Text from S.J. Res. 21, 68th Cong. (1923). See William Henry Chafe, *The American Woman* 112–13 (1972).

12. It was the League's defense of protectionist legislation that caused the wide postsuffrage split between the two groups of activists. According to one historian:

> [T]he two opposing camps were engaged in a bitter war. One side fought for the exclusive goal of female equality; the other side for social reform. One side believed that suffrage was only the first step in the campaign for freedom; the other that the Nineteenth Amendment had substantially finished the task of making women equal to men. Protective legislation became the crux of the differences between the two groups.

Id. at 119.

13. For a discussion of the principles underlying "equality feminism" and "difference feminism," see generally Carol Gilligan, *In a Different Voice* (1982).

14. The AFL-CIO and the International Ladies Garment Workers Union continued to oppose the amendment. See Babcock et al., supra note 10, at 132–33. Also opposing the amendment were fundamentalist religious groups and the John Birch Society, from which Phyllis Schlafly's Eagle Forum and its STOP ERA campaign later sprang. See Donald G. Matthews & Jane Sherron De Hart, *Sex, Gender, and the Politics of ERA* 59, 67, 153 (1990).

15. It is somewhat surprising that the time restriction on ratification of the proposed twenty-seventh amendment was not seriously challenged. Ironically, the Amendment that ultimately became the Twenty-Seventh was first passed and submitted to the states for ratification in 1789. See supra note 4.

16 . 404 U.S. 71 (1971).

17. *Reed,* 404 U.S. at 76.

18. Stephanie K. Seymour, "Women as Constitutional Equals: The Burger Court's Overdue Evolution," 33 Tulsa L.J. 23, 30 (1997) (quoting Joel B. Grossman, "Constitutional Policymaking in the Burger Years," 86 Mich. L. Rev. 1414, 1416 (1988)).

19. 411 U.S. 677 (1973).

20. See id. at 680. Ginsburg wrote the jurisdictional statement in *Frontiero,* filed an amicus brief for the Women's Rights Project, and jointly filed the reply brief with the Southern Poverty Law Center. Ginsburg, who was given ten minutes of the thirty-minute argument, urged the adoption of strict scrutiny. The principal lawyer for the appellant argued only that the statute was irrational. For background on Ginsburg's role in the case, see Deborah L. Markowitz, "In Pursuit of Equality: One Woman's Work to Change the Law," 14 Women's Rts. L. Rep. 335, 344–46 (1992).

21. See *Frontiero,* 411 U.S. at 690–91.

22. See id. at 691–92. In a separate concurring opinion, Justice Powell, writing for himself, Chief Justice Burger, and Justice Blackmun, also relied on rational basis analysis and added this tantalizing paragraph:

> There is another, and I find compelling, reason for deferring a general categorizing of sex classifications as invoking the strictest test of judicial scrutiny. The Equal Rights Amendment, which if adopted will resolve the substance of this precise question, has been approved by Congress and submitted for ratification by the States. If this Amendment is duly adopted, it will represent the will of the people accomplished in the manner prescribed by the Constitution.

> Id. at 692 (Powell, J., concurring). Justice Rehnquist dissented but did not file a separate opinion. See id. at 691 (Rehnquist, J., dissenting).

23. 416 U.S. 351 (1974).

24. 420 U.S. 636 (1975).

25. Unlike *Frontiero* and *Goldfarb,* see infra note 45, the Social Security Act was strictly a mother's benefit, and it did not rely on establishing dependence. Therefore, the plaintiff was automatically denied the benefit, even though his wife's salary had been greater than his own. See id. at 640–41, 645.

26. Id. at 648. The *Wiesenfeld* Court noted that "it is apparent both from the statutory scheme itself and from the legislative history . . . that Congress' purpose in providing benefits to young widows with children was . . . to permit women to elect not to work and to devote themselves to the care of children." Id. In 1977, in *California v. Goldfarb,* 430 US. 199 (1977), another of Ginsburg's successful equal protection lawsuits, the Supreme Court extended the ruling in *Wiesenfeld* to cover widowers without dependent children.

27. 429 U.S. 190 (1976).

28. 439 U.S. 357 (1979).

29. David Von Drehle, "A Trailblazer's Step-by-Step Assault on the Status Quo," Wash. Post (Nat'l Wkly. Ed.), July 26–Aug. 1, 1993, at 8.

30. 83 U.S. (16 Wall.) 130 (1873) (denying that Fourteenth Amendment guarantees women right to admission to practice in state courts). Justice Bradley, concurring, opined on the ill-suitedness of the female character to the practice of law: "The natural and proper timidity and delicacy which belongs to the female sex evidently unfits it for many of the occupations of civil life." Id. at 141 (Bradley, J., concurring).

31. 335 U.S. 464 (1948) (finding constitutional statute forbidding women from acting as bartenders, with exception of wives and daughters of male owners).

32. 368 U.S. 57 (1961) (holding that state statute permitting women to serve as jurors only if they explicitly waive their exemption from duty does not violate Fourteenth Amendment); see also discussion infra Part IV (placing *Hoyt* within development of Court's recognition of women's rights to serve on juries).

33. See Black's *Law Dictionary* 617 (6th ed. 1990) (defining "feme covert" as "A married woman. Generally used in reference to the former legal disabilities of a married woman").

34. La. Civ. Code Ann. art. 2404 (West 1971) (repealed 1979), invalidated by *Kirchberg v. Feenstra*, 450 U.S. 455, 458, 460–61 (1981) (holding that provision violated Equal Protection Clause).

35. See *Williams v. McNair*, 401 U.S. 951 (1971).

36. 458 U.S. 718 (1982) (holding that state statute excluding males from state-supported nursing school violates Equal Protection Clause).

37. 518 U.S. 515 (1996) (holding that exclusion of women from prestigious military school violates Equal Protection Clause and that violation cannot be cured by creation of parallel women's school).

38. See *Robinson v. Board of Regents*, 475 F.2d 707 (6th Cir. 1973).

39. Id. at 711.

40. Mary Cynthia Dunlap, Book Review, 27 J. Legal Educ. 120, 124 (1975) (reviewing Kenneth M. Davidson et al., *Sex-Based Discrimination: Text, Cases & Materials* (1974)). The review indicates that gender discrimination casebooks initially met with negative criticism and that, like courses on "Law and Native Americans" or "Race and Police," separate courses on "Women and the Law" were seen at the time by old-line teachers of "standard" law courses, such as Torts and Contracts, as pedagogically illegitimate. See id. at 123–24.

41. See id. at 733.

42. 518 U.S. 515 (1996).

43. Id. at 532–33 (citation omitted).

44. Id. at 559.

45. Linda Greenhouse, "From the High Court, A Voice Quite Distinctly a Woman's," N.Y. Times, May 26, 1999, at A1.

46. Baker, supra note 3, at 55. Justice Ginsburg, however, remains an ERA supporter. See David Harper, "Justice Assesses Gender Issue," Tulsa World, Aug. 29, 1997, available in Lexis, News Library ARCNWS file (quoting Justice Ginsburg on ERA: "[I]t belongs in our Constitution as a norm society embraces. It's what you'd like to teach ninth graders in civics class."); Jeffrey Rosen, "The New Look of Liberalism on the Court," N.Y Times, Oct. 5, 1997, § 6 (Magazine), at 60 (quoting Justice Ginsburg on ERA: "I would still like it as a symbol to see the E.R.A. in the Constitution for my granddaughter.").

47. Baker, supra note 3, at 53.

48. See Walter Dellinger, "The Legitimacy of Constitutional Change: Rethinking the Amendment Process," 97 Harv. L. Rev. 386, 427 (1983). For a history of the amendment process, see id. at 427–30.

49. See 145 Cong. Rec. H4486 (daily ed. June 17, 1999).

50. Colorado, Hawaii, Illinois, Maryland, Pennsylvania, Washington, and Wyoming.

51. California, Connecticut, Florida, Iowa, Louisiana, Massachusetts, Montana, New Hampshire, New Jersey, New Mexico, New York, Rhode Island, and Texas.

52. They included, in addition to Phyllis Schlafly's Eagle Forum members, representatives from the insurance industry, the armed services, and some labor organizations. There were also groups such as Utah's HOTDOG (Humanitarians Opposed To Degradation of Our Girls) and various offshoots of the John Birch Society.

53. Jill Ruckelshaus, Speech at the National Women's Political Caucus California State Convention, San Jose, California (1977) (on file with author).

Chapter 5

Civil Liberties

5-1

The Real World of Constitutional Rights

THE SUPREME COURT AND THE IMPLEMENTATION
OF THE ABORTION DECISIONS

Gerald N. Rosenberg

*When one considers how exposed the Constitution's "religious establish-
ment" clause is to continuous revision, it is not surprising to find other, less
established rights deeply enmeshed in politics as well. The next essay examines the right to an abortion, a controversial aspect of civil liberties policy that
has been defended as an application of the "right to privacy."*

*The Supreme Court began asserting the right to privacy in earnest with
Griswold v. Connecticut in 1965, when it ruled that a married couple's
decision to use birth control lay beyond the purview of the government. The
1973 Roe v. Wade decision establishing a woman's right to an abortion—the
best known and most controversial privacy right—has further established
privacy as a class of rights implicit in the Bill of Rights. But, as Gerald Rosenberg explains, Roe v. Wade left many aspects of abortion rights unresolved,
and a lively public debate on the subject continues today.*

Source: Gerald N. Rosenberg, "The Real World of Constitutional Rights: The Supreme Court and the
Implementation of the Abortion Decisions," in *Contemplating Courts*, ed. Lee Epstein (Washington, D.C.:
CQ Press, 1995), 390–419. Some notes and bibliographic references appearing in the original have been
deleted.

IN *ROE V. WADE* and *Doe v. Bolton* (1973) the Supreme Court held unconstitutional Texas and Georgia laws prohibiting abortions except for "the purpose of saving the life of the mother" (Texas) and where "pregnancy would endanger the life of the pregnant mother or would seriously and permanently injure her health" (Georgia). The Court asserted that women had a fundamental right of privacy to decide whether or not to bear a child. Dividing pregnancy roughly into three trimesters, the Court held that in the first trimester the choice of abortion was a woman's alone, in consultation with a physician. During the second trimester, states could regulate abortion for the preservation and protection of women's health, and in approximately the third trimester, after fetal viability, could ban abortions outright, except where necessary to preserve a woman's life or health. Although responding specifically to the laws of Texas and Georgia, the broad scope of the Court's constitutional interpretation invalidated the abortion laws of almost every state and the District of Columbia.[1] According to one critic, *Roe* and *Doe* "may stand as the most radical decisions ever issued by the Supreme Court" (Noonan 1973, 261).

Roe and *Doe* are generally considered leading examples of judicial action in support of relatively powerless groups unable to win legislative victories. In these cases, women were that politically disadvantaged group; indeed, it has been claimed, "No victory for women's rights since enactment of the 19th Amendment has been greater than the one achieved" in *Roe* and *Doe* ("A Woman's Right" 1973, A4). But women are not the only disadvantaged interests who have attempted to use litigation to achieve policy ends. Starting with the famous cases brought by civil rights groups, and spreading to issues raised by environmental groups, consumer groups, and others, reformers have over the past decades looked to the courts as important producers of political and social change. Yet, during the same period, students of judicial politics have learned that court opinions are not always implemented with the speed and directness that rule by law assumes. This is particularly the case with decisions that touch on controversial, emotional issues or deeply held beliefs, such as abortion.

This chapter contains an exploration of the effect of the Court's abortion decisions, both *Roe* and *Doe,* and the key decisions based on them. How did the public, politicians, medical professionals, and interest groups react to them? Were the decisions implemented? Did they bring safe and legal abortions to all American women? To some American women? If the answer turns out to be only some, then I want to know why. What are the factors that have led a constitutional right to be unevenly available? More generally, are there conditions under which Court decisions on behalf of relatively powerless groups are more or less likely to be implemented?[2]

The analysis presented here shows that the effect and implementation of the Court's abortion decisions have been neither straightforward nor simple. Political response has varied and access to legal and safe abortion has increased, but in an uneven and nonuniform way. These findings are best explained by two related factors. First, at the time of the initial decisions there was widespread support for legal abortion from several sets of actors, including relevant political and professional elites on both the national and local level, the public at large, and activists. Second, the Court's decisions, by allowing clinics to perform abortions, made it possible for women to obtain abortions in some places where hospitals refused to provide them. Implementation by private clinics, however, has led to uneven availability of abortion services and has encouraged local political opposition.

The Abortion Cases

Roe and *Doe* were the Court's first major abortion decisions, but they were not its last.[3] In response to these decisions, many states rewrote their abortion laws, ostensibly to conform with the Court's constitutional mandate but actually with the goal of restricting the newly created right. Cases quickly arose, and continue to arise, challenging state laws as inconsistent with the Court's ruling, if not openly and clearly hostile to it. In general, the Court's response has been to preserve the core holding of *Roe* and *Doe* that a woman has a virtually unfettered constitutional right to an abortion before fetal viability, but to defer to legislation in areas not explicitly dealt with in those decisions. These cases require brief mention.

Areas of Litigation

Since *Roe* and *Doe,* the Court has heard three kinds of cases on abortion. One type involves state and federal funding for abortion. Here, the Court has consistently upheld the right of government not to fund abortion services and to prohibit the provision of abortions in public hospitals, unless the abortion is medically necessary. In perhaps the most important case, *Harris v. McRae* (1980), the Court upheld the most restrictive version of the so-called Hyde Amendment, which barred the use of federal funds for even medically necessary abortions, including those involving pregnancies due to rape or incest.

A second area that has provoked a great deal of litigation is the degree of participation in the abortion decision constitutionally allowed to the spouse of a pregnant married woman or the parents of a pregnant single minor. The Court has consistently struck down laws requiring spousal involvement but has upheld laws requiring parental notification or consent, as long as there is a "judicial bypass" option allowing minors to bypass their parents and obtain permission from a court.

A third area generating litigation involves the procedural requirements that states can impose for abortions. Most of these cases have arisen from state attempts to make abortion as difficult as possible to obtain. Regulations include requiring all post–first trimester abortions to be performed in hospitals; the informed, written consent of a woman before an abortion can be performed; a twenty-four-hour waiting period before an abortion can be performed; a pathology report for each abortion and the presence of a second physician at abortions occurring after potential viability; the preservation by physicians of the life of viable fetuses; and restrictions on the disposal of fetal remains. The Court's most recent pronouncement on these issues, *Planned Parenthood of Southeastern Pennsylvania v. Casey* (1992), found informed consent, a twenty-four-hour waiting period, and certain reporting requirements constitutional.

Trends in Court Treatment of Abortion Cases

Since the late 1980s, as *Casey* suggests, the Court has upheld more restrictions on the abortion right. In *Webster v. Reproductive Health Services* (1989), the Court upheld a 1986 restrictive Missouri law, and in 1991, in *Rust v. Sullivan,* it upheld government regulations prohibiting family-planning organizations that receive federal funds from counseling patients about abortion or providing abortion referrals. Most important, in *Casey* the Court abandoned the trimester framework of *Roe.* Although the justices did not agree on the proper constitutional standard for assessing state restrictions on abortion, Justices Sandra Day O'Connor, Anthony M. Kennedy, and David H. Souter adopted an "undue burden" standard. Under this standard, states may regulate abortion but may not place an undue burden on women seeking an abortion of a nonviable fetus.

Many commentators expected *Casey* to generate an avalanche of litigation centering directly on the abortion rights. Given the ambiguity of the undue burden standard, they expected expanded state activity to limit abortion. These expectations may yet be fulfilled, but, interestingly, Court cases since *Casey* have not specifically focused on the abortion right per se. Rather, in recent litigation the Court has been asked to resolve questions concerning access to abortion; namely, what steps can courts take to prevent antiabortion advocates from interfering with public access to family-planning and abortion clinics? The reason these kinds of questions arose is not difficult to discern; the 1990s has seen the rise of militant tactics—ranging from boisterous protests to harassment of clinic workers and even to the murder of physicians performing abortions—by certain segments of the antiabortion movement.

These "access" cases have generated mixed Court rulings. In *Bray v. Alexandria Women's Health Clinic* (1993), the Court rejected an attempt by pro-choice groups to use the 1871 Ku Klux Klan Act as a way to bring federal courts into this area. But, in *Madsen v. Women's Health Center* (1994), the Court upheld parts of a Florida trial court injunction permanently enjoining antiabortion protesters from blocking access to an abortion clinic and from physically harassing persons leaving or entering it. With the enactment by Congress of the Freedom of Access to Clinic Entrances Act in 1994, and the immediate filing of a legal challenge, it is likely that the Court will have another opportunity to address this issue.

Implementing Constitutional Rights

How have the public, politicians, medical professionals, and interest groups reacted to the Court decisions since *Roe* and *Doe*? How has access to legal and safe abortion changed in the wake of these decisions? In other words, when the Supreme Court announces a new constitutional right, what happens?

Legal Abortions: The Numbers

An obvious way to consider this question, at least in the abortion realm, is to look at the number of legal abortions performed before and after the 1973 decisions. For, if the Court has had an important effect on society in this area, we might expect to find dramatic increases in the number of legal abortions obtained after 1973. Collecting statistics on legal abortion, however, is not an easy task. Record keeping is not as precise and complete as one would hope. Two organizations, the public Centers for Disease Control and Prevention in Atlanta and the private Alan Guttmacher Institute in New York, are the most thorough and reliable collectors of the information. The data they have collected on the number of legal abortions performed between 1966 and 1992 and the yearly percentage change are shown in Figure 1.

Interestingly, these data present a mixed picture of the effect of the abortion decisions. On the one hand, they suggest that after *Roe* the number of legal abortions increased at a strong pace throughout the 1970s (the solid line in Figure 1). On the other hand, they reveal that the changes after 1973 were part of a trend that started in 1970, three years before the Court acted. Strikingly, the largest increase in the number of legal abortions occurs between 1970 and 1971, two years before *Roe*! In raw numerical terms, the increase between 1972 and 1973 is 157,800, a full 134,500 fewer than the pre-*Roe* increase in 1970–1971. It is possible, of course, that the effect of *Roe* was not felt in 1973. Even though the decision

Figure 1. Legal Abortions, 1966–1992

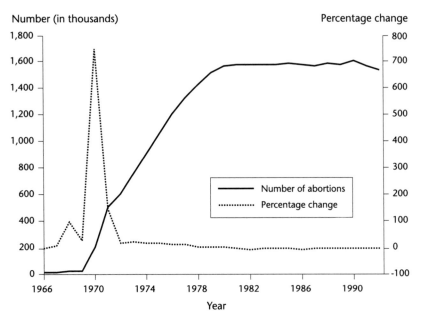

Sources: Estimates by the Alan Guttmacher Institute and the Centers for Disease Control and Prevention in Henshaw and Van Vort 1994, 100–106, 112; Lader 1973, 209; U.S. Congress 1974, 1976; Weinstock et al. 1975, 23. When sources differed, I have relied on data from the Alan Guttmacher Institute since its estimates are based on surveys of all known abortion providers and are generally more complete. Data points for 1983, 1986, and 1990 are estimates based on interpolations made by the Alan Guttmacher Institute.

was handed down in January, perhaps the 1973–1974 comparison gives a more accurate picture. If this is the case, the increase, 154,000, is still substantially smaller than the change during 1970–1971. And while the number of legal abortions continued to increase in the years immediately after 1974, that rate eventually stabilized and by the 1990s had actually declined. The dotted line in Figure 1 (representing the percentage change in the number of legal abortions performed from one year to the next) shows, too, that the largest increases in the number of legal abortions occurred in the years prior to *Roe*. . . .

The data presented above show that the largest numerical increases in legal abortions occurred in the years prior to initial Supreme Court action. . . . There was no steep or unusual increase in the number of legal abortions following *Roe*. To be sure, it is possible that without constitutional protection for abortion no more states would have liberalized or repealed their laws and those that had done so might have overturned their previous efforts. And the fact that the number of legal abortions continued to increase after 1973 suggests that the Court was effective in easing access to safe and legal abortion. But those increases, while large, were smaller than those of previous years. Hence, the growth in the number of legal abortions can be only partially attributed to the Court; it might even be the case that the increases would have continued without the Court's 1973 decisions.

What Happened?

Particularly interesting about the data presented above is that they suggest that *Roe* itself failed to generate major changes in the number of legal abortions. This finding is compatible with political science literature, in which it is argued that Supreme Court decisions, particularly ones dealing with emotional and controversial issues, are not automatically and completely implemented. It also appears to fit nicely with an argument I have made elsewhere (Rosenberg 1991), which suggests that several factors must be present for new constitutional rights to be implemented. These include widespread support from political and professional elites on both the national and local level, from the public at large, and from activists and a willingness on the part of those called on to implement the decision to act accordingly. This is true, as Alexander Hamilton pointed out two centuries ago, because courts lack the power of "either the sword or the purse." To a greater extent than other government institutions, courts are dependent on both elite and popular support for their decisions to be implemented.

To fill out my argument in greater detail, I examine both pre- and post-1973 actions as they relate to the implementation of the abortion right. In so doing, I reach two important conclusions. First, by the time the Court reached its decisions in 1973, little political opposition to abortion existed on the federal level, relevant professional elites and social activists gave it widespread support, it was practiced on a large scale (see Figure 1), and public support for it was growing. These positions placed abortion reform in the American mainstream. Second, in the years after 1973, opposition to abortion strengthened and grew.

Pre-*Roe* Support

In the decade or so prior to *Roe,* there was a sea change in the public position of abortion in American life. At the start of the 1960s, abortion was not a political issue. Abortions, illegal as they were, were performed clandestinely, and women who underwent the procedure did not talk about it.[4] By 1972, however, abortion had become a public and political issue. While little legislative or administrative action was taken on the federal level, a social movement, organized in the mid- and late 1960s, to reform and repeal prohibitions on abortion met with some success at the state level, and public opinion swung dramatically from opposition to abortion in most cases to substantial support.

Elites and Social Activists

Although abortions have always been performed, public discussion did not surface until the 1950s. In 1962 the American Law Institute (ALI) published its Model Penal Code on abortion, permitting abortion if continuing the pregnancy would adversely affect the physical or mental health of the woman, if there was risk of birth defects, or if the pregnancy resulted from rape or incest. Publicity about birth defects caused by Thalidomide, a drug prescribed in the 1960s to cure infertility, and a German measles epidemic in the years 1962–1965 kept the issue prominent. By November 1965 the American Medical Association Board of Trustees approved a report urging adoption of the ALI law.

In 1966, reform activists began making numerous radio and television appearances.[5] By then there were several pro-choice groups, including the Society for Humane Abortion in California; the Association for the Study of Abortion in New York, a prestigious board of doctors and lawyers; and the Illinois Committee for Medical Control of Abortion, which advocated repeal of all abortion laws. Abortion referral services were also started. Previously, pro-choice activists had made private referrals to competent doctors in the United States and Mexico, who performed illegal but safe abortions. But by the late 1960s, abortion referral groups operated publicly. In New York City, in 1967, twenty-two clergy announced the formation of their group, gaining front-page coverage in the *New York Times* (Fiske 1967). The Chicago referral service took out a full page ad in the *Sun-Times* announcing its services. In Los Angeles, the referral service was serving more than a thousand women per month. By the late 1960s pro-choice organizations, including abortion-referral services, were operating in many major U.S. cities. And by 1971, the clergy referral service operated publicly in eighteen states with a staff of about 700 clergy and lay people (Hole and Levine 1971, 299).

In order to tap this emerging support, the National Association for the Repeal of Abortion Laws (NARAL) was founded.[6] Protesting in the streets, lecturing, and organizing "days of anger" began to have an effect. Women who had undergone illegal abortions wrote and spoke openly about them. Seventy-five leading national groups endorsed the repeal of all abortion laws between 1967 and the end of 1972, including twenty-eight religious and twenty-one medical groups. Among the religious groups, support ranged from the American Jewish Congress to the American Baptist Convention. Medical groups included the American Public Health Association, the American Psychiatric Association, the American Medical Association, the National Council of Obstetrics-Gynecology, and the American College of Obstetricians and Gynecologists. Among other groups, support included the American Bar Association and a host of liberal organizations. Even the YWCA supported repeal (U.S. Congress 1976, 4:53–91).

The Federal Government

In the late 1960s, while the abortion law reform battle was being fought in the states, the federal arena was quiet. For example, although states with less restrictive laws received Medicaid funds that paid for some abortions, for "six years after 1967, not a single bill was introduced, much less considered, in Congress to curtail the use of federal funds for abortion" (Rosoff 1975, 13). The pace momentarily quickened in 1968 when the Presidential Advisory Council on the Status of Women, appointed by President Lyndon Johnson, recommended the repeal of all abortion laws (Lader 1973, 81–82).

Still, abortion was not a major issue in the 1968 presidential campaign. Despite his personal beliefs, the newly elected president, Richard M. Nixon, did not take active steps to limit abortion, and the U.S. government did not enter *Roe* nor, after the decision, did it give support to congressional efforts to limit abortion.[7] Although it is true that in 1973 and 1974 President Nixon was occupied with other matters, his administration essentially avoided the abortion issue.

In Congress there was virtually no abortion activity prior to 1973. In April 1970, Sen. Bob Packwood (R-Ore.) introduced a National Abortion Act designed to "guarantee and protect" the "fundamental constitutional right" of a woman "to control her own fertility" (U.S. Congress 1970a). He also introduced a bill to liberalize the District of Columbia's abortion law (U.S. Congress 1970b). Otherwise, Congress remained essentially inactive on the abortion issue.

The States

It is not at all surprising that the president and Congress did not involve themselves in the abortion reform movement of the 1960s. Laws banning abortion were state laws, so most of the early abortion law reform activity was directed at state governments. In the early and middle parts of the decade there was some legislative discussion in California, New Hampshire, and New York. By 1967, reform bills were introduced in twenty-eight states, including California, Colorado, Delaware, Florida, Georgia, Maryland, Oklahoma, New Jersey, New York, North Carolina, and Pennsylvania (Rubin 1982). The first successful liberalization drive was in Colorado, which adopted a reform bill, modeled on the ALI's Model Penal Code. Interestingly, another early reform state was California, where Gov. Ronald Reagan, despite intense opposition, signed a reform bill.

These victories further propelled the reform movement, and in 1968, abortion legislation was pending in some thirty states. During 1968–1969 seven states—Arkansas, Delaware, Georgia, Kansas, Maryland, New Mexico, and Oregon—enacted reform laws based on or similar to the ALI model (Lader 1973, 84). In 1970, four states went even further. In chronological order, Hawaii, New York, Alaska, and Washington essentially repealed prohibitions on abortions in the first two trimesters.

To sum up, in the five or so years prior to the Supreme Court's decisions, reform and repeal bills had been debated in most states, and seventeen plus the District of Columbia acted to liberalize their laws (Craig and O'Brien 1993, 75). State action had removed some obstacles to abortion, and safe and legal abortions were thus available in scattered states. And, as indicated in Figure 1, in 1972, nearly 600,000 legal abortions were performed. Activity was widespread, vocal, and effective.

Public Opinion

Another important element in the effectiveness of the Court is the amount of support from the population at large. By the eve of the Court's decision in 1973, public opinion had dramatically shifted from opposition to abortion in most cases to substantial, if not majority, support. Indeed, in the decades that have followed, opinion on abortion has remained remarkably stable.[8]

Looking at the 1960s as a whole, Blake (1971, 543, 544) found that opinions on discretionary abortion were "changing rapidly over time" and polls were recording "rapidly growing support." For example, relying on data from Gallup polls, Blake (1977b, 49) found that support for elective abortion increased approximately two and one-half times from 1968 to 1972. One set of Gallup polls recorded a fifteen-point drop in the percentage of respondents disapproving of abortions for financial reasons in the eight months between October 1969 and June 1970 (Blake 1977a, 58). . . . In 1971, a national poll taken for the Commission on Population Growth and the American Future found 50 percent of its respondents agreeing with the statement that the abortion "decision should be left up to persons involved and their doctor" (Rosenthal 1971, 22). Thus, in the words of one study, "[b]y the time the Supreme Court made its ruling, there was strong public support behind the legalization of abortion" (Ebaugh and Haney 1980, 493).

Much of the reason for the growth in support for the repeal of the laws on abortion, both from the public and from organizations, may have come from changes in opinion by the professional elite. Polls throughout the late 1960s reported that important subgroups of the American population were increasingly supportive of abortion law reform and repeal. Several nonscientific polls of doctors, for example, suggested a great deal of support for abortion reform. A scientific poll of nearly thirteen thousand respondents in nursing, medical, and social work schools in the autumn and winter of 1971 showed strong support for repeal. The poll found split opinions among nursing students and faculty but found that 69 percent of medical students, 71 percent of medical faculty, 76 percent of social work students, and 75 percent of social work faculty supported "freely accessible abortion" (Rosen et al. 1974, 165). And a poll by the American Council of Education of 180,000 college freshmen in 1970 found that 83 percent favored the legalization of abortion (Currivan 1970). It is clear that in the late 1960s and early 1970s, the public was becoming increasingly supportive of legal abortion.

Post-*Roe* Activity

The relative quiet of the early 1960s has yet to return to the abortion arena. Rather than settling the issue, the Court's decisions added even more controversy. On the federal level, legislative and administrative action dealing with abortion has swung back and forth, from more or less benign neglect prior to 1973 to open antipathy to modest support. State action has followed a different course. Legislative efforts in the 1960s and early 1970s to reform and repeal abortion laws gave way to efforts to limit access to abortions. Public opinion remained stable until the *Webster* decision, after which there was a noticeable shift toward the pro-choice position. Finally, the antiabortion movement grew both more vocal and more violent.

The Federal Government: The President

On the presidential level, little changed in the years immediately after *Roe*. Nixon, as noted, took no action, and Gerald R. Ford, during his short term, said little about abortion until the presidential campaign in 1976, when he took a middle-of-the-road, antiabortion position, supporting local option, the law before *Roe,* and opposing federal funding of abortion (Craig and O'Brien 1993, 160–161). His Justice Department, however, did not enter the case of *Planned Parenthood of Central Missouri v. Danforth*, in which numerous state restrictions on the provision of abortion were challenged, and the Ford administration took no major steps to help the antiabortion forces.[9]

The Carter administration, unlike its Republican predecessors, did act to limit access to abortion. As a presidential candidate Carter opposed federal spending for abortion, and as president, during a press conference in June 1977, he stated his support for the Supreme Court's decisions allowing states to refuse Medicaid funding for abortions (Rubin 1982, 107). The Carter administration also sent its solicitor general into the Supreme Court to defend the Hyde Amendment.

Ronald Reagan was publicly committed to ending legal abortion. Opposition to *Roe* was said to be a litmus test for federal judicial appointments, and Reagan repeatedly used his formidable rhetorical skills in support of antiabortion activists. Under his presidency, antiabortion laws enacted included prohibiting fetal tissue research by federal scientists, banning most abortions at military hospitals, and denying funding to organizations that counseled or provided abortion services abroad. His administration submitted amicus curiae cases in all the Court's abortion cases, and in two (*Thornburgh v. American College of Obstetricians and Gynecologists*, 1986, and *Webster*) urged that *Roe* be overturned. Yet, despite the rhetoric and the symbolism, these actions had little effect on the abortion rate. As Craig and O'Brien (1993, 190) put it, "in spite of almost eight years of antiabortion rhetoric, Reagan had accomplished little in curbing abortion."

The administration of George Bush was as, if not more, hostile to the constitutional right to abortion as its predecessor. It filed antiabortion briefs in several abortion cases and urged that *Roe* be overturned. During Bush's presidency, the Food and Drug Administration placed RU-486, a French abortion drug, on the list of unapproved drugs, making it ineligible to be imported for personal use. And, in the administration's most celebrated antiabortion action, the secretary of the Health and Human Services Department, Louis W. Sullivan, issued regulations prohibiting family-planning organizations that received federal funds from counseling patients about abortion or providing referrals (the "gag rule" upheld in *Rust*).

President Bill Clinton brought a sea change to the abortion issue. As the first pro-choice president since *Roe*, he acted quickly to reverse decisions of his predecessors. In particular, on the third day of his administration, and the twentieth anniversary of *Roe*, Clinton issued five abortion-related memos.

1. He rescinded the ban on abortion counseling at federally financed clinics (negating *Rust*).
2. He rescinded restrictions on federal financing of fetal tissue research.
3. He eased U.S. policy on abortions in military hospitals.
4. He reversed Reagan policy on aid to international family planning programs involved in abortion-related activities.
5. He called for review of the ban on RU-486, the French abortion pill (Toner 1993).

In addition, in late May 1994, he signed the Freedom of Access to Clinic Entrances Act, giving federal protection to facilities and personnel providing abortion services. And, in early August 1994, the U.S. Justice Department sent U.S. marshals to help guard abortion clinics in at least twelve communities around the country (Thomas 1994). Furthermore, his two Supreme Court appointees as of 1994, Ruth Bader Ginsburg and Stephen Breyer, are apparently both pro-choice.

The Federal Government: Congress

In contrast to the executive branch, Congress engaged in a great deal of antiabortion activity after 1973, although almost none of it was successful, and some supportive activity actually occurred in the late 1980s and early 1990s. By means of legislation designed to overturn *Roe*, riders to various spending bills, and constitutional amendments, many members of Congress made their opposition to abortion clear. Perhaps the most important congressional action was the passage of the Hyde Amendment, which restricted federal funding of abortion: First passed in 1976, and then in subsequent years, the amendment prohibited the use of federal funds for abortion except in extremely limited circumstances. Although the wording varied in some years, the least limited version allowed funding only to save the life of the woman, when rape or incest had occurred, or when some long-lasting health damage, certified by two physicians, would result from the pregnancy. The amendment has been effective and the number of federally funded abortions fell from 294,600 in 1977 to 267 in 1992 (Daley and Gold 1994, 250).

Despite the amount of congressional activity, the Hyde Amendment was the only serious piece of antiabortion legislation enacted.[10] And, in 1994, Congress actually enacted legislation granting federal protection to abortion clinics. Thus, Congress was hostile in words but cautious in action with abortion. While not supporting the Court and the right to abortion, congressional action did not bar legal abortion.[11]

The States

Prior to 1973 the states had been the main arena for the abortion battle, and Court action did not do much to change that. In the wake of the Court decisions, all but a few states had to rewrite their abortion laws to conform to the Court's constitutional mandate. Their reactions, like those on the federal level, varied enormously. Some states acted to bring their laws into conformity with the Court's ruling, while others reenacted their former restrictive laws or enacted regulations designed to impede access to abortion. Since abortion is a state matter, the potential for state action affecting the availability of legal abortion was high.

At the outset, a national survey reported that state governments "moved with extreme caution in implementing the Supreme Court's ruling" (Brody 1973, A1). By the end of 1973, Blake (1977b, 46) reports, 260 abortion-related bills had been introduced in state legislatures and 39 enacted. In 1974, 189 bills were introduced and 19 enacted. In total, in the two years immediately following the Court decisions, 62 laws relating to abortion were enacted by 32 states. And state activity continued, with more abortion laws enacted in 1977 than in any year since 1973 (Rubin 1982, 126, 136).

Many of these laws were hostile to abortion. "Perhaps the major share," Blake (1977b, 61 n. 2) believes, was "obstructive and unconstitutional." They included spousal and parental consent requirements, tedious written-consent forms describing the "horrors" of abortion, funding limitations, waiting periods, hospitalization requirements, elaborate statistical reporting requirements, and burdensome medical procedures. Other action undertaken by states was simple and directly to the point. North Dakota and Rhode Island, for example, responded to the Court's decisions by enacting laws allowing abortion only to preserve the life of the woman (Weinstock et al. 1975, 28; "Rhode Island" 1973). Virginia rejected a bill bringing its statutes into conformity with the Court's order (Brody 1973, 46). Arkansas enforced a state law allowing abortion only if the pregnancy threatened the life or health of the woman ("Abortions Legal for Year" 1973, A14). In Louisiana, the attorney general threatened to take away the license of any physician performing an abortion, and the state medical society declared that any physician who performed an abortion, except to save the woman's life, violated the ethical principles of medicine (Weinstock et al. 1975, 28). The Louisiana State Board of Medical Examiners also pledged to prevent physicians from performing abortions (Brody 1973). In Pennsylvania, the state medical society announced that it did "not condone abortion on demand" and retained its strict standards (King 1973, 35). And in Saint Louis, the city attorney threatened to arrest any physician who performed an abortion (King 1973). Given this kind of activity, it can be concluded that in many states the Court's intent was "widely and purposively frustrated" (Blake 1977b, 60–61).

Variation in state response to the constitutional right to an abortion continues to this day. Although legal abortions are performed in all states, the availability of abortion services varies enormously. As noted, a variety of restrictions on abortion have been enacted across the country. In the wake of the Court's decision in *Webster* (1989), which upheld a restrictive Missouri law, a new round of state restrictions on abortion was generally expected. Indeed, within two years of the decision nine states and Guam enacted restrictions. Nevertheless, four states enacted legislation protecting a woman's right to abortion (Craig and O'Brien 1993, 280). The Pennsylvania enactments were challenged in *Casey* (1992), in

Figure 2. Public Opinion and Abortion, Selected Years, 1975–1992

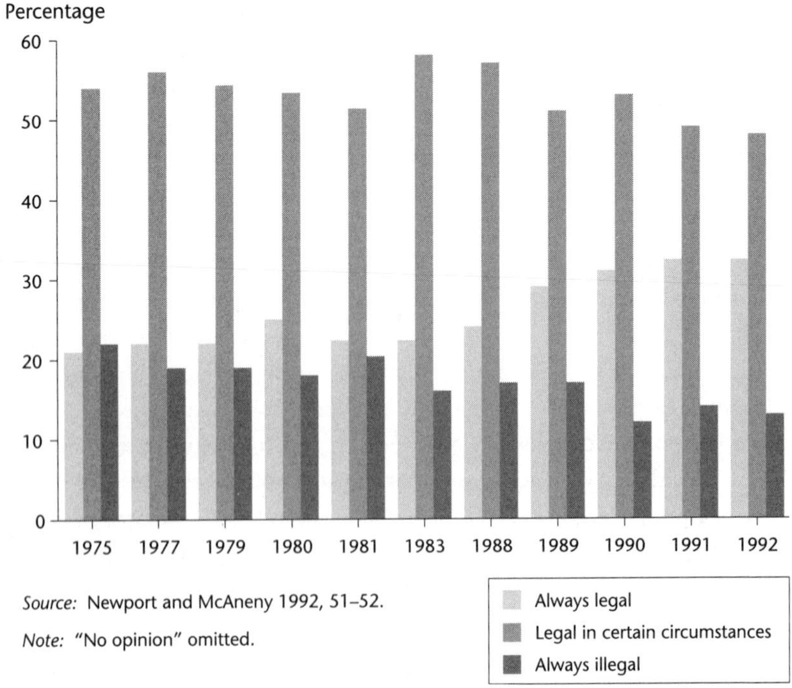

Percentage

Source: Newport and McAneny 1992, 51–52.

Note: "No opinion" omitted.

Always legal
Legal in certain circumstances
Always illegal

which the "undue burden" standard was announced. The lack of clarity in this standard virtually ensures that restrictions will continue to be enacted.

Public Opinion

As shown in Figure 2, public opinion changed little from the early 1970s (pre-*Roe*) until the *Webster* decision in 1989, after which a small but important growth in pro-choice support occurred. Although differently worded questions produce different results, it is clear that the American public remains strongly supportive of abortion when the woman's health is endangered by continuing the pregnancy, when there is a strong chance of a serious fetal defect, and when the pregnancy is the result of rape or incest. The public is more divided when abortion is sought for economic reasons, by single unmarried women unwilling to marry, and by married women who do not want more children. "The overall picture that emerges is that a majority supports leaving abortion legal and available to women unfortunate enough to need it, though many in the majority remain concerned about the moral implications" (Craig and O'Brien 1993, 269). . . .

Anti-Abortion Activity

Organized opposition to abortion increased dramatically in the years following the Court's initial decisions. National groups such as the American Life Lobby, Americans United for Life, the National Right to Life Committee, the Pro-Life Action League, and Operation Rescue and numerous local groups have adopted some of the tactics of the reformers. They have marched, lobbied, and protested, urging that abortion be made illegal in most or all circumstances. In addition, in the 1980s, groups like Operation Rescue began to adopt more violent tactics. And, since 1982, the U.S. Bureau of Alcohol, Tobacco and Firearms has reported 146 incidents of bombing, arson, or attempts against clinics and related sites in thirty states, causing more than $12 million in damages (Thomas 1994). The high level of harassment of abortion clinics is shown in Table 1.

The level of harassment appears to have increased over time. In just 1992 and 1993 the U.S. Bureau of Alcohol, Tobacco and Firearms recorded thirty-six incidents, which resulted in an estimated $3.8 million in damages (Thomas 1994). The National Abortion Federation, representing roughly half of the nation's clinics, noted that incidents of reported vandalism at its clinics more than doubled from 1991 to 1992 (Barringer 1993). From May 1992 to August 1993 the U.S. Bureau of Alcohol, Tobacco and Firearms reported that 123 family-planning clinics were bombed or burned (Baum 1993). In 1992 more than forty clinics were attacked with butyric acid (a chemical injected through key holes, under doors, or into ventilation shafts) forcing clinic closures and requiring costly repairs (Anderson and Binstein 1993, C27). One of the aims of this violence appears to be to raise the cost of operating abortion clinics to such an extent as to force their closure. In 1992 and 1993, for example, arson destroyed clinics in Missoula and Helena, Montana, and in Boise, Idaho. The clinics have either been unable to reopen or have had great difficulty in doing so because of the difficulty of finding owners willing to rent to them and obtaining insurance coverage. In 1990, in the wake of such violence, one major insurer, Traveler's Insurance Company, decided not to insure any abortion-related concerns (Baum 1993).

Another tactic aimed at shutting down abortion clinics is to conduct large, sustained protests. During the summer of 1991, for example, Operation Rescue staged forty-six days of protest in Wichita, Kansas, resulting in the arrest of approximately 2,700 people. During the summer of 1993, Operation Rescue launched a seven-city campaign with similar aims. In addition, there have been individual acts of violence against abortion providers. Dr. David Gunn was murdered in March 1993 outside an abortion clinic in Pensacola, Florida; Dr. George Tiller was shot in August 1993 in Wichita, Kansas; and Dr. John Britton and his escort, James Barrett, a retired air force lieutenant colonel, were murdered in late July 1994, also in Pensacola. Commenting on the murders of Dr. Britton and James

Table 1. Abortion Clinics Reporting Harassment,
1985 and 1988 (in percentage)

Activity	1985	1988
Picketing	80	81
Picketing with physical contact or blocking	47	46
Demonstrations resulting in arrests	—	38
Bomb threats	48	36
Vandalism	28	34
Picketing homes of staff members	16	17

Note: Dash = question not asked.

Source: Surveys of all abortion providers taken by the Alan Guttmacher Institute in Henshaw (1991, 246–252, 263).

Barrett, Don Treshman, director of the antiabortion group Rescue America, issued an ominous warning: "Up to now, the killings have been on one side, with 30 million dead babies and hundreds of dead and maimed mothers. On the other side, there are two dead doctors. Maybe the balance is going to shift" (quoted in Lewin 1994, A7).[12] In sum, as Forrest and Henshaw (1987, 13) concluded, "antiabortion harassment in the United States is widespread and frequent."

Two important facts can be gleaned from the foregoing discussion. First, at the time of the 1973 abortion decisions, large segments of the political and professional elite were either indifferent to or supported abortion reform. Second, after the decisions, many political leaders vociferously opposed abortion. Congress enacted antiabortion legislation as did some of the states. In addition, activist opposition was growing. How this opposition affected the implementation of the decisions is the focus of the next section.

The Effect of Opposition on the Implementation of Abortion Rights

On the eve of the abortion decisions, there was widespread support from critical professional elites, growing public support, successful reform in many states, and indifference from most national politicians. Is this sufficient for the implementation of constitutional rights?

Constitutional rights are not self-implementing. That is, to make a right a reality, the behavior of individuals and the policies of the institutions in which they work must change. Because abortion is a medical procedure, and because safe

Table 2. Hospitals Providing Abortions, Selected Years,
1973–1992 (percentage)

Year	Private, short-term non-Catholic, general	Public
1973	24	—
1974	27	17
1975	30	—
1976	31	20
1977	31	21
1978	29	—
1979	28	—
1980	27	17
1982	26	16
1985	23	17
1988	21	15
1992	18	13

Note: Dash = unavailable.

Sources: Forrest, Sullivan, and Tietze 1978, table 5; Henshaw 1986, 253; Henshaw et al. 1982, table 7; Henshaw, Forrest, and Van Vort 1987, 68; Henshaw and Van Vort 1990, 102–108, 142; Henshaw and Van Vort 1994, 100–106, 122; Rubin 1982, 154; Sullivan, Tietze, and Dryfoos, 1977, figure 10; Weinstock et al. 1975, 32.

abortion requires trained personnel, the implementation of abortion rights depends on the medical profession to provide abortion services. When done properly, first-term and most second-term abortions can be performed on an outpatient basis, and there is less risk of death in the procedure than there is in childbirth or in such routine operations as tonsillectomies. Thus, no medical or technical reasons stand in the way of the provision of abortion services. Following Supreme Court action, however, the medical profession moved with "extreme caution" in making abortion available (Brody 1973, 1). Coupled with the hostility of some state legislatures, barriers to legal abortion remained.

These barriers have proved to be strong. Perhaps the strongest barrier has been opposition from hospitals. In Table 2, I track the response of hospitals to the Court's decisions. The results are staggering. Despite the relative ease and safety of the abortion procedure, and the unambiguous holding of the Court, both public and private hospitals throughout America have refused to perform abortions. *The vast majority of public and private hospitals have never performed an abortion!* In 1973 and the first quarter of 1974, for example, slightly more than three-quarters of public and private non-Catholic general care short-term hospitals did not perform a single abortion (Weinstock et al. 1975, 31). As illustrated in the table, the passage of time has not improved the situation. By 1976, three years after the decision, at least 70 percent of hospitals provided no abortion services. By 1992 the situation had further deteriorated: only 18 percent of private non-Catholic general care short-term hospitals and only 13 percent of public hospitals provided abortions. As Stanley Henshaw (1986, 253, emphasis added) concluded, reviewing the data in 1986, "most hospitals have *never* performed abortions."

These figures mask the fact that even the limited availability of hospital abortions detailed here varies widely across states. In 1973, for example, only 4 percent of all abortions were performed in the eight states that make up the East South Central and West South Central census divisions (Weinstock et al. 1975, 25).[13] Two states, on the other hand, New York and California (which are home to about 20 percent of all U.S. women), accounted for 37 percent of all abortions in 1974 (Alan Guttmacher Institute 1976). In eleven states, "not a single public hospital reported performance of a single abortion for any purpose whatsoever in all of 1973" (Weinstock et al. 1975, 31). By 1976, three years after Court action, no hospitals, public or private, in Louisiana, North Dakota, and South Dakota performed abortions. The Dakotas alone had thirty public and sixty-two private hospitals. In five other states, which had a total of eighty-two public hospitals, not one performed an abortion. In thirteen additional states, less than 10 percent of each state's public hospitals reported performing any abortions (Forrest, Sullivan, and Tietze 1979, 46). Only in the states of California, Hawaii, New York, and North Carolina and in the District of Columbia did more than half the public hospitals perform any abortions during 1974–1975 (Alan Guttmacher Institute 1976, 30). By 1992, the situation was little better, with five states (California, New York, Texas, Florida, and Illinois) accounting for 49 percent of all legal abortions (Henshaw and Van Vort 1994, 102).

This refusal of hospitals to perform abortions means that women seeking them, particularly from rural areas, have to travel, often a great distance, to exercise their constitutional rights. In 1973, for example, 150,000 women traveled out of their state of residence to obtain abortions. By 1982 the numbers had dropped, but more than 100,000 women were still forced to travel to another state for abortion services. ...

Even when women can obtain abortions within their states of residence, they may still have to travel a great distance to do so. In 1974, the year after *Roe*, the Guttmacher Institute found that between 300,000 and 400,000 women left their home communities to obtain abortions (Alan Guttmacher Institute 1976). In 1980, across the United States, more than one-quarter (27 percent) of all women who had abortions had them outside of their home counties (Henshaw and O'Reilly 1983, 5). And in 1988, fifteen years after *Roe*, an estimated 430,000

(27 percent) women who had abortions in nonhospital settings traveled more than fifty miles from their home to reach their abortion provider. This includes over 140,000 women who traveled more than 100 miles to obtain a legal abortion (Henshaw 1991, 248).[14]

The general problem that faces women who seek to exercise their constitutional right to abortion is the paucity of abortion providers. From the legalization of abortion in 1973 to the present, at least 77 percent of all U.S. counties have been without abortion providers. And the problem is not merely rural. In 1980, seven years after Court action, there were still fifty-nine metropolitan areas in which no facilities could be identified that provided abortions (Henshaw et al. 1982, 5). The most recent data suggest that the problem is worsening. In 1992, 84 percent of all U.S. counties, home to 30 percent of all women of reproductive age, had no abortion providers. Ninety-one of the country's 320 metropolitan (28 percent) areas have no identified abortion provider, and an additional 14 (4 percent) have providers who perform fewer than fifty abortions per year....

Even when abortion service is available, providers have tended to ignore the time periods set out in the Court's opinions. In 1988, fifteen years after the decisions, only 43 percent of all providers perform abortions after the first trimester. More than half (55 percent) of the hospitals that perform abortions have refused to perform second-trimester procedures, a time in pregnancy at which hospital services may be medically necessary. Only at abortion clinics have a majority of providers been willing to perform abortions after the first trimester. Indeed, in 1988 a startling 22 percent of all providers refused to perform abortions past the tenth week of pregnancy, several weeks within the first trimester, during which, according to the Court, a woman's constitutional right is virtually all-encompassing (Henshaw 1991, 251).

Finally, although abortion is "the most common surgical procedure that women undergo" (Darney et al. 1987, 161) and is reportedly the most common surgical procedure performed in the United States, an *increasing* percentage of residency programs in obstetrics and gynecology do not provide training for it. A survey taken in 1985 of all such residency programs found that 28 percent of them offered no training at all, a nearly fourfold increase since 1976. According to the results of the survey, approximately one-half of the programs made training available as an option, while only 23 percent included it routinely (Darney et al. 1987, 160). By 1992 the percentage of programs requiring abortion training had dropped nearly to half, to 12 percent (Baum 1993). In a study done in 1992 of 216 of 271 residency programs, it was found that almost half (47 percent) of graduating residents had never performed a first-trimester abortion, and only 7 percent had ever performed one in the second trimester (Cooper 1993). At least part of the reason for the increasing lack of training is harassment by antiabortion activists. "Anti-abortion groups say these numbers prove that harassment of doctors, and in turn, medical schools which train residents in abortion procedures, is an effective tactic," Cooper reported. "'You humiliate the school. . . . We hope that in 10 years, there'll be none' that train residents how to perform abortions" (Randall Terry, founder of Operation Rescue, quoted in Cooper 1993, B3). . . .

It is clear that hospital administrators, both public and private, refused to change their abortion policies in reaction to the Court decisions. In the years since the Court's decisions, abortion services have remained centered in metropolitan areas and in those states that reformed their abortion laws and regulations prior to the Court's decisions. In 1976 the Alan Guttmacher Institute (1976, 13) concluded that "[t]he response of hospitals to the legalization of abortion continues to be so limited . . . as to be tantamount to no response." Jaffe, Lindheim, and Lee (1981, 15) concluded that "the delivery pattern for abortion services that has emerged since 1973 is distorted beyond precedent." Reviewing the data in the mid-1980s, Henshaw, Forrest, and Blaine (1984, 122) summed up the situation this way: "There is abundant evidence that many women still find it difficult or impossible to obtain abortion services because of the distance of their home to the nearest provider, the cost, a lack of information on where to go, and limitations on the circumstances under which a provider will make abortions available." Most recently, Henshaw (1991, 253) concluded that "an American woman seeking abortion services will find it increasingly difficult to find a provider who will serve her in an accessible location and at an affordable cost."

Implementing Constitutional Rights: The Market

The foregoing discussion presents a seeming dilemma. There has been hostility to abortion from some politicians, most hospital administrators, many doctors, and parts of the public. On the whole, in response to the Court, hospitals did not change their policies to permit abortions. Yet, as demonstrated in Figure 1, the number of legal abortions performed in the United States continued to grow. How is it, for example, that congressional and state hostility seemed effectively to prevent progress in civil rights in the 1950s and early 1960s but did not prevent abortion in the 1970s? The answer to this question not only removes the dilemma but also illustrates why the Court's abortion decisions were effective in making legal abortion more easily available. The answer, in a word, is *clinics*.

The Court's decisions prohibited the states from interfering with a woman's right to choose an abortion, at least in the first trimester. They did not uphold hospitalization requirements, and later cases explicitly rejected hospitalization requirements for second-trimester abortions.[15] Room was left for abortion reformers, population control groups, women's groups, and individual physicians to set up clinics to perform abortions. The refusal of many hospitals, then, to perform abortions could be countered by the creation of clinics willing to do the job. And that's exactly what happened.

In the wake of the Court's decisions the number of abortion providers sharply increased. In the first year after the decisions, the number of providers grew by nearly 25 percent. Over the first three years the percentage increase was almost 58 percent. The number of providers reached a peak in 1982 and has declined more than 18 percent since then. These raw data, however, do not indicate who these providers were.

... [T]he number of abortion providers increased because of the increase in the number of clinics. To fill the void that hospitals had left, clinics opened in large numbers. Between 1973 and 1974, for example, the number of nonhospital abortion providers grew 61 percent. Overall, between 1973 and 1976 the number of nonhospital providers grew 152 percent, nearly five times the rate of growth of hospital providers. In metropolitan areas . . . the growth rate was 140 percent between 1973 and 1976, five times the rate for hospital providers; in nonmetropolitan areas it was a staggering 304 percent, also about five times the growth rate for nonmetropolitan hospitals.

The growth in the number of abortion clinics was matched by the increase in the number of abortions performed by them. By 1974, nonhospital clinics were performing approximately 51 percent of all abortions, and nearly an additional 3 percent were being performed in physicians' offices. Between 1973 and 1974, the number of abortions performed in hospitals rose 5 percent, while the number performed in clinics rose 39 percent. By 1976, clinics accounted for 62 percent of all reported abortions, despite the fact that they were only 17 percent of all providers (Forrest, Sullivan, and Tietze 1979). From 1973 to 1976, the years immediately following Court action, the number of abortions performed in hospitals increased by only 8 percent, whereas the number performed in clinics and physicians' offices increased by a whopping 113 percent (Forrest et al. 1979).[16] The percentages continued to rise, and by 1992, 93 percent of all abortions were performed in nonhospital settings. Clinics satisfied the need that hospitals, despite the Court's actions, refused to meet.

In permitting abortions to be performed in clinics as well as hospitals, the Court's decisions granted a way around the intransigence of hospitals. The decisions allowed individuals committed to safe and legal abortion to make use of the market and create their own structures to meet the demand. They also provided a financial incentive for services to be provided. At least some clinics were formed solely as money-making ventures. As the legal activist Janice Goodman put it, "Some doctors are going to see a very substantial amount of money to be made on this" (quoted in Goodman, Schoenbrod, and Stearns 1973, 31). Nancy Stearns, who filed a pro-choice amicus brief in *Roe*, agreed: "[In the abortion cases] the people that are necessary to effect the decision are doctors, most of whom are not opposed, probably don't give a damn, and in fact have a whole lot to gain . . . because of the amount of money they can make" (quoted in Goodman et al. 1973, 29). Even the glacial growth of hospital abortion providers in the early and mid-1970s may be due, in part, to financial considerations. In a study of thirty-six general hospitals in Harris County (Houston), Texas, the need for increased income was found to be an important determinant of whether hospitals performed abortions. Hospitals with low occupancy rates, and therefore low income, the study reported, "saw changing abortion policy as a way to fill beds and raise income" (Kemp, Carp, and Brady 1978, 27).

Although the law of the land was that the choice of an abortion was not to be denied a woman in the first trimester, and regulated only to the extent necessary to preserve a woman's health in the second trimester, American hospitals, on the whole, do not honor the law. By allowing the market to meet the need, however, the Court's decisions resulted in at least a continuation of some availability of safe and legal abortion. Although no one can be sure what might have happened if clinics had not been allowed, if the sole burden for implementing the decisions had been on hospitals, hospital practice suggests that resistance would have been strong. After all, the Court did find abortion constitutionally protected, and most hospitals simply refused to accept that decision.

The implementation of constitutional rights, then, may depend a great deal on the beliefs of those necessary to implement them. The data suggest that without clinics the Court's decisions, constitutional rights notwithstanding, would have been frustrated.

Court Decisions and Political Action

It is generally believed that winning a major Supreme Court case is an invaluable political resource. The victorious side can use the decision to dramatize the issue, encourage political mobilization, and ignite a political movement. In an older view, however, this connection is dubious. Writing at the beginning of the twentieth century, Thayer (1901) suggested that reliance on litigation weakens political organizing. Because there have been more than twenty years of litigation in regard to abortion, the issue provides a good test of these competing views.

The evidence suggests that Roe and Doe may have seriously weakened the political effectiveness of the winners—pro-choice forces—and inspired the losers. After the 1973 decisions, many pro-choice activists simply assumed they had won and stopped their activity. According to J. Hugh Anwyl, then the executive director of Planned Parenthood of Los Angeles, pro-choice activists went "on a long siesta" after the abortion decisions (quoted in Johnston 1977, 1). Alfred F. Moran, an executive vice president at Planned Parenthood of New York, put it this way: "Most of us really believed that was the end of the controversy. The Supreme Court had spoken, and while some disagreement would remain, the issue had been tried, tested and laid to rest" (Brozan 1983, A17). These views were joined by a NARAL activist, Janet Beals: "Everyone assumed that when the Supreme Court made its decision in 1973 that we'd got what we wanted and the battle was over. The movement afterwards lost steam" (quoted in Phillips 1980, 3). By 1977 a survey of pro-choice and antiabortion activity in thirteen states nationwide revealed that abortion rights advocates had failed to match the activity of their opponents (Johnston 1977).[17] The political organization and momentum that had changed laws nationwide dissipated in reaction to Court victory. This may help explain why abortion services remain so unevenly available.

Reliance on Court action seems to have harmed the pro-choice movement in a second way. The most restrictive version of the Hyde Amendment, banning federal funding of abortions even where abortion is necessary to save the life of the woman, was passed with the help of a parliamentary maneuver by pro-choice legislators. Their strategy, as reported the following day on the front pages of the *New York Times* and the *Washington Post,* was to pass such a conservative bill that the Court would have no choice but to overturn it (Russell 1977; Tolchin 1977). This reliance on the Court was totally unfounded. With hindsight, Karen Mulhauser, a former director of NARAL, suggested that "had we made more gains through the legislative and referendum processes, and taken a little longer at it, the public would have moved with us" (quoted in Williams 1979, 12). By winning a Court case "without the organization needed to cope with a powerful opposition" (Rubin 1982, 169), pro-choice forces vastly overestimated the power and influence of the Court.

By the time of *Webster* (1989), however, pro-choice forces seemed to have learned from their mistakes, while right-to-life activists miscalculated. In early August 1989, just after *Webster,* a spokesperson for the National Right to Life Committee proclaimed: "[F]or the first time since 1973, we are clearly in a position of strength" (Shribman 1989, A8). Pro-choice forces, however, went on the offensive by generating a massive political response. Commenting on *Webster,* Nancy Broff, NARAL's legislative and political director, noted, "It finally gave us the smoking gun we needed to mobilize people" (quoted in Kornhauser 1989, 11). Membership and financial support grew rapidly. "In the year after *Webster,* membership in the National Abortion Rights Action League jumped from 150,000 to 400,000; in the National Organization for Women [NOW], from 170,000 to 250,000" (Craig and O'Brien 1993, 296). Furthermore, NARAL "nearly tripled" its income in 1989, and NOW "nearly doubled" its income, as did the Planned Parenthood Federation of America (Shribman 1989, A8). In May 1989 alone, NARAL raised $1 million (Kornhauser 1989).

This newfound energy was turned toward political action. In gubernatorial elections in Virginia and New Jersey in the fall of 1989, pro-choice forces played an important role in electing the pro-choice candidates L. Douglas Wilder and James J. Florio over antiabortion opponents. Antiabortion legislation was defeated in Florida, where Gov. Bob Martinez, an opponent of abortion, called a special session of the legislature to enact it. Congress passed legislation that allowed the District of Columbia to use its own tax revenues to pay for abortions and that essentially repealed the so-called gag rule, but President Bush vetoed both bills, and the House of Representatives failed to override the vetoes. As Paige Cunningham, of the antiabortion group Americans United for Life, put it: "The pro-life movement has been organized and active for twenty years, and some of us are tired. The pro-choice movement is fresh so they're operating with a much greater energy reserve. They've really rallied in light of *Webster*" (quoted in Berke 1989, 1).

This new understanding was also seen in *Casey*. Although pro-choice forces had seen antiabortion restrictions upheld in *Webster* and *Rust*, and the sure antiabortion vote of Justice Clarence Thomas had replaced the pro-choice vote of Justice Thurgood Marshall on the Supreme Court in the interim, pro-choice forces appealed the lower-court decision to the Supreme Court. As the *New York Times* reported, this was "a calculated move to intensify the political debate on abortion before the 1992 election" (Berke 1989, 1). Further increasing the stakes, they asked the Court either to reaffirm women's fundamental right to abortion or to overturn *Roe*. Berke (1991, B8) declared that "[t]he action marked an adjustment in strategy by the abortion rights groups, who seem now to be looking to the Court as a political foil rather than a source of redress."

All this suggests that Thayer may have the stronger case. That is, Court decisions do seem to have a mobilizing potential, but for the losers![18] Both winners and losers appear to assume that Court decisions announcing or upholding constitutional rights will be implemented, but they behave in different ways. Winners celebrate and relax, whereas losers redouble their efforts. Note, too, that in the wake of *Webster*, public opinion moved in a pro-choice direction, counter to the tenor of the opinion. Court decisions do matter, but in complicated ways.

Conclusion

"It does no good to have the [abortion] procedure be legal if women can't get it," stated Gwenyth Mapes, the executive director of the Missoula (Montana) Blue Mountain Clinic destroyed by arson in March 1993 (quoted in Baum 1993, A1).

Courts do not exist in a vacuum. Supreme Court decisions, even those finding constitutional rights, are not implemented automatically or in any straightforward or simple way. They are merely one part of the broader political picture. At best, they can contribute to the process of change. In and of themselves, they accomplish little.

The implementation of the Court's abortion decisions, partial though it has been, owes its success to the fact that the decisions have been made in a time when the role of women in American life is changing dramatically. Out of the social turmoil of the 1960s grew a women's movement that continues to press politically, socially, and culturally for ending restrictions on women's opportunities. Access to safe and legal abortion is part of this movement. In 1973 the Supreme Court lent its support by finding a constitutional right to abortion. And in the years since, it has maintained its support for that core constitutional right. Yet, I have argued that far more important in making safe and legal abortion available are the beliefs of politicians, relevant professionals, and the public. When these groups are supportive of abortion choice, that choice is available. Where they have opposed abortion, they have fought against the Court's decisions, successfully minimizing access to abortion. Lack of support from hospital administrators and some politicians and intense opposition from a small group of politicians and activists have limited the availability of abortion services. On the whole, in states that were supportive of abortion choice before Court action, access remains good. In the states that had the most restrictive abortion laws before *Roe,* abortion services are available but remain difficult to obtain. As Gwenyth Mapes put it, "It does no good to have the [abortion] procedure be legal if women can't get it."

This analysis suggests that in general, constitutional rights have a greater likelihood of being implemented when they reflect the preexisting beliefs of politicians, relevant professionals, and the public. When at least some of these groups are opposed, locally or nationally, implementation is less likely. The assumption that the implementation of Court decisions and constitutional rights is unproblematic both reifies and removes courts from the political, social, cultural, and economic systems in which they operate. Courts are political institutions, and their role must be understood accordingly. Examining their decisions without making the political world central to that examination may make for fine reading in constitutional-law textbooks, but it tells the reader very little about the lives people lead.

NOTES

1. Alaska, Hawaii, New York, and Washington had previously liberalized their laws. The constitutional requirements set forth in *Roe* and *Doe* were basically, although not completely, met by these state laws.

2. For a fuller examination, see Rosenberg 1991.

3. In 1971, before *Roe* and *Doe*, the Court heard an abortion case (*United States v. Vuitch*) from Washington, D.C. The decision, however, did not settle the constitutional issues involved in the abortion controversy.

4. Estimates of the number of legal abortions performed each year prior to *Roe* vary enormously, ranging from 50,000 to nearly 2 million. See Rosenberg 1991, 353–355.

5. The following discussion, except where noted, is based on Lader 1973.

6. After the 1973 decisions, NARAL kept its acronym but changed its name to the National Abortion Rights Action League.

7. Nixon's "own personal views" were that "unrestricted abortion policies, or abortion on demand" could not be squared with his "personal belief in the sanctity of human life" (quoted in Lader 1973, 176–177).

8. Franklin and Kosaki (1989, 762) argue that in the wake of *Roe* opinions hardened. That is, those who were pro-choice before the decision became even more so after; the same held true for those opposed to abortion. Court action did not change opinions; abortion opponents did not become abortion supporters (and vice versa). See Epstein and Kobylka 1992, 203.

9. Ford did veto the 1977 appropriations bill containing the Hyde Amendment. He stated that he did so for budgetary reasons (the bill was $4 billion over his budget request) and reasserted his support for "restrictions on the use of federal funds for abortion" (quoted in Craig and O'Brien 1993, 161).

10. The Congressional Research Service reports that Congress enacted thirty restrictive abortion statutes during 1973–1982 (Davidson 1983).

11. The growth in violent attacks on abortion clinics, and illegal, harassing demonstrations in front of them, may demonstrate a growing awareness of this point by the foes of abortion.

12. Treshman is not the only antiabortion activist to express such views. Goodstein (1994, A1) writes that "there is a sizable faction among the antiabortion movement's activists . . . who have applauded Hill [the convicted killer of Dr. Britton and Mr. Barrett] as a righteous defender of babies."

13. The East South Central states are Kentucky, Tennessee, Alabama, and Mississippi. The West South Central states are Arkansas, Louisiana, Oklahoma, and Texas. Together, these eight states contained 16 percent of the U.S. population in 1973.

14. It is possible, of course, that some women had personal reasons for not obtaining an abortion in their home town. Still, that seems an unlikely explanation as to why 100,000 women each year would leave their home states to obtain abortions.

15. *Akron v. Akron Center for Reproductive Health* (1983); *Planned Parenthood v. Ashcroft* (1983). The vast majority of abortions in the United States are performed in the first trimester. As early as 1976, the figure was 90 percent. See Forrest et al. 1979, 32.

16. The percentage for clinics is not artificially high because there were only a small number of clinic abortions in the years preceding Court action. In 1973, clinics performed more than 330,000 abortions, or about 45 percent of all abortions (see Alan Guttmacher Institute 1976, 27).

17. Others in agreement with this analysis include Tatalovich and Daynes (1981, 101, 164), participants in a symposium at the Brookings Institution (in Steiner 1983), and Jackson and Vinovskis (1983, 73), who found that after the decisions "state-level pro-choice grounds disbanded, victory seemingly achieved."

18. This also appears to have been the case in 1954 with the Court's school desegregation decision, *Brown v. Board of Education*. After that decision, the Ku Klux Klan was reinvigorated and the White Citizen's Councils were formed, with the aim of preserving racial segregation through violence and intimidation.

REFERENCES

"Abortions Legal for Year, Performed for Thousands." 1973. *New York Times*, December 31, sec. A.

Alan Guttmacher Institute. 1976. *Abortion 1974–1975: Need and Services in the United States, Each State and Metropolitan Area*. New York: Planned Parenthood Federation of America.

Anderson, Jack, and Michael Binstein. 1993. "Violent Shift in Abortion Battle." *Washington Post*, March 18, sec. C.

Barringer, Felicity. 1993. "Abortion Clinics Said to Be in Peril." *New York Times*, March 6, Sec. A.

Baum, Dan. 1993. "Violence Is Driving Away Rural Abortion Clinics." *Chicago Tribune*, August 21, Sec. A.

Berke, Richard L. 1989. "The Abortion Rights Movement Has Its Day." *New York Times*, October 15, Sec. 4.

_____.1991. "Groups Backing Abortion Rights Ask Court to Act." *New York Times*, November 8, Sec. A.

Blake, Judith. 1971. "Abortion and Public Opinion: The 1960–1970 Decade." *Science*, February 12.

_____.1977a. "The Abortion Decisions: Judicial Review and Public Opinion." In *Abortion: New Directions for Policy Studies*, edited by Edward Manier, William Liu, and David Solomon. Notre Dame, Ind.: University of Notre Dame Press.

_____.1977b. "The Supreme Court's Abortion Decisions and Public Opinion in the United States." *Population and Development Review* 3:45–62.

Brody, Jane E. 1973. "States and Doctors Wary on Eased Abortion Ruling." *New York Times*, February 16, Sec. A.

Brozan, Nadine. 1983. "Abortion Ruling: 10 Years of Bitter Conflict." *New York Times*, January 15, Sec. A.

Cooper, Helene. 1993. "Medical Schools, Students Shun Abortion Study." *Wall Street Journal*, Midwest edition, March 12, Sec. B.

Craig, Barbara Hinkson, and David M. O'Brien. 1993. *Abortion and American Politics*. Chatham, N.J.: Chatham House.

Currivan, Gene. 1970. "Poll Finds Shift to Left among College Freshmen." *New York Times*, December 20, Sec. 1.

Daley, Daniel, and Rachel Benson Gold. 1994. "Public Funding for Contraceptive, Sterilization, and Abortion Services, Fiscal Year 1992." *Family Planning Perspectives* 25:244–251.

Darney, Philip D., Uta Landy, Sara MacPherson, and Richard L. Sweet. 1987. "Abortion Training in U.S. Obstetrics and Gynecology Residency Programs." *Family Planning Perspectives* 19:158–162.

Davidson, Roger H. 1983. "Procedures and Politics in Congress." In *The Abortion Dispute and the American System*, edited by Gilbert Y. Steiner. Washington, D.C.: Brookings Institution.

Ebaugh, Helen Rose Fuchs, and C. Allen Haney. 1980. "Shifts in Abortion Attitudes: 1972–1978." *Journal of Marriage and the Family* 42:491–499.

Epstein, Lee, and Joseph F. Kobylka. 1992. *The Supreme Court and Legal Change.* Chapel Hill: University of North Carolina Press.

Fiske, Edward B. 1967. "Clergymen Offer Abortion Advice." *New York Times,* May 22, Sec. A.

Forrest, Jacqueline Darroch, and Stanley K. Henshaw. 1987. "The Harassment of U.S. Abortion Providers." *Family Planning Perspectives* 19:9–13.

Forrest, Jacqueline Darroch, Ellen Sullivan, and Christopher Tietze. 1978. "Abortion in the United States, 1976–1977." *Family Planning Perspectives* 10:271–279.

————. 1979. *Abortion 1976–1977: Need and Services in the United States, Each State and Metropolitan Area.* New York: Alan Guttmacher Institute.

Franklin, Charles H., and Liane C. Kosaki. 1989. "Republican Schoolmaster: The U.S. Supreme Court, Public Opinion, and Abortion." *American Political Science Review* 83:751–771.

Goodman, Janice, Rhonda Copelon Schoenbrod, and Nancy Stearns. 1973. "Doe and Roe." *Women's Rights Law Reporter* 1:20–38.

Goodstein, Laurie. 1994. "Life and Death Choices: Antiabortion Faction Tries to Justify Homicide." *Washington Post,* August 13, Sec. A.

Henshaw, Stanley K. 1986. "Induced Abortion: A Worldwide Perspective." *Family Planning Perspectives* 18:250–254.

————. 1991. "The Accessibility of Abortion Services in the United States." *Family Planning Perspectives* 23:246–252, 263.

Henshaw, Stanley K., and Kevin O'Reilly. 1983. "Characteristics of Abortion Patients in the United States, 1979 and 1980." *Family Planning Perspectives* 15:5.

Henshaw, Stanley K., and Jennifer Van Vort. 1990. "Abortion Services in the United States, 1987 and 1988." *Family Planning Perspectives* 22:102–108, 142.

————. 1994. "Abortion Services in the United States, 1991 and 1992." *Family Planning Perspectives* 26:100–106, 122.

Henshaw, Stanley K., Jacqueline Darroch Forrest, and Ellen Blaine. 1984. "Abortion Services in the United States, 1981 and 1982." *Family Planning Perspectives* 16:119–127.

Henshaw, Stanley K., Jacqueline Darroch Forrest, and Jennifer Van Vort. 1987. "Abortion Services in the United States, 1984 and 1985." *Family Planning Perspectives* 19:63–70.

Henshaw, Stanley K., Jacqueline Darroch Forrest, Ellen Sullivan, and Christopher Tietze. 1982. "Abortion Services in the United States, 1979 and 1980." *Family Planning Perspectives* 14:5–15.

Henshaw, Stanley K., Lisa M. Koonin, and Jack C. Smith. 1991. "Characteristics of U.S. Women Having Abortions, 1987." *Family Planning Perspectives* 23:75–81.

Hole, Judith, and Ellen Levine. 1971. *Rebirth of Feminism.* New York: Quadrangle.

Jackson, John E., and Maris A. Vinovskis. 1983. "Public Opinion, Elections, and the 'Single-Issue' Issue." In *The Abortion Dispute and the American System,* edited by Gilbert Y. Steiner. Washington, D.C.: Brookings Institution.

Jaffe, Frederick S., Barbara L. Lindheim, and Phillip R. Lee. 1981. *Abortion Politics.* New York: McGraw-Hill.

Johnston, Laurie. 1977. "Abortion Foes Gain Support as They Intensify Campaign." *New York Times,* October 23, Sec. 1.

Kemp, Kathleen A., Robert A. Carp, and David W. Brady. 1978. "The Supreme Court and Social Change: The Case of Abortion." *Western Political Quarterly* 31:19–31.

King, Wayne. 1973. "Despite Court Ruling, Problems Persist in Gaining Abortions." *New York Times,* May 20, Sec. 1.

Kornhauser, Anne. 1989. "Abortion Case Has Been Boon to Both Sides." *Legal Times,* July 3.

Lader, Lawrence. 1973. *Abortion II: Making the Revolution.* Boston: Beacon Press.

Lewin, Tamar. 1994. "A Cause Worth Killing For? Debate Splits Abortion Foes." *New York Times,* July 30, Sec. A.

Newport, Frank, and Leslie McAneny. 1992. "Whose Court Is It Anyhow? O'Connor, Kennedy, Souter Position Reflects Abortion Views of Most Americans." *Gallup Poll Monthly* 322 (July): 51–53.

Noonan, John T., Jr. 1973. "Raw Judicial Power." *National Review,* March 2.

Phillips, Richard. 1980. "The Shooting War over 'Choice' or 'Life' Is Beginning Again." *Chicago Tribune,* April 20, Sec. 12.

"Rhode Island Abortion Law Is Declared Unconstitutional." 1973. *New York Times,* May 17, Sec. A.

Rosen, R. A. Hudson, H. W. Werley Jr., J. W. Ager, and F. P. Shea. 1974. "Health Professionals' Attitudes toward Abortion." *Public Opinion Quarterly* 38:159–173.

Rosenberg, Gerald N. 1991. *The Hollow Hope: Can Courts Bring About Social Change?* Chicago: University of Chicago Press.

Rosenthal, Jack. 1971. "Survey Finds 50% Back Liberalization of Abortion Policy." *New York Times,* October 28, Sec. A.

Rosoff, Jeannie I. 1975. "Is Support for Abortion Political Suicide?" *Family Planning Perspectives* 7:13–22.

Rubin, Eva R. 1982. *Abortion, Politics, and the Courts.* Westport, Conn.: Greenwood Press.

Russell, Mary. 1977. "House Bars Use of U.S. Funds in Abortion Cases." *Washington Post,* June 18, Sec. A.

Shribman, David. 1989. "Abortion-Issue Foes, Preaching to the Converted in No Uncertain Terms, Step Up Funding Pleas." *Wall Street Journal,* December 26, Sec. A.

Steiner, Gilbert Y., ed. 1983. *The Abortion Dispute and the American System.* Washington, D.C.: Brookings Institution.

Sullivan, Ellen, Christopher Tietze, and Joy G. Dryfoos. 1977. "Legal Abortion in the United States, 1975–1976." *Family Planning Perspectives* 9:116.

Tatalovich, Raymond, and Byron W. Daynes. 1981. *The Politics of Abortion.* New York: Praeger.

Thayer, James Bradley. 1901. *John Marshall.* Boston: Houghton, Mifflin.

Thomas, Pierre. 1994. "U.S. Marshals Dispatched to Guard Abortion Clinics." *Washington Post,* August 2, Sec. A.

Tolchin, Martin. 1977. "House Bars Medicaid Abortions and Funds for Enforcing Quotas." *New York Times,* June 18, Sec. A.

Toner, Robin. 1993. "Clinton Orders Reversal of Abortion Restrictions Left by Reagan and Bush." *New York Times,* January 23, Sec. A.

United States. Congress. Senate. 1970a. *Congressional Record.* Daily ed. 91st Cong., 2d sess. April 23, S3746.

———. 1970b. *Congressional Record.* Daily ed. 91st Cong., 2d sess. February 24, S3501.

———. 1974. Committee on the Judiciary. *Hearings before the Subcommittee on Constitutional Amendments.* Vol. 2. 93d Cong., 2d sess.

———. 1976. Committee on the Judiciary. *Hearings before the Subcommittee on Constitutional Amendments.* Vol. 4. 94d Cong., 1st sess.

Weinstock, Edward, Christopher Tietze, Frederick S. Jaffe, and Joy G. Dryfoos. 1975. "Legal Abortions in the United States since the 1973 Supreme Court Decisions." *Family Planning Perspectives* 7:23–31.

Williams, Roger M. 1979. "The Power of Fetal Politics." *Saturday Review,* June 9.

"A Woman's Right." 1973. *Evening Star* (Washington, D.C.), January 27, Sec. A.

5-2

Competing Views of Civil Liberties and the War Against Terrorism

Michael Scardaville and Robert A. Levy

The possible existence of hidden terrorist cells in the United States led law enforcement and national security officials in 2002 to seek new authority to gather and act on information about both citizens and noncitizens residing within the United States. In response, critics raised the specter of a "Big Brother"—George Orwell's term for all-knowing government in his novel 1984—tracing everyone's economic and social behavior. Other commentators, however, dismissed this image and supported the government's efforts as a necessity for safeguarding the country. In the essays below, Michael Scardaville and Robert A. Levy explore the tradeoffs between antiterrorism efforts and civil liberties and come to differing conclusions. The articles appeared around the time Congress approved the creation of the new Department of Homeland Security, which is designed to be the lead agency for fighting domestic sources of terrorism by coordinating the activities of the FBI, the CIA, and other agencies.

"Targeting Terrorists . . . Not Privacy"

by Michael Scardaville

"A supersnoop's dream," the *Washington Times* calls it. It will give government agents "a computerized dossier on your private life," warns William Safire of the *New York Times*.

It's the federal government's Total Information Awareness (TIA) program, and if it's not positively Orwellian, say civil libertarians, it's at least X-Files. Worse yet, they argue, the program is being developed by John Poindexter—the professorial, pipe-smoking Reagan capo convicted (later overturned) of redirecting

Source: Michael Scardaville, "Targeting Terrorists . . . Not Privacy," *National Review Online,* November 25, 2002, http://www.nationalreview.com/comment/comment-scardaville112502.asp. Robert A. Levy, "The Federal Eye," *National Review Online,* November 26, 2002, http://www.nationalreview.com/comment/comment-levy112602.asp.

money to the contras trying to overthrow the communist government of Daniel Ortega in Nicaragua. If this goes forward, critics ask, will Poindexter and his beady-eyed bureaucrats know what Internet sites I like to frequent? That I've maxed out a credit card? That I play the office football pool? That my daughter has asthma?

Shouldn't I be worried about this?

Actually, only those already identified as terrorists have anything to fear.

What the government seeks to do with TIA is piece together the puzzles of terrorist networks before they launch their attacks. And it wants to do this in such a way—in fact, Poindexter and his staff spend much of their time on it—that our privacy and civil liberties are protected to the maximum extent possible.

And they are doing, if not the Lord's work, the work of the American people, who since Sept. 11, 2001, have called for some systematic way for various intelligence and other fact-gathering agencies to share and analyze information. Poindexter and his staff have gone to great pains to make their deliberations as public as possible. They have described the work of those seeking to launch TIA in symposia around the country, and they even post information on their website.

Even if they wanted to, TIA employees simply won't have time to monitor who plays football pools, who has asthma, who surfs what websites, or even who deals cocaine or steals cars. They'll begin with intelligence reports about people already suspected of terrorism, according to Ted Senator, project director of a component of TIA.

Those already identified as terrorists or potential terrorists by the intelligence community then could be monitored through existing public and private databases to build an in-depth portfolio, including contacts and frequent activities, Senator says. These portfolios should enable authorities to determine whom to watch and where to find them when they suspect a terror strike is imminent.

Access to this information should be limited to those with appropriate clearances as well as by need to know, and programmers are hard at work on filters for these purposes. Moreover, the Genisys program, another component of TIA, is being designed to separate identity information from transactions and match up the information "only when we have evidence and legal authority to do so," officials say.

The key to the program—both in terms of its effectiveness and its potential to gain acceptance from the millions of Americans who rightly worry about privacy and erosion of civil liberties—is to limit its use to detecting terrorists and preventing future attacks. That means the FBI, the CIA and the soon-to-be-created Department of Homeland Security intelligence arm.

It does not mean state and local law enforcement or even those who wish to use it for causes such as aviation security and health surveillance—monitoring for epidemics and biological warfare, etc. Americans must be able to trust that extremely few people will have access to these capabilities and that the punishment for misuse will be severe.

To meet the needs of these other agencies, Poindexter's group or the Homeland Security Advanced Research Projects Agency (HSARPA) could—and probably should—develop limited spin-offs dedicated to specific needs, such as linking city and state health surveillance networks to the Centers for Disease Control or cross-referencing airline passenger manifests with terrorist watch lists.

Americans are right to hold the government to a high standard on this. They are right to expect that officials won't comb through the records of everything they buy, every time they visit the doctor and so on.

But Americans also understand that technology exists to detect perhaps even entire terrorist cells, to prevent future Sept. 11–scale attacks, and that we'd be foolish not to take advantage of it. The trick, of course, is to strike the right balance between citizens' expectations of privacy and government's need to protect those citizens. Poindexter seems on track to do this.

Let's let him. It seems little enough to prevent another Sept. 11—or worse.

"The Federal Eye"

by Robert A. Levy

When a former Iran-Contra defendant gets appointed to run a little-known Defense Department operation called "Total Information Awareness," then posts a sign on his office stating that "Knowledge Is Power," civil libertarians, not surprisingly, are exercised. Admiral John Poindexter may be suited for the job, but is the job suited for a free society that has, until recently, fastidiously safeguarded the privacy of its citizens?

Reportedly, the new system will use high-tech "data mining" to gather information from multiple databases, link individuals and groups, and share information efficiently. Never mind that Pentagon computer scientists believe that terrorists could easily avoid detection, leaving bureaucrats with about 200 million dossiers on totally innocent Americans—instant access to e-mail, web surfing, and phone records, credit-card and banking transactions, prescription-drug purchases, travel data, and court records.

If Total Information Awareness were the first and only budding threat to civil liberties, opponents might be less apprehensive. But against a backdrop of multiple laws, executive orders, and proposals—all potentially troublesome to hardcore Bill of Rights devotees—our constitutional watchdogs are justifiably uneasy. Here are a few of their grievances:

The USA PATRIOT Act: Ordinarily, advance judicial authorization of executive actions, followed by judicial review to assure that officials haven't misbehaved, shields us from excessive concentrations of power in a single branch of government. Under the PATRIOT Act, however, the executive branch has overwhelming if not exclusive power. Judicial checks and balances are conspicuously absent.

Expansion of the FISA court's authority: The Foreign Intelligence Surveillance Act created a court that approves electronic surveillance of citizens and resident aliens allegedly serving a foreign power. Previously, the FISA court could act if foreign intelligence was the primary purpose of an investigation. Now, foreign intelligence need only be "a significant purpose." That is not a trivial change. It means easier government access to personal and business records, and relaxed authorization of Internet surveillance and wiretaps—even in criminal cases.

Domestic detention of non-citizens: Soon after 9/11, about 1,200 non-citizens were detained in secret without evidence linking a single one of them to al Qaeda. The recurring questions were pretty basic. How many remained in custody? Who were they? What were the charges against them? What was the status of their cases? Where and under what circumstances were they being held? The Justice Department adamantly refused to provide any answers.

Secret INS trials: Hundreds of deportation hearings have been held in secret by the Immigration and Naturalization Service—without a jury, and without access by the defendant to legal counsel. The U.S. Court of Appeals for the Sixth Circuit accused the INS of operating "in virtual secrecy in all matters dealing, even remotely, with national security." The court warned, "Democracies die behind closed doors."

Detention of U.S. citizens: The administration has unilaterally declared that two U.S. citizens are "enemy combatants," whisked them away, detained them indefinitely in a military brig, denied them legal counsel, filed no charges whatever, and prevented them from seeking meaningful judicial review.

Monitoring attorney-client communications: Attorney General John Ashcroft, armed only with "reasonable suspicion" that a communication would "facilitate acts of terrorism," invented Justice Department authority to monitor talks between detainees and their lawyers, without a court order, despite constitutional guarantees of an unimpeded right to counsel.

Military tribunals: The Bush executive order on military tribunals fell short in three respects. First, tribunals should be convened only outside the United States. Here, our criminal courts are a perfectly acceptable venue. Second, tribunals must be limited to prosecuting unlawful combatants, not merely someone tangentially related to international terrorism. Third, tribunals should be congressionally authorized, not decreed by the executive branch.

Terrorism Information and Prevention System: TIPS was the administration brainchild that would have transformed us into a nation of busybodies and snoops. About eleven million informants—especially mail carriers, utility employees and others with unique access to private homes—were to help the Justice Department build yet another database containing names of persons not charged with any wrongdoing.

Of course, advocates of expanded executive power remind civil libertarians that President Bush is an honorable man who understands that the Constitution is made of more than tissue paper. That argument is simply not persuasive—even to those who fervently share its underlying premise. The policies that are put in place by this administration are precedent-setting. Bush supporters need to reflect on the same powers in the hands of his predecessor or his successors.

Here's the guiding principle: In the post-9/11 environment, no rational person believes that civil liberties are inviolable. After all, government's primary obligation is to secure the lives of American citizens. But when government begins to chip away at our liberties, we must insist that it jump through a couple of hoops. First, government must offer compelling evidence that its new and intrusive programs will make us safer. Second, government must convince us that there is no less invasive means of attaining the same ends. In too many instances, those dual burdens have not been met.

If administration critics have a single overriding concern about policies adopted in the wake of 9/11, it is this: The president and the attorney general have concentrated too much unchecked authority in the hands of the executive branch—compromising the doctrine of separation of powers, which has been a cornerstone of our Constitution for more than two centuries. Those persons who would unhesitatingly tradeoff civil liberties in return for national security proclaim that concentrated power is necessary for Americans to remain free. Yet there's an obvious corollary that's too often missed: Unless Americans remain free, they will never be secure.

5-3

Miranda v. Arizona

Supreme Court of the United States

In their efforts to protect rights guaranteed by the Constitution, courts some-times establish rules of behavior for government officials. In 1966 the Supreme Court considered a number of instances in which police officers or prosecutors failed to give arrested individuals notice of their rights at the outset of the interrogations. The Court held that prosecutors could not use statements stem-ming from custodial interrogation unless they demonstrated the use of proce-dural safeguards "effective to secure the privilege again self-incrimination" as provided by the Fifth Amendment. To ensure that Fifth Amendment rights were protected, the Court outlined the specific warnings interrogators must give to suspects, including notice of the right to remain silent and the right to have counsel present during questioning.

MIRANDA v. ARIZONA

384 U.S. 436 (1966)

CERTIORARI TO THE SUPREME COURT OF ARIZONA.

Decided June 13, 1966.

MR. CHIEF JUSTICE WARREN delivered the opinion of the Court.

The cases before us raise questions which go to the roots of our concepts of American criminal jurisprudence: the restraints society must observe consistent with the Federal Constitution in prosecuting individuals for crime. More specifi-cally, we deal with the admissibility of statements obtained from an individual who is subjected to custodial police interrogation and the necessity for proce-dures which assure that the individual is accorded his privilege under the Fifth Amendment to the Constitution not to be compelled to incriminate himself. . . .

We dealt with certain phases of this problem recently in *Escobedo v. Illi-nois* . . . (1964). There, as in the four cases before us, law enforcement officials took the defendant into custody and interrogated him in a police station for the purpose of obtaining a confession. The police did not effectively advise him of his right to remain silent or of his right to consult with his attorney. Rather, they confronted him with an alleged accomplice who accused him of having perpetrated a murder. When the defendant denied the accusation and said "I didn't shoot Manuel, you did it," they handcuffed him and took him to an interrogation room. There, while handcuffed and standing, he was questioned for four hours until he confessed. During this interrogation, the police denied his request to speak to his attorney, and they prevented his retained attorney, who had come to the police station, from consulting with him. At his trial, the State, over his objection, introduced the confession against him. We held that the statements thus made were constitutionally inadmissible.

This case has been the subject of judicial interpretation and spirited legal debate since it was decided two years ago. Both state and federal courts, in assessing its implications, have arrived at varying conclusions. A wealth of scholarly material has been written tracing its ramifications and underpinnings. Police and prosecutor have speculated on its range and desirability. We granted certiorari in these cases . . . in order further to explore some facets of the problems, thus exposed, of applying the privilege against self-incrimination to in-custody interrogation, and to give concrete constitutional guidelines for law enforcement agencies and courts to follow.

We start here, as we did in Escobedo, with the premise that our holding is not an innovation in our jurisprudence, but is an application of principles long recognized and applied in other settings. We have undertaken a thorough re-examination of the Escobedo decision and the principles it announced, and we reaffirm it. That case was but an explication of basic rights that are enshrined in our Constitution—that "No person . . . shall be compelled in any criminal case to be a witness against himself," and that "the accused shall . . . have the Assistance of Counsel"—rights which were put in jeopardy in that case through official overbearing. These precious rights were fixed in our Constitution only after centuries of persecution and struggle. And in the words of Chief Justice Marshall, they were secured "for ages to come, and . . . designed to approach immortality as nearly as human institutions can approach it," *Cohens v. Virginia*, 6 Wheat. 264, 387 (1821).

Over 70 years ago, our predecessors on this Court eloquently stated:

> The maxim *nemo tenetur seipsum accusare* had its origin in a protest against the inquisitorial and manifestly unjust methods of interrogating accused persons, which [have] long obtained in the continental system, and, until the expulsion of the Stuarts from the British throne in 1688, and the erection of additional barriers for the protection of the people against the exercise of arbitrary power, [were] not uncommon even in England. While the admissions or

confessions of the prisoner, when voluntarily and freely made, have always ranked high in the scale of incriminating evidence, if an accused person be asked to explain his apparent connection with a crime under investigation, the ease with which the questions put to him may assume an inquisitorial character, the temptation to press the witness unduly, to browbeat him if he be timid or reluctant, to push him into a corner, and to entrap him into fatal contradictions, which is so painfully evident in many of the earlier state trials, notably in those of Sir Nicholas Throckmorton, and Udal, the Puritan minister, made the system so odious as to give rise to a demand for its total abolition. The change in the English criminal procedure in that particular seems to be founded upon no statute and no judicial opinion, but upon a general and silent acquiescence of the courts in a popular demand. But, however adopted, it has become firmly embedded in English, as well as in American jurisprudence. So deeply did the iniquities of the ancient system impress themselves upon the minds of the American colonists that the States, with one accord, made a denial of the right to question an accused person a part of their fundamental law, so that a maxim, which in England was a mere rule of evidence, became clothed in this country with the impregnability of a constitutional enactment. *Brown v. Walker,* 161 U.S. 591, 596–597 (1896).

In stating the obligation of the judiciary to apply these constitutional rights, this Court declared in *Weems v. United States* . . . (1910):

> . . . our contemplation cannot be only of what has been but of what may be. Under any other rule a constitution would indeed be as easy of application as it would be deficient in efficacy and power. Its general principles would have little value and be converted by precedent into impotent and lifeless formulas. Rights declared in words might be lost in reality. And this has been recognized. The meaning and vitality of the Constitution have developed against narrow and restrictive construction.

This was the spirit in which we delineated, in meaningful language, the manner in which the constitutional rights of the individual could be enforced against overzealous police practices. . . .

Our holding will be spelled out with some specificity in the pages which follow but briefly stated it is this: the prosecution may not use statements, whether exculpatory or inculpatory, stemming from custodial interrogation of the defendant unless it demonstrates the use of procedural safeguards effective to secure the privilege against self-incrimination. By custodial interrogation, we mean questioning initiated by law enforcement officers after a person has been taken into custody or otherwise deprived of his freedom of action in any significant way. As for the procedural safeguards to be employed, unless other fully effective means are devised to inform accused persons of their right of silence and to assure a continuous opportunity to exercise it, the following measures are required. Prior to any questioning, the person must be warned that he has a right to remain silent, that any statement he does make may be used as evidence against him, and that he has a right to the presence of an attorney, either retained or appointed. The defendant may waive effectuation of these rights, provided the waiver is made voluntarily, knowingly and intelligently. If, however, he indicates in any manner and at any stage of the process that he wishes to consult with an attorney before speaking there can be no questioning. Likewise, if the individual is alone and indicates in any manner that he does not wish to be interrogated, the police may not question him. The mere fact that he may have answered some questions or volunteered some statements on his own does not deprive him of the right to refrain from answering any further inquiries until he has consulted with an attorney and thereafter consents to be questioned. . . .

The constitutional issue we decide in each of these cases is the admissibility of statements obtained from a defendant questioned while in custody or otherwise deprived of his freedom of action in any significant way. In each, the defendant was questioned by police officers, detectives, or a prosecuting attorney in a room in which he was cut off from the outside world. In none of these cases was the defendant given a full and effective warning of his rights at the outset of the interrogation process. In all the cases, the questioning elicited oral admissions, and in three of them, signed statements as well which were admitted at their trials. They all thus share salient features—incommunicado interrogation of individuals in a police-dominated atmosphere, resulting in self-incriminating statements without full warnings of constitutional rights.

An understanding of the nature and setting of this in-custody interrogation is essential to our decisions today. The difficulty in depicting what transpires at such interrogations stems from the fact that in this country they have largely taken place incommunicado. From extensive factual studies undertaken in the early 1930's, including the famous Wickersham Report to Congress by a Presidential Commission, it is clear that police violence and the "third degree" flourished at that time. In a series of cases decided by this Court long after these studies, the police resorted to physical brutality—beating, hanging, whipping—and to sustained and protracted questioning incommunicado in order to extort confessions. The Commission on Civil Rights in 1961 found much evidence to indicate that "some policemen still resort to physical force to obtain confessions," 1961 Comm'n on Civil Rights Rep., Justice, pt. 5, 17. The use of physical brutality and violence is not, unfortunately, relegated to the past or to any part of the country. Only recently in Kings County, New York, the police brutally beat, kicked and placed lighted cigarette butts on the back of a potential witness under interrogation for the purpose of securing a statement incriminating a third party. . . .

The examples given above are undoubtedly the exception now, but they are sufficiently widespread to be the object of concern. Unless a proper limitation upon custodial interrogation is achieved—such as these decisions will advance—there can be no assurance that practices of this nature will be eradicated in the foreseeable future. . . .

Again we stress that the modern practice of in-custody interrogation is psychologically rather than physically oriented. As we have stated before, "Since *Chambers v. Florida,* 309 U.S. 227, this Court has recognized that coercion can be mental as well as physical, and that the blood of the accused is not the only hallmark of an unconstitutional inquisition." *Blackburn v. Alabama,* 361 U.S. 199, 206 (1960). Interrogation still takes place in privacy. Privacy results in secrecy and this in turn results in a gap in our knowledge as to what in fact goes on in the interrogation rooms. A valuable source of information about present police practices, however, may be found in various police manuals and texts which document procedures employed with success in the past, and which recommend various other effective tactics. These texts are used by law enforcement agencies themselves as guides. . . .

. . . the setting prescribed by the manuals and observed in practice becomes clear. In essence, it is this: To be alone with the subject is essential to prevent distraction and to deprive him of any outside support. The aura of confidence in his guilt undermines his will to resist. He merely confirms the preconceived story the police seek to have him describe. Patience and persistence, at times relentless questioning, are employed. To obtain a confession, the interrogator must "patiently maneuver himself or his quarry into a position from which the desired objective may be attained." When normal procedures fail to produce the needed result, the police may resort to deceptive stratagems such as giving false legal advice. It is important to keep the subject off balance, for example, by trading on his insecurity about himself or his surroundings. The police then persuade, trick, or cajole him out of exercising his constitutional rights. . . .

In the cases before us today, given this background, we concern ourselves primarily with this interrogation atmosphere and the evils it can bring. In No. 759, *Miranda v. Arizona,* the police arrested the defendant and took him to a special interrogation room where they secured a confession. In No. 760, *Vignera v. New York,* the defendant made oral admissions to the police after interrogation in the afternoon, and then signed an inculpatory statement upon being questioned by an assistant district attorney later the same evening. In No. 761, *Westover v. United States,* the defendant was handed over to the Federal Bureau of Investigation by local authorities after they had detained and interrogated him for a lengthy period, both at night and the following morning. After some two hours of questioning, the federal officers had obtained signed statements from the defendant. Lastly, in No. 584, *California v. Stewart,* the local police held the defendant five days in the station and interrogated him on nine separate occasions before they secured his inculpatory statement. . . .

It is obvious that such an interrogation environment is created for no purpose other than to subjugate the individual to the will of his examiner. This atmosphere carries its own badge of intimidation. To be sure, this is not physical intimidation, but it is equally destructive of human dignity. The current practice of incommunicado interrogation is at odds with one of our Nation's most cherished principles—that the individual may not be compelled to incriminate himself. Unless adequate protective devices are employed to dispel the compulsion inherent in custodial surroundings, no statement obtained from the defendant can truly be the product of his free choice. . . .

. . . unless we are shown other procedures which are at least as effective in apprising accused persons of their right of silence and in assuring a continuous opportunity to exercise it, the following safeguards must be observed.

At the outset, if a person in custody is to be subjected to interrogation, he must first be informed in clear and unequivocal terms that he has the right to remain silent. For those unaware of the privilege, the warning is needed simply to make them aware of it—the threshold requirement for an intelligent decision as to its exercise. More important, such a warning is an absolute prerequisite in overcoming the inherent pressures of the interrogation atmosphere. It is not just the subnormal or woefully ignorant who succumb to an interrogator's imprecations, whether implied or expressly stated, that the interrogation will continue until a confession is obtained or that silence in the face of accusation is itself damning and will bode ill when presented to a jury. Further, the warning will show the individual that his interrogators are prepared to recognize his privilege should he choose to exercise it.

The Fifth Amendment privilege is so fundamental to our system of constitutional rule and the expedient of giving an adequate warning as to the availability of the privilege so simple, we will not pause to inquire in individual cases whether the defendant was aware of his rights without a warning being given. Assessments of the knowledge the defendant possessed, based on information as to his age, education, intelligence, or prior contact with authorities, can never be more than speculation; a warning is a clearcut fact. More important, whatever the background of the person interrogated, a warning at the time of the interrogation is indispensable to overcome its pressures and to insure that the individual knows he is free to exercise the privilege at that point in time.

The warning of the right to remain silent must be accompanied by the explanation that anything said can and will be used against the individual in court. This warning is needed in order to make him aware not only of the privilege, but also of the consequences of forgoing it. It is only through an awareness of these consequences that there can be any assurance of real understanding and intelligent exercise of the privilege. Moreover, this warning may serve to make the individual more acutely aware that he is faced with a phase of the adversary system—that he is not in the presence of persons acting solely in his interest.

The circumstances surrounding in-custody interrogation can operate very quickly to overbear the will of one merely made aware of his privilege by his interrogators. Therefore, the right to have counsel present at the interrogation is indispensable to the protection of the Fifth Amendment privilege under the system we delineate today. Our aim is to assure that the individual's right to choose between silence and speech remains unfettered throughout the interrogation process. . . .

The presence of counsel at the interrogation may serve several significant subsidiary functions as well. If the accused decides to talk to his interrogators, the assistance of counsel can mitigate the dangers of untrustworthiness. With a lawyer present the likelihood that the police will practice coercion is reduced, and if coercion is nevertheless exercised the lawyer can testify to it in court. The presence of a lawyer can also help to guarantee that the accused gives a fully accurate statement to the police and that the statement is rightly reported by the prosecution at trial. . . .

An individual need not make a pre-interrogation request for a lawyer. While such request affirmatively secures his right to have one, his failure to ask for a lawyer does not constitute a waiver. No effective waiver of the right to counsel during interrogation can be recognized unless specifically made after the warnings we here delineate have been given. The accused who does not know his rights and therefore does not make a request may be the person who most needs counsel. . . .

If an individual indicates that he wishes the assistance of counsel before any interrogation occurs, the authorities cannot rationally ignore or deny his request on the basis that the individual does not have or cannot afford a retained attorney. The financial ability of the individual has no relationship to the scope of the rights involved here. The privilege against self-incrimination secured by the Constitution applies to all individuals. The need for counsel in order to protect the privilege exists for the indigent as well as the affluent. In fact, were we to limit these constitutional rights to those who can retain an attorney, our decisions today would be of little significance. . . .

In order fully to apprise a person interrogated of the extent of his rights under this system then, it is necessary to warn him not only that he has the right to consult with an attorney, but also that if he is indigent a lawyer will be appointed to represent him. Without this additional warning, the admonition of the right to consult with counsel would often be understood as meaning only that he can consult with a lawyer if he has one or has the funds to obtain one. . . .

Once warnings have been given, the subsequent procedure is clear. If the individual indicates in any manner, at any time prior to or during questioning, that he wishes to remain silent, the interrogation must cease. At this point he has shown that he intends to exercise his Fifth Amendment privilege; any statement taken after the person invokes his privilege cannot be other than the product of compulsion, subtle or otherwise. Without the right to cut off questioning, the setting of in-custody interrogation operates on the individual to overcome free choice in producing a statement after the privilege has been once invoked. If the individual states that he wants an attorney, the interrogation must cease until an attorney is present. At that time, the individual must have an opportunity to confer with the attorney and to have him present during any subsequent questioning. If the individual cannot obtain an attorney and he indicates that he wants one before speaking to police, they must respect his decision to remain silent. . . .

If the interrogation continues without the presence of an attorney and a statement is taken, a heavy burden rests on the government to demonstrate that the defendant knowingly and intelligently waived his privilege against self-incrimination and his right to retained or appointed counsel. *Escobedo v. Illinois*, 378 U.S. 478, 490, n. 14. . . .

An express statement that the individual is willing to make a statement and does not want an attorney followed closely by a statement could constitute a waiver. But a valid waiver will not be presumed simply from the silence of the accused after warnings are given or simply from the fact that a confession was in fact eventually obtained. . . .

The principles announced today deal with the protection which must be given to the privilege against self-incrimination when the individual is first subjected to police interrogation while in custody at the station or otherwise deprived of his freedom of action in any significant way. It is at this point that our adversary system of criminal proceedings commences, distinguishing itself at the outset from the inquisitorial system recognized in some countries. Under the system of warnings we delineate today or under any other system which may be devised and found effective, the safeguards to be erected about the privilege must come into play at this point. . . .

To summarize, we hold that when an individual is taken into custody or otherwise deprived of his freedom by the authorities in any significant way and is subjected to questioning, the privilege against self-incrimination is jeopardized. Procedural safeguards must be employed to protect the privilege, and unless other fully effective means are adopted to notify the person of his right of silence and to assure that the exercise of the right will be scrupulously honored, the following measures are required. He must be warned prior to any questioning that he has the right to remain silent, that anything he says can be used against him in a court of law, that he has the right to the presence of an attorney, and that if he cannot afford an attorney one will be appointed for him prior to any questioning if he so desires. Opportunity to exercise these rights must be afforded to him throughout the interrogation. After such warnings have been given, and such opportunity afforded him, the individual may knowingly and intelligently waive these rights and agree to answer questions or make a statement. But unless and until such warnings and waiver are demonstrated by the prosecution at trial, no evidence obtained as a result of interrogation can be used against him. . . .

5-4

Roe v. Wade

Supreme Court of the United States

To what extent can rights perceived by the people, but not explicitly protected by the Constitution, be recognized as constitutional principles by the courts? Judges often disagree on where the lines should be drawn. This question arose in Roe v. Wade, the Supreme Court's 1973 decision on abortion. The specific issue was, Does the Constitution embrace a woman's right to terminate her pregnancy by abortion? A 5–4 majority on the Supreme Court held that a woman's right to an abortion fell within the right to privacy protected by the Fourteenth Amendment. The decision gave a woman autonomy over the pregnancy during the first trimester and defined different levels of state interest for the second and third trimesters. The Court's ruling affected the laws of forty-six states. Justice Harry Blackmun, arguing for the majority, insisted that the Court had recognized such a right in a long series of cases and that it was appropriate to extend the right to a woman's decision to terminate a pregnancy. In a dissenting opinion, Justice William Rehnquist, who later became chief justice, argued that because abortion was not considered an implicit right at the time the Fourteenth Amendment, states must be allowed to regulate it.

ROE ET AL. v. WADE, DISTRICT ATTORNEY OF DALLAS COUNTY

410 U.S. 113

APPEAL FROM THE UNITED STATES DISTRICT COURT FOR THE NORTHERN DISTRICT OF TEXAS.

Decided January 22, 1973.

MR. JUSTICE BLACKMUN delivered the opinion of the Court.

This Texas federal appeal and its Georgia companion, *Doe v. Bolton, post,* . . . present constitutional challenges to state criminal abortion legislation. The Texas statutes under attack here are typical of those that have been in effect in many States for approximately a century. . . .

We forthwith acknowledge our awareness of the sensitive and emotional nature of the abortion controversy, of the vigorous opposing views, even among physicians, and of the deep and seemingly absolute convictions that the subject inspires. One's philosophy, one's experiences, one's exposure to the raw edges of human existence, one's religious training, one's attitudes toward life and family and their values, and the moral standards one establishes and seeks to observe, are all likely to influence and to color one's thinking and conclusions about abortion. . . .

Our task, of course, is to resolve the issue by constitutional measurement, free of emotion and of predilection. We seek earnestly to do this, and, because we do, we have inquired into, and in this opinion place some emphasis upon, medical and medical-legal history and what that history reveals about man's attitudes toward the abortion procedure over the centuries. We bear in mind, too, Mr. Justice Holmes' admonition in his now-vindicated dissent in *Lochner v. New York*, 198 U. S. 45, 76 (1905):

> [The Constitution] is made for people of fundamentally differing views, and the accident of our finding certain opinions natural and familiar or novel and even shocking ought not to conclude our judgment upon the question whether statutes embodying them conflict with the Constitution of the United States.

. . . Jane Roe [a pseudonym used to protect the identity of the woman], a single woman who was residing in Dallas County, Texas, instituted this federal action in March 1970 against the District Attorney of the county. She sought a declaratory judgment that the Texas criminal abortion statutes were unconstitutional on their face, and an injunction restraining the defendant from enforcing the statutes.

Roe alleged that she was unmarried and pregnant; that she wished to terminate her pregnancy by an abortion "performed by a competent, licensed physician, under safe clinical conditions"; that she was unable to get a "legal" abortion in Texas because her life did not appear to be threatened by the continuation of her pregnancy; and that she could not afford to travel to another jurisdiction in order to secure a legal abortion under safe conditions. She claimed that the Texas statutes were unconstitutionally vague and that they abridged her right of personal privacy, protected by the First, Fourth, Fifth, Ninth, and Fourteenth Amendments. By an amendment to her complaint Roe purported to sue "on behalf of herself and all other women" similarly situated. . . .

The principal thrust of appellant's attack on the Texas statutes is that they improperly invade a right, said to be possessed by the pregnant woman, to choose to terminate her pregnancy. Appellant would discover this right in the concept of personal "liberty" embodied in the Fourteenth Amendment's Due

Process Clause; or in personal, marital, familial, and sexual privacy said to be protected by the Bill of Rights or its penumbras, . . . or among those rights reserved to the people by the Ninth Amendment. . . .

It perhaps is not generally appreciated that the restrictive criminal abortion laws in effect in a majority of States today are of relatively recent vintage. Those laws, generally proscribing abortion or its attempt at any time during pregnancy except when necessary to preserve the pregnant woman's life, are not of ancient or even of common-law origin. Instead, they derive from statutory changes effected, for the most part, in the latter half of the 19th century. . . .

It is thus apparent that at common law, at the time of the adoption of our Constitution, and throughout the major portion of the 19th century, abortion was viewed with less disfavor than under most American statutes currently in effect. Phrasing it another way, a woman enjoyed a substantially broader right to terminate a pregnancy than she does in most States today. At least with respect to the early stage of pregnancy, and very possibly without such a limitation, the opportunity to make this choice was present in this country well into the 19th century. Even later, the law continued for some time to treat less punitively an abortion procured in early pregnancy. . . .

The Constitution does not explicitly mention any right of privacy. In a line of decisions, however, going back perhaps as far as *Union Pacific R. Co. v. Botsford* . . . (1891), the Court has recognized that a right of personal privacy, or a guarantee of certain areas or zones of privacy, does exist under the Constitution. In varying contexts, the Court or individual Justices have, indeed, found at least the roots of that right in the First Amendment . . . ; in the Fourth and Fifth Amendments . . . ; in the penumbras of the Bill of Rights . . . ; in the Ninth Amendment . . . ; or in the concept of liberty guaranteed by the first section of the Fourteenth Amendment. . . . These decisions make it clear that only personal rights that can be deemed "fundamental" or "implicit in the concept of ordered liberty," . . . are included in this guarantee of personal privacy. They also make it clear that the right has some extension to activities relating to marriage . . . ; procreation . . . ; contraception . . . ; family relationships . . . ; and child rearing and education. . . .

This right of privacy, whether it be founded in the Fourteenth Amendment's concept of personal liberty and restrictions upon state action, as we feel it is, or, as the District Court determined, in the Ninth Amendment's reservation of rights to the people, is broad enough to encompass a woman's decision whether or not to terminate her pregnancy. The detriment that the State would impose upon the pregnant woman by denying this choice altogether is apparent. Specific and direct harm medically diagnosable even in early pregnancy may be involved. Maternity, or additional offspring, may force upon the woman a distressful life and future. Psychological harm may be imminent. Mental and physical health may be taxed by child care. There is also the distress, for all concerned, associated with the unwanted child, and there is the problem of bringing a child into a family already unable, psychologically and otherwise, to care for it. In other cases, as in this one, the additional difficulties and continuing stigma of unwed motherhood may be involved. All these are factors the woman and her responsible physician necessarily will consider in consultation.

On the basis of elements such as these, appellant and some *amici* argue that the woman's right is absolute and that she is entitled to terminate her pregnancy at whatever time, in whatever way, and for whatever reason she alone chooses. With this we do not agree. Appellant's arguments that Texas either has no valid interest at all in regulating the abortion decision, or no interest strong enough to support any limitation upon the woman's sole determination, are unpersuasive. The Court's decisions recognizing a right of privacy also acknowledge that some state regulation in areas protected by that right is appropriate. As noted above, a State may properly assert important interests in safeguarding health, in maintaining medical standards, and in protecting potential life. At some point in pregnancy, these respective interests become sufficiently compelling to sustain regulation of the factors that govern the abortion decision. The privacy right involved, therefore, cannot be said to be absolute. . . .

We, therefore, conclude that the right of personal privacy includes the abortion decision, but that this right is not unqualified and must be considered against important state interests in regulation. . . .

Where certain "fundamental rights" are involved, the Court has held that regulation limiting these rights may be justified only by a "compelling state interest," . . . and that legislative enactments must be narrowly drawn to express only the legitimate state interests at stake. . . .

In the recent abortion cases . . . courts have recognized these principles. Those striking down state laws have generally scrutinized the State's interests in protecting health and potential life, and have concluded that neither interest justified broad limitations on the reasons for which a physician and his pregnant patient might decide that she should have an abortion in the early stages of pregnancy. Courts sustaining state laws have held that the State's determinations to protect health or prenatal life are dominant and constitutionally justifiable. . . .

The District Court held that the appellee [the district attorney, defending the Texas law] failed to meet his burden of demonstrating that the Texas statute's infringement upon Roe's rights was necessary to support a compelling state interest, and that, although the appellee presented "several compelling justifications for state presence in the area of abortions," the statutes outstripped these justifications and swept "far beyond any areas of compelling state interest." 314

F. Supp., at 1222–1223. Appellant and appellee both contest that holding. Appellant, as has been indicated, claims an absolute right that bars any state imposition of criminal penalties in the area. Appellee argues that the State's determination to recognize and protect prenatal life from and after conception constitutes a compelling state interest. As noted above, we do not agree fully with either formulation.

A. The appellee and certain *amici* argue that the fetus is a "person" within the language and meaning of the Fourteenth Amendment. In support of this, they outline at length and in detail the well-known facts of fetal development. If this suggestion of personhood is established, the appellant's case, of course, collapses, for the fetus' right to life would then be guaranteed specifically by the Amendment. The appellant conceded as much on reargument. On the other hand, the appellee conceded on reargument that no case could be cited that holds that a fetus is a person within the meaning of the Fourteenth Amendment.

The Constitution does not define "person" in so many words. Section 1 of the Fourteenth Amendment contains three references to "person." The first, in defining "citizens," speaks of "persons born or naturalized in the United States." The word also appears both in the Due Process Clause and in the Equal Protection Clause. "Person" is used in other places in the Constitution: in the listing of qualifications for Representatives and Senators, Art. I, § 2, cl. 2, and § 3, cl. 3; in the Apportionment Clause, Art. I, § 2, cl. 3; in the Migration and Importation provision, Art. I, § 9, cl. 1; in the Emolument Clause, Art. I, § 9, cl. 8; in the Electors provisions, Art. II, § 1, cl. 2, and the superseded cl. 3; in the provision outlining qualifications for the office of President, Art. II, § 1, cl. 5; in the Extradition provisions, Art. IV, § 2, cl. 2, and the superseded Fugitive Slave Clause 3; and in the Fifth, Twelfth, and Twenty-second Amendments, as well as in §§ 2 and 3 of the Fourteenth Amendment. But in nearly all these instances, the use of the word is such that it has application only postnatally. None indicates, with any assurance, that it has any possible pre-natal application.

All this, together with our observation, *supra,* that throughout the major portion of the 19th century prevailing legal abortion practices were far freer than they are today, persuades us that the word "person," as used in the Fourteenth Amendment, does not include the unborn. This is in accord with the results reached in those few cases where the issue has been squarely presented. . . . Indeed, our decision in *United States v. Vuitch,* 402 U. S. 62 (1971), inferentially is to the same effect, for we there would not have indulged in statutory interpretation favorable to abortion in specified circumstances if the necessary consequence was the termination of life entitled to Fourteenth Amendment protection.

This conclusion, however, does not of itself fully answer the contentions raised by Texas, and we pass on to other considerations.

B. The pregnant woman cannot be isolated in her privacy. She carries an embryo and, later, a fetus, if one accepts the medical definitions of the developing young in the human uterus. See Dorland's Illustrated Medical Dictionary 478–479, 547 (24th ed. 1965). The situation therefore is inherently different from marital intimacy, or bedroom possession of obscene material, or marriage, or procreation, or education, with which *Eisenstadt* and *Griswold, Stanley, Loving, Skinner,* and *Pierce* and *Meyer* were respectively concerned. As we have intimated above, it is reasonable and appropriate for a State to decide that at some point in time another interest, that of health of the mother or that of potential human life, becomes significantly involved. The woman's privacy is no longer sole and any right of privacy she possesses must be measured accordingly.

Texas urges that, apart from the Fourteenth Amendment, life begins at conception and is present throughout pregnancy, and that, therefore, the State has a compelling interest in protecting that life from and after conception. We need not resolve the difficult question of when life begins. When those trained in the respective disciplines of medicine, philosophy, and theology are unable to arrive at any consensus, the judiciary, at this point in the development of man's knowledge, is not in a position to speculate as to the answer.

It should be sufficient to note briefly the wide divergence of thinking on this most sensitive and difficult question. There has always been strong support for the view that life does not begin until live birth. This was the belief of the Stoics. It appears to be the predominant, though not the unanimous, attitude of the Jewish faith. It may be taken to represent also the position of a large segment of the Protestant community, insofar as that can be ascertained; organized groups that have taken a formal position on the abortion issue have generally regarded abortion as a matter for the conscience of the individual and her family. As we have noted, the common law found greater significance in quickening. Physicians and their scientific colleagues have regarded that event with less interest and have tended to focus either upon conception, upon live birth, or upon the interim point at which the fetus becomes "viable," that is, potentially able to live outside the mother's womb, albeit with artificial aid. Viability is usually placed at about seven months (28 weeks) but may occur earlier, even at 24 weeks. The Aristotelian theory of "mediate animation," that held sway throughout the Middle Ages and the Renaissance in Europe, continued to be official Roman Catholic dogma until the 19th century, despite opposition to this "ensoulment" theory from those in the Church who would recognize the existence of life from the moment of conception. The latter is now, of course, the official belief of the Catholic Church. As one brief *amicus* discloses, this is a view strongly held by many non-Catholics as well, and by many physicians. Substantial problems for precise definition of this view are posed, however, by new embryological data that purport to indicate that conception is a "process" over time, rather than an event, and by new medical techniques such as menstrual extraction, the "morning-after" pill, implantation of embryos, artificial insemination, and even artificial wombs. . . .

In view of all this, we do not agree that, by adopting one theory of life, Texas may override the rights of the pregnant woman that are at stake. We repeat, however, that the State does have an important and legitimate interest in preserving and protecting the health of the pregnant woman, whether she be a resident of the State or a nonresident who seeks medical consultation and treatment there, and that it has still *another* important and legitimate interest in protecting the potentiality of human life. These interests are separate and distinct. Each grows in substantiality as the woman approaches term and, at a point during pregnancy, each becomes "compelling." . . .

The judgment of the District Court as to intervenor Hallford is reversed, and Dr. Hallford's complaint in intervention is dismissed. In all other respects, the judgment of the District Court is affirmed. Costs are allowed to the appellee.

It is so ordered.

MR. JUSTICE REHNQUIST, dissenting.

The Court's opinion brings to the decision of this troubling question both extensive historical fact and a wealth of legal scholarship. While the opinion thus commands my respect, I find myself nonetheless in fundamental disagreement with those parts of it that invalidate the Texas statute in question, and therefore dissent. . . .

. . . I have difficulty in concluding, as the Court does, that the right of "privacy" is involved in this case. Texas, by the statute here challenged, bars the performance of a medical abortion by a licensed physician on a plaintiff such as Roe. A transaction resulting in an operation such as this is not "private" in the ordinary usage of that word. Nor is the "privacy" that the Court finds here even a distant relative of the freedom from searches and seizures protected by the Fourth Amendment to the Constitution, which the Court has referred to as embodying a right to privacy. *Katz v. United States,* 389 U. S. 347 (1967).

If the Court means by the term "privacy" no more than that the claim of a person to be free from unwanted state regulation of consensual transactions may be a form of "liberty" protected by the Fourteenth Amendment, there is no doubt that similar claims have been upheld in our earlier decisions on the basis of that liberty. I agree with the statement of MR. JUSTICE STEWART in his concurring opinion that the "liberty," against deprivation of which without due process the Fourteenth Amendment protects, embraces more than the rights found in the Bill of Rights. But that liberty is not guaranteed absolutely against depriva-tion, only against deprivation without due process of law. The test traditionally applied in the area of social and economic legislation is whether or not a law such as that challenged has a rational relation to a valid state objective. . . . The Due Process Clause of the Fourteenth Amendment undoubtedly does place a limit, albeit a broad one, on legislative power to enact laws such as this. If the Texas statute were to prohibit an abortion even where the mother's life is in jeopardy, I have little doubt that such a statute would lack a rational relation to a valid state objective under the test stated in *Williamson, supra.* But the Court's sweeping invalidation of any restrictions on abortion during the first trimester is impossi-ble to justify under that standard, and the conscious weighing of competing fac-tors that the Court's opinion apparently substitutes for the established test is far more appropriate to a legislative judgment than to a judicial one.

The Court eschews the history of the Fourteenth Amendment in its reliance on the "compelling state interest" test. . . . But the Court adds a new wrinkle to this test by transposing it from the legal considerations associated with the Equal Protection Clause of the Fourteenth Amendment to this case arising under the Due Process Clause of the Fourteenth Amendment. Unless I misapprehend the consequences of this transplanting of the "compelling state interest test," the Court's opinion will accomplish the seemingly impossible feat of leaving this area of the law more confused than it found it.

While the Court's opinion quotes from the dissent of Mr. Justice Holmes in *Lochner v. New York* . . . (1905), the result it reaches is more closely attuned to the majority opinion of Mr. Justice Peckham in that case. As in *Lochner* and similar cases applying substantive due process standards to economic and social welfare legislation, the adoption of the compelling state interest standard will inevitably require this Court to examine the legislative policies and pass on the wisdom of these policies in the very process of deciding whether a particular state interest put forward may or may not be "compelling." The decision here to break preg-nancy into three distinct terms and to outline the permissible restrictions the State may impose in each one, for example, partakes more of judicial legislation than it does of a determination of the intent of the drafters of the Fourteenth Amendment.

The fact that a majority of the States reflecting, after all, the majority senti-ment in those States, have had restrictions on abortions for at least a century is a strong indication, it seems to me, that the asserted right to an abortion is not "so rooted in the traditions and conscience of our people as to be ranked as funda-mental," *Snyder v. Massachusetts* . . . (1934). Even today, when society's views on abortion are changing, the very existence of the debate is evidence that the "right" to an abortion is not so universally accepted as the appellant would have us believe.

To reach its result the Court necessarily has had to find within the scope of the Fourteenth Amendment a right that was apparently completely unknown to the drafters of the Amendment. As early as 1821, the first state law dealing directly with abortion was enacted by the Connecticut Legislature. . . . By the time of the adoption of the Fourteenth Amendment in 1868, there were at least 36 laws enacted by state or territorial legislatures limiting abortion. While many States have amended or updated their laws, 21 of the laws on the books in 1868 remain in effect today. Indeed, the Texas statute struck down today was, as the majority notes, first enacted in 1857 and "has remained substantially unchanged to the present time." . . .

There apparently was no question concerning the validity of this provision or of any of the other state statutes when the Fourteenth Amendment was adopted. The only conclusion possible from this history is that the drafters did not intend to have the Fourteenth Amendment withdraw from the States the power to legislate with respect to this matter. . . .

For all of the foregoing reasons, I respectfully dissent.

Chapter 6

Congress

6-1

The Senate in Bicameral Perspective

Richard F. Fenno Jr.

Rules matter, and constitutional rules often matter most. The Framers of the Constitution created a bicameral national legislature and made the two houses of Congress different in their constituencies, size, and length of terms, with the expectation that they were shaping the way in which the House and Senate would behave. In the following essay, Richard Fenno introduces the differences between the House and the Senate that originated in the Constitution. He then traces the influence of the differences between the two chambers on the way representatives and senators campaign and govern.

BICAMERALISM WAS A bedrock element of the constitutional arrangement of 1787. A resolution "that the national legislature ought to consist of two branches" was the second one passed—"without debate or dissent"—at the federal convention.[1] When, later in the proceedings, several delegates defended the adequacy of the one-chamber Congress then existing under the Articles of Confederation, they did so as part of a strategic effort to secure the equal representation of states in the new system. The principle of bicameralism was never challenged. Twelve of the thirteen states already had bicameral legislatures. George Mason took this fact as evidence that "an attachment to more than one branch in the legislature"

Source: Richard F. Fenno Jr., *The United States Senate: A Bicameral Perspective* (Washington, D.C.: American Enterprise Institute, 1982), 1–6, 26–46.

was—along with "an attachment to republican government"—one of the two points on which "the mind of the people of America . . . was well settled."[2] When James Madison introduced the subject of a second chamber in *The Federalist,* he declared it to be "founded on such clear principles, and now so well understood in the United States that it would be more than superfluous to enlarge on it."[3] He and his colleagues did, of course, "enlarge" upon these "clear principles" in their debates and writings. And I shall do so briefly, to explicate the bicameral perspective.

The framers wanted to create a government, but at the same time they distrusted the power of government. To protect individual liberty, they believed, it was necessary to control the power of government, first through the electoral process and second by dividing authority among and within political institutions. Madison described the "principles" this way:

> In framing a government which is to be administered by men over men, the great difficulty lies in this: you must first enable the government to control the governed; and in the next place oblige it to control itself. A dependence on the people is, no doubt, the primary control on the government; but experience has taught mankind the necessity of auxiliary precautions.[4]

Bicameralism should be viewed most broadly as one of those "auxiliary precautions." Indeed, it is the first one mentioned by Madison after the paragraph quoted above. It came first because the framers believed that the most powerful institution of government and the one most likely to run out of control was the legislature. And they believed that "in order to control the legislative authority, you must divide it."[5]

"Is there no danger of legislative despotism?" James Wilson asked his convention colleagues rhetorically:

> Theory and practice both proclaim it. If the legislative authority be not restrained, there can be neither liberty nor stability; and it can only be restrained by dividing it within itself into distinct and independent branches.[6]

Madison elaborated in *The Federalist:*

> In republican government, the legislative authority necessarily predominates. The remedy for this inconveniency is to divide the legislature into different branches; and to render them, by different modes of election and different principles of action, as little connected with each other as the nature of their common functions and their common dependence on the society will admit.[7]

(Here we have enunciated the basic ideas of bicameralism: that the legislature consist of two "distinct and independent" bodies and that these bodies be "different" from one another.)

The framers, of course, had ideas about just what differences should exist between the Senate and the House. For one thing, they believed that the differences ought to be substantial. In Madison's words:

> As the improbability of sinister combinations will be in proportion to the dissimilarity in the genius of the two bodies, it must be politic to distinguish them from each other by every circumstance which will consist with a due harmony in all proper measures, and with the genuine principles of republican government.[8]

In pursuit of this goal, they determined that the Senate and the House should be structurally dissimilar with respect to their constituencies, their size, and the length of their terms. They also gave each chamber some distinctive policy prerogatives. The controversy over Senate and House constituencies very nearly broke up the entire enterprise. Once that was settled, however, the decisions of 1787 fixed the enduring agenda for discussions of bicameralism. For a long time the decision to establish different modes of election was also part of that agenda, but the Seventeenth Amendment, providing for the popular election of senators, removed it in 1913.

There is more, however, to the framers' conception of bicameralism than two legislative institutions differently constituted. They also believed that the two institutions should and would behave differently. The basic notion was simply that they would behave so as to check one another. In the very act of dividing power, the framers believed they had created two "different bodies of men who might watch and check each other."[9] Their favorite idea, that institutions should and would check one another, was a particularly strong element in their thinking about the Senate.

The House of Representatives was acknowledged to be "the grand repository of the democratic principle of the government."[10] That is why it was given the prerogative of initiating all legislation on taxes, where sensitivity to popular sentiment was deemed especially important. But the House was also thought likely to possess certain infirmities endemic to large, popularly elected legislatures—tendencies to instability in action, to impulsive, unpredictable, changeable decisions, and to a short-run view of good public policy. The Senate was thought of as providing a restraining, stabilizing counterweight, as being the source of a more deliberate, more knowledgeable, longer-run view of good public policy. Said Madison: "As a numerous body of Representatives was liable to err, also, from fickleness and passion, [a] necessary fence against this danger would be to select a portion of enlightened citizens, whose limited number, and firmness might reasonably interpose against impetuous councils." Madison also said: "The use of the Senate is to consist in its proceeding with more coolness, with more system and with more wisdom, than the popular branch."[11] On the basis of such a prediction, the Senate was granted prerogatives in foreign policy, where a steady view of the national interest and the respect of other nations was deemed especially important.

The framers based their predictions of House and Senate behavior on a set of assumptions about the importance of the structural differences they had prescribed. The superior "coolness," "system," and "wisdom" of the Senate, for example, were assumed to flow from its smaller size, the longer term of its members, and their election by state legislatures. If we ask whether the various predictions or their underlying assumptions have worked out as planned, the answer would be: not now—if ever. Some of the predicted differences—that the Senate would be "a more capable set of men" and would act with more "firmness"— seem almost quaint.[12] Research on the contemporary Congress has argued either that observable Senate-House differences do not follow the lines set forth by the framers or that those differences may be less important than the ever-growing similarities.[13] So there is evidence that the particular predictions and the particular linking assumptions of the framers do not hold true today.

Still, that is not a sufficient reason to abandon their original proposition: that structural differences would affect behavioral ones. The structural change to the popular election of senators, for instance, undoubtedly gave a major push to today's behavioral similarities. Other scholars, too, suggest that performance differences are related to structural differences.[14] So let us continue to assume that the enduring Senate-House differences—in constituency, size, and term—can have consequences for behavior, and let us consider such matters reasonable subjects for empirical investigation.

If encouragement be needed, it is provided by the existence of at least one crucial Senate-House difference in which the framers' assumptions about the effect of structures on behavior have been correct. By setting up two distinct and different bodies, they made it necessary that the Senate and the House take separate action. They wanted to make certain that the "concurrence of separate and dissimilar bodies is required in every public act."[15] Separate action means, at a minimum, sequential action, and sequential action very likely means different actions. That is because sequential action implies the passage of time and with it the changing of relevant contexts. Different contexts very likely lead to different behavior.

Not surprisingly, the exemplary anecdote about the Senate is an anecdote about sequence. It is the conversation between George Washington and Thomas Jefferson in which Jefferson, in France during the convention, asked Washington why he had consented to a second chamber. "Why," asked Washington, "did you pour that coffee into your saucer?" "To cool it," said Jefferson. "Even so," said Washington, "we pour legislation into the senatorial saucer to cool it." It was the Senate, of course, that was designed to contribute "coolness." But in the execution, it has been the existence of two separate legislative stages that has brought coolness to the legislative process. The anecdote is an exemplary one not just for the Senate, but for the Congress as a whole, for what it illustrates is the importance of separate, sequential action by the two chambers. The Senate is as likely to initiate heatedly as the House; the House is as likely to be the cooling saucer as the Senate.

If this is so, then the analysis of sequence becomes basic to an understanding of bicameral behavior—more basic than an analysis of whether the Senate is more liberal or more conservative than the House. The framers did not so much create one precipitate chamber and one stabilizing chamber as they did force decision making to move across two separate chambers, however those chambers might be constituted. The strategic maneuverings necessitated by such a process become a subject for empirical investigation—as in the analysis of conference committee behavior by Gerald Strom and Barry Rundquist.[16] For reasons of strategy, it would be important for members of the two chambers to assess each other's relative liberalism or conservatism. But analysts of sequencing strategies must recognize the more general proposition that the actions and reactions, the expectations and anticipations, of the two-stage process are as likely to flow one way across the two chambers as the other. The idea of two legislative institutions acting separately and sequentially and thereby having an effect on each other is another ingredient of a bicameral perspective. Although it is not pursued in this essay, it gives additional purpose to what is pursued here.

In sum, the framers of the constitution consciously created a bicameral legislature. They tried to create two different institutions, to construct them so that they would behave differently, and to provide for legislative action at two separate stages. Their legacy leaves us with two questions. What, if any, are the differences between the Senate and House? What, if any, difference do the differences make? To research these questions is a tall order. It calls for observation and description of both houses of Congress and of legislators both individually and collectively, both in and outside Washington. This essay attempts a beginning. Because its ultimate interest is in the Senate, it treats the Senate more than the House. Further, it treats senators more individually than collectively, and it treats them more outside than inside Washington. But it tries to do what it does comparatively—in accordance with a bicameral perspective. . . .

A Bicameral Perspective: Campaigning and Governing

The Six-Year Term

. . . House members campaign continuously. Although an analytical distinction can be drawn between the campaign and the rest of their term, the activity of campaigning never stops. The typical House member's attitude was expressed by one who said, "If an incumbent doesn't have the election won before the campaign begins, he's in trouble. It's hard for me to step up my campaign. I've never been home less than forty times a year since I've been in Congress." When I traveled during the campaign with House members, I rarely had the sense that they were doing anything extraordinary. Their schedules might be a bit more crowded and might include a larger number of partisan events than during an off-year visit, but I felt that they were engaging in their familiar, year-round routines. Two weeks before election one of them remarked, typically, "We are doing now just about the same thing—I'll say the very same thing—I do when I come home weekends." My visits to their districts in nonelection years confirmed this view.

But a researcher does not get the same feeling during incumbent senators' campaigns. There one senses that they have geared up for a qualitatively different effort from anything they have engaged in recently. House members talk a lot about "last time." They campaign "the way we did it last time." Memories of "last time," that is, the last election, are vivid. In a senator's campaign, however, there is noticeably less talk about "last time." The campaign workers tend not to have been involved "last time." Last time is much less of a benchmark for this time; to the degree that it is, recollections of it are vague. In other words, although House members never stop campaigning, senators do. That is why it is impossible to make the easy inferences from campaign styles to home styles for senators that can be made for House members. For senators, campaign styles are not necessarily home styles. There is undoubtedly a relation between them, stronger in some instances than in others. I shall have something to say about this later. Now I propose to examine the underlying structural feature that gives rise to this observed House-Senate difference: the six-year term. It is another legacy of the decisions of 1787.

Traveling the two campaign trails sensitizes the researcher to the difference between the two-year term and the six-year term. It is a big difference. This statement may come as no surprise, but it is not self-evident. The most widely read and reprinted political science treatment of Senate-House differences, by Lewis Froman, contains not one word about the difference in the length of terms. In his chapter "Differences between the House and the Senate," Froman writes:

> Probably the two most important differences between the House and the Senate, and the two from which most of the others are derived, are that the House is more than four times as large as the Senate and that Senators represent sovereign states in a federal system, whereas most congressmen represent smaller and sometimes shifting parts of states.[17]

And in the chart that follows, entitled "Major Differences between the House and the Senate," Froman lists eleven major differences, not one of which has anything to do with the difference between the two-year term and the six-year term. It is largely a matter of research perspective. Froman studied the House and Senate from the inside, in Washington, and he saw only internal, organizational differences. One who begins research in the constituencies at campaign time sees other differences and carries other perspectives to Capitol Hill.

From the perspective of a Senate campaign, six years seems like a long time. Incumbent candidates talk less about last time precisely because it was so long ago—long enough to render the last campaign irrelevant, even if it could be remembered. A defeated senator discussed the six-year change in his state's policy climate:

> When I went in, the war was still on—Vietnam. The fellow I ran against was very closely associated with that. That was of interest to people. There was not building up, then, that avalanche of antigovernment feeling, in the sense that the government could not solve problems. There was a suspicion of people in government, the sense that government was remote. That feeling was there. But the lack of faith in government has grown enormously in six years. [Six years ago] there was a lot more support for farm price supports. There was more support for government programs to help *me*. . . . Now there's the Goldwater spirit, that government never has done anything right and never will. . . . So the mood changed in six years. There's no doubt about that. The impact was very great, I think. People said about me, "He is not a bad guy. He works hard at it. He's honest. He comes back. But he's just too liberal. He hasn't kept up with this change and is holding out for old ideas. There's nothing wrong with him but his views."

This comment about change is not meant to explain an electoral outcome, although perhaps it does. Nor is it meant to explain why campaigning senators have difficulty delineating their supportive constituencies, although perhaps it may. It is meant, rather, to convey some sense of just how long a six-year term can be. Six years, especially six years without any electoral feedback, is plenty of time to get out of touch with one's constituency. Six years, in short, can be a political lifetime.

We cannot understand the Senate without examining the effects of this lengthy term. Six years between elections is long enough to encourage a senator to stop campaigning for a while and do something else with his or her time. House members, too, have this option, but they are constrained by the two-year term to a degree that senators are not—constrained to devote their time and energies fairly continuously and fairly heavily to campaigning for reelection. It is not happenstance that the hardest Senate campaigner I have traveled with was one who was serving a two-year term—a senator with a House member's term of office. "We started running four years ago and we have been running ever since," he said. "I have visited 165 cities and towns, places where no sitting senator has ever been."

He came home every weekend for a year and a half. And he was introduced, everywhere, as "a man who is accessible." "Our campaign organization never shut down," said his campaign manager. He campaigned, in other words, like a House member; he did so because of the constraints of the two-year term. Like a House member, he had no choice. Even more, he had to cultivate a constituency much larger than that of a House member.

All senators, I assume, worry a lot about reelection, too. I also assume, however, that their reelection concerns are less immediate, less central, and less overwhelming than they are for House members, at least for some of the time. The amplitude of the six-year cycle gives senators more of a choice. To the degree that they choose to campaign less than continuously, it should be easier for outsiders to disentangle their campaign activities from their noncampaign activities. It gives us an incentive to analyze the effect of one kind of activity on the other and to examine the choices senators make about their noncampaign activity. That is what I propose to do. As I proceed, the focus of description will shift gradually from the constituencies to Washington, from outside the Senate into the Senate, and from the processes of campaigning to the processes of governing.

The Electoral Cycle

A two-year term compresses campaign activity and noncampaign activity so that they appear, to the observer, to proceed simultaneously. A six-year term makes it easier to separate the two kinds of activities and view them sequentially. It invites a view in which the mixture of campaign and noncampaign activity changes over the course of the six years, campaign activity visibly increasing as election time approaches and visibly decreasing afterward. Senators themselves speak in the language of cycles. "Your life has a six-year cycle to it," said one eighteen-year veteran:

> We say in the Senate that we spend four years as a statesman and two years as a politician. You should get cracking as soon as the last two years open up. You should take a poll on the issues, identify people to run your campaign in different parts of the states, raise money, start your PR, and so forth.

A five-term senator, Russell Long, said, "My usual pattern in the first three years of a term is to stick close to the job here and in the last three years to step up the pace in Louisiana."[18] Some evidence, both cross-sectional and longitudinal, exists in support of this cyclical view of senatorial behavior.

The presence of three distinct classes of senators, each with a different reelection date, makes possible some cross-sectional analysis. At the constitutional convention James Wilson noted, "As one-third would go out triennially, there would always be divisions holding their places for unequal terms and consequently

Table 1. Average Amount Raised per Senator, 1977 and 1979 (in dollars)

	Reelection Date		
	One year away	Three years away	Five years away
1977	250,000 (22)	5,000 (34)	32,000 (30)
1979	391,000 (29)	64,000 (29)	112,000 (33)

Source: Federal Election Commission.

Note: Senators who did not file reports have been omitted. Numbers of senators in each group in parentheses.

acting under the influence of different views and different impulses."[19] Among those "different views and different impulses" is the impulse to campaign for reelection. In a cyclical view of the matter, the impulse would be strongest in that class for which election day was closest at hand.

I have examined the campaign contributions of all senators for the years 1977 and 1979, the years before the 1978 and 1980 Senate elections. The amount of money raised by each senator is taken to be a measure of that senator's campaign activity in that year. The results, reported in Table 1, do indeed indicate that the senators one year away from reelection campaign harder, that is, raise more money, than the senators for whom election day is either three years or five years away. The average amounts raised by the three classes (one year, three years, and five years away from reelection) were $250,000, $5,000, and $32,000 for 1978 and $391,000, $64,000, and $112,000 for 1980. In each year senators whose next election was furthest away ranked second in average amount collected. The pattern, then, is curvilinear. Those whose reelection was five years away "campaigned harder" than those whose reelection was only three years away. But they did so presumably because they were paying off the debts of a campaign just concluded. They were looking backward to the previous election, not forward to the next one.

Two changes between 1978 and 1980 are worth noting. Senators in all classes raised more money in 1979 than they did in 1977; campaigning is getting more expensive for everyone. The largest proportionate increase in fund raising occurred in the middle group, the class whose reelection was three years away. The average amount collected in this middle group jumped from $5,000 in 1977 to $64,000 in [1979], and the total amount collected by that one-third of the Senate jumped from $170,000 in 1977 to $1.9 million in 1979. This may indicate that senators are beginning their fund raising earlier than previously. As Robert Peabody has recently written:

> Few Senators can afford the proverbial luxury of serving as statesmen for four years, then reverting to the political role for the remaining two years of the

term. Many of the younger group of Senators appear to be following the practice of running hard through most of the six-year term, not unlike the experience of House incumbents.[20]

Table 1 contains some evidence of this change and at the same time demonstrates that some behavior still follows the electoral cycle.

The table indicates that there is a perceptible quickening of fund raising around the fifth year. Students of campaign finance have noted the same phenomenon. Herbert Alexander has observed, "It's becoming almost imperative for senators to spend the fifth year of their term to sew up the following year's elections."[21] Gary Jacobson has shown, for House races, that once a challenger starts spending large amounts of money, the incumbent cannot win simply by raising more money than the challenger.[22] It may be necessary, of course, for the incumbent to raise money in the sixth year to combat a strong challenger. But it can be even more important for an incumbent to use his or her fund-raising ability earlier, so as to keep a strong challenger from emerging. The appearance of electoral vulnerability can be disastrous for an incumbent, since potential challengers and the elites who fund them base their decisions partly on the perceived vulnerability of an incumbent.[23] Moreover, they will be making their calculations in the fifth year. One way to appear invulnerable is to raise a lot of money early. Such is the logic of fifth-year fund raising: at least, be prepared; at most, ward off a strong challenge. The logic of the preemptive strike may be even more important in the Senate than in the House, given the greater ability of Senate challengers to get media attention and to raise money once they have become committed to the race.

Two weeks before election, one incumbent senator talked about his fifth-year campaigning activity:

> Eighteen months ago, we started thinking about the strategy of the campaign. Our first strategy was to scare off other people from running by showing strength. And we did many interesting things to show our strength. . . . It worked in scaring off the governor and a congressman. It didn't work on my opponent. Whether or not we scared off the right people, we'll know on election day.

One of the "interesting things" this senator had done in the year before the election was to raise over $300,000. His press secretary talked about some of the others:

> In June of last year, we made a major strategic decision—to put an aura of invincibility around the senator. We collected money from all segments of the population of the state. We brought him and his family back home to the state. We ran a spring primary campaign as if we had an opponent—a heavy-schedule television campaign. In June of this year, we took a poll. He was ahead of his opponent by over twenty points.

This fifth-year activity may well have been the key to what turned out to be a narrow victory. Back in Washington after his reelection, the senator commented:

> Here's something that would interest you from your professional standpoint. All the political leaders in the state, on both sides, thought my opponent was in a hopeless race. They believed the polls. The other party's leaders believed it so much that they gave up on him. They didn't dig down and help him. That may have hurt him more than anything else.

He believes the strategy worked. Although it is not my purpose to explain election outcomes, this case illustrates the rationale behind one cyclical pattern of campaign activity.

A second, less direct indicator of cyclical campaign activity might be the frequency with which the different classes of senators return to their home states. We would expect that those senators whose reelection was less than two years away would return home to campaign more often than those whose reelection was more than two years away. We have already noted that senators as a group return to their electoral constituencies a good deal less frequently than House members do. Among senators, however, do those up for reelection behave differently from those who are not? In general, there is some evidence that they do. Such patterns as there are run in the expected direction: more attentiveness to their constituencies by senators in the reelection class than by those in the other two classes. The differences are not overwhelming, however, and the small numbers in many categories argue against strong assertions. Still, the evidence is weakly supportive.

In 1977 the twenty-two incumbents facing reelection in 1978 averaged twenty-three trips to their home states, those whose reelection was three years away averaged sixteen trips, and those whose reelection was five years away averaged eighteen trips. Senators who retired in 1978, a group totally lacking in electoral incentives, averaged twelve trips home in 1977 (see Table 2). The difference between this group and their colleagues running for reelection is substantial. It surely testifies to a relationship between the proximity of reelection and trips home, if not to any great strength in its cyclical nature.

Among the three nonretiring groups, the findings resemble those for campaign finance activity. Senators up for reelection are most active, and recently elected senators seem to engage in more electorally related activity than senators in the middle of their term. In the area of campaign finance, the newly elected senators are still paying off their debts. In the matter of trips home, they are probably slow to throttle down from their recent campaigns. This might be particularly true of senators elected for the first time, whose sense of electoral insecurity might remain with them. In any case, it is the first-term senators whose performance accounts for the slightly higher average among the newly elected

Table 2. Trips Home by Senate Class, 1977

Number of trips home	Reelection 1978		Reelection 1980		Reelection 1982		Retiring 1978	
	Number	Percent	Number	Percent	Number	Percent	Number	Percent
31+	5	23	3	9	5	18	0	0
21–30	7	32	6	19	4	14	2	29
11–20	9	41	13	41	12	43	1	14
0–10	1	5	10	31	7	25	4	57
Total	22	100	32	100	28	100	7	100
Average	23		16		18		12	

Source: Travel vouchers submitted to the secretary of the Senate.

Note: Excludes senators from Delaware, Maryland, and Virginia; senators who had served less than a full year; and senators whose records were obviously incomplete.

class. Veteran senators in that class, that is, those elected in 1976, did not go home any more frequently in 1977 than those senators who had been elected in 1974. There is thus some evidence, although it is not overwhelming, for a cyclical explanation of senatorial attentiveness to home.

Table 2 presents further evidence for an electoral cycle. The distribution of trips home within the reelection class differs from that of the other two classes and the retiring senators. Senators running for reelection are clustered more heavily in the top two categories than are senators in the other two classes or those who are retiring. The differences are greatest in the category of ten or fewer trips home; only one reelection-bound senator dared risk such infrequent visits. The retiring senators, of course, look very different from all other senators, but there is no clear pattern differentiating between the two classes of senators not running for reelection. Although reelection concerns have some effect on one class of senators, then, Table 2 conveys no information about other phases of a more defined electoral cycle.

A confounding circumstance affecting the distribution of trips home is the simple matter of distance from Washington, D.C. Among House members, it was found that distance, that is, the expenditure of time, money, and energy, was strongly related to trips home.[24] There is no reason to believe that this would not be true of the Senate, and it is. Table 3 presents a distribution of trips home by senators according to the region from which they come, region being employed as a surrogate for distance, as it was with House members. The farther senators live from Washington, the more difficult it is for them to get home. Senators from the East go home more often than any other group; those from the Far West go home less often than any other group. No senator from the Far West is

Table 3. Trips Home by Senators, by Region, 1977

Number of trips home	East	South	Border	Midwest	Far West
31+	8	3	0	2	0
21–30	5	7	5	2	0
11–20	3	5	1	12	14
0–10	1	3	2	5	11
Total	17	18	8	21	25
Average	27	21	19	16	11

Source: Travel vouchers submitted to the secretary of the Senate.

Note: Excludes senators from Delaware, Maryland, and Virginia; senators who had served less than a full year; and senators whose records were obviously incomplete.

to be found in the highest two categories of trips home. Senators from the Midwest also go home markedly less often than those from the East and South. So striking are these patterns that the question arises whether or not they overwhelm such evidence as supports the notion of a reelection effect. Perhaps region explains all the differences observed in Table 2. Senate classes may be skewed toward one region or another; thus an apparent reelection effect may mask what really is a distance effect.

The 1980 and 1982 Senate classes, for example, are more skewed toward the Far West, 31 percent and 32 percent respectively, than is the class of 1978, only 21 percent of whose members are from the Far West. These regional differences could account for the higher average number of trips among the group of senators running for reelection. One way to check for independent reelection effects would be to see whether, within each region, senators running for reelection were more attentive than senators in the two other classes to their home states. When this calculation is made, the effect of the electoral cycle remains. Of the twenty-two senators running for reelection, sixteen exceeded the average of all senators from their region, and six averaged fewer trips than their regional colleagues. Thus, although distance has an important effect on the frequency of senators' visits home, the proximity to reelection has an independent effect.

Other factors that might be thought to affect a cyclical-reelection explanation for trips home but do not do so—at least in terms of a bivariate relationship— include election margin, seniority, size of state, and previous service in the House. A more idiosyncratic factor, home style, probably does take an additional toll on the cyclical rationale of trips home. Consider, for example, the twenty cases where a senator faced reelection and his or her colleague from the same state did not. With distance thus held constant, we would expect, according to a cyclical rationale, that the campaigning senator would return home more often than his noncampaigning colleague. In ten cases he clearly did; but in six cases he clearly did not, and four cases were virtual ties. It seems likely, therefore, that some senators adopt and maintain a home style calling for frequent personal appearances back home and much personal attentiveness to the electorate. It is a decision having nothing to do with the amplitude of the electoral cycle or the proximity of reelection. Such a style may be adopted to make a deliberate contrast with the senator's same-state colleague. It is worth noting that in all six cases in the non-cyclical pattern, it was the junior senator (five of whom were in their first term) who went home most often, even though the senior senator was the one running for reelection. Support for a cyclical-reelection explanation of behavior is weakened a bit more by this finding, and the importance of decisions about home style, taken independent of reelection proximity, is reasserted.

A final strand of research gives some support to a cyclical view of senatorial behavior. It is the body of work that demonstrates that the roll-call or other policy-related behavior of senators changes in the direction of the policy sentiments of their constituents as their reelection approaches. Since these changes are calculated to improve a senator's electoral prospects, we can think of this as another form of campaign activity. The prototype for this research is not about the U.S. Senate at all; it is James Kuklinski's study of California legislators. He found that the voting of state senators, who serve four-year terms, moved toward the policy preferences of their constituents as reelection time approached and moved away from those preferences after their reelection, while the voting of assemblymen, who serve two-year terms, showed no such cyclical change. Ryan Amacher and William Boyes argue a similar conclusion for the Senate. "Long terms, such as the U.S. Senate, seem to produce cycles in which the representative is able to behave independently when first elected and then becomes more representative as reelection approaches."[25] Their conclusion, unfortunately, rests on a methodology far less convincing than Kuklinski's.

John Jackson found that among senators whose 1963 constituency-related voting behavior was not consistent with their previously observed constituency-related voting behavior, the change could be explained by increased attention to the constituency among those whose reelection was closest at hand and decreased attention among those just reelected. Keith Poole has shown that senators' roll-call behavior, as measured by interest group ratings, becomes more ambiguous, or less consistent ideologically, the closer they get to reelection. Finally, Warren Kostroski and Richard Fleisher found that the voting behavior of senators up for reelection was more responsive to the policy wishes of their supportive constituencies than the voting behaviors of senators not up for reelection.[26]

In all these studies there is evidence, produced cross-sectionally, in support of a cyclical effect on campaign activity. Still, the evidence is not strong. The first study was not about the Senate at all. The second study, where the finding is the most applicable, used very questionable methods. The presence of cyclical effects was not the major finding of the last three studies but a subsidiary result. Their major findings emphasized behavioral consistency. Thus the body of evidence leaves us just about where we were at the conclusion of the discussion of trips home. There is weakly supportive evidence for the operation of an electoral cycle and for its systematic effect on campaign activity.

Evidence that constituency-related voting increases at the end of the cycle is buttressed a bit, however, by evidence that such voting can be diluted at the beginning of the electoral cycle. Evidence for the proposition—the "statesman" proposition—is fragmentary, but several senators talked about it. Said one in his first year, "I wouldn't have voted against food stamps as I did last Saturday if I had to run in a year. The six-year term gives you insurance. Well, not exactly—it gives you a cushion. It gives you some squirming room." Said another newcomer:

> It [the six-year term] helps you to take politically unpopular positions. Right now I'm trying to think of a way to change cost-of-living indexing. I'm convinced we've got to find a way of turning that process around. I don't know whether I'll get anywhere. Indexing is very popular. None of the people running for reelection next year will tackle it. I wouldn't either if I had to get reelected next year.

The idea is, of course, that such political actions would not be possible if the senator were near the end of his term. House members, by contrast, are always near the end of their term. As a House member put it, "You are tied down a lot closer to your constituency here than in the Senate. . . . Over there at least one-third of the senators can afford to be statesmen. Here you have to be a politician all the time because you have to run every two years." A third senator reflected, similarly, on the Senate's passage of the Panama Canal treaty:

> Two years is a much shorter leash. I think it makes a real difference. I don't think you would ever have gotten the Panama Canal treaty through the House. Not with the election coming up and the mail coming in so heavily against it. The sentiment in the House might not have been any different from what it was in the Senate. But you could never have passed it.

The implication is that some portion of the Senate was freed from the intense reelection pressure by the insulating effect of the length of term. Patterned action taken near the beginning of the cycle thus testifies to its existence as much as patterned action taken at the end of the cycle.

All this puts us a little bit in mind of an observation by H. Douglas Price: "Cycles have a deservedly bad reputation in most of the social sciences, but they seem to exercise an irresistible pull on explorers of poorly understood subjects."[27]

Perhaps when we understand more about the Senate, the appeal of the electoral cycle will vanish. But until such time, it will continue to seem a useful way of exploring the consequences of the six-year term.

The Adjustment from Campaigning to Governing

There is a cycle-related admonition that senators repeat to one another: "Your most important years here are your first and your fifth." They sometimes argue over which is the more important. We know why the fifth year is important. It is the reelection year. We can guess why the first year is important. It is the adjustment year. Political scientists have devoted a great deal of attention to the adjustment period in the Senate, much more than they have paid to the reelection period. In the 1960s the writing about adjustment was dominated by the idea that newly elected senators had to attune themselves to the informal "folkways" of the institution. Especially prominent among those folkways was the notion that first-term senators should observe an apprenticeship. Donald Matthews, in his classic 1960 study, called it "the first rule of Senate behavior" that a newcomer "is expected to keep his mouth shut, not to take the lead in floor fights, to listen and to learn."[28] Recent writings on the Senate, however, have demonstrated beyond any doubt that this "norm of apprenticeship" is dead.[29] That does not mean, however, that the period of adjustment is any the less crucial for a newly elected senator—either in his eyes or in the eyes of those who make judgments about him. Political scientists, therefore, face the problem of confronting a crucial period in the life of a senator at the same time that they have undermined their favorite intellectual framework for studying it.

The suggestion offered here is to view the adjustment period from the perspective of the campaign and the electoral cycle. Newly elected senators can be seen as making a transition from campaign activity, during which time their noncampaign activity will be affected to varying degrees by their campaign activity. The adjustment they make is not so much something that takes place in Washington as it is an adjustment that takes place between constituency behavior and Washington behavior. The relationship, from this perspective, between campaign activity and noncampaign activity has long been deemed important by students of Congress. "It is difficult, really, to understand the Senators, how they act and why," asserted Matthews, "without considering what happens to them while they are running for office."[30] John Bibby and Roger Davidson have written, "The relationship of the campaign to the legislator's total world is of special fascination to students of the legislative process."[31] Yet both works make particular mention of the need for scholarly research into the relationship. Matthews, indeed, admits that his book has little to say on the subject.[32]

Senate newcomers are emerging from their campaigns and are positioned at the beginning of a six-year electoral cycle. From a cyclical view, they should be gearing down their campaign activity and stepping up their noncampaign activity. The six-year senatorial term relaxes their electoral constraints sufficiently so that they can, at some point, stop their campaigning and devote their time and energy to something else. Or, at least, they can alter the mixture of their activities. Indeed, it could be argued that all senators must make some such adjustment. If the amplitude of the electoral cycle is not a sufficient inducement, outsiders—particularly the media—will doubtless fix a set of noncampaign expectations for them. Just what is meant by "noncampaign activity" remains purposely vague, but it has something to do with the conduct of the legislature's business, with governing the country. Senators will make the adjustment from campaigning to governing at different rates of speed, in different ways, and with different consequences.

A senator's early days in office provide the observer with a natural setting in which to explore the variety of ways in which the campaign just concluded can impinge on the legislative behavior just taking shape. On the first visit to a newly elected senator's office, for example, an observer is struck by the number of familiar faces there, by the presence of acquaintances from the campaign trail. Whatever their ultimate adjustment to life in the Senate may be, newly elected senators want some people from the campaign with them in Washington.

I followed six neophyte senators from their campaigns into the Senate. On the average, one-third of their Senate staffs—in Washington and back home—were people who had worked in their campaigns. All six campaign managers became members of the Washington staffs, three as chief administrative assistants, two as chief legislative assistants. All six campaign press secretaries became senatorial press secretaries, five in Washington and one in the home state. This direct exchange of jobs, greater than for any other staff position, testifies to the continuing importance of the media for senators as well as for Senate candidates. One method, therefore, of coping with the adjustment period is to maintain some continuity in personnel, some "binding ties."[33]

The presence of people from the campaign ensures the continuance of some campaign activity throughout the six-year term—or if not campaign activity, at least what might be called a campaign metabolism. Senators want some people around who have the requisite metabolic makeup. They want people who have a first-hand sensitivity to electoral forces and electoral problems in the state. They want people who have proven political skill, proven political loyalty, and proven ability to function under pressure. They want people who can understand the senator's political obligations and assess his political risks. All these qualities are best discovered, developed, and tested in the crucible of a campaign. All will be needed to conduct whatever campaign activity is conducted over the next six years, and all will affect noncampaign activity as well. If we, on the outside, are to understand a senator's noncampaign activity, we shall have to know that some members of his staff possess this campaign metabolism. They will automatically factor into all their judgments perceptions of the last campaign and considerations of the next campaign, even as they go about their noncampaign activity. Looking back over six years, an administrative assistant to a first-term senator, the man who also managed the first campaign, provided an example:

> I started worrying the day after his election. He was the first member of the party elected from our state in many years. His reelection was never out of my mind. I thought everything we did here meant something could be done about our political situation or our political base. The senator may not have seen it that way. He's not a political guy. He's the least political senator around.

Staffers with a campaign metabolism will join the senator in making decisions about what is politically wise or politically feasible. Indeed, it may not even be possible to understand certain decisions made by senators unless we know that they have been made by people who had been campaigners.

Another set of continuing influences flows from the events and the rhetoric (I hesitate to say dialogue) of the campaign. At the most obvious level, there are the policy positions taken during the campaign that must now be addressed in office. "The problems I talked about in the campaign are the problems I'm still interested in—the auto industry," said one senator two months into his first term. "It's a continuum," said another, at the same stage:

> There are a lot of campaign promises to be fulfilled. We have to look after the export of coal, coal regulation, steel, pollution issues, Japanese imports, textiles. The NEA [National Education Association], which was a big help to me in the campaign, want more recognition on education matters. There are Jewish issues. There are the problems of [particular cities]. . . . I'm interested in a full plate of things.

John Bibby and Roger Davidson wrote of Senator Abraham Ribicoff that "the Senate campaign provided an important testing ground for the issues and themes that were to mark his early Senate career."[34] During their campaigns Senate candidates emphasize certain public policy concerns, and they carry the emphasis with them into the Senate.

How long the policy emphases of the campaign remain on the senator's "plate of things" is a matter of conjecture. Donald Matthews suggests that "the Senator's initial mandate—partly self-defined, partly reflecting popular sentiment . . . may be a major influence on his voting record many years after it was received."[35] One implication is that policy positions taken in the campaign may persist for so long that eventually the senator can get badly out of touch with his constituency—and, of course, lose. Another implication is that the duration of the campaign emphasis will depend on just how strong the senator believes the initial mandate to be. The finding of Alan Abramowitz that some Senate campaigns are more ideological than others and that voters respond ideologically to the more ideological campaigns may help to sort out the kinds of campaigns that have the most lasting effects on victorious senators.[36] I have already noted that Senate campaigns tend to be more policy oriented than House campaigns, but Senate campaigns can vary widely in the amount of policy controversy they contain.

One way to maintain a campaign policy interest is to institutionalize it by obtaining membership on the committee that deals with it. In an after-dinner campaign speech at a rural high school, I heard one Senate candidate say to the growers of a particular farm product, "I hope I become a member of the Agriculture Committee. I want to become a member of that committee. If I get to the Senate, I'm going to make the point loud and clear that in all the Department of Agriculture there's not one advocate of your industry." It was a campaign promise made to a group of his very strongest supporters. In Washington, in January, he was somewhat less enthusiastic. "The Agriculture Committee is a shambles. . . . When I told other senators I wanted it, they said 'too bad' or 'maybe we can reduce the size of the committee so you won't have to go on.'" But he felt constrained to do so. As his administrative assistant put it, "He's going to go on Agriculture whether he wants to or not." The first legislative staff person he hired was an agricultural expert. The first bill he introduced was an agricultural bill. Altogether it was a very direct, specific, and continuing influence of the campaign on this senator's subsequent legislative work.

To the degree that the adjustment period follows the presumed pattern of the electoral cycle, newly elected senators should gradually subordinate campaign-related behavior to behavior related to legislative work. But they will not all act to do so with the same speed or produce the same degree of subordination. We now know, for example, that some senators must remain active for a while in fund raising to pay off campaign debts. Moreover, some senators enjoy campaigning and are therefore less likely to ease up on it.

Candidate A—now Senator A—is such a person. He likes to campaign. During the campaign he had exclaimed at one point, "I like what we are doing here better than what I do in Washington. The House is a zoo. People say the Senate is much better. . . . [They say] 'you'll even enjoy it.'" Whereas a number of his former House colleagues saw in the six-year term a welcome opportunity to stop their incessant campaigning, he saw nothing attractive in that particular feature of Senate life. Three months into his term, he commented:

I never gave the six-year term one minute's thought. People say to me, "Aren't you glad you're in for six years?" I say, "No." I always liked campaigning. I always won big in elections. I'll campaign just as often as a senator as I did in the House and in exactly the same way. I was back there over the recess, traveled over the state and made fifteen speeches in five days. Campaigning is the best part of the job. It's the most fun. The six-year term makes absolutely no difference to me.

It will be interesting to see whether, in spite of himself, the six-year term has some effect on his campaign rhythms. Certainly the mixture of activities will be far different for him than for some others, and the play of cyclical effects will be diminished. It seems very likely that, just as his established campaign style did not change when he ran for the Senate, his established home style will not change much while he is in the Senate.

Candidate B—now Senator B—experienced a different adjustment period. When I talked with him three months into his first term, he said, "Nobody talks about their campaigns. It's over. You start fresh. It's the same as your being in the House. That doesn't matter over here either. It's a clean slate." And that was the way he wanted it. Unlike Senator A, he was trying to establish a clean slate with his constituents. "I set a certain standard of expectation when I was in the House, going home every weekend, but I'm not going to do that now. One of the reasons I ran for the Senate was so I wouldn't have to go home every weekend." His determination to disengage quickly from campaign activities was not just a matter of personal preference. It was a decision that emerged out of the dynamics of the campaign itself. His election opponents had called him a "show horse" and had described the contest as "a show horse against a work horse." He was sufficiently affected by this campaign rhetoric that he worked hard to negate it during his early days in office. Two and a half months into his term, he commented:

> Yesterday I got a call from the editor of the state's largest paper asking me why I was keeping such a low profile back in the state. They are going to write a criticism of me for not appearing at every bean supper back home. I've been studying hard, doing my homework, showing up on time. During the campaign, I had to confront the show horse–work horse argument. I've been trying to be a work horse. I've been down here for a month and a half without going home.

Senator B was moving along the cycle in the direction we would normally expect, but his movement was accelerated by his experience in the campaign. It seems likely that Senator B's campaign may have an effect on his home style, changing it from what it was in the House; but we shall have to wait and see.

In general, when the campaign rhetoric emphasizes policy matters, policy concerns can be expected to have an important effect on the adjustment period. When the rhetoric of the campaign emphasizes stylistic matters, however, stylistic concerns can be expected to have an important effect on the adjustment period. Whether the effect is to speed up or retard the movement toward non-campaign activity by the newly elected senator depends entirely on the substantive content of the campaign rhetoric.

The case of candidate C—now Senator C—is instructive. Senator C was a person who wanted to gear down his campaigning during the adjustment period but found it nearly impossible to do so. When I originally asked candidate C why he wanted to leave the House, he answered, "You run for election all the time. You win one month, and a month later you find out who your opponent will be. You go to bean suppers eight days in a row." One month after his election, I asked him what he would miss least about the House. He answered quickly and with a smile. "The two-year term. Now I can do what I want to do well." He is a highly issue-oriented person, and he was impatient to begin some sustained legislative work. Yet, in the first four months of his tenure, he made thirteen trips home and spent thirty-one days there. Senator B, in that same period, went home five times and spent nine days there. Why the contrast?

Once again, we must look to the dynamics of the campaign itself. Candidate C's main line of attack against the incumbent senator had been a stylistic one—his lack of accessibility. "When was the last time you saw your senator?" he would ask. "He hasn't been in my district more than twice in six years. . . . He's very much of a Washingtonian and all that implies. He's on the Washington-overseas shuttle." The implied campaign promise was, of course, to be accessible—as accessible, he sometimes said, as he had been when he was in the House. "I will hold town meetings like I did as a congressman—twenty a year," he told a reporter in January. "I'll also do 'work days': spend a day doing what people do for a living. My wife will go back once a month and go around meeting people and giving speeches." It seemed easy to contemplate. "I was more involved in my congressional district than any congressman ever; so it's nothing more than an extension of what I'm into already. I'm comfortable with it, and I think it will work." In his early days, he tried to make it work. Indeed, he did not stop campaigning.

In May, he exclaimed:

> In the House, I tried to do everything I was asked to do, go everywhere I was invited. The problem is: How do you learn to say no? I'm doing fourteen commencements this spring. Can you believe it? Part of it is my own doing. After the campaign, I never stopped. I went around thanking everybody. So I never recouped from the campaign. And I haven't stopped since. The result is I'm tired all the time.

As we drove around the state one day in June, he revealed another reason for his continuing campaign activity—a degree of electoral insecurity evidenced by neither Senator A nor Senator B. They, however, represented states the same size and twice the size of their House districts whereas Senator C was trying to digest a vastly larger statewide constituency. "There are so many places I haven't been where I want to get established," he said that day. Passing through one small town, he said, "This could be a good place for a town meeting. They would appreciate it. I haven't been here before." In the car, he leafed through a pile of "thank you" letters. "When you accept appearances like these and do them well, the recognition is tremendous. So the temptation is to keep it up. . . . Politically it's fantastic; but personally it's devastating." He added, "I can't keep up the pace." A couple of years later he looked back on his adjustment period:

> There was a definite period of confusion and wandering. It lasted for about a year. We didn't know what we were doing. We didn't know what issues to work on. I was running around the state like a madman. The problem was that I still thought of myself as a congressman; but I wasn't a congressman, and I had ten times the territory to cover. You need to make judgments about what you want to do here, and we began to do that.

Finally he had begun to enjoy the fruits of the six-year term he had so coveted in the beginning. In the Senate Office Building he told a group of college students that same day, "This is the best job there is. The six-year term gives you time to think. In the House, you just finish packing away the decorations from the victory celebration when someone announces against you, and you have to start campaigning all over again." By that time he had subordinated his campaign activity to his noncampaign activity. But as one of his chief campaigners and chief Senate staffers said, "It took us a long time to get over the campaign."

There is a lot more to any senator's adjustment period than the campaign effects I have discussed. There are a whole series of adjustments to be made to one's fellow senators, to the internal routines of legislative work, and to the other actors in the Washington political community. All adjustment problems, however, can be seen as matters of choice. Senators will choose—in accordance with their personal goals, their perception of their political world, and the objective constraints within which they operate—their modes of adjustment. They will decide what kind of senators they want to be and how they will spend their resources of time, intelligence, energy, and support. I have discussed a few such senatorial adjustment choices, concerning staff, policy, committee, style, as they are affected by the campaign. I have suggested that the campaign perspective will help us understand the adjustment period, but I suggest no more than that. Just as the senators themselves gradually subordinate campaign activity to noncampaign activity, so must the observer subordinate the campaign perspective to other perspectives in order to comprehend a fuller range of Senate activities. For us as for them, there is a transition from the matter of campaigning to the matter of governing. But that is for another essay.

NOTES

1. James Madison, *Notes of Debates in the Federal Convention of 1787* (New York: W. W. Norton, 1969), pp. 38–39.

2. Ibid., p. 158.

3. *The Federalist Papers* (New York: New American Library, 1969), no. 62, p. 379.

4. Ibid., no. 51, p. 322

5. Madison, *Notes*, p. 127.

6. Ibid., pp. 126–27.

7. *Federalist*, no. 51, p. 322.

8. Ibid., no. 62, p. 379.

9. Madison, *Notes*, p. 193.

10. Ibid., p. 39.

11. Ibid., pp. 194, 83.

12. Ibid., pp. 113, 194.

13. Gary E. Gammon, "The Role of the United States: Its Conception and Its Performance" (Ph.D. diss., Claremont Graduate School, 1978); and Norman J. Ornstein, "The House and the Senate in a New Congress," in Thomas E. Mann and Norman J. Ornstein, eds., *The New Congress* (Washington, D.C.: American Enterprise Institute, 1981).

14. Joseph M. Bessette, "Deliberative Democracy: The Majority Principle in Republican Government," in Robert A. Goldwin and William A. Schambra, eds., *How Democratic Is the Constitution?* (Washington, D.C.: American Enterprise Institute, 1980); and Nelson W. Polsby, "Strengthening Congress in National Policymaking," *Yale Review* (Summer 1970), pp. 481–97.

15. *Federalist*, no. 63, p. 386.

16. Gerald S. Strom and Barry S. Rundquist, "A Revised Theory of Winning in House-Senate Conferences," *American Political Science Review* (June 1997).

17. Lewis A. Froman Jr., *The Congressional Process: Strategies, Rules, and Procedures* (Boston: Little, Brown, 1967), pp. 7–8.

18. *New York Times*, April 15, 1979.

19. James Madison, *Notes of Debates in the Federal Convention of 1787* (New York: W. W. Norton, 1969), p. 198.

20. Robert Peabody, "Senate Party Leadership: From the 1950s to the 1980s" (unpublished manuscript, Baltimore, 1980), p. 27; see also, Norman J. Ornstein, "The House and the Senate in a New Congress," in Thomas E. Mann and Norman J. Ornstein, eds., *The New Congress* (Washington, D.C.: American Enterprise Institute, 1981).

21. *Congressional Quarterly Weekly Report*, July 28, 1979, p. 1539.

22. Gary Jacobson, *Money in Congressional Elections* (New Haven, Conn.: Yale University Press, 1980).

23. Gary Jacobson and Samuel Kernell, *Strategy and Choice in Congressional Elections* (New Haven, Conn.: Yale University Press, 1982).

24. Richard F. Fenno Jr., *Home Style: House Members in Their Districts* (Boston: Little, Brown, 1978).

25. James H. Kuklinski, "Representativeness and Elections: A Political Analysis," *American Political Science Review* (March 1978), pp. 165–77; and Ryan C. Amacher and William J. Boyes, "Cycles in Senatorial Voting Behavior: Implications for the Optimal Frequency of Elections," *Public Choice* (1978), pp. 5–13.

26. John Jackson, *Constituencies and Leaders in Congress* (Cambridge, Mass.: Harvard University Press, 1974), chap. 5; Keith T. Poole, "Dimensions of Interest Group Evaluation of the U.S. Senate, 1969–1978," *American Journal of Political Science* (February 1981), pp. 49–67; and Warren Kostroski and Richard Fleisher, "Competing Models of Electoral Linkage: Senatorial Voting Behavior, 1963–1964" (unpublished manuscript, 1977?).

27. H. Douglas Price, "'Critical Elections' and Party History: A Critical Review," *Polity* (1971), pp. 236–42, at p. 239.

28. Donald R. Matthews, *U.S. Senators and Their World* (Chapel Hill: University of North Carolina Press, 1960), pp. 92–99.

29. David Rohde, Norman Ornstein, and Robert Peabody, "Political Change and Legislative Norms in the U.S. Senate" (paper delivered at the annual meeting of the American Political Science Association, Chicago, 1974); Ross Baker, *Friend and Foe in the U.S. Senate* (New York: Free Press, 1980); and Michael Foley, *The New Senate* (New Haven, Conn.: Yale University Press, 1980).

30. Matthews, *U.S. Senators,* p. 68.

31. John Bibby and Roger Davidson, *On Capitol Hill* (New York: Holt, Rinehart, 1967), p. 51.

32. Matthews, *U.S. Senators,* p. 50; see also Bibby and Davidson, *On Capitol Hill,* p. 52.

33. Robert Salisbury and Kenneth Shepsle, "Congressional Staff Turnover and the Ties-That-Bind," *American Political Science Review* (June 1981), pp. 381–96.

34. Bibby and Davidson, *On Capitol Hill,* p. 52.

35. Matthews, *U.S. Senators,* pp. 234–35.

36. Alan Abramowitz, "Choices and Echoes in the 1978 U.S. Senate Elections: A Research Note," *American Journal of Political Science* (February 1981), pp. 112–118.

6-2

from *Congress: The Electoral Connection*

David R. Mayhew

Many unflattering stereotypes permeate public thinking about members of Congress. Legislators are sometimes viewed as partisans who are preoccupied with scoring political points against the opposition party. At other times, they are treated as ideologues pursuing their personal policy interests at the expense of the nation's collective interest. Sometimes they are even considered to be a special psychological type—power-hungry politicians. In the following essay, David Mayhew explores the implications of a more realistic assumption—that legislators seek reelection. He argues that legislators' efforts to gain reelection produce predictable behavior while in office. In particular, legislators seek to claim credit for legislation that sends money for projects in their constituencies back home, they find taking positions on issues more important than passing bills, and, of course, they advertise themselves.

THE DISCUSSION TO COME will hinge on the assumption that United States congressmen are interested in getting reelected—indeed, in their role here as abstractions, interested in nothing else. Any such assumption necessarily does some violence to the facts, so it is important at the outset to root this one as firmly as possible in reality. A number of questions about that reality immediately arise.

First, is it true that the United States Congress is a place where members wish to stay once they get there? ...

In the modern Congress the "congressional career" is unmistakably upon us. Turnover figures show that over the past century increasing proportions of members in any given Congress have been holdovers from previous Congresses—members who have both sought reelection and won it. Membership turnover noticeably declined among southern senators as early as the 1850s, among senators generally just after the Civil War. The House followed close behind, with turnover dipping in the late nineteenth century and continuing to decline throughout the twentieth. Average number of terms served has gone up

Source: David R. Mayhew, *Congress: The Electoral Connection* (New Haven: Yale University Press, 1974), 13–27, 49–77. Notes appearing in the original have been deleted.

and up, with the House in 1971 registering an all-time high of 20 percent of its members who had served at least ten terms. It seems fair to characterize the modern Congress as an assembly of professional politicians spinning out political careers. The jobs offer good pay and high prestige. There is no want of applicants for them. Successful pursuit of a career requires continual reelection.

A second question is this: even if congressmen seek reelection, does it make sense to attribute that goal to them to the exclusion of all other goals? Of course the answer is that a complete explanation (if one were possible) of a congressman's or any one else's behavior would require attention to more than just one goal. There are even occasional congressmen who intentionally do things that make their own electoral survival difficult or impossible. . . . The electoral goal has an attractive universality to it. It has to be the *proximate* goal of everyone, the goal that must be achieved over and over if other ends are to be entertained. One former congressman writes, "All members of Congress have a primary interest in getting re-elected. Some members have no other interest." Reelection underlies everything else, as indeed it should if we are to expect that the relation between politicians and public will be one of accountability. What justifies a focus on the reelection goal is the juxtaposition of these two aspects of it—its putative empirical primacy and its importance as an accountability link. . . .

. . . Congressmen must constantly engage in activities related to reelection. There will be differences in emphasis, but all members share the root need to do things—indeed, to do things day in and day out during their terms. The next step here is to present a typology, a short list of the *kinds* of activities congressmen find it electorally useful to engage in. The case will be that there are three basic kinds of activities. . . .

One activity is *advertising,* defined here as any effort to disseminate one's name among constituents in such a fashion as to create a favorable image but in messages having little or no issue content. A successful congressman builds what amounts to a brand name, which may have a generalized electoral value for other politicians in the same family. The personal qualities to emphasize are experience, knowledge, responsiveness, concern, sincerity, independence, and the like. Just getting one's name across is difficult enough; only about half the electorate, if asked, can supply their House members' names. It helps a congressman to be known. . . . A vital advantage enjoyed by House incumbents is that they are much better known among voters than their November challengers. They are better known because they spend a great deal of time, energy, and money trying to make themselves better known. There are standard routines—frequent visits to the constituency, nonpolitical speeches to home audiences, the sending out of infant care booklets and letters of condolence and congratulation. . . . Anniversaries and other events aside, congressional advertising is done largely at public expense. Use of the franking privilege has mushroomed in recent years; in early 1973 one estimate predicted that House and Senate members would send out about 476 million pieces of mail in the year 1974, at a public cost of $38.1 million—or about 900,000 pieces per member with a subsidy of $70,000 per member. By far the heaviest mailroom traffic comes in Octobers of even-numbered years. There are some differences between House and Senate members in the ways they go about getting their names across. House members are free to blanket their constituencies with mailings for all boxholders; senators are not. But senators find it easier to appear on national television—for example, in short reaction statements on the nightly news shows. Advertising is a staple congressional activity, and there is no end to it. For each member there are always new voters to be apprised of his worthiness and old voters to be reminded of it.

A second activity may be called *credit claiming*, defined here as acting so as to generate a belief in a relevant political actor (or actors) that one is personally responsible for causing the government, or some unit thereof, to do something that the actor (or actors) considers desirable. The political logic of this, from the congressman's point of view, is that an actor who believes that a member can make pleasing things happen will no doubt wish to keep him in office so that he can make pleasing things happen in the future. The emphasis here is on individual accomplishment (rather than, say, party or governmental accomplishment) and on the congressman as doer (rather than as, say, expounder of constituency views). Credit claiming is highly important to congressmen, with the consequence that much of congressional life is a relentless search for opportunities to engage in it.

Where can credit be found? If there were only one congressman rather than 535, the answer would in principle be simple enough. Credit (or blame) would attach in Downsian fashion to the doings of the government as a whole. But there are 535. Hence it becomes necessary for each congressman to try to peel off pieces of governmental accomplishment for which he can believably generate a sense of responsibility. For the average congressman the staple way of doing this is to traffic in what may be called "particularized benefits." Particularized governmental benefits, as the term will be used here, have two properties: (1) Each benefit is given out to a specific individual, group, or geographical constituency, the recipient unit being of a scale that allows a single congressman to be recognized (by relevant political actors and other congressmen) as the claimant for the benefit (other congressmen being perceived as indifferent or hostile). (2) Each benefit is given out in apparently ad hoc fashion (unlike, say, social security checks) with a congressman apparently having a hand in the allocation. A particularized benefit can normally be regarded as a member of a class.

That is, a benefit given out to an individual, group, or constituency can normally be looked upon by congressmen as one of a class of similar benefits given out to sizable numbers of individuals, groups, or constituencies. Hence the impression can arise that a congressman is getting "his share" of whatever it is the government is offering. (The classes may be vaguely defined. Some state legislatures deal in what their members call "local legislation.")

In sheer volume the bulk of particularized benefits come under the heading of "casework"—the thousands of favors congressional offices perform for supplicants in ways that normally do not require legislative action. High school students ask for essay materials, soldiers for emergency leaves, pensioners for location of missing checks, local governments for grant information, and on and on. Each office has skilled professionals who can play the bureaucracy like an organ—pushing the right pedals to produce the desired effects. But many benefits require new legislation, or at least they require important allocative decisions on matters covered by existent legislation. Here the congressman fills the traditional role of supplier of goods to the home district. It is a believable role; when a member claims credit for a benefit on the order of a dam, he may well receive it. Shiny construction projects seem especially useful. In the decades before 1934, tariff duties for local industries were a major commodity. In recent years awards given under grant-in-aid programs have become more useful as they have become more numerous. Some quests for credit are ingenious; in 1971 the story broke that congressmen had been earmarking foreign aid money for specific projects in Israel in order to win favor with home constituents. It should be said of constituency benefits that congressmen are quite capable of taking the initiative in drumming them up; that is, there can be no automatic assumption that a congressman's activity is the result of pressures brought to bear by organized interests. Fenno shows the importance of member initiative in his discussion of the House Interior Committee.

A final point here has to do with geography. The examples given so far are all of benefits conferred upon home constituencies or recipients therein (the latter including the home residents who applauded the Israeli projects). But the properties of particularized benefits were carefully specified so as not to exclude the possibility that some benefits may be given to recipients outside the home constituencies. Some probably are. Narrowly drawn tax loopholes qualify as particularized benefits, and some of them are probably conferred upon recipients outside the home districts. (It is difficult to find solid evidence on the point.) Campaign contributions flow into districts from the outside, so it would not be surprising to find that benefits go where the resources are.

How much particularized benefits count for at the polls is extraordinarily difficult to say. But it would be hard to find a congressman who thinks he can afford to wait around until precise information is available. The lore is that they count—furthermore, given home expectations, that they must be supplied in regular quantities for a member to stay electorally even with the board. Awareness of favors may spread beyond their recipients, building for a member a general reputation as a good provider. "Rivers Delivers." "He Can Do More For Massachusetts." ...

... Is credit available elsewhere for governmental accomplishments beyond the scale of those already discussed? The general answer is that the prime mover role is a hard one to play on larger matters—at least before broad electorates. A claim, after all, has to be credible. If a congressman goes before an audience and says, "I am responsible for passing a bill to curb inflation," or "I am responsible for the highway program," hardly anyone will believe him. There are two reasons why people may be skeptical of such claims. First, there is a numbers problem. On an accomplishment of a sort that probably engaged the supportive interest of more than one member it is reasonable to suppose that credit should be apportioned among them. But second, there is an overwhelming problem of information costs. For typical voters Capitol Hill is a distant and mysterious place; few have anything like a working knowledge of its maneuverings. Hence there is no easy way of knowing whether a congressman is staking a valid claim or not. The odds are that the information problem cuts in different ways on different kinds of issues. On particularized benefits it may work in a congressman's favor; he may get credit for the dam he had nothing to do with building. Sprinkling a district with dams, after all, is something a congressman is supposed to be able to do. But on larger matters it may work against him. For a voter lacking an easy way to sort out valid from invalid claims the sensible recourse is skepticism. Hence it is unlikely that congressmen get much mileage out of credit claiming on larger matters before broad electorates.

Yet there is an obvious and important qualification here. For many congressmen credit claiming on nonparticularized matters is possible in specialized subject areas because of the congressional division of labor. The term "governmental unit" in the original definition of credit claiming is broad enough to include committees, subcommittees, and the two houses of Congress itself. Thus many congressmen can believably claim credit for blocking bills in subcommittee, adding on amendments in committee, and so on. The audience for transactions of this sort is usually small. But it may include important political actors (e.g., an interest group, the president, the *New York Times*, Ralph Nader) who are capable of both paying Capitol Hill information costs and deploying electoral resources. There is a well-documented example of this in Fenno's treatment of post office politics in the 1960s. The postal employee unions used to watch very closely the activities of the House and Senate Post Office Committees and supply valuable electoral resources (money, volunteer work) to members who did their bidding on salary bills. . . .

The third activity congressmen engage in may be called *position taking*, defined here as the public enunciation of a judgmental statement on anything likely to be of interest to political actors. The statement may take the form of a roll call vote. The most important classes of judgmental statements are those prescribing American governmental ends (a vote cast against the war; a statement that "the war should be ended immediately") or governmental means (a statement that "the way to end the war is to take it to the United Nations"). The judgments may be implicit rather than explicit, as in: "I will support the president on this matter." But judgments may range far beyond these classes to take in implicit or explicit statements on what almost anybody should do or how he should do it: "The great Polish scientist Copernicus has been unjustly neglected"; "The way for Israel to achieve peace is to give up the Sinai." The congressman as position taker is a speaker rather than a doer. The electoral requirement is not that he make pleasing things happen but that he make pleasing judgmental statements. The position itself is the political commodity. Especially on matters where governmental responsibility is widely diffused it is not surprising that political actors should fall back on positions as tests of incumbent virtue. For voters ignorant of congressional processes the recourse is an easy one. . . .

The ways in which positions can be registered are numerous and often imaginative. There are floor addresses ranging from weighty orations to mass-produced "nationality day statements." There are speeches before home groups, television appearances, letters, newsletters, press releases, ghostwritten books, . . . articles, even interviews with political scientists. On occasion congressmen generate what amount to petitions; whether or not to sign the 1956 Southern Manifesto defying school desegregation rulings was an important decision for southern members. Outside the roll call process the congressman is usually able to tailor his positions to suit his audiences. A solid consensus in the constituency calls for ringing declarations; for years the late Senator James K. Vardaman (D., Miss.) campaigned on a proposal to repeal the Fifteenth Amendment. Division or uncertainty in the constituency calls for waffling; in the late 1960s a congressman had to be a poor politician indeed not to be able to come up with an inoffensive statement on Vietnam ("We must have peace with honor at the earliest possible moment consistent with the national interest"). On a controversial issue a Capitol Hill office normally prepares two form letters to send out to constituent letter writers—one for the pros and one (not directly contradictory) for the antis. . . .

. . . Versatility of this sort is occasionally possible in roll call voting. For example a congressman may vote one way on recommittal and the other on final passage, leaving it unclear just how he stands on a bill. Members who cast identical votes on a measure may give different reasons for having done so. Yet it is on roll calls that the crunch comes; there is no way for a member to avoid making a record on hundreds of issues, some of which are controversial in the home constituencies. Of course, most roll call positions considered in isolation are not likely to cause much of a ripple at home. But broad voting patterns can and do; member "ratings" calculated by the Americans for Democratic Action, Americans for Constitutional Action, and other outfits are used as guidelines in the deploying of electoral resources. And particular issues often have their alert publics. Some national interest groups watch the votes of all congressmen on single issues and ostentatiously try to reward or punish members for their positions; over the years some notable examples of such interest groups have been the Anti-Saloon League, the early Farm Bureau, the American Legion, the American Medical Association, and the National Rifle Association. On rare occasions single roll calls achieve a rather high salience among the public generally. This seems especially true of the Senate, which every now and then winds up for what might be called a "showdown vote," with pressures on all sides, presidential involvement, media attention given to individual senators' positions, and suspense about the outcome. Examples are the votes on the nuclear test-ban treaty in 1963, civil rights cloture in 1964, civil rights cloture again in 1965, the Haynsworth appointment in 1969, the Carswell appointment in 1970, and the ABM in 1970. Controversies on roll calls like these are often relived in subsequent campaigns, the southern Senate elections of 1970 with their Haynsworth and Carswell issues being cases in point.

Probably the best position-taking strategy for most congressmen at most times is to be conservative—to cling to their own positions of the past where possible and to reach for new ones with great caution where necessary. Yet in an earlier discussion of strategy the suggestion was made that it might be rational for members in electoral danger to resort to innovation. The form of innovation available is entrepreneurial position taking, its logic being that for a member facing defeat with his old array of positions it makes good sense to gamble on some new ones. It may be that congressional marginals fulfill an important function here as issue pioneers—experimenters who test out new issues and thereby show other politicians which ones are usable. An example of such a pioneer is Senator Warren Magnuson (D., Wash.), who responded to a surprisingly narrow victory in 1962 by reaching for a reputation in the area of consumer affairs. Another example is Senator Ernest Hollings (D., S.C.), a servant of a shaky and racially heterogeneous southern constituency who launched "hunger" as an issue in 1969—at once pointing to a problem and giving it a useful nonracial definition. One of the most successful issue entrepreneurs of recent decades was the late

Senator Joseph McCarthy (R., Wis.); it was all there—the close primary in 1946, the fear of defeat in 1952, the desperate casting about for an issue, the famous 1950 dinner at the Colony Restaurant where suggestions were tendered, the decision that "Communism" might just do the trick.

The effect of position taking on electoral behavior is about as hard to measure as the effect of credit claiming. Once again there is a variance problem; congressmen do not differ very much among themselves in the methods they use or the skills they display in attuning themselves to their diverse constituencies. All of them, after all, are professional politicians. . . .

There can be no doubt that congressmen believe positions make a difference. An important consequence of this belief is their custom of watching each other's elections to try to figure out what positions are salable. Nothing is more important in Capitol Hill politics than the shared conviction that election returns have proven a point. . . .

These, then, are the three kinds of electorally oriented activities congressmen engage in—advertising, credit claiming, and position taking. It remains only to offer some brief comments on the emphases different members give to the different activities. No deterministic statements can be made; within limits each member has freedom to build his own electoral coalition and hence freedom to choose the means of doing it. Yet there are broad patterns. For one thing senators, with their access to the media, seem to put more emphasis on position taking than House members; probably House members rely more heavily on particularized benefits. But there are important differences among House members. Congressmen from the traditional parts of old machine cities rarely advertise and seldom take positions on anything (except on roll calls), but devote a great deal of time and energy to the distribution of benefits. In fact they use their office resources to plug themselves into their local party organizations. . . .

. . . [A] difference appears if the initial assumption of a reelection quest is relaxed to take into account the "progressive" ambitions of some members—the aspirations of some to move up to higher electoral offices rather than keep the ones they have. There are two important subsets of climbers in the Congress—House members who would like to be senators (over the years about a quarter of the senators have come up directly from the House), and senators who would like to be presidents or vice presidents (in the Ninety-third Congress about a quarter of the senators had at one time or another run for these offices or been seriously "mentioned" for them). In both cases higher aspirations seem to produce the same distinctive mix of activities. For one thing credit claiming is all but useless. It does little good to talk about the bacon you have brought back to a district you are trying to abandon. And, as Lyndon Johnson found in 1960, claiming credit on legislative maneuvers is no way to reach a new mass audience;

it baffles rather than persuades. Office advancement seems to require a judicious mixture of advertising and position taking. Thus a House member aiming for the Senate heralds his quest with press releases; there must be a new "image," sometimes an ideological overhaul to make ready for the new constituency. Senators aiming for the White House do more or less the same thing—advertising to get the name across, position taking ("We can do better"). In recent years presidential aspirants have sought Foreign Relations Committee membership as a platform for making statements on foreign policy.

There are these distinctions, but it would be a mistake to elevate them over the commonalities. For most congressmen most of the time all three activities are essential. . . .

6-3

Congressional Trends

Steven S. Smith

Congress is the world's most powerful national legislature, in large part because of the formal powers granted to it by the U.S. Constitution more than two centuries ago. Yet as political scientist Steven Smith explains in this essay, Congress still is a rapidly changing institution. New-style politics, the new media, an evolving membership, new policy demands, election outcomes, and most recently the war against terrorism have changed virtually every aspect of congressional politics—the setting, the players, institutional advantages, and the issue arenas. Smith argues that members of Congress suffer from their inability to act efficiently, to prevent occasional scandals, to resist the pressures of constituency demands and campaigns, to avoid intense partisanship, and to compete effectively with the president, particularly in the area of national security.

THE UNITED STATES Congress is an amazing institution. It is the most powerful national legislature. It serves as an important check on one-man rule by the president. Many dedicated individuals, both elected and unelected, work in Congress. To be sure, there is much about congressional politics that is distasteful— partisanship infuses it, large egos roam the halls of Capitol Hill, and the formalities often seem stuffy and antiquated. Still, the ability of 535 elected representatives to peacefully resolve the conflicts that arise in a society approaching 300 million people remains an amazing feat.

Perhaps the most fascinating aspect of Congress is that it is always changing. New problems, whatever their sources, invariably create new demands on it. Elections bring new members, who often alter the balance of opinion in the House and the Senate. And each new president asks for support for a new policy program. Members of Congress usually respond to these demands by passing new legislation. But as they pursue their personal political goals, compete with each other for control over policy, and react to pressure from presidents, constituents, and lobbyists, lawmakers sometimes seek to gain advantage or to remove impediments to action by altering the procedures and organization of Congress itself. This is made easier by the fact that the Constitution outlines only a few key features of congressional decision-making processes: both houses must agree to legislation before it is sent to the president for signature or veto;

one-fifth of each house may demand the yeas and nays (a recorded vote); an elected Speaker presides over the House of Representatives, while the vice president serves as the president of the Senate.

The purpose of this essay is to highlight modern trends in congressional politics and explore the reasons behind them. Overall, Congress has become a more representative institution, but the ability of its members to exercise independent judgment in policy making has been challenged by a number of recent developments in American politics. Open government, divided-party control of the policy-making institutions, new technologies, and new issues make the lawmakers' tasks more challenging. In spite of their great collective power, members of Congress suffer from their inability to act efficiently, to prevent occasional scandals, to resist the pressures of constituency demands and campaigns, to avoid intense partisanship, and to compete effectively with the president, particularly in the area of national security.

Self-Inflicted Wounds

For James Madison, representative government served two purposes—to make the law responsive to the values and interests of the people and to allow representatives to make law. The second purpose was, and is, controversial. Madison explained in *Federalist* No. 10 (see chapter 2) that he hoped representatives would rise above the inevitable influence of public opinion to make policy for the public "good." Arguing in favor of representative government for a large country, Madison insisted that America would be best served by "representatives whose enlightened views and virtuous sentiments" would "render them superior to local prejudices and schemes of injustice." Representatives, not the people themselves, were more likely to be good policy makers.

Modern Americans do not share Madison's view. A poll conducted in 2001 by Princeton Survey Research Associates for the Kaiser Foundation showed that 68 percent of the respondents said the views of the majority should have a great deal of influence on policy. Thus while Madison believed legislators should be *trustees*—representing their constituents by exercising independent judgment about the interests of the nation—only a minority of modern Americans would agree. Most seem to expect elected representatives to faithfully present their constituents' views—that is, to be *delegates* for their constituents. A delegate-legislator, however, would not have an easy job because constituents often have conflicting or ambiguous views (or none at all) about the issues before Congress.

People's views about Congress itself are not ambiguous, however. Political scientists John R. Hibbing and Elizabeth Theiss-Morse have discovered that while Americans do show an appreciation for Congress as an institution, they have

Figure 1. Percent of Respondents Saying That They Have a "Great Deal" of Confidence in National Political Institutions (Gallup Poll)

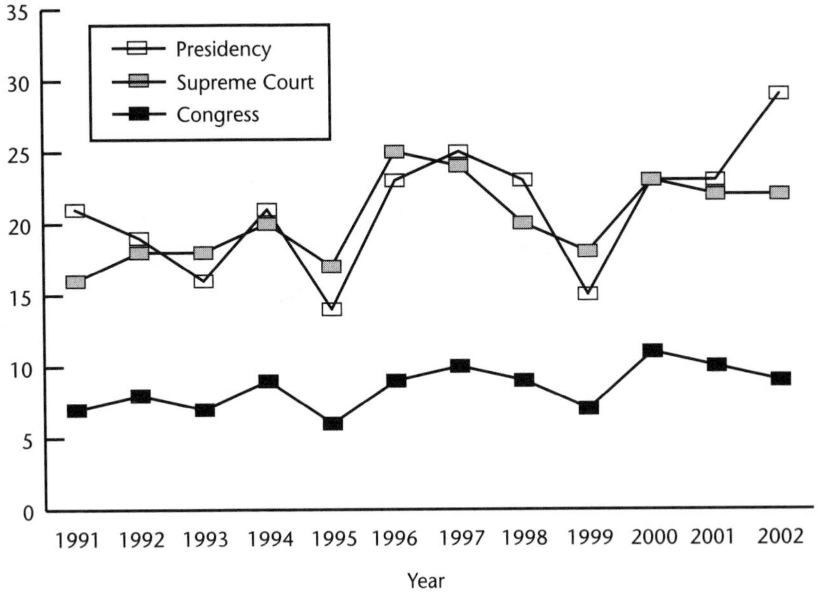

Source: http://roperweb.ropercenter.uconn.edu/cgi-bin/hsrun.exe/roperweb/pom/pom.htx;start=HS_special_topics?Topic=congress.

little confidence in its members collectively.[1] Congress is seldom given high marks by the general public; in fact, its ratings are often very, very low. Confidence in Congress ebbs and flows with the public's confidence in government generally, but seldom do more than a few Americans have a great deal of it. For many years, the Gallup organization has asked a sample of respondents how much confidence they have in Congress, the president, and the Supreme Court. As Figure 1 shows, Americans always report less confidence in Congress than in the other institutions.

Congress's openness to the media and the public, in contrast to the closed decision-making meetings of the White House and Supreme Court, may make it especially vulnerable to unfavorable comparisons. The legislative process is easy to dislike—it often generates political posturing and grandstanding, it necessarily involves compromise and deal making, and it frequently leaves broken campaign promises in its trail.

Still, members of Congress themselves often are responsible for the disparagement and ridicule directed at their institution. Scandals, which involve only a tiny fraction of the membership, add to the public's frustration with Congress and seem to regularly contribute to the institution's low ratings in opinion polls.

Highlights of congressional scandals from the past decade or so are listed in Box 1.

Political scientist Norman J. Ornstein worries that the media has placed an increasing emphasis on the negative and sensational side of Congress, which he labels the "tabloidization" of media coverage. "The drive to emulate the *National Enquirer* and the *Star* has spread to the most respectable newspapers and magazines," Ornstein argues, "while network news divisions have begun to compete with tabloids like 'Inside Edition' and 'Hard Copy' with their own tabloid shows like 'Prime Time Live' and 'Dateline: NBC,' and with changed coverage on the nightly news." Stories or rumors of scandal—both individual and institutional—have dominated news coverage of politics and politicians in recent decades more than at any other time in modern history, and not just in terms of column inches or broadcast minutes but in emphasis as well. Ornstein explains that "the expansion of radio and cable television talk shows also seems to have increased the speed with which bad news about Congress is disseminated and the frequency with which bad news is repeated. On many of these programs, there is a premium on a quick wit and a good one-liner and little time for sober, balanced commentary."[2]

Candidates for Congress quickly exploit themes that resonate with the public. As a result, running *for* Congress by running *against* Congress, an old art form in American politics, has gained an even more prominent place in recent campaigns. Indeed, many recent arrivals on Capitol Hill promised to end "business as usual" in Washington and to push through reforms to "fix" Congress—to end the system of congressional perks, to stop the influence of special interests, and so on. Among each new cohort of legislators are members who complained about the "inside-the-beltway" (referring, of course, to the freeway that encircles the District of Columbia) mentality of their predecessors. The repetition of anti-Congress themes by its own members has contributed, no doubt, to the declining ratings for Congress and its lawmakers in public opinion polls.

The Plebiscitary Syndrome

Congress suffers from the increasingly plebiscitary nature of American politics, according to political scientist Robert A. Dahl. By a movement toward plebiscitary politics, Dahl means more direct communication between the public and elected officials and the demise of intermediaries—such as parties, civic groups, and membership organizations—that once served to represent public opinion to elected officials.[3] New technologies facilitate communication and feedback. For example, public opinion polls have become more affordable because of advancements in telephone and computer technology. Radio and television call-in shows enable nearly every constituent to talk directly to a member of Congress from

Box 1. Congressional Scandals since 1989

- In 1989 House Speaker James Wright, D-Texas, resigned after Republicans charged him with ethics violations in connection with his royalties on a book.

- In 1991 Sen. David Durenburger, R-Minn., in a unanimously approved Senate resolution, was condemned for a book deal and for seeking reimbursement for expenses for staying in a condo he owned.

- The Senate's handling of Anita Hill's charges of sexual harassment against Supreme Court nominee Clarence Thomas raised questions about fairness and sensitivity in the Senate.

- The disclosure that many House members had repeatedly overdrawn their accounts at the House bank led people to believe that members enjoyed special privileges, and it led to news stories about cheap haircuts, special parking privileges, and other perks for lawmakers.

- Questions about the propriety of campaign contributions were raised in the "Keating Five" affair, which concerned the relationship between five senators and a prominent savings-and-loan owner seeking to block an investigation of his financial dealings.

- Two top House employees pleaded guilty to charges of taking money from operations they had supervised.

- In 1995 a long investigation of sexual harassment charges against Sen. Robert Packwood, R-Ore., led to his forced resignation from office.

- In 1995 Rep. Dan Rostenkowski, D-Ill., former chairman of the House Ways and Means Committee, was found guilty of illegally receiving cash for personal use from the House post office. He later served a prison term.

- In 1995 Rep. Enid Waldholtze, R-Utah, retired after her husband was charged with felonies in conjunction with raising funds for her campaign.

- In 1997 Speaker Newt Gingrich, R-Ga., agreed to pay $300,000 in fines based on charges that he used nonprofit organizations for political purposes and misled the House Committee on Standards of Official Conduct.

- In 1998 Rep. Jay Kim, R-Calif., pleaded guilty to charges involving more than $250,000 in illegal campaign contributions.

- In 2001 Rep. Gary Condit, D-Calif., was embarrassed by disclosure of an affair with an office intern who later disappeared and was found murdered (authorities did not associate Condit with the murder).

- In 2002 Rep. James A. Traficant Jr., D-Ohio, was found guilty of receiving brides in exchange for helping businesses get government contracts and of engaging in a pattern of racketeering since taking office in 1985.

- In 2002 Sen. Robert Torricelli, D-N.J., dropped out of a bid for reelection after it became clear that he would be defeated because of Senate ethics committee condemnation for accepting money and gifts from a donor.

- In 2002 the bankruptcy of the energy market giant Enron brought attention to the fact that the company had donated about $1.1 million to congressional candidates in the previous eleven years, including donations to 188 representatives and 71 senators of that Congress.

time to time. "Town meetings" broadcast on radio and television serve the same function. Computerized mass mailings flow in and out of Washington every day. Satellite technology allows members to easily and inexpensively communicate with groups in their districts or home states. Constituents can reach most members by electronic mail. And advances in air travel allow a large number of representatives and senators to be back in their districts and states for most weekends. For elected officials, the urge to exploit the new technologies is irresistible.

Plebiscitary politics may appear to be an encouraging development. It seems better to have public opinion influencing members' decisions than to have highly paid lobbyists representing organized interests swaying congressional votes. But as Dahl notes, the effects of direct communication between the people and their representatives on Capitol Hill may not be so desirable for several reasons. First, elected officials and special interests could manipulate direct communication to their advantage. If the politicians are the ones who choose the time and place for direct communication, the process could create nothing more than a deceiving appearance of responsiveness. Second, the "public" likely to communicate directly with members may not be representative of the members' larger constituencies. They would probably be people intensely interested in either politics in general or a single issue who can afford, and know how to use, new information technologies. If so, then members' impressions of public opinion could be distorted by such communication. And third, as Madison might have argued, direct communication with more constituents could lead members to make premature public commitments on more issues and reduce their flexibility in negotiating compromises in the legislative arena. The likely result would be that demagoguery and grandstanding would take precedence over resolving conflicts and solving problems. Public opinion could win out over the public interest.

If Dahl is right, then new information technologies could further intensify public frustration with Congress and encourage even more catering to public opinion by members. The emergence of a plebiscitary syndrome in Congress—marked by hypersensitivity to public opinion, grandstanding, rigidity, and paralysis, with new policy enacted only when the risk of inaction becomes too severe—could be the result. The natural response of elected officials and their challengers to such circumstances could be to encourage even more plebiscitary democracy and make matters worse.

The Campaign Complex

A close cousin to the plebiscitary syndrome is the campaign complex—the merging of campaigning and governing. Of course, we hope for a strong linkage between governing and campaigning as a basis for holding policy makers accountable. Broadly speaking, campaign promises are (and should be) related to governing, and election outcomes are (and should be) shaped by performance in office. Inevitably, then, the line between governing and campaigning becomes blurred. Yet in recent decades campaigning has become more fully integrated with governing. No longer is governing done in Washington and campaigning done at home. Members and top leaders now gear their daily routines to the demands of campaigning, and decisions by policy makers appear to be an extension of campaigns.

The costs of modern campaigns are staggering. Today a victor in a Senate race in an average-size state can spend nearly $10 million; the number of House victors spending more than a million dollars is high and rising. (Many races in recent years actually have been far more expensive—those totals exclude money spent by parties and outside groups.) For an incumbent seeking reelection, that is an average of more than $32,000 for each week served during a six-year Senate term and about $10,000 for each week served during a two-year House term. These figures reflect a rapid rise in campaign expenditures in the 1970s and early 1980s, some leveling off in the mid-1980s, and escalating costs since the early 1990s. Competitive pressures, between incumbents and challengers and between the two parties, have produced a never-ending search for cash. In the view of many observers, the need for money reduces time for other activities, including time for the give-and-take of legislating.

The campaign complex extends beyond the rank-and-file members to congressional leaders. Party leaders spend many evenings and weekends at fundraising events. Many leaders have developed their own political action committees (leadership PACs, they have been called) to raise and distribute money. Leaders have formed public relations task forces within their parties, and the campaign committees of the congressional parties have greatly expanded their activities. Perhaps most important, congressional leaders now often use political and information technology developed for campaigning in legislative battles. Professional consultants and pollsters help fashion legislative priorities and tactics. Opposition research—digging up dirt on your election opponent—is conducted against congressional colleagues of the opposite party. Media campaigns are planned for major legislative proposals, with the assistance of television-advertising specialists. Money, media, and partisanship feed on each other.

The Lobbying Cauldron

In recent decades the number of interest groups in Washington and the rest of the country has multiplied many times over. By one count, groups increased from about one thousand in the late 1940s to more than seven thousand in the early 1980s. This is primarily a byproduct of the expanding scope of the federal government's activity—as federal programs affected more interests, more interests sought representation in Washington. Technological developments in transportation, information management, and communications have enabled scattered people, corporations, and even state and local governments to easily organize, raise money, and set up offices and staff in Washington. The process feeds on itself, with new groups forming to counter the influence of other groups. As a result, there has been a tremendous increase in the demands placed on members of Congress by lobbyists from organized groups.

Interest groups have not only multiplied but also become more diverse. In addition to groups associated with economic interests, many of them representing new industries, "citizens'" groups sprouted in the 1960s and 1970s and continue to grow in number. These groups are often outgrowths of national movements—such as those for civil rights, women's rights, children's rights, the elimination of hunger, consumers' rights, welfare rights, gay rights, environmental protection, and helping the homeless. Many of these groups attract funding from foundations and philanthropists, and some enjoy memberships numbering in the hundreds of thousands.

In recent years groups also have become more skilled in camouflaging their true identities—and thereby the exact nature of their interests. For most major legislative battles, coalitions of groups and corporations form under appealing all-American names and pool their resources to fund mass media campaigns to generate support; they often dissolve as quickly as they were created. Many coalitions are the handiwork of entrepreneurs in law firms, consulting outfits, and public relations shops who are paid to coordinate the activity of the coalitions they spearhead.

Campaign finance reforms in the early 1970s enabled all interest groups, both profit and nonprofit, to create political action committees and become active contributors to legislators' election campaigns. Needless to say, campaign contributors have an edge over others in gaining the attention of legislators. More than that, the availability of money from political action committees has greatly reduced candidates' reliance on parties for the resources critical to winning elections. In the past decade unregulated contributions—called soft money—to parties and other political entities have exceeded direct, regulated contributions to candidates, but such contributions may soon be banned by law.

The roots have been taken out of grassroots lobbying. New technologies provide the ability to make highly targeted, highly efficient appeals to stimulate constituency demands on Washington. By the late 1980s computerized telephone messages allowed groups to communicate with many thousands of people within a few hours. Technology now allows a group to telephone its own members, a targeted group (such as one House member's constituency), or the general public; briefly interview the respondents about their views on a subject; and for respondents who favor the group's position, provide a few more facts to reinforce their views, solicit them to write letters to members of Congress, and quickly transfer the calls to the appropriate Capitol Hill offices before the respondents hang up. Several groups have developed television programs—some shown on the many cable television channels available in most communities—as a way of reaching specific audiences. Lobbyists are already planning ways to take advantage of electronic mail and interactive video technologies to flood Congress with constituents' messages. As a result, for a group with money, the absence of a large membership is not much of an obstacle to generating public pressure on members of Congress.

It would be a mistake, however, to conclude that all the pressuring in Washington comes from lobbyists. Members of Congress, particularly the most powerful, expect their friends in the lobbying community to provide campaign contributions. Furthermore, powerful members often call on the lobbyists to employ their own resources—such as ad campaigns, campaign contributions, and person-to-person lobbying—to support the lawmakers in their legislative battles. Thus in the cauldron of political relationships between legislators and organized interests, influence runs in many directions.

The Unexpected and the Complex

New issues—such as the war against terrorism—always present some difficulty for Congress. They often create problems for congressional committees, whose official jurisdictions were defined years earlier when no one anticipated those issues. Committees scramble to assert jurisdiction, and committee leaders or the parent chambers are asked to referee. After a certain amount of infighting and delay, committees eventually manage to adjust. In the view of some observers, however, new issues are surfacing at an increasing rate, and Congress's ability to adjust in a timely manner is becoming more and more strained.

The issues facing Congress are also becoming more technical and complex. Increasingly, expertise in science, engineering, information technology, economics, or other specialized fields is required to understand policy problems and alternatives. Congress often solves this problem, political scientist Theodore J. Lowi emphasizes, by setting broad policy goals and delegating the power to

Figure 2. Number of Bills Enacted and Pages Enacted

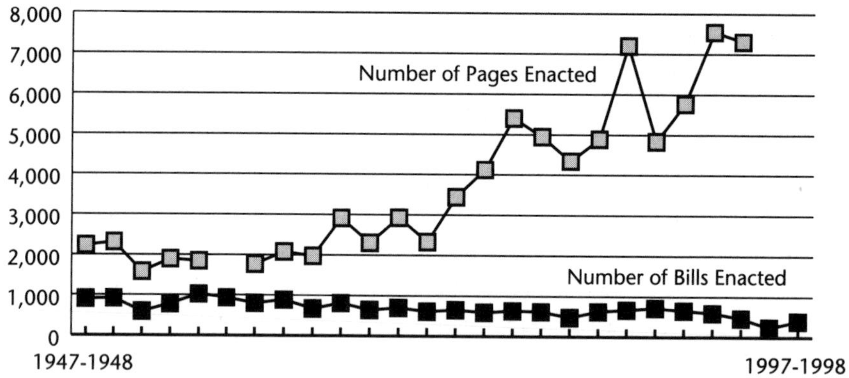

Source: *United States Statutes at Large* (Washington, D.C.: Government Printing Office, 1937–)

make the necessary technical decisions to experts in the executive branch.[4] In this way, Congress is able to respond to demands for action—but it does so at the cost of enhancing the executive branch's power over the details of public policy. At other times, Congress seeks to legislate the technical details, but the cost then is that only a few members and staff assistants can understand the legislation and participate effectively in making important decisions. Scientific and medical research, defense programs, environmental protection, the regulation of financial institutions, international trade, and many other fields of public policy are no longer within the common experiences of elected officials. Thus most members must look to competing interpretations of proposed legislation offered by staff specialists, lobbyists, and a wide array of outside experts.

The increasing complexity of the issues facing Congress is a result of the increasing complexity of American society, of technological and organizational innovation, and of the integration of the international and domestic economies. Fewer major policies can be debated in isolation from other major policies. For example, health care reform concerns issues such as employer-employee relations, economic growth, welfare reform, and tax policy. This complexity leads Congress to craft unwieldy bills, often written by multiple committees, laden with technical language, and comprising several hundred pages. Other factors, such as the desire to consolidate legislation into omnibus bills, have contributed to bill size as well. Figure 2 shows the increasing length of the average bill enacted in recent decades. The length of bills presents a serious challenge to legislators who might want to understand the legislation on which they are asked to cast votes.

Political scientist Lawrence L. Dodd believes that Congress, at least as it now operates, cannot cope with the important issues of our time. In his view, the problem lies in the relationship between members and their constituents:

> The voters may see the decay of urban infrastructure, sense the declining educational and job opportunities of their children, acknowledge the ecological damage of industrial pollution, and worry about the long-term effects of a mounting deficit. But as they consider their vote for senator and representative, the citizens override any broad concerns they may have with collective issues and vote in accord with ensuring immediate benefits; they do so by voting for the powerful local incumbent who can assist with a desired local defense contract or who can help them with their veterans claim or Medicare benefits. They do so because of the immediate influence that a powerful incumbent legislator can have on their particularized interests. Likewise, the legislators may share a growing concern with collective societal and economic reversals. But their efforts to maintain electoral security and exercise personal influence in Congress are best served by focusing on those particularized programs that mobilize group support, that help them build a solid reputation as effective legislators, and that ensure election. The emerging collective problems of the new era thus go unacknowledged and tear away at the fabric of society.[5]

If Dodd is right, then the public's ratings of congressional performance will be low for many years to come.

Congress's tendency is to allow the president to define solutions to the nation's problems and then to criticize those solutions from narrow, often parochial, perspectives. Unfortunately, plebiscitary politics, the proliferation of interest groups, and the new ways technology has provided for influencing members of Congress reinforce this tendency. Modern politics puts more pressure than ever on members to explain themselves in terms readily understood by the folks back home. Scholar and congressman David E. Price, D-N.C., observes, "Members must constantly explain themselves and their actions in terms of ordinary knowledge. A decision that does not lend itself to such an explanation often has a heavy burden of proof against it. In the era of television journalism, of thirty-second ads and negative advertising, a defensive deference to ordinary knowledge has probably become more important in congressional behavior than it was before."[6] The gap between what legislators do and what they can explain seems to be widening.

Regional and Group Representation

In recent decades demographic and social changes in American society have altered the composition of Congress in important ways. One significant change

Table 1. Changes in the Apportionment of House Seats,
by Region, 1960–2000

Region	Post-1960 Seats	Post-2000 Seats	Difference
East	108	83	−25
Midwest	125	100	−25
South	133	154	21
West	69	98	29
Total	435	435	

Source: Census Bureau, http://www.census.gov/population/www/censusdata/
apportionment.html.

has been in the allocation of House seats to the states. The 435 seats of the House are reapportioned every ten years to reflect changes in the distribution of the nation's population across the states. A formula in law guides the Census Bureau, which calculates the number of districts for each state every ten years after the decennial census. Population shifts have allowed certain states in the South and West to gain seats in the House of Representatives at the expense of several eastern and midwestern states. The regional shifts are visible in Table 1. Census Bureau projections suggest that the South and West will gain even more seats after the national census in the year 2000—again at the expense of the industrial Northeast and Midwest.

The redistribution of seats away from the northern industrial states has reduced their political clout at a time when they could use it. The need for infrastructure repairs, worker retraining, low-income housing, and other government services is more severe in the old industrial states than in other regions of the country. Yet these states' declining influence in the House is reducing their ability to acquire financial assistance from the federal government. Indeed, the shift of power to the more conservative regions of the country has undercut congressional support for a major federal role in the rehabilitation of the industrial cities of the northern-tier states.

Economic growth, an influx of workers from the older industrial states, and the expansion of the middle class in the South and West have all spurred the population growth there. The most obvious consequence of these developments is that the South is no longer a one-party region, as it was just three decades ago. Republicans are now competitive in Senate races throughout the South and hold many House seats as well. As recently as 1960 Republicans held no Senate seats and only 6 of 104 House seats in the states of the old Confederacy. After the 1992 elections Republicans held 13 of the 22 Senate seats and 48 of the 125 House seats in the region, with the largest numbers in Florida and Texas. The southern Senate seats were critical to Republicans between 1981 and 1986, when they controlled the Senate, and again after 1994.

The houses of Congress have also acquired a sizable contingent of women and minorities. The growing strength of women's and minority groups, the acquisition of political experience by women and minority politicians in state and local government, and new voting laws have contributed to the recent improvement in congressional representation. In 1993 the Senate gained its first black woman, Carol Moseley-Braun, D-Ill., and its first Native American, Ben Nighthorse Campbell, D-Colo. (who later switched parties). Table 2 shows the gains that women, African Americans, and Hispanics have made in Congress in recent years. Even more—many more—women and minorities have been running for Congress. More than one hundred women have been major party candidates for Congress in each election since 1992.

Though women and minorities remain greatly underrepresented in Congress, most observers agree that female and minority lawmakers have already had a substantial impact. Most obviously, the Congressional Caucus for Women's Issues (fifty-six members in 2001), the Congressional Black Caucus (thirty-seven members in 2001), and, to a lesser extent, the Congressional Hispanic Caucus (twenty-one members in 2001) have become important factions within the House Democratic party—although all three have Republican members. More generally, issues important to these groups have been given higher priority by party leaders, and the interests of women and minorities have been given greater prominence in debates on many pieces of legislation. Indeed, social and economic problems seem to be more frequently discussed in the first person today— that is, more members refer to their personal experiences when addressing their colleagues and constituents. Two women have held first-tier positions (Rep. Nancy Pelosi of California was elected House Democratic whip in 2001 and then minority leader in 2002; Rep. Deborah Pryce of Ohio was elected House Republican Conference chair in 2002) and others have held second-tier party positions, and even more have gained sufficient seniority to chair important committees and subcommittees. Only one African American, J. C. Watts of Oklahoma, who served as House Republican Conference chair in 1998–2002, has held a first-tier position. When Rep. Robert Menendez of New Jersey became the House Democratic Caucus chair in 2002, he became the highest-ranking Hispanic legislator in the history of Congress.

Notable changes have occurred as well in members' occupational profiles. Though lawyers and business executives still predominate (with nearly 250

Table 2. Number of Women and Minorities in the House
and Senate, 1971–2002

Congress (First Year)	Women		African Americans		Hispanic Americans	
	House	Senate	House	Senate	House	Senate
92d (1971)	12	1	12	1	5	1
93d (1973)	14	0	15	1	5	1
94th (1975)	18	0	16	1	5	1
95th (1977)	18	0	16	1	5	0
96th (1979)	16	1	16	0	6	0
97th (1981)	19	2	16	0	6	0
98th (1983)	21	2	20	0	10	0
99th (1985)	22	2	19	0	11	0
100th (1987)	23	2	22	0	11	0
101st (1989)	25	2	23	0	11	0
102d (1991)	29	2	25	0	10	0
103d (1993)	48	6	38	1	17	0
104th (1995)	49	8	39	1	18	0
105th (1997)	51	9	37	1	18	0
106th (1999)	58	9	39	0	19	0
107th (2001)	49	13	36	0	19	0
108th (2003)	60	14	37	0	22	0

Sources: *Vital Statistics on American Politics* (Washington, D.C.: CQ Press, 2000), 201; 107th and
108th Congresses data collected by the author.

lawyers and 150 executives) and the number of farmers has declined (down from
about seventy-five in the 1950s to about twenty-five in 1994), the occupational
backgrounds of members overall are now somewhat more diverse than three or
four decades ago. Educators, for instance, have become more numerous.

These trends in the membership of Congress—the shift to the Sunbelt, the
growing numbers of women and minority members, and the greater diversity in
members' previous experience—are likely to continue well into this century.
They will probably continue to be sources of change in the way Congress con-
ducts its business and in the policy choices Congress makes.

Oscillating Party Control

Shifting majority control has been perhaps the most conspicuous change in Congress in recent years—the advent of Republican control of both houses after the
1994 elections, the switch back to Democratic control in the Senate in 2001 after
Senator James Jeffords of Vermont gave up his Republican affiliation, and the

Republicans' victories in 2002 that allowed them to regain a Senate majority. With an evenly divided electorate, we have experienced a prolonged period of narrow majorities in both houses in the last decade.

Political scientist Richard F. Fenno Jr. argues that frequent changes in party control keep the arrogance of the majority party in check.[7] It may also reduce the temptation for a new majority to overreach itself once in office. For instance, according to Fenno because in 1994 it had been 40 years since the Republicans had controlled the House, when they took over they were both inexperienced and impatient. This led them to overstate their mandate from the 1994 elections, translate that inflated mandate into rigid and ultimately unsuccessful legislative strategies, and perhaps contributed to the reelection of Democrat Bill Clinton to the presidency in 1996.

Fenno also observes that the long era of Democratic rule led the Republicans, prior to their 1994 takeover, to adopt radical measures to end it. The Republicans assumed an uncompromising stance in Congress, making legislating more difficult and heightening partisanship. Then after the Republicans gained control, Speaker Gingrich led a rhetorical assault on the very institution his party had fought to control, contributing to a further loss of public support for Congress.

If Fenno is correct, frequently alternating control of Congress will produce greater flexibility in Democratic and Republican policy positions, more pragmatic party strategies, greater civility in political discourse, and perhaps greater public support for the institution. A political "uncertainty principle"—that an uncertain electoral future breeds political moderation—may be at work. It is too early to tell whether Fenno is right. A reasonable argument can be made that split-party control, even with occasional change in party control, has contributed to intensified partisanship and a politics of blame that has hardly bred moderation and civility.

Revived Centralization

During most of the twentieth century, the standard assessment of Congress was that most policy decisions were really made by committees and ratified by the parent house. Analysts described reliance on committees as "decentralized" decision making, which contrasted with a hypothetical "centralized" pattern in which leaders of the majority party orchestrated policy making. The decentralized pattern seemed appropriate—legislators who specialized in the subject matter of their committees would guide policy making. In fact, the decentralized-centralized continuum always fit the larger House of Representatives better than the Senate. In the Senate, with the possibility of floor filibusters and the ability of senators to offer amendments on nearly any subject to most bills, more decisions were effectively decided on the floor. Decision making in the Senate might better have been called "collegial" rather than either centralized or decentralized.

The House and Senate went through a period of reform in the early 1970s that led observers of the day to warn about the dangers of fragmentation in congressional policy making. In the House, majority party Democrats guaranteed that most legislation would originate in well-staffed subcommittees under the guidance of chairs who operated independently of full committee chairs. The coordinating and integrating influence of the central leaders and committee chairs appeared to be waning, and Congress seemed to be losing whatever ability it had to enact coherent policy. All of this happened at a time when the pressures brought by new interest groups, new lobbying strategies, and new issues were mounting. Although Congress had become a more open and democratic institution, its capacity to manage the nation's affairs seemed diminished.

By the mid-1980s, however, Congress—again, particularly the House—had not turned out as many observers expected. The congressional agenda had become more focused, the parties more polarized and central party leaders more assertive, and the decentralization of power to the subcommittees had been tempered. Although Congress did not revert to its old ways, it acquired a new mix of characteristics that justified a new label—the postreform Congress. The root causes seemed to be changes in the parties' electoral coalitions, the dominance of budget politics, divided party control of the houses of Congress and the presidency, and the associated intensification of partisanship.

Perhaps the most important electoral trend of the late twentieth century was the replacement of some conservative southern Democrats with conservative Republicans. The partisan replacement made the Democrats in Congress more liberal on balance and reinforced the conservatism of congressional Republicans. This polarization of congressional parties led members to turn to party leaders for more central coordination of legislative and electoral strategies and contributed to sharpened partisanship in Washington.

The large federal budget deficit was a dominant force in legislative politics from 1980 to 1995. Few new federal programs were initiated, and much, if not most, of the period's important legislation consisted of large budget bills, particularly budget-reconciliation bills, which are the handiwork of many congressional committees and affect the full range of federal programs over multiple years. This emphasis on large, all-encompassing budget bills further reduced the ability of committees and individual members to pursue policy initiatives. The great electoral importance of such comprehensive bills required that top leaders—the president and congressional party leaders—be intimately involved in the negotiations.

Renewed large deficits, with the advent of the war against terrorism, guarantee that centralized strategizing and negotiations will continue.

Divided party control of the House, Senate, and the presidency has appeared to further intensify partisanship since the 1970s, as each institution and party has tried to avoid blame for ballooning deficits, unmet demands for action on social problems, and economic hard times. In the past three decades, top party leaders have begun to speak more authoritatively for their parties, and party regulars have looked to these leaders to define a legislative program and more aggressively promote party views in the media. For at least a year or so after the Republicans gained a majority of House seats in 1994, Speaker Gingrich came to be recognized as the most powerful Speaker since Joseph Cannon, R-Ill., in the first decade of the twentieth century. Gingrich's successor, Speaker Dennis Hastert, R-Ill., remains remarkably active in all major policy decisions. Even Senate party leaders—Republican Trent Lott and Democrat Tom Daschle—are deeply involved in defining and promoting legislative programs originating in party, rather than committee, deliberations.

Secret Government and Transparent Policy Making

Perhaps the most serious challenge to Congress's role in the American constitutional system is secret government necessitated by national security. The war against terrorism has revived fears that secrecy in the national security agencies will undermine Congress's ability to influence the direction of policy, to oversee the expenditure of public funds, and to hold executive officials accountable. Executive branch officials are hesitant to reveal certain information to members of Congress because they do not trust the legislators to keep it secret. For their part, legislators cannot know what information is being withheld from Congress, so secret government tends to breed distrust on Capitol Hill.

In the 1970s, in the aftermath of the Vietnam War and disclosures of misdeeds by intelligence agencies, Congress enacted various laws that required notification of Congress before the commitment of armed forces abroad, arms sales, and covert operations. Congress also granted itself the power to approve or disapprove such actions in certain cases. In addition, Congress created intelligence committees and established other mechanisms for handling classified information. Yet since then, many members of Congress have been unwilling to assume some responsibility for national security policy by exploiting the new laws or insisting on presidential cooperation. Presidents of both parties have disliked being constrained by these laws, arguing at times that the laws unconstitutionally impinge on presidential powers. The result is continuing uncertainty about when congressional approval is required. Congressional participation in national security policy making varies from case to case, driven as much by political considerations as by legal ones.

The fight against terrorism poses special challenges for members of Congress. More classified activity, more covert action, and a bewildering array of technologies are involved. More domestic police activity is conducted under the umbrella of national security. The need for quick, coordinated, multi-agency action has intensified. Congress is not well suited to effectively checking such executive action. It is open and slow, its division of labor among committees not well matched to the executive agencies involved, and its members hesitant to challenge the executive branch on high-risk policies and in areas where the public is likely to defer to the president.

A Resilient Institution

The ways in which representation and lawmaking are pursued in Congress have evolved in important ways in recent decades. As this essay has implied, not all of these developments have improved representation or lawmaking. Plebiscitary politics, interest group pressure, media coverage, and secret government present new challenges to members of Congress. They risk being so politically constrained in their decision making that their potential for creative, independent policy making will be undermined.

Still, however serious we judge the problems of today's Congress, we should remember that it is a remarkably resilient institution. Its place in the political process is not threatened. It is rich in resources; critics even charge that it is too strong. The legitimacy of its decisions is not seriously questioned by the chief executive, the courts, the states, or the American people, and Congress remains a vital check on the exercise of power by other institutions of government.

NOTES

1. John R. Hibbing and Elizabeth Theiss-Morse, *Congress as Public Enemy: Public Attitudes toward American Political Institutions* (New York: Cambridge University Press, 1995).

2. Norman J. Ornstein, "Congress Inside Out: Here's Why Life on the Hill Is Meaner Than Ever," *Roll Call,* September 20,1993, 27.

3. Robert A. Dahl, "Americans Struggle to Cope with a New Political Order That Works in Opaque and Mysterious Ways," *Public Affairs Report* (Institute of Governmental Studies, University of California, Berkeley, September 1993), 1, 4–6.

4. See Theodore J. Lowi, "Toward a Legislature of the First Kind," in *Knowledge, Power, and the Congress,* ed. William H. Robinson and Clay H. Wellborn (Washington, D. C.: Congressional Quarterly, 1991), 9–36.

5. Lawrence C. Dodd, "Congress and the Politics of Renewal: Redressing the Crisis of Legitimation," in *Congress Reconsidered,* 5th ed., ed. Lawrence C. Dodd and Bruce I. Oppenheimer (Washington, D. C.: CQ Press, 1993), 426.

6. David E. Price, "Comment," in Robinson and Wellborn, *Knowledge, Power, and the Congress,* 128.

7. Richard F. Fenno Jr., *Learning to Govern: An Institutional View of the 104th Congress* (Washington, D.C.: Brookings Institution, 1997).

Chapter 7

The Presidency

———◆———

7-1

from *Presidential Power*

Richard E. Neustadt

In his classic treatise Presidential Power, *Richard E. Neustadt presents a problem that confronts every occupant of the White House: His authority does not match the expectations for his performance. We expect our presidents to be leaders, Neustadt tells us, but the office guarantees no more than that they will be clerks. In the following excerpt, Neustadt explains that the key to presidential success lies in persuasion and shows how the ability to persuade depends on bargaining.*

THE LIMITS ON COMMAND suggest the structure of our government. The Constitutional Convention of 1787 is supposed to have created a government of "separated powers." It did nothing of the sort. Rather, it created a government of separated institutions *sharing* powers.[1] "I am part of the legislative process," Eisenhower often said in 1959 as a reminder of his veto.[2] Congress, the dispenser of authority and funds, is no less part of the administrative process. Federalism adds another set of separated institutions. The Bill of Rights adds others. Many public purposes can only be achieved by voluntary acts of private institutions; the press, for one, in Douglass Cater's phrase, is a "fourth branch of government."[3]

Source: Richard Neustadt, *Presidential Power and the Modern Presidents: The Politics of Leadership from Roosevelt to Reagan* (1960; New York: Simon & Schuster, 1990), 29–49.

And with the coming of alliances abroad, the separate institutions of a London, or a Bonn, share in the making of American public policy.

What the Constitution separates our political parties do not combine. The parties are themselves composed of separated organizations sharing public authority. The authority consists of nominating powers. Our national parties are confederations of state and local party institutions, with a headquarters that represents the White House, more or less, if the party has a President in office. These confederacies manage presidential nominations. All other public offices depend upon electorates confined within the states.[4] All other nominations are controlled within the states. The President and congressmen who bear one party's label are divided by dependence upon different sets of voters. The differences are sharpest at the stage of nomination. The White House has too small a share in nominating congressmen, and Congress has too little weight in nominating presidents for party to erase their constitutional separation. Party links are stronger than is frequently supposed, but nominating processes assure the separation.[5]

The separateness of institutions and the sharing of authority prescribe the terms on which a President persuades. When one man shares authority with another, but does not gain or lose his job upon the other's whim, his willingness to act upon the urging of the other turns on whether he conceives the action right for him. The essence of a President's persuasive task is to convince such men that what the White House wants of them is what they ought to do for their sake and on their authority. (Sex matters not at all; for *man* read *woman*.)

Persuasive power, thus defined, amounts to more than charm or reasoned argument. These have their uses for a President, but these are not the whole of his resources. For the individuals he would induce to do what he wants done on their own responsibility will need or fear some acts by him on his responsibility. If they share his authority, he has some share in theirs. Presidential "powers" may be inconclusive when a President commands, but always remain relevant as he persuades. The status and authority inherent in his office reinforce his logic and his charm.

Status adds something to persuasiveness; authority adds still more. When Truman urged wage changes on his secretary of commerce [Charles Sawyer] while the latter was administering the [recently seized] steel mills, he and Secretary Sawyer were not just two men reasoning with one another. Had they been so, Sawyer probably would never have agreed to act. Truman's status gave him special claims to Sawyer's loyalty or at least attention. In Walter Bagehot's charming phrase, "no man can *argue* on his knees." Although there is no kneeling in this country, few men—and exceedingly few cabinet officers—are immune to the impulse to say "yes" to the President of the United States. It grows harder to say "no" when they are seated in his Oval Office at the White House, or in his study on the second floor, where almost tangibly he partakes of the aura of his physical surroundings. In Sawyer's case, moreover, the President possessed formal authority to intervene in many matters of concern to the secretary of commerce. These matters ranged from jurisdictional disputes among the defense agencies to legislation pending before Congress and, ultimately, to the tenure of the secretary, himself. There is nothing in the record to suggest that Truman voiced specific threats when they negotiated over wage increases. But given his formal powers and their relevance to Sawyer's other interests, it is safe to assume that Truman's very advocacy of wage action conveyed an implicit threat.

A President's authority and status give him great advantages in dealing with the men he would persuade. Each "power" is a vantage point for him in the degree that other men have use for his authority. From the veto to appointments, from publicity to budgeting, and so down a long list, the White House now controls the most encompassing array of vantage points in the American political system. With hardly an exception, those who share in governing this country are aware that at some time, in some degree, the doing of *their* jobs, the furthering of *their* ambitions, may depend upon the President of the United States. Their need for presidential action, or their fear of it, is bound to be recurrent if not actually continuous. Their need or fear is his advantage.

A President's advantages are greater than mere listing of his "powers" might suggest. Those with whom he deals must deal with him until the last day of his term. Because they have continuing relationships with him, his future, while it lasts, supports his present influence. Even though there is no need or fear of him today, what he could do tomorrow may supply today's advantage. Continuing relationships may convert any "power," any aspect of his status, into vantage points in almost any case. When he induces other people to do what he wants done, a President can trade on their dependence now and later.

The President's advantages are checked by the advantages of others. Continuing relationships will pull in both directions. These are relationships of mutual dependence. A President depends upon the persons whom he would persuade; he has to reckon with his need or fear of them. They too will possess status or authority, or both, else they would be of little use to him. Their vantage points confront his own; their power tempers his.

Persuasion is a two-way street. Sawyer, it will be recalled, did not respond at once to Truman's plan for wage increases at the steel mills. On the contrary, the secretary hesitated and delayed and only acquiesced when he was satisfied that publicly he would not bear the onus of decision. Sawyer had some points of vantage all his own from which to resist presidential pressure. If he had to reckon with coercive implications in the President's "situations of strength," so had Truman to be mindful of the implications underlying Sawyer's place as a department head, as steel administrator, and as a cabinet spokesman for business. Loyalty is reciprocal. Having taken on a dirty job in the steel crisis, Sawyer had strong claims to loyal support. Besides, he had authority to do some things that the White House could ill afford. . . . [H]e might have resigned in a huff (the removal power also works two ways). Or . . . he might have declined to sign necessary orders. Or he might have let it be known publicly that he deplored what he was told to do and protested its doing. By following any of these courses Sawyer almost surely would have strengthened the position of management, weakened the position of the White House, and embittered the union. But the whole purpose of a wage increase was to enhance White House persuasiveness in urging settlement upon union and companies alike. Although Sawyer's status and authority did not give him the power to prevent an increase outright, they gave him capability to undermine its purpose. If his authority over wage rates had been vested by a statute, not by revocable presidential order, his power of prevention might have been complete. So Harold Ickes [Sr.] demonstrated in the famous case of helium sales to Germany before the Second World War.[6]

The power to persuade is the power to bargain. Status and authority yield bargaining advantages. But in a government of "separated institutions sharing power," they yield them to all sides. With the array of vantage points at his disposal, a President may be far more persuasive than his logic or his charm could make him. But outcomes are not guaranteed by his advantages. There remain the counter pressures those whom he would influence can bring to bear on him from vantage points at their disposal. Command has limited utility; persuasion becomes give-and-take. It is well that the White House holds the vantage points it does. In such a business any President may need them all—and more.

THIS VIEW OF POWER as akin to bargaining is one we commonly accept in the sphere of congressional relations. Every textbook states and every legislative session demonstrates that save in times like the extraordinary Hundred Days of 1933—times virtually ruled out by definition at mid-century—a President will often be unable to obtain congressional action on his terms or even to halt action he opposes. The reverse is equally accepted: Congress often is frustrated by the President. Their formal powers are so intertwined that neither will accomplish very much, for very long, without the acquiescence of the other. By the same token, though, what one demands the other can resist. The stage is set for that great game, much like collective bargaining, in which each seeks to profit from the other's needs and fears. It is a game played catch-as-catch-can, case by case. And everybody knows the game, observers and participants alike.

The concept of real power as a give-and-take is equally familiar when applied to presidential influence outside the formal structure of the federal government. . . . When he deals with [governors, union officials, company executives and even citizens or workers] a President draws bargaining advantage from his status or authority. By virtue of their public places or their private rights they have some capability to reply in kind.

In spheres of party politics the same thing follows, necessarily, from the confederal nature of our party organizations. Even in the case of national nominations a President's advantages are checked by those of others. In 1944 it is by no means clear that Roosevelt got his first choice as his running mate. In 1948 Truman, then the President, faced serious revolts against his nomination. In 1952 his intervention from the White House helped assure the choice of Adlai Stevenson, but it is far from clear that Truman could have done as much for any other candidate acceptable to him.[7] In 1956 when Eisenhower was President, the record leaves obscure just who backed Harold Stassen's efforts to block Richard Nixon from renomination as vice president. But evidently everything did not go quite as Eisenhower wanted, whatever his intentions may have been.[8] The outcomes in these instances bear all the marks of limits on command and of power checked by power that characterize congressional relations. Both in and out of politics these checks and limits seem to be quite widely understood.

Influence becomes still more a matter of give-and-take when Presidents attempt to deal with allied governments. A classic illustration is the long unhappy wrangle over Suez policy in 1956. In dealing with the British and the French before their military intervention, Eisenhower had his share of bargaining advantages but no effective power of command. His allies had their share of counterpressures, and they finally tried the most extreme of all: action despite him. His pressure then was instrumental in reversing them. But had the British government been on safe ground at home, Eisenhower's wishes might have made as little difference after intervention as before. Behind the decorum of diplomacy—which was not very decorous in the Suez affair—relationships among allies are not unlike relationships among state delegations at a national convention. Power is persuasion, and persuasion becomes bargaining. The concept is familiar to everyone who watches foreign policy.

In only one sphere is the concept unfamiliar: the sphere of executive relations. Perhaps because of civics textbooks and teaching in our schools, Americans instinctively resist the view that power in this sphere resembles power in all others. Even Washington reporters, White House aides, and congressmen are not immune to the illusion that administrative agencies comprise a single structure, "the" executive branch, where presidential word is law, or ought to be. Yet . . . when a President seeks something from executive officials his persuasiveness is subject to the same sorts of limitations as in the case of congressmen, or governors, or national committeemen, or private citizens, or foreign governments. There are no generic differences, no differences in kind and only sometimes in degree. The incidents preceding the dismissal of [General Douglas]

MacArthur and the incidents surrounding seizure of the steel mills make it plain that here as elsewhere influence derives from bargaining advantages; power is a give-and-take.

Like our governmental structure as a whole, the executive establishment consists of separated institutions sharing powers. The President heads one of these; cabinet officers, agency administrators, and military commanders head others. Below the departmental level, virtually independent bureau chiefs head many more. Under mid-century conditions, federal operations spill across dividing lines on organization charts; almost every policy entangles many agencies; almost every program calls for interagency collaboration. Everything somehow involves the President. But operating agencies owe their existence least of all to one another—and only in some part to him. Each has a separate statutory base; each has its statutes to administer; each deals with a different set of subcommittees at the Capitol. Each has its own peculiar set of clients, friends, and enemies outside the formal government. Each has a different set of specialized careerists inside its own bailiwick. Our Constitution gives the President the "take-care" clause and the appointive power. Our statutes give him central budgeting and a degree of personnel control. All agency administrators are responsible to him. But they also are responsible to Congress, to their clients, to their staffs, and to themselves. In short, they have five masters. Only after all of those do they owe any loyalty to each other.

"The members of the cabinet," Charles G. Dawes used to remark, "are a president's natural enemies." Dawes had been Harding's budget director, Coolidge's vice president, and Hoover's ambassador to London; he also had been General Pershing's chief assistant for supply in World War I. The words are highly colored, but Dawes knew whereof he spoke. The men who have to serve so many masters cannot help but be somewhat the "enemy" of any one of them. By the same token, any master wanting service is in some degree the "enemy" of such a servant. A President is likely to want loyal support but not to relish trouble on his doorstep. Yet the more his cabinet members cleave to him, the more they may need help from him in fending off the wrath of rival masters. Help, though, is synonymous with trouble. Many a cabinet officer, with loyalty ill rewarded by his lights and help withheld, has come to view the White House as innately hostile to department heads. Dawes's dictum can be turned around.

A senior presidential aide remarked to me in Eisenhower's time: "If some of these cabinet members would just take time out to stop and ask themselves, 'What would I want if I were President?' they wouldn't give him all the trouble he's been having." But even if they asked themselves the question, such officials often could not act upon the answer. Their personal attachment to the President is all too often overwhelmed by duty to their other masters.

Executive officials are not equally advantaged in their dealings with a President. Nor are the same officials equally advantaged all the time. Not every officeholder can resist like a MacArthur or Sawyer. . . . The vantage points conferred upon officials by their own authority and status vary enormously. The variance is heightened by particulars of time and circumstance. In mid-October 1950, Truman, at a press conference, remarked of the man he had considered firing in August and would fire the next April for intolerable insubordination:

> Let me tell you something that will be good for your souls. It's a pity that you . . . can't understand the ideas of two intellectually honest men when they meet. General MacArthur . . . is a member of the Government of the United States. He is loyal to that Government. He is loyal to the President. He is loyal to the President in his foreign policy. . . . There is no disagreement between General MacArthur and myself.[9]

MacArthur's status in and out of government was never higher than when Truman spoke those words. The words, once spoken, added to the general's credibility thereafter when he sought to use the press in his campaign against the President. And what had happened between August and October? Near victory had happened, together with that premature conference on postwar plans, the meeting at Wake Island.

If the bargaining advantages of a MacArthur fluctuate with changing circumstances, this is bound to be so with subordinates who have at their disposal fewer powers, lesser status, to fall back on. And when officials have no powers in their own right, or depend upon the President for status, their counterpressure may be limited indeed. White House aides, who fit both categories, are among the most responsive men of all, and for good reason. As a director of the budget once remarked to me, "Thank God I'm here and not across the street. If the President doesn't call me, I've got plenty I can do right here and plenty coming up to me, by rights, to justify my calling him. But those poor fellows over there, if the boss doesn't call them, doesn't ask them to do something, what *can* they do but sit?" Authority and status so conditional are frail reliances in resisting a President's own wants. Within the White House precincts, lifted eyebrows may suffice to set an aide in motion; command, coercion, even charm aside. But even in the White House a President does not monopolize effective power. Even there persuasion is akin to bargaining. A former Roosevelt aide once wrote of cabinet officers:

> Half of a President's suggestions, which theoretically carry the weight of orders, can be safely forgotten by a Cabinet member. And if the President asks about a suggestion a second time, he can be told that it is being investigated. If he asks a third time, a wise Cabinet officer will give him at least part of what he suggests. But only occasionally, except about the most important matters, do Presidents ever get around to asking three times.[10]

The rule applies to staff as well as to the cabinet, and certainly has been applied *by* staff in Truman's time and Eisenhower's.

Some aides will have more vantage points than a selective memory. Sherman Adams, for example, as the assistant to the President under Eisenhower, scarcely deserved the appellation "White House aide" in the meaning of the term before his time or as applied to other members of the Eisenhower entourage. Although Adams was by no means "chief of staff" in any sense so sweeping—or so simple—as press commentaries often took for granted, he apparently became no more dependent on the President than Eisenhower on him. "I need him," said the President when Adams turned out to have been remarkably imprudent in the Goldfine case, and delegated to him, at least nominally, the decision on his own departure.[11] This instance is extreme, but the tendency it illustrates is common enough. Any aide who demonstrates to others that he has the President's consistent confidence and a consistent part in presidential business will acquire so much business on his own account that he becomes in some sense independent of his chief. Nothing in the Constitution keeps a well-placed aide from converting status into power of his own, usable in some degree even against the President—an outcome not unknown in Truman's regime or, by all accounts, in Eisenhower's.

The more an officeholder's status and his powers stem from sources independent of the President, the stronger will be his potential pressure on the President. Department heads in general have more bargaining power than do most members of the White House staff; but bureau chiefs may have still more, and specialists at upper levels of established career services may have almost unlimited reserves of the enormous power which consists of sitting still. As Franklin Roosevelt once remarked:

> The Treasury is so large and far-flung and ingrained in its practices that I find it almost impossible to get the action and results I want—even with Henry [Morgenthau] there. But the Treasury is not to be compared with the State Department. You should go through the experience of trying to get any changes in the thinking, policy, and action of the career diplomats and then you'd know what a real problem was. But the Treasury and the State Department put together are nothing compared with the Na-a-vy. The admirals are really something to cope with—and I should know. To change anything in the Na-a-vy is like punching a feather bed. You punch it with your right and you punch it with your left until you are finally exhausted, and then you find the damn bed just as it was before you started punching.[12]

In the right circumstances, of course, a President can have his way with any of these people. . . . [But] as between a President and his "subordinates," no less than others on whom he depends, real power is reciprocal and varies markedly with organization, subject matter, personality and situation. The mere fact that persuasion is directed at executive officials signifies no necessary easing of his way. Any new congressman of the Administration's party, especially if narrowly elected, may turn out more amenable (though less useful) to the President than any seasoned bureau chief "downtown." *The probabilities of power do not derive from the literary theory of the Constitution.*

THERE IS a widely held belief in the United States that were it not for folly or for knavery, a reasonable President would need no power other than the logic of his argument. No less a personage than Eisenhower has subscribed to that belief in many a campaign speech and press-conference remark. But faulty reasoning and bad intentions do not cause all quarrels with Presidents. The best of reasoning and of intent cannot compose them all. For in the first place, what the President wants will rarely seem a trifle to the people he wants it from. And in the second place, they will be bound to judge it by the standard of their own responsibilities, not his. However logical his argument according to his lights, their judgment may not bring them to his view.

Those who share in governing this country frequently appear to act as though they were in business for themselves. So, in a real though not entire sense, they are and have to be. When Truman and MacArthur fell to quarreling, for example, the stakes were no less than the substance of American foreign policy, the risks of greater war or military stalemate, the prerogatives of Presidents and field commanders, the pride of a proconsul and his place in history. Intertwined, inevitably, were other stakes as well: political stakes for men and factions of both parties; power stakes for interest groups with which they were or wished to be affiliated. And every stake was raised by the apparent discontent in the American public mood. There is no reason to suppose that in such circumstances men of large but differing responsibilities will see all things through the same glasses. On the contrary, it is to be expected that their views of what ought to be done and what they then should do will vary with the differing perspectives their particular responsibilities evoke. Since their duties are not vested in a "team" or a "collegium" but in themselves, as individuals, one must expect that they will see things for themselves. Moreover, when they are responsible to many masters and when an event or policy turns loyalty against loyalty—a day-by-day occurrence in the nature of the case—one must assume that those who have the duties to perform will choose the terms of reconciliation. This is the essence of their personal responsibility. When their own duties pull in opposite directions, who else but they can choose what they will do?

When Truman dismissed MacArthur, the latter lost three posts: the American command in the Far East, the Allied command for the occupation of Japan, and the United Nations command in Korea. He also lost his status as the senior officer on active duty in the United States armed forces. So long as he held those positions and that status, though, he had a duty to his troops, to his profession, to himself (the last is hard for any man to disentangle from the rest). As a public figure and a focus for men's hopes he had a duty to constituents at home, and in Korea and Japan. He owed a duty also to those other constituents, the UN governments contributing to his field forces. As a patriot he had a duty to his country. As an accountable official and an expert guide he stood at the call of Congress. As a military officer he had, besides, a duty to the President, his constitutional commander. Some of these duties may have manifested themselves in terms more tangible or more direct than others. But it would be nonsense to argue that the last negated all the rest, however much it might be claimed to override them. And it makes no more sense to think that anybody but MacArthur was effectively empowered to decide how he himself would reconcile the competing demands his duties made upon him.

. . . Reasonable men, it is so often said, *ought* to be able to agree on the requirements of given situations. But when the outlook varies with the placement of each man, and the response required in his place is for each to decide, their reasoning may lead to disagreement quite as well—and quite as reasonably. Vanity, or vice, may weaken reason, to be sure, but it is idle to assign these as the cause of . . . MacArthur's defiance. Secretary Sawyer's hesitations, cited earlier, are in the same category. One need not denigrate such men to explain their conduct. For the responsibilities they felt, the "facts" they saw, simply were not the same as those of their superiors; yet they, not the superiors, had to decide what they would do.

Outside the executive branch the situation is the same, except that loyalty to the President may often matter *less*. There is no need to spell out the comparison with governors of Arkansas, steel company executives, trade union leaders, and the like. And when one comes to congressmen who can do nothing for themselves (or their constituents) save as they are elected, term by term, in districts and through party structures differing from those on which a President depends, the case is very clear. An able Eisenhower aide with long congressional experience remarked to me in 1958: "The people on the Hill don't do what they might *like* to do, they do what they think they *have* to do in their own interest as *they* see it." This states the case precisely.

The essence of a President's persuasive task, with congressmen and everybody else, is to induce them to believe that what he wants of them is what their own appraisal of their own responsibilities requires them to do in their interest, not his. Because men may differ in their views on public policy, because differences in outlook stem from differences in duty—duty to one's office, one's constituents, oneself—that task is bound to be more like collective bargaining than like a reasoned argument among philosopher kings. Overtly or implicitly, hard bargaining has characterized all illustrations offered up to now. This is the reason why: Persuasion deals in the coin of self-interest with men who have some freedom to reject what they find counterfeit.

A PRESIDENT DRAWS influence from bargaining advantages. But does he always need them? . . . [S]uppose most players of the governmental game see policy objectives much alike, then can he not rely on logic (or on charm) to get him what he wants? The answer is that even then most outcomes turn on bargaining. The reason for this answer is a simple one: Most who share in governing have interests of their own beyond the realm of policy objectives. The sponsorship of policy, the form it takes, the conduct of it, and the credit for it separate their interest from the President's despite agreement on the end in view. In political government the means can matter quite as much as ends; they often matter more. And there are always differences of interest in the means.

Let me introduce a case externally the opposite of my previous examples: the European Recovery Program of 1948, the so-called Marshall Plan. This is perhaps the greatest exercise in policy agreement since the Cold War began. When the then secretary of state, George Catlett Marshall, spoke at the Harvard commencement in June 1947, he launched one of the most creative, most imaginative ventures in the history of American foreign relations. What makes this policy most notable for present purposes, however, is that it became effective upon action by the Eightieth Congress, at the behest of Harry Truman, in the election year 1948.[13]

Eight months before Marshall spoke at Harvard, the Democrats had lost control of both houses of Congress for the first time in fourteen years. Truman, whom the secretary represented, had just finished his second troubled year as President-by-succession. Truman was regarded with so little warmth in his own party that in 1946 he had been urged not to participate in the congressional campaign. At the opening of Congress in January 1947, Senator Robert A. Taft, "Mr. Republican," had somewhat the attitude of a President-elect. This was a vision widely shared in Washington, with Truman relegated thereby to the role of caretaker-on-term. Moreover, within just two weeks of Marshall's commencement address, Truman was to veto two prized accomplishments of Taft's congressional majority: the Taft-Hartley Act and tax reduction.[14] Yet scarcely ten months later the Marshall Plan was under way on terms to satisfy its sponsors, its authorization completed, its first-year funds in sight, its administering agency in being: all managed by as thorough a display of executive-congressional cooperation as any we have seen since the Second World War. For any President at any time this would have been a great accomplishment. In years before mid-century it would have been enough to make the future reputation of his term. And for a Truman, at this time, enactment of the Marshall Plan appears almost miraculous.

How was the miracle accomplished? How did a President so situated bring it off? In answer, the first thing to note is that he did not do it by himself. Truman had help of a sort no less extraordinary than the outcome. Although each stands for something more complex, the names of Marshall, Vandenberg, Patterson, Bevin, Stalin tell the story of that help.

In 1947, two years after V-J Day, General Marshall was something more than secretary of state. He was a man venerated by the President as "the greatest living American," literally an embodiment of Truman's ideals. He was honored at the Pentagon as an architect of victory. He was thoroughly respected by the secretary of the Navy, James V. Forrestal, who that year became the first secretary of defense. On Capitol Hill, Marshall had an enormous fund of respect stemming from his war record as Army chief of staff, and in the country generally no officer had come out of the war with a higher reputation for judgment, intellect, and probity. Besides, as secretary of state, he had behind him the first generation of matured foreign service officers produced by the reforms of the 1920s, and mingled with them, in the departmental service, were some of the ablest of the men drawn by the war from private life to Washington. In terms both of staff talent and staff use, Marshall's years began a State Department "golden age" that lasted until the era of McCarthy. Moreover, as his under secretary, Marshall had, successively, Dean Acheson and Robert Lovett, men who commanded the respect of the professionals and the regard of congressmen. (Acheson had been brilliantly successful at congressional relations as assistant secretary in the war and postwar years.) Finally, as a special undersecretary Marshall had Will Clayton, a man highly regarded, for good reason, at both ends of Pennsylvania Avenue.

Taken together, these are exceptional resources for a secretary of state. In the circumstances, they were quite as necessary as they obviously are relevant. The Marshall Plan was launched by a lame-duck Administration "scheduled" to leave office in eighteen months. Marshall's program faced a congressional leadership traditionally isolationist and currently intent upon economy. European aid was viewed with envy by a Pentagon distressed and virtually disarmed through budget cuts, and by domestic agencies intent on enlarged welfare programs. It was not viewed with liking by a Treasury intent on budget surpluses. The plan had need of every asset that could be extracted from the personal position of its nominal author and from the skills of his assistants.

Without the equally remarkable position of the senior senator from Michigan, Arthur H. Vandenberg, it is hard to see how Marshall's assets could have been enough. Vandenberg was chairman of the Senate Foreign Relations Committee.

Actually, he was much more than that. Twenty years a senator, he was the senior member of his party in the chamber. Assiduously cultivated by FDR and Truman, he was a chief Republican proponent of bipartisanship in foreign policy and consciously conceived himself its living symbol to his party, to the country, and abroad. Moreover, by informal but entirely operative agreement with his colleague Taft, Vandenberg held the acknowledged lead among Senate Republicans in the whole field of international affairs. This acknowledgment meant more in 1947 than it might have meant at any other time. With confidence in the advent of a Republican administration two years hence, most of the gentlemen were in a mood to be responsive and responsible. The war was over, Roosevelt dead, Truman a caretaker, theirs the trust. That the senator from Michigan saw matters in this light his diaries make clear.[15] And this was not the outlook from the Senate side alone; the attitudes of House Republicans associated with the Herter Committee and its tours abroad suggest the same mood of responsibility. Vandenberg was not the only source of help on Capitol Hill. But relatively speaking his position there was as exceptional as Marshall's was downtown.

Help of another sort was furnished by a group of dedicated private citizens who organized one of the most effective instruments for public information seen since the Second World War: the Committee for the Marshall Plan, headed by the eminent Republicans whom FDR in 1940 had brought to the Department of War: Henry L. Stimson as honorary chairman and Robert P. Patterson as active spokesman. The remarkable array of bankers, lawyers, trade unionists, and editors, who had drawn together in defense of "internationalism" before Pearl Harbor and had joined their talents in the war itself, combined again to spark the work of this committee. Their efforts generated a great deal of vocal public support to buttress Marshall's arguments, and Vandenberg's, in Congress.

But before public support could be rallied, there had to be a purpose tangible enough, concrete enough, to provide a rallying ground. At Harvard, Marshall had voiced an idea in general terms. That this was turned into a hard program susceptible of presentation and support is due, in major part, to Ernest Bevin, the British foreign secretary. He well deserves the credit he has sometimes been assigned as, in effect, coauthor of the Marshall Plan. For Bevin seized on Marshall's Harvard speech and organized a European response with promptness and concreteness beyond the State Department's expectations. What had been virtually a trial balloon to test reactions on both sides of the Atlantic was hailed in London as an invitation to the Europeans to send Washington a bill of particulars. This they promptly organized to do, and the American Administration then organized in turn for its reception without further argument internally about the pros and cons of issuing the "invitation" in the first place. But for Bevin there might have been trouble from the secretary of the treasury and others besides.[16]

If Bevin's help was useful at that early stage, Stalin's was vital from first to last. In a mood of self-deprecation Truman once remarked that without Moscow's "crazy" moves "we would never have had our foreign policy . . . we never could have got a thing from Congress."[17] George Kennan, among others, had deplored the anti-Soviet overtone of the case made for the Marshall Plan in Congress and the country, but there is no doubt that this clinched the argument for many segments of American opinion. There also is no doubt that Moscow made the crucial contributions to the case.

By 1947 events, far more than governmental prescience or open action, had given a variety of publics an impression of inimical Soviet intentions (and of Europe's weakness) and a growing urge to "do something about it." Three months before Marshall spoke at Harvard, Greek-Turkish aid and promulgation of the Truman Doctrine had seemed rather to crystallize than to create a public mood and a congressional response. The Marshall planners, be it said, were poorly placed to capitalize on that mood, nor had the secretary wished to do so. Their object, indeed, was to cut across it, striking at the cause of European weakness rather than at Soviet aggressiveness, per se. A strong economy in Western Europe called, ideally, for restorative measures of continental scope. American assistance proffered in an anti-Soviet context would have been contradictory in theory and unacceptable in fact to several of the governments that Washington was anxious to assist. As Marshall, himself, saw it, the logic of his purpose forbade him to play his strongest congressional card. The Russians then proceeded to play it for him. When the Europeans met in Paris, Molotov walked out. After the Czechs had shown continued interest in American aid, a Communist coup overthrew their government while Soviet forces stood along their borders within easy reach of Prague. Molotov transformed the Marshall Plan's initial presentation; Czechoslovakia assured its final passage, which followed by a month the takeover in Prague.

Such was the help accorded Truman in obtaining action on the Marshall Plan. Considering his politically straitened circumstances he scarcely could have done with less. Conceivably some part of Moscow's contribution might have been dispensable, but not Marshall's or Vandenberg's or Bevin's or Patterson's or that of the great many other men whose work is represented by their names in my account. Their aid was not extended to the President for his own sake. He was not favored in this fashion just because they liked him personally or were spellbound by his intellect or charm. They might have been as helpful had all held him in disdain, which some of them certainly did. The Londoners who seized the ball, Vandenberg and Taft and the congressional majority, Marshall and his planners, the officials of other agencies who actively supported them or "went along," the host of influential private citizens who rallied to the cause—all these played the parts they did because they thought they had to, in their interest, given their responsibilities, not Truman's. Yet they hardly would have found it in their interest to collaborate with one another or with him had he not furnished them precisely what they needed from the White House. Truman could not do without their help, but he could not have had it without unremitting effort on his part.

The crucial thing to note about this case is that despite compatibility of views on public policy, Truman got no help he did not pay for (except Stalin's). Bevin scarcely could have seized on Marshall's words had Marshall not been plainly backed by Truman. Marshall's interest would not have comported with the exploitation of his prestige by a president who undercut him openly or subtly or even inadvertently at any point. Vandenberg, presumably, could not have backed proposals by a White House that begrudged him deference and access gratifying to his fellow partisans (and satisfying to himself). Prominent Republicans in private life would not have found it easy to promote a cause identified with Truman's claims on 1948—and neither would the prominent New Dealers then engaged in searching for a substitute.

Truman paid the price required for their services. So far as the record shows, the White House did not falter once in firm support for Marshall and the Marshall Plan. Truman backed his secretary's gamble on an invitation to all Europe. He made the plan his own in a well-timed address to the Canadians. He lost no opportunity to widen the involvements of his own official family in the cause. Averell Harriman, the secretary of commerce; Julius Krug, the secretary of the interior; Edwin Nourse, the Economic Council chairman; James Webb, the director of the budget—all were made responsible for studies and reports contributing directly to the legislative presentation. Thus these men were committed in advance. Besides, the President continually emphasized to everyone in reach that he did not have doubts, did not desire complications and would foreclose all he could. Reportedly his emphasis was felt at the Treasury, with good effect. And Truman was at special pains to smooth the way for Vandenberg. The senator insisted on "no politics" from the Administration side; there was none. He thought a survey of American resources and capacity essential; he got it in the Krug and Harriman reports. Vandenberg expected advance consultation; he received it, step by step, in frequent meetings with the President and weekly conferences with Marshall. He asked for an effective liaison between Congress and agencies concerned; Lovett and others gave him what he wanted. When the senator decided on the need to change financing and administrative features of the legislation, Truman disregarded Budget Bureau grumbling and acquiesced with grace. When, finally, Vandenberg desired a Republican to head the new administering agency, his candidate, Paul Hoffman, was appointed despite the President's own preference for another. In all these ways Truman employed the sparse advantages his "powers" and his status then accorded him to gain the sort of help he had to have.

Truman helped himself in still another way. Traditionally and practically, no one was placed as well as he to call public attention to the task of Congress (and its Republican leadership). Throughout the fall and winter of 1947 and on into the spring of 1948, he made repeated use of presidential "powers" to remind the country that congressional action was required. Messages, speeches, and an extra session were employed to make the point. Here, too, he drew advantage from his place. However, in his circumstances, Truman's public advocacy might have hurt, not helped, had his words seemed directed toward the forthcoming election. Truman gained advantage for his program only as his own endorsement of it stayed on the right side of that fine line between the "caretaker" in office and the would-be candidate. In public statements dealing with the Marshall Plan he seems to have risked blurring this distinction only once, when he called Congress into session in November 1947 asking both for interim aid to Europe and for peacetime price controls. The second request linked the then inflation with the current Congress (and with Taft), becoming a first step toward one of Truman's major themes in 1948. By calling for both measures at the extra session he could have been accused—and was—of mixing home-front politics with foreign aid. In the event no harm was done the European program (or his politics). But in advance a number of his own advisers feared that such a double call would jeopardize the Marshall Plan. Their fears are testimony to the narrowness of his advantage in employing his own "powers" for its benefit.[18]

It is symptomatic of Truman's situation that bipartisan accommodation by the White House then was thought to mean congressional consultation and conciliation on a scale unmatched in Eisenhower's time. Yet Eisenhower did about as well with opposition congresses as Truman did, in terms of requests granted for defense and foreign aid. It may be said that Truman asked for more extraordinary measures. But it also may be said that Eisenhower never lacked for the prestige his predecessor had to borrow. It often was remarked, in Truman's time, that he seemed a split personality, so sharply did his conduct differentiate domestic politics from national security. But personality aside, how else could he, in his first term, gain ground for an evolving foreign policy? The plain fact is that Truman had to play bipartisanship as he did or lose the game.

HAD TRUMAN LACKED the personal advantages his "powers" and his status gave him, or if he had been maladroit in using them, there probably would not have been a massive European aid program in 1948. Something of the sort, perhaps quite different in its emphasis, would almost certainly have come to pass before the end of 1949. Some American response to European weakness and to Soviet expansion was as certain as such things can be. But in 1948 temptations to await a Taft plan or a Dewey plan might well have caused at least a year's postponement of response had the outgoing Administration bungled its congressional or public or allied or executive relations. Quite aside from the specific virtues of their plan, Truman and his helpers gained that year, at least, in timing the American response. As European time was measured then, this was a precious gain. The President's own share in this accomplishment was vital. He made his contribution by exploiting his advantages. Truman, in effect, lent Marshall and the rest the perquisites and status of his office. In return they lent him their prestige and their own influence. The transfer multiplied his influence despite his limited authority in form and lack of strength politically. Without the wherewithal to make this bargain, Truman could not have contributed to European aid.

Bargaining advantages convey no guarantees. Influence remains a two-way street. In the fortunate instance of the Marshall Plan, what Truman needed was actually in the hands of men who were prepared to "trade" with him. He personally could deliver what they wanted in return. Marshall, Vandenberg, Harriman, et al., possessed the prestige, energy, associations, staffs essential to the legislative effort. Truman himself had a sufficient hold on presidential messages and speeches, on budget policy, on high-level appointments, and on his own time and temper to carry through all aspects of his necessary part. But it takes two to make a bargain. It takes those who have prestige to lend it on whatever terms. Suppose that Marshall had declined the secretaryship of state in January 1947; Truman might not have found a substitute so well equipped to furnish what he needed in the months ahead. Or suppose that Vandenberg had fallen victim to a cancer two years before he actually did; Senator Wiley of Wisconsin would not have seemed to Taft a man with whom the world need be divided. Or suppose that the secretary of the treasury had been possessed of stature, force, and charm commensurate with that of his successor in Eisenhower's time, the redoubtable George M. Humphrey. And what if Truman then had seemed to the Republicans what he turned out to be in 1948, a formidable candidate for President? It is unlikely that a single one of these "supposes" would have changed the final outcome; two or three, however, might have altered it entirely. Truman was not guaranteed more power than his "powers" just because he had continuing relationships with cabinet secretaries and with senior senators. Here, as everywhere, the outcome was conditional on who they were and what he was and how each viewed events, and on their actual performance in response.

Granting that persuasion has no guarantee attached, how can a President reduce the risks of failing to persuade? How can he maximize his prospects for effectiveness by minimizing chances that his power will elude him? The Marshall Plan suggests an answer: He guards his power prospects in the course of making choices. Marshall himself, and Forrestal and Harriman, and others of the sort held office on the President's appointment. Vandenberg had vast symbolic value partly because FDR and Truman had done everything they could, since 1944, to build him up. The Treasury Department and the Budget Bureau—which together might have jeopardized the plans these others made—were headed by officials whose prestige depended wholly on their jobs. What Truman needed from those "givers" he received, in part, because of his past choice of men and measures. What they received in turn were actions taken or withheld by him, himself. The things they needed from him mostly involved his own conduct where his current choices ruled. The President's own actions in the past had cleared the way for current bargaining. His actions in the present were his trading stock. Behind each action lay a personal choice, and these together comprised his control over the give-and-take that gained him what he wanted. In the degree that Truman, personally, affected the advantages he drew from his relationships with other men in government, his power was protected by his choices.

By "choice" I mean no more than what is commonly referred to as "decision": a President's own act of doing or not doing. Decision is so often indecisive, and indecision is so frequently conclusive, that *choice* becomes the preferable term. "Choice" has its share of undesired connotations. In common usage it implies a black-and-white alternative. Presidential choices are rarely of that character. It also may imply that the alternatives are set before the choice maker by someone else. A President is often left to figure out his options for himself. . . .

If Presidents could count upon past choices to enhance their current influence, as Truman's choice of men had done for him, persuasion would pose fewer difficulties than it does. But Presidents can count on no such thing. Depending on the circumstances, prior choices can be as embarrassing as they were helpful in the instance of the Marshall Plan. . . . Truman's hold upon MacArthur was weakened by his deference toward him in the past.

Assuming that past choices have protected influence, not harmed it, present choices still may be inadequate. If Presidents could count on their own conduct to provide them enough bargaining advantages, as Truman's conduct did where Vandenberg and Marshall were concerned, effective bargaining might be much easier to manage than it often is. In the steel crisis, for instance, Truman's own persuasiveness with companies and union, both, was burdened by the conduct of an independent wage board and of government attorneys in the courts, to say nothing of Wilson, Arnall, Sawyer, and the like. Yet in practice, if not theory, many of *their* crucial choices never were the President's to make. Decisions that are legally in others' hands, or delegated past recall, have an unhappy way of proving just the trading stock most needed when the White House wants to trade. One reason why Truman was consistently more influential in the instance of the Marshall Plan than in the steel case or the MacArthur case is that the Marshall Plan directly involved Congress. In congressional relations there are some things that no one but the President can do. His chance to choose is higher when a message must be sent, or a nomination submitted, or a bill signed into law, than when the sphere of action is confined to the executive, where all decisive tasks may have been delegated past recall.

But adequate or not, a President's choices are the only means in his own hands of guarding his own prospects for effective influence. He can draw power from continuing relationships in the degree that he can capitalize upon the needs of others for the Presidency's status and authority. He helps himself to do so, though, by nothing save ability to recognize the preconditions and the chance advantages and to proceed accordingly in the course of the choice making that comes his way. To ask how he can guard prospective influence is thus to raise a further question: What helps him guard his power stakes in his own acts of choice?

NOTES

1. The reader will want to keep in mind the distinction between two senses in which the word *power* is employed. When I have used the word (or its plural) to refer to formal constitutional, statutory, or customary authority, it is either qualified by the adjective "formal" or placed in quotation marks as "power(s)." Where I have used it in the sense of effective influence on the conduct of others, it appears without quotation marks (and always in the singular). Where clarity and convenience permit, *authority* is substituted for "power" in the first sense and *influence* for power in the second.

2. See, for example, his press conference of July 22, 1959, as reported in the *New York Times*, July 23, 1959.

3. See Douglass Cater, *The Fourth Branch of Government* (Boston: Houghton Mifflin, 1959).

4. With the exception of the vice presidency, of course.

5. See David B. Truman's illuminating study of party relationships in the Eighty-first Congress, *The Congressional Party* (New York: Wiley, 1959), especially chaps. 4, 6, 8.

6. As secretary of the interior in 1939, Harold Ickes refused to approve the sale of helium to Germany despite the insistence of the State Department and the urging of President Roosevelt. Without the secretary's approval, such sales were forbidden by statute. See *The Secret Diaries of Harold L. Ickes* (New York: Simon & Schuster, 1954), vol. 2, especially pp. 391–93, 396–99.

In this instance the statutory authority ran to the secretary as a matter of his discretion. A President is unlikely to fire cabinet officers for the conscientious exercise of such authority. If the President did so, their successors might well be embarrassed both publicly and at the Capitol were they to reverse decisions previously taken. As for a President's authority to set aside discretionary determinations of this sort, it rests, if it exists at all, on shaky legal ground not likely to be trod save in the gravest of situations.

7. Truman's *Memoirs* indicate that having tried and failed to make Stevenson an avowed candidate in the spring of 1952, the President decided to support the candidacy of Vice Presi-

dent Barkley. But Barkley withdrew early in the convention for lack of key northern support. Though Truman is silent on the matter, Barkley's active candidacy nearly was revived during the balloting, but the forces then aligning to revive it were led by opponents of Truman's Fair Deal, principally Southerners. As a practical matter, the President could not have lent his weight to their endeavors and could back no one but Stevenson to counter them. The latter's strength could not be shifted, then, to Harriman or Kefauver. Instead the other Northerners had to be withdrawn. Truman helped withdraw them. But he had no other option. See Harry S Truman, *Memoirs*, vol. 2, *Years of Trial and Hope* (Garden City, N.Y.: Doubleday, Time Inc., 1956), pp. 495–96.

8. The reference is to Stassen's public statement of July 23, 1956, calling for Nixon's replacement on the Republican ticket by Governor Herter of Massachusetts, the later secretary of state. Stassen's statement was issued after a conference with the President. Eisenhower's public statements on the vice-presidential nomination, both before and after Stassen's call, permit of alternative inferences: either that the President would have preferred another candidate, provided this could be arranged without a showing of White House dictation, or that he wanted Nixon on condition that the latter could show popular appeal. In the event, neither result was achieved. Eisenhower's own remarks lent strength to rapid party moves that smothered Stassen's effort. Nixon's nomination thus was guaranteed too quickly to appear the consequence of popular demand. For the public record on this matter see reported statements by Eisenhower, Nixon, Stassen, Herter, and Leonard Hall (the National Republican Chairman) in the *New York Times* for March 1, 8, 15, 16; April 27; July 15, 16, 25–31; August 3, 4, 17, 23, 1956. See also the account from private sources by Earl Mazo in *Richard Nixon: A Personal and Political Portrait* (New York: Harper, 1959), pp. 158–87

9. Stenographic transcript of presidential press conference, October 19, 1950, on file in the Truman Library at Independence, Missouri.

10. Jonathan Daniels, *Frontier on the Potomac* (New York: Macmillan, 1946), pp. 31–32.

11. Transcript of presidential press conference, June 18, 1958, in *Public Papers of the Presidents Dwight D. Eisenhower, 1958* (Washington, D.C.: National Archives, 1959), p. 479. In the summer of 1958, a congressional investigation into the affairs of a New England textile manufacturer, Bernard Goldfine, revealed that Sherman Adams had accepted various gifts and favors from him (the most notoriety attached to a vicuna coat). Adams also had made inquiries about the status of a Federal Communications Commission proceeding in which Goldfine was involved. In September 1958 Adams was allowed to resign. The episode was highly publicized and much discussed in that year's congressional campaigns.

12. As reported in Marriner S. Eccles (*Beckoning Frontiers*, New York: Knopf, 1951), p. 336.

13. In drawing together these observations on the Marshall Plan, I have relied on the record of personal participation by Joseph M. Jones, *The Fifteen Weeks* (New York: Viking, 1955), especially pp. 89–256; on the recent study by Harry Bayard Price, *The Marshall Plan and Its Meaning* (Ithaca: Cornell University Press, 1955), especially pp. 1–86; on the Truman *Memoirs*, vol. 2, chaps. 7–9; on Arthur H. Vandenberg, Jr., ed., *The Private Papers of Senator Vandenberg* (Boston: Houghton Mifflin, 1952), especially pp. 373 ff.; and on notes of my own made at the time. This is an instance of policy development not covered, to my knowledge, by any of the university programs engaged in the production of case studies.

14. Secretary Marshall's speech, formally suggesting what became known as the Marshall Plan, was made at Harvard on June 5, 1947. On June 20 the President vetoed the Taft-Hartley

Act; his veto was overridden three days later. On June 16 he vetoed the first of two tax reduction bills (HR 1) passed at the first session of the Eightieth Congress; the second of these (HR 3950), a replacement for the other, he also disapproved on July 18. In both instances his veto was narrowly sustained.

15. *Private Papers of Senator Vandenberg*, pp. 378–79, 446.

16. The initial reluctance of the Secretary of the Treasury, John Snyder, to support large-scale spending overseas became a matter of public knowledge on June 25, 1947. At a press conference on that day he interpreted Marshall's Harvard speech as a call on Europeans to help themselves, by themselves. At another press conference the same day, Marshall for his own part had indicated that the United States would consider helping programs on which Europeans agreed. The next day Truman held a press conference and was asked the inevitable question. He replied, "General Marshall and I are in complete agreement." When pressed further, Truman remarked sharply, "The secretary of the treasury and the secretary of state and the President are in complete agreement." Thus the President cut Snyder off, but had programming gathered less momentum overseas, no doubt he would have been heard from again as time passed and opportunity offered.

The foregoing quotations are from the stenographic transcript of the presidential press conference June 26, 1947, on file in the Truman Library at Independence, Missouri.

17. A remark made in December 1955, three years after he left office, but not unrepresentative of views he expressed, on occasion, while he was President.

18. This might also be taken as testimony to the political timidity of officials in the State Department and the Budget Bureau where that fear seems to have been strongest. However, conversations at the time with White House aides incline me to believe that there, too, interjection of the price issue was thought a gamble and a risk. For further comment see my "Congress and the Fair Deal: A Legislative Balance Sheet," *Public Policy*, vol. 5 (Cambridge: Harvard University Press, 1954), pp. 362–64.

7-2

from *Going Public*

Samuel Kernell

Richard Neustadt, writing in 1960, judged that the president's ability to lead depended on skill at the bargaining table in cutting deals with other politicians. In the following essay Samuel Kernell examines how the leadership strategy of modern presidents has evolved. He finds that, rather than limiting their leadership to quiet diplomacy with fellow Washingtonians, modern presidents often "go public," a set of activities borrowed from presidential election campaigns and directed toward persuading other politicians to adopt their policy preferences. Some examples of going public are a televised press conference, a special prime-time address to the nation, traveling outside Washington to deliver a speech to a business or professional convention, and a visit to a day care center with network cameras trailing behind.

Introduction: Going Public in Theory and Practice

WHEN PRESIDENT BUSH delivered his State of the Union address to the joint assembly of the mostly Democratic Congress in January 1992, he assumed what has become a familiar stance with Congress:

> I pride myself that I am a prudent man, and I believe that patience is a virtue. But I understand that politics is for some a game. . . . I submit my plan tomorrow. And I am asking you to pass it by March 20. And I ask the American people to let you know they want this action by March 20.
>
> From the day after that, if it must be: The battle is joined.
>
> And you know when principle is at stake, I relish a good fair fight.

Once upon a time, these might have been fighting words, but in this era of divided government, with the legislative and executive branches controlled by different parties, and presidents who therefore routinely enlist public support in their dealings with other Washington politicians, such rhetoric caused hardly a ripple in Congress.

Source: Samuel Kernell, *Going Public: New Strategies of Presidential Leadership,* 3d ed. (Washington, D.C.: CQ Press, 1997), 1–12, 17–26, 34–38, 57–64.

By 1992, presidential appeals for public support had, in fact, become commonplace. Jimmy Carter delivered four major television addresses on the energy crisis alone and was about to give a fifth when his pollster convinced him that he would be wasting his time. Richard Nixon employed prime-time television so extensively to promote his policies on Vietnam that the Federal Communications Commission (FCC) took an unprecedented step when it applied the "fairness doctrine" to a presidential appeal and granted critics of the war response time on the networks.[1] (In the past, the FCC had occasionally invoked the "equal time" rule during presidential campaigns.) More than any other of Bush's predecessors, Ronald Reagan excelled in rallying public opinion behind presidential policies, but by the end of his second term, he had worn out his welcome with the networks, who stood to lose at least $200,000 in advertising each time he delivered one of his prime-time addresses. They instituted an independent assessment of the likely newsworthiness of the president's address, thereby managing to pare down the frequency of Reagan's televised speeches.[2]

I call the approach to presidential leadership that has come into vogue at the White House "going public." It is a strategy whereby a president promotes himself and his policies in Washington by appealing to the American public for support. Forcing compliance from fellow Washingtonians by going over their heads to appeal to their constituents is a tactic not unknown during the first half of the century, but it was seldom attempted. Theodore Roosevelt probably first enunciated the strategic principle of going public when he described the presidency as the "bully pulpit." Moreover, he occasionally put theory into practice with public appeals for his Progressive reforms. During the next thirty years, other presidents also periodically summoned public support to help them in their dealings with Congress. Perhaps the most famous such instance is Woodrow Wilson's ill-fated whistle-stop tour of the country on behalf of his League of Nations treaty. Another historic example is Franklin D. Roosevelt's series of radio "fireside chats," which were designed less to subdue congressional opposition than to remind politicians throughout Washington of his continuing national mandate for the New Deal.

These historical instances are significant in large part because they were rare. Unlike President Nixon, who thought it important "to spread the White House around" by traveling and speaking extensively,[3] these earlier presidents were largely confined to Washington and obliged to speak to the country through the nation's newspapers. The concept and legitimizing precedents of going public may have been established during these years, but the emergence of presidents who *routinely* do so to promote their policies in Washington awaited the development of modern systems of transportation and mass communications. Going public should be appreciated as a strategic adaptation to the information age.

The regularity with which recent presidents have sought public backing for their Washington dealings has altered the way politicians both inside and outside the White House regard the office. The following chapters of this book present numerous instances of presidents preoccupied with public relations, as if these activities chiefly determined their success. Cases are recounted of other Washington politicians intently monitoring the president's popularity ratings and his addresses on television, as if his performance in these realms governed their own behavior. Also examined are testimonials of central institutional figures, such as those from various Speakers of the House of Representatives, citing the president's prestige and rhetoric as they explain Congress's actions. If the public ruminations of politicians are to be believed, the president's effectiveness in rallying public support has become a primary consideration for those who do business with him.

Presidential Theory

Going public merits study because presidents now appeal to the public routinely. But there is another reason as well. Compared with many other aspects of the modern presidency, scholarship has only recently directed its attention toward this feature of the president's repertoire. Although going public had not become a keystone of presidential leadership in the 1950s and 1960s when much of the influential scholarship on the subject was written, sufficient precedents were available for scholars to consider its potential for presidential leadership in the future.

Probably the main reason presidential scholarship has shortchanged going public is its fundamental incompatibility with bargaining. Presidential power is the "power to bargain," as Richard E. Neustadt taught a generation of students of the presidency.[4] When Neustadt gave this theme its most evocative expression in 1960, the "bargaining president" had already become a centerpiece of pluralist theories of American politics. Nearly a decade earlier, Robert A. Dahl and Charles E. Lindblom had described the politician in America generically as "the human embodiment of a bargaining society." They made a special point to include the president in writing that despite his possessing "more hierarchical controls than any other single figure in the government . . . like everyone else . . . the President must bargain constantly."[5] Since Neustadt's landmark study, other major works in the field have reinforced and elaborated on the concept of the bargaining president.[6]

Going public violates bargaining in several ways. First, it rarely includes the kinds of exchanges necessary, in pluralist theory, for the American political system to function properly. At times, going public will be merely superfluous—

fluff compared with the substance of traditional political exchange. Practiced in a dedicated way, however, it can threaten to displace bargaining.

Second, going public fails to extend benefits for compliance, but freely imposes costs for noncompliance. In appealing to the public to "tell your senators and representatives by phone, wire, and Mailgram that the future hangs in balance," the president seeks the aid of a third party—the public—to force other politicians to accept his preferences.[7] If targeted representatives are lucky, the president's success may cost them no more than an opportunity at the bargaining table to shape policy or to extract compensation. If unlucky, they may find themselves both capitulating to the president's wishes and suffering the reproach of constituents for having resisted him in the first place. By imposing costs and failing to offer benefits, going public is more akin to force than to bargaining. Nelson W. Polsby makes this point when he says that members of Congress may "find themselves ill disposed toward a president who prefers to deal indirectly with them [by going public] through what they may interpret as coercion rather than face-to-face in the spirit of mutual accommodation."[8] The following comment of one senator may well sum up commonly felt sentiments, if not the actions, of those on Capitol Hill who find themselves repeatedly pressured by the president's public appeals: "A lot of Democrats, even if they like the President's proposal, will vote against him because of his radio address on Saturday."[9]

Third, going public entails public posturing. To the extent that it fixes the president's bargaining position, posturing makes subsequent compromise with other politicians more difficult. Because negotiators must be prepared to yield some of their clients' preferences to make a deal, bargaining proverbially proceeds best behind closed doors. Consider the difficulty Ronald Reagan's widely publicized challenge "My tax proposal is a line drawn in dirt" posed for subsequent budget negotiations in Washington.[10] Similarly, during his nationally televised State of the Union address in 1994, President Bill Clinton sought to repair his reputation as someone too willing to compromise away his principles by declaring to the assembled joint session of Congress, "If you send me [health care] legislation that does not guarantee every American private health insurance that can never be taken away, you will force me to take this pen, veto the legislation, and we'll come right back here and start all over again."[11] Not only did these declarations threaten to cut away any middle ground on which a compromise might be constructed, they probably stiffened the resolve of the president's adversaries, some of whom would later be needed to pass the administration's legislative program.

Finally, and possibly most injurious to bargaining, going public undermines the legitimacy of other politicians. It usurps their prerogatives of office, denies their role as representatives, and questions their claim to reflect the interests of their constituents. For a traditional bargaining stance with the president to be restored, these politicians would first have to reestablish parity, probably at a cost of conflict with the White House.[12]

Given these fundamental incompatibilities, one may further speculate that by spoiling the bargaining environment, going public renders the president's future influence ever more dependent upon his ability to generate popular support for himself and his policies. The degree to which a president draws upon public opinion determines the kind of leader he will be.

Presidential Practice

Bargaining and going public have never been, in principle, particularly congenial styles of leadership. One can imagine, however, that in an earlier era, when technology limited the capacity and tendency of presidents to engage in public relations, these two strategies of leadership might have coexisted in quiet tension. In modern times, though, when going public is likely to take the form of a political campaign which engages the energies of numerous presidential aides and the president's attention, the choice has become clear: to choose one strategy of leadership makes it increasingly difficult to undertake the other. And since they cannot be naively combined, the decision to go public at one juncture may preclude and undermine the opportunity to bargain at another, and vice versa. All this means that the decision to bargain or to go public must be carefully weighed.

The two case studies below reveal that modern presidents and their advisers carefully attend to this strategic issue. As we shall do throughout this book, we compare instances of presidential success and failure in order to understand the potential gains and losses embedded in presidents' choices.

Ronald Reagan Enlists Public Opinion as a Lever

No president has enlisted public strategies to better advantage than did Ronald Reagan. Throughout his tenure, he exhibited a full appreciation of bargaining and going public as the modern office's principal strategic alternatives. The following examples from a six-month survey of White House news coverage show how entrenched this bifurcated view of presidential strategy has become. The survey begins in late November 1984, when some members of the administration were pondering how the president might exploit his landslide victory and others were preparing a new round of budget cuts and a tax reform bill for the next Congress.

November 29, 1984. Washington Post columnist Lou Cannon reported the following prediction from a White House official: "We're going to have confrontation on spending and consultation on tax reform." The aide explained, "We have somebody to negotiate with us on tax reform, but may not on budget cuts."[13] By "confrontation" he was referring to the president's success in appealing to the public on national television, that is, in going public. By "consultation" he meant bargaining.

January 25, 1985. The above prediction proved accurate two months later when another staffer offered as pristine an evocation of going public as one is likely to find: "We have to look at it, in many ways, like a campaign. He [Reagan] wants to take his case to the people. You have a constituency of 535 legislators as opposed to 100 million voters. But the goal is the same—to get the majority of voters to support your position."[14]

February 10, 1985. In a nationally broadcast radio address, President Reagan extended an olive branch inviting members of Congress to "work with us in the spirit of cooperation and compromise" on the budget. This public statement probably did little to allay the frequently voiced suspicion of House Democratic leaders that such overtures were mainly intended for public consumption. One Reagan aide insisted, however, that the president simply sought to reassure legislators that "he would not 'go over their heads' and campaign across the country for his budget without trying first to reach a compromise."[15] In this statement the aide implicitly concedes the harm public pressure can create for bargaining but seeks to incorporate it advantageously into the strategic thinking of the politicians with whom the administration must deal by not forswearing its use.

March 9, 1985. After some public sparring, the administration eventually settled down to intensive budget negotiations with the Republican-led Senate Finance Committee. Failing to do as well as he would like, however, Reagan sent a message to his party's senators through repeated unattributed statements to the press that, if necessary, he would "go to the people to carry our message forward."[16] Again, public appeals, though held in reserve, were threatened.

March 11, 1985. In an interview with a *New York Times* correspondent, a senior Reagan aide sized up his president: "He's liberated, he wants to get into a fight, he feels strongly and wants to push his program through himself. . . . Reagan never quite believed his popularity before the election, never believed the polls. Now he has it, and he's going to push . . . ahead with our agenda."[17]

May 16, 1985. To avoid entangling tax reform with budget deliberations in Congress, Reagan, at the request of Republican leaders, delayed unveiling his tax reform proposal until late May. A couple of weeks before Reagan's national television address on the subject, White House aides began priming the press with leaks on the proposal's content and promises that the president would follow it with a public relations blitz. In the words of one White House official, the plan was to force Congress to make a "binary choice between tax reform or no tax reform."[18] The administration rejected bargaining, as predicted nearly six months earlier by a White House aide, apparently for two strategic reasons. First, Reagan feared that in a quietly negotiated process, the tax reform package would unravel under the concerted pressure of the special interests. Second, by taking the high profile approach of "standing up for the people against the special interests," in the words of one adviser, tax reform might do for Republicans what social security did for Democrats—make them the majority party.[19]

During these six months when bargaining held out promise—as it had during negotiations with the Senate Finance Committee—public appeals were held in reserve. The White House occasionally, however, threatened an appeal in trying to gain more favorable consideration. On other occasions, when opponents of the president's policies appeared capable of extracting major concessions—House Democrats on the budget and interest groups on tax reform, for example—the White House disengaged from negotiation and tried through public relations to force Congress to accept his policies. Although by 1985 news items such as the preceding excerpts seemed unexceptional as daily news, they are a recent phenomenon. One does not routinely find such stories in White House reporting twenty years earlier when, for example, John Kennedy's legislative agenda was stalled in Congress.

President Clinton Snares Himself by Bargaining

Shortly after assuming office, President Clinton received some bad news. The Bush administration had underestimated the size of the next year's deficit by $50 billion. The president's campaign promises of new domestic programs and a middle-class tax cut would have to be put on hold in favor of fulfilling his third, now urgent pledge to trim $500 billion from the deficit over the next five years. On February 17, 1993, President Clinton appeared before a joint session of Congress and a national television audience to unveil his deficit reduction package. The president's deficit-cutting options were constrained by two considerations: he wanted to include minimal stimulus spending to honor his campaign promise, and he faced a Congress controlled by fellow Democrats who were committed to many of the programs under the budget ax. Even with proposed cuts in defense spending, the only way the budget could accommodate these constraints was through a tax increase. The package raised taxes on the highest income groups and introduced a broad energy consumption tax. During the following weeks, the president and his congressional liaison team quietly lobbied Congress. He would not again issue a public appeal until the eve of the final vote in August.

The president soon learned that Republicans in both chambers had united in opposition to the administration proposal. Led by Newt Gingrich in the House of Representatives and Bob Dole in the Senate, Republicans retreated to the sidelines and assumed the role of Greek chorus, ominously chanting "tax and spend liberals." This meant that the administration needed virtually every Democratic vote to win. Democratic members appreciated this, and many began exploiting the rising value of their votes to extract concessions that would make the legislation more favorable to their constituents.

By June the president's bargaining efforts had won him a watered down bill that even he had difficulty being enthusiastic about. Meanwhile, the Republicans' public relations campaign had met with success. The American public had come to regard President Clinton as a "tax and spend liberal." Whereas shortly after the speech, the Los Angeles Times had found half of their polling respondents willing to describe the president's initiative as "bold and innovative" and only 35 percent of them willing to describe it as "tax and spend," by June these numbers had reversed. Now, 53 percent labeled it "tax and spend" and only 28 percent still regarded it as "bold and innovative."[20] Given this turnaround in the public's assessment of the initiative, it was not surprising that the public also downgraded its evaluation of the initiative's sponsor. During the previous five months, President Clinton's approval rating had plunged from 58 to 41 percent.

This was the situation when several of Clinton's senior campaign consultants sounded the alarm in a memo: in only six months the president had virtually exhausted his capacity for leadership. If he did not turn back the current tide of public opinion, he would be weakened beyond repair. In response, the president assembled his senior advisers to evaluate current strategy. This set the stage for a confrontation between those advisers who represented the president in bargaining with other Washingtonians and those staffers who manned the White House public relations machinery. The argument that erupted between these advisers should disabuse anyone of the notion that bargaining and cultivating public support are separate, self-contained spheres of action that do not encroach on one another.[21]

The president's chief pollster, Stanley Greenberg, opened the discussion by stating his and his fellow consultants' position: "We do not exaggerate when we say that our current course, advanced by our economic team and Congressional leaders, threatens to sink your popularity further and weaken your presidency." "The immediate problem," Greenberg explained, "is that thanks to the Republican effort no one views your economic package as anything other than a tax scheme. You must exercise a 'bold zero option,' which is consultant talk for 'rid your policy of any taxes that affect the middle class.'" (In fact, the only tax still in the bill was a 4.3-cent-per-gallon gasoline tax that would raise a modest $20 billion.) Greenberg then unveiled polling data that found broad public support for such a move. He closed by warning everyone in the room, "We have a very short period of time. And if we don't communicate something serious and focused in the period, we're going to be left with what our detractors used to characterize our plan. . . . Don't assume we can fix it in August." This concluded the case for going public. And in order to use this strategy, Clinton had to change course on taxes.

According to those present, the economic and congressional advisers had listened to this argument "with a slow burn." Finally, the president's chief lobbyist, Howard Paster, blurted out, "This isn't an election! The Senate breaks its ass to get a 4.3-cent-a-gallon tax passed, and we can't just abandon it." Besides, they needed the $20 billion provided by the tax to offset other concessions that would be necessary to get the bill passed. "I need all the chips that are available," Paster pleaded. "Don't bargain them away here. Let me have maximum latitude."

From here, the discussion deteriorated into name calling and assignment of blame. It stopped when Clinton started screaming at everyone—"a purple fit" is the way one participant described it. In the end the president decided that he had to stay the course but that he would begin traveling around the country to explain to the public that his economic package was the "best" one that could be enacted. In mid-August, after a concerted public relations campaign that concluded with a nationally televised address, the legislation barely passed. (In the Senate, Vice President Al Gore cast the tie-breaking vote.) The new administration's first legislative initiative had drained its resources both in Congress and across the nation. From here, the Clinton administration limped toward even more difficult initiatives represented by the North American Free Trade Agreement (NAFTA) and health care reform.

Clearly, as both case studies show, going public appears to foster political relations that are quite at odds with those traditionally cultivated through bargaining. One may begin to examine this phenomenon by asking, what is it about modern politics that would inspire presidents to go public in the first place?

How Washington and Presidents Have Changed

The incompatibility of bargaining and going public presents a pressing theoretical question. Why should presidents come to favor a strategy of leadership that appears so incompatible with the principles of pluralist theory? Why, if other Washington elites legitimately and correctly represent the interests of their clients and constituents, would anything be gained by going over their heads? The answers to these questions are several and complex, having to do with the ways Washington and presidents have changed. All in all, bargaining has shown declining efficiency, and opportunities to go public have increased. . . .

There is another, more fundamental reason for the discrepancy between theory and current practice. Presidents have preferred to go public in recent years perhaps because the strategy offers a better prospect of success than it did in the past. Politicians in Washington may no longer be as tractable to bargaining as they once were. We are in an era of divided government, with one party controlling Congress and the other holding the presidency. Each side frequently finds political advantage in frustrating the other. On such occasions, posturing in preparation for the next election takes precedence over bargaining.

The decoupling of voters from political parties across the nation, which makes possible the occurrence of divided government, has also had more pervasive consequences for political relations among politicians in Washington. Weaker leaders, looser coalitions, more individualistic politicians, and stronger public pressure are among the developments reworking political relations in Washington that may inspire presidents to embrace a strategy of leadership antithetical to that prescribed by theory....

The President's Place in Institutionalized Pluralism

Constructing coalitions across the broad institutional landscape of Congress, the bureaucracy, interest groups, courts, and state governments requires a politician who possesses a panoramic view and commands the resources necessary to engage the disparate parochial interests of Washington's political elites. Only the president enjoys such vantage and resources. Traditional presidential scholarship leaves little doubt as to how they should be employed....

> Status and authority yield bargaining advantages. But in a government of "separated institutions sharing powers," they yield them to all sides. With the array of vantage points at his disposal, a President may be far more persuasive than his logic or his charm could make him. But outcomes are not guaranteed by his advantages. There remain the counter pressures those whom he would influence can bring to bear on him from vantage points at their disposal. Command has limited utility; persuasion becomes give-and-take....[22]

Bargaining is thus the essence of presidential leadership, and pluralist theory explicitly rejects unilateral forms of influence as usually insufficient and ultimately costly. The ideal president is one who seizes the center of the Washington bazaar and actively barters with fellow politicians to build winning coalitions. He must do so, according to this theory, or he will forfeit any claim to leadership....

The President's Calculus

... No politician within Washington is better positioned than the president to go outside of the community and draw popular support. With protocoalitions in disarray and members more sensitive to influences from beyond Washington, the president's hand in mobilizing public opinion has been strengthened. For the new Congress—indeed, for the new Washington generally—going public may at times be the most effective course available.

Under these circumstances, the president's prestige assumes the currency of power. It is something to be spent when the coffers are full, to be conserved when low, and to be replenished when empty. As David Gergen remarked when he was President Reagan's communications director, "Everything here is built on the idea that the President's success depends on grassroots support."[23]

Sixteen years later White House officials continue to adhere to this view. Early in 1997, when asked by campaign-weary news reporters why President Clinton maintained such a heavy travel schedule after the election victory, press secretary Michael D. McCurry lectured them on modern political science: "Campaigns are about framing a choice for the American people. . . . When you are responsible for governing you have to use the same tools of public persuasion to advance your program, to build public support for the direction you are attempting to lead."[24]

Modern presidents must be attentive to the polls, but they need not crave the affection of the public. Their relationship with it may be purely instrumental. However gratifying public approval may be, popular support is a resource the expenditure of which must be coolly calculated. As another Clinton aide explained, "Clinton has come to believe that if he keeps his approval ratings up and sells his message as he did during the campaign, there will be greater accept-ability for his program. . . . The idea is that you have to sell it as if in a campaign."[25]

Bargaining presidents require the sage advice of politicians familiar with the bargaining game; presidents who go public need pollsters. Compare the relish with which President Nixon was reported by one of his consultants to have approached the polls with the disdain Truman expressed. "Nixon had all kinds of polls all the time; he sometimes had a couple of pollsters doing the same kind of survey at the same time. He really studied them. He wanted to find the thing that would give him an advantage."[26] The confidant went on to observe that the president wanted poll data "on just about anything and everything" throughout his administration.

Indicative of current fashion, presidents from Carter through Clinton have all had in-house pollsters taking continuous—weekly, even daily—readings of pub-lic opinion.[27] When George Bush reportedly spent $216,000 of Republican National Committee money on in-house polling in one year, many Washington politicians probably viewed the president's use of this resource as excessive. But this figure looked modest after Bill Clinton spent nearly ten times that amount in 1993. That year he averaged three or four polls and an equal number of focus groups each month.[28]

Pollsters vigilantly monitor the pulse of opinion to warn of slippage and to identify opportunities for gain. Before recommending a policy course, they assess its costs in public support. Sometimes, as with Clinton's pollsters, they go so far as to ask the public whether the president should bargain with Congress's leaders or challenge them by mobilizing public opinion.[29] These advisers' regular and frequently unsolicited denials that they affected policy belie their self-effacement.

To see how the strategic prescriptions of going public differ from those of bargaining, consider the hypothetical case of a president requiring additional votes if he is to prevail in Congress. If a large number of votes is needed, the most obvious and direct course is to go on prime-time television to solicit the public's active support. Employed at the right moment by a popular president, the effect may be dramatic. This tactic, however, has considerable costs and risks. A real debit of lost public support may occur when a president takes a forthright position. There is also the possibility that the public will not respond, which damages the president's future credibility. Given this, a president understandably finds the *threat* to go public frequently more attractive than the *act*. To the degree such a threat is credible, the anticipated responses of some representatives and senators may suffice to achieve victory.

A more focused application of popular pressure becomes available as an election nears. Fence-sitting representatives and senators may be plied with promises of reelection support or threats of presidential opposition. This may be done privately and selectively, or it may be tendered openly to all who may vote on the president's program. Then there is the election itself. By campaigning, the president who goes public can seek to alter the partisan composition of Congress and thereby gain influence over that institution's decisions in the future.

All of these methods for generating publicity notwithstanding, going public offers fewer and simpler stratagems than does its pluralist alternative. At the heart of the latter lies bargaining, which above all else involves choice: choice among alternative coalitions, choice of specific partners, and choice of the goods and services to be bartered. The number and variety of choices place great demands upon strategic calculation, so much so that pluralist leadership must be understood as an art. In Neustadt's schema, the president's success ultimately reduces to intuition, an ability to sense "right choices."[30]

Going public also requires choice, and it leaves ample room for the play of talent. (One need only compare the television performance of Carter and Reagan.) Nonetheless, public relations appears to be a less obscure matter. Going public promises a straightforward presidency—its options fewer, its strategy simpler, and consequently, its practitioner's behavior more predictable.

Thus there is a rationale for modern presidents to go public in the emerging character of Washington politics. As Washington comes to depend on looser, more individualistic political relations, presidents searching for strategies that work will increasingly go public.

So far, I have said little about the individual in the White House or the personal character of leadership. To consider these ingredients important does not violate any of the assumptions made here. Rationality does not leave choice to be determined strictly by the environment. To the degree occupants of the Oval Office differ in their skills and conceptions of leadership, one may expect that similar circumstances will sometimes result in different presidential behavior.

Perhaps, as has frequently been suggested, presidents go public more today because of who they are. What did Jimmy Carter and Ronald Reagan have in common? The answer is their lack of interest in active negotiation with fellow politicians and their confidence in speaking directly to the voters.

The Calculus of Those Who Deal with the President

Those Washingtonians who conduct business with the president observe his behavior carefully. Their judgment about his leadership guides them in their dealings with him. Traditionally, the professional president watchers have asked themselves the following questions: What are his priorities? How much does he care whether he wins or loses on a particular issue? How will he weigh his options? Is he capable of winning?

Each person will answer these questions about the president's will and skill somewhat differently, of course, depending upon his or her institutional vantage. The chief lobbyist for the United Auto Workers, a network White House correspondent, and the mayor of New York City may size up the president differently depending upon what they need from him. Nonetheless, they arrive at their judgments about the president in similar ways. Each observes the same behavior, inspects the same personal qualities, evaluates the views of the same recognized opinion leaders—columnists and commentators, among others—and tests his or her own tentative opinions with those of fellow community members. Local opinion leaders promote a general agreement among Washingtonians in their assessments of the president. Their agreement is his reputation.[31]

A president with a strong reputation does better in his dealings largely because others expect fewer concessions from him. Accordingly, he finds them more compliant; an orderly marketplace prevails. Saddled with a weak reputation, conversely, a president must work harder. Because others expect him to be less effective, they press him harder in expectation of greater gain. Comity at the bargaining table may give way to contention as other politicians form unreasonable expectations of gain. Through such expectations, the president's reputation regulates community relations in ways that either facilitate or impede his success. In a world of institutionalized pluralism, bargaining presidents seldom actively traded upon their prestige, leaving it to influence Washington political elites only through their anticipation of the electorate's behavior. As a consequence, prestige remained largely irrelevant to other politicians' assessments of the president.[32] Once presidents began going public and interjecting prestige directly into their relations with fellow politicians, and once these politicians found their resistance to this pressure diminished because of their own altered circumstances, the president's ability to marshal public opinion soon became an important ingredient of his reputation. New questions were added to traditional ones. Does the president feel strongly enough about an issue to go public? Will he follow through on his threats to do so? Does his standing in the country run so deep that it will likely be converted into mail to members of Congress, or is it so shallow that it will expire as he attempts to use it?

In today's Washington, the answers to these questions contribute to the president's reputation. As a consequence, his prestige and reputation have lost much of their separateness. The community's estimates of Carter and Reagan rose and fell with the polls. Through reputation, prestige has begun to play a larger role in regulating the president's day-to-day transactions with other community members. Grappling with the unclear causes of Carter's failure in Washington, Neustadt arrived at the same conclusion:

> A President's capacity to draw and stir a television audience seems every bit as interesting to current Washingtonians as his ability to wield his formal powers. This interest is his opportunity. While national party organizations fall away, while congressional party discipline relaxes, while interest groups proliferate and issue networks rise, a President who wishes to compete for leadership in framing policy and shaping coalitions has to make the most he can out of his popular connection. Anticipating home reactions, Washingtonians . . . are vulnerable to any breeze from home that presidential words and sights can stir. If he is deemed effective on the tube they will anticipate. That is the essence of professional reputation.[33]

The record supports Neustadt's speculation. In late 1978 and early 1979, with his monthly approval rating dropping to less than 50 percent, President Carter complained that it was difficult to gain Congress's attention for his legislative proposals. As one congressional liaison official stated, "When you go up to the Hill and the latest polls show Carter isn't doing well, then there isn't much reason for a member to go along with him."[34] A member of Congress concurred: "The relationship between the President and Congress is partly the result of how well the President is doing politically. Congress is better behaved when he does well. . . . Right now, it's almost as if Congress is paying no attention to him."[35]

NOTES

1. Newton N. Minow, John Bartlow Martin, and Lee M. Mitchell, *Presidential Television* (New York: Basic Books, 1973), 84–87.

2. Peter J. Boyer, "Networks Refuse to Broadcast Reagan's Plea," *New York Times*, February 3, 1988.

3. Robert B. Semple Jr., "Nixon Eludes Newsmen on Coast Trip," *New York Times*, August 3, 1970, 16.

4. Richard E. Neustadt, *Presidential Power* (New York: John Wiley and Sons, 1980).

5. Robert A. Dahl and Charles E. Lindblom, *Politics, Economics, and Welfare* (New York: Harper and Row, 1953), 333.

6. Among them are Aaron Wildavsky, *The Politics of the Budgetary Process* (Boston: Little, Brown, 1964); Graham T. Allison, *The Essence of Decision: Explaining the Cuban Missile Crisis* (New York: HarperCollins, 1987); Hugh Heclo, *The Government of Strangers* (Washington, D.C.: Brookings Institution, 1977); and Nelson W. Polsby, *Consequences of Party Reform* (New York: Oxford University Press, 1983).

7. From Ronald Reagan's address to the nation on his 1986 budget. Jack Nelson, "Reagan Calls for Public Support of Deficit Cuts," *Los Angeles Times*, April 25, 1985, 1.

8. Nelson W. Polsby, "Interest Groups and the Presidency: Trends in Political Intermediation in America," in *American Politics and Public Policy*, ed. Walter Dean Burnham and Martha Wagner Weinbey (Cambridge: MIT Press, 1978), 52.

9. Hedrick Smith, "Bitterness on Capitol Hill," *New York Times*, April 24, 1985, 14.

10. Ed Magnuson, "A Line Drawn in Dirt," *Time*, February 22, 1982, 12–13.

11. William J. Clinton, *Public Papers of the Presidents of the United States: William J. Clinton, 1994*, vol. 1 (Washington, D.C.: Government Printing Office, 1995), 126–135.

12. See David S. Broder, "Diary of a Mad Majority Leader," *Washington Post*, December 13, 1981, C1, C5; David S. Broder, "Rostenkowski Knows It's His Turn," *Washington Post National Weekly Edition*, June 10, 1985, 13.

13. Lou Cannon, "Big Spending-Cut Bill Studied," *Washington Post*, November 29, 1984, A8.

14. Bernard Weinraub, "Reagan Sets Tour of Nation to Seek Economic Victory," *New York Times*, January 25, 1985, 43.

15. Bernard Weinraub, "Reagan Calls for 'Spirit of Cooperation' on Budget and Taxes," *New York Times*, February 10, 1985, 32. On Democratic suspicions of Reagan's motives see Hedrick Smith, "O'Neill Reflects Democratic Strategy on Budget Cuts and Tax Revisions," *New York Times*, December 6, 1984, B20; and Margaret Shapiro, "O'Neill's New Honeymoon with Reagan," *Washington Post National Weekly Edition*, February 11, 1985, 12.

16. Jonathan Fuerbringer, "Reagan Critical of Budget View of Senate Panel," *New York Times*, March 9, 1985, 1. Senate Majority Leader Bob Dole told reporters that if the president liked the Senate's final budget package he would campaign for it "very vigorously . . . going to television, whatever he needs to reduce federal spending." Karen Tumulty, "Reagan May Get Draft of Budget Accord Today," *Los Angeles Times*, April 4, 1985, 1.

17. Bernard Weinraub, "In His 2nd Term, He Is Reagan the Liberated," *New York Times*, March 11, 1985, 10.

18. David E. Rosenbaum, "Reagan Approves Primary Elements of Tax Overhaul," *New York Times*, May 16, 1985, 1.

19. Robert W. Merry and David Shribman, "G.O.P. Hopes Tax Bill Will Help It Become Majority Party Again," *Wall Street Journal*, May 23, 1985, 1. See also Rosenbaum, "Reagan Approves Primary Elements of Tax Overhaul," 14. Instances such as those reported here continued into summer. See, for example, Jonathan Fuerbringer, "Key Issues Impede Compromise on Cutting Deficit," *New York Times*, June 23, 1985, 22.

20. These figures are reported in Richard E. Cohen, *Changing Course in Washington* (New York: Macmillan, 1994), 180.

21. The account of this meeting comes from Bob Woodward, *The Agenda* (New York: Simon and Schuster, 1994).

22. Richard E. Neustadt, *Presidential Power*, 28–29. Compare with Dahl and Lindblom's earlier observation: "The President possesses more hierarchical controls than any other single figure in the government; indeed, he is often described somewhat romantically and certainly ambiguously as the most powerful democratic executive in the world. Yet like everyone else in the American policy process, the President must bargain constantly—with Congressional leaders, individual Congressmen, his department heads, bureau chiefs, and leaders of nongovernmental organizations" (Dahl and Lindblom, *Politics, Economics, and Welfare*, 333).

23. Sidney Blumenthal, "Marketing the President," *New York Times Magazine*, September 13, 1981, 110.

24. Alison Mitchell, "Clinton Seems to Keep Running Though the Race Is Run and Won," *New York Times*, February 12, 1997, A1, A12.

25. Ibid., A12.

26. Cited in George C. Edwards III, *The Public Presidency* (New York: St. Martin's Press, 1983), 14.

27. B. Drummond Ayres Jr., "G.O.P. Keeps Tabs on Nation's Mood," *New York Times*, November 16, 1981, 20.

28. These figures are cited in George C. Edwards III, "Frustration and Folly: Bill Clinton and the Public Presidency," in *The Clinton Presidency: First Appraisals*, ed. Colin Campbell and Bert A. Rockman (Chatham, N.J.: Chatham House, 1996), 234.

29. In 1993 Clinton's chief pollster, Stanley Greenberg, added such a question to one of his national surveys. Unsurprisingly, a sizable majority favored cooperation with Congress. Bob Woodward, *The Agenda* (New York: Simon and Schuster, 1994), 268–269.

30. Neustadt, *Presidential Power*, especially chap. 8; and Peter Sperlich, "Bargaining and Overload: An Essay on Presidential Power," in *Perspectives on the Presidency*, ed. Aaron Wildavsky (Boston: Little, Brown, 1975).

31. This discussion of reputation follows closely that of Neustadt in *Presidential Power* (New York: John Wiley and Sons, 1980), chap. 4.

32. Neustadt observed that President Truman's television appeal for tighter price controls in 1951 had little visible effect on how Washington politicians viewed the issue. This is the only mention of a president going public in the original eight chapters of the book. Neustadt, *Presidential Power*, 45.

33. Neustadt, *Presidential Power*, 238.

34. Cited in Gary C. Jacobson, *The Politics of Congressional Elections*, 4th ed. (New York: Longman, 1997), 193–194.

35. Statement by Rep. Richard B. Cheney cited in Charles O. Jones, "Congress and the Presidency," in *The New Congress*, eds. Thomas E. Mann and Norman J. Ornstein (Washington, D.C.: American Enterprise Institute, 1981), 241.

7-3

How 3 Weeks of War in Iraq Looked from the Oval Office

Elisabeth Bumiller, David E. Sanger, and Richard W. Stevenson

The constitutional role as commander in chief gives the president extraordinary authority over a narrow range of public policy. When at war presidents have adopted a variety of postures. They may delegate authority (and, presumably, responsibility) to their military commanders, while they shore up the domestic flank against critics in Congress, the press, and the streets. Or they may become their own commanders—pouring over charts, deploying troops, and issuing orders to their field generals. Some presidents began as strong delegators but, finding that they ultimately bore responsibility for failure, eventually came to participate more actively in military strategy. Abraham Lincoln and Harry S. Truman did so successfully. By contrast, Lyndon B. Johnson, trying to contain the Vietnam War to preserve his ambitious and unfinished domestic policy agenda, second-guessed his generals and sometimes rescinded their actions. George W. Bush opted for the hands-off delegator role in Iraq. With the luxury of overwhelming military superiority and near certain victory, he could afford this course. And according to this summary news report of his actions during the three-week war, the posture served him well. Perhaps reflecting the easy access of field commanders to the several hundred journalists "embedded" in the troops, those generals who had expected instant success were the president's earliest doubters.

WASHINGTON, APRIL 13—It was the morning of March 19 in the White House Situation Room, just hours before President Bush's 48-hour ultimatum to Saddam Hussein to get out of Iraq was to expire. President Bush had just polled his war council for any last-minute reservations about the war plan. Hearing none, he issued the "execute" command to Gen. Tommy R. Franks, who saluted back via a flickering video screen from his headquarters in Qatar.

But in a White House that invariably seeks to project unwavering confidence and to portray the commander in chief as always resolute, what participants in the room that morning say they remember was the anxiety.

Source: Elisabeth Bumiller, David E. Sanger, and Richard W. Stevenson, "How 3 Weeks of War in Iraq Looked From the Oval Office," *New York Times*, April 14, 2003.

"You could have heard a pin drop in that room," said a senior administration official who was there. "It was silent for a couple minutes." Then the administration's warrior-turned-diplomat, Secretary of State Colin L. Powell, reached out to touch the president's hand. It was a gesture of support, but it was born, perhaps, of an understanding that the risks ahead were beyond the president's experience.

So much rested on the answer to the question that one of Mr. Bush's top national security aides had posed a few weeks before.

"How long will this go on?" he asked. "Three days, three weeks, three months, three years?" Duration, they all knew, would probably determine casualties, the risk of attacks using chemical or biological weapons, the stability of the Middle East, relations with allies. And, of course, the presidency of George W. Bush, who, some of his advisers acknowledged, was gambling his political future on a quick victory.

The past 25 days have been among the most stressful, emotional and turbulent of the second Bush White House, from the first, audacious attempt to kill Mr. Hussein to the toppling of his statue to the discovery today of seven prisoners of war. A White House that worships order had to react to the chaos of war and a script that kept changing. Sandstorms, unexpected resistance from the enemy and verbal grenades lobbed at the war plan by armchair generals at times forced the White House into a defensive crouch. . . .

Those 25 days have shown Mr. Bush to be short-tempered with criticism of the war plan in the days when the campaign did not appear to be going well, and downcast when confronted with American battlefield deaths and the capture of women as prisoners of war. With disgust, he told a member of his war council that the Iraqis "fight like terrorists."

But he has also shown patience in giving the plan a chance to work, . . . and in his determination to leave battlefield tactics in the hands of his battlefield commander, General Franks.

As always, he was a creature of the routines that make his own world orderly, even as chaos streamed across the television screen. He stuck to his rituals: first briefings by 6 a.m., war council meetings, daily exercise, regular prayer, early bedtimes, weekends at Camp David. His travel was limited to military bases, where he could rally the troops and comfort their families, and to a trip to Northern Ireland as a payback to his most faithful foreign ally, Prime Minister Tony Blair of Britain.

By this past Wednesday, as Mr. Bush stepped out of a meeting in the Oval Office with the president of Slovakia and watched on television as celebrating Iraqis dragged Mr. Hussein's statue through the streets, the war routine seemed to break. "They got it down!" Mr. Bush exclaimed. One of the aides with him said, "He knew it wasn't the end, but he could finally see the beginning of the end."

By this afternoon, stepping out of his helicopter, Mr. Bush looked happier than he had in weeks. . . .

The First Hours: A Plan Is Put in Motion, Quickly

The war plan that Mr. Bush approved in the situation room on the morning of March 19 remained intact for about six hours.

By early afternoon, George J. Tenet, the director of central intelligence, had learned of a stunning tip from an Iraqi spy: Mr. Hussein was very likely to be in a bunker in southern Baghdad that night. Mr. Tenet raced to the Pentagon to discuss the information with Secretary of Defense Donald H. Rumsfeld and Gen. Richard B. Myers, the chairman of the joint chiefs of staff. General Franks, meanwhile, had received the same information from C.I.A. officers in the field, and ordered two F-117 stealth fighter-bombers aloft in case the president ordered a strike.

By 3:30 p.m., all three men had gathered in the Oval Office, along with Condoleezza Rice, the national security adviser, and Andrew H. Card Jr., the White House chief of staff. Mr. Bush listened impassively, advisers said, as the group discussed the source of the information and the risks of the operation. "It had huge possibilities," one of the participants in the conversation said. "You know, huge, positive outcomes." But they spent time, this participant said, discussing how an early strike would "affect the rest of what is planned"—and the damage that could be done if the information was wrong.

For hours the group talked through the possibilities. "You know—that the Iraqis might do the baby-milk factory thing again," the participant said, a reference to a famous moment in the 1991 gulf war when Western reporters were taken to see the injuries at a supposed civilian location.

The president worried that there would be propaganda that "you struck women and children."

Ms. Rice, according to the official who was at the meeting, reminded the group that Iraqis "love to propagandize and lie about what's just taken place."

By 7:12 p.m., three minutes before what General Franks said was the deadline for making a decision, Mr. Bush determined it was worth the risk. "Let's go," he said, according to an aide. By 9:30 p.m. Washington time, the bunker had been bombed. Some 45 minutes later, Mr. Bush addressed the nation. "On my orders, coalition forces have begun striking selected targets of military importance," he said in a four-minute speech from the Oval Office.

At least outwardly, Mr. Bush took it all in stride. Before his Oval Office address that Wednesday night, he gave a little pump of his fist and said "feel good" to an aide in the room. By 10:40 p.m., he was back in the White House residence watching television with his wife, Laura. At one point a crawl line on one of the cable news channels informed viewers that the president and first lady had gone to sleep—the it's-all-under-control spin being dispensed downstairs in the press room.

"Whoops, we'd better go to bed," Mrs. Bush said, according to a friend who spoke to her afterward.

That Friday, March 21, just as his father had done on the first weekend of the first gulf war, Mr. Bush went to Camp David. He asked Roland W. Betts, his old fraternity rush chairman from Yale and one of his closest friends, to come along. The two spent hours that Saturday walking the trails, working out in the Camp David gym, watching the battle news on television and talking of little else but the war.

"He is just totally immersed," Mr. Betts said after coming off the mountain.

Lowering Expectations: A Rolling Start Turns Rough

But it turned out that Mr. Bush was entering the tactical and emotional low point of the war. He was awakened early in his cabin at Camp David that Sunday, March 22, and informed that American soldiers had apparently been captured in the Iraqi town of Nasiriya, and that one of them was a woman, Specialist Shoshana N. Johnson. "That troubled him," Mr. Betts said. Specialist Johnson was one of the P.O.W.'s found alive today.

The president returned to the White House that afternoon as scheduled, and in his first give-and-take with reporters since the start of the war he tried to lower expectations. "It is evident that it's going to take a while to achieve our objective, but we're on course, we're determined and we're making good progress," he said. But he seemed almost too emphatic, and inside the White House some aides were already concerned that the warm welcome Mr. Cheney had predicted for the troops in the south was not materializing.

By midweek, critics were beginning to question the relatively small size of the allied force in Iraq and to ask why the C.I.A. had not foreseen the fierce paramilitary resistance in the south. Mr. Bush's aides say the president never shared those doubts, even as he was pressing them incessantly for updates. When a reporter was visiting one top aide for 20 minutes that Tuesday, the president called twice pressing for new details.

On Wednesday, on his way to a speech at the headquarters of the United States Central Command in Tampa, Fla., Mr. Bush scratched from his remarks an assessment that the battle plan was ahead of schedule. Instead, he changed tones.

"The path we are taking is not easy, and it may be long," he said in the speech.

On Thursday, Mr. Bush seemed peevish during a news conference at Camp David with Mr. Blair, whose combination of passion and artful articulation dominated the event. At one point, Mr. Bush was reduced to standing by silently as Mr. Blair made an ardent speech about the success of the war. "I have nothing more to add to that," the president said.

By Friday, explosive comments made in Iraq by the commander of the Army forces in the Persian Gulf, Lt. Gen. William S. Wallace, were all over the front pages of the newspapers. "The enemy we're fighting is a bit different than the one we war-gamed against," General Wallace said, an assessment that was widely interpreted to be supportive of the criticism that Mr. Rumsfeld had ignored his generals' warnings that they did not have enough troops.

The White House went into public relations attack mode. A senior administration official described the president as "irritated" and said that Mr. Bush thought questions about whether the conflict was going more slowly than planned were "silly."

The administration was annoyed in part at the news media for filling empty air time with doubts—"Imagine if F.D.R. had to put up with this between D-Day and the fall of Berlin," one snapped—but also at retired officers who were offering critical assessments as part of the round-the-clock television coverage.

At 2 p.m. that Friday, March 28, Mr. Bush stepped out of the Oval Office and across the hall to the Roosevelt Room to meet with a group of veterans—and everyone in the room knew that American forces were now heading toward Baghdad, which was defended by much-feared Iraqi units like the Medina division of the Republican Guard.

"I don't know when the Medina battle will begin; Tommy hasn't told me yet," Mr. Bush told the veterans, referring to General Franks.

The president's point, aides said, was that he was not going to micromanage the war the way Lyndon B. Johnson had during Vietnam—and he was not going to bow to pressure to rewrite the plan every time it hit a bump.

"We don't second-guess out of the White House," Mr. Bush told the veterans. "We don't adjust the plan based on editorials." Then he headed for Camp David.

The Turnaround: Fighting Words and Good News

By Monday, Mr. Bush was fighting back. He traveled to Philadelphia and told cheering members of the Coast Guard that in just 11 days, "coalition forces have taken control of most of western and southern Iraq." "Day by day," he said, "we are moving closer to Baghdad. Day by day, we are moving closer to victory."

The next day, the turnaround began. Shortly before 5 p.m., Mr. Rumsfeld called Mr. Bush to inform him that Pfc. Jessica D. Lynch had been safely rescued from a hospital in Nasiriya. "That's great!" the president said, according to an aide. The news of the rescue saturated coverage the next day, and was treated at the White House as a harbinger that the terms of the conflict were in flux. The following day, April 3, American troops seized parts of Baghdad's international airport, an enormous strategic and psychological victory, putting the forces within sight of the capital. The rapid progress inspired a buoyant mood.

"Our task now is changing from managing irrational skepticism to managing irrational exuberance," a senior administration official said. That same day, an obviously more ebullient Mr. Bush traveled to Camp Lejeune, N.C., to tell 12,000 cheering marines that "a vise is closing" on Mr. Hussein.

He also met privately with the families of some of the marines who had died, hearing their stories, going through family pictures, talking to children whose fathers would never return. "It broke his heart," said one aide who was there. "It's the hardest moment of the job."

The next day, troops from the Army's Third Infantry Division were in control of the airport as Mr. Bush met in the Roosevelt Room with a dozen Iraqi exiles eager for a financial and political stake in a new Baghdad. Mr. Bush, his mood chipper, told the group that the United States was "slowly peeling" the hands of Saddam Hussein and his "thugs" off Iraqi throats, a participant in the meeting said.

After nearly an hour, the participant said, Mr. Bush concluded the meeting by saying, "Listen, I've got to hop," and then headed quickly for the door. But before leaving the room, he turned to the group and, unasked, gave what the visitors took to be a reference to when he thought the war would be over.

"Soon," he said, before disappearing down the hall.

Internal Debate: Battling over Who Runs Iraq

The start of the war suspended several debates within the White House, notably the one between Mr. Powell and the administration's hawks over how to disarm Iraq without wreaking more harm than necessary on America's strained alliances.

But quickly, a new argument took its place. It was about postwar Iraq—who should run it, who should determine which Iraqi leaders should emerge from the seed-corn democracy the United States intended to sow. "Same players, same departments, just a different version of the same fight," one senior White House official said.

The plan Mr. Bush approved before the war called for an interim authority that had a mix of all kinds of Iraqis—the exiles and the "newly liberated." But in the first week of April Mr. Rumsfeld reopened the issue, writing a letter to Mr. Bush saying that he wanted to fly the exiles into the country and give them control of the south. That would give Pentagon favorites, including Ahmad Chalabi, the head of the Iraqi National Congress, a huge advantage in the eventual leadership of the country.

Mr. Powell was alarmed. "He saw this as an effort by the hawks to get their own guys on the ground where they could dominate events," one of Mr. Powell's senior aides said. The C.I.A., also suspicious of the exiles, had similar concerns, though it had ways—including money and advice on the ground in Iraq—to help its favorites.

The revelation of the Rumsfeld letter forced Ms. Rice to come into the White House press room on April 4 to describe what the new government would look like. "She had to set down the law for a lot of these guys," one senior official said. No sooner had she done so, though, than Mr. Chalabi was flown to southern Iraq with a group of lightly armed supporters, to the surprise of American diplomats. "This will get nastier," one senior diplomat predicted.

Meanwhile, a parallel fight broke out over how to describe the role of the United Nations. Ms. Rice said that only countries that had spilled "blood and treasure" would run Iraq. She said the United Nations would have a "major role," but one limited to humanitarian relief. "She was clearly speaking for the president," one official said. "The U.N. doesn't have the juice to get this done. And he's not about to hand the place over to French and Germans."

Yet Mr. Blair needed to show that he had a firm hand on the process. Meeting in Northern Ireland early last week, the president and the Prime Minister finally settled on the words "vital role" to describe the United Nations' future in Iraq—although even Mr. Powell has said he does not know what that means.

Then and Now: The Father, the Son and the Legacy

In some important ways, Mr. Bush's conduct of the war over its first three weeks was about trying to correct mistakes made by his father during and after the first gulf war.

On the afternoon after the first strike against Mr. Hussein, Mr. Bush convened a cabinet meeting to set out the plan for the early stages of the war—and to keep his domestic agenda alive. He warned against focusing so much on the war that issues like education, Medicare and above all the economy got lost or forgotten.

It has become a political cliché to say the current president is obsessed with avoiding the fate of his father, who was turned out of office after one term in part because he was perceived as ignoring the economy. But the story's familiarity does not make it any less compelling to this White House.

Throughout the war, the administration has not only tracked the economic fallout closely but has also tried to keep up the pressure on Congress to pass the centerpiece of Mr. Bush's economic plan, his $726 billion tax cut proposal. But with Mr. Bush consumed by the conflict in Iraq and Democrats hanging together despite pressure from the White House not to buck a wartime president, the administration lost a big round in Congress. It failed, for now at least, to stop the Senate from cutting his tax cut to $350 billion. . . .

Chapter 8

The Bureacracy

8-1

from *Bureaucracy*

James Q. Wilson

When Congress and the president create new programs and assign responsibility for implementing them to executive agencies, they are delegating power that might be used arbitrarily by unelected bureaucrats. To avoid the arbitrary use of power—one of the prime objectives of democracy—they impose rules on agencies. These rules, which serve as beneficial constraints, may limit bureaucrats' options and create inefficiencies in the implementation of policy. In the following essay James Q. Wilson examines the causes and consequences of discretion and arbitrariness and of rules and inefficiencies.

ON THE MORNING of May 22, 1986, Donald Trump, the New York real estate developer, called one of his executives, Anthony Gliedman, into his office. They discussed the inability of the City of New York, despite six years of effort and the expenditure of nearly $13 million, to rebuild the ice-skating rink in Central Park. On May 28 Trump offered to take over the rink reconstruction, promising to do the job in less than six months. A week later Mayor Edward Koch accepted the offer and shortly thereafter the city appropriated $3 million on the understanding that Trump would have to pay for any cost overruns out of his own pocket.

Source: James Q. Wilson, *Bureaucracy: What Government Agencies Do and Why They Do It* (New York: Basic Books, 2000), 315–345. Notes appearing in the original have been deleted.

On October 28, the renovation was complete, over a month ahead of schedule and about $750,000 under budget. Two weeks later, skaters were using it.

For many readers it is obvious that private enterprise is more efficient than are public bureaucracies, and so they would file this story away as simply another illustration of what everyone already knows. But for other readers it is not so obvious what this story means; to them, business is greedy and unless watched like a hawk will fob off shoddy or overprices goods on the American public, as when it sells the government $435 hammers and $3,000 coffeepots. Trump may have done a good job in this instance, but perhaps there is something about skating rinks or New York City government that gave him a comparative advantage; in any event, no larger lessons should be drawn from it.

Some lessons can be drawn, however, if one looks closely at the incentives and constraints facing Trump and the department of Parks and Recreation. It becomes apparent that there is not one "bureaucracy problem" but several, and the solution to each in some degree is incompatible with the solution to every other. First there is the problem of accountability—getting agencies to serve agreed-upon goals. Second there is the problem of equity—treating all citizens fairly, which usually means treating them alike on the basis of clear rules known in advance. Third there is the problem of responsiveness—reacting reasonably to the special needs and circumstances of particular people. Fourth there is the problem of efficiency—obtaining the greatest output for a given level of resources. Finally there is the problem of fiscal integrity—assuring that public funds are spent prudently for public purposes. Donald Trump and Mayor Koch were situated differently with respect to most of these matters.

Accountability. The Mayor wanted the old skating rink refurbished, but he also wanted to minimize the cost of the fuel needed to operate the rink (the first effort to rebuild it occurred right after the Arab oil embargo and the attendant increase in energy prices). Trying to achieve both goals led city hall to select a new refrigeration system that as it turned out would not work properly. Trump came on the scene when only one goal dominated: get the rink rebuilt. He felt free to select the most reliable refrigeration system without worrying too much about energy costs.

Equity. The Parks and Recreation Department was required by law to give every contractor an equal chance to do the job. This meant it had to put every part of the job out to bid and to accept the lowest without much regard to the reputation or prior performance of the lowest bidder. Moreover, state law forbade city agencies from hiring a general contractor and letting him select the subcontractors; in fact, the law forbade the city from even discussing the project in advance with a general contractor who might later bid on it—that would have been collusion. Trump, by contrast, was free to locate the rink builder with the best reputation and give him the job.

Fiscal Integrity. To reduce the chance of corruption or sweetheart deals the law required Parks and Recreation to furnish complete, detailed plans to every contractor bidding on the job; any changes after that would require renegotiating the contract. No such law constrained Trump; he was free to give incomplete plans to his chosen contractor, hold him accountable for building a satisfactory rink, but allow him to work out the details as he went along.

Efficiency. When the Parks and Recreation Department spent over six years and $13 million and still could not reopen the rink, there was public criticism but no city official lost money. When Trump accepted a contract to do it, any cost overruns or delays would have come out of his pocket and any savings could have gone into his pocket (in this case, Trump agreed not to take a profit on the job).

Gliedman summarized the differences neatly: "The problem with government is that government can't say, 'yes' . . . there is nobody in government that can do that. There are fifteen or twenty people who have to agree. Government has to be slower. It has to safeguard the process."

Inefficiency

The government can't say "yes." In other words, the government is constrained. Where do the constraints come from? From us.

Herbert Kaufman has explained red tape as being of our own making: "Every restraint and requirement originates in somebody's demand for it." Applied to the Central Park skating rink Kaufman's insight reminds us that civil-service reformers demanded that no city official benefit personally from building a project; that contractors demanded that all be given an equal chance to bid on every job; and that fiscal watchdogs demanded that all contract specifications be as detailed as possible. For each demand a procedure was established; viewed from the outside, those procedures are called red tape. To enforce each procedure a manager was appointed; those managers are called bureaucrats. No organized group demanded that all skating rinks be rebuilt as quickly as possible, no procedure existed to enforce that demand, and no manager was appointed to enforce it. The political process can more easily enforce compliance with constraints than the attainment of goals.

When we denounce bureaucracy for being inefficient we are saying something that is half true. Efficiency is a ratio of valued resources used to valued outputs produced. The smaller that ratio the more efficient the production. If the valued output is a rebuilt skating rink, then whatever process uses the fewest dollars or the least time to produce a satisfactory rink is the most efficient process. By this test Trump was more efficient than the Parks and Recreation Department.

But that is too narrow a view of the matter. The economic definition of efficiency (efficiency in the small, so to speak) assumes that there is only one valued output, the new rink. But government has many valued outputs, including a reputation for integrity, the confidence of the people, and the support of important interest groups. When we complain about skating rinks not being built on time we speak as if all we cared about were skating rinks. But when we complain that contracts were awarded without competitive bidding or in a way that allowed bureaucrats to line their pockets we acknowledge that we care about many things besides skating rinks; we care about the contextual goals—the constraints—that we want government to observe. A government that is slow to build rinks but is honest and accountable in its actions and properly responsive to worthy constituencies may be a very efficient government, *if* we measure efficiency in the large by taking into account *all* of the valued outputs.

Calling a government agency efficient when it is slow, cumbersome, and costly may seem perverse. But that is only because we lack any objective way for deciding how much money or time should be devoted to maintaining honest behavior, producing a fair allocation of benefits, and generating popular support as well as to achieving the main goal of the project. If we could measure these things, and if we agreed as to their value, then we would be in a position to judge the true efficiency of a government agency and decide when it is taking too much time or spending too much money achieving all that we expect of it. But we cannot measure these things nor do we agree about their relative importance, and so government always will appear to be inefficient compared to organizations that have fewer goals.

Put simply, the only way to decide whether an agency is truly inefficient is to decide which of the constraints affecting its action ought to be ignored or discounted. In fact that is what most debates about agency behavior are all about. In fighting crime are the police handcuffed? In educating children are teachers tied down by rules? In launching a space shuttle are we too concerned with safety? In building a dam do we worry excessively about endangered species? In running the Postal Service is it important to have many post offices close to where people live? In the case of the skating rink, was the requirement of competitive bidding for each contract on the basis of detailed specifications a reasonable one? Probably not. But if it were abandoned, the gain (the swifter completion of the rink) would have to be balanced against the costs (complaints from contractors who might lose business and the chance of collusion and corruption in some future projects).

Even allowing for all of these constraints, government agencies may still be inefficient. Indeed, given the fact that bureaucrats cannot (for the most part) benefit monetarily from their agencies' achievements, it would be surprising if they were not inefficient. Efficiency, in the large or the small, doesn't pay. . . .

Military procurement, of course, is the biggest source of stories about waste, fraud, and mismanagement. There cannot be a reader of this book who has not heard about the navy paying $435 for a hammer or the air force paying $3,000 for a coffeepot, and nobody, I suspect, believes Defense Department estimates of the cost of a new airplane or missile. If ever one needed evidence that bureaucracy is inefficient, the Pentagon supplies it.

Well, yes. But what kind of inefficiency? And why does it occur? To answer these questions one must approach the problem just as we approached the problem of fixing up a skating rink in New York City: We want to understand why the bureaucrats, all of whom are rational and most of whom want to do a good job, behave as they do.

To begin, let us forget about $435 hammers. They never existed. A member of Congress who did not understand (or did not want to understand) government accounting rules created a public stir. The $3,000 coffeepot existed, but it is not clear that it was overpriced. But that does not mean there are no problems; in fact, the real problems are far more costly and intractable than inflated price tags on hammers and coffeemakers. They include sticking too long with new weapons of dubious value, taking forever to acquire even good weapons, and not inducing contractors to increase their efficiency. What follows is not a complete explanation of military procurement problems; it is only an analysis of the contribution bureaucratic systems make to those problems.

When the military buys a new weapons system—a bomber, submarine, or tank—it sets in motion a procurement bureaucracy comprised of two key actors, the military program manager and the civilian contract officer, who must cope with the contractor, the Pentagon hierarchy, and Congress. To understand how they behave we must understand how their tasks get defined, what incentives they have, and what constraints they face.

Tasks

The person nominally in charge of buying a major new weapon is the program manager, typically an army or air force colonel or a navy captain. Officially, his job is to design and oversee the acquisition strategy by establishing specifications and schedules and identifying problems and tradeoffs. Unofficially, his task is somewhat different. For one thing he does not have the authority to make many important decisions; those are referred upward to his military superiors, to Defense Department civilians, and to Congress. For another, the program he oversees must constantly be sold and resold to the people who control the resources (mostly, the key congressional committees). And finally, he is surrounded by inspectors and auditors looking for any evidence of waste, fraud, or abuse and by the advocates of all manner of special interests (contractors' representatives, proponents of small and minority business utilization, and so on). As the Packard Commission observed, the program manager, "far from being the manager of the program . . . is merely one of the participants who can influence it."

Under these circumstances the actual task of the program manager tends to be defined as selling the program and staying out of trouble. Harvard Business School professor J. Ronald Fox, who has devoted much of his life to studying and participating in weapons procurement, found that a program manager must spend 30 to 50 percent of his time defending his program inside DOD and to Congress. It is entirely rational for him to do this, for a study by the General Accounting Office showed that weapons programs with effective advocates survived (including some that should have been terminated) and systems without such advocates were more likely to be ended (even some that should have been completed). Just as with the New York City skating rink, in the Pentagon there is no one who can say "yes" and make it stick. The only way to keep winning the support of the countless people who must say "yes" over and over again is to forge ahead at full speed, spending money at a rate high enough to prevent it from being taken away.

The program manager's own background and experience reinforce this definition of his task. He is a military officer, which means he cares deeply about having the best possible airplane, tank, or submarine. In recommending any trade-offs between cost and performance, his natural inclination is to favor performance over savings. After all, someday he may have to fly in that airplane or sail on that ship. This often leads to what is commonly called "goldplating": seeking the best possible, most sophisticated weapon and making frequent changes in the contract specifications in order to incorporate new features. The program manager, of course, does not make these decisions, but he is an integral part of a user-dominated process that does make them.

The civilian counterpart to the program manager is the contracting officer. What is clear is that he or she, and not the program manager, is the only person legally authorized to sign the contract. In addition, the contracting officer administers the contract and prepares a report on contractor performance. Everything else is unclear. In principle, contracting officers are supposed to be involved in every step of the acquisition process, from issuing an invitation to bid on the contract through the completion of the project. In practice, as Ronald Fox observes, contracting officers often play only a small role in designing the acquisition strategy or in altering the contracts (this tends to be dominated by the program manager) and must share their authority over enforcing the terms of the contract with a small army of auditors and advocates.

What dominates the task of the contract officer are the rules, the more than 1,200 pages of the Federal Acquisition Regulation and Defense Acquisition Regulation in addition to the countless other pages in DOD directives and congressional authorization legislation and the unwritten "guidance" that arrives with every visit to a defense plant where a contracting officer works. Contract officers are there to enforce constraints, and those constraints have grown exponentially in recent years.

Incentives

In theory, military program managers are supposed to win promotions if they have done a good job supervising weapons procurement. In fact, promotions to the rank of general or admiral usually have been made on the basis of their reputation as combat officers and experience as military leaders. . . . The perceived message is clear: Traditional military specialties are a surer route to the top than experience as a program manager.

Reinforcing this bias against acquisition experience is the generalist ethos of the armed services—good officers can do any job; well-rounded officers have done many jobs. As a result, the typical program manager has a brief tenure in a procurement job. In 1986, the GAO found that the average program manager spent twenty-seven months on the job, and many spent less than two years. By contrast, it takes between eleven and twenty years to procure a major new weapons system, from concept to deployment. This means that during the acquisition of a new aircraft or missile, the identity of the program will change five or ten times.

In 1987, the services, under congressional prodding, established career paths for acquisition officers so that they could rise in rank while continuing to develop experience in procurement tasks. It is not yet clear how significant this change will be. If it encourages talented officers to invest ten or twenty years in mastering procurement policies it will be a major gain, one that will enable program managers from DOD to deal more effectively with experienced industry executives and encourage officers to make tough decisions rather than just keeping the program alive.

Civilian contract officers do have a distinct career path, but as yet not one that produces in them much sense of professional pride or organizational mission. Of the more than twenty thousand civilian contract administrators less than half have a college degree and the great majority are in the lower civil-service grades (GS-5 to GS-12). Even the most senior contract officers rarely earn (in 1988) more than $50,000 a year, less than half or even one-third of what their industry counterparts earn. Moreover, all are aware that they work in offices where the top posts usually are held by military officers; in civil-service jargon, the "head room" available for promotions is quite limited. . . .

The best evidence of the weakness of civilian incentives is the high turnover rate. Fox quotes a former commander of the military acquisition program as saying that "good people are leaving in droves" because "there is much less psychic income today" that would make up for the relatively low monetary income. The Packard Commission surveyed civilian procurement personnel and found that over half would leave their jobs if offered comparable jobs elsewhere in the federal government or in private industry.

In short, the incentives facing procurement officials do not reward people for maximizing efficiency. Military officers are rewarded for keeping programs alive and are encouraged to move on to other assignments, civilian personnel have weak inducements to apply a complex array of inconsistent constraints to contract administration.

Constraints

These constraints are not designed to produce efficiency but to reduce costs, avoid waste, fraud, and abuse, achieve a variety of social goals, and maintain the productive capacity of key contractors.

Reducing costs is not the same thing as increasing efficiency. If too little money is spent, the rate of production may be inefficient and the managerial flexibility necessary to cope with unforeseen circumstances may be absent. Congress typically appropriates money one year at a time. If Congress wishes to cut its spending or if DOD is ordered to slash its budget requests, the easiest thing to do is to reduce the number of aircraft, ships, or missiles being purchased in a given year without reducing the total amount purchased. This stretch-out has the effect of increasing the cost of each individual weapon as manufacturers forgo the economies that come from large-scale production. As Fox observes (but as many critics fail to understand), the typical weapons program in any given year is not overfunded, it is *under*funded. Recognizing that, the Packard Commission called for adopting a two-year budget cycle.

Reducing costs and eliminating fraud are not the same as increasing efficiency. There no doubt are excessive costs and there may be fraud in military procurement, but eliminating them makes procurement more efficient only if the costs of eliminating the waste and fraud exceed the savings thereby realized. To my knowledge no one has systematically compared the cost of all the inspectors, rules, and auditors with the savings they have achieved to see if all the checking and reviewing is worth it. Some anecdotal evidence suggests that the checking does not always pay for itself. In one case the army was required to spend $5,400 to obtain fully competitive bids for spare parts that cost $11,000. In exchange for the $5,400 and the 160 days it took to get the bids, the army saved $100. In short, there is an optimal level of "waste" in any organization, public or private: It is that level below which further savings are worth less than the cost of producing them.

The weapons procurement system must serve a number of "social" goals mandated by Congress. It must support small business, provide opportunities for minority-owned businesses, buy American-made products whenever possible, rehabilitate prisoners, provide employment for the handicapped, protect the environment, and maintain "prevailing" wage rates. One could lower the cost of procurement by eliminating some or all of the social goals the process is obliged to honor; that would produce increases in efficiency, narrowly defined. But what interest group is ready to sacrifice its most cherished goal in the name of efficiency? And if none will volunteer, how does one create a congressional majority to compel the sacrifice?

Weapons procurement also is designed to maintain the productive capacity of the major weapons builders. There is no true market in the manufacture of missiles, military aircraft, and naval vessels because typically there is only one buyer (the government) and no alternative uses for the production lines established to supply this buyer. Northrop, Lockheed, Grumman, McDonnell Douglas, the Bath Iron Works, Martin Marietta—these firms and others like them would not exist, or would exist in very different form, if they did not have a continuous flow of military contracts. As a result, each new weapons system becomes a do-or-die proposition for the executives of these firms. Even if the Pentagon cared nothing about their economic well-being it would have to care about the productive capacity that they represent, for if it were ever lost or much diminished the armed services would have nowhere else to turn when the need arose for a new airplane or ship. And if by chance the Pentagon did not care, Congress would; no member believes he or she was elected to preside over the demise of a major employer.

This constraint produces what some scholars have called the "follow-on imperative": the need to give a new contract to each major supplier as work on an old contract winds down. If one understands this it is not necessary to imagine some sinister "military-industrial complex" conspiring to keep new weapons flowing. The armed services want them because they believe, rightly, that their task is to defend the nation against real though hard to define threats; the contractors want them because they believe, rightly, that the nation cannot afford to dismantle its productive capacity; Congress wants them because its members believe, rightly, that they are elected to maintain the prosperity of their states and districts.

When these beliefs encounter the reality of limited resources and the need to make budget choices, almost everyone has an incentive to overstate the benefits and understate the costs of a new weapons system. To do otherwise—to give a cautious estimate of what the weapon will achieve and a candid view of what it will cost—is to invite rejection. And none of the key actors in the process believe they can afford rejection.

The Bottom Line

The incentives and constraints that confront the military procurement bureaucracy push its members to overstate benefits, understate costs, make frequent and detailed changes in specifications, and enforce a bewildering array of rules designed to minimize criticism and stay out of trouble. There are hardly any incentives pushing officials to leave details to manufacturers or delegate authority to strong program managers whose career prospects will depend on their ability to produce good weapons at a reasonable cost.

In view of all this, what is surprising is that the system works as well as it does. In fact, it works better than most people suppose. The Rand Corporation has been studying military procurement for over thirty years. A summary of its findings suggests some encouraging news, most of it ignored amidst the headlines about hammers and coffeepots. There has been steady improvement in the performance of the system. Between the early 1960s and the mid-1980s, cost overruns, schedule slippages, and performance shortfalls have all decreased. Cost overruns of military programs on the average are now no greater than they are for the civil programs of the government such as highway and water projects and public buildings. Moreover, there is evidence that for all its faults the American system seems to work as well or better than that in many European nations. . . .

Arbitrary Rule

Inefficiency is not the only bureaucratic problem nor is it even the most important. A perfectly efficient agency could be a monstrous one, swiftly denying us our liberties, economically inflicting injustices, and competently expropriating our wealth. People complain about bureaucracy as often because it is unfair or unreasonable as because it is slow or cumbersome.

Arbitrary rule refers to officials acting without legal authority, or with that authority in a way that offends our sense of justice. Justice means, first, that we require the government to treat people equally on the basis of clear rules known in advance: If Becky and Bob both are driving sixty miles per hour in a thirty-mile-per hour zone and the police give a ticket to Bob, we believe they also should give a ticket to Becky. Second, we believe that justice obliges the government to take into account the special needs and circumstances of individuals: If Becky is speeding because she is on her way to the hospital to give birth to a child and Bob is speeding for the fun of it, we may feel that the police should ticket Bob but not Becky. Justice in the first sense means fairness, in the second it means responsiveness. Obviously, fairness and responsiveness often are in conflict.

The checks and balances of the American constitutional system reflect our desire to reduce the arbitrariness of official rule. That desire is based squarely on the premise that inefficiency is a small price to pay for freedom and responsiveness. Congressional oversight, judicial review, interest-group participation, media investigations, and formalized procedures all are intended to check administrative discretion. It is not hyperbole to say that the constitutional order is animated by the desire to make the government "inefficient."

This creates two great tradeoffs. First, adding constraints reduces the efficiency with which the main goal of an agency can be attained but increases the chances that the agency will act in a nonarbitrary manner. Efficient police departments would seek out criminals without reading them their rights, allowing them to call their attorneys, or releasing them in response to a writ of habeas corpus. An efficient building department would issue construction permits on demand without insisting that the applicant first show that the proposed building meets fire, safety, sanitation, geological, and earthquake standards.

The second great tradeoff is between nonarbitrary governance defined as treating people equally and such governance defined as treating each case on its merits. We want the government to be both fair and responsive, but the more rules we impose to insure fairness (that is, to treat all people alike) the harder we make it for the government to be responsive (that is, to take into account the special needs and circumstances of a particular case).

The way our government manages these tradeoffs reflects both our political culture as well as the rivalries of our governing institutions. Both tend toward the same end: We define claims as rights, impose general rules to insure equal treatment, lament (but do nothing about) the resulting inefficiencies, and respond to revelations about unresponsiveness by adopting new rules intended to guarantee that special circumstances will be handled with special care (rarely bothering to reconcile the rules that require responsiveness with those that require equality). And we do all this out of the best of motives: a desire to be both just and benevolent. Justice inclines us to treat people equally, benevolence to treat them differently; both inclinations are expressed in rules, though in fact only justice can be. It is this futile desire to have a rule for every circumstance that led Herbert Kaufman to explain "how compassion spawns red tape."

Discretion at the Street Level

We worry most about arbitrary rule at the hands of those street-level bureaucracies that deal with us as individuals rather than as organized groups and that touch the more intimate aspects of our lives: police, schools, prisons, housing inspectors, mental hospitals, welfare offices, and the like. That worry is natural; in these settings we feel helpless and The State seems omnipotent. We want these bureaucracies to treat us fairly but we also want them to be responsible to our particular needs. The proper reconciliation of these competing desires requires a careful understanding of the tasks of these organizations.

There are at least two questions that must be answered: What constitutes in any specific organization the exercise of arbitrary or unjust power? Under what circumstances will the elaboration of rules reduce at an acceptable cost the unjust use of power? Police officers act unjustly when they arrest people without cause. "Equality before the law" is the bedrock principle of our criminal justice system, however imperfectly it may be realized. And so we create rules defining when people can be arrested. . . .

Discretion at the Headquarters Level

Interest groups also complain about arbitrariness, especially when they deal with regulatory agencies that have either no clear rules (and so the groups do not know whether policies in effect today will be in effect tomorrow) or rules so clear and demanding that there is no freedom to adjust their activities to conform to economic or technological imperatives.

The exercise of discretion by regulatory agencies does not occur because their activities are invisible or their clients are powerless but because these agencies and their legislative supporters have certain beliefs about what constitutes good policy. For many decades after the invention of the regulatory agency, Progressives believed that good decisions were the result of empowering neutral experts to decide cases on the basis of scientifically determined facts and widely shared principles. No one took it amiss that these "principles" often were so vague as to lack any meaning at all. The Federal Communications Commission (FCC) was directed to issue broadcast licenses as the "public interest, convenience, and necessity" shall require. A similar "standard" was to govern the awarding of licenses to airline companies by the now-defunct Civil Aeronautics Board (CAB). The Antitrust Division of the Justice Department was charged with enforcing the Sherman Act that made "combinations in restraint of trade" illegal.

What the statute left vague "experts" were to imbue with meaning. But expert opinion changes and some experts in fact are politicians who bow to the influence of organized interests or ideologues who embrace the enthusiasms of zealous factions. The result was an invitation for interests to seek particular results in the absence of universal standards.

One might suppose that the agencies, noticing the turmoil caused by having to decide hard cases on the basis of vacuous standards, would try to formulate and state clear policies that would supply to their clients the guidance that the legislature was unwilling to provide; but no. For the most part regulatory agencies with ambiguous statutes did not clarify their policies. I conjecture that this is because the agencies realized what Michel Crozier has stated: Uncertainty is power. If one party needs something from another and cannot predict how that second party will behave, the second party has power over the first. In the extreme case we will do almost anything to please a madman with life-or-death power over us because we cannot predict which behavior will produce what reaction. . . .

Conclusions

Neither inefficiency nor arbitrariness is easily defined and measured. Inefficiency in the small, that is, the excessive use of resources to achieve the main goal of an agency, is probably commonplace; but inefficiency in the large—the excessive use of resources to achieve all the goals, including the constraints—may not be so common. To evaluate the efficiency of a government agency one first must judge the value of the constraints under which it operates; to improve its efficiency one must decide which constraints one is willing to sacrifice. The best way to think about this is to ask whether we would be willing to have the same product or service delivered by a private firm.

If we decide that the constraints are important then we should be clear-eyed about the costs of retaining them. Those costs arise chiefly from the fact that most bureaucrats will be more strongly influenced by constraints than by goals. Constraints apply early in the process: You know from day one what will get you into trouble. Goals apply late in the process (if then): You must wait to see if the goal is achieved, assuming (a big assumption) that you can state the goal or confirm its achievement. Constraints are strongly enforced by attentive interest groups and their allies in Congress, the White House, the courts, and the media; goal attainment is weakly enforced because an agency head can always point to factors beyond one's control that prevented success. Constraints dissipate managerial authority; every constraint is represented in the organization by someone who can say no. Goals, if they exist and can be attained, are the basis for increasing managerial authority; a clear and attainable goal provides an opportunity for one person to say yes.

Bureaucracies will differ in their vulnerability to the tradeoff between goal attainment and constraint observance. Production organizations, having clear and attainable goals, are more easily evaluated from the standpoint of economic efficiency and thus the cost of any given constraint is more easily assessed. Coping and procedural organizations are impossible to evaluate in terms of economic efficiency and so the cost of a constraint is hard to assess. Craft organizations are a mixed case; because their outputs are observable, we know if they are attaining their goal, but because their work is hard to observe we may think mistakenly that we can alter those work procedures without paying a cost in goal attainment.

The Social Security Administration and the Postal Service are not hard to judge in efficiency terms, though the latter presents a more difficult case than the former because we want the USPS to serve a number of partially inconsistent purposes. The State Department and public schools are impossible to evaluate in efficiency terms, and so we regularly pile on more constraints without any sense that we are paying a price. Police detectives or the Army Corps of Engineers can be evaluated, but only after the fact—the crook is caught, the bridge completed—but we are at somewhat of a loss to know what alteration in procedures would have what effect on these outcomes. Prisons can be evaluated in terms of the resources they consume and the complaints they engender, but ordinarily we have little information as to whether changes in resources or complaints have any effect on such objectives as security, rehabilitation, or deterrence.

Arbitrariness means acting without legal authority, or with such authority in ways that treat like cases in an unlike manner or unlike cases in a similar manner. Deciding what constitutes a "like case" is the heart of the problem. Prisons require rules, but what ends should the rules serve—custody? Security? Self-governance? Rehabilitation? Regulatory agencies formulate rules, but under what circumstances can those rules be clear and comprehensive as opposed to vague and partial? The next [section] will not answer all these questions, but it will suggest how Americans have tried to use rules, as well as the problems with rule-oriented bureaucracy.

Rules

On February 8, 1967, Robert H. Weaver, the secretary of the Department of Housing and Urban Development, announced that henceforth persons applying for apartments in federally financed public housing projects would be given such apartments on a first-come, first-serve basis. Weaver, who is black, issued the new rule in response to the criticism of civil-rights organizations (including a group he once headed) that the local managers of these projects practiced or condoned segregation.

Under the old rules the city agencies that ran these projects gave to individual project managers great discretion to pick their tenants. The effect of that discretion, combined with the preferences of the tenants, was that projects tended to be all-white or all-black. In Boston, for example, there were twenty-five public housing projects built for low-income tenants. Thirteen of these were more than 96 percent white, two were entirely black, and the rest were predominately of one race or the other. These differences could not be explained entirely by neighborhood considerations. The Mission Hill project was 100 percent white; across the street from it, the Mission Hill Extension project was 80 percent black.

Weaver's order became known as the "1-2-3 Rule." It worked this way: All housing applicants would be ranked in numerical order based on the date they applied for housing, their need for housing, and the size of their families. When a vacancy became available it would be offered to the family at the top of the list. If there were more than one vacancy the one offered first would be drawn from the project with the most vacancies. If the family turned it down it would be offered another, and then a third. If all three vacancies were rejected the family would go to the bottom of the list and the next family in line would receive the offer. The Weaver order was an effort, typical of many in government, to prevent the arbitrary use of discretion by replacing discretion with a rule.

Eight years later a group of tenants sued the Boston Housing Authority (BHA). In his findings, the Housing Court judge determined that public housing in Boston still was being allocated in a way that perpetuated racial segregation, a view confirmed by a 1976 report of the Department of Housing and Urban Development. What had gone wrong? How could a discriminatory pattern of tenant assignment persist for so long after the BHA had implemented, albeit reluctantly, a clear federal rule that on its face did not allow race to be taken into account in choosing tenants?

The answer, supplied by the research of Jon Pynoos and Jeffrey M. Prottas, suggests the limit to rules as a means for controlling the discretion of bureaucrats. First, the 1-2-3 Rule combined three criteria: date, need, and family size. To rank applicants by these criteria someone had to decide how to measure "need" and then how much weight to give to need as opposed to family size or date of application. The evaluation of need inevitably was subjective. Moreover, the neediest families almost by definition were those who had been on the waiting list for the least time. For example, a family living on the street because its home had burned down the night before clearly is going to be regarded as needier than one whose home is livable but who may have been on the waiting list for many months. Second, the rules were inconsistent with the incentives facing the applicants. Applicants wanted to live in the "nicest" projects, but these usually had few vacancies. The worst projects, those with the most crime, litter, and graffiti, had the most vacancies. Applicants would rather turn down a bad project, even if it meant going to the bottom of the list. Since the bad projects often were all-black, this meant that hardly any families, especially any white families, were willing to move in, and so they tended to remain all-black. Third, the rules were inconsistent with the incentives facing the project managers. Managers were exposed to pressure from the tenants in the buildings they operated to keep out the "bad element"—drug users, prostitutes, families with noisy children—and to attract the "good element," such as retired couples and the elderly. The managers bent to these pressures by various stratagems such as concealing the existence of vacancies from the central office or finding ways to veto the applications of certain tenants.

Rules and Discretion

Max Weber said that the great virtue of bureaucracy—indeed, perhaps its defining characteristic—was that it was an institutional method for applying general rules to specific cases, thereby making the actions of government fair and predictable. Weber's belief in the superiority of rule-based governance has been echoed by Theodore J. Lowi, who has criticized the exercise of administrative discretion in the modern American state on the grounds that it leads to the domination of the state by interest groups, thereby weakening popular control and creating new structures of privilege. To restore democratic accountability he called for replacing discretionary authority with what he termed "juridical democracy": governance based on clear legislative standards for bureaucratic action or, failing that, on clear rules formulated by the bureaucracies themselves. When rules are clear, governance is better. Lawrence Friedman has argued that welfare and public housing programs are especially suitable for governance by rule because they involve the simple allocation of resources on an equitable basis. . . .

On occasion, Americans have temporarily abandoned their fear of discretion and their insistence on rules. During the New Deal a number of regulatory agencies—the Securities and Exchange Commission, the National Labor Relations Board, the Federal Communications Commission—were endowed with great powers and vague standards. But in time we have returned to our natural posture, insisting that the powers of any new agencies carefully be circumscribed by law (as they were with the Environmental Protection Agency) and that the powers of existing agencies be if not precisely defined then at least judicially reviewable. But the love of rules has obscured the question of the circumstances under which rules will work. Clearly, an apparently simple rule did not solve the problems of the Boston Housing Authority.

As we saw, the first-come, first-served rule had several defects. Those defects suggest some of the properties a workable and fair rule should have. First, a good rule should treat equals equally. The BHA rule attempted to allocate dissimilar things among dissimilar claimants. Not all apartments were the same: They varied in size, amenity, and, above all, location. Not all clients were the same: Some were law-abiding, some lawless; some were orderly, some disorderly. Second, an effective rule will specify the tradeoffs to be made among the criteria governing the application of the rule. The BHA rule did not do this and in fact could not have done it. Need and time on the waiting list often were in conflict and there was no nonarbitrary way to resolve the conflict. Third, a workable rule will be consistent with the incentives operating on the administrators and on at least some of the clients. Neither the BHA clients nor its managers had many incentives to conform to the rules. The clients wanted to move into "nice" housing; very few wanted to integrate housing, whatever the cost in amenity. The managers wanted to get "nice" clients; very few wanted problem families. We want rules to be clear, but the BHA rule only seemed to be clear.

Rules and Tasks

When the work and the outcomes of a government agency are observable and unambiguous some but not all of the conditions for management by rule are present. I have called such bureaus production agencies. . . . Processing claims for old-age and survivors' insurance in the Social Security Administration (SSA) is subject to very detailed rules. These rules seem to work well. This happens not only because the work (processing claims) and the outcomes (who gets how much money) are easily observed, but also because the rules meet or come very close to meeting the tests described in the preceding section: They refer to comparable cases (people of a defined age and marital status), they do not involve difficult tradeoffs (unless the Social Security Trust Fund runs out of money, everybody who meets certain tests gets money), and they conform to the natural incentives of the agency members (the service ethos of the SSA leads its employees to want to give money to every eligible person).

SSA also manages the disability insurance program. This makes the use of rules a bit more complicated because the definition of a disabled person is much more ambiguous than that of an elderly or retired one. In his excellent book on SSA management of the disability program [*Bureaucratic Justice: Managing Social Security Claims* (1983)], Jerry Mashaw concluded that despite the ambiguity the program works reasonably well. One reason is that every disabled person is entitled to benefits whatever his or her financial need; thus the definition of "disabled," although vague, does not have to be traded off against an even vaguer definition of need. Moreover, the lack of clarity in the rules defining disability is made up for by the working environment of the operators. The examiners who review claims for disability payments work elbow-to-elbow with their peers and supervisors. The claims are all in writing, there is no need to make snap judgments, and the decisions are reviewable by quality assurance inspectors. Dissatisfied claimants can appeal the decisions to administrative law judges. Out of this deliberate process there has emerged a kind of common law of disability, a set of precedents that reflects pooled experience and shared judgments.

The use of rules becomes more difficult in local welfare offices. These agencies administer the federal Aid to Families with Dependent Children program that, until it was changed in 1988, authorized the states to pay money to needy women who had children but no husbands and were otherwise fit but unemployable parents. It is very hard to make clear rules on these matters. What is a "fit" or an "employable" parent? How much does a given woman "need"? Some countries such as Great Britain do not try to solve these problems by rule; instead they empower welfare workers to make a judgment about each case and to use their discretion in approving payments.

In the United States, we use rules—up to a point. Since many of the rules are inevitably vague, the welfare workers who administer them have a significant amount of discretion. An intake worker could use that discretion to deny benefits to women on grounds of fitness or employability. But in fact they rarely do. Joel Handler, who studied welfare administration in Wisconsin in the 1960s, described how welfare workers used the rules they were given: In essence they focused on what was measurable. In each of the six counties investigated by Handler, the questions asked of applicants chiefly involved assessing the women's financial resources. The rule that was enforced was the means test: "Are your resources sufficiently inadequate as to justify your participation in this program?" If the applicant passed the means test the rest of the interview was about her budget—how much money she needed and for what. In only a minority of the cases were any questions asked about employability, marriage plans, or childcare practices. Though the federal government once tried by a law passed in 1962 to get welfare workers to deliver "social services" to their clients, the workers did not deliver them.

Welfare workers could get in trouble for allowing ineligible clients to get on the welfare rolls. But only *financial* ineligibility was easily determined, and so the rules governing money were the rules that were enforced. The workers had little incentive to find out how the clients led their lives and even less to tell them how they ought to lead those lives.

If rules are such an imperfect guide to action even in welfare and housing agencies (where according to Friedman their application was supposed to be straightforward), it is not hard to imagine how much more imperfect their use will be in coping, procedural, or craft agencies. Consider police patrol officers. We expect them to prevent disorderly conduct, but it is virtually impossible to define disorderly (or orderly) conduct. Behavior that is frightening to an old woman or nerve-wracking to a diamond-cutter is fun to a teenager or necessary to a garbage collector. Because we cannot produce a clear rule by which to guide the police control of disorderly conduct does not mean that the police should do nothing about disorder. But what they will do always will be a matter of dispute.

Or consider the "rules" contained in the Education for All Handicapped Children Act passed by Congress in 1975. It required each state to guarantee by a certain date a free and appropriate education for all handicapped children between the ages of three and twenty-one. That goal, however laudable, strained the capacity of every state's educational system. But if tight timetables and scarce resources were the only problems the law would not have raised any fundamental administrative problems. What made matters worse was that the law did not leave the selection of means to local authorities; instead it required the schools to develop for each eligible child an Individualized Education Program, or IEP, that specified short-term and annual instructional goals as well as the services that were to be supplied to attain those goals. Each IEP was to be developed jointly by a team comprised of the child's teacher and parents together with specialists in education for the handicapped and others "as necessary." If a parent disagreed with the IEP, he or she was afforded a due-process hearing. Here, a bureaucracy—the public school—the work and outputs of which can barely be observed (much less measured) was obliged to follow a rule that called for the education of every handicapped child (but not every "normal" one) on the basis of an individual plan that could be shaped and enforced by going to court.

Rules, like ideas, have consequences. When there is a mismatch between legal rules and bureaucratic realities, the rules get subverted. The subversion in this case took two forms. First, teachers struggling to find the time and energy for their daily tasks would not refer potentially eligible children to the special-education program. And when they did refer them they often made the decision on the basis not of which child most needed special education but of which child was giving the teacher the most trouble in the classroom. Second, some parents but not others took advantage of their due-process rights. Most observers agree that competent, middle-class parents were more effective at using the legal system than less competent, lower-class parents.

Because of the law, more is being done today for handicapped children than was once the case, but how it is being done cannot readily be inferred from the IEP rules. If some critics are right the insistence on defining education by means of formal, legally enforceable rules has led to substituting paperwork and procedure for services and results. This should not be surprising. A rule is a general statement prescribing how a class of behaviors should be conducted. Using a general statement to produce an individualized result is almost a contradiction in terms. We tailor behavior in accordance with individual circumstances precisely in those cases when the circumstances defy classification by rule.

The bureaucratic behaviors that most easily can be defined by rule tend to be those that are frequent, similar, and patterned—those that are routine. SSA easily applied rules in advance to its retirement benefits; with somewhat more difficulty it began to develop rules for disability claims. By contrast, the National Labor Relations Board (NLRB) has few rules. "Neither the fulminations of commentators nor the prodding of courts," Mashaw writes, "has convinced it that any of its vague adjudicatory doctrines can bear particularization or objectification in regulatory form." The Federal Communications Commission (FCC) for a long time resisted demands that it formulate into clear rules the standards it would use for awarding broadcast licenses. The NLRB and the FCC saw themselves as quasi-judicial bodies that decided each unique case on its individual merits. In fact, many NLRB and FCC policies probably could have been reduced to rule. The FCC did this when it finally announced what it had long practiced: that broadcast licenses routinely would be renewed absent some showing that they should not be. Commissions, like courts, resist routinization, perhaps because they delve so deeply into the matters before them that they see differences where others see similarities.

Rules and Impermissible Outcomes

Even where bureaucratic behavior is not so routinized that it can be conveniently prescribed by rule, we insist on rules when there is a significant risk of an impermissible outcome. There is no reason in principle why we could not repeal the laws against homicide and create in their stead a Commission on Life Enhancement and Preservation (CLEP) that would hear complaints about persons who had killed other persons. It would consider evidence about the character of the deceased: Was he lazy or dutiful, decent or disorderly, likable or hateful? On the basis of this evaluation of the lost life and relying on the professional judgment of its staff, the CLEP would decide whether the life lost was worth losing and, if not, whether the person who took it was justified in doing so. By thus decriminalizing homicide, we surely would experience a reduction in the number of events officially labeled murders since the CLEP would undoubtedly conclude that many who had been killed richly deserved their fate.

Most of us would not vote for such a proposal because we attach so high a value to human life that we are unwilling to trust anyone, especially any bureaucrat employed by CLEP, to decide who should die and who should live. We hold this view despite our belief that there are probably some (perhaps many) that the world would be better off without. In short, the risk of error—in this case, wrongly deciding that a worthy life had been a worthless one—is so great that we allow no discretion to the government. If a person who kills another is to escape punishment, it must be for particular excusing conditions (for example, self-defense) and not because of a government-assessed valuation of the lost life.

The laws of this country have multiplied beyond measure the number of outcomes that are deemed impermissible. From 1938 to 1958, the Food and Drug Administration (FDA) had the authority to prevent the sale or distribution of any drug unless it was shown by "adequate tests" to be safe. In 1958 new legislation was passed that directed it to bar from sale or distribution any food additive, food color, or drug administered to food animals if "it is found to induce cancer when ingested by man or animal." This was the so-called Delaney Amendment, named after the New York congressman who sponsored it.

Ignoring for the moment certain exceptions, the Delaney Amendment implied that we should swallow nothing that might cause cancer in the kinds of laboratory animals on which scientists test foods. In principle, this meant that the FDA was hostage to progress in analytical chemistry: As scientists improved their ability to detect cancer-causing chemicals, the FDA would be obliged to ban those chemicals (and the foods they contained) from the supermarket shelves. Cancer was a risk, the FDA was told, that it was impermissible to run, whatever the costs. Thus it was to enforce the rule, "no cancer."

But when the FDA in 1979 used this rule to ban saccharin, the artificial sweetener used in such products as "Sweet 'n Low," it suddenly discovered that Congress did not mean what it had said—at least in this case. "All hell broke loose," recalled one representative. Consumers wanted to use saccharin in order to lose weight, even if scientists had discovered that in very high dosages it induced bladder cancer in laboratory animals. Faced with this popular revolt, Congress swiftly passed a law delaying (and ultimately prohibiting) the FDA ban on saccharin. But Congress did not review the Delaney Amendment: It stood as a rule that could not (with certain minor exceptions) be traded off against any other rule. . . .

The United States relies on rules to control the exercise of official judgment to a greater extent than any other industrialized democracy. The reason, I think, has little to do with the kinds of bureaucrats we have and everything to do with the political environment in which those bureaucrats must work. If we wish to complain about how rule-ridden our government agencies seem to be, we should direct those complaints not to the agencies but to the Congress, the courts, and the organized interests that make effective use of Congress and the courts.

Rules: Gains and Losses

The difficulty of striking a reasonable balance between rules and discretion is an age-old problem for which there is no "objective" solution any more than there is to the tension between other competing human values such as freedom and order, love and discipline, or change and stability. At best we can sensitize ourselves to the gains and losses associated with governance by rule rather than by discretion.

Rules, if they are clear, induce agencies to produce certain observable outcomes: nursing homes must have fire sprinklers, hotels must have smoke alarms, dairy products may not contain polychorinated biphenyls (PCBs), automobiles must be equipped with crashworthy bumpers and steering wheels. But rules often cannot induce organizations to improve hard-to-observe processes. A nursing home may be safer because it has certain equipment installed, but it will not be well run unless it has competent head nurses. Eugene Bardach and Robert Kagan make this point by comparing public and private factory inspections. An inspector from OSHA charged with enforcing rules will evaluate the physical aspects of a factory: the ventilation, guardrails, and safety devices. By contrast, an inspector from an insurance company charged with assessing the insurability of the firm will evaluate the attitude and policies of management: its safety consciousness. The difference in approaches is important because, if John Mendeloff is correct, "most workplace injuries are not caused by violations of standards [i.e., rules], and even fewer are caused by violations that inspectors can detect."

Rules create offices, procedures, and claims inside an organization that can protect precarious values. An automobile company is required to comply with OSHA rules. If the only effect of the rules were the company's fear of inspectors, not much would happen. But to cope with the inspectors the company will hire its own industrial safety experts, and these in turn will establish procedures and generate pressures that alter the company's behavior even when it is not being inspected. At the same time, rules generate paperwork and alter human relationships in ways that can reduce the ability of the organization to achieve its goals and its incentives to cooperate with those who enforce the rules. To verify that military aircraft are built according to government specifications, hundreds of pounds of forms must be filled out that document each operation on each aircraft; these forms, one set for every individual airplane, must be stored for twenty years. Nurses must record every step in medical treatments. Personnel officers must document the grounds for every hiring and promotional decision. Teachers must fill out sign-in sheets, absence slips, attendance records, textbook requests, lesson plans, student evaluations, questionnaires, ethnic and language surveys, free-lunch applications, time cards, field-trip requests, special-needs assessments, and parental conference reports. Rarely does anybody read these forms. They are, after all, what Bardach and Kagan call a "declaration of innocence"; no aircraft company, charge nurse, personnel officer, or schoolteacher will use these forms to admit their wrongdoing, and so no government inspector will read them. The rules and the forms contribute to the adversarial relationship that so often characterizes the relationship between regulator and regulatee.

Rules specify minimum standards that must be met. This is a clear gain when an organization, public or private, is performing below the minimum. But minimum standards often become maximum standards. Alvin Gouldner first noticed this in his study of a private firm, the General Gypsum Company (a pseudonym). Suppose workers were expected to "get the day's job done." Some would work less than eight hours, some much longer. Now suppose that a rule is announced—

"everybody will work eight hours"—and a device (the time clock) is installed to enforce it. Laggards would now work eight hours but zealots would stop working more than eight. Bardach and Kagan observed this in the case of OSHA rules: At one time, a company would improve ventilating or lighting systems when workers or union leaders complained about these matters; later, the company would make no changes unless required by OSHA rules.

To decide whether the gains from imposing a rule outweigh the costs you must carefully judge the particular circumstances of a given organization. In other words, no rule can be promulgated that tells you when promulgating rules is a good idea. But at least the tensions highlighted in this section should make you aware that rules have risks and teach you to be sensitive to the fact that the American political system is biased toward solving bureaucratic problems by issuing rules. Given that bias, people who worry about the costs of rules usually will not be heard very clearly in the hubbub of concern about an unmet need or a bureaucratic failure.

Talented, strongly motivated people usually will find ways of making even rule-ridden systems work. This is especially the case when complying with the rules is seen as a mere formality; a form to be filled out, a box to be checked, a file to be kept. Teachers, nurses, police officers, and housing project managers can find ways of getting the job done—if they want to.

The managerial problem arises from two facts: First, talented, strongly motivated workers are a minority in any organization. People who can cope with rules will be outnumbered by people who hide behind them. . . .

Second, whatever behavior will get an agency executive in trouble will get a manager in trouble; whatever gets a manager in trouble will get an operator in trouble. Or put another way: Agency executives have a strong incentive to enforce on their subordinates those rules the violation of which create external political difficulties for the executive. This means that even talented and motivated operators will not be free to violate rules that threaten their agency, even if the rule itself is silly. Many agency executives do not understand this. They are eager to deflect or mollify critics of their agencies. In their eagerness they suppose that announcing a rule designed to forbid whatever behavior led to the criticism actually will work. Their immediate subordinates, remote from field pressures (and perhaps eager to ingratiate themselves with the executive) will assure their bosses that the new rule will solve the problem. But unless the rule actually redefines the core tasks of the operators in a meaningful and feasible way, or significantly alters the incentives those operators value, the rule will be seen as just one more constraint on getting the job done (or, more graphically, as "just another piece of chicken——t").

8-2

The Politics of Bureaucratic Structure

Terry M. Moe

Legislators, presidents, and other political players care about the content and implementation of policy. They also care about the way executive agencies are structured: Where in the executive branch are new agencies placed? What kind of bureaucrat will be motivated to aggressively pursue, or to resist the pursuit of, certain policy goals? Who should report to whom? What rules should govern bureaucrats' behavior? In the following essay, Terry M. Moe observes that these questions are anticipated and answered by politicians as they set policy. They are the subjects of "structural" politics. The federal bureaucracy is not structured on the basis of a theory of public administration, Moe argues, but should instead be viewed as the product of politics.

AMERICAN PUBLIC BUREAUCRACY is not designed to be effective. The bureaucracy arises out of politics, and its design reflects the interests, strategies, and compromises of those who exercise political power.

This politicized notion of bureaucracy has never appealed to most academics or reformers. They accept it—indeed, they adamantly argue its truth—and the social science of public bureaucracy is a decidedly political body of work as a result. Yet, for the most part, those who study and practice public administration have a thinly veiled disdain for politics, and they want it kept out of bureaucracy as much as possible. They want presidents to stop politicizing the departments and bureaus. They want Congress to stop its incessant meddling in bureaucratic affairs. They want all politicians to respect bureaucratic autonomy, expertise, and professionalism.[1]

The bureaucracy's defenders are not apologists. Problems of capture, inertia, parochialism, fragmentation, and imperialism are familiar grounds for criticism. And there is lots of criticism. But once the subversive influence of politics is mentally factored out, these bureaucratic problems are understood to have bureaucratic solutions—new mandates, new rules and procedures, new personnel systems, better training and management, better people. These are the quintes-

Source: John E. Chubb and Paul E. Peterson, eds., *Can the Government Govern?* (Washington, D.C.: Brookings Institution Press, 1989), 267–285. Some notes appearing in the original have been deleted.

sential reforms that politicians are urged to adopt to bring about effective bureaucracy. The goal at all times is the greater good: "In designing any political structure, whether it be the Congress, the executive branch, or the judiciary, it is important to build arrangements that weigh the scale in favor of those advocating the national interest." [2]

The hitch is that those in positions of power are not necessarily motivated by the national interest. They have their own interests to pursue in politics—the interests of southwest Pennsylvania or cotton farmers or the maritime industry—and they exercise their power in ways conducive to those interests. Moreover, choices about bureaucratic structure are not matters that can be separated off from all this, to be guided by technical criteria of efficiency and effectiveness. Structural choices have important consequences for the content and direction of policy, and political actors know it. When they make choices about structure, they are implicitly making choices about policy. And precisely because this is so, issues of structure are inevitably caught up in the larger political struggle. Any notion that political actors might confine their attention to policymaking and turn organizational design over to neutral criteria or efficiency experts denies the realities of politics.

This essay is an effort to understand bureaucracy by understanding its foundation in political choice and self-interest. The central question boils down to this: what sorts of structures do the various political actors—interest groups, presidents, members of Congress, bureaucrats—find conducive to their own interests, and what kind of bureaucracy is therefore likely to emerge from their efforts to exercise political power? In other words, why do they build the bureaucracy they do? . . .

A Perspective on Structural Politics

Most citizens do not get terribly excited about the arcane details of public administration. When they choose among candidates in elections, they pay attention to such things as party or image or stands on policy. If pressed, the candidates would probably have views or even voting records on structural issues—for example, whether the Occupational Safety and Health Administration should be required to carry out cost-benefit analysis before proposing a formal rule or whether the Consumer Product Safety Commission should be moved into the Commerce Department—but this is hardly the stuff that political campaigns are made of. People just do not know or care much about these sorts of things.

Organized interest groups are another matter. They are active, informed participants in their specialized issue areas, and they know that their policy goals are crucially dependent on precisely those fine details of administrative structure that cause voters' eyes to glaze over. Structure is valuable to them, and they have every incentive to mobilize their political resources to get what they want. As a result, they are normally the only source of political pressure when structural issues are at stake. Structural politics is interest group politics.

Interest Groups: The Technical Problem of Structural Choice

Most accounts of structural politics pay attention to interest groups, but their analytical focus is on the politicians who exercise public authority and make the final choices. This tends to be misleading. It is well known that politicians, even legislators from safe districts, are extraordinarily concerned about their electoral popularity and, for that reason, are highly responsive to their constituencies. To the extent this holds true, their positions on issues are not really their own, but are induced by the positions of others. If one seeks to understand why structural choices turn out as they do, then, it does not make much sense to start with politicians. The more fundamental questions have to do with how interest groups decide what kinds of structures they want politicians to provide. This is the place to start.

In approaching these questions about interest groups, it is useful to begin with an extreme case. Suppose that, in a given issue area, there is a single dominant group (or coalition) with a reasonably complex problem—pollution, poverty, job safety, health—it seeks to address through governmental action, and that the group is so powerful that politicians will enact virtually any proposal the group offers, subject to reasonable budget constraints. In effect, the group is able to exercise public authority on its own by writing legislation that is binding on everyone and enforceable in the courts.

The dominant group is an instructive case because, as it makes choices about structure, it faces no political problems. It need not worry about losing its grip on public authority or about the influence of its political opponents—considerations which would otherwise weigh heavily in its calculations. Without the usual uncertainties and constraints of politics, the group has the luxury of concerning itself entirely with the technical requirements of effective organization. Its job is to identify those structural arrangements that best realize its policy goals.

It is perhaps natural to think that, since a dominant group can have anything it wants, it would proceed by figuring out what types of behaviors are called for by what types of people under what types of conditions and by writing legislation spelling all this out in the minutest detail. If an administrative agency were necessary to perform services, process applications, or inspect business operations, the jobs of bureaucrats could be specified with such precision that they would have little choice but to do the group's bidding.

For simple policy goals—requiring, say, little more than transfer payments—these strategies would be attractive. But they are quite unsuited to policy problems of any complexity. The reason is that, although the group has the political power to impose its will on everyone, it almost surely lacks the knowledge to do it well. It does not know what to tell people to do.

In part, this is an expertise problem. Society as a whole simply has not developed sufficient knowledge to determine the causes of or solutions for most social problems; and the group typically knows much less than society does, even when it hires experts of its own. These knowledge problems are compounded by uncertainty about the future. The world is subject to unpredictable changes over time, and some will call on specific policy adjustments if the group's interests are to be pursued effectively. The group could attempt to specify all future contingencies in the current legislation and, through continuous monitoring and intervention, update it over time. But the knowledge requirements of a halfway decent job would prove enormously costly, cumbersome, and time-consuming.

A group with the political power to tell everyone what to do, then, will typically not find it worthwhile to try. A more attractive option is to write legislation in general terms, put experts on the public payroll, and grant them the authority to "fill in the details" and make whatever adjustments are necessary over time. This compensates nicely for the group's formidable knowledge problems, allowing it to pursue its own interests without knowing exactly how to implement its policies and without having to grapple with future contingencies. The experts do what the group is unable to do for itself. And because they are public officials on the public payroll, the arrangement economizes greatly on the group's resources and time.

It does, however, raise a new worry: there is no guarantee the experts will always act in the group's best interests. Experts have their own interests—in career, in autonomy—that may conflict with those of the group. And, due largely to experts' specialized knowledge and the often intangible nature of their outputs, the group cannot know exactly what its expert agents are doing or why. These are problems of conflict of interest and asymmetric information, and they are unavoidable. Because of them, control will be imperfect.

When the group's political power is assured, as we assume it is here, these control problems are at the heart of structural choice. The most direct approach is for the group to impose a set of rules to constrain bureaucratic behavior. Among other things, these rules might specify the criteria and procedures bureaucrats are to use in making decisions; shape incentives by specifying how bureaucrats are to be evaluated, rewarded, and sanctioned; require them to collect and report certain kinds of information on their internal operations, and set up oversight procedures by which their activities can be monitored. These are basic components of bureaucratic structure.

But some slippage will remain. The group's knowledge problems, combined with the experts' will and capacity to resist (at least at the margins), make perfect control impossible. Fortunately, though, the group can do more than impose a set of rules on its agents. It also has the power to choose who its agents will be— and wise use of this power could make the extensive use of rules unnecessary.

The key here is reputation. Most individuals in the expert market come with reputations that speak to their job-relevant traits: expertise, intelligence, honesty, loyalty, policy preferences, ideology. "Good" reputations provide reliable information. The reason is that individuals value good reputations, they invest in them—by behaving honestly, for instance, even when they could realize short-term gains through cheating—and, having built up reputations, they have strong incentives to maintain them through consistent behavior. To the group, therefore, reputation is of enormous value because it allows predictability in an uncertain world. And predictability facilitates control.

To see more concretely how this works, consider an important reputational syndrome: professionalism. If individuals are known to be accountants or securities lawyers or highway engineers, the group will immediately know a great deal about their "type." They will be experts in certain issues. They will have specialized educations and occupational experiences. They will analyze issues, collect data, and propose solutions in characteristic ways. They will hew to the norms of their professional communities. Particularly when professionalism is combined with reputational information of a more personal nature, the behavior of these experts will be highly predictable.

The link between predictability and control would seem especially troublesome in this case, since professionals are widely known to demand autonomy in their work. And, as far as restrictive rules and hierarchical directives are concerned, their demand for autonomy does indeed pose problems. But the group is forced to grant experts discretion anyway, owing to its knowledge problems. What professionalism does—via reputation—is allow the group to anticipate how expert discretion will be exercised under various conditions; it can then plan accordingly as it designs a structure that takes best advantage of their expertise. In the extreme, one might think of professionals as automatons, programmed to behave in specific ways. Knowing how they are programmed, the group can select those with the desired programs, place them in a structure designed to accommodate them, and turn them loose to exercise free choice. The professionals would see themselves as independent decisionmakers. The group would see them as under control. And both would be right.

The purpose of this illustration is not to emphasize professionalism per se, but to clarify a general point about the technical requirements of organizational design. A politically powerful group, acting under uncertainty and concerned with solving a complex policy problem, is normally best off if it resists using its power to tell bureaucrats exactly what to do. It can use its power more productively by selecting the right types of bureaucrats and designing a structure that affords them reasonable autonomy. Through the judicious allocation of bureaucratic roles and responsibilities, incentive systems, and structural checks on bureaucratic choice, a select set of bureaucrats can be unleashed to follow their expert judgment, free from detailed formal instructions.

Interest Groups: The Political Problem of Structural Choice

Political dominance is an extreme case for purposes of illustration. In the real world of democratic politics, interest groups cannot lay claim to unchallenged legal authority. Because this is so, they face two fundamental problems that a dominant group does not. The first I will call political uncertainty, the second political compromise. Both have enormous consequences for the strategic design of public bureaucracy—consequences that entail substantial departures from effective organization.

Political uncertainty is inherent in democratic government. No one has a perpetual hold on public authority nor, therefore, a perpetual right to control public agencies. An interest group may be powerful enough to exercise public authority today, but tomorrow its power may ebb, and its right to exercise public authority may then be usurped by its political opponents. Should this occur, they would become the new "owners" of whatever the group had created, and they could use their authority to destroy—quite legitimately—everything the group had worked so hard to achieve.

A group that is currently advantaged, then, must anticipate all this. Precisely because its own authority is not guaranteed, it cannot afford to focus entirely on technical issues of effective organization. It must also design its creations so that they have the capacity to pursue its policy goals in a world in which its enemies may achieve the right to govern. The group's task in the current period, then, is to build agencies that are difficult for its opponents to gain control over later. Given the way authority is allocated and exercised in a democracy, this will often mean building agencies that are insulated from public authority in general—and thus insulated from formal control by the group itself.

There are various structural means by which the group can try to protect and nurture its bureaucratic agents. They include the following:

- It can write detailed legislation that imposes rigid constraints on the agency's mandate and decision procedures. While these constraints will tend to be flawed, cumbersome, and costly, they serve to remove important types of decisions from future political control. The reason they are so attractive is rooted in the American separation-of-powers system, which sets up obstacles that make formal legislation extremely difficult to achieve—and, if achieved, extremely difficult to overturn. Should the group's opponents gain in political power, there is a good chance they would still not be able to pass corrective legislation of their own.

- It can place even greater emphasis on professionalism than is technically justified, since professionals will generally act to protect their own autonomy and resist political interference. For similar reasons, the group can be a strong supporter of the career civil service and other personnel systems that insulate bureaucratic jobs, promotion, and pay from political intervention. And it can try to minimize the power and number of political appointees, since these too are routes by which opponents may exercise influence.

- It can oppose formal provisions that enhance political oversight and involvement. The legislative veto, for example, is bad because it gives opponents a direct mechanism for reversing agency decisions. Sunset provisions, which require reauthorization of the agency after some period of time, are also dangerous because they give opponents opportunities to overturn the group's legislative achievements.

- It can see that the agency is given a safe location in the scheme of government. Most obviously, it might try to place the agency in a friendly executive department, where it can be sheltered by the group's allies. Or it may favor formal independence, which provides special protection from presidential removal and managerial powers.

- It can favor judicialization of agency decisionmaking as a way of insulating policy choices from outside interference. It can also favor making various types of agency actions—or inactions—appealable to the courts. It must take care to design these procedures and checks, however, so that they disproportionately favor the group over its opponents.

The driving force of political uncertainty, then, causes the winning group to favor structural designs it would never favor on technical grounds alone: designs that place detailed formal restrictions on bureaucratic discretion, impose complex procedures for agency decisionmaking, minimize opportunities for oversight, and otherwise insulate the agency from politics. The group has to protect itself and its agency from the dangers of democracy, and it does so by imposing structures that appear strange and incongruous indeed when judged by almost any reasonable standards of what an effective organization ought to look like.

But this is only part of the story. The departure from technical rationality is still greater because of a second basic feature of American democratic politics: legislative victory of any consequence almost always requires compromise. This means that opposing groups will have a direct say in how the agency and its mandate are constructed. One form that this can take, of course, is the classic compromise over policy that is written about endlessly in textbooks and newspapers. But there is no real disjunction between policy and structure, and many of the opponents' interests will also be pursued through demands for structural concessions. What sorts of arrangements should they tend to favor?

- Opponents want structures that work against effective performance. They fear strong, coherent, centralized organization. They like fragmented authority, decentralization, federalism, checks and balances, and other structural means of promoting weakness, confusion, and delay.
- They want structures that allow politicians to get at the agency. They do not want to see the agency placed within a friendly department, nor do they favor formal independence. They are enthusiastic supporters of legislative veto and reauthorization provisions. They favor onerous requirements for the collection and reporting of information, the monitoring of agency operations, and the review of agency decisions—thus laying the basis for active, interventionist oversight by politicians.
- They want appointment and personnel arrangements that allow for political direction of the agency. They also want more active and influential roles for political appointees and less extensive reliance on professionalism and the civil service.
- They favor agency decisionmaking procedures that allow them to participate, to present evidence and arguments, to appeal adverse agency decisions, to delay, and, in general, to protect their own interests and inhibit effective agency action through formal, legally sanctioned rules. This means that they will tend to push for cumbersome, heavily judicialized decision processes, and that they will favor an active, easily triggered role for the courts in reviewing agency decisions.
- They want agency decisions to be accompanied by, and partially justified in terms of, "objective" assessments of their consequences: environmental impact statements, inflation impact statements, cost-benefit analysis. These are costly, time-consuming, and disruptive. Even better, their methods and conclusions can be challenged in the courts, providing new opportunities for delaying or quashing agency decisions.

Political compromise ushers the fox into the chicken coop. Opposing groups are dedicated to crippling the bureaucracy and gaining control over its decisions, and they will pressure for fragmented authority, labyrinthine procedures, mechanisms of political intervention, and other structures that subvert the bureaucracy's performance and open it up to attack. In the politics of structural choice, the inevitability of compromise means that agencies will be burdened with structures fully intended to cause their failure.

In short, democratic government gives rise to two major forces that cause the structure of public bureaucracy to depart from technical rationality. First, those currently in a position to exercise public authority will often face uncertainty about their own grip on political power in the years ahead, and this will prompt them to favor structures that insulate their achievements from politics. Second, opponents will also tend to have a say in structural design, and, to the degree they do, they will impose structures that subvert effective performance and politicize agency decisions.

Legislators and Structural Choice

If politicians were nothing more than conduits for political pressures, structural choice could be understood without paying much attention to them. But politicians, especially presidents, do sometimes have preferences about the structure of government that are not simple reflections of what the groups want. And when this is so, they can use their control of public authority to make their preferences felt in structural outcomes.

The conduit notion is not so wide of the mark for legislators, owing to their almost paranoid concern for reelection. In structural politics, well informed interest groups make demands, observe legislators' responses, and accurately assign credit and blame as decisions are made and consequences realized. Legislators therefore have strong incentives to do what groups want—and, even in the absence of explicit demands, to take entrepreneurial action in actively representing group interests. They cannot satisfy groups with empty position taking. Nor can they costlessly "shift the responsibility" by delegating tough decisions to the bureaucracy. Interest groups, unlike voters, are not easily fooled.

This does not mean that legislators always do what groups demand of them. Autonomous behavior can arise even among legislators who are motivated by nothing other than reelection. This happens because politicians, like groups, recognize that their current choices are not just means of responding to current pressures, but are also means of imposing structure on their political lives. This will sometimes lead them to make unpopular choices today in order to reap political rewards later on.

It is not quite right, moreover, to suggest that legislators have no interest of their own in controlling the bureaucracy. The more control legislators are able to exercise, the more groups will depend on them to get what they want; and this, in itself, makes control electorally attractive. But the attractiveness of control is diluted by other factors. First, the winning group—the more powerful side—will pressure to have its victories removed from political influence. Second, the capacity for control can be a curse for legislators in later conflict, since both sides will descend on them repeatedly. Third, oversight for purposes of serious policy control is time-consuming, costly, and difficult to do well; legislators typically have much more productive ways to spend their scarce resources.

The result is that legislators tend not to invest in general policy control. Instead, they value "particularized" control: they want to be able to intervene quickly, inexpensively, and in ad hoc ways to protect or advance the interests of particular clients in particular matters. This sort of control can be managed by an individual legislator without collective action; it has direct payoffs; it will generally be carried out behind the scenes; and it does not involve or provoke conflict. It generates political benefits without political costs. Moreover, it fits in quite nicely with a bureaucratic structure designed for conflict avoidance: an agency that is highly autonomous in the realm of policy yet highly constrained by complex procedural requirements will offer all sorts of opportunities for particularistic interventions.

The more general point is that legislators, by and large, can be expected either to respond to group demands in structural politics or to take entrepreneurial action in trying to please them. They will not be given to flights of autonomous action or statesmanship.

Presidents and Structural Choice

Presidents are motivated differently. Governance is the driving force behind the modern presidency. All presidents, regardless of party, are expected to govern effectively and are held responsible for taking action on virtually the full range of problems facing society. To be judged successful in the eyes of history—arguably the single most important motivator for presidents—they must appear to be strong leaders. They need to achieve their policy initiatives, their initiatives must be regarded as socially valuable, and the structures for attaining them must appear to work.

This raises two basic problems for interest groups. The first is that presidents are not very susceptible to the appeals of special interests. They want to make groups happy, to be sure, and sometimes responding to group demands will contribute nicely to governance. But this is often not so. In general, presidents have incentives to think in grander terms about what is best for society as a whole, or at least broad chunks of it, and they have their own agendas that may depart substantially from what even their more prominent group supporters might want. Even when they are simply responding to group pressures—which is more likely, of course, during their first term—the size and heterogeneity of their support coalitions tend to promote moderation, compromise, opposition to capture, and concern for social efficiency.

The second problem is that presidents want to control the bureaucracy. While legislators eagerly delegate their powers to administrative agencies, presidents are driven to take charge. They do not care about all agencies equally, of course. Some agencies are especially important because their programs are priority items on the presidential agenda. Others are important because they deal with sensitive issues that can become political bombshells if something goes wrong. But most all agencies impinge in one way or another on larger presidential responsibilities—for the budget, for the economy, for national defense—and presidents must have the capacity to direct and constrain agency behavior in basic respects if these larger responsibilities are to be handled successfully. They may often choose not to use their capacity for administrative control; they may even let favored groups use it when it suits their purposes. But the capacity must be there when they need it.

Presidents therefore have a unique role to play in the politics of structural choice. They are the only participants who are directly concerned with how the bureaucracy as a whole should be organized. And they are the only ones who actually want to run it through hands-on management and control. Their ideal is a rational, coherent, centrally directed bureaucracy that strongly resembles popular textbook notions of what an effective bureaucracy, public or private, ought to look like.

In general, presidents favor placing agencies within executive departments and subordinating them to hierarchical authority. They want to see important oversight, budget, and policy coordination functions given to department superiors—and, above them, to the Office of Management and Budget and other presidential management agencies—so that the bureaucracy can be brought under unified direction. While they value professionalism and civil service for their contributions to expertise, continuity, and impartiality, they want authority in the hands of their own political appointees—and they want to choose appointees whose types appear most conducive to presidential leadership.

This is just what the winning group and its legislative allies do not want. They want to protect their agencies and policy achievements by insulating them from politics, and presidents threaten to ruin everything by trying to control these agencies from above. The opposing groups are delighted with this, but they cannot always take comfort in the presidential approach to bureaucracy either. For presidents will tend to resist complex procedural protections, excessive judicial review, legislative veto provisions, and many other means by which the losers try to protect themselves and cripple bureaucratic performance. Presidents want agencies to have discretion, flexibility, and the capacity to take direction. They do not want agencies to be hamstrung by rules and regulations—unless, of course, they are presidential rules and regulations designed to enhance presidential control.

Legislators, Presidents, and Interest Groups

Obviously, presidents and legislators have very different orientations to the politics of structural choice. Interest groups can be expected to anticipate these differences from the outset and devise their own strategies accordingly.

Generally speaking, groups on both sides will find Congress a comfortable place in which to do business. Legislators are not bound by any overarching notion of what the bureaucracy as a whole ought to look like. They are not intrinsically motivated by effectiveness or efficiency or coordination or management or any other design criteria that might limit the kind of bureaucracy they are willing to create. They do not even want to retain political control for themselves.

The key thing about Congress is that it is open and responsive to what the groups want. It willingly builds, piece by piece—however grotesque the pieces, however inconsistent with one another—the kind of bureaucracy interest groups incrementally demand in their structural battles over time. This "congressional bureaucracy" is not supposed to function as a coherent whole, nor even to constitute one. Only the pieces are important. That is the way groups want it.

Presidents, of course, do not want it that way. Interest groups may find them attractive allies on occasion, especially when their interests and the presidential agenda coincide. But, in general, presidents are a fearsome presence on the political scene. Their broad support coalitions, their grand perspective on public policy, and their fundamental concern for a coherent, centrally controlled bureaucracy combine to make them maverick players in the game of structural politics. They want a "presidential bureaucracy" that is fundamentally at odds with the congressional bureaucracy everyone else is busily trying to create.

To the winning group, presidents are a major source of political uncertainty over and above the risks associated with the future power of the group's opponents. This gives it even greater incentives to pressure for structures that are insulated from politics—and, when possible, disproportionately insulated from presidential politics. Because of the seriousness of the presidency's threat, the winning group will place special emphasis on limiting the powers and numbers of political appointees, locating effective authority in the agency and its career personnel, and opposing new hierarchical powers—of review, coordination, veto—for units in the Executive Office or even the departments.

The losing side is much more pragmatic. Presidents offer important opportunities for expanding the scope of conflict, imposing new procedural constraints on agency action, and appealing unfavorable decisions. Especially if presidents are not entirely sympathetic to the agency and its mission, the losing side may actively support all the trappings of presidential bureaucracy—but only, of course, for the particular case at hand. Thus, while presidents may oppose group efforts to cripple the agency through congressional bureaucracy, groups may be able to achieve much the same end through presidential bureaucracy. The risk, however, is that the next president could turn out to be an avid supporter of the agency, in which case presidential bureaucracy might be targeted to quite different ends indeed. If there is a choice, sinking formal restrictions into legislative concrete offers a much more secure and permanent fix.

Bureaucracy

Bureaucratic structure emerges as a jerry-built fusion of congressional and presidential forms, their relative roles and particular features determined by the powers, priorities, and strategies of the various designers. The result is that each agency cannot help but begin life as a unique structural reflection of its own politics.

Once an agency is created, the political world becomes a different place. Agency bureaucrats are now political actors in their own right. They have career and institutional interests that may not be entirely congruent with their formal missions, and they have powerful resources—expertise and delegated authority—that might be employed toward these selfish ends. They are new players whose interests and resources alter the political game.

It is useful to think in terms of two basic types of bureaucratic players: political appointees and careerists. Careerists are the pure bureaucrats. As they carry out their jobs, they will be concerned with the technical requirements of effective organization, but they will also face the same problem that all other political actors face: political uncertainty. Changes in group power, committee composition, and presidential administration represent serious threats to things that bureaucrats hold dear. Their mandates could be restricted, their budgets cut, their discretion curtailed, their reputations blemished. Like groups and politicians, bureaucrats cannot afford to concern themselves solely with technical matters. They must take action to reduce their political uncertainty.

One attractive strategy is to nurture mutually beneficial relationships with groups and politicians whose political support the agency needs. If these are to provide real security, they must be more than isolated quid pro quos; they must be part of an ongoing stream of exchanges that give all participants expectations of future gain and thus incentives to resist short-term opportunities to profit at one another's expense. This is most easily done with the agency's initial supporters. Over time, however, the agency will be driven to broaden its support base, and it may move away from some of its creators—as regulatory agencies sometimes have, for example, in currying favor with the business interests they are supposed to be regulating. All agencies will have a tendency to move away from presidents, who, as temporary players, are inherently unsuited to participation in stable, long-term relationships.

Political appointees are also unattractive allies. They are not long-term participants, and no one will treat them as though they are. They have no concrete basis for participating in the exchange relationships of benefit to careerists.

Indeed, they may not want to, for they have incentives to pay special attention to White House policy, and they will try to forge alliances that further those ends. Their focus is on short-term presidential victories, and relationships that stabilize politics for the agency may get in the way and have to be challenged.

As this begins to suggest, the strategy of building supportive relationships is inherently limited. In the end, much of the environment remains out of control. This prompts careerists to rely on a second, complementary strategy of uncertainty avoidance: insulation. If they cannot control the environment, they can try to shut themselves off from it in various ways. They can promote further professionalization and more extensive reliance on civil service. They can formalize and judicialize their decision procedures. They can base decisions on technical expertise, operational experience, and precedent, thus making them "objective" and agency-centered. They can try to monopolize the information necessary for effective political oversight. These insulating strategies are designed, moreover, not simply to shield the agency from its political environment, but also to shield it from the very appointees who are formally in charge.

All of this raises an obvious question: why can't groups and politicians anticipate the agency's alliance and insulationist strategies and design a structure ex ante that adjusts for them? The answer, of course, is that they can. Presidents may push for stronger hierarchical controls and greater formal power for appointees than they otherwise would. Group opponents may place even greater emphasis on opening the agency up to political oversight. And so on. The agency's design, therefore, should from the beginning incorporate everyone's anticipations about its incentives to form alliances and promote its own autonomy.

Thus, however active the agency is in forming alliances, insulating itself from politics, and otherwise shaping political outcomes, it would be a mistake to regard the agency as a truly independent force. It is literally manufactured by the other players as a vehicle for advancing and protecting their own interests, and their structural designs are premised on anticipations about the roles the agency and its bureaucrats will play in future politics. The whole point of structural choice is to anticipate, program, and engineer bureaucratic behavior. Although groups and politicians cannot do this perfectly, the agency is fundamentally a product of their designs, and so is the way it plays the political game. That is why, in our attempt to understand the structure and politics of bureaucracy, we turn to bureaucrats last rather than first.

Structural Choice as a Perpetual Process

The game of structural politics never ends. An agency is created and given a mandate, but, in principle at least, all of the choices that have been made in the formative round of decisionmaking can be reversed or modified later.

As the politics of structural choice unfolds over time, three basic forces supply its dynamics. First, group opponents will constantly be on the lookout for opportunities to impose structures of their own that will inhibit the agency's performance and open it up to external control. Second, the winning group must constantly be ready to defend its agency from attack—but it may also have attacks of its own to launch. The prime reason is poor performance: because the agency is burdened from the beginning with a structure unsuited to the lofty goals it is supposed to achieve, the supporting group is likely to be dissatisfied and to push for more productive structural arrangements. Third, the president will try to ensure that agency behavior is consistent with broader presidential priorities, and he will take action to impose his own structures on top of those already put in place by Congress. He may also act to impose structures on purely political grounds in response to the interests of either the winning or opposing group.

All of this is going on all the time, generating pressures for structural change that find expression in both the legislative and executive processes. These are potentially of great importance for bureaucracy and policy, and all the relevant participants are intensely aware of it. However, the choices about structure that are made in the first period, when the agency is designed and empowered with a mandate, are normally far more enduring and consequential than those that will be made later. They constitute an institutional base that is protected by all the impediments to new legislation inherent in separation of powers, as well as by the political clout of the agency's supporters. Most of the pushing and hauling in subsequent years is likely to produce only incremental change. This, obviously, is very much on everyone's minds in the first period.

NOTES

1. Harold Seidman and Robert Gilmour, *Politics, Position, and Power: From the Positive to the Regulatory State*, 4th ed. (Oxford University Press, 1986); and Frederick C. Mosher, *Democracy and the Public Service*, 2d ed. (Oxford University Press, 1982).

2. Seidman and Gilmour, *Politics, Position, and Power*, p. 330.

8-3

Assessing the Department of Homeland Security

Ivo H. Daalder et al.

In November 2002 Congress passed, and President George W. Bush signed, legislation creating a new Department of Homeland Security (DHS). The massive new department represents an effort to improve the government's ability to prevent and respond to terrorism occurring within the United States. In an essay written before the DHS legislation was enacted, Brookings Institution scholars discuss the difficulty of designing a department that effectively coordinates the resources of the federal government in the fight against domestic terrorism. The authors are mildly critical of the range of offices incorporated in the DHS and provide an overview of the sources of continuing difficulties in running such a large department. The administration faces ongoing challenges in coordinating DHS's work with the FBI, the CIA, the Department of Defense, and other still independent agencies.

PRESIDENT GEORGE W. BUSH went on nationwide television June 6 [2002] to urge Congress to create a new Department of Homeland Security. It would, in his words, be "charged with four primary tasks": controlling our borders; responding to terror-driven emergencies; developing technologies to detect weapons of mass destruction and protect citizens against their use; and "review[ing] intelligence and law enforcement information . . . to produce a single daily picture of threats against our homeland." The President's proposal, which is far more ambitious in scope than any legislative or other existing alternative for consolidating agencies and functions dealing with homeland security, would pull together some 200,000 government officials now associated with more than twenty government agencies. If approved by Congress in anything like the form proposed, it would be, as the President stated, "the most extensive reorganization of the federal government since the 1940s." Only the creation of the Department of Energy a quarter century ago offers a more recent parallel.

The President's announcement came as a surprise. For months, he and his senior aides had argued against a fundamental reorganization of the federal

Source: Ivo H. Daalder, I. M. Destler, James M. Lindsay, Paul C. Light, Robert E. Litan, Michael E. O'Hanlon, Peter R. Orsag, and James B. Steinberg, *Assessing the Department of Homeland Security* (Washington, DC: Brookings Institution, July 2002).

government. In March, the President's spokesman, Ari Fleischer, asserted that "creating a Cabinet post doesn't solve anything." Instead, "the White House needs a coordinator to work with the agencies, wherever they are." And such a coordinating structure had been put in place shortly after September 11, when President Bush appointed his old friend, Pennsylvania Governor Tom Ridge, as the director of a new Office of Homeland Security (OHS). The President also established a Homeland Security Council (HSC), modeled after its national security namesake, to coordinate homeland security efforts throughout the government. For President Bush and his senior advisers, the combination of Ridge, a 100-person White House office, and a Cabinet-level coordinating council represented the best organizational response to the new challenge of securing the nation against future terrorist attacks. As a result, the White House continued to reject efforts on the Hill to legislate more far-reaching organizational changes—including the idea of creating a Department of Homeland Security.

All that changed on June 6, when the President not only announced his support for just such a reorganization, but proposed a merger far more ambitious than anything anyone else had proposed. What had changed? President Bush and his advisers stress that their proposal flows logically from their efforts to review overall requirements for securing the country against attack. They also insist that the reforms reflect the strategic priorities of their national homeland security strategy, which Ridge's office has for many months labored to produce by early summer 2002. But the strategy had not been completed by the time the reorganization decisions were made. And while the proposed department's four pillars of border and transportation security, information analysis and infrastructure protection, consequence management, and countering chemical, biological, radiological or nuclear (CBRN) weapons threats may reflect the administration's priorities, these tasks do not themselves constitute a coherent homeland security strategy.

Additional factors were therefore important in convincing the President of the need for a bold organizational initiative. One of these, clearly, was a sense that the original organizational setup was not working. By early spring 2002, Ridge's operation was encountering substantial difficulties. Ridge had lobbied his Cabinet colleagues to reorganize the border security effort—proposing the merger of the Coast Guard, Customs Service, the Immigration and Naturalization Service's enforcement arm (including the Border Patrol), and the Animal and Plant Health Inspection Service—but was rebuffed and forced to settle for something far short of what he believed necessary. The color-coded advisory system developed by Ridge's office created as much uncertainty as clarity. And the White House's refusal to allow Ridge to testify before Congress, even to defend the administration's integrated homeland security budget request that his office had pulled together, significantly undermined his credibility on Capitol Hill.

In light of these problems, President Bush's Chief of Staff Andrew Card proposed in April that a small group of senior White House aides look into ways the federal government might be reorganized. Bush agreed. "Start with a clean piece of paper," he reportedly told Card. Within days, the aides had developed eight different options. By late May, Bush had accepted the recommendation from Card, Ridge, and others to go with one of the more extensive reorganization options. That decision was communicated to President Bush's Cabinet secretaries, including those immediately affected, only hours before he addressed the nation on June 6.

Widespread support for a major reorganization on Capitol Hill provided another reason for Bush's decision. In early May [2002], Senators Joe Lieberman (D-Conn.), Arlen Specter (R-Pa.), and Bob Graham (D-Fla.) had joined forces with Representatives Mac Thornberry (R-Tex.), Jane Harman (D-Calif.), Jim Gibbons (R-Nev.), and Ellen Tauscher (D-Calif.) to introduce a bipartisan, bicameral proposal for creating a Department of Homeland Security by combining the border agencies, the Federal Emergency Management Agency, and various entities responsible for protecting the nation's critical infrastructure. Lieberman pushed his bill through the Governmental Affairs Committee, which he chairs, on a party-line vote in mid-May. When soon thereafter news broke about various potential intelligence lapses and information sharing problems involving the FBI and CIA, support mounted for a dramatic reorganization effort along the lines Lieberman and his colleagues were advocating. As June began, the Bush administration appeared to be losing the initiative on the homeland security front that it had enjoyed since September 11.

The President's speech of June 6 proposing creation of a new Department of Homeland Security was therefore timely and politically astute. Democrats who had long supported a major reorganization—and had unsuccessfully pressed the White House and the Republican leadership on Capitol Hill to join them—quickly rallied behind the President's proposal. Some, like House Minority Leader Dick Gephardt (D-Mo.), went further, proposing that Congress pass a bill creating a new department by the time of the one-year anniversary of the World Trade Center and Pentagon attacks. Republicans, most of whom had resisted calls for major reorganization, quickly fell in line, their unease about expanding the size of government assuaged by the President's assurance that the reorganization would require no additional expenditures.

The Administration's Proposal

On June 18, Tom Ridge traveled to Capitol Hill to present the House and Senate leadership with legislation detailing the administration's reorganization proposals. The proposed department's primary mission would be to "prevent terrorist attacks within the United States; reduce the vulnerability of the United States to terrorism; and minimize the damage, and assist, in the recovery, from terrorist attacks that do occur" (sec. 101). It would consist of five divisions, each headed by an undersecretary for homeland security. . . . The Secret Service would be moved from Treasury and report directly to the secretary. Another six assistant secretaries and the commandant of the Coast Guard would be subject to Senate confirmation. The President would appoint an additional fourteen people, including up to ten assistant secretaries, none of whom would be subject to confirmation.

The secretary of homeland security would also have unprecedented powers under the administration's proposal. He would be able to transfer functions and responsibilities among subordinates and reorganize the structure of the entire department at will (the Hill would have to be notified 90 days in advance of any change affecting an agency established by an act of Congress). He would be allowed to reprogram appropriated funds from one program to another without congressional approval if it involved less than five percent of any appropriation available to the secretary. The administration's proposed legislation would also provide the secretary with broad latitude in personnel policy, exempt the department from key provisions of the Freedom of Information Act, and limit the ability of the inspector general to be an independent watchdog within the department.

The proposed department would rest on four substantive pillars—border and transportation security, emergency preparedness and response, chemical, biological, radiological, and nuclear countermeasures, and information analysis and infrastructure protection.

Border and Transportation Security. This division would be responsible for preventing the entry into the United States of terrorists and materials that they could use to do the nation harm. This would include responsibility for protecting the country's "borders, territorial waters, ports, terminals, waterways and air, land, and sea transportation systems of the United States" (sec. 401(2)). The division would also become responsible for administrating U.S. immigration and naturalization laws and U.S. customs laws. The main components of the proposed division would be four: [the Coast Guard from the Department of Transportation; Border Security from the Department of Justice, Transportation Security from the Department of Transportation and elsewhere, and Immigration Services from the Department of Justice and elsewhere. . .]

Emergency Preparedness and Response. This division would lead and coordinate the efforts by federal, state, and local government as well as the private sector to prepare for and respond to possible terrorist attacks, natural disasters, and other major emergencies. In the event of a terrorist attack or major disaster, the division would direct the federal government's entire response effort. To assist in that effort, it would be responsible for building a comprehensive national incident management system to coordinate federal, state, and local activities, including by developing interoperable communications technology to enable all those involved in a response effort to communicate effectively. The division would be divided into four components—addressing preparedness, mitigation, response, and recovery—and would be formed by transferring the following agencies to the new department: [*Federal Emergency Management Agency,* which now coordinates the federal preparedness; domestic preparedness offices from Justice and the FBI; the *Strategic National Stockpile,* transferred from the Department of Health and Human Services (HHS), which consists of pallets with pharmaceuticals, antidotes and medical supplies that can be transferred to any point in the United States within 12 hours; *Office of the Assistant Secretary for Public Health Emergency Preparedness,* which was created within HHS as part of bioterrorism legislation signed into law in June and would be responsible for preparing for, protecting against, responding to, and recovering from all acts of bioterrorism; *Nuclear Incident Response Team,* which, . . . remains housed in the Department of Energy. . . .

Chemical, Biological, Radiological and Nuclear Countermeasures. This division would be responsible for "securing the people, infrastructures, property, resources, and systems in the United States from acts of terrorism involving chemical, biological, radiological, or nuclear weapons or other emerging threats" (sec. 301 (1)). It would accomplish this task primarily by conducting and leading national efforts to develop effective countermeasures. These would focus both on preventing the importation of such weapons and materials and detecting, preventing, protecting against, and responding to terrorist attacks that employ them. The division would be subdivided into four components dealing with science and technology development, chemical, biological/agricultural, and radiological/nuclear weapons and materials. It would accomplish its mission by transferring the . . . agencies and programs [from the Departments of Agriculture, Energy, and Health and Human Services. . . .]

Information Analysis and Infrastructure Protection. The mission of this division would be to assess terrorist threats in the United States, determine the vulnerabilities of key resources and critical infrastructure to possible terrorist attack, and then develop protective measures designed to prevent attacks from taking place or to mitigate their harm. In order to accomplish this mission, the legislation proposes that the secretary "shall have access to all reports, assessments, and analytical information relating to threats of terrorism in the United States" (sec. 203), but has limited access to raw intelligence unless the Secretary requests and the President approves the access. The division would also administer the new homeland security advisory system, exercise primary responsibility for public threat advisories, and with other agencies provide warning information to state and local authorities, the private sector, and the public. To accomplish these tasks, the division would be divided into an infrastructure protection and a threat analysis sections, which would be composed of the following agencies: [*National Infrastructure Protection Center*, transferred from the FBI and responsible for assessing, warning, investigating, and responding to threats or attacks against the country's critical infrastructures; infrastructure and computer security offices from the Departments of Commerce and Energy and the General Services Administration; *National Communications System*, transferred from the Defense Department and responsible for maintaining federal communication systems in the event of a national emergency]. . . .

In all, the Bush administration proposes to create a Department of Homeland Security by transferring twenty-two agencies that currently reside in eight of the thirteen federal departments. . . . The projected personnel size of the new department is said to be about 170,000, but this probably underestimates the overall size by the 30–40,000 additional people the Transportation Security Administration expects to hire over the next few months as well as other missions which are given to the new department but not currently staffed (such as the terrorist threat assessment function) and overall department management. . . .

[Our view is that there is a] need for a more focused Homeland Security Department, which would be centered on Border and Transportation Security, Infrastructure Protection, and Domestic Terrorism Assessment and Analysis. It would exclude, at least initially, FEMA and units responsible for CBRN countermeasures. Including the Secret Service (not addressed in this chapter), it would incorporate 12 of the 22 agencies or offices in the original White House plan, roughly 185,000 employees (compared to the administration plan's estimate of 200,000 once the larger number of likely TSA employees are counted), and roughly $26 billion (two-thirds) of the $37.5 billion the administration projected as the current budget of the new department. It would, therefore, be very large. But it would be substantially more focused than what the administration proposes to do, and hence easier to manage. Above all, it would center on those functions whose consolidation seems likely to offer substantial gains to homeland security. . . .

Managing the Department

New executive departments are rare. Even less frequent are those that do not simply elevate or separate a previously existing agency (Education, Veterans

Affairs) but combine a number of relatively equal, formerly independent entities (such as Defense, Transportation, and Energy). The Department of Homeland Security falls clearly into this latter category. And it will not just be the largest reorganization since 1947; it is also likely to be the most difficult to manage.

The numbers are stunning. Alongside its 200,000 employees, which will include at least 30,000 baggage screeners not counted in the President's initial proposal, the proposed department (or the more focused alternative we advocate) will contain a vast array of largely incompatible management systems, including at least 80 different personnel systems mixed in and among the agencies. There are, for example, special pay rates for the Transportation Security Administration, the Secret Service, and the Biomedical Research Service; higher overtime rates for air marshals, the Secret Service, and immigration inspectors; guaranteed minimum overtime for Customs officers and immigration inspectors; Sunday, night, and premium pay for the Secret Service, Customs Service, and immigration inspectors; and foreign language awards and death benefits for Customs officers.

The secretary will also oversee labor contracts with at least 18 separate employee unions, including 33,000 members of the American Federation of Government Employees, 12,000 members of the National Treasury Employees Union, and many others in the National Association of Agriculture Employees, the Metal Trades Council, International Association of Machinists and Aerospace Workers, Fraternal Order of Police, Boilermakers Brotherhood, and International Brotherhood of Police Officers.

Some of this administrative complexity reflects the sheer size of the reorganization, which involves a multitude of highly customized systems. Some of these, in turn, are the product of successful efforts to escape the federal government's ossified personnel system, most notably the pay caps on hard-to-recruit positions in the scientific, technical, and law enforcement markets. Some also reflects the prevailing wisdom of the 1990s. Convinced that one administrative size does not fit all, Vice President Al Gore and his reinventing campaign let a thousand management flowers bloom. As Gore argued in 1993, Washington was filled with big, wasteful bureaucracies that paid a premium for centralization. Left to their own devices, however, many agencies opted for highly customized solutions, replacing old systems with highly stylized alternatives that fit what they saw as unique missions and very different customers.

There is much to admire in the reinventing effort, including significant gains in customer satisfaction at agencies such as the Customs Service and of the Federal Emergency Management Agency. But many of the new systems were implemented without a common template. Agencies had to develop strategic plans under the Government Performance and Results Act, for example, but they did so using different measures with uneven rigor. They also had to generate annual financial statements, but they did so with incompatible financial management systems. And they had to become conversant in e-government, as it is now called, but they did so with customized computer hardware and software.

DHS clearly represents a re-centralizing instinct. The secretary, not the 22 agency heads or Congress, will approve the financial statements, oversee a unified information system, and, with help from the director of the Office of Personnel Management, create an integrated personnel system that might well be the prototype for the rest of government in coming years. Even with this authority, it will take years, if not decades, to create common management systems to govern the department, and perhaps just as long to break down the competing cultures those systems currently protect. The department's strategic plan will be centralized, but its implementation will rely almost entirely on systems that were designed more for difference than commonality. It takes only a moment to decentralize, but decades to recentralize. . . .

The new secretary does not have to resolve every challenge on the first day, however. Congress often goes back into reorganizations to fine-tune, reconsider, and rearrange its work long after passage. Congress has returned to the Department of Defense reorganization at least six times since 1947, starting with the National Security Act of 1949, which gave the Pentagon departmental status and downgraded the service secretaries. In 1958, it passed the Department of Defense Reorganization Act, which strengthened coordination among the armed services. In 1980, it enacted the Defense Officer Personnel Management Act, which revised military promotion and retirement practices. Five years later, it legislated the Defense Procurement Improvement Act, which was a direct response to the procurement scandals of the early 1980s, and the following year it passed the Goldwater-Nichols Department of Defense Reorganization Act, which once again sought to strengthen coordination. Finally, in 1989, Congress passed the Base Closure and Realignment Act.

Congress has also returned to the Health, Education, and Welfare reorganization, most notably with the Department of Education Organization Act in 1979, which set asunder what President Eisenhower had joined together in 1953, and the 1994 Social Security Independence and Improvement Act, which split the Social Security Administration from what had been renamed the Department of Health and Human Services in 1979. Indeed, there is not a single reorganization over the past seventy years that has not been changed in some material way later on. The *U.S. Government Manual* provides more than 50 pages of executive organizations terminated, transferred, or changed in name since March 4, 1933, the date of Franklin Roosevelt's inauguration. We create new agencies, then rearrange, downsize, coordinate, and terminate them. Then, more often than not, we create them again.

Congress and the President will almost certainly begin thinking about how to reorganize DHS on the day they create it. Indeed, the President has anticipated just that in proposing for the new secretary extraordinary authority to "establish, consolidate, alter, or discontinue such organization units within the Department, as he may deem necessary or appropriate." Given the evolving nature of the homeland security challenge, some flexibility is likely to be essential to the success of the new department. As we discuss below, however, the flexibility the administration seeks is somewhat excessive and needs to be constrained to assure better accountability.

The repeated fiddling with organizational structure underscores an important point: a new department is not a panacea. Merely combining similar units will not produce coherent policy, for example, nor will it produce greater performance, increase morale, or raise budgets. Twenty-five years after the establishment of the Department of Energy, the nation still has no coherent energy policy. Consolidating efforts most certainly will not make broken agencies whole. If an agency is not working in another department, there is no reason to believe that it will work well in the new agency. Bluntly put, garbage in, garbage out. Conversely, if an agency is working well in another department or on its own as an independent agency, there is no guarantee that it will continue to work well in the new agency. Given these challenges, it is hardly surprising that the President and his advisers would ask for the fullest possible authority to act quickly. The waivers and exemptions from current law show up early in the President's . . . proposal:

- [The proposal] creates up to 28 senior positions in the department, including the secretary, deputy secretary, five under secretaries, an inspector general, a commandant of the Coast Guard, a director of the Secret Service, a chief financial officer, a chief information officer, and up 16 assistant secretaries. The number is not unusual given the department's size and scope, but the President's appointing authority is unprecedented. Of the 28 homeland security positions, only 14 would be subject to Senate confirmation.

- [The proposal gives] the secretary of homeland security . . . complete freedom to determine the titles, duties, and qualifications for all 16 assistant secretaries. Congress has not given such broad authority since creating the Department of Transportation in 1966.

- [The proposal] gives the secretary the authority to reorganize the department at will. In the case of any entity established by statute, the statute merely requires that the secretary give the House and Senate ninety days notice.

- The President's proposal would also give the secretary and director of the Office of Personnel Management full authority to create a personnel system that is "flexible and contemporary." Although the two words are never defined, the implication is obvious: the new department would be free to design a new system from scratch. The rules governing this system would be subject to the notice and comment requirements of the Administrative Procedure Act, which would provide an opportunity for the deliberative consideration and public input that such a redesign would require.

It is hard to blame the President for wanting this last waiver. The current civil service personnel system underwhelms at virtually every task it is asked to do. It is slow at hiring, interminable at firing, permissive at promoting, useless at disciplining, and penurious at rewarding. The vast majority of federal employees describe the hiring process as slow and confusing, a quarter do not call it fair, and less than a third say that the federal government does a good job at disciplining poor performers. [This provision was very controversial, but a modified version of this waiver that left the President's discretion largely intact was included in the final bill.]

Tempting though it is to give the secretary maximum authority to move quickly, Congress should modify the waivers to assure greater accountability and appropriate oversight. Congress would be well advised, for example, to reduce the President's appointment burden by simply cutting the number of appointees from 28 to a number nearer 14, which is roughly the same number that launched the departments of Energy and Education. Even at the size the President proposes, the Department of Homeland Security will be thick enough with 14 presidential appointees. Where the President wishes to avoid the burdensome Senate confirmation process, he already has ample authority to appoint non-career members of the Senior Executive Service and personal and confidential assistants. In any case, Congress should not allow the precedent of authorizing appointment of up to ten assistant secretaries not subject to Senate confirmation.

Similarly, Congress as a whole should not give the new secretary the unfettered civil-service waivers imagined in the legislation. [It did, however.] The secretary needs a workforce that hits the ground running, not one that spends its first days asking how the words "flexible" and "contemporary" might affect each worker's future. At the same time, however, the secretary needs a workforce that does not spend its first days figuring out how to jump from lower-paying jobs in one homeland security agency such as the Border Patrol to higher-paying jobs in another such as the Air Marshals program. . . .

Beyond Reorganization

. . . [M]anaging even a relatively compact new Department of Homeland Security will be a daunting challenge. Yet this could prove to be the easy part of the larger problem of organizing to make America safer. The core function of border security is, in principle, amenable to organizational consolidation and centralization.

The task is discrete, and the units responsible can be brought together, appropriately instructed, and provided the information and the staff needed to do their job.

Matters become more complicated when attention turns inside U.S. borders. Whether the issue is preventing terrorist attacks from individuals already inside the country or responding to the damage such terrorists can wreak, we come up against a stubborn fact: homeland security is, by its very nature, a highly decentralized activity, with success depending on a multitude of actors—both in government at all levels and in the private sector having the resources, the tools and the information that will enable them to make good, timely decisions. Recent events have illustrated this point dramatically—an alert border inspector in Washington helped thwart a major terrorist threat to the United States at the time of the Millennium celebrations. A flight instructor found it suspicious that a student was interested only in steering a commercial jetliner, not in taking off or landing, and then reported his suspicion to law enforcement authorities. A doctor re-examined the X-ray of a postal worker and diagnosed inhalation anthrax in time for an effective antibiotic treatment to be administered. In some cases, these "first responders" will be working for the DHS, but often they will be employees of other agencies, state and local governments, or even the private sector.

Yet a comprehensive homeland security strategy must take into account the broad range of actors who are essential to an effective response. Information must flow down to the operators in field: the local policeman making an arrest needs to be able to learn, quickly, whether the offender is on a terrorist watch list. Information must flow up: a doctor who diagnoses an anthrax case must be able, and motivated, to report this immediately to those monitoring potential bioterrorism. Information must flow across: local FBI, police and fire officials must have the will *and* the technical capacity to communicate—rapidly—with one another. The July 4th murders at Los Angeles International Airport highlighted, for example, how responsibility for security at the airport taken as a whole is dispersed among the FBI, local police, airport authorities, and the TSA without any single organization being actually in charge.

This brings front-and-center the issue of federal-state-local relations. The administration proposal recognizes this in [its proposal], which "specifies responsibilities of the Secretary of Homeland Security relating to coordination with state and local officials" as well as the private sector. To this end an "intergovernmental affairs office" would be created, reporting directly to the secretary, to "consolidate and streamline relations" among officials at the three governmental levels and "give state and local officials one primary contact instead of many on training, equipment, planning, and other critical needs such as emergency response."

The primary contact role rightly encourages state and local initiatives, for communities must see themselves as "owning" the local homeland security problem, not just responding to Washington. But Washington needs to help them develop coordinated and effective homeland security systems. Since September 11, every state has appointed a homeland security coordinator. These state "homeland security czars" have regular conference calls with each other and with the Office of Homeland Security. In most cases, however, the czar position is merely a second job for a leading police official, emergency management director, or the commander of the state National Guard.

Furthermore, in many states, the "homeland security office" has no separate staff or budget. To enhance local coordination, the federal government should take the lead in creating, for each state, and major city and / or metropolitan area, an interagency task force, involving federal, state, local and key private sector actors. These task forces would address the full range of issues from the local perspective (prevention, protection, response), and establish related committees for key areas (*e.g.*, on law enforcement, chaired by the FBI). Federal homeland security funds would be provided to subsidize the costs associated with these task forces. Further federal support should also be tied to coordinated plans which they develop. And as stressed in our prior Brookings study, federal financing should be directly linked to fighting terrorism—training and equipment devoted to that purpose, such as advanced, compatible communications devices to be distributed across agencies that need to coordinate, rather than general increases in firefighters, police, etc. There should also be a federally-sponsored assessment of state and local progress in homeland security, setting minimum (floor) standards of performance and rating states and communities on their performance.

If an enhanced FEMA is maintained outside the DHS, as we recommend . . . , then it should take the lead in federal-state-local relations. It has important ties on which to build, and much of the necessary work—training of first responders, information-sharing during crises events—falls into the category of consequence management. If FEMA is brought into the department, then the responsibility should rest there. In either case, each of the task forces should be chaired by a federal official (FEMA or DHS) stationed in the region.

The Role of the White House

Whether Congress establishes the broad ranging department the Bush administration proposes or the more focused department we advocate, there will remain a need for White-House coordination. By the administration's own reckoning, more than 100 U.S. government agencies are involved in the homeland security effort. It proposes to merge twenty-two of them. So even if the administration's proposal is adopted in its entirety, fully three-quarters of the federal government entities involved in homeland security will remain outside the DHS. Among these are most of the critical agencies—FBI, CIA, Defense, CDC, etc. There is a critical need to coordinate their actions with those of DHS and to develop and implement a government-wide homeland security strategy.

Arguably, the secretary of homeland security could take on these responsibilities. But interagency coordination led by individual Cabinet secretaries has seldom worked well in the past and it is not likely to do so now. The secretaries of Defense, Treasury, Justice, State, and HHS are unlikely to defer to directives from another Cabinet agency that is a competitor for funds and presidential attention. That means a White House-led coordination system must be retained.

Under current arrangements, set up by Executive Order last October [2001], this structure consists of a Homeland Security Council composed of the President and his senior advisers, and an Office of Homeland Security and director who advise the President and manage the interagency process (including that of the HSC). It is a process that can, in principle, work effectively, as the national security decision-making process (on which it is modeled) has shown. But so far it hasn't. Ten months after the terrorist attacks, OHS still has not delivered to the President and the country the national homeland security strategy that, according to the President's Executive Order, is its number one job. Director Tom Ridge proposed a major border security reorganization over six months ago, but that proposal was opposed by other Cabinet agencies and not adopted. The limitations of the current interagency arrangements were glaringly exposed by the fact that the President chose to use an ad hoc, largely secretive approach to developing his reorganization proposal rather than using the interagency arrangements he so recently established for considering homeland security policy. . . .

Conclusion

Our assessment provides powerful arguments for the core of the President's DHS proposal—the merger of the border and transportation security agencies. They address the common problem of securing the perimeter of the United States: the urgent need to prevent, in the wake of September 11, the entry of individuals and cargoes intended to do catastrophic harm. Consolidating these agencies should enable more efficient sharing of information, more complete evaluation of potential threats, and more effective actions to block them. Moreover, the administration has, for the most part, included the right agencies for this function in its draft legislation. The Customs Service and the Immigration and Naturalization Service are critical, though the INS's nonenforcement, immigration service-related functions should not transfer to the new department. DHS is also a more appropriate home for the Coast Guard than the Department of Transportation. The Animal and Plant Health Inspection Service also protects against threats on terrorists' potential menu, though an assessment is needed on just where to draw the line between security-related and other Agriculture inspection functions. In all of these cases, the cost of severing formal ties with the current departmental home is modest: in no case is a border agency's mission central to its department's prime functions, and Cabinet secretaries paid their work little heed prior to September 11.

On the matter of issuing visas, the administration bill rightly transfers control from the Department of State to the new department, but it keeps the implementation of this authority in the State Department and its overseas embassies and consulates. We go further, and have officials of the new department issue the visas themselves, working in U.S. embassies and consulates. (All other consular functions would remain with the Department of State.)

The Transportation Security Agency is also appropriate for transfer to DHS. It oversees travel within the United States as well as from abroad, and the potential synergies between the border protection function and airline screening clearly argue for consolidation. In proposing to combine border and transportation security into a single whole, the administration rightly recognizes that this security function extends both beyond our frontiers and into the heartland along the land, air, rail, and shipping transportation lines.

Overall protection of the nation's critical infrastructure is another function that belongs in the new department. As noted previously, "infrastructure" encompasses an enormous range of structures, networks, and institutions, from buildings or dams or port facilities located in a single place to internet-linked control systems governing everything from transmission of electricity to management of financial accounts. Given that infrastructure protection is a relatively new sphere of government activity, with no single, integrated home within existing agencies, the decision to consolidate it within DHS is compelling.

There is also a clear need for the new department to develop its own independent analytic capacity. However, rather than limiting this capacity to assessing threats to critical infrastructure as the administration proposes, we believe the department should have the lead responsibility for fusing all sources of intelligence analysis of terrorist threats to the United States—including raw intelligence derived from foreign intelligence sources and domestic law enforcement operations. The unit will be able to both provide the comprehensive analysis that has until now been sorely lacking and connect this analysis directly to key operational agencies carrying out homeland security functions. Its responsibilities would include some elements of information and intelligence collection through the department's own organic units (such as the border and transportation security agencies), but it would not subsume the foreign intelligence collection of the CIA, NSA, etc., nor the legal authorities currently exercised by the FBI for domestic intelligence collection. Further reform of the intelligence community may well be warranted, but it should be postponed, as Congress now intends, until completion of the intelligence committees' review of the causes of September 11 and the administration's own further assessment of intelligence reorganization needs.

If one "limited" the new department to the missions of border and infrastructure agencies, plus this overall analytic function, it would still be an enormous organization. It would have about 185,000 employees (including newly federalized airport security screeners), over 90 percent of those in the administration's proposed structure, and more than in any current department save Defense and Veterans Affairs. Its budget would be two-thirds that of the administration-proposed department. Consolidating the border and infrastructure functions and adding the intelligence-law enforcement fusion center would represent a huge step forward—one that Congress can and should take sooner rather than later. . . .

The case for creating a department of homeland security is strong, and Congress is almost certain to do so. But legislators need to scrutinize closely what kind of department will be most effective. Our analysis leads strongly to the conclusion that a more modest and clearly-focused consolidation of homeland security functions is preferable to the more complicated, multi-function merger proposed by the President. A DHS concentrating on border and transportation security, infrastructure protection, and intelligence assessment would be functionally more coherent—and hence easier to manage. It would allow its secretary and management team to focus on issues where the need for organizational consolidation is clear and defer for future consideration the inclusion of functions where the benefits of consolidation are yet to be proven.

Chapter 9

The Judiciary

9-1

from *The Choices Justices Make*

Lee Epstein and Jack Knight

When deciding cases before the Supreme Court, the justices weigh the argu-
ments offered by the plaintiffs and defendants. But, as Lee Epstein and Jack
Knight tell us below, the merits of a case are rarely all that the justices con-
sider. Since the outcome will be decided by a majority of the Court, rather
than by an individual justice, each justice can be expected to strategically
adapt his or her expressed preferences to attract the support and votes of the
other justices. In a very real sense, successful Supreme Court justices must be
good "politicians."

DRIVING WHILE INTOXICATED (DWI) and driving under the influence (DUI) are
now familiar terms to most Americans, but that was not true during the 1960s.
With the Vietnam War and the civil rights movement monopolizing the media,
drunk driving was just not one of the pressing issues of the day.

Even so, various researchers and government agencies began to explore the
problem as early as 1968.[1] Although these initial studies differed in design and
sampling, they reached the same general conclusion: teens, particularly males,
had a greater tendency than the general population to be involved in alcohol-
related traffic incidents. A 1972 FBI report, for example, indicated that between

Source: Lee Epstein and Jack Knight, *The Choices Justices Make* (Washington, D.C.: CQ Press, 1998), 1–21.

1967 and 1972 national drunk driving arrests among those under eighteen increased 138 percent and that 93 percent of those arrested were males.

Despite the accumulation of statistical evidence, another decade elapsed before most states even considered raising the legal drinking age. Oklahoma was a notable exception. In 1972 it passed a law prohibiting men from purchasing beer until they reached the age of twenty-one, but allowing women to buy low alcohol-content beer at eighteen.

Regarding the Oklahoma law as a form of sex discrimination, Curtis Craig, a twenty-year-old male who wanted to buy beer, and Carolyn Whitener, a beer vendor who wanted to sell it, brought suit in a federal trial court. Among the arguments they made was that laws discriminating on the basis of sex should be subject, at least according to rulings by the U.S. Supreme Court, to a "strict scrutiny" test.[2] Under this standard of review, as Table 1 shows, a court presumes a law to be unconstitutional, and, to undermine that assumption, the government must demonstrate that its legislation is the least restrictive means available to achieve a *compelling* state interest. As one might imagine, laws reviewed under this standard almost never survived tests in court.[3] In Craig and Whitener's opinion, the Oklahoma statute was no exception: no compelling state interest was achieved by establishing different drinking ages for men and women.

In response, the state argued that the U.S. Supreme Court had never explicitly applied the strict scrutiny test to laws discriminating on the basis of sex. Rather, the justices had ruled that such laws ought to be subject to a lower level of review—a test called "rational basis" (Table 1). Under this test the state need demonstrate only that the law is a *reasonable* measure designed to achieve a *legitimate* (as opposed to compelling) government purpose. Surely, Oklahoma contended, its law met this standard because statistical studies indicated that men "drive more, drink more, and commit more alcohol-related offenses."

The trial court held for the state. While it acknowledged that U.S. Supreme Court precedent was murky, it felt that the weight of case law supported the state's reliance on the lower standard.* Moreover, the state had met its obligation of establishing a rational basis for the law: given the statistical evidence, Oklahoma's goal of reducing drunk driving seemed legitimate.

---

*The problem was that a majority of the justices had not backed a particular standard of review since 1971, when a unanimous Court used the rational basis test to strike down an Idaho law that gave preference to men as estate administrators. *Reed v. Reed*, 404 U.S. 71 (1971). Two years later, however, a plurality adopted the strict scrutiny approach saying that the military could not force women officers to prove that their husbands were dependent on them while presuming that wives were financially dependent on their male officer spouses. *Frontiero v. Richardson*, 411 U.S. 677 (1973). But, in *Stanton v. Stanton*, 421 U.S. 7 (1975), the case most proximate to *Craig,* the Court seemed to give up the search for an appropriate standard. At issue in *Stanton* was a Utah law specifying that, for purposes of receiving child support payments, boys

Table 1. Arguments in *Craig v. Boren* over the Appropriate Test
to Assess Sex-Based Classifications

Party	Test Advanced	Policy Implications
Craig/Whitener	*Strict Scrutiny:* The law must be the least restrictive means available to achieve a compelling state interest.	If adopted, the Court would almost never uphold a sex-based classification. It would (presumably) strike down the Oklahoma law.
Oklahoma	*Rational Basis:* The law must be a reasonable measure designed to achieve a legitimate government purpose.	If adopted, the Court would (presumably) uphold most sex-based classifications, including the Oklahoma law.
ACLU	Something "in between" strict scrutiny and rational basis.[a]	If adopted, the Court would sometimes strike down laws discriminating on the basis of sex and sometimes uphold them. The ACLU argued that application of this test should lead the Court to strike down the Oklahoma law.

a. This test is now called "heightened scrutiny": the law must be substantially related to the achievement of an important government objective.

Refusing to give up the battle, Craig and Whitener appealed to the U.S. Supreme Court. While they and the state continued to press the same claims they had at trial, a third party advanced a somewhat different approach. The American Civil Liberties Union entered the case as an amicus curiae, a friend of the court, on behalf of Craig (see Table 1).* ACLU attorneys Ruth Bader Ginsburg and Melvin Wulf argued that the Oklahoma law "could not survive review

---

reach adulthood at age twenty-one and girls at eighteen. The Court held that the law constituted impermissible sex discrimination, but it failed to articulate a standard of review. Instead, the majority opinion concluded that "under any test—compelling state interest, rational basis, or something in between—[the Utah law] does not survive . . . attack."

It is no wonder that trial court judges were confused over the appropriate standard of review. As one district court judge wrote, "Lower courts searching for guidance in the 1970s Supreme Court sex discrimination precedents [prior to *Craig*] have 'an uncomfortable feeling'—like players at a shell game who are 'not absolutely sure there is a pea.'" Quoted in Herma H. Kay, *Sex-Based Discrimination* (St. Paul: West, 1981), 70.

*Despite the literal meaning of amicus curiae, most amici are not friends of the court; rather, they support one party over the other. Nearly 85 percent of all orally argued Supreme Court cases contain at least one amicus curiae brief, and the average is 4.4. See Lee Epstein, "Interest Group Litigation During the Rehnquist Court Era," *9 Journal of Law and Politics* (1993): 639–717. In *Craig*, however, the ACLU was the only group to file an amicus curiae brief.

whatever the appropriate test": strict scrutiny or rational basis or "something in between." This argument, which Ginsburg and Wulf had taken directly from the Court's decision in *Stanton v. Stanton,* was interesting in two regards: it suggested that (1) the Court could apply the lower rational basis standard and still hold for Craig, or (2) the Court might consider developing a standard "in between" strict scrutiny and rational basis.

What would the Supreme Court do? That question loomed large during the justices' conference, held a few days after oral arguments.[4] As it is traditional for the chief justice to speak first, Warren Burger led off the discussion. He asserted that *Craig* was an "isolated case" that the Court should dismiss on procedural grounds. The problem was that, because Curtis Craig had turned twenty-one after the Court agreed to hear the case, his claim was moot. So, to Burger, the . . . issue was whether Whitener, "the saloon keeper," had standing to bring the suit. Burger thought that she did not.* But, if his colleagues disagreed and thought Whitener had standing, Burger said he was willing to find for Craig if the majority opinion was narrowly written. By this, Burger meant that he did not want to apply strict scrutiny to classifications based on sex.†

Once Burger had spoken, the other justices presented their views in order of seniority, another of the Court's norms.†† They were, as Table 2 shows, all over the map. Lewis Powell and Harry Blackmun agreed with the chief justice: both would dismiss on the standing issue, and both thought they could find for Craig. William Rehnquist also wanted to dismiss on standing, but would hold for Oklahoma should the Court resolve the dispute. The remaining five justices would rule in Craig's favor, but disagreed on the appropriate standard. Thurgood Marshall favored strict scrutiny, as did William Brennan, but Brennan suggested that a standard in between rational and strict might be viable.[5] Byron White seemed to go along with Brennan. Potter Stewart intimated that the Court need only apply the rational basis test to find in Craig's favor. John Paul Stevens argued that

---

*The doctrine of standing prohibits the Court from resolving a dispute if the party bringing the litigation is not the appropriate one. The Court has said that Article III of the U.S. Constitution requires that litigants demonstrate "such a personal stake in the outcome of the controversy as to assure that concrete adverseness which sharpens the presentation of issues upon which the Court so largely depends for illumination of difficult constitutional questions." *Baker v. Carr,* 369 U.S. 186 at 204 (1962). In *Craig,* Burger felt that Whitener, being over the age of twenty-one and female, did not have the requisite personal stake.

†He made this point again in an October 18, 1976, memo to Brennan: "I may decide to join you in reversal, particularly if we do not expand the 'equal advantage' clause or 'suspect' classifications! In short, I am 'available.'" He reiterated this position in two subsequent memos dated November 11 and November 15.

††The order of speaking is a norm, as is the tradition of the chief justice speaking first at conference. Norms structure social interactions (here, among the justices) and are known to the community (the justices) to serve this function. See Jack Knight, *Institutions and Social Conflict* (Cambridge: Cambridge University Press, 1992).

Table 2. Justices' Conference Positions on the Issues in *Craig v. Boren*

	Conference Position		
Justice	Standing	Standard	Disposition
Burger	No	Rational?	Dismiss/Lean toward Craig if decided on merits
Brennan	Yes	[Strict]/ In-between*	Craig
Stewart	Yes	Rational	Craig
White	Yes	Strict/ In-between?	Craig
Marshall	Yes	Strict	Craig
Blackmun	No	Undeclared	Dismiss/Lean toward Craig if decided on merits
Powell	No	Rational?	Dismiss/Lean toward Craig if decided on merits
Rehnquist	No	Rational	Dismiss/Lean toward Oklahoma if decided on merits
Stevens	Yes	Above rational	Craig

? = Implicit but not explicit from conference discussion. * "Strict" represented Brennan's most preferred position, but at conference he offered the "in-between" standard.

Data Sources: Docket sheets and conference notes of Justice William J. Brennan Jr., Library of Congress; and conference notes and vote tallies of Justice Lewis F. Powell Jr., Washington and Lee University School of Law.

some "level of scrutiny above mere rationality has to be applied," but he was not clear on what that standard should be.

According to the Court's procedures, if the chief justice is in the majority after the conference vote, he decides who will write the opinion of the Court. If he is not part of the majority, the most senior member of the majority—Brennan, in the *Craig* case—takes on that responsibility. According to Court records, Brennan assigned the *Craig* opinion to himself. When he took on the responsibility, Brennan knew, as do all justices, that he needed to obtain the signatures of at least four others if his opinion was to become the law of the land. If he failed to get a majority to agree to its contents, his opinion would become a judgment of the Court and would lack precedential value.

The majority requirement for precedent is another of the Court's many norms, which for Brennan, in *Craig*, must have seemed imposing. Only three others—Marshall and possibly White and Stevens—tended to agree with his *most* preferred positions in the case: (1) Whitener had standing; (2) a strict scrutiny standard should be used; and (3) the Court should rule in Craig's favor. From

Table 3. Major Voting and Opinion Options

Option	Meaning
1. Join the majority or plurality	The justice is a "voiceless" member of the majority or plurality; the justice writes no opinion but agrees with the opinion of the Court.[a]
2. Write or join a regular concurrence	The justice writes or joins an opinion and is also a member of the majority or plurality opinion coalition.
3. Write, join, or note[b] a special concurrence	The justice agrees with the disposition made by the majority or plurality but disagrees with the reasons in the opinion. The justice is not a member of the majority or plurality opinion coalition.[c]
4. Write, join, or note a dissent	The justice disagrees with the disposition made by the majority or plurality. The justice is not a member of the majority or plurality opinion coalition.

Note: A justice may be assigned to write the opinion of the Court. But, with the exception of self-assignment, a justice does not make this decision for himself or herself. It is the responsibility of the chief justice, if he is in the majority, or the senior associate in the majority, if the chief justice is not, to assign the opinion of the Court.

a. Or the judgment of the Court, which results when the opinion writer cannot get a majority of the participating justices to agree to the opinion's contents.

b. To note is to speak, without opinion, as in "Justice Stewart concurs in the judgment of the Court."

c. At least one justice must cast such a concurrence to produce a judgment of the Court.

Source: Jeffrey A. Segal and Harold J. Spaeth, *The Supreme Court and the Attitudinal Model* (New York: Cambridge University Press, 1993), 276.

whom would the fourth vote come? Rehnquist seemed out of the question because his position was diametrically opposed to Brennan's on all the main points, and he would surely dissent. Blackmun, Powell, and Burger also favored dismissal but were closer to Brennan on point 3.

That left Stewart. He, as do all justices, had several feasible courses of action, as shown in Table 3: join the majority opinion, concur "regularly," concur "specially," or dissent. Based on his conference position—he had voted in favor of both standing and Craig, but was not keen on the strict scrutiny approach—it was possible that Stewart, as well as Blackmun, Powell, and Burger, might join Brennan's disposition of the case (that Craig should win) but disagree with the strict scrutiny standard the opinion articulated. This situation would not be good news from Brennan's perspective because such (dis)agreement—called a "special" concurrence—meant that Stewart would fail to provide the crucial fifth signature. Stewart might, however, join the majority opinion coalition and write a regular concurrence. A regular concurrence, in contrast to a special concurrence, counts as an opinion "join," and Brennan would have his fifth vote.*

After several opinion drafts, all revised to accommodate the many suggestions of his colleagues, Brennan succeeded in marshaling a Court. The final version took up the ACLU's invitation, as well as Brennan's conference alternative, and articulated a new test for sex discrimination cases. Called "heightened" or midlevel scrutiny, it lies somewhere between strict scrutiny and rational basis.† From there, the votes and positions fell out as Table 4 indicates. Note that Powell, Burger, and Blackmun did not join opinions that coincided with their conference positions; that Marshall signed an opinion advocating a standard that was less than ideal from his point of view; and that Brennan's writing advanced a sex discrimination test that fell short of his most preferred standard. Even the votes changed. Powell, Blackmun, and Burger switched their positions, but in different directions.

In the end, *Craig* leaves us with many questions. Why did Powell, Blackmun, and Burger alter their votes? Why did Brennan advance the heightened scrutiny test when he clearly favored strict scrutiny? Why did Marshall join Brennan's opinion, when it adopted a standard he found less than appealing? More generally, why did *Craig* come out the way it did?

These questions become more interesting when we consider that *Craig* is not an anomaly. In more than half of all orally argued cases, the justices switch their votes, make changes in their opinions to accommodate the suggestions of colleagues, and join writings that do not necessarily reflect their sincere preferences.[6]

Overview of the Strategic Account

How might we answer the questions raised by *Craig* and many other Court cases? Certainly, we should begin by acknowledging the voluminous body of literature that has attempted to address them. For more than fifty years scholars have tried to develop theories to explain why justices behave in particular ways, and they have had a modicum of success or, at the very least, they have come to some

---

*When justices agree to sign on to an opinion draft, they typically write a memo to the writer saying that they "join" the opinion. Many simply write "I join" or "Join me."

†Brennan outlined the heightened scrutiny approach as follows: "classifications by gender must serve important governmental objectives and must be substantially related to the achievement of those objectives." *Craig v. Boren,* 429 U.S. 190 at 197 (1976). Using this approach, the Court sometimes strikes down sex-based classifications, such as the law in *Craig,* and sometimes upholds them. One law it upheld is the federal policy limiting the military draft to men. See *Rostker v. Goldberg,* 453 U.S. 57 (1981).

Table 4. Comparison of Justices' Conference and
Final Positions in *Craig v. Boren*

Justice	Conference Position			Final Position		
	Standing	Standard	Disposition	Standing	Standard	Disposition
Burger	No	Rational?	Dismiss/ Craig	No	Rational	Oklahoma[a]
Brennan	Yes	[Strict]/ In-between*	Craig	Yes	Heightened	Craig
Stewart	Yes	Rational	Craig	Yes	Unclear	Craig[b]
White	Yes	Strict/ In-between?	Craig	Yes	Heightened	Craig
Marshall	Yes	Strict	Craig	Yes	Heightened	Craig
Blackmun	No	Undeclared	Dismiss/ Craig	Yes	Heightened	Craig[c]
Powell	No	Rational?	Dismiss/ Craig	Yes	Heightened[d]	Craig[e]
Rehnquist	No	Rational	Dismiss/ Oklahoma	No	Rational	Oklahoma[a]
Stevens	Yes	Above rational	Craig	Yes	Heightened[d]	Craig[e]

? = Implicit but not explicit from conference discussion. * "Strict" represented Brennan's most preferred position, but, at conference, he offered the "in-between" standard.

a. Wrote dissenting opinion.
b. Wrote opinion concurring in judgment (special concurrence).
c. Wrote opinion concurring in part.
d. With reservations or qualifications.
e. Wrote concurring opinion (regular concurrence).

Data Sources: Docket sheets and conference notes of Justice William J. Brennan Jr., Library of Congress; and conference notes and vote tallies of Justice Lewis F. Powell Jr., Washington and Lee University School of Law.

agreement over the fundamentals. Among the most important of these is the primacy of policy preferences; that is, judicial specialists generally agree that justices, first and foremost, wish to see their policy preferences etched into law. They are, in the opinion of many, "single-minded seekers of legal policy."[7]

Craig illustrates this point. During conference discussion, almost every justice expressed some preference about the way he wanted the case to come out and what he hoped the opinion would say. For example, we know that Marshall wanted the Court to hold that Whitener had standing, to apply a strict scrutiny standard to sex discrimination claims, and to rule in Craig's favor. But, as we also know, his preferences alone did not drive Marshall's behavior: he signed an opinion articulating a standard of review that fell short of his most preferred position.

So it seems that something is missing from this basic story of Court decisions. Even after we take preferences into account, important questions linger, suggesting the need for a more comprehensive approach—a strategic account of judicial decisions. This account rests on a few simple propositions: justices may be primarily seekers of legal policy, but they are not unconstrained actors who make decisions based only on their own ideological attitudes. Rather, justices are strategic actors who realize that their ability to achieve their goals depends on a consideration of the preferences of other actors, the choices they expect others to make, and the institutional context in which they act. We call this a *strategic account.* ...

Major Components of the Strategic Account

As we have set it out, the strategic account of judicial decision making comprises three main ideas: justices' actions are directed toward the attainment of goals; justices are strategic; and institutions structure justices' interactions. ...

Goals

A central assumption of strategic explanations is that actors make decisions consistent with their goals and interests. We say that an actor makes a rational decision when she takes a course of action that satisfies her desires most efficiently. What this means is that when a political actor chooses between two courses of action, she will select the one she thinks is most likely to help her attain her goals. ... [I]n terms of *Craig,* because Marshall preferred the establishment of a strict scrutiny standard more than a heightened scrutiny standard, and heightened scrutiny more than a rational basis standard, we would say he acted rationally if he made those individual choices that led to a decision by the full Court that established a standard closest to the strict scrutiny criterion. ...

Strategic Interaction

The second part of the strategic account is tied to the first: for justices to maximize their preferences, they must act strategically in making their choices. By "strategic," we mean that judicial decision making is interdependent. From *Craig,* we learn that it is not enough to say that Justice Brennan chose heightened scrutiny over rational basis or strict scrutiny because he preferred heightened scrutiny; we know he actually preferred strict scrutiny. Rather, interdependency suggests that Brennan chose heightened scrutiny because he believed that the other relevant actors—including his colleagues—would choose rational basis, and, given this choice, heightened scrutiny led to a better outcome for Brennan than the alternatives.[8]

To put it plainly, strategic decision making is about *interdependent* choice: an individual's action is, in part, a function of her expectations about the actions of others.* To say that a justice acts strategically is to say that she realizes that her success or failure depends on the preferences of other actors and the actions she expects them to take, not just on her own preferences and actions.[9]

Occasionally, strategic calculations lead justices to make choices that reflect their sincere preferences. Suppose, in *Craig*, that all of the justices agreed on all of the important issues: Whitener had standing; a strict scrutiny standard should be used; and the Court should rule in Craig's favor. If those conditions held, Brennan would have been free to write an opinion that reflected his true preferences, for they were the same as the Court's. In other instances, strategic calculations lead a justice to act in a sophisticated fashion; that is, he acts in a way that does not accurately reflect his true preferences so as to avoid the possibility of seeing his colleagues reject his most preferred policy in favor of his least preferred. Brennan may have followed this line of thinking in *Craig*. We know that he had to choose among three possible standards, but preferred strict scrutiny over heightened scrutiny over rational basis. Yet, he did not select his most preferred standard, opting instead for his second choice. Why? A possibility is that Brennan thought an opinion advancing strict scrutiny would be completely unacceptable to certain members of the Court, who would push for a rational basis standard, his least preferred standard. He may have chosen heightened scrutiny because, based on his knowledge of the preferences of other justices, it allowed him to avoid his least preferred position, not because it was his first choice.

Brennan chose the course of action that any justice concerned with maximizing his policy preferences would take. In other words, for Brennan to set policy as close as possible to his ideal point, strategic behavior was essential. In *Craig* he needed to act in a sophisticated fashion, given his beliefs about the preferences of the other actors and the choices he expected them to make. . . .

Institutions

According to the strategic account, we cannot fully understand the choices justices make unless we also consider the institutional context in which they operate. By institutions, we mean sets of rules that "structure social interactions in particular ways." . . . [I]nstitutions can be formal, such as laws, or informal, such as norms and conventions.[10]

---

*Some believe that such a broad (and simple) conception of strategic decision making undermines the value of the approach. See, for example, Howard Gillman, "Placing Judicial Motives in Context," 7 *Law and Courts* (1997): 10–13. We, however, see it as what underlies its importance because it acknowledges the breadth of the phenomena that might be explained.

To see how central institutions are to this account of judicial decisions, consider two examples. First, think about how the norm governing the creation of precedent—a majority of justices must sign an opinion for it to become the law of the land—affected the resolution of *Craig*. Had Brennan believed that four other justices shared his preference for the strict scrutiny standard, he would have written an opinion that adopted that standard. However, only three justices at the most were firmly behind him. If a different threshold for the establishment of precedent had existed, if four justices were enough, perhaps Brennan would have pushed for strict scrutiny. But such was not the case, which may explain, in part, why he was willing to consider the heightened standard: given the norm for precedent, he thought heightened was the best he could do.

Second, another institution of some importance is Article III of the U.S. Constitution, which states that justices "hold their Offices during good Behaviour." What this phrase means is that, barring an impeachment by Congress, justices have life tenure; unlike members of legislatures and even judges in many states, they do not have to face the voters to retain their jobs. The institution of life tenure also influences justices' goals. Instead of acting to maximize their chances for reelection, justices act to maximize policy.[11] To understand the effect of this institution, one has only to think about the kinds of activities in which a justice running for office would engage as opposed to a justice attempting to influence policy. In deciding *Craig*, for example, rather than considering the preferences of his colleagues and Congress over what test to use in sex discrimination cases, Justice Brennan would have been taking the pulse of his "constituents," talking with lobbyists, holding press conferences, and otherwise behaving in the ways we associate with members of Congress, not justices of the Supreme Court.[12]

Conclusion

As we have set it out, the strategic account of judicial decisions has several implications for the way we think about the development of law in American society. We argue that it suggests that law, as it is generated by the Supreme Court, is the result of short-term strategic interactions among the justices and between the Court and other branches of government.[13] But before we think about the implications of the strategic account, we must consider whether it is plausible and whether it provides us with any real leverage to understand judicial decisions.

To accomplish these tasks, we follow essentially the same path that David Mayhew did in *Congress: The Electoral Connection*: we develop a "picture" of justices as strategic seekers of legal policy and explore how justices so motivated go about making choices.[14] . . .

NOTES

1. See Mark Wolfson, "The Legislative Impact of Social Movement Organizations: The Anti-Drunken-Driving Movement and the 21-Year-Old Drinking Age," 76 *Social Science Quarterly* (1995): 311–327.

2. The material in the next few paragraphs comes from *U.S. Supreme Court Records and Briefs*, BNA's Law Reprints, no. 75-628.

3. Susan Gluck Mezey, *In Pursuit of Equality* (New York: St. Martin's, 1992), 17.

4. The next few paragraphs draw on the papers, including case files, docket books, and transcriptions of conference discussions, of Justices William J. Brennan Jr., Lewis F. Powell Jr., and Thurgood Marshall. The Brennan and Marshall collections are located in the Library of Congress; the Powell papers, in the Law Library at Washington and Lee University.

5. Typically, Brennan's case files contain memos of the remarks he made at conferences. Unfortunately, his *Craig* conference memo was missing, so we rely on Bernard Schwartz, who writes that Brennan wanted to adopt the strict scrutiny approach (see Brennan's opinion for the Court in *Frontiero v. Richardson*), but at conference he offered the "in between" standard. See Bernard Schwartz, *The Ascent of Pragmatism* (Reading, Mass.: Addison-Wesley, 1990), 226. For now, the important point is that "strict scrutiny" represented Brennan's most preferred position.

6. See, for example, Lee Epstein and Jack Knight, "Documenting Strategic Interaction on the U.S. Supreme Court" (paper presented at the 1995 annual meeting of the American Political Science Association, Chicago). Vote shifts are already the object of extensive investigation. For the latest and best installment, see Forrest Maltzman and Paul J. Wahlbeck, "Strategic Considerations and Vote Fluidity on the Burger Court," 90 *American Political Science Review* (1996): 581–592.

7. Tracey E. George and Lee Epstein, "On the Nature of Supreme Court Decision Making," 86 *American Political Science Review* (1990): 325.

8. See, generally, Peter C. Ordeshook, *A Political Theory Primer* (New York: Routledge, 1992).

9. See Charles M. Cameron, "Decision-Making and Positive Political Theory (Or, Using Game Theory to Study Judicial Politics)" (paper presented at the 1994 Columbus Conference, Columbus, Ohio).

10. See Jack Knight, *Institutions and Social Conflict* (Cambridge: Cambridge University Press, 1992), 2–3.

11. See Jeffrey A. Segal and Harold J. Spaeth, *The Supreme Court and the Attitudinal Model* (New York: Cambridge University Press, 1993), 69–72.

12. See, generally, David Mayhew, *Congress: The Electoral Connection* (New Haven: Yale University Press, 1974).

13. Knight makes this argument in *Institutions and Social Conflict*, and we explore it in an essay on *Marbury v. Madison*, 1 Cr. 137 (1803). Jack Knight and Lee Epstein, "On the Struggle for Judicial Supremacy," 30 *Law and Society Review* (1996): 87–130.

14. After proclaiming that representatives and senators were "single-minded seekers of reelection," Mayhew (*Congress: The Electoral Connection*, 9) went on to develop a "picture of what the United States Congress looks like if the reelection quest is examined seriously."

The Most Dangerous Branch?

Simon Lazarus

Over the past couple of decades Supreme Court doctrine has drifted in a conservative direction, particularly in the area of police procedures and states' rights. The following article identifies several of the prominent cases that have changed national policy and restored some parity to federal-state relations. Beyond this change in policy preferences, Simon Lazarus also discerns the emergence of a more activist judicial posture in which judges are no longer so reluctant to overrule acts of Congress or to spurn attempts by Congress and the presidency to define the kinds of laws the Constitution allows.

ON SATURDAY, DECEMBER 9, 2000, literally minutes before the United States Supreme Court issued its startling 5–4 decision to stay the Florida presidential-ballot recount, I happened to be chatting about the case after tennis with a senior Clinton Administration legal official. Without hesitation my tennis partner, a canny political insider and a seasoned Supreme Court litigator, forecast victory for Gore. The Florida court, he assured a rapt locker-room audience, had "bullet-proofed" its opinion with an elaborate exegesis of the state's complex electoral statutes; no way would conservative justices, whose deference to state prerogatives was well known, second-guess a state supreme court's painstaking interpretation of its own state's laws.

My friend turned out to be wrong, of course—and he wasn't alone. Nearly all mainstream legal experts were blindsided by *Bush v. Gore.*

The decision should not have come as a surprise. For several years now judicial conservatives have been marching to a new and very different drummer, but to date only a tiny, mostly academic cadre of astute Court watchers has grasped the content and the implications of the Supreme Court majority's agenda. To be sure, the intense partisan struggle over President Bush's judicial nominees has not gone unnoticed. But the media and most politicians simply assume that they're witnessing a recycling of the high-decibel constitutional controversies and judicial-nomination struggles of the 1970s and 1980s. Indeed, President Bush

Source: Simon Lazarus, "The Most Dangerous Branch?" *The Atlantic Monthly,* June 2002.

has constantly reiterated his goal of naming "strict constructionists" to the federal bench, and has cited Supreme Court Justices Antonin Scalia and Clarence Thomas as model nominees. In fact, however, Scalia, Thomas, and their ideological followers on and off the Court have a very different view of their judicial philosophy. "I am not a strict constructionist," Scalia has written, "and no one ought to be."

Most observers surmise that the President has in mind candidates who would overturn *Roe v. Wade,* the landmark 1973 decision that made abortion a constitutional right, and other bold Bill of Rights interpretations of that era. But the architects of *Bush v. Gore* have a radically different set of priorities. Their focus is not on dismantling the edifice of "rights" built by "activist" liberal judges when Earl Warren and Warren Burger presided over the Supreme Court—indeed, this majority has often defended free-speech, privacy, and due-process safeguards against the claims of aggressive legislatures and prosecutors. Rather, their focus is on the scope of government power. Brandishing a starkly devolutionist concept of federalism, these new conservatives question decisions as far back as the 1930s that legitimated the New Deal and the Great Society, and that empower Congress to legislate on essentially any matter of national concern. The new credo differs sharply from the judicial restraint practiced by conservative justices such as Burger and Lewis Powell and articulated by the late Yale professor Alexander M. Bickel in his landmark treatise, *The Least Dangerous Branch* (1962).

Clarence Thomas is almost invariably allied with Scalia in expounding and extending this new federalist agenda. Joining in nearly as frequently, but with independent views, is Chief Justice William Rehnquist. More often than not this trio brings Justices Anthony Kennedy and Sandra Day O'Connor with it— though both sometimes balk at the philosophical claims and practical objectives of their colleagues. Off the Court the majority's themes resonate in the rulings of certain federal appellate judges, in conferences and publications of the conservative lawyers' Federalist Society, and in voluminous published works of conservative scholars at think tanks and universities.

Broad attention to the ideas propounded in these quarters is overdue. If those ideas are substantially realized, they will threaten the viability of major programs in fields as diverse as civil rights, environmental protection, health, and education—in particular the national testing requirements that form the core of President Bush's new No Child Left Behind law. Equally at risk are pending or likely proposals for federal action on such pressing national concerns as cloning and homeland security.

Champions of this new federalism first proclaimed its far-reaching scope and signaled their intense commitment to its principles in two 1995 cases—neither of which stirred significant public attention at the time. In *United States v. Lopez* the

5–4 majority that went on to decide *Bush v. Gore* ruled that Congress's constitutional power to regulate interstate commerce did not justify the Gun Free School Zones Act of 1990, which banned possession of a firearm within a thousand feet of a school. The specific holding of this case was narrow enough to permit Congress to salvage the law with minor technical changes. Nevertheless, the decision provoked an impassioned intramural debate on the Court, spanning six opinions and ninety-five pages in the *United States Supreme Court Reports*. Writing for the majority, Rehnquist dwelt only briefly on the gun ban itself; his real concern, he made clear, was to ensure that this federal remedy for school violence not set a precedent for "direct" federal regulation of the "educational process," such as a "mandate[d] federal curriculum for local elementary and secondary schools."

In dissent, Justice Stephen Breyer argued that Congress could readily find a "direct economic link between basic education and industrial productivity." (And indeed, six years after *Lopez*, precisely because of the widely perceived link between education standards and economic productivity, Bush proposed and Congress enacted mandatory national testing requirements to upgrade public school performance.) But to Rehnquist, it was simply irrelevant that Congress might rationally conclude that education materially affects the economy. In terms calculated to reverberate through decades of opinions to come, he wrote, "We start with first principles. The Constitution creates a Federal Government of enumerated powers." The enumerated powers do not include non-economic subjects, such as the regulation of local school curricula, over which the states "historically have been sovereign," and which "the States may regulate but Congress may not."

Rehnquist's zeal to wall off traditional state responsibilities from federal authority was reinforced by Thomas in a dissent to a second 1995 decision, *U.S. Term Limits, Inc. v. Thornton*. In this case a 5–4 majority—in which Kennedy voted with the four "liberal" members of the Court—barred states from imposing term limits on their congressional representatives. In his opinion, which was joined by Scalia, Rehnquist, and O'Connor, Thomas wrote that the concept of exclusive state jurisdiction, described by Rehnquist in *Lopez*, extends, "either expressly or by necessary implication," to all areas that the original Framers of the Constitution neglected to name. Elaborating, he asserted that "the notion of popular sovereignty that undergirds the Constitution does not erase state boundaries, but rather tracks them." In other words, when the Framers wrote "We the People," they meant not we the people of a unified nation but we the people of each state. This theory reduces "We the People" to a meaningless rhetorical flourish; the Constitution and the federal government it creates are not instruments of the American people but creatures exclusively of—and hence decidedly junior to—the states and their governments.

Although eye-catching, such attempts to recast the theoretical limits of federal power are less significant than the operational question of who—Congress or the Court—should decide what those limits are. If there is, to use Rehnquist's term, a "first principle" of the post-New Deal concept of constitutional governance, surely it is that the people's elected representatives, not life-tenured judicial appointees, should determine what problems the federal government will address and where in the federal system to assign responsibility.

For the first third of the twentieth century a conservative Supreme Court enforced a laissez-faire ideology by blocking federal regulatory initiatives on federalist grounds. But in 1937, under pressure from President Franklin Roosevelt, the Court changed its tune. Since that time the nation has engaged in innumerable debates about the proper allocation of power between federal and state governments. These debates have spanned virtually all areas of domestic policy—health, education, environmental protection, discrimination, law enforcement, and, currently, euthanasia, abortion, and cloning. But the debates have never been about whether Congress *can* impose national standards; they have been about whether it *should*. All sides have assumed that Congress has the constitutional authority to address any problem of national importance.

This was the bedrock assumption that the *Lopez* majority challenged as a violation of constitutional "first principles." It is a challenge that has brought the nation close to a point where Congress could find itself virtually unable to pass laws regulating any non-economic matters. The majority opinion in *Lopez* indicated that such matters are inherently those that "States may regulate but Congress may not." Combine that with the February 2001 decision in *Board of Trustees of the University of Alabama v. Garrett,* which barred application of the Americans With Disabilities Act to state employees, and which ruled that even meticulously documented default by state governments will not necessarily permit federal intrusion on state sovereignty to enforce the Fourteenth Amendment. Add the notion—sometimes invoked by the Court majority and frequently repeated by advocates of federalism on the lower federal courts and elsewhere—that control of areas such as education and law enforcement is the states' "sovereign" prerogative. The result could be that non-economic regulatory laws such as the ADA and the Endangered Species Act become flatly unconstitutional.

As the Yale scholar Bruce Ackerman has shown, the United States has several times cast aside one working model of the Constitution and replaced it with another, each time through a highly political process that has involved Congress, the presidency, and elections as well as the Supreme Court. The most recent makeover occurred in the late 1930s and the 1940s, when the Supreme Court was driven to accommodate the New Deal.

The nation may have arrived at a new constitutional watershed. The question of the moment is whether the confirmation process for Bush's judicial nominees will spark a vigorous debate on the merits of the new conservative jurisprudence. The issue is not achieving "balance" on the courts between "liberal" and "conservative" judges, as some Democratic senators and liberal professors have suggested. If Americans elect Republican Presidents, they can expect Republican judges. The issue is the specific agenda of this particular genre of judicial conservatives. Their predecessors were more hard-nosed about the Bill of Rights than their liberal counterparts, but they preached deference to the political branches, and they worked within the post-New Deal constitutional regime. Rehnquist, Scalia, Thomas, and their allies consider themselves outside the consensus that supports that regime. They are working to change it.

At some point groups across the political spectrum will be forced to recalibrate their interest in this debate as they grasp their stakes in such questions as, Is the United States a unified democratic nation or, as the Federalist Society claims, a "Federal Republic," in which autonomous state governments are the sole forum for addressing a wide range of issues? Can the electorate discipline the federal establishment, or is active Court intervention necessary, as the libertarian Cato Institute contends, to "constrain government growth"? Is it unrealistic to retain James Madison's belief, expressed in *The Federalist* No. 46, that in allocating federal and state functions the people should be free to give "most of their confidence where they may discover it to be most due"? May Congress determine that effective education requires national testing standards, or that antiterrorist measures require background checks by local police departments on arrestees, gun buyers, or other groups? Do the states need the courts to protect them from congressional overreaching?

Ultimately, this debate is about democracy—about what the defining elements of our constitutional scheme are and, in particular, what place democracy occupies in it. In a recent speech at New York University, Justice Breyer suggested that the Constitution should be understood primarily as an engine for promoting "democratic self-government." The Constitution itself (and, implicitly, a Court administering it), Breyer said, "does not resolve, and was not intended to resolve, society's problems" but rather "provides a *framework* for the creation of *democratically determined solutions* [italics added]."

Many observers may wonder, What's the big deal? Isn't this obvious? But one suspects that Breyer felt compelled to make this statement because three of his colleagues on the Court disagree and two others are not sure where they stand.

As the New York University professor Larry Kramer has noted, activist conservatives argue that it is *exclusively* the province of the judiciary—not of Congress, the President, or the states—to say what the Constitution means. They do not view federal lawmaking as a process in which the various interests, including state governments and agencies, arrive at "democratically determined solutions." On the contrary, they view Congress through the lens of economic libertarianism and its cousin, "public-choice theory," which cast legislatures as irredeemably warped by the parochial machinations of interest groups and self-seeking officials. New federalists treat the legislative process as merely a first step toward giving the courts the final word on what the law is.

How far will the Court pursue its federalist project? Will it ultimately align the law with the conservative Northwestern law professor Gary Lawson's view that "the post-New Deal administrative state is unconstitutional"? Will the velocity of change increase if the current, shaky 5–4 majority becomes a rock-solid 6–3 or 7–2? Or will Justice O'Connor or Justice Kennedy team with pragmatic conservative appointees and centrists in the current minority to shape a moderate, "mend it, don't end it" approach to federal regulatory excess? The bet here is that the new federalists will continue on their way without missing a beat absent engagement in the issue by the President or Congress. And if *Bush v. Gore* taught us anything, it is that when Justices Rehnquist, Scalia, and Thomas know their destination, they will not worry about breaking doctrinal china to get there.

9-3

Federalist No. 78

Alexander Hamilton
May 28, 1788

Of the several branches laid out in the Constitution, the judiciary is the least democratic—that is, the least responsive to the expressed preferences of the citizenry. Indeed, it is hard to imagine an institution designed to be less responsive to the public than the Supreme Court, whose unelected judges enjoy lifetime appointments. During the Constitution's ratification, this fact exposed the judiciary to all sorts of wild speculation from opponents about the dire consequences the judiciary would have for the new republic. In one of the most famous passages of The Federalist, *Alexander Hamilton seeks to calm fears by declaring the judiciary to be "the least dangerous branch." Unlike the president, the Court does not control a military force, and unlike Congress, it cannot confiscate citizens' property through taxation. At the same time, Hamilton does not shrink from assigning the judiciary a critical role in safeguarding the Constitution against congressional and presidential encroachments he sees as bound to occur from time to time. By assigning it this role, he assumed that the Supreme Court has the authority of "judicial review" even though there was no provision for it in the Constitution.*

WE PROCEED now to an examination of the judiciary department of the proposed government. In unfolding the defects of the existing Confederation, the utility and necessity of a federal judicature have been clearly pointed out. It is the less necessary to recapitulate the considerations there urged, as the propriety of the institution in the abstract is not disputed; the only questions which have been raised being relative to the manner of constituting it, and to its extent. To these points, therefore, our observations shall be confined.

The manner of constituting it seems to embrace these several objects: 1st. The mode of appointing the judges. 2d. The tenure by which they are to hold their places. 3d. The partition of the judiciary authority between different courts, and their relations to each other.

First.

As to the mode of appointing the judges; this is the same with that of appointing the officers of the Union in general, and has been so fully discussed . . . that nothing can be said here which would not be useless repetition.

Second.

As to the tenure by which the judges are to hold their places; this chiefly concerns their duration in office; the provisions for their support; the precautions for their responsibility.

According to the plan of the convention, all judges who may be appointed by the United States are to hold their offices during good behavior. . . . The standard of good behavior for the continuance in office of the judicial magistracy, is certainly one of the most valuable of the modern improvements in the practice of government. In a monarchy it is an excellent barrier to the despotism of the prince; in a republic it is a no less excellent barrier to the encroachments and oppressions of the representative body. And it is the best expedient which can be devised in any government, to secure a steady, upright, and impartial administration of the laws.

Whoever attentively considers the different departments of power must perceive, that, in a government in which they are separated from each other, the judiciary, from the nature of its functions, will always be the least dangerous to the political rights of the Constitution; because it will be least in a capacity to annoy or injure them. The Executive not only dispenses the honors, but holds the sword of the community. The legislature not only commands the purse, but prescribes the rules by which the duties and rights of every citizen are to be regulated. The judiciary, on the contrary, has no influence over either the sword or the purse; no direction either of the strength or of the wealth of the society; and can take no active resolution whatever. It may truly be said to have neither FORCE nor WILL, but merely judgment; and must ultimately depend upon the aid of the executive arm even for the efficacy of its judgments.

This simple view of the matter suggests several important consequences. It proves incontestably, that the judiciary is beyond comparison the weakest of the three departments of power [1]; that it can never attack with success either of the other two; and that all possible care is requisite to enable it to defend itself against their attacks. It equally proves, that though individual oppression may now and then proceed from the courts of justice, the general liberty of the people can never be endangered from that quarter; I mean so long as the judiciary remains truly distinct from both the legislature and the Executive. For I agree, that "there is no liberty, if the power of judging be not separated from the legislative and executive powers." [2] And it proves, in the last place, that as liberty can have nothing to fear from the judiciary alone, but would have every thing to fear from its union with either of the other departments; that as all the effects of such a union must ensue from a dependence of the former on the latter, notwithstanding a nominal and apparent separation; that as, from the natural feebleness of the judiciary, it is in continual jeopardy of being overpowered, awed, or influenced by its co-ordinate branches; and that as nothing can contribute so much to its firmness and independence as permanency in office, this quality may therefore be justly regarded as an indispensable ingredient in its constitution, and, in a great measure, as the citadel of the public justice and the public security.

The complete independence of the courts of justice is peculiarly essential in a limited Constitution. By a limited Constitution, I understand one which contains certain specified exceptions to the legislative authority; such, for instance, as that it shall pass no bills of attainder, no ex post facto laws, and the like. Limitations of this kind can be preserved in practice no other way than through the medium of courts of justice, whose duty it must be to declare all acts contrary to the manifest tenor of the Constitution void. Without this, all the reservations of particular rights or privileges would amount to nothing.

Some perplexity respecting the rights of the courts to pronounce legislative acts void, because contrary to the Constitution, has arisen from an imagination that the doctrine would imply a superiority of the judiciary to the legislative power. It is urged that the authority which can declare the acts of another void, must necessarily be superior to the one whose acts may be declared void. As this doctrine is of great importance in all the American constitutions, a brief discussion of the ground on which it rests cannot be unacceptable.

There is no position which depends on clearer principles, than that every act of a delegated authority, contrary to the tenor of the commission under which it is exercised, is void. No legislative act, therefore, contrary to the Constitution, can be valid. To deny this, would be to affirm, that the deputy is greater than his principal; that the servant is above his master; that the representatives of the people are superior to the people themselves; that men acting by virtue of powers, may do not only what their powers do not authorize, but what they forbid.

If it be said that the legislative body are themselves the constitutional judges of their own powers, and that the construction they put upon them is conclusive upon the other departments, it may be answered, that this cannot be the natural presumption, where it is not to be collected from any particular provisions in the Constitution. It is not otherwise to be supposed, that the Constitution could intend to enable the representatives of the people to substitute their will to that of their constituents. It is far more rational to suppose, that the courts were designed to be an intermediate body between the people and the legislature, in order, among other things, to keep the latter within the limits assigned to their authority. The interpretation of the laws is the proper and peculiar province of the courts. A constitution is, in fact, and must be regarded by the judges, as a fundamental law. It therefore belongs to them to ascertain its meaning, as well as the meaning of any particular act proceeding from the legislative body. If there should happen to be an irreconcilable variance between the two, that which has the superior obligation and validity ought, of course, to be preferred; or, in other words, the Constitution ought to be preferred to the statute, the intention of the people to the intention of their agents.

Nor does this conclusion by any means suppose a superiority of the judicial to the legislative power. It only supposes that the power of the people is superior to both; and that where the will of the legislature, declared in its statutes, stands in opposition to that of the people, declared in the Constitution, the judges ought to be governed by the latter rather than the former. They ought to regulate their decisions by the fundamental laws, rather than by those which are not fundamental.

This exercise of judicial discretion, in determining between two contradictory laws, is exemplified in a familiar instance. It not uncommonly happens, that there are two statutes existing at one time, clashing in whole or in part with each other, and neither of them containing any repealing clause or expression. In such a case, it is the province of the courts to liquidate and fix their meaning and operation. So far as they can, by any fair construction, be reconciled to each other, reason and law conspire to dictate that this should be done; where this is impracticable, it becomes a matter of necessity to give effect to one, in exclusion of the other. The rule which has obtained in the courts for determining their relative validity is, that the last in order of time shall be preferred to the first. But this is a mere rule of construction, not derived from any positive law, but from the nature and reason of the thing. It is a rule not enjoined upon the courts by legislative provision, but adopted by themselves, as consonant to truth and propriety, for the direction of their conduct as interpreters of the law. They thought it reasonable, that between the interfering acts of an EQUAL authority, that which was the last indication of its will should have the preference.

But in regard to the interfering acts of a superior and subordinate authority, of an original and derivative power, the nature and reason of the thing indicate the converse of that rule as proper to be followed. They teach us that the prior act of a superior ought to be preferred to the subsequent act of an inferior and subordinate authority; and that accordingly, whenever a particular statute contravenes the Constitution, it will be the duty of the judicial tribunals to adhere to the latter and disregard the former.

It can be of no weight to say that the courts, on the pretense of a repugnancy, may substitute their own pleasure to the constitutional intentions of the legislature. This might as well happen in the case of two contradictory statutes; or it might as well happen in every adjudication upon any single statute. The courts must declare the sense of the law; and if they should be disposed to exercise WILL instead of JUDGMENT, the consequence would equally be the substitution of their pleasure to that of the legislative body. The observation, if it prove any thing, would prove that there ought to be no judges distinct from that body.

If, then, the courts of justice are to be considered as the bulwarks of a limited Constitution against legislative encroachments, this consideration will afford a strong argument for the permanent tenure of judicial offices, since nothing will contribute so much as this to that independent spirit in the judges which must be essential to the faithful performance of so arduous a duty.

This independence of the judges is equally requisite to guard the Constitution and the rights of individuals from the effects of those ill humors, which the arts of designing men, or the influence of particular conjunctures, sometimes disseminate among the people themselves, and which, though they speedily give place to better information, and more deliberate reflection, have a tendency, in the meantime, to occasion dangerous innovations in the government, and serious oppressions of the minor party in the community. . . . Until the people have, by some solemn and authoritative act, annulled or changed the established form, it is binding upon themselves collectively, as well as individually; and no presumption, or even knowledge, of their sentiments, can warrant their representatives in a departure from it, prior to such an act. But it is easy to see, that it would require an uncommon portion of fortitude in the judges to do their duty as faithful guardians of the Constitution, where legislative invasions of it had been instigated by the major voice of the community.

But it is not with a view to infractions of the Constitution only, that the independence of the judges may be an essential safeguard against the effects of occasional ill humors in the society. These sometimes extend no farther than to the injury of the private rights of particular classes of citizens, by unjust and partial laws. Here also the firmness of the judicial magistracy is of vast importance in mitigating the severity and confining the operation of such laws. It not only serves to moderate the immediate mischiefs of those which may have been passed, but it operates as a check upon the legislative body in passing them; who, perceiving that obstacles to the success of iniquitous intention are to be expected from the scruples of the courts, are in a manner compelled, by the very motives of the injustice they meditate, to qualify their attempts. . . .

That inflexible and uniform adherence to the rights of the Constitution, and of individuals, which we perceive to be indispensable in the courts of justice, can certainly not be expected from judges who hold their offices by a temporary commission. Periodical appointments, however regulated, or by whomsoever made, would, in some way or other, be fatal to their necessary independence. If the power of making them was committed either to the Executive or legislature, there would be danger of an improper complaisance to the branch which possessed it; if to both, there would be an unwillingness to hazard the displeasure of either; if to the people, or to persons chosen by them for the special purpose, there would be too great a disposition to consult popularity, to justify a reliance that nothing would be consulted but the Constitution and the laws.

There is yet a further and a weightier reason for the permanency of the judicial offices, which is deducible from the nature of the qualifications they require. It has been frequently remarked, with great propriety, that a voluminous code of laws is one of the inconveniences necessarily connected with the advantages of a free government. To avoid an arbitrary discretion in the courts, it is indispensable that they should be bound down by strict rules and precedents, which serve to define and point out their duty in every particular case that comes before them; and it will readily be conceived from the variety of controversies which grow out of the folly and wickedness of mankind, that the records of those precedents must unavoidably swell to a very considerable bulk, and must demand long and laborious study to acquire a competent knowledge of them. Hence it is, that there can be but few men in the society who will have sufficient skill in the laws to qualify them for the stations of judges. And making the proper deductions for the ordinary depravity of human nature, the number must be still smaller of those who unite the requisite integrity with the requisite knowledge. . . .

NOTES

1. The celebrated Montesquieu, speaking of them, says: "Of the three powers above mentioned, the judiciary is next to nothing." "Spirit of Laws." vol. i., page 186. [See Charles de Secondat, Baron de Montesquieu, *The Spirit of Laws,* trans. Thomas Nugent, rev. J. V. Pritchard (London: G. Bell & Sons Ltd., 1914]

2. Idem, page 181.

9-4

The Power of the Fourth

Deborah Sontag

This article explores further the emergence of conservative judicial activism, but in this instance at the next level of the federal judiciary below the Supreme Court, the circuit courts of appeal. Specifically, Deborah Sontag reports efforts by conservative judges on the Fourth Circuit Court to promote major revisions in national policy in the cases they accept and the arguments underwriting their revisionist rulings. That a cohort of active, conservative judges is appearing at every level reflects the political process that selects them. A couple of decades of mostly Republican presidents and, more recently, Republican Senates has favored recruitment of conservatives to the bench, just as decades of Democratic dominance of Congress and the presidency had staffed the federal judiciary with a preponderance of liberals by the late 1960s. This examination of the Fourth Circuit's decisions also offers insight into the complex relationships between the circuits and the Supreme Court, relationships that cannot be elucidated with a simple description of the hierarchical structure of the courts.

THE 19TH-CENTURY courthouse that houses the United States Court of Appeals for the Fourth Circuit sits across from a CVS and a Dress Barn on a desultory stretch of Main Street in Richmond, Va. The entrance—peeling "Pull" sign, metal detector, dim lobby—is not awe-inspiring. But upstairs in the courtrooms, beneath the pendulous chandeliers and the oil portraits of former jurists, a hush prevails. Whether or not the judges are on the bench, people whisper. It is as if they tacitly accept that the atmosphere should continue to be rarefied even as the judicial process becomes increasingly polluted by politics.

This 148-year-old building, once the site of the Confederate Treasury, is where you go if you are appealing the decisions of federal judges or juries in Virginia, West Virginia, Maryland, North Carolina or South Carolina. It's the last stop before the Supreme Court, which, given how few cases the highest court actually hears, essentially makes it the court of last resort for those seeking justice in this region. Let the plaintiff beware, though; the Fourth Circuit is considered the shrewdest, most aggressively conservative federal appeals court in the nation.

Source: Deborah Sontag, "The Power of the Fourth," *The New York Times Magazine*, March 9, 2003.

396

On the last Tuesday in February, Lisa Ocheltree of Lexington, S.C., settled warily onto a hardwood bench in a courtroom carpeted in billiard-table green. Several years ago, Ocheltree won a substantial jury verdict in a sexual-harassment suit against her former employer. The jury found that vulgar language, crude sexual commentary and sexual acting-out created an extremely hostile working environment for Ocheltree as the sole woman in a costume-production workshop. But a three-judge panel of the Fourth Circuit overturned that verdict late last year. "Were they telling me that I should have just sucked it up?" Ocheltree asked. She petitioned the full court to reconsider the panel's 2-to-1 decision, and the judges agreed to take her case en banc, which they hardly ever do.

And so all 12 judges were about to file in and take the bench, affording a rare glimpse at the dynamic of the entire court. Ocheltree's lawyer was nervous: a three-judge panel of the Fourth Circuit provides a grilling, but this would be a full-court press. Ocheltree, however, was determined not to be intimidated. "Just because I'm a blue-collar worker doesn't mean I'm gonna let the black robes scare me," she said. "It may be the South, but it's the 21st century."

Geographically, the Fourth Circuit, one of 13 federal courts of appeals, is not the most southern. But it is singularly genteel: its judges descend from the bench to shake lawyers' hands after oral arguments. And as recently as 1999, Chief Justice William H. Rehnquist led the Fourth Circuit's annual judicial conference in a traditional rousing sing-along that included "Dixie." This always offended civil rights lawyers and the few African-American lawyers in attendance. But it never surprised them.

It was not until the year 2001 that the Fourth Circuit, which has the largest African-American population of any appellate jurisdiction, became the final federal appeals court to be racially or ethnically integrated. Many consider the court to be a legacy of Strom Thurmond and Jesse Helms because the former senators from the Carolinas played a key role in shaping it through patronage appointments and obstructionism. Indeed, President Bush's most recent appointment to the Fourth Circuit, Dennis W. Shedd, is a former chief of staff to Thurmond; his pending nominee, Terrence Boyle, is a former Helms aide unsuccessfully nominated by Bush's father more than 10 years ago.

Although President Bush may or may not get the chance to name a new Supreme Court justice this year, he is busy trying to fill 25 federal appeals court vacancies, including 3 on the Fourth Circuit, with the backing of a newly Republican Senate. He already has 16 nominees waiting for confirmation. And despite the occasional Democratic filibuster, he appears poised to transform the federal judiciary—which includes 179 appeals judges at full strength—back into an overwhelmingly conservative bench. In 12 years between them, Ronald Reagan and George H. W. Bush established a Republican majority on every appeals court.

Clinton, facing stiff resistance from an opposition Senate for six of his eight years, pushed that back somewhat so that Bush inherited a Republican majority on 8 of the 13 appellate courts, with 3 more poised to swing Republican through his appointments. And those appointments, because they are for life, could reverberate for generations. Judge H. Emory Widener Jr. of the Fourth Circuit, who is 79, was named by Richard Nixon 31 years ago.

As Bush makes his selections, his staunch conservative supporters tout the Fourth Circuit as a model to emulate, and liberals view it anxiously as a harbinger of doom. That's because the Fourth Circuit, which has eight Republican and four Democratic appointees, is not only conservative but also bold and muscular in its conservatism. It is confident enough to strike down acts of Congress when it finds them stretching the limits of the federal government's power and hardheaded enough to rule against nearly every death-row defendant who comes before it.

To critics, the Fourth Circuit lacks compassion for the individual. To admirers, the Fourth Circuit is a welcome corrective after years of soft, liberally activist benches, a brilliant court with a healthy respect for the concerns of prosecutors, of business owners, of state officials—and of the Bush administration, which received deference from the court to treat a United States citizen captured in Afghanistan as an "enemy combatant" who could be detained without charges even on American soil.

Helms once told a North Carolina newspaper that the furor in Washington over judicial nominations was out of whack with the sentiments of the public: "You go out on the street of Raleigh, N.C., and ask 100 people, 'Do you give a damn who is on the Fourth Circuit Court of Appeals?' They'll say, 'What's that?'"

He had a point. Few pay much attention to federal courts below the Supreme Court level. But they should. The appellate courts, created in the late 19th century to relieve overcrowding of the Supreme Court's docket, decide about 28,000 cases a year compared with the highest court's 75 or so. Practically speaking, they have the final say in most matters of law; their reach is broader, if not deeper, than the Supreme Court's itself.

Judges on the Fourth Circuit say that they just follow the Supreme Court's lead. And it is true that the Fourth Circuit is the appellate court closest in thinking to the Rehnquist Court. But the relationship is symbiotic: the Fourth Circuit does not just imitate; it also initiates. It pushes the envelope, testing the boundaries of conservative doctrine in the area of, say, reasserting states' rights over big government. Sometimes, the Supreme Court reins in the Fourth Circuit, reversing its more experimental decisions, but it also upholds them or leaves them alone to become the law of the land. There is a cross-fertilization, which could see its apotheosis this spring: the Fourth Circuit is dominated intellectually by two very different conservative judges, J. Harvie Wilkinson 3rd and J. Michael Luttig, both of whom are leading candidates for the next Supreme Court vacancy.

Judge Karen J. Williams, 52, a tall, slender woman with delicate features and a regal carriage, wrote the decision overturning the jury verdict in *Lisa Ocheltree v. Scollon Productions*. The federal law that prohibits sexual harassment in the workplace, as she phrased it ever so piquantly, is not a "neo-Victorian chivalry code designed to protect" the "tender sensitivities of contemporary women."

Williams eloped at 17 with her teenage sweetheart, gave birth to four children, taught school, commuted to law school and eventually became a lawyer in her husband's private practice in Orangeburg, S.C. She was appointed by former President Bush in 1992 on the recommendation of Strom Thurmond, a friend of her father-in-law's, then the president of the South Carolina State Senate. At Williams's investiture, Thurmond and her father-in-law reminisced about how they used to double-date.

Once a month, the judges, whose annual salary of $164,000 is higher than that of senators, travel from their home states to Richmond to hear a week of oral arguments. They sit in three-judge panels randomly selected by a computer program and invariably encounter a rich menu of human dramas and hot-button issues. They hear everything from bankruptcy cases to international child-custody disputes, from race discrimination claims to environmental battles over wetlands. In the January hearings, they debated whether Norfolk, Va., could use an anti-loitering statute to keep an elderly couple from protesting abortion on a bridge over a highway and whether animal-control officers in High Point, N.C., were stripping pit bull owners of their Fourth Amendment rights by killing their dogs. They examined three cadets' contention that the mealtime prayer at the Virginia Military Institute was unconstitutional and an Israeli immigrant's appeal of his conviction for interfering with a flight crew when, on the three-month anniversary of 9/11, he behaved so oddly that the pilots made an emergency landing.

The full Fourth Circuit rarely sits to review the decision of one of its three-judge panels. When it does, though, critics say that it uses this en banc procedure to overturn liberal decisions that slip through, and there are plenty of supporting examples. But with Ocheltree, the judges were sitting in reconsideration of a quite conservative decision, one that would greatly limit the ability of employees in the region to make successful claims of sexual harassment. They were also addressing the sensitive issue of the sanctity of jury decisions.

Williams was the author of an infamous decision several years ago. The Fourth Circuit ruled that the liberal Warren Court's landmark 1966 ruling in *Miranda v. Arizona* was not constitutionally based, and as such that an obsolete

Congressional statute trumped it. More than 30 years ago, the statute was a still-born attempt to overrule the court's holding that criminal suspects must be apprised of their rights through what have become known as Miranda warnings. It was never enforced and largely forgotten until the Fourth Circuit resurrected it. And Williams's decision helped cement the Fourth Circuit's reputation as a judicially active conservative court. But the Supreme Court reversed it, 7 to 2, with Antonin Scalia and Clarence Thomas, the two most conservative justices and President Bush's self-proclaimed favorites, dissenting. In that instance and several others, the Fourth Circuit's effort to nudge the Supreme Court toward greater conservatism backfired. Still, the Supreme Court has upheld 36.5 percent of the Fourth Circuit's decisions over the last decade, infinitesimally better than the average. It is, at the very least, a dialogue.

The Fourth Circuit does not march in conservative lock step, however, and its intellectually vibrant judges do not constitute an ideological cabal. The court often reaches consensus across the ideological divide; some of its work is non-ideological in nature. Sometimes the majority lets liberal decisions stand; other times even the most conservative judges issue opinions that seem to betray their ideological stripes. And often the fiercest legal arguments are not between the liberals and the conservatives but between conservatives themselves.

Yet when it comes to high-profile decisions, the Fourth Circuit tends to divide neatly along party lines. And taken together, those decisions not only bespeak a conservative philosophy of law but also serve a conservative political agenda. Among its many decisions, the Fourth Circuit has upheld the minute of silence in Virginia schools; ended court-ordered busing in Charlotte; upheld state laws that stringently regulate abortion clinics or require parental notification or ban so-called partial-birth abortions; ruled that the Virginia Military Institute could remain all male as long as there was a separate but comparable education for women; upheld a Charleston, S.C., program that tested maternity patients for illegal drug use without their consent and turned the results over to the police; overturned a Virginia prohibition against license plates bearing the Confederate flag; ruled that the F.D.A. didn't have the authority to regulate nicotine as a drug; and, most recently, overruled a West Virginia federal judge's efforts to strictly limit mountaintop mining that buries Appalachian streams beneath piles of fill and waste.

As the Ocheltree hearing opened in a packed courtroom, the bailiff intoned the traditional blessing: "God save the United States and this honorable court." The judges took their seats in leather swivel chairs, with the brand-new chief judge, William W. Wilkins Jr. of South Carolina, in the center. Wilkins started his career as a clerk to Judge Clement Haynsworth of the Fourth Circuit (whose Supreme

Court nomination by Nixon was rejected by Congress) and then went on to become an aide and campaign director for Thurmond. He was the first federal judge appointed by Reagan.

J. Harvie Wilkinson 3rd had technically stepped down as chief judge after seven years, as required by law. But he was sitting just off-center, and he still dominated, he and Luttig, each in his own way.

A warm, gracious and patrician Virginian, Wilkinson, 58, appears slight and owlish in his civilian clothes—blue blazer, gold buttons—yet commanding in his robes. The son of a banker, the future judge attended boarding school at Lawrenceville and college at Yale before returning to Virginia to study law. While a law student, he ran as a Republican candidate for Congress; when he got 30 percent of the vote, he jokes, he took it as a mandate to finish law school. He eventually taught law and served as editorial-page editor of *The Norfolk Virginian-Pilot*. (This didn't keep *The Pilot* from editorializing against his appointment to the bench in 1983, saying that he lacked courtroom experience.)

The two judges both clerked for Supreme Court justices they still revere—Wilkinson for Lewis F. Powell Jr. and Luttig for Chief Justice Warren Burger as well as for Antonin Scalia when Scalia was an appeals court judge. Both worked for Republican Justice Departments and participated in judicial selections, Wilkinson under Reagan and Luttig under the first Bush. Luttig shepherded Clarence Thomas through his contentious confirmation, and pictures of Thomas hang on his chambers' walls, including one inscribed "This would not have been possible without you! Thanks so much, buddy!" (Luttig's three clean-cut male clerks will head to the Supreme Court next year to clerk for Thomas, Scalia and Anthony M. Kennedy.)

These similarities between Wilkinson and Luttig, and their keen legal minds, initially created a natural alliance between them. Luttig, a native of Tyler, Tex., said that he used to spend more time talking with Wilkinson than with any other judge on the court. They are still friends, he said. But the years have clarified the differences in the two judges' styles and their jurisprudence, and they often parry and thrust in their decisions, with Luttig going for the direct and Wilkinson the indirect jabs. Often Wilkinson and Luttig end up voting the same way, but "there's this very antagonistic sideshow," said Rodney Smolla, a University of Richmond law professor.

Many lawyers assume that Luttig is more conservative than Wilkinson. But the law journal *Judicature* recently evaluated the decisions of six possible Bush nominees for the Supreme Court and found Wilkinson to be furthest to the right—exceptionally conservative. It found Luttig the second least conservative of the six. "Did you see the *Judicature* article?" Luttig asked me, and he also made sure that I had read some cases in which he took unexpectedly liberal positions.

He is loath to be predictable and eager to be perceived as more moderate in anticipation of a Supreme Court opening.

Wilkinson and Luttig do not like to talk about the possibility that they will be competing for a nomination as soon as this spring if, say, Chief Justice Rehnquist, 78, or Justice Sandra Day O'Connor, 72, steps down. But during Ocheltree's hearing at the Richmond courthouse, the subject was in the air.

Since 1995, for so long that she is beginning to feel and sound like a crusader, Lisa Ocheltree, 41, has been pursuing her claim against Scollon Productions, a manufacturer of life-size costumes for mascots like the South Carolina Gamecock and characters like Tommy Pickles.

She filed suit under a civil rights law, Title VII, that sees sexual harassment as a violation of the prohibition against workplace discrimination because of sex. Some sexual-harassment claims involve a quid pro quo; others, like Ocheltree's, assert a hostile work environment. Unfortunately for Ocheltree, she has ended up before the appeals court least likely to be sympathetic to any such claims.

Plaintiffs in sexual-harassment suits prevail in only 21 percent of their appeals before the Fourth Circuit, according to a recent *Cornell Law Review* article. They win, in contrast, 80 percent of the time in the New York-based Second Circuit, which is dominated by Democratic appointees, and 39 percent of the time nationwide.

When Ocheltree, now a U.P.S. employee, worked at Scollon Productions, she was the only woman in an otherwise all-male production shop. Over time, the atmosphere grew more coarse, she said, until it was dominated by sexually explicit conversation and behavior.

A co-worker pinched the nipples of a mannequin while another fell to his knees and simulated oral sex on it. A co-worker teased her with a dirty song while others, including her supervisor, laughed at the show. A colleague tried to get her to react to a photograph of a man with his genitalia pierced. During Ocheltree's trial, a male co-worker said that the other men would routinely fondle the mannequins because they knew it bothered Ocheltree.

Ocheltree complained about the environment during an employee meeting, and she was rebuffed repeatedly when she tried to get an audience with the company's senior executives. After about 18 months at Scollon, she was fired. A federal judge summarily dismissed her complaint, but, representing herself, she appealed that judgment to the Fourth Circuit, which determined that she had grounds for trial. A jury awarded Ocheltree $7,280 in compensatory damages and $400,000 in punitive damages. The judge reduced the damages to $50,000 because Scollon is a small business. Nonetheless, Ocheltree said that her victory restored her "sense of honor and dignity," even though the men at the plant "are laughing to this day."

Scollon Productions appealed the jury's verdict to the Fourth Circuit, contending that Ocheltree's description of the workplace environment was exaggerated and that the crude behavior wasn't directed at Ocheltree anyway. The three-judge panel assigned the case included Williams, Paul V. Niemeyer, appointed by Bush in 1990, and M. Blane Michael, a bow-tie-wearing Clinton appointee from West Virginia. Williams and Niemeyer voted to reverse the jury's decision, and Michael was the dissenter.

It is a role that Michael, who keeps a large photograph of Clinton's inauguration on his chambers' walls, often exercises. There have been other instances in which it has pitted him against Williams too, although he told me that their personal relations are cordial. Still, Michael wrote the dissent in the Miranda case and in one in which Williams found that people with symptom-free H.I.V. are not protected by the Americans With Disabilities Act.

Michael said that Williams and Niemeyer chose "again and again" to see the evidence in a light favorable to Ocheltree's employer rather than to Ocheltree. They were ignoring the fact that the jury found Ocheltree to be the credible party, and they were ignoring their obligation to respect a jury's finding, he said. There is, he wrote, "a profound difference in our respective approaches to reviewing a jury verdict."

In a spirited opinion, Williams wrote that there was no reason to believe that the vulgar atmosphere in the workshop had anything to do with Ocheltree's presence or the fact that she was a woman. The incidents were isolated, and the rest was banter, she said. The courts shouldn't treat women preferentially by insulating them from everyday insults. And further, she added, there was some indication that Ocheltree herself was not a "model of femininity."

In his dissent, Michael wrote that a reasonable jury would conclude that the men at Scollon Productions resented Ocheltree's intrusion into their workplace and had set out to make her unwelcome. He said that the "overall tenor of the workplace banter conveyed the message that women exist primarily to gratify male desires for oral sex." In a workplace suffused with representations of women as sexual objects, a female worker "would doubtless wonder," he wrote, whether her male co-workers were looking at her and asking themselves "whether she 'swallows'" or whether she could "'suck a golf ball through a garden hose.'"

Franklin Delano Roosevelt famously set out to overhaul the federal judiciary ideologically. Confronting courts that were thwarting his New Deal projects, he strove to create liberal ones that would grant the government more power to regulate the economy. Decades later, Reagan displayed a similar purposefulness, screening judicial candidates using ideological "litmus tests" in order to choose jurists who were strict constructionists, tough on crime, anti-abortion and pro-family.

Between them, Reagan and the first President Bush named six judges to the Fourth Circuit; those six joined Nixon's appointee, Widener, to form a solid conservative core. On other courts, the transformation to conservative has been more startling. The two Deep South appellate courts, for instance, used to be civil rights crusaders. But until the Carter judges retired, the Fourth Circuit was, if not liberal, at least more balanced.

Clinton put a priority on diversifying the federal bench, picking up where Carter had left off. Despite an uncooperative Senate, he succeeded in getting a record 9 black, 7 Hispanic and 20 female judges confirmed.

Yet the Clinton administration never saw its role as reasserting ideological balance on the courts. When Clinton took office, the appeals courts were solidly Republican, but his administration did not feel compelled to find liberal powerhouses to counter the conservative heavyweights appointed by Reagan and Bush. "Some in the White House argued very forcefully that their job was not to put on the federal bench the liberal equivalents of the Luttigs and the Wilkinsons," said Nan Aron, president of Alliance for Justice, a liberal coalition. Clinton was not a die-hard liberal himself, and he tended to nominate centrist legal professionals in tune with his more centrist politics. Still, he faced intense partisan battles, particularly over his minority appointees, and the acrimony continued through Bush's first two years, affecting not just the political arena but also the courts themselves.

Luttig told me that he thinks the politics surrounding judicial appointments makes judges hyperconscious of their political sponsors. "Judges are told, 'You're appointed by us to do these things.' So then judges start thinking, Well, how do I interpret the law to get the result that the people who pushed for me to be here want me to get?" he said. "I believe that there's a natural temptation to line up as political partisans that is reinforced by the political process. And it has to be resisted, by the judiciary and by the politicians."

Clinton named four white judges to the Fourth Circuit without much battle, including one, William B. Traxler Jr., of Greenville, S.C., who was first elevated to the federal bench, on Thurmond's recommendation, by former President Bush. Traxler votes so often with the conservative majority that court watchers forget he's a Democratic appointee. The other three—Blane Michael and Robert B. King of West Virginia and Diana Gribbon Motz of Maryland—are unofficially the dissenters.

In contrast to his smooth experience with getting the white judges confirmed, Clinton tried at least four times to name an African-American to the Fourth

Circuit. His nominees were blocked every time. Jesse Helms still bore a grudge from Clinton's failure to renominate his former aide Terrence Boyle, after Boyle's nomination by the first Bush had elapsed. Helms then blocked, as is the home state senator's power, every Clinton nominee from North Carolina, including two African-American judges. As a result, there is no one from North Carolina on the Fourth Circuit now, although proving that even a retired Helms can get his way, President Bush has a pending nominee from North Carolina—and that is Boyle.

During his period of obstructionism, Helms insisted, and Thurmond publicly concurred, that the matter had nothing to do with race or politics. It would simply be a waste of taxpayer money, Helms said repeatedly, to fill vacancies on the Fourth Circuit when the chief judge, Wilkinson, thought the court would function less efficiently if it were bigger. (And clearly it would have if it became less ideologically homogeneous.)

Clinton finally tried an end run around Helms by nominating a Virginian, a soft-spoken African-American lawyer named Roger L. Gregory. Gregory comes from a small town in rural Virginia where his parents worked in the local tobacco factory. He grew up to found a Richmond law firm with L. Douglas Wilder, the former governor of Virginia. He gives inspirational speeches to black youths. His nomination had bipartisan support. But even Gregory couldn't get a hearing scheduled.

So Clinton resorted to an extraordinary tactic. During his last days in office, after Congress had recessed, Clinton unilaterally appointed Gregory to the bench. President Bush, eager to demonstrate bipartisanship and win support for his own candidates, eventually allowed Gregory's temporary appointment to become permanent. In July 2001, the Senate confirmed him 93 to 1, with Trent Lott casting the dissenting vote. The Fourth Circuit Court of Appeals was officially integrated.

In a study of capital convictions and appeals between 1973 and 1995, Prof. James S. Liebman of Columbia University Law School found that the Fourth Circuit granted relief to death-row inmates less frequently than any other appeals court in the country. Even at that point, and it has gotten more restrictive since, the Fourth Circuit was overturning 12 percent of the death sentences it reviewed: that compared with an average 40 percent reversal rate for federal appeals courts. "There are other conservative courts of appeal but none that are a black hole of capital litigation like the Fourth Circuit," said John H. Blume, director of the Cornell Death Penalty Project, who represents South Carolina prisoners.

When Kevin Wiggins's case came up before the Fourth Circuit in January 2002, he was on death row in Maryland, trying not to get his hopes up. A federal district chief judge had invalidated his death sentence and voided his conviction for murder. Theoretically, he should have gone free. But the state appealed. And Wiggins knew, because death-row prisoners know these things, that the odds of winning in the Fourth Circuit weren't good.

In February, I visited Wiggins in the C-pod of the Maryland Correctional Adjustment Center in downtown Baltimore. When a guard unlocked the door to a narrow concrete visiting cell, Wiggins was already there, staring blankly through a scratched glass partition. Wearing a white undershirt, his face round with a wisp of a mustache, he was itching to get talking. And talk he did, like a balloon releasing air, his words a jumble as he dizzyingly flicked back and forth in time.

Matter-of-factly, Wiggins described himself as "a nobody with no family and no skills." He had a nightmarish childhood, according to information gathered by a forensic social worker hired by his present lawyer. His mother was alcoholic, neglectful and abusive. When he was 6, Wiggins was removed from his mother's home after she burned him severely with a hot plate in punishment for playing with matches. He then endured a series of foster homes in which he was beaten, locked in closets and repeatedly raped. He emerged into adulthood as a barely educated loner who lived in rented rooms and worked at minimum-wage jobs. He was of "borderline intelligence," according to state social-service records.

Wiggins had no criminal record when he was arrested at age 27 for the murder of an elderly woman. The State of Maryland maintained that Wiggins drowned Florence Lacs, 77, in her bathtub in 1988: he was working as a painter in her building, and he and his girlfriend were found in possession of Lacs's credit cards and car. There was no forensic evidence linking Wiggins to the murder, though there was unidentified forensic evidence—fingerprints, hair, fibers and a baseball cap left at the scene. Still, in a bench trial, a state judge convicted Wiggins of robbery and murder.

During the subsequent sentencing trial, Wiggins's inexperienced public defenders decided to reargue his innocence instead of presenting a case for why he should get life not death. They did not even bother to investigate his background to discover whether he possessed the kind of "social history" that is routinely used to humanize a defendant and mitigate against the imposition of the death penalty.

Wiggins has now been on death row since 1989. In 1993, a high-powered Washington lawyer, Donald B. Verrilli, Jr., took on Wiggins's case pro bono, and it began wending its way through the postconviction review and then the state appeals process. Verrilli found the case against Wiggins to be weakly circumstantial at best, offering evidence only that Wiggins was a logical suspect. Verrilli said he came to believe that Wiggins did not commit the crime but rather served as the "fall guy for people more clever than him." Specifically, there is a plausible alternative to the course of events involving Wiggins's girlfriend, who was 15 years his elder. All charges against her were dropped, and she testified against Wiggins; her brother, it seemed, lived in an apartment below the victim's.

The case's first stop in federal court was at the bench of Maryland's United States chief district judge, J. Frederick Motz, who happens to be married to Judge Diana Motz, a Clinton appointee on the Fourth Circuit. Judge Frederick Motz is a former federal prosecutor appointed by Reagan; he is not, as he said in court one day, "an anti-capital punishment person." In a 55-page opinion, he concluded, "No rational finder of fact could have found Wiggins guilty of murder beyond a reasonable doubt." He invalidated the murder conviction and threw out the death sentence too.

I asked Wiggins whether he was happy when Motz took his side. "It's hard for me to be happy about anything," he said. Wiggins told me that he could remember only one joyful time in his life. It was after his mother burned him. Six years old, he awoke in a hospital bed, surrounded by nurses who clucked over him, petting his hair and bringing him cookies.

When Maryland prosecutors decided to appeal to the Fourth Circuit, Motz publicly questioned their desire to continue pursuing what he characterized as a flimsy case. "Why isn't this case of moral concern to the state?" he asked. "Or don't you care?"

At the Fourth Circuit, Wiggins drew a panel of three Republican appointees— Wilkinson, Widener and Niemeyer. In a hearing last winter, the judges appeared to be wrestling with the case; they doubled the time they usually allot attorneys to present their arguments. Last May, however, in a decision written by the 79-year-old Judge Widener, the panel ended up reinstating Wiggins's conviction and his death sentence. The panel gave the original trial judge the benefit of the doubt; it deferred to his assertion that he based his decision of Wiggins's guilt on a totality of evidence and that he did not infer Wiggins's guilt from his possession of the victim's property. And it ruled that the public defenders' failure to present Wiggins's background during the sentencing hearing was a trial tactic rather than negligence.

And yet the panel had some hesitations. Judge Wilkinson wrote that he couldn't "say with certainty" that Wiggins committed the murder. And Judge Niemeyer acknowledged that it was something of a close call to find that Wiggins had adequate counsel.

"I think that most circuit courts, if they have real doubts about what has happened in a capital case, they will reverse," Professor Liebman said. "The Fourth Circuit doesn't have the same threshold. In this case, they saw the tripwire and stepped right over it."

Generally, the Supreme Court upholds the Fourth Circuit's tough stance in death-penalty cases by a 5-to-4 vote, dividing ideologically.

Many, if not most, appeals judges show a pattern to their judging over time.

Wilkinson has granted a new hearing to a death-row prisoner once in 19 years, according to a *South Carolina Law Review* article. In contrast, Judge Francis D. Murnaghan Jr. of Maryland, who used to be the Fourth Circuit's pre-eminent liberal, granted relief to about one out of three death-row prisoners who came before him.

Yet no judge wants to be seen as tailoring his decisions to his ideology, as bending the law to determine preconceived results. Every judge will tell you that he or she comes to each case with an open mind, seeing a distinct set of facts that raises distinct legal questions.

Wilkinson said he feels strongly that judges should never be rated and ranked as if they were politicians whose votes could be counted. He said that the statistical analyses of judges' decisions, followed by the affixing of a label of liberal or conservative, is reductive.

"I don't go on the bench as liberal or conservative," Wilkinson said. And yet he does not dispute that he is a conservative jurist. He acknowledges his place among those who came of age concerned about "the excessive activism" of the Warren Court. The Warren Court was seen as having overstepped its bounds with rulings that expanded equal protection, the right to vote, criminal defendants' rights and the right to privacy. Conservatives, in contrast, preached judicial restraint.

Yet with conservatives now controlling most of the nation's federal appeals courts, Wilkinson is one among many who have come to a new appreciation of judicial activism. Like the "new federalists" whose conservative thinking increasingly influences the legal mainstream, Wilkinson said he believes that the Constitution is more than just the Bill of Rights. He doesn't think that the Bill of Rights has been overemphasized, he is quick to say, but that what he calls "the structural Constitution" has been underemphasized.

"That body of the document that spells out the relationship between the federal government and the states was neglected for far too long," he said. "The power of Congress was seen as unlimited and that of the states as a virtual nullity." Wilkinson has found it exciting, he said, to be engaged in redressing this imbalance, which sometimes means striking down Congressional acts that seem to usurp state power unconstitutionally.

But he notes, because he is of judicious temperament, that judicial activism is "heady wine" and that restraint is still the greater virtue. Everything in moderation. Luttig takes exception to the view that striking down Congressional laws necessarily constitutes judicial activism. "Remember, it's sophomoric to think that invalidation of a statute equals judicial activism," he said. "Judicial activism means deciding a case based on one's own personal predilections, regardless. It might well take the form of sustaining a law that should be stricken." Several years ago, in an opinion written by Luttig, the Fourth Circuit struck down a key provision of the Violence Against Women Act. As Luttig saw it, Congress had established a federal civil right that didn't exist in the Constitution—the right to be free of crimes of violence motivated by gender—and then established the additional right for victims of such violence to sue their aggressors for damages in federal court. Congress had justified the law based on the idea—which Luttig clearly finds ridiculous—that gender-motivated violence is a national problem with a dampening effect on the economy and interstate commerce and that states have not risen to the task of tackling this problem.

Luttig ruled that Congress had overstepped its authority. A three-judge panel of the Fourth Circuit originally heard the appeal, upholding the constitutionality of the Violence Against Women Act, as had 17 of 18 federal district judges who had reviewed it. But the full Fourth Circuit vacated the liberal decision, taking the case en banc. Motz, the Clinton appointee, hinted in her dissent that her colleagues were motivated by their distaste for the act itself. "Judges' policy choices provide no basis for finding a statute unconstitutional," she wrote.

The case went up to the Supreme Court, and the Supreme Court agreed with the Fourth Circuit, 5 to 4, striking down the right of rape victims and abused women to sue in federal court under this statute. The Supreme Court version of the Fourth Circuit's ruling became the law of the land, and the Fourth Circuit and the Supreme Court jointly reinforced the principle that Congress's powers are limited.

Luttig's opinion, though, went beyond the Supreme Court's rhetorically. He began, "We the People, distrustful of power, and believing that government limited and dispersed protects freedom best, provided that our federal government would be one of enumerated powers, and that all power unenumerated would be reserved to the several States and to ourselves."

Cass Sunstein, a University of Chicago law professor, said that no court had issued such a battle cry for states' rights since before the New Deal.

During the nearly two hours that the Fourth Circuit debated her case, Ocheltree, dressed in a pin-striped pants suit with a white handkerchief sewed into the breast pocket, sat anonymously on a pewlike bench, holding her husband's hand in a tight grip. The judges didn't even know she was there. Her feathered dirty blond hair fell over her eyes a few times, and she tossed it back. Other than that, she was frozen, riveted by the theater of the bench, which veered occasionally into *Grand Guignol*.

Chuck Thompson, the lawyer for Scollon Productions, who used to clerk for Senior Judge Clyde H. Hamilton, a Republican appointee to the Fourth Circuit, wore a red bow tie. "May it please the court," he said. He didn't get a chance to say very much more. This was the judges' show. Karen Williams, author of the pro-employer decision, spent more time arguing Scollon's case than Thompson did. Michael, the dissenter, rolled his eyes and defended Ocheltree; Motz fired a few one-line zingers. Luttig, wagging his finger, told his fellow judges where their legal reasoning proved inadequate and instructed the lawyers for both sides what their arguments should be. "I'd have to disagree with you," Thompson ventured at one point.

"You can't!" Luttig retorted. "You can't disagree!" Wilkinson, perennially concerned with civility, exuded disgust at the locker-room atmosphere being described and exasperation with his colleagues for rehashing the ugly details of the case. "Who enjoys what and who enjoys whom," he said, his voice booming, "that's not for an appellate court to decide." For Wilkinson, the bottom line seemed to be that there was a jury verdict, and his remarks hinted that he was disinclined to overturn it.

Luttig, however, didn't seem certain that the jury verdict was defensible, and he scolded Ocheltree's lawyer, William Elvin Hopkins Jr., 36, for failing to make his best case. As Luttig saw it, the crux of Hopkins's challenge was to explain why Ocheltree was discriminated against if the locker-room atmosphere predated her arrival at Scollon. "You'll lose if you don't better answer that before this panel," he said. Luttig suggested this theory: Most men would stop such salacious talk once a woman was in their midst and if they didn't, it was precisely *because* she was there. Their behavior may not have changed, but their motivation did, he said.

When the conversation became graphic, Widener, whose eyes had been closed, seemed to startle into participation. "You're asking us to hold that when there's an all-male shop, a woman can walk in and say, 'Give me the money!'"

Williams agreed: there was no reason for Ocheltree to have been any more offended than her male colleagues by sexually explicit conversation, not in an age when magazines feature articles about how much women enjoy oral sex.

As in most oral arguments I observed, Gregory, the African-American judge who joined the court in 2001, didn't grandstand. When he speaks, though, he doesn't mince words, slices to the core and if the subject is discrimination, he gets it. Title VII is not about sex or race, he said; it's about power. And the incidents with the mannequin speak volumes, he said: "The problem with the mannequin is that it became almost an effigy, if you will, of the plaintiff."

As Ocheltree left the courthouse, still holding her husband's hand, she said that she felt the court would do the right thing when it issued its decision later this year. There was no real basis for her optimism, though, not in the court's track record or in the questions the judges asked at her hearing. It could go either way, but the odds are not with the Lisa Ocheltrees or the Kevin Wigginses, not in the Fourth Circuit or, for that matter, in an ever increasing number of appellate courts in this country.

Legal scholars talk about the pendulum swinging from liberal to conservative, from a preoccupation with individuals' rights to a preoccupation with states' rights, and suggest that, in time, it will swing back once more. It would certainly help many Americans sustain their faith in the system if the courts could find their equilibrium, if they could become less ideological, less predictable and less political. That doesn't appear to be on the horizon, though, not in the foreseeable future. In the historic site in Richmond where the Confederacy once thrived, the United States Court of Appeals for the Fourth Circuit is ushering in the 21st century.

Chapter 10

Public Opinion

10-1

Analyzing and Interpreting Polls

Herbert Asher

Public opinion polls have gained a prominent place in modern American politics. Polls themselves often are newsworthy, particularly during campaigns and times of political crisis. Unfortunately, as Herbert Asher shows in the following essay, polls are open to misinterpretation and misuse. The wording of questions, the construction of a sample, the choice of items to analyze and report, the use of surveys to measure trends, and the examination of subsets of respondents all pose problems of interpretation. Every consumer of polling information must understand these issues to properly use the information polls provide.

. . . INTERPRETING A POLL is more an art than a science, even though statistical analysis of poll data is central to the enterprise. An investigator examining poll results has tremendous leeway in deciding which items to analyze, which sample subsets or breakdowns to present, and how to interpret the statistical results. Take as an example a poll with three items that measure attitudes toward arms control negotiations. The investigator may construct an index from these three items. . . . Or the investigator may emphasize the results from one question, perhaps because of space and time constraints and the desire to keep matters simple, or because

Source: Herbert Asher, *Polling and the Public: What Every Citizen Should Know,* 4th ed. (Washington, D.C.: CQ Press, 1998), 141–169.

those particular results best support the analyst's own policy preferences. The investigator may examine results from the entire sample and ignore subgroups whose responses deviate from the overall pattern. Again time and space limitations or the investigator's own preferences may influence these choices. Finally, two investigators may interpret identical poll results in sharply different ways depending on the perspectives and values they bring to their data analysis; the glass may indeed be half full or half empty.

As the preceding example suggests, the analysis and interpretation of data entail a high degree of subjectivity and judgment. Subjectivity in this context does not mean deliberate bias or distortion, but simply professional judgments about the importance and relevance of information. Certainly, news organizations' interpretations of their polls are generally done in the least subjective and unbiased fashion. But biases can slip in—sometimes unintentionally, sometimes deliberately—when, for example, an organization has sponsored a poll to promote a particular position. Because this final phase of polling is likely to have the most direct influence on public opinion, this chapter includes several case studies to illustrate the judgmental aspects of analyzing and interpreting poll results.

Choosing Items to Analyze

Many public opinion surveys deal with multifaceted, complex issues. For example, a researcher querying Americans about their attitudes toward tax reform might find initially that they overwhelmingly favor a fairer tax system. But if respondents are asked about specific aspects of tax reform, their answers may reflect high levels of confusion, indifference, or opposition. And depending upon which items the researcher chooses to emphasize, the report might convey support, indifference, or opposition toward tax reform. American foreign policy in the Middle East is another highly complex subject that can elicit divergent reactions from Americans depending on which aspects of the policy they are questioned about.

Some surveys go into great depth on a topic through multiple items constructed to measure its various facets. The problem for an investigator in this case becomes one of deciding which results to report. Moreover, even though an extensive analysis is conducted, the media might publicize only an abbreviated version of it. In such a case the consumer of the poll results is at the mercy of the media to portray accurately the overall study. Groups or organizations that sponsor polls to demonstrate support for a particular position or policy option often disseminate results in a selective fashion which enables them to put the organization and its policies in a favorable light.

In contrast with in-depth surveys on a topic, *omnibus surveys* are superficial in their treatment of particular topics because of the need to cover many subjects in the same survey. Here the problem for an investigator becomes one of ensuring that the few questions employed to study a specific topic really do justice to the substance and complexity of that topic. It is left to the consumer of both kinds of polls to judge whether they receive the central information on a topic or whether other items might legitimately yield different substantive results.

The issue of prayer in public schools is a good example of how public opinion polling on a topic can be incomplete and potentially misleading. Typically, pollsters ask Americans whether they support a constitutional amendment that would permit voluntary prayer in public schools, and more than three-fourths of Americans respond that they would favor such an amendment. This question misses the mark. Voluntary prayer by individuals is in no way prohibited; the real issue is whether there will be *organized* voluntary prayer. But many pollsters do not include items that tap this aspect of the voluntary prayer issue. Will there be a common prayer? If so, who will compose it? Will someone lead the class in prayer? If so, who? Under what circumstances and when will the prayer be uttered? What about students who do not wish to participate or who prefer a different prayer?

The difficulty with both the in-depth poll and the omnibus survey is that the full set of items used to study a particular topic is usually not reported and thus the consumer cannot make informed judgments about whether the conclusions of the survey are valid. Recognizing this, individuals should take a skeptical view of claims by a corporate executive or an elected officeholder or even a friend that the polls demonstrate public support for or opposition to a particular position. The first question to ask is: What is the evidence cited to support the claim? From there one might examine the question wording, the response alternatives, the screening for nonattitudes, and the treatment of "don't know" responses. Then one might attempt the more difficult task of assessing whether the questions used to study the topic at hand were really optimal. Might other questions have been used? What aspects of the topic were not addressed? Finally, one might ponder whether different interpretations could be imposed on the data and whether alternative explanations could account for the reported patterns.

In evaluating poll results, there is always the temptation to seize upon those that support one's position and ignore those that do not. The problem is that one or two items cannot capture the full complexity of most issues. For example, a *Newsweek* poll conducted by the Gallup Organization in July 1986 asked a number of questions about sex laws and lifestyles. The poll included the following three items (Alpern 1986, 38):

Do you approve or disapprove of the Supreme Court decision upholding a state law against certain sexual practices engaged in privately by consenting adult homosexuals? [This question was asked of the 73 percent who knew about the Supreme Court decision.]

Disapprove	47%
Approve	41%

In general, do you think that states should have the right to prohibit particular sexual practices conducted in private between consenting adult homosexuals?

No	57%
Yes	34%

Do you think homosexuality has become an accepted alternative lifestyle or not?

Yes	32%
No	61%
Don't know	7%

Note that the first two items tap citizens' attitudes toward the legal treatment of homosexuals, while the third addresses citizens' views of homosexuality as a lifestyle. Although differently focused, all three questions deal with aspects of gay life. It would not be surprising to see gay rights advocates cite the results of the first two questions as indicating support for their position. Opponents of gay rights would emphasize the results of the third question.

An Eyewitness News/*Daily News* poll of New York City residents conducted in February 1986 further illustrates how the selective use and analysis of survey questions can generate very different impressions of popular opinion on an issue. This poll asked a number of gay rights questions:

On another matter, would you say that New York City needs a gay rights law or not?

Yes, need gay rights law	39%
No, do not need gay rights law	54%
Don't know/no opinion	8%

On another matter, do you think it should be against the law for landlords or private employers to deny housing or a job to someone because that person is homosexual or do you think landlords and employers should be allowed to do that if they want to?

Yes, should be against law	49%
No, should not be against law	47%
Volunteered responses	
Should be law only for landlord	1%
Should be law only for employers	8%
Don't know/no opinion	3%

Although a definite majority of the respondents oppose a gay rights law in response to the first question, a plurality also believe that it should be illegal for landlords and employers to deny housing and jobs to persons because they are homosexual. Here the two questions both address the legal status of homosexuals, and it is clear which question gay rights activists and gay rights opponents would cite in support of their respective policy positions. It is not clear, however, which question is the better measure of public opinion. The first question is unsatisfactory because one does not know how respondents interpreted the scope of a gay rights law. Did they think it referred only to housing and job discrimination, or did they think it would go substantially beyond that? The second question is inadequate if it is viewed as equivalent to a gay rights law. Lumping housing and jobs together constitutes another flaw since citizens might have divergent views on these two aspects of gay rights.

Additional examples of the importance of item selection are based on polls of Americans' attitudes about the Iraqi invasion of Kuwait in 1990. Early in the Persian Gulf crisis, various survey organizations asked Americans, using different questions, how they felt about taking military action against Iraq. Not surprisingly, the organizations obtained different results.

Do you favor or oppose direct U.S. military action against Iraq at this time? (Gallup, August 3–4, 1990)

Favor	23%
Oppose	68%
Don't know/refused	9%

Do you agree or disagree that the U.S. should take all actions necessary, including the use of military force, to make sure that Iraq withdraws its forces from Kuwait? (ABC News/*Washington Post*, August 8, 1990)

Agree	66%
Disagree	33%
Don't know	1%

Would you approve or disapprove of using U.S. troops to force the Iraqis to leave Kuwait? (Gallup, August 9–12, 1990, taken from *Public Perspective*, September/October 1990, 13)

| Approve | 64% |
| Disapprove | 36% |

(I'm going to mention some things that may or may not happen in the Middle East and for each one, please tell me whether the U.S. should or should not take military action in connection with it). . . . If Iraq refuses to withdraw from Kuwait? (NBC News/*Wall Street Journal*, August 18–19, 1990, taken from *Public Perspective*, September/October 1990, 13)

| No military action | 51% |
| Military action | 49% |

Note that the responses to these questions indicate varying levels of support for military action even though most of the questions were asked within two weeks of each other. The first question shows the most opposition to military action. This is easily explained: the question concerns military action *at this time,* an alternative that many Americans may have seen as premature until other means had been tried. The other three questions all indicate majority support for military action, although that support ranges from a bare majority to about two-thirds of all Americans. It is clear which question proponents and opponents of military action would cite to support their arguments.

Throughout the Persian Gulf crisis, public opinion was highly supportive of President Bush's policies; only in the period between October and December 1990 did support for the president's handling of the situation drop below 60 percent. For example, a November 1990 CBS News/*New York Times* poll showed the following patterns of response:

Do you approve or disapprove of the way George Bush is handling Iraq's invasion of Kuwait?

Approve	50%
Disapprove	41%
Don't know/NA	8%

Likewise, an ABC News/*Washington Post* poll in mid-November reported:

Do you approve or disapprove of the way George Bush is handling the situation caused by Iraq's invasion of Kuwait?

Approve	59%
Disapprove	36%
Don't know/NA	5%

Some opponents of the military buildup tried to use these and similar polls to demonstrate that support for the president's policies was decreasing, since earlier polls had indicated support levels in the 60–70 percent range. Fortunately, the *Washington Post* poll cited above asked respondents who disapproved of Bush's policy whether the president was moving too slowly or too quickly. It turned out that 44 percent of the disapprovers said "too slowly" and 37 percent "too quickly." Thus, a plurality of the disapprovers preferred more rapid action against Iraq—a result that provided little support for those critics of the president's policies who were arguing against a military solution.

Shortly before the outbreak of the war, the *Washington Post* conducted a survey of American attitudes about going to war with Iraq. To assess the effects of question wording, the *Post* split its sample in half and used two different versions of the same question followed by the identical follow-up question to each item.

Version 1

As you may know, the U.N. Security Council has authorized the use of force against Iraq if it doesn't withdraw from Kuwait by January 15. If Iraq does not withdraw from Kuwait, should the United States go to war against Iraq to force it out of Kuwait at some point after January 15 or not?

Go to war sometime after January 15	62%
No, do not go to war	32%

How long after January 15 should the United States wait for Iraq to withdraw from Kuwait before going to war to force it out?

Do not favor war at any point	32%
Immediately	18%
Less than one month	28%
1–3 months	8%
4 months or longer	2%

Version 2

The United Nations has passed a resolution authorizing the use of military force against Iraq if they do not withdraw their troops from Kuwait by January 15. If Iraq does not withdraw from Kuwait by then, do you think the United States should start military actions against Iraq, or should the United States wait longer to see if the trade embargo and economic sanctions work?

U.S. should start military actions	49%
U.S. should wait longer to see if sanctions work	47%

How long after January 15 should the United States wait for Iraq to withdraw from Kuwait before going to war to force it out?

U.S. should start military actions	49%

For those who would wait:

Less than a month	15%
1–3 months	17%
4 months or longer	9%

Morin (1991) points out how very different portraits of the American public can be painted by examining the two versions with and without the follow-up question. For example, version 1 shows 62 percent of Americans supporting war against Iraq, while version 2 shows only 49 percent. These different results stem from inclusion of the embargo and sanctions option in the second version. Thus it appears that version 2 gives a less militaristic depiction of the American public. Responses to the follow-up question, however, provide a different picture of the public. For example, the first version shows that 54 percent of Americans (18 + 28 + 8) favor going to war within three months. But the second version shows that 81 percent of Americans (49 + 15 + 17) favor war within three months. The point, of course, is that the availability of different items on a survey can generate differing descriptions of the public's preferences.

The importance of item selection is illustrated in a final example on the Gulf War from an April 3, 1991, ABC News/*Washington Post* poll conducted just after the conflict. It included the following three questions:

Do you approve or disapprove of the way that George Bush is handling the situation involving Iraqi rebels who are trying to overthrow Saddam Hussein?

Approve	69%
Disapprove	24%
Don't know	7%

Please tell me if you agree or disagree with this statement: The United States should not have ended the war with Iraqi President Saddam Hussein still in power.

Agree	55%
Disagree	40%
Don't know	5%

Do you think the United States should try to help rebels overthrow Hussein or not?

Yes	45%
No	51%
Don't know	4%

Note that the responses to the first item indicate overwhelming approval for the president. But if one analyzed the second question in isolation, one might conclude that a majority of Americans did not support the president and indeed wanted to restart the war against Saddam Hussein. But the third item shows that a majority of Americans oppose helping the rebels. The lesson of this and the previous examples is clear. Constructing an interpretation around any single survey item can generate a very inaccurate description of public opinion. Unfortunately, advocates of particular positions have many opportunities to use survey results selectively and misleadingly to advance their cause.

The health care debate in 1993 and 1994 also provides examples of how the selection of items for analysis can influence one's view of American public opinion. *Washington Post* polls asked Americans whether they thought the Clinton health plan was better or worse than the present system (Morin 1994). In one version of the question, the sample was given the response options "better" or "worse," while in the other version respondents could choose among "better," "worse," or "don't know enough about the plan to say." The following responses were obtained:

Version 1		Version 2	
better	52%	better	21%
worse	34%	worse	27%
don't know (volunteered)	14%	don't know enough	52%

Clearly, very different portrayals of American public opinion are presented by the two versions of the question. The first version suggests that a majority of Americans believed that the Clinton plan was better than the status quo, while the second version suggests that a plurality of citizens with opinions on the issue felt that the Clinton plan was worse. It is obvious which version of the question supporters and opponents of the Clinton health plan would be more likely to cite.

Another example from the health care reform area deals with Americans' feelings about the seriousness of the health care problem. Certainly, the more seriously the problem was viewed, the greater the impetus for changing the health care system. Different polling organizations asked a variety of questions designed to tap the importance of the health care issue (questions taken from the September/October 1994 issue of *Public Perspective*, 23, 26):

> Louis Harris and Associates (April 1994): Which of the following statements comes closest to expressing your overall view of the health care system in this country? . . . There are some good things in our health care system, but fundamental changes are needed to make it better. . . . Our health care system has so much wrong with it that we need to completely rebuild it. . . . On the whole, the health care system works pretty well and only minor changes are necessary to make it work.
>
> | Fundamental changes needed | 54% |
> | Completely rebuild it | 31% |
> | Only minor changes needed | 14% |
>
> NBC/*Wall Street Journal* (March 1994): Which of the following comes closest to your belief about the American health care system—the system is in crisis; the system has major problems, but is not in crisis; the system has problems, but they are not major; or the system has no problems?
>
> | Crisis | 22% |
> | Major problems | 50% |
> | Minor problems | 26% |
>
> Gallup (June 1994): Which of these statements do you agree with more: The country has health care problems, but no health care crisis, or, the country has a health care crisis?
>
> | Crisis | 55% |
> | Problems but no crisis | 41% |
> | Don't know | 4% |
>
> Gallup (June 1994): Which of these statements do you agree with more: The country has a health care crisis, or the country has health care problems, but no health care crisis?
>
> | Crisis | 35% |
> | Problems but no crisis | 61% |
> | Don't know | 4% |

Certainly if one were trying to make the case that health care reform was an absolute priority, one would cite the first version of the Gallup question in which

55 percent of the respondents labeled health care a crisis. But if one wanted to move more slowly and incrementally on the health care issue, one would likely cite the NBC News/*Wall Street Journal* poll in which only 22 percent of Americans said there was a crisis. Health care reform is the kind of controversial public policy issue that invites political leaders to seize upon those poll results to advance their positions. In such situations, citizens should be sensitive to how politicians are selectively using the polls.

Schneider (1996) has provided an excellent example of how examination of a single trial heat question may give a misleading impression of the electoral strength of presidential candidates. A better sense of the candidates' true electoral strength is achieved by adding to the analysis information about the incumbent's job approval rating. For example, in a trial heat question in May 1980 incumbent president Jimmy Carter led challenger Ronald Reagan by 40 to 32 percent, yet at the time Carter's job rating was quite negative: 38 percent approval and 51 percent disapproval. Thus Carter's lead in the trial heat item was much more fragile than it appeared; indeed, Reagan went on to win the election. Four years later, in May of 1984, President Reagan led challenger Walter Mondale by 10 percentage points in the trial heat question. But Reagan's job rating was very positive: 54 percent approval compared with 38 percent disapproval. Thus Reagan's 10-point lead looked quite solid in view of his strong job ratings, and he won overwhelmingly in November. Finally, in April 1992, incumbent president George Bush led challenger Bill Clinton by 50 to 34 percent in the trial heat question, a huge margin. But Bush's overall job rating was negative—42 percent approval versus 48 percent disapproval. Bush's lead over Clinton, then, was not as strong as it appeared, and Clinton ultimately won the election.

By collecting information on multiple aspects of a topic, pollsters are better able to understand citizens' attitudes (Morin and Berry 1996). One of the anomalies of 1996 was the substantial number of Americans who were worried about the health of the economy at a time when by most objective indicators the economy was performing very well. Part of the answer to this puzzle was Americans' ignorance and misinformation about the country's economic health. For example, even though unemployment was substantially lower in 1996 than in 1991, 33 percent of Americans said it was higher in 1996 and 28 percent said the same. The average estimate of the unemployment rate was 20.6 percent when in reality it was just over 5 percent. Americans' perceptions of inflation and the deficit were similar; in both cases Americans thought that the reality was much worse than it actually was. It is no wonder that many Americans expressed economic insecurity during good economic times; they were not aware of how strongly the economy was performing.

The final example in this section focuses on how the media selects what we learn about a poll even when the complete poll and analyses are available to the citizenry. The example concerns a book entitled *Sex in America: A Definitive Survey* by Robert T. Michael et al., published in 1994, along with a more specialized and comprehensive volume, *The Social Organization of Sexuality: Sexual Practices in the United States* by Edward O. Laumann et al. Both books are based on an extensive questionnaire administered by the National Opinion Research Center to 3,432 scientifically selected respondents. . . .

Because of the importance of the subject matter and because sex sells, media coverage of the survey was widespread. How various media reported the story indicates how much leeway the media have and how influential they are in determining what citizens learn about a given topic. For example, the *New York Times* ran a front-page story on October 7, 1994, entitled "Sex in America: Faithfulness in Marriage Thrives After All." Less prominent stories appeared in subsequent issues, including one on October 18, 1994, inaccurately entitled "Gay Survey Raises a New Question."

Two of the three major news magazines featured the sex survey on the covers of their October 17, 1994, issues. The *Time* cover simply read "Sex in America: Surprising News from the Most Important Survey since the Kinsey Report." The *U.S. News & World Report* cover was more risqué, showing a partially clad man and woman in bed; it read "Sex in America: A Massive New Survey, the Most Authoritative Ever, Reveals What We Do Behind the Bedroom Door." In contrast, *Newsweek* simply ran a two-page story with the lead "Not Frenzied, But Fulfilled. Sex: Relax. If you do it—with your mate—around twice a week, according to a major new study, you basically wrote the book of love."

Other magazines and newspapers also reported on the survey in ways geared to their readership. The November issue of *Glamour* featured the survey on its cover with the teaser "Who's doing it? And how? MAJOR U.S. SEX SURVEY." The story that followed was written by the authors of the book. While the cover of the November 15, 1994, *Advocate* read "What That Sex Survey Really Means," the story focused largely on what the survey had to say about the number of gays and lesbians in the population. The lead stated "10%: Reality or Myth? There's little authoritative information about gays and lesbians in the landmark study *Sex in America*—but what there is will cause big trouble." Finally, the *Chronicle of Higher Education*, a weekly newspaper geared to college and university personnel, in its October 17, 1994, issue headlined its story "The Sex Lives of Americans. Survey that had been target of conservative attacks produces few startling results."

Both books about the survey contain a vast amount of information and a large number of results and findings. But most of the media reported on such topics as marital fidelity, how often Americans have sex, how many sex partners people have, how often people experience orgasm, what percentages of the population are gay and lesbian, how long sex takes, and the time elapsed between a couple's first meeting and their first sexual involvement. Many of the reports also presented results for married vs. singles, men vs. women, and other analytical groupings. While most of the media coverage cited above was accurate in reporting the actual survey results, it also was selective in focusing on the more titillating parts of the survey, an unsurprising outcome given the need to satisfy their readerships.

Examining Trends with Polling Data

Researchers often use polling data to describe and analyze trends. To isolate trend data, a researcher must ensure that items relating to the topic under investigation are included in multiple surveys conducted at different points in time. Ideally, the items should be identically worded. But even when they are, serious problems of comparability can make trend analysis difficult. Identically worded items may not mean the same thing or provide the same stimulus to respondents over time because social and political changes in society have altered the meaning of the questions. For example, consider this question:

> Some say that the civil rights people have been trying to push too fast. Others feel they haven't pushed fast enough. How about you? Do you think that civil rights leaders are trying to push too fast, are going too slowly, or are they moving at about the right speed?

The responses to this item can be greatly influenced by the goals and agenda of the civil rights leadership at the time of the survey. A finding that more Americans think that the civil rights leaders are moving too fast or too slowly may reflect not a change in attitude from past views about civil rights activism but a change in the civil rights agenda itself. In this case, follow-up questions designed to measure specific components of the civil rights agenda are needed to help define the trend.

There are other difficulties in achieving comparability over time. For example, even if the wording of an item were to remain the same, its placement within the questionnaire could change, which in turn could alter the meaning of a question. Likewise, the definition of the sampling frame and the procedures used to achieve completed interviews could change. In short, comparability entails much more than simply wording questions identically. Unfortunately, consumers of poll results seldom receive the information that enables them to judge whether items are truly comparable over time.

Two studies demonstrate the advantages and disadvantages of using identical items over time. Abramson (1990) complained that the biennial National Election Studies (NES) conducted by the Survey Research Center at the University of

Michigan, Ann Arbor, were losing their longitudinal comparability as new questions were added to the surveys and old ones removed. Baumgartner and Walker (1988), in contrast, complained that the use of the same standard question over time to assess the level of group membership in the United States had systematically underestimated the extent of such activity. They argued that new measures of group membership should be employed, which, of course, would make comparisons between past and present surveys more problematic. Although both the old and the new measures can be included in a survey, this becomes very costly if the survey must cover many other topics.

Two other studies show how variations in question wording can make the assessment of attitude change over time difficult. Borrelli and colleagues (1987) found that polls measuring Americans' political party loyalties in 1980 and in 1984 varied widely in their results. They attributed the different results in these polls to three factors: whether the poll sampled voters only; whether the poll emphasized "today" or the present in inquiring about citizens' partisanship; and whether the poll was conducted close to election day, which would tend to give the advantage to the party ahead in the presidential contest. The implications of this research for assessing change in party identification over time are evident—that is, to conclude that genuine partisan change occurred in either of the two polls, other possible sources of observed differences, such as modifications in the wording of questions, must be ruled out. In a study of support for aid to the Nicaraguan contras between 1983 and 1986, Lockerbie and Borrelli (1990) argue that much of the observed change in American public opinion was not genuine. Instead, it was attributable to changes in the wording of the questions used to measure support for the contras. Again, the point is that one must be able to eliminate other potential explanations for observed change before one can conclude that observed change is genuine change.

Smith's (1993) critique of three major national studies of anti-Semitism conducted in 1964, 1981, and 1992 is an informative case study of how longitudinal comparisons may be undermined by methodological differences across surveys. The 1981 and 1992 studies were ostensibly designed to build upon the 1964 effort, thereby facilitating an analysis of trends in anti-Semitism. But, as Smith notes, longitudinal comparisons among the three studies were problematic because of differences in sample definition and interview mode, changes in question order and question wording, and insufficient information to evaluate the quality of the sample and the design execution. In examining an eleven-item anti-Semitism scale, he did find six items highly comparable over time that indicated a decline in anti-Semitic attitudes.

Despite the problems of sorting out true opinion change from change attributable to methodological factors, there are times when public opinion changes markedly and suddenly in response to a dramatic occurrence and the observed change is indeed genuine. Two examples from CBS News/ *New York Times* polls in 1991 about the Persian Gulf war illustrate dramatic and extensive attitude change. The first example concerns military action against Iraq. Just before the January 15 deadline imposed by the UN for the withdrawal of Iraq from Kuwait, a poll found that 47 percent of Americans favored beginning military action against Iraq if it did not withdraw; 46 percent were opposed. Two days after the deadline and after the beginning of the allied air campaign against Iraq, a poll found 79 percent of Americans saying the United States had done the right thing in beginning military action against Iraq. The second example focuses on people's attitudes toward a ground war in the Middle East. Before the allied ground offensive began, only 11 percent of Americans said the United States should begin fighting the ground war soon; 79 percent said bombing from the air should continue. But after the ground war began, the numbers shifted dramatically: 75 percent of Americans said the United States was right to begin the ground war, and only 19 percent said the nation should have waited longer. Clearly, the Persian Gulf crisis was a case in which American public opinion moved dramatically in the direction of supporting the president at each new stage.

Examining Subsets of Respondents

Although it is natural to want to know the results from an entire sample, often the most interesting information in a poll comes from examining the response patterns of subsets of respondents defined according to certain theoretically or substantively relevant characteristics. For example, a January 1986 CBS News/*New York Times* poll showed President Reagan enjoying unprecedented popularity for a six-year incumbent: 65 percent approved of the president's performance, and only 24 percent disapproved. But these overall figures mask some analytically interesting variations. For example, among blacks only 37 percent approved of the president's performance; 49 percent disapproved. The sexes also differed in their views of the president, with men expressing a 72 percent approval rate compared with 58 percent for women. (As expected among categories of party loyalists, 89 percent of the Republicans, 66 percent of the independents, and only 47 percent of the Democrats approved of the president's performance.) Why did blacks and whites—and men and women—differ in their views of the president?

There is no necessary reason for public opinion on an issue to be uniform across subgroups. Indeed, on many issues there are reasons to expect just the opposite. That is why a fuller understanding of American public opinion is gained by taking a closer look at the views of relevant subgroups of the sample. In doing so, however, one should note that dividing the sample into subsets increases the sampling error and lowers the reliability of the sample estimates. For example, a sample of 1,600 Americans might be queried about their attitudes on abortion. After the overall pattern is observed, the researcher might wish to break down the sample by religion—yielding 1,150 Protestant, 400 Catholic, and 50 Jewish respondents—to determine whether religious affiliation is associated with specific attitudes toward abortion. The analyst might observe that Catholics on the whole are the most opposed to abortion. To find out which Catholics are most likely to oppose abortion, she might further divide the 400 Catholics into young and old Catholics or regular church attenders and nonregular attenders, or into four categories of young Catholic churchgoers, old Catholic churchgoers, young Catholic nonattenders, and old Catholic nonattenders. The more breakdowns done at the same time, the quicker the sample size in any particular category plummets, perhaps leaving insufficient cases in some categories to make solid conclusions.

Innumerable examples can be cited to demonstrate the advantages of delving more deeply into poll data on subsets of respondents. An ABC News/*Washington Post* poll conducted in February 1986 showed major differences in the attitudes of men and women toward pornography; an examination of only the total sample would have missed these important divergences. For example, in response to the question "Do you think laws against pornography in this country are too strict, not strict enough, or just about right?" 10 percent of the men said the laws were too strict, 41 percent said not strict enough, and 47 percent said about right. Among women, only 2 percent said the laws were too strict, a sizable 72 percent said they were not strict enough, and 23 percent thought they were about right (Sussman 1986b, 37).

A CBS News/*New York Times* poll of Americans conducted in April 1986 found widespread approval of the American bombing of Libya; 77 percent of the sample approved of the action, and only 14 percent disapproved. Despite the overall approval, differences among various subgroups are noteworthy. For example, 83 percent of the men approved of the bombing compared with 71 percent of the women. Of the white respondents, 80 percent approved in contrast to only 53 percent of the blacks (Clymer 1986). Even though all of these demographically defined groups gave at least majority support to the bombing, the differences in levels of support are both statistically and substantively significant.

Polls showed dramatic differences by race in the O. J. Simpson case, with blacks more convinced of Simpson's innocence and more likely to believe that he could not get a fair trial. For example, a field poll of Californians (*U.S. News & World Report*, August 1, 1994) showed that only 35 percent of blacks believed that

Simpson could get a fair trial compared with 55 percent of whites. Also, 62 percent of whites thought Simpson was "very likely or somewhat likely" to be guilty of murder compared with only 38 percent for blacks. Comparable results were found in a national *Time*/CNN poll (*Time*, August 1, 1994): 66 percent of whites thought Simpson got a fair preliminary hearing compared with only 31 percent of black respondents, while 77 percent of the white respondents thought the case against Simpson was "very strong" or "fairly strong" compared with 45 percent for blacks. A *Newsweek* poll (August 1, 1994) revealed that 60 percent of blacks believed that Simpson was set up (20 percent attributing the setup to the police); only 23 percent of whites believed in a setup conspiracy. When asked whether Simpson had been treated better or worse than the average white murder suspect, whites said better by an overwhelming 52 to 5 percent margin, while blacks said worse by a 30 to 19 percent margin. These reactions to the Simpson case startled many Americans who could not understand how their compatriots of another race could see the situation so differently.

School busing to achieve racial integration has consistently been opposed by substantial majorities in national public opinion polls. A Harris poll commissioned by *Newsweek* in 1978 found that 85 percent of whites opposed busing (Williams 1979, 48). An ABC News/*Washington Post* poll conducted in February 1986 showed 60 percent of whites against busing (Sussman 1986a). The difference between the two polls might reflect genuine attitude change about busing in that eight-year period, or it might be a function of different question wording or different placement within the questionnaire. Whatever the reason, additional analysis of both these polls shows that whites are not monolithic in their opposition to busing. For example, the 1978 poll showed that 56 percent of white parents whose children had been bused viewed the experience as "very satisfactory." The 1986 poll revealed sharp differences in busing attitudes among younger and older whites. Among whites age thirty and under, 47 percent supported busing and 50 percent opposed it, while among whites over age thirty, 32 percent supported busing and 65 percent opposed it. Moreover, among younger whites whose families had experienced busing firsthand, 54 percent approved of busing and 46 percent opposed it. (Of course, staunch opponents of busing may have moved to escape busing, thereby guaranteeing that the remaining population would be relatively more supportive of busing.)

Another example of the usefulness of examining poll results within age categories is provided by an ABC News/*Washington Post* poll conducted in May 1985 on citizens' views of how the federal budget deficit might be cut. One item read, "Do you think the government should give people a smaller Social Security cost-of-living increase than they are now scheduled to get as a way of reducing the budget deficit, or not?" Among the overall sample, 19 percent favored granting a smaller cost-of-living increase and 78 percent opposed. To test the widespread view that young workers lack confidence in the Social Security system and doubt they will ever get out of the system what they paid in, Sussman (1985c) investigated how different age groups responded to the preceding question. Basically, he found that all age groups strongly opposed a reduction in cost-of-living increases. Unlike the busing issue, this question showed no difference among age groups— an important substantive finding, particularly in light of the expectation that there would be divergent views among the old and young. Too often people mistakenly dismiss null (no difference) results as uninteresting and unexciting; a finding of no difference can be just as substantively significant as a finding of a major difference.

An example where age does make a difference in people's opinions is the topic of physician-assisted suicide. A *Washington Post* poll conducted in 1996 asked a national sample of Americans, "Should it be legal or illegal for a doctor to help a terminally ill patient commit suicide?" (Rosenbaum 1997). The attitudes of older citizens and younger citizens were markedly different on this question—the older the age group, the greater the opposition to doctor-assisted suicide. For example, 52 percent of respondents between ages eighteen and twenty-nine thought doctor-assisted suicide should be legal; 41 percent said it should be illegal. But for citizens over age seventy, the comparable figures were 35 and 58 percent. Even more striking were some of the racial and income differences on this question. Whites thought physician involvement in suicide should be legal by a 55 to 35 percent margin; blacks opposed it 70 to 20 percent. At the lowest income levels, doctor-assisted suicide was opposed by a 54 to 37 percent margin; at the highest income level it was supported by a 58 to 30 percent margin.

In many instances the categories used for creating subgroups are already established or self-evident. For example, if one is interested in gender or racial differences, the categories of male and female or white and black are straightforward candidates for investigation. Other breakdowns require more thought. For example, what divisions might one use to examine the effects of age? Should they be young, middle-aged, and old? If so, what actual ages correspond to these categories? Is middle age thirty-five to sixty-five, forty to sixty, or what? Or should more than three categories of age be defined? In samples selected to study the effects of religion, the typical breakdown is Protestant, Catholic, and Jewish. But this simple threefold division might overlook some interesting variations; that is, some Protestants are evangelical, some are fundamentalist, and others are considered mainline denominations. Moreover, since most blacks are Protestants, comparisons of Catholics and Protestants that do not also control for race may be misleading.

Establishing categories is much more subjective and judgmental in other situations. For example, religious categories can be defined relatively easily by denominational affiliation, as mentioned earlier, but classifying respondents as evangelicals or fundamentalists is more complicated. Those who actually belong to denominations normally characterized as evangelical or fundamentalist could be so categorized. Or an investigator might identify some evangelical or fundamentalist beliefs, construct some polling questions around them, and then classify respondents according to their responses to the questions. Obviously, this would require some common core of agreement about the definition of an evangelical or fundamentalist. Wilcox (1984, 6) argues:

> Fundamentalists and evangelicals have a very similar set of religious beliefs, including the literal interpretation of the Bible, the need for a religious conversion known as being "born-again," and the need to convert sinners to the faith. The evangelicals, however, are less anti-intellectual and more involved in the secular world, while the fundamentalists criticize the evangelicals for failing to keep themselves "pure from the world."

Creating subsets by ideology is another common approach to analyzing public opinion. The most-often-used categories of ideology are liberal, moderate, and conservative, and the typical way of obtaining this information is to ask respondents a question in the following form: "Generally speaking, do you think of yourself as a liberal, moderate, or conservative?" However, one can raise many objections to this procedure, including whether people really assign common meanings to these terms. Indeed, the levels of ideological sophistication and awareness have been an ongoing topic of research in political science.

Journalist Kevin Phillips (1981) has cited the work of political scientists Stuart A. Lilie and William S. Maddox, who argue that the traditional liberal-moderate-conservative breakdown is inadequate for analytical purposes. Instead, they propose a fourfold classification of liberal, conservative, populist, and libertarian, based on two underlying dimensions: whether one supports or opposes governmental intervention in the economy and whether one supports or opposes expansion of individual behavioral liberties and sexual equality. They define liberals as those who support both governmental intervention in the economy and expansion of personal liberties, conservatives as those who oppose both, libertarians as citizens who favor expanding personal liberties but oppose governmental intervention in the economy, and populists as persons who favor governmental economic intervention but oppose the expansion of personal liberties. According to one poll, populists made up 24 percent of the electorate, conservatives 18 percent, liberals 16 percent, and libertarians 13 percent, with the rest of the electorate not readily classifiable or unfamiliar with ideological terminology.

This more elaborate breakdown of ideology may help us to better understand public opinion, but the traditional categories still dominate political discourse. Thus, when one encounters citizens who oppose government programs that affect the marketplace but support pro-choice court decisions on abortion, proposed gay rights statutes, and the Equal Rights Amendment, one feels uncomfortable calling them liberals or conservatives since they appear to be conservative on economic issues and liberal on lifestyle issues. One might feel more confident in classifying them as libertarians.

Additional examples of how an examination of subsets of respondents can provide useful insights into the public's attitudes are provided by two CBS News/*New York Times* surveys conducted in 1991, one dealing with the Persian Gulf crisis and the other with attitudes toward police. Although the rapid and successful conclusion of the ground war against Iraq resulted in widespread approval of the enterprise, before the land assault began there were differences of opinion among Americans about a ground war. For example, in the February 12–13 CBS News/*New York Times* poll, Americans were asked: "Suppose several thousand American troops would lose their lives in a ground war against Iraq. Do you think a ground war against Iraq would be worth the cost or not?" By examining the percentage saying it would be worth the cost, one finds the following results for different groups of Americans:

All respondents	45%	Independents	46%
Men	56%	Republicans	54%
Women	35%	Eighteen to twenty-nine year-olds	50%
Whites	47%	Thirty to forty-four year-olds	44%
Blacks	30%	Forty-five to sixty-four year-olds	51%
Democrats	36%	Sixty-five years and older	26%

Note that the youngest age group, the one most likely to suffer the casualties, is among the most supportive of a ground war. Note also the sizable differences between men and women, whites and blacks, and Democrats and Republicans.

Substantial racial differences in opinion also were expressed in an April 1–3, 1991, CBS News/*New York Times* poll on attitudes toward local police. Overall, 55 percent of the sample said they had substantial confidence in the local police, and 44 percent said little confidence. But among whites the comparable percentages were 59 percent and 39 percent, while for blacks only 30 percent had substantial confidence and fully 70 percent expressed little confidence in the police. Even on issues in which the direction of white and black opinion was the same, there were still substantial racial differences in the responses. For example, 69 percent of whites said that the police in their own community treat blacks and whites the same, and only 16 percent said the police were tougher on blacks than on whites. Although a plurality—45 percent—of blacks agreed that the police treat blacks and whites equally, fully 42 percent of black respondents felt that the police were tougher on blacks. Certainly if one were conducting a study to ascertain citizens' attitudes about police performance, it would be foolish not to examine the opinions of relevant subgroups.

Another example of the importance of examining subsets of respondents is provided by a January 1985 ABC News/*Washington Post* poll that queried Americans about their attitudes on a variety of issues and presented results not only for the entire sample but also for subsets of respondents defined by their attentiveness to public affairs (Sussman 1985b). Attentiveness to public affairs was measured by whether the respondents were aware of four news events: the subway shooting in New York City of four alleged assailants by their intended victim; the switch in jobs by two key Reagan administration officials, Donald Regan and James Baker; the Treasury Department's proposal to simplify the tax system; and protests against South African apartheid held in the United States. Respondents then were divided into four levels of awareness, with 27 percent in the highest category, 26 percent in the next highest, 25 percent in the next category, and 22 percent falling in the lowest. The next step in the analysis was to compare the policy preferences of the highest and lowest awareness subsets.

There were some marked differences between these two groups. For example, on the issue of support for the president's military buildup, 59 percent of the lowest awareness respondents opposed any major cuts in military spending to lessen the budget deficit. In contrast, 57 percent of the highest awareness group said that military spending should be limited to help with the budget deficit. On the issue of tax rates, a majority of both groups agreed with the president that taxes were too high, but there was a difference in the size of the majority. Among the lowest awareness respondents, 72 percent said taxes were too high and 24 percent said they were not, while among the highest awareness respondents, 52 percent said taxes were too high and 45 percent said they were not (Sussman 1985b).

Opinions about the future of Social Security and Medicare also are affected by citizens' knowledge about the two programs (Pianin and Brossard 1997). In one poll, the more people knew about Social Security and Medicare, the more likely they were to believe that these programs were in crisis and that major governmental action was needed. For example, among highly knowledgeable respondents, 88 percent believed that Social Security either was in crisis or had major problems; only 70 percent of respondents with little knowledge agreed. Likewise, 89 percent of the highly knowledgeable respondents believed Social Security would go bankrupt if Congress did nothing compared to only 61 percent for the less-informed respondents.

All these findings raise some interesting normative issues about public opinion polls. . . . [T]he methodology of public opinion polls is very democratic. All citizens have a nearly equal chance to be selected in a sample and have their views counted; all respondents are weighted equally (or nearly so) in the typical data analysis. Yet except at the polls all citizens do not have equal influence in shaping public policy. The distribution of political resources, whether financial or informational, is not uniform across the population. Polls themselves become a means to influence public policy, as various decision makers cite poll results to legitimize their policies. But should the views of all poll respondents be counted equally? An elitist critic would argue that the most informed segments of the population should be given the greatest weight. Therefore, in the preceding example of defense spending, more attention should be given to the views of the highest awareness subset (assuming the validity of the levels of awareness), which was more supportive of reducing military spending. An egalitarian argument would assert that all respondents should be counted equally. . . .

Interpreting Poll Results

An August 1986 Gallup poll on education showed that 67 percent of Americans would allow their children to attend class with a child suffering from AIDS, while 24 percent would not. What reaction might there be to this finding? Some people might be shocked and depressed to discover that almost one-fourth of Americans could be so mean-spirited toward AIDS victims when the scientific evidence shows that AIDS is not a disease transmitted by casual contact. Others might be reassured and relieved that two-thirds of Americans are sufficiently enlightened or tolerant to allow their children to attend school with children who have AIDS. Some people might feel dismay: How could 67 percent of Americans foolishly allow their children to go to school with a child who has AIDS when there is no absolute guarantee that AIDS cannot be transmitted casually?

Consider this example from a 1983 poll by the National Opinion Research Center (NORC): "If your party nominated a black for President, would you vote for him if he were qualified for the job?" Eighty-five percent of the white respondents said yes. How might this response be interpreted? One might feel positive about how much racial attitudes have changed in the United States. A different perspective would decry the fact that in this supposedly tolerant and enlightened era, 15 percent of white survey respondents could not bring themselves to say they would vote for a qualified black candidate.

In neither example can we assign a single correct meaning to the data. Instead, the interpretation one chooses will be a function of individual values and beliefs, and purposes in analyzing the survey. This is demonstrated in an analysis of two national surveys on gun control, one sponsored by the National Rifle Association (NRA) and conducted by Decision/Making/Information, Inc., and the other sponsored by the Center for the Study and Prevention of Handgun Violence and conducted by Cambridge Reports, Inc. (pollster Patrick Caddell's firm). Although the statistical results from both surveys were comparable, the two reports arrived at substantially different conclusions. The NRA's analysis concluded:

Majorities of American voters believe that we do *not* need more laws governing the possession and use of firearms and that more firearms laws would *not* result in a decrease in the crime rate. (Wright 1981, 25)

In contrast, the center's report stated:

It is clear that the vast majority of the public (both those who live with handguns and those who do not) want handgun licensing and registration. . . . The American public wants some form of handgun control legislation. (Wright 1981, 25)

Wright carefully analyzed the evidence cited in support of each conclusion and found that

the major difference between the two reports is not in the findings, but in what is said about or concluded about the findings: what aspects of the evidence are emphasized or de-emphasized, what interpretation is given to a finding, and what implications are drawn from the findings about the need, or lack thereof, for stricter weapons controls. (Wright 1981, 38)

In essence, it was the interpretation of the data that generated the difference in the recommendations.

Two polls on tax reform provide another example of how poll data can be selectively interpreted and reported (Sussman 1985a). The first poll, sponsored by the insurance industry, was conducted by pollster Burns Roper. Its main conclusion, reported in a press conference announcing the poll results, was that 77 percent of the American public "said that workers should not be taxed on employee benefits" and that only 15 percent supported such a tax, a conclusion very reassuring to the insurance industry. However, Roper included other items in the poll that the insurance industry chose not to emphasize. As Sussman points out, the 77 percent opposed to the taxing of fringe benefits were then asked, "Would you still oppose counting the value of employee benefits as taxable income for employees if the additional tax revenues went directly to the reduction of federal budget deficits and not into new spending?" Twenty-six percent were no longer opposed to taxing fringe benefits under this condition, bringing the overall opposition down to 51 percent of the sample.

A second follow-up question asked, "Would you still oppose counting the value of employee benefits as taxable income for employees if the additional tax revenues permitted an overall reduction of tax rates for individuals?" (a feature that was part of the Treasury Department's initial tax proposals). Now only 33 percent of the sample was opposed to taxing fringes, 50 percent supported it, and 17 percent were undecided. Thus, depending upon which results one used, one could show a majority of citizens supportive of or opposed to taxing fringe benefits.

The other poll that Sussman analyzed also tapped people's reactions to the Treasury Department's tax proposal. A number of questions in the survey demonstrated public hostility to the Treasury proposal. One item read:

> The Treasury Department has proposed changing the tax system. Three tax brackets would be created, but most current deductions from income would be eliminated. Non-federal income taxes and property taxes would not be deductible, and many deductions would be limited. Do you favor or oppose this proposal? (Sussman 1985a)

Not surprisingly, 57 percent opposed the Treasury plan, and only 27 percent supported it. But as Sussman points out, the question is highly selective and leading since it focuses on changes in the tax system that hurt the taxpayer. For example, nowhere does it inform the respondent that a key part of the Treasury plan was to reduce existing tax rates so that 80 percent of Americans would be paying either the same amount or less in taxes than they were paying before. Clearly, this survey was designed to obtain a set of results compatible with the sponsor's policy objectives.

Morin (1995) describes a situation in which polling data were misinterpreted and misreported in the *Washington Post* because of faulty communication between a *Post* reporter and a local polling firm that was conducting an omnibus survey in the Washington, D.C., area. Interested in how worried federal employees were about their jobs given the budgetary battles between the Clinton White House and the Republican Congress in 1995, the reporter commissioned the polling firm to include the following questions in its survey: "Do you think your agency or company will probably be affected by federal budget cutbacks? Do you think your own job will be affected?" The poll discovered that 40 percent of the federal workers interviewed believed their own jobs might be affected. Unfortunately, when the polling outfit prepared a report for its client, the reporter, the report concluded that these federal workers felt their jobs were jeopardized. And then the reporter's story stated, "Four out of every 10 federal employees fear losing their jobs because of budget reductions." As Morin points out, this conclusion does not follow from the polling questions asked. The belief that one's job will likely be affected is not equivalent to the fear of losing one's job. Instead, the effects might be lower salary increases, decreased job mobility, increased job responsibilities, and the like. A correction quickly appeared in the *Post* clarifying what the polling data actually had said. One lesson of this example is the responsibility that pollsters have to clients to communicate carefully and accurately what poll results mean. Another lesson is that one should not try to read too much into the responses to any single survey item. In this case, if the reporter wanted to know exactly how federal workers thought their jobs would be affected, a specific question eliciting this information should have been included in the survey.

Weighting the Sample

Samples are selected to be representative of the population from which they are drawn. Sometimes adjustments must be made to a sample before analyzing and reporting results. These adjustments may be made for substantive reasons or because of biases in the characteristics of the selected sample. An example of adjustments made for substantive reasons is pollsters' attempts to determine who the likely voters will be and to base their election predictions not on the entire sample but on a subset of likely voters.

To correct for biases, weights can be used so that the sample's demographic characteristics more accurately reflect the population's overall properties. Because sampling and interviewing involve statistics and probability theory as well as logistical problems of contacting respondents, the sample may contain too few blacks, or too few men, or too few people in the youngest age category. Assuming that one knows the true population proportions for sex, race, and age, one can adjust the sample by the use of weights to bring its numbers into line with the overall population values. For example, if females constitute 60 percent of the sample but 50 percent of the overall population, one might weight each female respondent by five-sixths, thereby reducing the percentage of females in the sample to 50 percent (five-sixths times 60 percent).

A 1986 *Columbus Dispatch* preelection poll on the gubernatorial preferences of Ohioans illustrates the consequences of weighting. In August 1986 the *Dispatch* sent a mail questionnaire to a sample of Ohioans selected from the statewide list of registered voters. The poll showed that incumbent Democratic governor Richard Celeste was leading former GOP governor James Rhodes, 48 percent to 43 percent, with Independent candidate and former Democratic mayor of Cleveland Dennis Kucinich receiving 9 percent; an undecided alternative was not provided to respondents (Curtin 1986a). Fortunately, the *Dispatch* report of its poll included the sample size for each category (unlike the practice of the national media). One table presented to the reader showed the following relationship between political party affiliation and gubernatorial vote preference (Curtin 1986b):

Gubernatorial preference	Democrat	Republican	Independent
Celeste	82%	14%	33%
Rhodes	9	81	50
Kucinich	9	5	17
Total %	100	100	100
(N)	(253)	(245)	(138)

Given the thrust of the news story that Celeste was ahead, 48 to 43 percent, the numbers in the table were surprising because Rhodes was running almost as well among Republicans as Celeste was among Democrats, and Rhodes had a substantial lead among Independents. Because the N's were provided, one could calculate the actual number of Celeste, Rhodes, and Kucinich votes in the sample as follows:

Celeste votes $= .82(253) + .14(245) + .33(138) = 287$

Rhodes votes $= .09(253) + .81(245) + .50(138) = 291$

Kucinich votes $= .09(253) + .05(245) + .17(138) = 58$

The percentages calculated from these totals show Rhodes slightly *ahead*, 46 to 45 percent, rather than trailing. At first I thought there was a mistake in the poll or in the party affiliation and gubernatorial vote preference. In rereading the news story, however, I learned that the sample had been weighted. The reporter wrote, "Results were adjusted, or weighted, slightly to compensate for demographic differences between poll respondents and the Ohio electorate as a whole" (Curtin 1986b). The reporter did inform the reader that the data were weighted, but nowhere did he say that the adjustment affected who was ahead in the poll.

The adjustment probably was statistically valid since the poll respondents did not seem to include sufficient numbers of women and blacks, two groups that were more supportive of the Democratic gubernatorial candidate. However, nowhere in the news story was any specific information provided on how the weighting was done. This example illustrates that weighting can be consequential, and it is probably typical in terms of the scant information provided to citizens about weighting procedures.

When Polls Conflict: A Concluding Example

A variety of factors can influence poll results and their subsequent interpretation. Useful vehicles for a review of these factors are the polls that led up to the 1980, 1984, 1988, 1992, and 1996 presidential elections—polls that were often highly inconsistent. For example, in the 1984 election, polls conducted at comparable times yielded highly dissimilar results. A Harris poll had Reagan leading Mondale by 9 percentage points, an ABC News / *Washington Post* poll had Reagan ahead by 12 points, a CBS News / *New York Times* survey had Reagan leading by 13 points, a *Los Angeles Times* poll gave Reagan a 17-point lead, and an NBC News poll had the president ahead by 25 points (Oreskes 1984). In September 1988 seven different polls on presidential preference were released within a three-day period with results ranging from Bush ahead by 8 points to a Dukakis lead of 6 points (Morin 1988). In 1992 ten national polls conducted in the latter part of August showed

Clinton with leads over Bush ranging from 5 to 19 percentage points (Elving 1992). And in 1996, the final preelection polls showed Clinton leading Dole by margins ranging from 7 to 18 percentage points. How can polls on an ostensibly straightforward topic such as presidential vote preference differ so widely? Many reasons can be cited, some obvious and others more subtle in their effects.

Among the more subtle reasons are the method of interviewing and the number of callbacks that a pollster uses to contact respondents who initially were unavailable. According to Lewis and Schneider (1982, 43), Patrick Caddell and George Gallup in their 1980 polls found that President Reagan received less support from respondents interviewed personally than from those queried over the telephone. Their speculation about this finding was that weak Democrats who were going to desert Carter found it easier to admit this in a telephone interview than in a face-to-face situation.

With respect to callbacks, Dolnick (1984) reports that one reason a Harris poll was closer than others in predicting Reagan's sizable victory in 1980 was that it made repeated callbacks, which at each stage "turned up increasing numbers of well-paid, well-educated Republican-leaning voters." A similar situation occurred in 1984. Traugott (1987) found that persistence in callbacks resulted in a more Republican sample, speculating that Republicans were less likely to have been at home or available initially.

Some of the more obvious factors that help account for differences among compared polls are question wording and question placement. Some survey items mention the presidential and vice-presidential candidates, while others mention only the presidential challengers. Some pollsters ask follow-up questions of undecided voters to ascertain whether they lean toward one candidate or another; others do not. Question order can influence responses. Normally, incumbents and better known candidates do better when the question on vote intention is asked at the beginning of the survey rather than later. If vote intention is measured after a series of issue and problem questions have been asked, respondents may have been reminded of shortcomings in the incumbent's record and may therefore be less willing to express support for the incumbent.

Comparable polls also can differ in how the sample is selected and how it is treated for analytical purposes. Some polls sample registered voters; others query adult Americans. There are differences as well in the methods used to identify likely voters. As Lipset (1980) points out, the greater the number of respondents who are screened out of the sample because they do not seem to be likely voters, the more probable it is that the remaining respondents will be relatively more Republican in their vote preferences. Some samples are weighted to guarantee demographic representativeness; others are not.

It is also possible that discrepancies among polls are not due to any of the above factors, but may simply reflect statistical fluctuations. For example, if one poll with a 4 percent sampling error shows Clinton ahead of Dole, 52 to 43 percent, this result is statistically congruent with other polls that might have a very narrow Clinton lead of 48 to 47 percent or other polls that show a landslide Clinton lead of 56 to 39 percent.

Voss et al. (1995) summarized and compared many of the methodological differences among polls conducted by eight polling organizations for the 1988 and 1992 presidential elections. Even though all eight organizations were studying the same phenomenon, there were enough differences in their approaches that polls conducted at the same time using identical questions might still get somewhat different results for reasons beyond sampling error. One feature Voss et al. examined was the sampling method—how each organization generated a list of telephone numbers from which to sample. Once the sample was selected, polling organizations conducting telephone interviews still had to make choices about how to handle "busy signals, refusals, and calls answered by electronic devices, how to decide which household members are eligible to be interviewed, and how to select the respondent from among those eligible" (Voss et al. 1995). The investigators also examined the various weighting schemes used by each survey operation to ensure a representative sample. Much of this methodological information is not readily available to the consumer of public opinion polls, and if it were many consumers would be overwhelmed by the volume of methodological detail. Yet these factors can make a difference. For example, the eight polling organizations analyzed by Voss et al. treated refusals quite differently. Some of the outfits did not call back after receiving a refusal from a potential respondent; other organizations did make callbacks. One organization generally tried to call back but with a different interviewer, but then gave up if a second refusal was obtained.

Just as different methodological features can affect election polls, they also can influence other surveys. One prominent example dealt with the widely divergent estimates of rape obtained from two different national surveys. Much of this discrepancy stemmed from the methodological differences between the two surveys (Lynch 1996). Because the poll consumer is unaware of many of the design features of a survey, he or she must assume the survey design was appropriate for the topic at hand. Then the consumer can ask whether the information collected by the survey was analyzed and interpreted correctly.

REFERENCES

Abramson, Paul R., Brian Silver, and Barbara Anderson. 1990. "The Decline of Overtime Comparability in the National Election Studies." *Public Opinion Quarterly* 54 (summer): 177–190.

Alpern, David M. 1986. "A *Newsweek* Poll: Sex Laws." *Newsweek*, 14 July, 38.

Baumgartner, Frank R., and Jack L. Walker. 1988. "Survey Research and Membership in Voluntary Associations." *American Journal of Political Science* 32 (November): 908–928.

Borrelli, Stephen, Brad Lockerbie, and Richard G. Niemi. 1987. "Why the Democrat-Republican Partisan Gap Varies from Poll to Poll." *Public Opinion Quarterly* 51 (spring): 115–119.

Clymer, Adam. 1986. "A Poll Finds 77% in U.S. Approve Raid on Libya." *New York Times*, 17 April, A-23.

Curtin, Michael. 1986a. "Celeste Leading Rhodes 48% to 43%, with Kucinich Trailing." *Columbus Dispatch*, 10 August, 1-A.

———. 1986b. "Here Is How Poll Was Taken." *Columbus Dispatch*, 10 August, 8-E.

Dolnick, Edward. 1984. "Pollsters Are Asking: What's Wrong." *Columbus Dispatch*, 19 August, C-1.

Elving, Ronald D. 1992. "Polls Confound and Confuse in This Topsy-Turvy Year." *Congressional Quarterly Weekly Report*, 12 September, 2725–2727.

Laumann, Edward O., et al. 1994. *The Social Organization of Sexuality.* Chicago: University of Chicago Press.

Lewis, I. A., and William Schneider. 1982. "Is the Public Lying to the Pollsters?" *Public Opinion* 5 (April/May): 42–47.

Lipset, Seymour Martin. 1980. "Different Polls, Different Results in 1980 Politics." *Public Opinion* 3 (August/September): 19–20, 60.

Lockerbie, Brad, and Stephen A. Borrelli. 1990. "Question Wording and Public Support for Contra Aid, 1983–1986." *Public Opinion Quarterly* 54 (summer): 195–208.

Lynch, James P. 1996. "Clarifying Divergent Estimates of Rape from Two National Surveys." *Public Opinion Quarterly* 60 (winter): 558–619.

Michael, Robert T., John H. Gagnon, Edward O. Laumann, and Gina Kolata. 1994. *Sex in America: A Definitive Survey.* Boston: Little, Brown.

Morin, Richard. 1988. "Behind the Numbers: Confessions of a Pollster." *Washington Post*, 16 October, C-1, C-4.

———. 1991. "2 Ways of Reading the Public's Lips on Gulf Policy." *Washington Post*, 14 January, A-9.

———. 1994. "Don't Know Much About Health Care Reform." *Washington Post* National Weekly Edition, 14–20 March, 37.

———. 1995. "Reading between the Numbers." *Washington Post* National Weekly Edition, 4–10 September, 30.

Morin, Richard, and John M. Berry. 1996. "Economic Anxieties." *Washington Post* National Weekly Edition, 4–10 November, 6–7.

Oreskes, Michael. 1984. "Pollsters Offer Reasons for Disparity in Results." *New York Times*, 20 October, A-8.

Phillips, Kevin P. 1981. "Polls Are Too Broad in Analysis Divisions." *Columbus Dispatch*, 8 September, B-3.

Pianin, Eric, and Mario Brossard. 1997. "Hands Off Social Security and Medicare." *Washington Post* National Weekly Edition, 7 April, 35.

Rosenbaum, David E. 1997. "Americans Want a Right to Die. Or So They Think." *New York Times*, 8 June, E3.

Schneider, William. 1996. How to Read a Trial Heat Poll." Transcript, CNN "Inside Politics Extra," 12 May (see AllPolitics Web site).

Smith, Tom W. 1993. "Actual Trends or Measurement Artifacts? A Review of Three Studies of Anti-Semitism." *Public Opinion Quarterly* 57 (fall): 380–393.

Sussman, Barry. 1985a. "To Understand These Polls, You Have to Read the Fine Print." *Washington Post* National Weekly Edition, 4 March, 37.

———. 1985b. "Reagan's Support on Issues Relies Heavily on the Uninformed." *Washington Post* National Weekly Edition, 1 April, 37.

———. 1985c. "Social Security and the Young." *Washington Post* National Weekly Edition, 27 May, 37.

———. 1986a. "It's Wrong to Assume that School Busing Is Wildly Unpopular." *Washington Post* National Weekly Edition, 10 March, 37.

———. 1986b. "With Pornography, It All Depends on Who's Doing the Looking." *Washington Post* National Weekly Edition, 24 March, 37.

Traugott, Michael W. 1987. "The Importance of Persistence in Respondent Selection for Pre-election Surveys." *Public Opinion Quarterly* 51 (spring): 48–57.

Voss, D. Stephen, Andrew Gelman, and Gary King. 1995. "Preelection Survey Methodology: Details from Eight Polling Organizations, 1988 and 1992." *Public Opinion Quarterly* 59 (spring): 98–132.

Wilcox, William Clyde. 1984. "The New Christian Right and the White Fundamentalists: An Analysis of a Potential Political Movement." Ph.D. diss., Ohio State University.

Williams, Dennis A. 1979. "A New Racial Poll." *Newsweek*, 26 February, 48, 53.

Wright, James D. 1981. "Public Opinion and Gun Control: A Comparison of Results from Two Recent National Surveys." *Annals of the American Academy of Political and Social Science* 455 (May): 24–39.

10-2

Dynamic Representation

James A. Stimson, Michael B. MacKuen, and Robert S. Erikson

The relationship between public opinion and government action is complex. In the United States, with single-member congressional districts, we often consider relationship at the "micro" level—that is, whether individual elected officials are following the wishes of their home constituencies. But the overall relationship between public preferences and government behavior, the "macro" level, is more difficult to assess. In the following essay, James Stimson, Michael MacKuen, and Robert Erikson provide a look at this relationship with the help of a creative invention. These scholars use a statistical technique to build an aggregate measure of public opinion from dozens of polls. The technique allows them to measure change in the liberalism of views expressed in the polls over several decades. Then, using similarly aggregated measures of the behavior of Congress, the president, and the Supreme Court, they evaluate the relationship between the liberalism of public opinion and the behavior of the institutions. Government as a whole proves responsive to public opinion, and Congress and the presidency prove more responsive to public opinion than the Supreme Court.

... WHAT DOES IT mean that a government represents public feelings? Responsiveness must be a central part of any satisfactory answer. Representative governments respond to—meaning act as a consequence of—changes in public sentiment. To "act as a consequence of" changes in public sentiment implies a sequence, inherently structured in time. We may say that if, by knowing about earlier changes in public sentiment, we can improve the prediction of public policy over what we could have done from knowing only the history of public policy itself, then opinion causes policy, and this is dynamic representation. ...

The *dynamic* character of representation has a second aspect. Most political decisions are about change or the prevention of change. Governments decide to change health care systems, to reduce environmental regulations, to develop new weapons systems, or to increase subsidies for long staple cotton growers. Or not. Thus, political decisions have a directional force to them, and their incremental

Source: James A. Stimson, Michael B. MacKuen, and Robert S. Erikson, "Dynamic Representation," *American Political Science Review* 89 (September 1995): 543–564. Notes appearing in the original have been deleted.

character is inherently dynamic. Further, most public opinion judgments concern change as well. The public expresses preferences for "more" or "less" governmental action across different spheres: "faster school integration," "cuts in welfare spending," "getting tougher on crime," and so on. The main difference is that public sentiment is generally more vague, diffuse, than the more concrete government action.

This understanding suggests something akin to the familiar "thermostat" analogy. The public makes judgments about current public policy—most easily that government's actions need to be enhanced or trimmed back. These judgments will change as policy changes, as real-world conditions change, or as "politically colored" perceptions of policy and conditions change. And as the simple model indicates, politicians and government officials sense these changes in public judgment and act accordingly. Thus, when public policy drifts away from the public's demands for policy, the representation system acts as a control mechanism to keep policy on course.

The question now is how. If public opinion governs, how does it find its way into the aggregation of acts that come to be called public policy.

The Mechanisms of Dynamic Representation

Start with a politician facing a policy choice. With both preferences over policy options and a continuing need to protect the electoral career from unwanted termination, the elected official will typically need to balance personal preference against electoral expediency. We presume that politicians have personal preferences for and against particular policies and also that they value reelection. Then for each choice, we can define (1) a personal ideal point in the space of policy options and (2) an *expediency point* (that position most likely to optimize future reelection changes). The expediency point might be the median voter of the relevant constituency or some similar construct. We are not concerned here about particular rules. All that matters is that the politician have a *perception* of the most expedient position.

. . . Politicians create an appropriate margin of safety: those who highly value policy formulation or who feel safe at home choose policy over security; those who face competitive challenge in the next election lean toward "expediency" and security. . . .

. . . [E]lectoral turnover stems from events that overwhelm the margin of safety that the politicians select. Campaign finance, personal scandals, challenger tactics, the framing of electoral choice—all affect outcomes. The victims come both from those who take electoral risk by pursuing policy and also from those who ignore personal preference and concentrate solely on reelection: what matters is the force of electoral events relative to the politician's expectations. . . .

To breathe life into this system, let us put it into motion to see its aggregate and dynamic implications. Assume that public opinion—global attitudes toward the role of government in society—moves over time. Immediately we can expect greater turnover as the force of public opinion augments the normal electoral shocks to upset incumbent politicians' standard calculus. Now, the changes in personnel will prove systematic: rightward shifts in public opinion will replace Democrats with Republicans, and leftward shifts Republicans with Democrats. . . .

Rational Anticipation, Turnover, and Policy Consequence

Turnover from elections works most transparently with politicians who are neither well informed (until hit on the head by the club of election results) nor strategic. But that does not look at all like the politicians we observe. The oft-painted picture of members of Congress, for example, as people who read five or six daily newspapers, work 18-hour days, and leave no stone unturned in anticipating the electoral problems that might arise from policy choices does not suggest either limited information or naïveté.

We explicitly postulate the reverse of the dumb and naïve politician: (1) elected politicians are rational actors; (2) they are well informed about movements in public opinion; and (3) they agree with one another about the nature of those movements. This was well said by John Kingdon: "People in and around government sense a national mood. They are comfortable discussing its content, and believe they know when the mood shifts. The idea goes by different names. . . . But common to all . . . is the notion that a rather large number of people out in the country are thinking along certain common lines, that this national mood changes from one time to another in discernible ways, and that these changes in mood or climate have important impacts on policy agendas and policy outcomes" (1984, 153). . . .

Elected politicians, we believe, sense the mood of the moment, assess its trend, and anticipate its consequence for future elections. Changes in opinion, correctly perceived, will lead politicians to revise their beliefs about future election opportunities and hazards. Revised beliefs imply also revised expedient positions. Such strategic adjustment will have two effects: (1) it will dampen turnover, the conventional path of electoral influence; and (2) it will drive policy through rational anticipation.

When politicians perceive public opinion change, they adapt their behavior to please their constituency and, accordingly, enhance their chances of reelection. Public opinion will still work through elections, however. When they are surprised by the suddenness or the magnitude of opinion change or when they are unable credibly to alter their policies, politicians, despite their best efforts, will occasionally face defeat at the polls. Rather more fitfully than was the case with dumb politicians, public preferences will operate on electoral institutions by changing the personnel and thus the aggregated preferences of elected officials.

But that is not the only public opinion effect. Changing policy from shifting perceptions of what is electorally expedient we will refer to as *rational anticipation*. In a world of savvy politicians, rational anticipation produces dynamic representation without need for actual electoral defeats.

Politicians modify their behavior at the margin. Liberals and conservatives do not change their stripes, but they do engage in strategic behavior either to minimize risk from movements adverse to their positions or to maximize electoral payoff from movements supportive of their positions. For example, in a conservative era, such as the early 1980s, conservative Democrats found it easier to break with their party and did it more often, while liberal Republicans found it more difficult and dangerous and did it less often. The result of such conditions can be substantial shifts in winning and losing coalitions without any change of personnel.

Moreover, such direct anticipation of the electoral future does not exhaust the possibilities. For other actors also anticipate the effects of future elections on the current behavior of elected officials. Those who advance policy proposals— bureaucrats, lobbyists, judges, and citizens—are concerned with what can be done successfully, be it administrative act, judicial decision, or legislative proposal. And other politicians—those who pursue a leadership role or advocate particular policies—may choose to push ahead of the curve, to multiply the effects of even marginal shifts in opinion by anticipating others' anticipated reactions.

The impact of rational anticipation is thus a net shift in policy outputs from the aggregation of all these smallish strategic decisions, which (responding to the same signal) tend to move all in the same direction. It should be observable as the direct response of policy to opinion change, when election turnover effects are controlled.

A Design for Assessing Representation

This two-part setup permits three possible empirical outcomes: (1) two-stage representation may occur through the mechanism of electoral turnover, where candidate success depends upon the public opinion of the moment, which is then reflected in policy behavior; (2) movements in policy acts may reflect opinion without changes in elite personnel, the rational anticipation scheme; and (3) no representation might occur if both schemes fail. The alternatives are laid out

Figure 1. The Pathways to Dynamic Representation

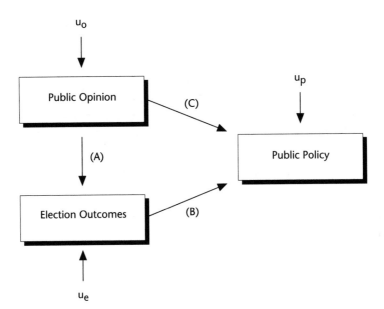

in Figure 1. There we can see three testable linkages. The first, A, is the first stage of the electoral sequence. The question to be answered is, Does public opinion affect election outcomes? The second stage, B, is not much in doubt. Its question is no cliff-hanger: Is there a difference in policy behavior between liberals and conservatives? The third linkage, C, is rational anticipation. Its question is, Does public policy move with public opinion independently of the effects of (past) elections? . . .

. . . The scheme of Figure 1 takes account of reality by positing other sets of causes of all phenomena as disturbances. The first, u_o, is the exogenous factors that account for changes in opinion. Not a focus of attention here (but see Durr 1993), they are such plausible forces as national optimism or pessimism arising from economic performance and reactions to past policies as experienced in daily life.

Elections are influenced by factors such as incumbent party performance, incumbency, macropartisanship, and so forth. Those factors appear as u_e on Figure 1. And finally, u_p captures sets of causes of public policy other than representation—such things as the events and problems to which policy is response or solution. Some of these "disturbances" are amenable to modeling, and will be. Some are irreducible, and must remain unobserved. . . .

Measurement

The raw materials of dynamic representation are familiar stuff: public opinion, elections, and public policy together form the focus of a major proportion of our scholarly activity. But familiar as these concepts are, longitudinal measures of them are (excepting elections) ad hoc at best and more often nonexistent. It is easy to think of movements of public opinion over time and public policy over time. It is not easy to quantify them. The situation—familiar concepts but novel measures—requires more than the usual cursory attention to measurement concerns. We begin with public opinion.

The Measures: Public Opinion and Elections

To tap public opinion over time we have the measure domestic policy mood (Stimson 1991). Mood is the major dimension underlying expressed preferences over policy alternatives in the survey research record. It is properly interpreted as left versus right—more specifically, as global preferences for a larger, more active federal government as opposed to a smaller, more passive one across the sphere of all domestic policy controversies. Thus our public opinion measure represents the public's sense of whether the political "temperature" is too hot or too cold, whether government is too active or not active enough. The policy status quo is the baseline, either explicit or implicit, in most survey questions. What the questions (and the mood measure) tap then is relative preference—the preferred direction of policy change.

Displayed in Figure 2, the *policy mood* series portrays an American public opinion that moves slowly back and forth from left (up on the scale) to right (down) over time and is roughly in accord with popular depictions of the eras of modern American politics. It reaches a liberal high point in the early 1960s, meanders mainly in the liberal end of its range through the middle 1970s, moves quite dramatically toward conservatism approaching 1980, and then begins a gradual return to liberalism over the 1980s. Note as well that the neutral point (50% liberal, 50% conservative) means something: points above 50 mean that the public wants more conservative policy. Thus, while the public's conservatism peaked in 1980, the public continued to demand more conservative policy (though by smaller margins) until 1984. (Thus we may think of our mood measure as a signal to politicians about the intensity and the direction of political pressure. It represents a demand for change.) . . .

The Measures: Policy Change

What is policy liberalism, and how can we measure it? What we observe is decisions such as congressional votes—not quite "policy." Our view is that each

Figure 2. Public Opinion over Time: Domestic Policy Mood, 1956–1993

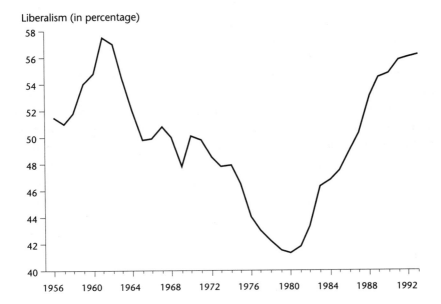

involves policy *change* at the margin. The issue as it is typically confronted is, Should we move current government policy in more liberal (expansive) directions or in more conservative ones? What we observe is who votes how. We see, for example, a particular vote in which the liberal forces triumph over conservative opponents. We take such a vote to mean that in fact the (unobserved) content of the vote moves policy in a liberal direction—or resists movement in the conservative direction.

This is a direct analogy to public opinion as we measure it. We ask the public whether government should "do more" or "spend more" toward some particular purpose. We take the response, "do more," "do less," "do about the same" to indicate the preferred direction of policy *change*. In both cases direction of change from the status quo is the issue.

Measuring this net liberalism or conservatism of global policy output seems easy enough in concept. We talk about some Congresses being more or less liberal than others as if we knew what that meant. But if we ask how we know, where those intuitions come from, the answer is likely to be nonspecific. The intuitions probably arise from fuzzy processing of multiple indicators of, for example, congressional action. And if none of them by itself is probably "the" defensible measure, our intuitions are probably correct in netting out the sum of many of them, all moving in the same direction. That, at least, is our strategy here. We will exploit several indicators of annual congressional policy output, each by itself dubious. But when they run in tandem with one another, the set will seem much more secure than its members.

Congressional Rating Scales. Rating scales are a starting point. Intended to tap the policy behaviors of individual House members and Senators, scales produced by groups such as Americans for Democratic Action (ADA) and Americans for Constitutional Action (ACA), later American Conservative Union (ACU), are now available for most of the period in question. Neither of these is intended to be a longitudinal measure of congressional action; and from a priori consideration of the properties such a measure would want, this is not how we would derive one. But if scales move similarly across chambers and scales from different organizations move in common over time, then we begin to believe that whatever it is they are measuring is probably global liberalism or conservatism of roll-call voting. Thus, as a measure of *net group rating*, we take the yearly average of the House's (or Senate's) ADA score and (100 minus) the ACA/ACU score.

Congressional Roll-Call Outcomes. The strength of the rating scales is their cross-sectional validity: they discriminate liberals from moderates from conservatives in any given year. Their weakness is longitudinal validity: we are less confident that they discriminate liberal from moderate from conservative Congresses. For greater face validity, we turn to the roll calls themselves as measures of policymaking. A quite direct measure is the answer to the questions, On ideological votes, who wins? and By how much do they win? Provided that we can isolate a set of roll calls that polarize votes along the left-versus-right main dimension of American domestic politics, measuring the degree of, say, liberalism is as easy as counting the votes. If we know which position on the vote is liberal and which conservative, then all that remains is to observe who won and by how much (and then aggregate that roll-call information to the session).

We exploit the cross-sectional strength of the rating scales (specifically, ADA) to classify roll calls. For each of the 25,492 roll-call votes in both houses for 1956–90, we classify the vote as left-right polarized or not (and then in which direction). The criterion for the classification as polarized is that the vote must show a greater association with member ADA scores than a hypothetical party-line vote for the particular members of each Congress. The intuition of this criterion is that we know we are observing a left-right cleavage when defection from party lines is itself along left–right lines—conservative Democrats voting with Republicans, liberal Republicans voting with Democrats. Although the party vote itself might be ideological, we cannot know that it is. One measure of the net liberalism of the session (for each house separately) is then simply the median size of the liberal coalition (on votes where the liberal and conservative sides are defined). A second approach to the same raw data is to focus on winning and losing, rather than coalition size. In this set of measures we simply count the percentage of liberal wins. We are observing quite directly then who wins, who loses, and by how much.

The Dramatic Acts of Congress: Key Votes. Scales of roll-call votes tell us about the overall tenor of public policy. Probably an excellent basis for inference about the net direction of policy movement, they do not distinguish between minor matters and those of enormous public consequence and visibility. Getting a good measure of "importance" presents a formidable challenge, requiring great numbers of subtle judgments about content and context. It is nonetheless desirable to have some indication of whether legislative activity produces something of import. A particular subset of legislation, the *Congressional Quarterly* "key votes" for each session of Congress, does attempt to distinguish the crucial from the trivial. The virtues of this set of votes are that it reflects the wisdom of expert observers of Congress at the time about what was important, and the measures are readily coded into liberal or conservative actions (and some that are neither).

We quantify the key votes as a combination of who wins and by how much. Accordingly, we average (1) the percentage of liberal wins and (2) the size of the liberal winning coalition. Crude, the measures nonetheless tap the issue in question, the direction of highly visible outcomes. The resulting time series are noisy (as would be expected from the small numbers of votes for each year), evincing a good deal of year-to-year fluctuation that seems meaningless. But they also show a picture of episodes of major policy change occurring exactly when expected for the Great Society (liberalism, peaking in 1965) and the Reagan Revolution (conservatism, peaking in 1981) periods respectively.

To get a sense of how legislative policy has moved over the years, look at Figure 3. (Figure 3a) presents our four measures for the House of Representatives. (To keep the eye on systematic movement, we have smoothed the graphs by taking a centered three-year moving average for each series. Note that we smooth only in this graph: we use the measured data for the statistical analysis.) It is clear that each indicator (wins, coalition size, ADA–ACA ratings, and key votes) contains both a common component and an idiosyncratic component. The lines move together, with a bit of zig and zag around the main flow. The panel for the Senate (Figure 3b) carries a similar message. Peaks of liberalism came during the early 1960s and the late 1980s, with conservatism at its height around 1980. While thus similar in outline, the patterns are not quite identical.

Presidential Policy Liberalism. The beginning point of dealing with the presidency is noting the near impossibility of direct measures of presidential liberalism from what presidents say and do. While we have an intuition about various acts and speeches, any attempt to quantify that intuition, to extract acts from the context of actions, quickly becomes hopelessly subjective. The alternative is to

Figure 3. Indicators of Public Policy Change in Four Parts of American Government (Three Year Moving Averages)

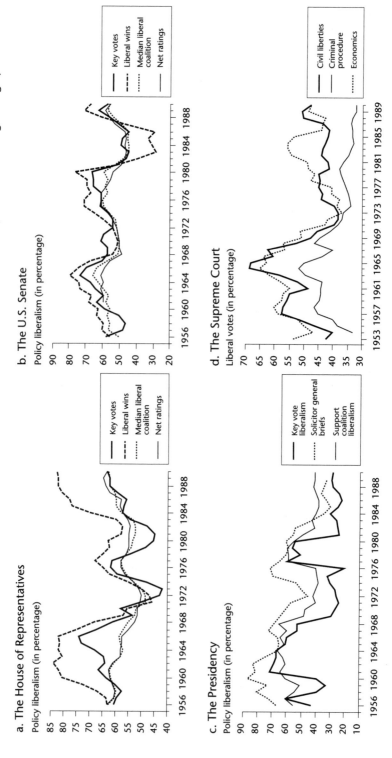

a. The House of Representatives

Policy liberalism (in percentage)

Key votes
Liberal wins
Median liberal coalition
Net ratings

b. The U.S. Senate

Policy liberalism (in percentage)

Key votes
Liberal wins
Median liberal coalition
Net ratings

c. The Presidency

Policy liberalism (in percentage)

Key vote liberalism
Solicitor general briefs
Support coalition liberalism

d. The Supreme Court

Liberal votes (in percentage)

Civil liberties
Criminal procedure
Economics

look instead at presidents through their quantifiable records of interacting with the legislature and judiciary.

We know how often particular members of Congress support and oppose the president. And we can measure the liberalism of individual members in several ways. The most convenient of these is ADA scores, which are present for the entire period, as other comparable indicators are not. And we know that ADA ratings are very highly correlated with other ratings when available—positively or negatively—so that they can serve as a useful instrument of the underlying concept.

How then to combine these different pieces of information? A first approach is to ask the question, How liberal are the regular supporters of the president each year?, and then adopt that standard as a reflection of what the president wanted from Congress. That, however, is confounded by shared partisanship between president and member. We expect members of the president's party to be more likely to be regular supporters—independent of ideological agreement with the president's program. To deal with shared party ties as a confounding factor in presidential support, we opt instead to focus on presidential support within party. The strategy is first to divide each party into support and opposition groups based upon whether member presidential support is above or below the average for the party. The mean ADA rating of each party's "support" group is then an estimate of the president's ideological position. The opposition groups similarly measure the reverse. The measurement question then may be reduced to how such separate estimates are to be combined. For a summary measure of presidential position we perform a principal components analysis of the eight indicators (*support* vs. *oppose*, by party, by house). That analysis shows decisively that each of the eight taps a single underlying dimension. Such a dimension is estimated with a factor score and rescaled . . . to approximate the ADA scales from which it was derived.

For a second legislative presidential position measure we simply take the recorded presidential position for the key votes and compute the percentage of presidential stands each year that are liberal, where again the votes are classified by polarization with individual ADA ratings.

Presidential Interaction with the Court. With less regularity and on a quite different set of issues, presidents make their policy views known to the U.S. Supreme Court. The mechanism for doing so formally is the amicus curiae brief filed by the presidency's designated agent to the courts, the solicitor general. On over 700 occasions in the 1953–89 terms, the solicitor general went on record with the Court, arguing that the holdings of particular judicial decisions ought to be affirmed or reversed. About 90% of these briefs take positions on cases that are themselves classifiably liberal or conservative.

We employ the solicitor general briefs data as leverage to measure presumed presidential position on judicial issues. Using the direction coding from the Spaeth Supreme Court data base for the case and our knowledge of whether the solicitor general argued to affirm or reverse, we code each of the briefs as to direction—liberal, conservative, or nonideological. It is then an easy matter to produce aggregated annual scales as percentage liberal of the ideological positions taken.

A quick comparison of the presidential series with the legislative series (in Figure 3) suggests less coherence in the presidential measures. Much of the discord comes from the *Solicitor General* series (which we retain, nevertheless, for its substantive value). Note also that the presidential series is typically more conservative than the two congressional series, as we might reasonably expect from the historical party control of the two institutions.

Supreme Court Liberalism. For data we have the Supreme Court data base for the period 1953–90. From that, we can content-classify the majority position in individual cases as liberal, conservative, or neither; and from that, the lifetime liberalism or conservatism of individual justices is readily derived. Then we return to the individual cases and scale the majority and dissenting votes by the justices who cast them. This allows a content-free second classification of the majority position as liberal, conservative, or not ideological. From this we build annual measures of the major-case content categories. We have chosen four such categories—*civil rights and liberties, criminal procedure, economics,* and *other*—the number a compromise between separating matters which might in principle produce different alignments and grouping broadly enough to have sufficient cases in each for reliable annual measures.

For each measure we construct a time series consisting of the percentage of all votes cast by the justices on the liberal side of the issue, whichever that is, for the year. This focus on justice decisions, rather than aggregate outcomes of the Court, appears to produce a more moderate measure over time than the alternative. . . .

We examine the first three domains in Figure 3. There we see that the issue domains move pretty much in tandem. All domains show the famous liberalism of the Warren Court in the mid-1960s and the conservative reaction of the Burger Court. Most show a modest rebound of liberalism in the early 1980s, which then reverses from the influence of new Reagan justices.

The pattern of more substantive notice is that the *"criminal procedure"* cases produce no liberal rebound in the 1980s. This is an interesting exception, for public attitudes toward crime and criminals are themselves an exception to the growing liberalism of the 1980s (Stimson 1991). This is a case where the conservative message ("The solution is more punitive law enforcement") is still dominant. . . .

Figure 4. Global Public Opinion and Global Public Policy:
Predicted and Actual Policy

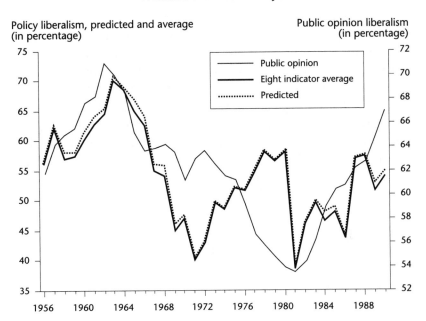

Policy liberalism, predicted and average
(in percentage)

Public opinion liberalism
(in percentage)

Public opinion
Eight indicator average
Predicted

A Summary Analysis of Governmental Responsiveness

For a summation of dynamic representation we slice across the institutional structure of American politics, returning to the familiar questions, Does public opinion influence public policy? and By what process? Our combining the policy output of the four institutions is, of course, a fiction: a single national public policy
is not the average of independent branches. We "average" across different
branches to provide a rough answer to a rough question. Here we select two indicators from each of the four prior analyses (president, House, Senate, and
Supreme Court) and then estimate representation as it works on the American
national government as a whole. . . .

We get a better sense of the historical dynamic by examining Figure 4. Plotted
here are measures of public opinion, public policy and predicted policy. The first
(in the light, solid line) is public opinion, with its liberal peaks during the early
1960s and late 1980s and its conservative peak around 1980. The dark, solid line
represents policy, a simple average of our eight policy indicators. Without much
work, it is clear that the two series are basically similar: policy reflects the timing
and range of public opinion change.

Yet the two paths are not identical. Policy turned much more conservative dur-ing the late 1960s and early 1970s than the public demanded. Then, contrary to the continuing turn to the right, policy temporarily shifted leftward under Carter's leadership. Now look at the small dots that show predicted policy. . . . The exceptionally good fit is apparent. More important, the model is now able to account for the otherwise surprising conservatism just before 1972 and the liber-alism of the late 1970s by including the Vietnam War and the composition vari-ables. Thus, while the main part of policy moves in accord with public prefer-ences, significant deviations can and do occur. Those deviations seem explicable but not by public preferences. Public opinion is powerful but not all-powerful.

Figure 4 takes us back to where we started, public policy preferences, and for-ward to the end of the story, the policy liberalism of American government, 1956–90. The point is that the two are a lot alike. . . .

Some Reflections on American Politics

The past four decades of United States history show that politicians translate changes in public opinion into policy change. Further, the evidence suggests that this translation varies by institution, both in the mechanisms that produce the link and in the nature of the dynamics.

Most important, dynamic representation finds strong support. Our work indi-cates that when the public asks for a more activist or a more conservative gov-ernment, politicians oblige. The early peak of public opinion liberalism during the early 1960s produced liberal policy; the turn away from activism and the steady move toward conservatism was similarly reflected in national policy; and the recent 1980s upsurge of public demand for action was also effective (with the exception of the Court). To be sure, other things matter too. We have modeled a late 1960s shift rightward in policy (beyond that driven by public opinion) as a function of the Vietnam War's dominance over domestic political agendas. In addition, we modeled the shift leftward during the years of the Carter presidency (a shift contrary to the prevailing movement in public opinion) as a coincidence of compositional factors.

While we are confident that the basic result holds, we know that we do not yet fully understand movement in public policy. Nevertheless, the main story is that large-scale shifts in public opinion yield corresponding large-scale shifts in gov-ernment action.

The link between opinion and policy is undoubtedly more complicated. While concentrating on policy response to opinion, we have seen little evidence of opinion reaction to policy. Elementary analyses generate contradictory infer-ences: the matter is subtle, the timing probably complex. We do know enough to assert that opinion reaction cannot explain the structural associations we uncover. We do not know enough to characterize the fuller relationship. This, of course, is a compelling subject for hard work.

Beyond the basic result, we can say that American national institutions vary in the mechanisms that produce responsiveness. It is the Senate, not the House of Representatives, that most clearly mimics the eighteenth-century clockwork meant to produce electoral accountability. When comparing the effectiveness of turnover and rational anticipation, we find that for the Senate (and also for the presidency), the most important channel for governmental representation is electoral replacement. Equally responsive, however, is the House of Representatives. Its members employ rational anticipation to produce a similarly effective public policy response, without the overt evidence of personnel change. The Supreme Court appears to reflect public opinion far more than constitutionally expected; but, in comparison, it is the institution that responds least.

Finally, the dynamics prove interesting. Each of the electoral institutions translates immediately public opinion into public policy. That is to say, when electoral politicians sense a shift in public preferences, they act directly and effectively to shift the direction of public policy. We find no evidence of delay or hesitation. The Court, not surprisingly, moves at a more deliberate speed. But equally important, rational anticipation is based not only on the long-term trends in public opinion but also on year-to-year shifts. That is to say, politicians constantly and immediately process public opinion changes in order to stay ahead of the political curve. Understanding politics well, the constitutional framers were correct in expecting short-term politics to be a fundamental part of dynamic representation.

The United States government, as it has evolved over the years, produces a complex response to public demands. The original constitutional design mixed different political calculations into different institutions so that no personal ambition, no political faction, no single political interest, or no transient passion could dominate. We now see the founders' expectations about complexity manifest in contemporary policymaking. Constitutional mechanisms harness politicians' strategies to the public's demands. In the end, the government combines both short- and long-term considerations through both rational anticipation and compositional change to produce a strong and resilient link between public and policy. . . .

REFERENCES

Durr, Robert H. 1993. "What Moves Policy Sentiment?" *American Political Science Review* 87:158–70.

Kingdon, John W. 1984. *Agendas, Alternatives, and Public Policies*. Boston: Little, Brown.

Stimson, James A. 1991. *Public Opinion in America: Moods, Cycles, and Swings*. Boulder: Westview.

10-3

The People's Craving for Unselfish Government

John R. Hibbing

Public opinion polls appear to show increasing dissatisfaction with government among Americans in recent decades. Political scientist John Hibbing argues that survey data, properly interpreted, demonstrate that the source of dissatisfaction is the belief that governmental decisions are made by self-serving politicians and greedy special interests. Consequently, the public favors reforms that limit the influence of special interests on elected officials. The media feed distrust of government, and the Constitution limits the kinds of reforms that are possible, Hibbing notes, so greater public involvement in politics and government is the only approach likely to enhance public confidence in government.

THE STUDY OF public opinion typically focuses on people's attitudes toward particular candidates, parties, ideologies, and issues, as is indicated by the subject matter of most chapters in this book. Such an orientation is perfectly appropriate since people's candidate, party, ideological, and issue preferences undoubtedly form the core of their political worldviews. As important as these topics are, they unfortunately obscure another central component of political public opinion: people's attitudes toward governing structures and processes. After all, if it is deemed important to understand what people think of the candidates and parties in government, is it not important to understand what people think about the government in which these candidates and parties serve?

Why Care About Public Attitudes Toward Government?

If the structure and operation of government were immutable—that is, if government were merely an unshakable arena in which candidates, parties, ideologies, and issue positions clashed—then determining people's attitudes toward government would be unnecessary. Government would simply operate in a neutral, deep-background fashion and people's attitudes toward it would be unin-

Source: Barbara Norrander and Clyde Wilcox, eds., *Understanding Public Opinion*, 2d ed. (Washington, D.C.: CQ Press, 2002), 301–318. Bibliographic references in the original have been deleted.

teresting and of little consequence. But perceptions of the structure and operation of government are anything but inconsequential. Public opinion of government affects its operation and, therefore, understanding why people view government as they do becomes a crucial task.

Until the late 1960s, little thought was given to the American public's views of
its government. Indeed, what was there to say? Americans revered the Constitution, thought their government was the best in the world, harbored few desires
for serious systemic reform, and were quite deferential to the people in government. A famous comparative study published in 1963 revealed that 82 percent of
the people in the United States were proud of American governmental institutions, even as only 23 percent were proud of the American economic system and
a minuscule 7 percent were proud of the American people. Of the other countries included in the survey, none came close to the pride in government possessed by Americans. To be specific, the highest percentage of residents outside
of the United States taking pride in their government was in the United King-
dom, where only 46 percent did so. In Italy, only 3 percent of the people were
proud of their government; Germany was not much better, at 7 percent. To a
great extent, it was Americans' pride in their form of government that helped to
fuel the intense feelings of the cold war. The American way of government was
best, people thought, and it was essential that it triumph over other ways.

But then came urban unrest, the Vietnam War, civil rights, rising crime rates,
and Watergate. Government no longer had the solutions and sometimes
appeared to cause the problems. Presidents lied to the American people about
the status of the war in Southeast Asia and, while in the Oval Office, gave permission for hush money to be paid to criminals. Governors and members of
Congress tried to block the pathways to real civil rights for African Americans
and, more generally, were increasingly seen as grossly insensitive to the changes
that were sweeping society. Starting around 1967, people's confidence in government began to drop. This drop was especially evident among liberals, traditionally the group most inclined to see government favorably. But by the 1970s, as
conservatives continued their usual lament that governmental collective decisions were inferior to individual decisions in a marketplace environment, liberals
became convinced that government was little more than a cheerleader for the
military-industrial complex. Government was left with few defenders anywhere
on the ideological spectrum.

Scholarly research eventually noticed the decline in confidence. In a famous
exchange in 1974, Arthur Miller and Jack Citrin agreed that major changes had
occurred in the way people looked at government, but they disagreed on the exact
meaning of these changes. Miller contended that "pervasive and enduring distrust
of government . . . [can] . . . increase the potential for radical change", but Citrin

felt survey respondents were merely voicing frustration with incumbent office-holders and that they still supported (and even took pride in) the political system in a general sense. In other words, Miller implied that dissatisfaction could lead to serious systemic disruptions whereas Citrin believed it would probably result in nothing more than voting out the ins and voting in the outs.

It would appear that Citrin's position has better withstood the passage of time. Although the country has experienced occasional periods of increased satisfaction with government, mostly in the mid-1980s and late 1990s, governmental approval has generally been quite low ever since the decline of the 1970s; yet the American political system has never seemed seriously threatened by a lack of popular support. In academic jargon, people may not have approved of specific actions by the government but they mostly retained a "diffuse support" for the political system.

Since the revolution never came—indeed, the United States did not even experience a full-fledged party realignment—does this mean no systemic consequences flow from people's loss of confidence in government? This is where the original Miller–Citrin exchange may have done a disservice. If the issue is cast as one in which diffuse support is either present or absent, many of the possible consequences of unfavorable attitudes toward government are defined away. The truth of the matter is that the concept of diffuse support is not particularly useful beyond reminding us of the obvious point that it is possible for people to be upset with a particular action of government and still respect the existing governmental system at a more basic level. What is now apparent is that even if people do not want the current political system to go away, negative attitudes toward government have implications far beyond a desire to vote for the out party.

For example, research has indicated that when the public has little confidence in institutions of government like Congress, prospective officeholders are less likely to be willing to serve. Incumbents are more likely to quit and potential challengers are less likely to start when the public mood is palpably sour. One member of Congress who retired after serving just a few terms said: "People just presume we are dishonorable. . . . Imagine living under a cloud of suspicion all the time. If you can do that, you can understand why some of us think serving in Congress isn't enjoyable." Another said, "The vilification of the average politician in the eyes of the public is a very alarming trend. . . . Some people seem to think I should be ashamed to have served in the U.S. Congress." This last remark calls to mind former representative Pat Schroeder's favorite plea to reporters: "Please don't tell my mother I am in Congress; she thinks I am a prostitute and I would hate to disappoint her."

Other problems also accrue when people think ill of government. Sometimes, elected officials are so concerned about public attitudes toward their institution that they avoid tackling tough policy problems. Usually the way for a political institution to preserve popularity is to avoid dealing with contentious issues, so the temptation is to leave the challenging problems for a later date. Another danger is that people who are unhappy with government may seek to change or reform various aspects of the political system without thoroughly considering whether those changes will in fact make people feel better about the government. Finally, research in psychology has indicated that people who lack confidence in an institution will be less likely to comply with the laws (or other outputs) of that institution.

These are serious issues. If a decline in confidence in government leads to a lower quality of elected officials, to timidity rather than temerity in addressing serious problems, to counterproductive reforms, and to cavalier public attitudes toward compliance with government edicts, the health of our society will be affected. In short, the fact that a lack of confidence may not lead people to want to overthrow the existing governmental regime does not mean that a lack of confidence does not have deleterious consequences. People's attitudes toward government serve as important institutional constraints. If the attitudes are sufficiently negative, government will have more difficulty doing what it is supposed to do. But the extent to which public attitudes impinge upon the ability of the governmental system to do its job depends on the precise nature of the people's dissatisfaction. For that reason determining which aspect of government is responsible for the downturn in public approval becomes an important task.

Differences in Attitudes Toward Institutions and Officials

For quite some time now research has indicated that while most people are supportive of their own member of Congress they may at the same time think little of Congress itself. (In this respect, politics may be quite similar to the law and medicine since people tend to be fond of their own attorney and their own doctor but think less highly of the legal and medical professions generally.) Because a single representative is such a small part of the governmental system, a more fruitful distinction may be between the institutions (and overall institutional structure) of government and the collections of officials working within those institutions.

Americans are actually quite supportive of the governmental system when they are asked to focus on institutions in the abstract or, especially, on the constitutionally provided arrangement of institutions. It is only when people's attention turns to the elected officials and bureaucrats who labor within these institutions that opinion turns negative. This distinction is captured in Figure 1, which reports results from a national survey conducted in 1992.[1] In this survey, respondents were first presented with the following item: "Thinking about people in

Figure 1. Contrasting Public Approval of Institutions

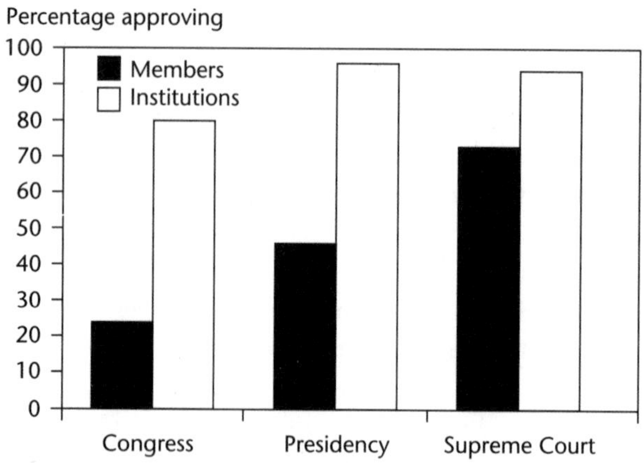

Percentage approving

Source: 1992 Public Attitues Toward Political Institutions. Survey in John R. Hibbing and Elizabeth Theiss-Morse, *Congress as Public Enemy: Public Attitudes Toward American Political Institutions* (New York: Cambridge University Press, 1995)

government, please tell me if you strongly approve, approve, disapprove, or strongly disapprove of the way the people in the Congress [in the Presidency; in the Supreme Court] are handling their jobs." Thus, in the case of Congress, for example, the referent was not just Congress generally but rather the people in Congress. Respondents were then told: "Now, sometimes when we talk about parts of the government, like the Supreme Court, the Presidency, and the Congress, we don't mean the people currently serving in office, we mean the institutions themselves, no matter who is in office. These institutions have their own buildings, historical traditions, and purposes." Then, they were asked whether they strongly approved, approved, disapproved, or strongly disapproved of each institution.

The results show a tremendous disparity between approval levels of the institutions on the one hand and of the people in those institutions on the other. The gap is especially large for Congress: three times as many respondents approved of the institution of Congress as of the members of Congress. (To simplify the figure, strongly approve and approve responses were collapsed, as were strongly disapprove and disapprove.) Well over twice as many people approved of the institution of the presidency as approved of President George H. W. Bush (remember, the survey was conducted in 1992). Even in the Supreme Court, which (predictably) had the smallest differential, it was still the case that the percent approving of the institution was 1.3 times the percent approving of the justices. Not surprisingly, then, when people are asked if they want "major change" in the structure of government, they say they do not. When in a 1998 national survey respondents were asked to agree or disagree with the statement that "our basic governmental structures are the best in the world and should not be changed in a major fashion," 65.7 agreed, leaving barely one-third supporting major change—and even at that many of the "major" changes the one-third had in mind turned out to be quite minor.[2] Surveys done in the early to mid-1970s (unfortunately, the item was not asked in the 1960s) show similar levels of public support for existing arrangements and opposition to major change.[3]

Attitudes That Have Not Become More Negative

To this point, the results suggest it is incorrect to leave the impression that people dislike everything about politics and government. They actually are remarkably approving of government (and government institutions) in the abstract. It is only when living, breathing human beings get involved that approval tends to dissipate. But what is it about the actions of government officials as a group that tends to upset modern Americans? In attempting to answer this question, it is useful to see how perceptions of those officials have changed over the years. To do so, I draw on data collected by the National Election Studies (NES) at the University of Michigan. The advantage of these data is that similar questions have been asked repeatedly, sometimes since the late 1950s. The repetition of identical items makes it possible to draw conclusions about the manner in which officials have lost much of the public trust.[4]

Perhaps the best way to proceed is to identify those potential sources of dissatisfaction that have not changed and therefore cannot be responsible for declining levels of trust. For example, some might suspect that the decline in public faith in government is explained by a growing perception that public officials waste a lot of taxpayers' money. This hypothesis does not withstand analytical scrutiny. In every election year since 1968, with the exception of 1986, NES's national sample has been asked whether "people in government waste tax money." It is true that a majority of respondents admit to believing that people in government waste "a lot" of money, but the percent responding in such a fashion did not change much from 1968 to 1998. As can be seen in Figure 2, after increasing in the second half of the 1970s, perceptions of the level of profligacy among people in government dropped back to levels present in the late 1960s. People tend to think governmental officials waste tax money, but this perception has not become more common over the past thirty years so would not seem to be at the core of people's decreased confidence in government.

Much the same thing can be said for the amount of attention people in government pay to ordinary people. Given the shrill populist tone of modern political rhetoric, it might reasonably be thought that the public has the perception

Figure 2. How Much Taxpayer Money Do Public Officials Waste? 1968–1998

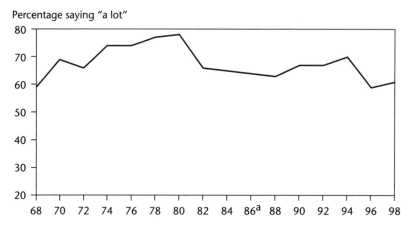

Percentage saying "a lot"

Source: National Election Studies.
[a]Data for 1986 are missing; the number reported here is the average of 1984 and 1988.

that ordinary people are being ignored and that this perception is why many are upset with the political system. Once again, the sentiment is not supported by the data. The NES pollsters frequently ask respondents, "How much does the government listen to the people?" Permitted responses are "not much," "some," and "a good deal"; for simplicity's sake, Figure 3 presents the percent of respondents selecting the most negative answer—"not much." Unfortunately, this item has not been consistently posed in midterm elections so I present results only for presidential election years. The overall results speak surprisingly well for people's perception of government attentiveness, as only about one-fourth to one-third of those in the samples expressed the belief that government does not listen much. But with regard to the more telling matter of how perceptions have changed since the late 1960s, the pattern is similar to that appearing in Figure 2. After an increase in the late 1970s, perceptions that government officials do not listen much dropped and by the late 1990s were actually lower than they were in the late 1960s. People's frustration with governmental officials apparently cannot be traced to the perception that those officials are unwilling or unable to listen to the people.

These findings about "listening" are not an aberration. The people at NES compile something they call a government responsiveness index, which is computed by combining responses to two items: "How much attention do you feel the government pays to what the people think when it decides what to do," and "How much do you feel that having elections makes the government pay attention to

Figure 3. How Much Does the Government Listen to the People? 1968–1996

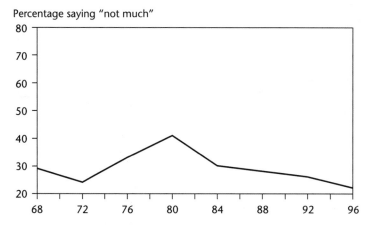

Percentage saying "not much"

Source: National Election Studies.

what the people think?" As can be seen in Figure 4, this index was at 62 in 1968 and, while it is true that perceptions of governmental responsiveness have declined since then, the extent of this decline was minuscule over the thirty years covered, with the 1996 figure only a few points lower, at 55. To the extent people have become more hostile toward government it is not because they now perceive government to be much less responsive to the needs of the people than did those surveyed a few decades ago.

Finally, maybe people are upset with governmental officials because they have allowed politics to become too complicated. When officials exult in the nuances of issues and try to highlight their issue differences with other politicians, ordinary people might feel cut out of government. But, as it turns out, the people do not believe politics has become more complicated (see Figure 5). In fact, save for an unusual spike in 1998, the trend seems to be toward popular perceptions that politics is less complicated than it was in the past. No doubt, a majority of Americans has always agreed that politics was "too complicated," but no growth in this perception is apparent in Figure 5. To find the source of people's loss of confidence in governmental officials, our attention must be directed elsewhere.

People are not upset with the institutions of government and certainly not with the constitutional structure that holds these institutions together. They *are* upset with elected officials and other people in government, but what is the source of their displeasure? We have just seen that, compared with those of the late 1960s, people at the end of the millennium were not more likely to perceive government

Figure 4. Government Responsiveness Index, 1968–1996

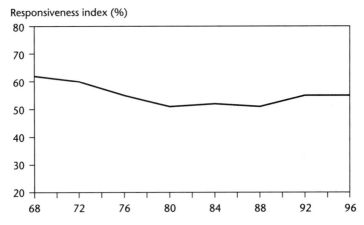

Responsiveness index (%)

Source: National Election Studies.

officials as greater spendthrifts, as less responsive, or as more likely to obfuscate and complicate issues. What, then, is it about these elected officials that has led to the alleged crisis of confidence in American government?

Attitudes That Have Become More Negative

The answer is surprisingly simple. People have become much more likely to believe that government officials are serving their own interests rather than the interests of the people. This simple change is at the core of any serious effort to come to terms with the decline in favorable public attitudes toward government. How are officials acting selfishly? By carrying water for special interests who then lavish benefits including campaign contributions, gifts, trips to warm countries, and lucrative postgovernment positions on those public officials. The people are convinced that government is now controlled by an unholy collusion of special interests and elected officials. Evidence for the prevalence of this perception is easy to muster.

Returning to the National Election Studies data, a useful and frequently asked item is this: "Is the government run for the benefit of all or is it run for the benefit of a few big interests?" Unlike the other time-series findings reported to this point (which showed remarkable over-time stability), perceptions that the government is run for a few big interests have increased dramatically, as shown in Figure 6. In the 1960s, a clear minority of respondents said government was run

Figure 5. Is Politics Too Complicated? 1968–1998

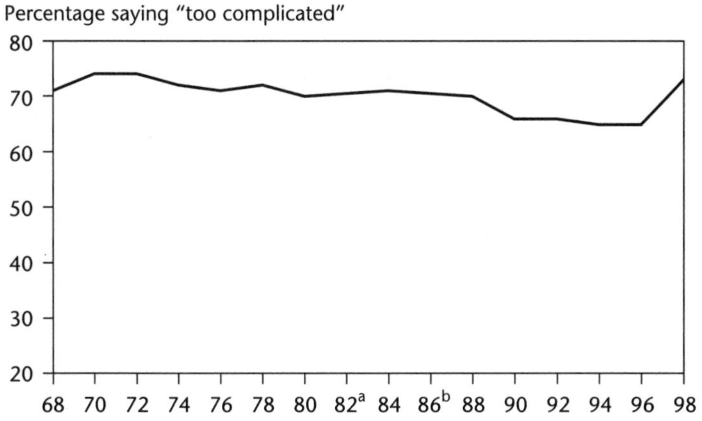

Percentage saying "too complicated"

Source: National Election Studies.

[a]Data for 1982 are missing; the number reported here is the average of 1980 and 1984.

[b]Data for 1986 are missing; the number reported here is the average of 1984 and 1988.

by a few big interests. By 1975, over half believed that big interests ruled, and by the early to mid-1990s three out of four Americans believed government was run by a few big interests. These figures dropped a little in the late 1990s but were still 25–30 percentage points above the levels present in the late 1960s.

Many people have even come to the conclusion that government officials commonly cross the line of legality in their self-serving actions. Survey respondents were asked how many "government officials are crooked." Believing officials to be crooked has serious implications for the state of democracy. In 1968 only one out of four people believed "quite a few" government officials were crooked (see Figure 7). By the time of Watergate, in the mid-1970s, the proportion of respondents who thought many officials were crooked had increased from 25 to 45 percent. While the data are not complete for the 1980s, it would appear there was a modest drop in perceptions of the extent to which officials were crooked (many attitudes toward government improved in the mid-1980s in conjunction with what has been referred to as the era of Reagan "feel goodism") before the early 1990s witnessed a resumption of negative perceptions. In 1994 we even had the unprecedented situation wherein a majority of the American people believed that "quite a few" of the people in government were crooked. Not only do the people believe that the government is being run for the sake of big interests, they believe that quite a few government officials are breaking the law in order to assist their special-interest friends.

Figure 6. Is Government Run for the Benefit of a Few Big Interests? 1968–1998

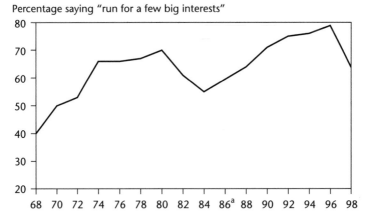

Percentage saying "run for a few big interests"

Source: National Election Studies.

[a]Data for 1986 are missing; the number reported here is the average of 1984 and 1988.

In the light of these perceptions, is it any surprise that the people do not have much trust in government? How can government be trusted if those in it are trying only to help themselves and are willing even to break the law in order to achieve that goal? NES gives people the chance to say whether they trust the federal government only some of the time, most of the time, or just about always. In Figure 8, the percentage responding either "most of the time," or "just about always" is summed and presented for every election year survey since 1968. The pattern is similar to that evident in Figures 6 and 7. In 1968, the government was in good shape in the eyes of the people: 61 percent believed it could be trusted at least most of the time, a startling level of trust given all that was going on in 1968. But the salad days did not last long, and by the end of the 1970s trust was at just 25 percent, less than half the levels of just a decade before. The mid-1980s provided a modest resurgence in trust only to give way in the early to mid-1990s to the lowest levels ever. Trust, as with several other indicators of public attitudes toward government, improved markedly from the early 1990s to the late 1990s, but even so, levels remained 20 to 25 percentage points lower than at the beginning of the time period.[5]

Focus Group Comments

Teasing people's attitudes from survey data is not always possible to do, particularly on matters such as the aspects of government they may like and dislike, and

Figure 7. Are Government Officials Crooked? 1968–1998

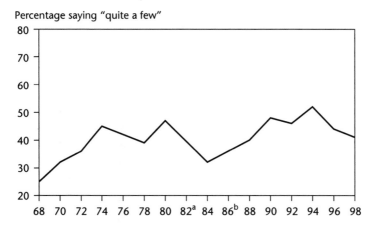

Source: National Election Studies.
[a]Data for 1982 are missing; the number reported here is the average of 1980 and 1984.
[b]Data for 1986 are missing; the number reported here is the average of 1984 and 1988.

why they feel the way they do. Accordingly, some scholars have been turning to focus groups in order to allow people more liberties in explaining their true sentiments. Closed-ended survey questions are better suited to discerning cut-and-dried preferences regarding candidates and issues than to fleshing out people's sometimes sketchy thoughts about changes that might move the governing process closer to the kind they prefer. A well-known danger of using focus groups in public opinion research is the possibility that the group moderator could be in a position to lead participants toward certain statements, particularly when the topic is one the people have not thought much about. Although the same is true of survey questions, the more structured format of survey instruments makes it easier at least to determine when question wording or question order has artificially influenced respondents. In focus groups, the best way to minimize the potential for external influence is for the moderator to play a minimalist role, to stick to a publicized script, and to make transcripts available so that interested researchers can check for possible moderator influence.

Focus groups that meet these criteria and that deal with the topic of public attitudes toward government were conducted in late 1997 at various places across the country.[6] In each of the eight sessions, groups of ten to thirteen previously unacquainted individuals were brought together for approximately two hours to discuss the aspects of government they liked and disliked. The following are some typical quotations from these focus group sessions, beginning with those highlighting people's dissatisfaction with the power of special interests

Figure 8. How Much Can Government Be Trusted? 1968–1998

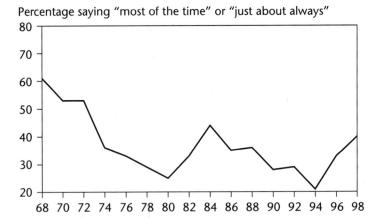

Percentage saying "most of the time" or "just about always"

Source: National Election Studies.

over elected officials. Only first names are used since participants were promised anonymity.

> (Robert) I think interest groups have too much control of what our elected officials say in our government. And congress people are basically just like, well this guy gave me ten million dollars so ... I've got to vote this way. They're bought, you know, bought by the interest group.
>
> (Lisa) [Politicians] seem so easily influenced by lobbyists. .... Money and influential groups shouldn't be able to influence the decisions that the law-makers make so easily.
>
> (Maria) [Politicians] think about who's in power, who's the dominant group. And they do the laws according to who's going to benefit from it.

Although this antipathy toward special interests and selfish politicians will surprise few who have been listening to the American people of late, it is more surprising to learn that ordinary people are not eager to supplant special interests in the influence-peddling department. Though politicians and elite observers are forever striving to get the people more involved in politics, the people are at best ambivalent and at worst fearful of greater popular involvement. They are definitely averse to more direct forms of democracy that would require the public to spend more time on politics, such as town hall meetings, and they even prefer to avoid reforms in indirect democracy that attempt to heighten accountability and representation, thereby putting more of a burden on the people to communicate their preferences to, and then to monitor the actions of, elected officials, perhaps via the Internet or interactive cable television. Consider the following focus group comments.

> (Alfredo) [Ordinary] people are not very intelligent relating to what's going on in politics [and] would be swayed by a couple of dollars.
>
> (Eric) We have avenues to contact our representatives. I don't think that structurally we lack the ability to let our representatives know what we want; we just choose not to do so.
>
> (Michelene) When I leave here, when I walk out this door, I'm not going to volunteer for anything. I'm not going to get involved in anything. I mean I know this. I'm not going to pretend I'm some political activist. I'm lazy. I'm not going to do it. I'm too busy obsessing on other things going on in my life. . . . So somebody's got to do it and I don't care how much money they make, you know. . . . I don't want the job. I'm not interested in it.
>
> (John) People are satisfied with their way of life and everything . . . and they're going to let someone else take care of [politics].
>
> (Linda) Part of the problem is that [politicians] . . . have to have something that drives them to make them even run for office these days. And so sometimes you get the wrong kind of people in government. . . . He's got his own agenda. . . . He's not doing it for service to the people.

The composite picture is not one of a public champing at the bit to get into the political arena. Focus group participants lacked confidence in their own ability and the ability of people like them to play a more active role in government. They doubted people's political capabilities as well as their motivation. Eric remarks that people have plenty of opportunities to contact representatives but that they just "choose not to do so." Linda goes even further. She dislikes it when politicians offer an agenda that they believe would improve society. In Linda's mind, having an agenda prohibits politicians from being in a position to serve the people. But, of course, if politicians are not taking stances and offering ideas, people will not be able to choose officials on the basis of their positions or to hold them accountable for the successes and failures of those positions. If the people are not upset by a perceived lack of policy accountability, what has upset them?

Why People Dislike Officials

To the extent the focus group comments are accurate reflections of public sentiments, people do not seek more representation or greater systemic sensitivity to the policy preferences of ordinary people, even as people simultaneously plead for a reduction in the power of special interests. This combination of attitudes may seem puzzling but is actually a perfect parallel to the survey results indicating that respondents do not perceive that government officials fail to listen to the people (see Figure 3) but are convinced that government officials *are* listening to special interests. The explanation for this puzzling combination of views is that, contrary to much writing in the popular press and elsewhere, people are not eager for their own voices to be heard. People are not convinced they have much to say about most policy choices. Thus, negative views of government do not tend to sprout from perceptions of a lack of responsiveness. Many, many citizens do not want the government to be more responsive to them because this change would require them to follow issues and politics more carefully, and this is the last thing they want to do. But just because people do not want to play a bigger role in government themselves does not mean they cannot want special interests to play less of a role. In fact, this is precisely what the people do want.

More than anything, people dislike government when it is perceived to make suckers out of them, and people have become increasingly convinced that government can and does take advantage of the people.[7] Elected officials are believed to luxuriate in a pool of taxpayer-provided perquisites while they service the interests of the rich, the powerful, and the demanding, all the while growing increasingly out of touch with real people. This sentiment was apparent in the remarks of Robert, Lisa, and Maria. They believed that rich and loud groups are controlling members of Congress. Taxpayers pay for members' salaries and perquisites while special interests reap all the rewards. Oh, sure, elected officials may pay ritualistic attention to the regular people. They may hold town meetings and attend the occasional high school graduation and Kiwanis Club meeting, but they only engage in such activities because they want to be returned to office where they and their special interest chums can continue the cycle. This is why people do not like government.

Recognizing that people want to reduce the power of special interests but do not wish to increase their own power helps to solve several puzzles of public opinion. It explains why people sound so stridently populist in discussing the influence of special interests but are so reluctant to push out these interests if it means taking power in their own hands. It explains why people can support legislative term limits even though they recognize that limits reduce representation and accountability. (People's logic seems to be that, if we are unable to stop legislators from taking advantage of us, at least we can limit the length of time they are able to do so.) And it explains why people have so much more confidence in the Supreme Court than in Congress (justices may make stupid decisions but they are not enriching themselves in the process and so are much more likely to be forgiven than members of Congress).

Why did negativity toward government become so noticeable in the early 1970s and why did it moderate in the mid-1980s and the late-1990s even though aversion to being taken advantage of is likely to be relatively stable over time? Of course, societal conditions still have much to do with public attitudes toward government.[8] Society seemed to be coming apart in the late 1960s, and economic conditions were unsettled throughout much of the 1970s. By the mid-1980s and then again in the late 1990s conditions—especially economic conditions—were improved and attitudes toward government became more favorable. But societal conditions are only part of the explanation. The United States has never had a longer run of economic prosperity than from 1993 to 2000, yet public confidence in government in 2000 was still well beneath what it had been in the 1950s and 1960s. Why? Because government has become visibly a high-stakes endeavor. It was not until the end of the 1960s that big money began playing a consistent role in anything other than presidential elections. It was not until the end of the 1960s that the professionalization of politics, with its accompanying high salaries, pension plans, private banks, commissaries, health clubs, and oversized staffs, soaked into public awareness. It was not until the 1960s that government became involved in such a large number of issue areas that interest groups saw the advantage of setting up permanent residence in Washington. It was not until the 1960s that societal diversity really began to make itself felt, thus contributing to people's sense that somebody was out there on the other side of the issue ready to seek advantage through the political system. All these things make it possible for politicians to play the people for suckers and make it less likely that even a prosperous economy will return perceptions of government to the favorable levels of the 1950s and early 1960s. The change is not in people's sensitivity to being played for a sucker or in the perceived willingness of people to play others for suckers but rather in the perceived *ability* of those in and around government to play us for suckers, thanks largely to the growth and professionalization of government as well as to the increasingly evident diversity of society.

How to Improve Public Attitudes Toward Government

Traditionally, those who have studied public attitudes toward government have lumped together a variety of measures (several of these measures were presented in Figures 2 through 8) into an index of trust. By combining these diverse items, however, scholars are left unable to identify the real cause of dissatisfaction with government. More careful inspection indicates that the core source of popular dissatisfaction is not the policies government produces, the lack of responsiveness to the people's wishes, erroneous decisions, or even the perception that government wastes taxpayer dollars. Instead, dissatisfaction springs mainly from the perception that governmental decisions—whatever those decisions may be—are being made for the wrong reasons. Self-serving politicians and greedy but politically astute and connected special interests play the people for suckers and this is the aspect of government that bothers people more than anything else.

The widely reported spike in Americans' support for government that followed the September 11, 2001, attacks on the World Trade Center in New York City and the Pentagon in the suburbs of Washington, D.C., although predictable, is also perfectly consistent with the interpretation of public attitudes offered here. (Levels of trust, for example, reached their highest levels since the mid-1960s.) It certainly was not the case that in the wake of the tragedy the American people had more input into government than usual; so that cannot be the reason they became so much more approving of government. Rather, what happened was that all public officials—Republicans and Democrats, the president, and members of Congress—for a time at least, refrained from arguing in public. Special interests were not visible, and it was hard for people to imagine how any particular actions of politicians could be designed for their own ends. Instead, officials' attention was focused on getting the country through those horrible days. That is how the public wanted those in government to behave.

Of course, the cost of this increase in public support for American government was far too high. Short of major threats to the security of the country and to the lives of its people, what can be done to lessen people's sense that government insiders are taking advantage of them? One solution would be to attempt to locate and empanel elected officials who are completely unselfish, but people are understandably dubious that such saints exist. When asked if the country has just been unlucky in ending up with greedy politicians or if it is instead the system that turns good people into self-serving public officials, a strong majority of survey respondents choose the latter. Focus group participants agree. Several even felt that if ordinary people were in Congress they would begin behaving just as current members of Congress do. For example, one said: "I really feel like it wouldn't matter if we were in Congress. I think we would more or less act just as they're acting". Rather than waiting for a group of saints to arrive, the public prefers the more proactive strategy of making it impossible, or at least much more difficult, for elected officials to benefit themselves. Thus, new campaign finance laws, gift-giving restrictions, salary cuts, staff reductions, perquisite eliminations, outside earnings bans, term limits, and restrictions on postgovernment employment are all extremely popular with citizens.

Making it more difficult for people in government to feather their own nests directly addresses the aspect of government that most troubles the people, but it is unlikely that even herculean reforms would convince the people that governmental decisions were largely devoid of self-interest on the part of the decision makers. People are just too cynical, the press is just too eager to connect every governmental action to a self-interested motive, and the Constitution would seem to stand in the way of several changes that would be needed, such as banning independent spending that helps (or hinders) a candidate's campaign or prohibiting certain types of employment once an individual leaves government service. As a result, a central part of improving public attitudes toward government would be to educate people to the hard reality that they cannot have it both ways. People need to be taught that if they want to bring special interests to heel, they will probably need to become more involved. As much as the people would like a system that both allows collective decisions to be made by unselfish officials *and* lets ordinary people stay relatively uninvolved, such a government is a logical impossibility, assuming the people also wish for the government to be somewhat democratic.

NOTES

1. This survey was conducted by the Bureau of Sociological Research at the University of Nebraska for John Hibbing and Elizabeth Theiss-Morse from late July till early October of 1992 using standard random digit dialing techniques. There were 1,433 respondents. Full information is contained in Hibbing and Theiss-Morse 1995. [See John R. Hibbing and Elizabeth Theiss-Morse, *Congress as Public Enemy: Public Attitudes Toward American Political Institutions* (New York: Cambridge University Press, 1995).]

2. This survey was conducted by Gallup for John Hibbing and Elizabeth Theiss-Morse from mid-April till mid-May of 1998 using Gallup's standard three-call, "youngest male-oldest female" respondent selection procedure with 1,266 respondents. Full information is contained in Hibbing and Theiss-Morse forthcoming. [See John R. Hibbing and Elizabeth Theiss-Morse, *Stealth Democracy: Americans' Beliefs About How Government Should Work* (New York: Cambridge University Press, 2002).]

3. In 1972, the National Election Studies survey instrument included an item asking whether "a big change was needed in our form of government or should it be kept pretty much as is." Only 25 percent said that a big change was needed. In a 1976 NES item that speaks directly to the Miller-Citrin controversy, respondents were asked: "There has been some talk recently about how people have lost faith and confidence in the government in Washington. Do you think this lack of trust is just because of the individuals in office or is there something more seriously wrong with government in general and the way it operates?" Even right after Watergate, better than two-thirds of the respondents (68.1 percent) felt the lack of trust was due to the individuals in office. In the same survey, 80 percent claimed to be "proud of many things about our form of government." People may be dissatisfied with government but are skeptical of the need for major change.

4. The National Election Studies surveys are conducted every two years in conjunction with the federal elections, usually in a postelection survey. Interviews are conducted in person and the number of cases varies between 1,000 and 3,000. For further information, see www.umich.edu/~nes>.

5. For excellent efforts to account for the decline in confidence and trust in government, see Lipset and Schneider 1987; Orren 1997; Alford 2001; Citrin and Luks 2001; and Chanley, Rahn, and Rudolph 2001. [See Seymour Martin Lipset and William Schneider, *The Confidence Gap* (Baltimore: Johns Hopkins University Press, 1987); Gary Orren, "Fall from Grace: The Public's

Loss of Faith in Government," in *Why People Don't Trust Government,* ed. Joseph S. Nye Jr., Philip D. Zelikow, and David C. King (Cambridge: Harvard University Press, 1997); John R. Alford, "We're All in This Together: The Decline of Trust in Government, 1958–1996," in *What Is It About Government That Americans Dislike?* ed. John R. Hibbing and Elizabeth Theiss-Morse (Cambridge: Cambridge University Press, 2001); Jack Citrin and Samantha Luks, "Political Trust Revisited: Déjà Vu All Over Again?" in *What Is It About Government That Americans Dislike?*; and Virginia Chanley, Wendy Rahn, and Thomas Rudolph, "The Origins and Consequences of Public Views about Government," in *What Is It About Government That Americans Dislike?*

6. Two sessions each were held in Omaha, Nebraska; Bangor, Maine; San Diego, California; and Atlanta, Georgia. Participants were recruited by advertisements, flyers, random telephone calls, and announcements at various civic and social meetings, and they were paid a small fee for their cooperation. Further details are available in Hibbing and Theiss-Morse forthcoming. [See note 2 for reference.]

7. Experimental research even indicates that people are willing to sacrifice monetary gain to avoid being a sucker. In the ultimatum bargaining game, Player 1 divides $20 with another player, Player 2. Player 2 can accept or reject Player 1's proposed allocation, but if it is rejected neither player gets anything. The findings of this experiment consistently show that when Player 2 feels Player 1 was too self-serving, say by proposing to keep $18 while giving only $2 to Player 2, Player 2 typically rejects the allocation even though doing so costs $2. Better to not be played for a sucker than to reap a monetary gain (see, for example, Guth and Tietz 1990). [See Werner Guth and Reihard Tietz, "Ultimatum Bargaining Behavior: A Survey and Comparison of Experimental Results," *Journal of Economic Psychology* 11: 417–449.]

8. Evidence of the importance of economic conditions in explaining variations in approval of government is decidedly mixed. For an overview, see Lawrence 1997. When the focus is on individual institutions rather than government generally, it appears that approval of the president is quite sensitive to societal conditions, Congress somewhat, and the Supreme Court very little (see Hibbing and Theiss-Morse 1995, chap. 2, for a more thorough discussion). All in all, the message is that economic conditions are only one of many factors that explain governmental approval.

Chapter 11

Voting, Campaigns, and Elections

11-1

from *The Reasoning Voter*

Samuel L. Popkin

Voters confront difficult choices with incomplete and usually biased informa-
tion. Many voters are not strongly motivated to learn more. Even if they want
to learn more, the information they need is often not available in a convenient
form. In the following essay, Samuel L. Popkin argues that this predicament
does not necessarily lead voters to make irrational decisions. Voters instead
rely on low-cost shortcuts to obtain information and make decisions. Popkin's
analysis can help us to better understand the role of campaigns in voters'
decision-making processes as well as other features of American politics.

IN RECENT DECADES, journalists and reformers have complained with increasing
force about the lack of content in voting and the consequent opportunities for
manipulating the electorate. And yet over the same period academic studies of
voting have begun to expose more and more about the substance of voting decisions and the limits to manipulation of voters. The more we learn about what
voters know, the more we see how campaigns matter in a democracy. And the
more we see, the clearer it becomes that we must change both our critiques of
campaigns and our suggestions for reforming them.

Source: Samuel L. Popkin, *The Reasoning Voter: Communication and Persuasion in Presidential Campaigns,* 2d
ed. (Chicago: University of Chicago Press, 1994), 212–219. Notes appearing in the original have been
deleted.

In this [essay] I summarize my findings about how voters reason and show how some modest changes which follow from my theory could ameliorate some defects of the campaign process.

I have argued . . . that the term *low-information rationality,* or "gut" rationality, best describes the kind of practical reasoning about government and politics in which people actually engage. . . . [L]ow-information reasoning is by no means devoid of substantive content, and is instead a process that economically incorporates learning and information from past experiences, daily life, the media, and political campaigns. . . .

Gut rationality draws on the information shortcuts and rules of thumb that voters use to obtain and evaluate information and to choose among candidates. These information shortcuts and rules of thumb must be considered when evaluating an electorate and considering changes in the electoral system.

How Voters Reason

It is easy to demonstrate that Americans have limited knowledge of basic textbook facts about their government and the political debates of the day. But evaluating citizens only in terms of such factual knowledge is a misleading way to assess their competence as voters.

Because voters use shortcuts to obtain and evaluate information, they are able to store far more data about politics than measurements of their textbook knowledge would suggest. Shortcuts for obtaining information at low cost are numerous. People learn about specific government programs as a by-product of ordinary activities, such as planning for retirement, managing a business, or choosing a college. They obtain economic information from their activities as consumers, from their workplace, and from their friends. They also obtain all sorts of information from the media. Thus they do not need to know which party controls Congress, or the names of their senators, in order to know something about the state of the economy or proposed cuts in Social Security or the controversies over abortion. And they do not need to know where Nicaragua is, or how to describe the Politburo, in order to get information about changes in international tensions which they can relate to proposals for cutting the defense budget.

When direct information is hard to obtain, people will find a proxy for it. They will use a candidate's past political positions to estimate his or her future positions. When they are uncertain about those past positions, they will accept as a proxy information about the candidate's personal demographic characteristics and the groups with which he or she has associated. And since voters find it difficult to gather information about the past competence of politicians who have performed outside their district or state, they will accept campaign competence as a proxy for competence in elected office—as an indication of the political skills needed to handle the issues and problems confronting the government.

Voters use evaluations of personal character as a substitute for information about past demonstrations of political character. They are concerned about personal character and integrity because they generally cannot infer the candidate's true commitments from his past votes, most of which are based on a hard-to-decipher mixture of compromises between ideal positions and practical realities. Evaluating any sort of information for its relevance to politics is a reasoning process, not a reflex projection directly from pocketbook or personal problems to votes. But in making such evaluations, voters use the shortcut of relying on the opinions of others whom they trust and with whom they discuss the news. These opinions can serve as fire alarms that alert them to news deserving more than their minimal attention. As media communities have developed, voters have the additional shortcut of validating their opinions by comparing them with the opinions of political leaders whose positions and reputations people grow to know over time.

People will use simplifying assumptions to evaluate complex information. A common simplifying assumption is that a politician had significant control over an observable result, such as a loss of jobs in the auto industry. This saves people the trouble of finding out which specific actions really caused the result. Another example of a simplifying assumption is the notion that "My enemy's enemy is my friend."

People use party identification as running tallies of past information and shortcuts to storing and encoding their past experiences with political parties. They are able to encode information about social groups prominent in the party, the priorities of the party, and the performance of the party and its president in various policy areas. This generalized information about parties provides "default values" from which voters can assess candidates about whom they have no other information. In keeping generalized tallies by issue area, they avoid the need to know the specifics of every legislative bill.

As a shortcut in assessing a candidate's future performance, without collecting more data, people assemble what data they have about the candidate into a causal narrative or story. Because a story needs a main character, they can create one from their knowledge of people who have traits or characteristics like those of the candidate. This allows them to go beyond the incomplete information they have about a candidate, and to hold together and remember more information than they otherwise could. Because these stories are causal narratives, they allow voters to think about government in causal terms and to evaluate what it will do. Narratives thus help people incorporate their reasoning about government into their projections about candidates; their assumptions "confer political significance on some facts and withhold it from others." They offer people a way to connect personal and political information, to project that information into the future, and to make a complete picture from limited information.

Finally, people use shortcuts when choosing between candidates. When faced with an array of candidates in which some are known well and some are known poorly, and all are known in different and incomparable ways, voters will seek a clear and accessible criterion for comparing them. This usually means looking for the sharpest differences between the candidates which can be related to government performance. Incorporating these differences into narratives allows them to compare the candidates without spending the calculation time and the energy needed to make independent evaluations of each candidate.

Working Attitudes

People do not and cannot use all the information they have at one time. What they use will depend in part on the point of view or frame with which they view the world; attitudes and information are brought to bear if they fit the frame. Of the attitudes and bits of information available, people tend to use those they consider important or those they have used recently. As the changes in voter attitudes entailed by the emergence of new candidates in primaries suggest, attitudes and information will also be brought to the foreground when they fit with what is *expected* in a situation. Our realizations, the thoughts that come clearly to mind, depend in part on what others say about their own thoughts and perceptions.

Thus, as options change, expectations change. If a Democrat were asked in early 1984 what he or she thought of Walter Mondale as a presidential candidate, and the reply was "He'll be all right," that response could be interpreted as coming from a nonthinking voter who was passively following a media report about the thinking of others. But the same response could also be interpreted as an indication of a complex ability to come to grips with the available choices, with issue concerns that cannot be satisfied simultaneously, and with the compromises considered necessary to reach consensus with other people. Similarly, if the same voter were asked a few weeks later what he or she thought about Gary Hart and the reply was "He's just what we need," the response could be interpreted to mean that this voter was simply following the media-reported bandwagon. On the other hand, it could be interpreted to mean that reported changes in public expectations had brought other attitudes and concerns forward in the voter's mind. As this example suggests, the information voters use depends on the reasoning they do, and the reasoning they do depends in part on their expectations. It also indicates that the way in which the content of a voter's response is interpreted depends on a theory about how voters use information and make choices. And I am convinced that any such theory must account for the "working attitudes" of voters—the combinations of feeling, thought, and information they bring to bear when they make their choices at the polls.

Why Campaigns Matter

Changes in government, in society, and in the role of the mass media in politics have made campaigns more important today than they were fifty years ago, when modern studies of them began. Campaign communications make connections between politics and benefits that are of concern to the voter; they offer cognitive focal points, symbolic "smoking guns," and thus make voters more aware of the costs of misperception. Campaigns attempt to achieve a common focus, to make one question and one cleavage paramount in voters' minds. They try to develop a message for a general audience, a call that will reach beyond the "disinterested interest" of the highly attentive, on one hand, and the narrow interests of issue publics, on the other. Each campaign attempts to organize the many cleavages within the electorate by setting the political agenda in the way most favorable to its own candidates. . . .

The spread of education has both broadened and segmented the electorate. Educated voters pay more attention to national and international issues and they are now connected in many more electronic communities—groups of people who have important identifications maintained through media rather than direct, personal contact. There are also today more government programs— Medicare, Social Security, welfare, and farm supports are obvious examples— that have a direct impact on certain groups, which become issue publics. Other issue publics include coalitions organized around policies toward specific countries, such as Israel or Cuba; various conservation and environmental groups; and groups concerned with social issues, such as abortion and gun control. Furthermore, there are now a great many more communications channels with which these people can keep in touch with those outside their immediate neighborhoods or communities. Such extended groups are not new, and modern communications technology is not necessary to mobilize them, as the abolitionist and temperance movements remind us; but the channels to mobilize such groups are more available today, and I believe that the groups they have nurtured are more numerous. When the national political conventions were first telecast in 1952, all three networks showed the same picture at the same time because there was only one national microwave relay; today, with the proliferation of cable systems and satellite relays, television and VCRs can now show over a hundred channels. Furthermore, as channels and options have proliferated, and as commuting time has increased and two-career families become more common, the proportion of people watching mainstream networks and network news is also dropping.

Over the past fifty years, as surveys have become increasingly available to study public opinion, there have been many gains in knowledge about voting and elections. There have also been losses, as national surveys have replaced the detailed community orientation of the original Columbia studies. We know much more about individuals and much less about extended networks, and we have not adequately examined the implications for society and campaigning of the transitions from face-to-face to electronic communities.

Both primaries and the growth of media communication have increased the amount of exposure people get to individual candidates, particularly the quantity of personal information they get about the candidates. This increases the importance of campaigns because it gives voters more opportunities to abandon views based on party default values in favor of views based on candidate information, and also more opportunities to shift from views based on a candidate's record to views based on his or her campaign image. Moreover, as primaries have expanded, parties have had to deal with the additional task of closing ranks after the campaign has pitted factions within the party against each other. Primaries have also changed the meaning of political party conventions. Conventions no longer deliberate and choose candidates; instead, they present the electorate with important cues about the social composition of the candidate's coalition and about the candidate's political history and relations with the rest of the party. The more primaries divide parties, the more cues are needed to reunite parties and remind supporters of losing candidates about their differences with the other party.

The Implications of Shortcuts

Recognizing the role of low-information rationality in voting behavior has important implications for how we measure and study attitudes, how we evaluate the effects of education, and how we evaluate electoral reforms. To begin with, we must acknowledge that the ambivalence, inconsistency, and changes in preference that can be observed among voters are not the result of limited information. They exist because as human beings we can never use all of what we know at any one time. We can be as ambivalent when we have a lot of information and concern as when we have little information and limited concern. Nor do inconsistency, ambivalence, and change result from a lack of education (especially civic education) or a lack of political interest. Ambivalence is simply an immutable fact of life. Economists and psychologists have had to deal with the inconsistencies people demonstrate in cognitive experiments on framing and choice: preference reversals and attitude changes can no longer be attributed to a lack of information, a lack of concern, a lack of attention, low stakes, or the existence of "non-attitudes."

The use of information shortcuts is likewise an inescapable fact of life, and will occur no matter how educated we are, how much information we have, and how much thinking we do. Professionals weighing résumés and past accomplishments against personal interviews, or choosing from an array of diverse objects, have the same problems and use the same shortcuts as voters choosing presidents. What we have called Gresham's law of information—that new and personal information, being easier to use, tends to drive old and impersonal political information out of circulation—applies not only to the inattentive and the uneducated but to all of us. We must therefore stop considering shortcuts pejoratively, as the last refuge of citizens who are uneducated, lacking in the political experience and expertise of their "betters," or cynically content to be freeloaders in our democracy.

Drunkard's Searches and information shortcuts provide an invaluable part of our knowledge and must therefore be considered along with textbook knowledge in evaluating any decision-making process. As Abraham Kaplan has noted, the Drunkard's Search—metaphorically, looking for the lost keys under the nearest streetlight—seems bothersome because of the assumption that we should begin any search rationally, in the most likely places rather than in those that are the best lit and nearest to hand. He adds, "But the joke may be on us. It may be sensible to look first in an unlikely place just *because* 'it's lighter there.' ... The optimal pattern of search does not simply mirror the pattern of probability density of what we seek. We accept the hypothesis that a thing sought is in a certain place because we remember having seen it there, or because it is usually in places of that kind, or for like reasons. But ... we look in a certain place for additional reasons: we happen to be in the place already, others are looking elsewhere." At least when people look under the streetlight, they will almost certainly find their keys if they are there; if they look by the car, in the dark, they are far less likely to find them even if they are there.

... [W]e should keep in mind the main features about how voters obtain information and reason about their political choices. The Drunkard's Search is an aid to calculation as well as an information shortcut. By telling us where to look, it also tells us how to choose, how to use easily obtained information in making comparisons and choices. As long as this is how we search and choose, people will neither have nor desire all the information about their government that theorists and reformers want them to have.

The faith that increased education would lead to higher levels of textbook knowledge about government, and that this knowledge in turn would enable the electorate to measure up to its role in democratic theory, was misplaced. Education doesn't change *how* we think. Education broadens the voter, because educated voters pay attention to more problems and are more sensitive to connections between their lives and national and international events. However, educated voters still *sample* the news, and they still rely on shortcuts and calculation aids in assessing information, assembling scenarios, and making their choices. Further, an educated, broadened electorate is a more diffuse electorate, an electorate segmented by the very abundance of its concerns. Such an electorate will be harder to form into coalitions. The more divided an electorate, the more time and communication it takes to assemble people around a single cleavage.

Since all citizens sample the news and use shortcuts, they must be judged in part by the quality of the "fire alarms" to which they respond. They must be judged in part by *who* they know and respond to, not simply by *what* they know. Furthermore, this use of fire alarms has an important implication. Since people can only respond to the fire alarms they hear, it matters how the fire alarms to which they are exposed are chosen. If it matters whether the responses to a policy or crisis are mediated electronically by Jesse Jackson and Jesse Helms, or by Bill Bradley and Robert Dole, then attention must be given to how the mediators are chosen by the networks.

11-2

Promises and Persuasion

L. Sandy Maisel

The nature of modern campaigns makes them a primary source of Americans' frustration about politics. Distortion and disrespect are common features of campaign advertising. In this essay, L. Sandy Maisel, a political scientist and former candidate for Congress, outlines his views on the ethical standards that candidates and their campaign organizations should follow. While acknowledging that shades of gray exist in campaign practices, Maisel argues that we need to demand higher ethical standards from candidates for public office. Codes of conduct for campaigns can be helpful, but ultimately the public must hold candidates personally accountable for unethical practices.

THE IDEALIST WOULD respond to the original subtitle of this chapter—The Twin Dilemmas of Campaign Ethics—simply: "At last someone is talking about ethics in campaigns. It's about time!" The cynic would respond: *"Candidate ethics* is an oxymoron. Campaigns are all about being unethical; everyone knows that!" The pragmatist would respond: "Here we go again. Candidate ethics are all well and good in theory, but they can never work in practice!" ...

This chapter is written by a student of politics, one who has observed campaigns for more than three decades and one who has been involved in a number of different campaigns—as candidate, as campaign staffer, as political commentator. To be sure, I am a pragmatist, and I have my cynical side. But I am also an idealist. I think campaigns can be made better from an ethical perspective, within either the civic responsibility or the self-interest conception of that term, but only after difficult questions are asked and answered. This chapter is an attempt to lay out some of those questions and to suggest some answers.

I start from one basic assumption: *Candidates for public office are generally ethical individuals.* They seek public office in order to advance policies that they believe will benefit the polity as a whole. To be sure, they have personal goals—to advance their own careers, to obtain benefits for their communities, to reset societal directions they feel those in office have imposed on our society in error—but generally

Source: Candice J. Nelson, David A. Dulio, and Stephen Medvic, eds., *Shades of Gray: Perspectives on Campaign Ethics* (Washington, D.C.: Brookings Institution Press, 2002), 39–59. Notes and bibliographic references appearing in the original have been deleted.

they want to "do good." I do not deny that on occasion an individual enters or uses politics for personal gain, but those individuals are the rare exception, the rotten apples that in many ways do spoil the barrel. They sully the reputation of thousands of others from whose good efforts our country has benefited.

The argument in this chapter also depends on a second assumption: *Most candidates do not give a great deal of thought to ethical considerations before they enter a campaign, and many campaign decisions are made without explicit discussion of the ethical considerations involved.* Candidates want to win office; they believe that they are better suited for office than the individuals they oppose; they believe that their views of appropriate public policy will lead to a better future than the alternatives their opponents propose. And they run for office for those reasons. Their opponent is unqualified. The country will be better off if their party is in power. Their community will be better served if they and their party set the agenda for the city, state, or nation.

If the motives are not always totally pure, they are not badly tainted. Politics is about power. Ambition is needed to get ahead. Partisanship is central to the electoral process. But power, ambition, and partisanship are used primarily to forward a vision of the future. The campaign is an effort to convince the citizens that one individual's vision, one party's sense of direction, is preferable to those of another individual or another party.

Ethical Problems in Modern Campaigning

A corollary of these two assumptions is that ethical problems in campaigns sneak in unexamined. And the logical question to pursue is: What is the nature of the ethical problems about which we worry? . . . What is it about campaigns and the roles of candidates that make certain kinds of actions unethical?

The cynic's response to this chapter's original subtitle is instructive. One cannot use *ethics* and *campaigning* in the same phrase without an inherent contradiction. Our citizens expect the worst of our candidates. The assumption is that candidates will say anything and do anything in order to get elected. Every political observer can point to practices considered unethical—questionable advertisements, unsubstantiated accusations, misleading telephone calls, venomous personal attacks, unfulfilled promises. Examples are given that are really code words—the girl with the daisy; Willie Horton; Helms-Gantt; a secret plan to end the Vietnam War.

Let us look at each of these for a moment. In the 1964 presidential campaign, the Democrats ran an ad—just once, as is often pointed out—implying that the Republican candidate, Barry Goldwater, would use nuclear weapons without due care for the enormity of such an act. The advertisement—showing a little girl counting daisy petals as she picked them off a stem while a voice-over gave the countdown to a nuclear explosion—was deemed as having gone too far to make the point. The scare tactics were considered beyond some acknowledged but unspecified limit. Verdict: The Democrats had made an unethical use of advertising. Result: The Democratic campaign, the candidate for whom the ad was made, and the firm making the ad were widely criticized, and the ad was quickly withdrawn.

In the 1988 presidential campaign the Republicans attacked the gubernatorial record of Democratic candidate Michael Dukakis. As governor of Massachusetts, Dukakis had been responsible for a prisoner furlough program for those not eligible for parole. One of the black prisoners on furlough, Willie Horton, committed a murder. The ad used by the Republicans showed a revolving prison door with convicts leaving, seemingly at will. The implication was that the program was a failure, that Dukakis was responsible for that failure, and that he would be equally inept as president of the United States. Verdict: There was no consensus on an ethical standard. Result: The ad ran its course, the Democrats cried foul and claimed that the ad sought to inspire racial fear, but the Republicans did not back down.

In 1990 North Carolina senator Jesse Helms, seeking reelection to a fourth term, was opposed by Harvey Gantt, the African American mayor of Charlotte. In what was at the time the most expensive Senate campaign in history, Helms, who trailed in early polls, viciously attacked Gantt, drawing out the racial and sexual prejudices of his constituents. In one such attack, Helms stated that Gantt was campaigning in out-of-state gay communities in order to raise campaign funds. In another he misrepresented Gantt's views of abortion. And in a particularly egregious example, he played on racial prejudice in an ad that showed a white pair of hands crumpling a job rejection letter. The voice-over said that "you" lost the job because of racial quotas that Harvey Gantt says are fair. The ad clearly implied that whites had to fear the election of a black senator. Verdict: Helms's tactics were roundly criticized as unethical. Result: Helms narrowly won the race, his campaign unethical but successful.

Finally, during the 1968 Republican primaries, former vice president Richard Nixon implied that he had a secret plan to bring about peace in Vietnam. While he never said explicitly that he had such a plan in place, Nixon implied as much by refusing to answer questions about it on the grounds he should not reveal in advance a bargaining position he would use if elected. The secret plan never materialized; in fact, it had never existed. Verdict: The public should be aware of campaign promises; it might not be ethical to make promises one has no intention of keeping, but it certainly is a common practice of successful politicians.

Result: Nixon won the election and the war dragged on, despite the American public's fervent wish for peace.

The ethical problem, then, involves what our campaigns have become and what we expect of those campaigns. The public expects exaggeration, innuendo, broken promises, whatever tactics are necessary to win. I do not believe that Lyndon Johnson or George H. W. Bush or Richard Nixon or even Jesse Helms went into a campaign thinking that they or their operatives would act unethically. I do not believe that they ever debated the ethics of the question. Evidence indicates that the Johnson campaign was surprised by the response to the daisy commercial; they withdrew the ad quickly in light of the negative response. Nixon made his statement on Vietnam to distinguish himself from his fellow Republican contestants for the party nomination and to demonstrate his criticism of the Democrats' war policy. George H. W. Bush thought that Dukakis was vulnerable on the crime issue and sought to exploit his differences with the Massachusetts governor on that spectrum of issues. Helms had a very different vision of America from Gantt's; I believe he genuinely (but wrongly) feared the consequences for North Carolina of a Gantt victory. Thus he fought by whatever means he could to whip up the enthusiasm of his followers. In my view—and I think in the eyes of most objective observers—serious ethical questions are legitimately raised in each of these situations. But they were not raised by the participants at the time.

The Democratic Principles behind the Electoral Process

Ethical questions are raised if an action violates accepted mores for action in a society; ethical principles should apply in virtually any context, including political campaigns. But Dennis Thompson notes that there are often conflicts between ethical behavior, which is inherently individual-based, and political behavior, when an individual is working with others and often acting on behalf of others. Political ethics, according to Thompson, "joins ethics and politics without supposing that it can eliminate the conflict between them." . . .

To demonstrate this point, let us return to the example of Richard Nixon's secret plan to end the war. And let us apply some assumptions that may or may not be true. First, let us assume that no secret plan in fact existed (an assumption that conforms with known facts). Second, let us assume that Nixon needed to distinguish himself from his Republican opponents and also from the Democrats in order to be elected (also conforming with known facts). Third, let us assume that Nixon believed that the Democrats had no plans for either winning or ending the Vietnam crisis and that the military had lost all faith in Democratic leadership (a hypothetical assumption with no basis in known facts). Fourth, let us assume that this country's most powerful enemies were poised to take advantage of significant vulnerabilities caused by our involvement in the Vietnam quagmire and that they were only waiting for a Democratic victory and the extension of the war that would follow to exploit our weaknesses (another hypothetical assumption without factual basis). Under those circumstances, Nixon decided that he had to lie to the American people in order to preserve the nation. He violated one ethical principle—that one should not lie—in order to prevent extreme harm to the country.

If those assumptions were accurate, should Nixon's unethical act be considered appropriate? Would he not have been more wrong to allow harmful consequences without taking any action? It is not difficult to pose similar hypothetical situations, but they are just that—hypothetical. And it is frequently easy to rationalize unethical behavior if one assumes the worst consequences of not taking that action. What is more difficult, but also necessary, is to set standards of political ethics against which to judge individual behavior.

To begin to propose these standards, we return to basic democratic theory. ... We hold elections in order to choose those who are to govern. We hold frequent elections in order to hold those whom we have elected accountable for their actions. We have campaigns so that citizens can judge the record of those in office against the prospects of what would be done by those seeking office. The question of why we have campaigns is at the center of the discussion of what ethical standards should be applied to candidates for office. In the simplest terms, candidates should act in such a way that allows the electoral system to operate as it should within the framework of our polity. Further, they should be compelled to act in a manner that does no harm to the polity as a whole.

Our concern, therefore, is about actions that do not allow citizens to make informed judgments. Return to the Nixon example above. Under the hypothetical assumptions, Nixon's action would not be considered ethical unless he knew somehow that the citizenry would choose his solution with its consequences over the Democrats' course of action with the consequences that would follow from that. We assumed such dire consequences that one might also conclude that Nixon would know that, but situations in politics are rarely so black and white. And the difficulty is in the shades of gray.

Most of those running for office honestly believe that the country or state or city would be better off if they were in office than if their opponent won. Even most cynics would grant that assumption. But candidates cannot act to achieve that end if their actions deny the citizenry the information needed to reach that same conclusion. That is, the campaigns must be open and honest about what a candidate stands for and what the opponent stands for—and then the voters can decide. Candidates cannot act in such a way as to deny the voters information to make their decision without violating the very reason we have elections.

But that minimalist answer will not suffice. Campaigns and elections give legitimacy to our representative democracy. Candidates cannot act in such a manner as to undermine that legitimacy. If citizens do not believe in the sanctity of the electoral process, if they do not believe that their views are really determinative, if they believe that the entire process is corrupt, then that basic sense of legitimacy is lost and the critical connection between those who govern and the governed so necessary for a representative democracy is also lost. If the views of the cynic are prevalent, if most citizens believe that the process is basically corrupt, if the common view is that all politicians act unethically so why bother to vote, then our democracy is in jeopardy. And those politicians who have acted in a manner to encourage those views have violated the basic principles of political ethics.

Candidates for office thus must navigate along a narrow path. They want to win and feel that their victory is important. Thus they should campaign vigorously, make their best case, appeal to as many voters as possible, and demonstrate to those voters why electing them is preferable to electing their opponents. But they must do so in such a way that the process remains unscathed, that the citizens in fact can decide, and that the citizens understand their power so that they want to decide. In the remaining sections of this chapter we will look at two aspects of campaigns in which, whether they acknowledge it or not, candidates confront ethical dilemmas—the promises they make and the means they use to persuade voters to support them.

Promises: What Should Candidates Promise to Do if Elected?

If the purpose of a campaign is for the candidates to state to the citizenry what they will do if elected, so that voters can decide between alternative policy agendas, then the content of campaign promises is critical to the electoral process. Candidates realize this and work hard to propose policies that will appeal to the electorate. They want to put their best foot forward, to talk about those issues that will convince the electorate to support them. That is as it should be.

However, making campaign promises that appeal to the voters can be too easy. The ethical problem arises if candidates make proposals that are not possible or not genuine in order to win an election. Certainly, the first amendment to the Constitution, if it does nothing else, guarantees those involved in politics the right to say what they please. We are not talking about regulations of what can be said, what can be promised. But we are talking about what is ethical for a candidate to promise.

We should start with the easiest aspects of campaign promises. It is appropriate, beyond ethical question—and, in fact, necessary if campaigns are to serve the function they are designed to serve in a representative democracy—for candidates to state what they favor as policy alternatives and how they would implement those policies. "If I am elected, I will introduce legislation to outlaw practice X, and I will work as hard as I can to achieve passage of that legislation." The candidate's goal is clear; the candidate's actions if elected are clear. The candidate does not make promises that cannot be kept, and the voter can evaluate both the proposed policy and the candidate's likely chances for success.

Now take the next step. What if the candidate states his or her position on a policy and promises action. "If I am elected, I will introduce legislation to outlaw practice X, and I will see that that legislation is passed." The difference between these two promises might seem a small one, but it is important. In the second case, the candidate can guarantee the first part of what is promised but is powerless to achieve the second. How can an individual legislator—or even a president or governor—"see that legislation is passed"? No one official in our system of government has that power. Is it ethical to make that promise?

What is the ethical tenet that is violated? Put simply, the candidate lied. Lying is unethical; we could not successfully live in a society in which people routinely lied, and no one could accept the word of a fellow citizen as truthful. But "lying" is not a unidimensional concept. Some lies are clearly more serious than others. How seriously should we take candidate lies during a campaign? Do lies like the one in the second statement of campaign promises violate our society's sense of appropriate behavior?

A lie is a statement that conveys a false impression. . . . Truth is not so important as truthfulness; that is, [the] concern about lying is with the intent of the person promulgating the lie, not with the absolute truth of the statement. In addition, . . . a statement must also be viewed from the perspective of the person to whom that statement is directed. A statement is deceptive and action is unethical if the person making the statement knows that statement to be false and intends for the listener to accept it as true.

We can go further in differentiating among campaign promises that are not entirely truthful. Are there untruthful campaign promises that are the equivalent of "white lies," slight exaggerations of the truth that do no harm? I think that there are. A candidate for Congress says that she will come home to the district every weekend in order to stay in touch but knows that at times the House is in session on a weekend, such a trip will be impossible. Her statement was not truthful, but the point of the promise was to demonstrate that the candidate would not lose touch with the people who sent her to Washington. Those who heard the statement understood its intent. No harm, no foul.

Many candidates make promises during campaigns that they honestly believe to be true, but that are in fact not true. "If I am elected to the Senate, I will contribute to the Democratic majority, and we will prevent the president from fundamentally changing the ideological composition of the Supreme Court." The candidate might well have believed that his election would swing the Senate in his party's direction. But, lo and behold, it did not. The campaign statement was not true, but the candidate was not being deceptive. He was clear to the voters about his position (on Supreme Court nominations), his desired outcome (no change in the ideological composition of the Court), and his potential role in it (working with his party to halt undesirable presidential nominations). He was wrong about which party would control the Senate and thus about his ability to achieve his goal. In this case, no deception, no foul.

A third level of lying involves clear deception. The candidate knows that what he says is not true, and the reason he says it is to convince the voters to support him. Candidates cross the line of ethical behavior in two possible ways. First, if they make statements they do not really believe. If a candidate for the U.S. Senate says that he will not use a litmus test of an individual's position on abortion in weighing whether to confirm a nominee for a judicial post, and if that Senate candidate knows that he would never support a nominee who does not favor a woman's right to choose (or one who does), that candidate has intentionally deceived the voters with the goal of convincing them that he stands for or against a policy when he in fact feels the opposite. The candidate's action is clearly unethical.

But some actions are not that clear-cut. Candidates also cross into unethical territory if they try to convince voters to favor their candidacy with promises that they know or come to believe to be false. If a candidate questions the validity of her own statement, she should not make that statement or she should retract it. "If I am elected governor, I will improve the quality of education in our state's schools, from the elementary level to our state university." Fair enough— the candidate wants better education for citizens of the state. But then she meets with her advisers on educational matters and comes to understand the complexity of the problem facing the state's university. She wants a better university, but she is not willing to commit the time or money necessary to make significant changes in the short run. The candidate owes it to the people to discuss what she really can and cannot do. The problem here is not lack of good intentions, but rather exaggeration of what can be done. Like the guarantee that the candidate discussed above would "see to it that legislation is passed," this candidate undermines the electoral system by giving citizens reasons to be cynical.

Two decades ago Morris Fiorina wrote an eloquent defense of why rational citizens should vote retrospectively (based on a candidate's or a party's past performance) rather than prospectively (based on their promises of future action).

Essentially, he argued that voting prospectively is more costly and less rational—it is more difficult to evaluate the worth of promises than to judge past performance, and what evidence is there that candidates keep their promises in any case? One need not be a cynic to claim that politicians make promises that they cannot keep. We as a nation expect that most promises will not be kept. To the extent that this is so, candidates act unethically by undermining the system that is at the theoretical heart of representative democracy.

Is there an ethical lesson to be learned from this discussion of various types of campaign promises and of various types of lies? Is there an ethical principle that candidates should seek to follow? I think there is. At the most obvious level, candidates should not speak falsely; they should not equivocate on key issues. They should be called to task by objective observers, not just by their opponents, if they are professing positions in a campaign that are popular with the voters but opposite of those they have taken earlier in their careers and are likely to take again if elected.

But more than that, candidates should be held accountable for their promises and for the ways in which they express those promises. We should praise candidates for the specificity of their promises and for making promises that they have the capability to fulfill if elected. We should criticize those who word promises vaguely, whose pledges lack specificity, who choose words carefully to cloud issues, not to clarify them. The democratic process cannot function if citizens paying attention to a campaign still do not know what a candidate intends to do and will be capable of doing when elected. The responsibility lies with the candidates (and those who report on candidate campaigns) more than it does with the electorate, for the voters are only able to process what is given to them. In an important sense, candidates who do not live up to this responsibility are not acting ethically because they undermine the legitimacy of the representative system in which they seek to serve.

Persuasion: How Can Candidates Contrast Their Records with Their Opponents'?

Political campaigns are not softball. Candidates do not simply say, "I'm a good guy, so vote for me!" The whole point of campaigns is to convince the electorate that one candidate and policies are better than the other candidate and policies. One way to do that is through campaign platforms and campaign promises. The other way to do that is by campaigning *against* your opponent. While ethical considerations should be raised about promises made, most ethical concerns deal with what is said about the other candidate.

Negative Advertising: Comparisons or Attacks

Saying something about one's opponent is not necessarily a bad thing to do. Many candidates talk frequently about their opponents. Some even praise them for what they have done, for their distinguished service, for their dedication to the public. But then they have to give the voters a reason to reject this upstanding public servant in favor of someone else.

The generic term often applied to candidate efforts to make their case over their opponent's is *negative campaigning* or *negative advertising*. The latter is a misused and poorly conceived term. First of all, much of what is said about an opponent is not said in advertising. It is said on the stump, in debates, in media interviews. So the use of the word *advertising* overstates the importance of that one way of campaigning. But it is more important to note that a difference exists between *comparative appeals* and *attacks*. Comparative appeals stress that one should favor one candidate over another because of differences that can be objectively observed—between their records, their experiences, their platforms, and so on. Attack appeals seek to undermine the opponent, to create a negative image about the individual or what consequences would follow from that person's election. Comparative appeals differ from attacks in tone and content; either can deal with policy differences between the candidates or with personal matters. I argue below that comparative appeals are appropriate and in fact central to the electoral process; on the contrary, attacks cross the line into unethical behavior.

Policy Differences

What could be more basic to the electoral process than one candidate comparing his stands on the issues to those of his opponent? That is the essence of comparative campaigning. That kind of comparison is how voters know what to expect when a candidate becomes an officeholder. That type of campaigning allows voters to hold officeholders accountable for prior actions. There is no ethical problem involved in straightforward comparisons of voting records or of policy differences as they have been expressed in campaign promises. In fact, . . . this type of negative campaigning "provides voters with a lot of valuable information they definitely need to have when deciding how to cast their ballots." One could even argue that a candidate has an obligation to make appropriate comparisons to give the voters the data they need to make informed choices.

However, differences that are presented as stark by one candidate may be seen as nuanced by another. Votes that one candidate says reflect certain ideological positions might be interpreted differently by his opponent. Campaigning is about politics, about gaining an advantage, not about civics lessons. Any campaign manager worth her pay will present comparisons that put her candidate in the most favorable light. The ways in which comparisons are made, in which policy differences are presented to the electorate, can in fact raise serious ethical questions. The questions raised are of two types: the accuracy not only of the information posed but also of the implications one intends the listener to draw from that information by the way it is presented; and who is sponsoring an advertisement and what the responsibility of the candidate favored in an ad is, if the ad itself is questionable. We will deal with these separately.

In recent years various media outlets, in virtually every corner of the country, have begun airing or printing "ad watch" segments in which journalists assess the accuracy of the claims made in political advertisements. This development is clearly beneficial and has resulted in campaign after campaign literally footnoting claims made in their advertisements. If a candidate is involved in outright lying, he stands a good chance of exposure; most campaigns are careful on this point.

But political campaigns run against those with long voting records have a real advantage if they intend to "go negative." It is almost always possible to find an example of a vote cast by an officeholder that can be interpreted in a number of different ways. A congressman casts a vote against a large raise in the minimum wage because he knows that a bill with that number in it will fail while one with a slightly lower raise will pass. An opponent reports that the congressman cast a vote against raising the minimum wage to the higher level, implying that the vote was antilabor. Is that advertisement strictly accurate? Yes. Is it truthful? No. The opponent knew or should have known why the incumbent cast the vote that he did. Context is crucial in voting in any legislative body that relies on compromise and negotiation to reach results that approximate an optimal outcome. The opponent implied other motivations, knowing they were false. As with lying about campaign promises, the intent of the person making the claim is the relevant factor. One cannot legislate against such practices, but they are clearly unethical.

But this issue is even more complex. Political ads are all about tone and image as well as content. Let us look at two examples. First, when Leon Panetta (D) first ran for the U.S. House of Representatives in 1976, his opponent was the incumbent, Burt Talcott (R), who presented himself as a hardworking fourteen-year veteran. In point of fact, Talcott had missed about half the votes in his principal House committee. Panetta was certainly justified in pointing out that his opponent was less than honest in his claim, that he was in fact an absentee representative much of the time. But one of Panetta's own campaign workers wondered if they "were wrong to point that out in a spot with arresting music and dramatic close ups of an empty chair." If the candidate or his staff raises these questions themselves, [the questions] are clearly meat for a discussion of ethical considerations.

Mitch McConnell's (R) 1984 Senate campaign in Kentucky against incumbent Walter "Dee" Huddleston (D) featured one of the most effective (and funniest) ads in the history of modern television campaigning. McConnell's ad mentioned a series of votes in the Senate that Huddleston had missed, all accurately documented. The visual was a pack of bloodhounds roaming over the Capitol grounds in search of Huddleston, with the voice-over asking, "Where's Senator Huddleston?" The ad effectively portrayed Huddleston as a deadbeat who was not doing his job; the image stuck, and McConnell won. The ad was given a great deal of credit for that victory. The problem is that Huddleston had over a 90 percent voting participation record during his Senate career. McConnell's staff surely knew that. McConnell has expressed no qualms about his tactics. Should he? Again, no one questions McConnell's right to have run this advertisement, nor were the specific claims in the advertisement inaccurate. But the implication was inaccurate—and the intent of the ad was to create the implication. It is difficult to imagine a definition of ethical behavior that would incorporate deliberate distortion of a record in order to deceive the voters.

The issue becomes somewhat murkier when it is not a candidate but rather a surrogate for a candidate who is sponsoring the offensive advertisement or carrying on a campaign that is ethically questionable. During the 1996 congressional elections, questionable negative campaigns run by surrogates dominated the political landscape. The AFL-CIO ran a $35 million advertising campaign directed against sixty-four Republican incumbents deemed to be vulnerable. The generic ads, which merely plugged in the incumbent's name and picture for a specific district, noted that the minimum wage had remained the same for five years while corporate profits and executive salaries had both increased dramatically. The ad stated that the viewer should send a message to Congressman X, never mentioning the name of the Democrat.

In the same year the Republican National Committee and the National Republican Senatorial Committee joined together to produce and sponsor generic ads criticizing incumbent Democratic senators in five states. These ads dubbed the incumbents as liberals who favored increasing taxes on working families while they raised their own salaries and voted for wasteful programs. The Republican candidates in those races did not openly state that the incumbents were against "workfare" and in favor of wasteful programs, but they all referred to the implications in the ads as if they were factual.

These examples are not unique. Surrogate campaigning has become one of the principal tools of election efforts in recent years. The two national party committees (the Democratic National Committee and the Republican National Committee) and their Hill committees (the Democratic Senatorial Campaign Committee, the National Republican Senatorial Committee, the Democratic Congressional

Campaign Committee, and the National Republican Congressional Committee), labor and business groups, and single-issue advocacy groups of all kinds take on incumbents without coordinating their efforts with the candidate they support. They operate within the limits of the campaign finance laws as they are currently written and interpreted, but that does not absolve either these groups or the candidates they favor of acknowledging ethical considerations.

Distortion of a candidate's record or position on issues, campaigning by innuendo, and intentional deceit may all have proven to be successful in the campaign context, but that does not make them acceptable from an ethical point of view. It is difficult—if not impossible—to draw a line precisely. Again, the intent of the person making the appeal is the relevant variable. But a system that accepts unfettered actions deemed clearly detrimental to the process as a whole because legal language cannot be found to draw what are obviously fuzzy lines contains within it the seeds of its own destruction. And those who participate in such a system have an ethical obligation, within the framework of ethics concerned with civic responsibility, to observe self-restraint in order to preserve the democratic process.

Personal Attacks

If ethical questions are raised about questionable campaign appeals that deal with policy positions or a candidate's record of service, even more serious questions are raised about negative campaigning that involves personal attacks on a candidate. The basic ethical dilemma in this instance is whether politicians' private lives are relevant to their ability to represent the public and to exercise their official duties. . . .

Intimate details of a candidate's life—or of the lives of his family—should under normal circumstances remain protected. The public does not necessarily have the right to know everything about an individual just because that individual seeks public office. However, the candidate does forfeit some degree of privacy. . . .

How can those boundaries be delineated? Richard Scher is among those who believe that truth is the only factor relevant in deciding whether to disclose private information about an opponent: "Calling a person a spouse abuser, if true, is not negative campaigning, as it reflects on the worthiness of the person to be given the public trust." The argument is made that any personal misconduct is relevant, because the individual seeks to represent us all. If the public really needs to judge a candidate, they need to know everything about that candidate. If the public does not think previous misbehavior is relevant, they will ignore the charges and vote based on other considerations. Therefore, no holds are barred; everything is aboveboard.

That argument fails to meet standards for ethical behavior for two reasons. First, individuals do have a zone of privacy that demands respect. If an action represents a youthful indiscretion, if the behavior is that of a family member who is not seeking office (but will be hurt by its revelation), if the incident in question is a private matter that does not bear on official duties, that zone of privacy should be maintained, and those who violate it should be accountable for their actions. What is their motive? Is it truly to guard the public from representation by unfit individuals or is it to further their own careers?

Second, the argument that all should be revealed disregards the impact on the polity. If the nature of campaigning is merely to discredit the character of one's opponent, then the result will be representation by individuals who are in fact held in low regard by the public. Evidence exists that the public responds to negative personal attacks by thinking less of both the individual attacked and the individual making the attack. No one questions the strategic impact of personal attacks, but the overall result is increased public disapproval of politicians as a group and of the political process in general. That result is detrimental to our system of government, and those whose actions lead to that result are acting unethically in undermining the very system they seek to serve.

If the "no holds barred" standard fails the ethical test, what standard should a candidate use in evaluating whether to use negative personal information about her opponent? The standard should be that of relevance. If her opponent is running a campaign based on "return to family values," then his aberrant sexual behavior or his lack of concern for his children would be relevant. If a candidate is running as "tough on crime," then efforts to help a misbehaving friend out of a legal jam would be relevant. But if a candidate is running on economic issues, then a five-year-old affair that he and his family have put behind them is not relevant.

Moral standards are highly personal. Candidates themselves must make the judgments about relevancy, and they must make judgments about their own motives. And it is in making these judgments that campaign ethics is involved. In the case of campaigning against an opponent based on his personal behavior in the past, candidates and their campaigns must be particularly aware of the consequences of their actions not only for their immediate campaign but for the process in which they participate. That is, not only their self-interest in winning an election is at stake; they have a responsibility to the system and the polity for the consequences of their campaign tactics as well. Candidates must ask the difficult ethical questions: Why am I doing this? Does the importance of this issue overweigh the costs I am inflicting on another person and her family? Does this issue really define the difference between me and my opponent on a criterion that the public should be using to judge us? The principle that candidates must consider involves looking beyond the campaign to ask whether they want to be the type of person who lowers the level of debate in this manner—and if they do, do they deserve to serve the public any more than their opponent? What will be the impact on the polity, on how citizens view all public officials? Rarely are candidates that introspective, and the polity suffers accordingly.

The Means of Campaigning

To this point we have discussed the messages that campaigns convey and the ethical implications of those messages. At least a word should be said about the means of campaigning. Most campaign tactics—leafleting, paid media advertising, speeches, debates, and so on—do not merit any comment; while they may be unethical under certain circumstances, normally they are not. But some techniques deserve special attention.

In recent years it has become quite common for campaigns to hire so-called "opposition research firms," political consultants charged with finding any information that might be in the public record regarding an opponent. The firms look at voting records of candidates who have previously held elective office, credit ratings, tax filings, divorce records, campaign finance reports, any and all information that can be made available to the public. Such efforts lower the level of campaigning; they are essentially looking for anything at all to exploit rather than assessing if some information on an opponent's personal life is relevant. The practice serves no positive purpose and, while certainly legal, is ethically inappropriate.

Second, and equally reprehensible, is the practice of push polling. Push polls are conducted by telephone and seek to implant doubt in the voter's mind about an opponent. "Would you be more likely to vote for or against Candidate X if you knew he had been accused of failure to pay child support?" The question does not say that the opponent has failed to pay child support, or even that he has been so accused. But the implication is there and the seed of doubt is planted. Push polls have appeared in various campaigns in recent years. Often the polling firm is an independent contractor from a different region of the country than the voters it is contacting. The organization sponsoring these polls is all but impossible to ascertain. The practice is reprehensible and should be denounced in the strongest possible terms. Candidates willing to have push polls used in their campaigns fail to meet the most rudimentary tests of ethical behavior.

Conclusions

Is it possible to set standards for candidate ethics during a campaign? Perhaps before answering this question we should point to some difficulties. First, this problem is not a new one. Candidates since the beginning of the Republic have attacked their opponents on personal grounds, criteria unrelated to the duties of the office sought. When James G. Blaine ran for president against Grover Cleveland, his campaign slogan was "Ma, Ma, where's my Pa? He's in the White House, Ha! Ha! Ha!" And the response quickly came back, "Blaine, Blaine, James G. Blaine! Continental liar from the State of Maine!" It is difficult to think of a more disingenuous campaign slogan than Woodrow Wilson's claim in 1916: "He kept us out of war!" Not for long. The examples of personal attacks and half-truths in campaigns throughout the nation's history could fill books (and have).

Furthermore, we should point out that all things are not what they seem. Should a candidate be blamed for changing his mind on an issue because circumstances have changed? Many analysts claim that George H. W. Bush lost his re-election bid in 1992 because he went back on the promise made during his acceptance speech at the 1988 Republican National Convention, "The Congress will push me to raise taxes, and I'll say no, they'll push and I'll say no, and they'll push again. And all I can say to them is: Read my lips: no new taxes." His words were clear; the context was specified; and the time between his promise and his reneging on the promise was short—eighteen months. Perhaps he deserved his fate, because he knew, or should have known, that he was making a pledge he could not keep and was courting voters based on that pledge.

But was Bush's action really so different from that of Franklin Delano Roosevelt, who pledged in a speech in Pittsburgh in 1932 that he would balance the budget if he were elected president? Upon taking office, FDR was won over to the side of Keynesian economics and the desirability of deficit spending to combat the Great Depression. When FDR asked his aides how he could justify that action in light of his campaign promise in the Pittsburgh speech, Samuel I. Rosenman reports that he replied, "Mr. President, the only thing you can say about that 1932 speech is to deny categorically that you ever made it." To be sure, there were differences. Roosevelt was spouting accepted doctrine in his Pittsburgh speech, not staking claim to a position that would distinguish him from his opponent. And evidence certainly points to the fact that he did not knowingly deceive the public; he believed what he said and had not engaged in extended debate over whether it was in fact true. But FDR did not keep his promise and was praised for his flexibility; George H. W. Bush reneged on his and was vilified. The lines are not easy to draw.

Having said that, we as a society can do better. We can expect more of our candidates; we can demand more of our candidates. And candidates should expect more of themselves. Many candidates around the country have pledged to run clean campaigns and have been successful. Those who have shunned entreaties to go negative, even at difficult times in their campaigns, are especially deserving of praise.

A number of state bar associations, including those of Pennsylvania and Delaware, have proposed codes of ethics for judicial campaigns. In Maine, the Institute of Global Ethics, the Margaret Chase Smith Library, and the Margaret Chase Smith Institute for Public Policy at the University of Southern Maine proposed a code of election ethics that has been in place since 1996 and has been signed by all candidates for congressional and statewide office in the last three election cycles.

The Maine Code of Election Ethics is based on three assumptions—that negativism and attack advertising demean representative democracy; that negative campaigns contribute to citizen cynicism, alienation, and decreasing participation; and that candidates should be responsible for their own campaigns. The code specifies that campaigns will be based on four principles: (1) honesty and fairness, including not employing surrogates to use subtle deceptions or half-truths and denouncing those who do so without the candidate's knowledge; (2) respect for one's opponent, including no use or permitting of personal attacks, innuendo, or stereotyping; (3) acceptance of responsibility by the candidate for the actions of campaign staffers and for openness and publicity in discussing issues frankly and sincerely, including any criticism of the opponent; and (4) compassion for the opponent, including recognition that a candidate's behavior in a campaign affects the integrity of the society in which the election is held.

Like most codes of ethics, this one carries no enforcement mechanisms; however, citizens are encouraged to report violations to a toll-free number. While no one who has lived in Maine during the last three election cycles would rate them as flawless, the level of negativity has seemed to decrease and the extent to which the campaigns are issue-oriented has increased. These are clearly good signs. But not many states run elections on as high a level as those in Maine are run.

In the final analysis, there is little in the Maine Code of Election Ethics, nor in any other code of ethics, that one would not hope candidates would do on their own. That is, we expect our political candidates to act ethically, to act in a manner to bring credit to the process in which they participate and to the office they seek to hold, to work to better representative democracy. Not all candidates meet these expectations. One test of the success of a civil society such as ours is the extent to which we reject those who do not meet our expectations. To date, we have not passed that test. But the fact that we are asking the questions and discussing the issues is a hopeful sign.

11-3

Party Polarization in National Politics: The Electoral Connection

Gary C. Jacobson

A popular notion among political scientists and other observers is that national politicians have become more polarized and partisan because the electorate has become more polarized. The behavior of elected officials merely reflects the differences in the parties' electoral bases. The map of the nation's congressional districts appears to confirm this supposition. It shows that Democrats win in urban areas while Republicans win in suburban and rural areas, suggesting that a cultural divide in the American electorate has produced partisan polarization among elected members of Congress. In this essay, Gary C. Jacobson describes the polarization of the electorate and Congress but observes that the partisan polarization of Congress seems to have emerged before the polarization of the electorate. He argues that leaders in Congress contributed to the polarization of public opinion.

. . . IN DECEMBER 1998 the House of Representatives voted to impeach President Bill Clinton. The vote was radically partisan: all but four Republicans voted for at least one of the four articles of impeachment, and only five Democrats voted for any of them. Grant every member's claim of a conscience vote, and it becomes all the more remarkable that 98 percent of Republican consciences dictated a vote to impeach the president, while 98 percent of Democratic consciences dictated the opposite. The Senate's verdict after the impeachment trial was only slightly less partisan. Every Democrat voted for acquittal, and 91 percent of the Republicans voted for conviction on at least one article.

Research on congressional roll call voting, notably by several authors represented in this volume, makes it clear that party line voting on the impeachment issue was not an aberration, but the culmination of a trend nearly two decades old. The proportion of partisan roll call votes and party loyalty on these votes have been increasing in both houses of Congress since the 1970s, reflecting growing ideological polarization of the congressional parties. To appreciate how dramatically the parties have diverged since the 1970s, look at Figure 1, which displays the

Source: Jon R. Bond and Richard Fleisher, eds., *Polarized Politics: Congress and the President in a Partisan Era* (Washington, D.C.: CQ Press, 2000), 9–30. Notes and bibliographical references appearing in the original have been deleted.

Figure 1. Ideological Positions on Roll-Call Votes

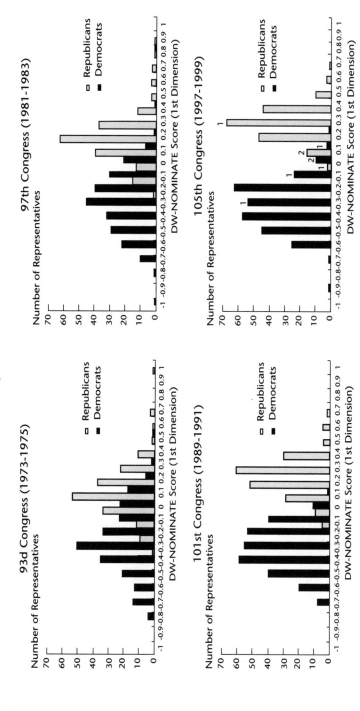

Source: Compiled by the author from Poole and Rosenthal DW-NOMINATE Scores (http://voteview.gsia.cmu.edu.dwnl.htm).

Note: The entries are frequency distributions of Republican and Democratic members of Congress on a liberal-conservative dimension based on non-unanimous roll call votes in which 1 represents the most conservative position and –1 represents the most liberal. Each bar indicates the number of representatives falling into the specified range. For example, in the 105th Congress, sixty-two Republicans had scores between .03 and .04 on the scale.

Figure 2. Difference in Median and Mean DW-NOMINATE Scores of Republicans and Democrats, 83d through 105th Congresses

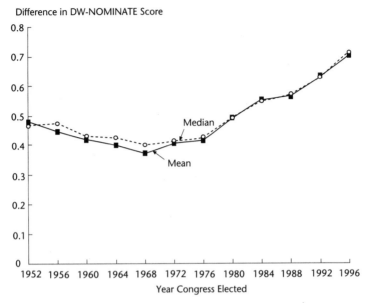

Note: The entries are the difference between the mean and the median positions on the DW-NOMINATE scale of House Republicans and Democrats in the specified Congress. The larger the difference, the farther apart the two parties are ideologically.

distribution of House members' scores on a common measure of political ideology in selected Congresses spanning the past three decades. These scores, known as dw-nominate scores, are calculated from all non-unanimous roll call votes cast from the 80th Congress through the 105th Congress. Each member's pattern of roll call votes locates him or her on a liberal-conservative dimension ranging from −1.0 (most liberal) to 1.0 (most conservative), allowing us to compare the distribution of positions along the dimension taken by Democrats and Republicans in different Congresses.

In the 93d Congress, the ideological locations of House Democrats and Republicans overlapped across the middle half of the scale, and the gap between the two parties' modal locations was comparatively small. In the 97th Congress, the overlap was a bit less extensive but still sizable. By the 101st Congress, the parties had become noticeably more polarized. The 105th Congress, which voted on Clinton's impeachment, was the most sharply polarized of all, with not a single Republican falling below zero on the scale, and only four Democrats scoring above zero.

Trends in partisan polarization in the House over a somewhat longer period are summarized in Figure 2, which displays the difference in median and mean dw-nominate scores of House Republicans and Democrats in the Congress immediately following each presidential election from 1952 through 1996. Note particularly how dramatically the gap between the parties' average ideological locations grew in the 1990s; in the 105th Congress, the parties' medians and means were more than 0.7 points apart on this 2-point scale. According to Keith Poole and Howard Rosenthal, the first dw-nominate dimension captures, in addition to liberal-conservative ideology, the primary cleavage that distinguishes the two parties, and hence the scores also serve as measures of party loyalty. From this perspective, party unity on the House impeachment vote was simply a manifestation of a broader pattern of partisan polarization highlighted by the nearly complete disappearance of conservative Democrats and liberal Republicans (although a few moderates remain in both parties). The numbers above the columns in the last panel of Figure 1 show how many members bolted their party on impeachment. Note that all but two of the nine who defected on impeachment belong to the small set of members who still have dw-nominate scores adjacent to or overlapping those of members of the opposing party.

The Republicans persisted in their attempts to impeach and remove Clinton even though every one of the myriad national polls taken from the eruption of the Monica Lewinsky scandal in January 1998 through the end of the trial in February 1999 found the public opposed to impeachment and conviction, typically by margins of about two to one. Yet the public, like Congress, was from start to finish sharply polarized on the issue. In poll after poll, a solid majority of self-identified Republicans favored Clinton's impeachment and removal, while more than 80 percent of self-identified Democrats remained opposed. In the end, 68 percent of Republicans wanted the Senate to convict and remove Clinton, while only 30 percent favored acquittal; among Democrats, 89 percent favored acquittal, while only 10 percent preferred conviction. Members of Congress may have voted their consciences, but their consciences were wonderfully in tune with the preferences of their core supporters. Congressional Republicans acted against the manifest preferences of a majority of Americans on a highly salient issue, and they may yet pay for it in the 2000 election by losing the House and—much less likely—the Senate. But they voted the way the majority of Republican voters wanted them to.

Partisan voting on impeachment thus reflected, albeit in an exaggerated and skewed fashion, sharply divided electoral constituencies. It also reflected the power of majority party leaders in the contemporary House to enforce discipline, notably on the adoption of a rule governing the impeachment bill that did not permit consideration of a censure resolution. Moderate Republicans were left with no alternative short of impeachment. These two forces—the emergence of distinct and increasingly homogenous electoral coalitions in both parties and, in consequence, the greater willingness of members to submit to party discipline—are the chief explanations that have been offered for the broader rise in party unity and ideological divergence since the 1970s. Respect for the power of the electoral connection usually concedes causal priority to electoral change. Yet voters can respond only to the options presented by the parties' candidates. If legislative parties become more dissimilar and unified as their respective electoral coalitions become more dissimilar and homogenous, it is also true that the choices offered by more polarized, unified parties encourage polarized electoral responses.

My goal in this chapter is to review the electoral changes that both underlie and reflect the more unified and divergent congressional parties of the 1990s. The story contains few surprises, but fresh observations from the most recent elections point uniformly to a near-term future that is, if anything, substantially more conducive to partisan coherence and division, intensifying conflicts not only within the legislature, but especially—under divided government—between the president and Congress.

Most of the analysis is presented graphically, for this is the most efficient way to summarize and appreciate the various interrelated trends. I begin with some observations on changes in partisanship and voting behavior since the 1970s. Next, I show how the electoral coalitions of House Democrats and Republicans have consequently diverged. The circle is completed by an examination of how patterns of roll call voting have become increasingly predictable from electoral decisions, fulfilling one major condition for responsible party government. An ironic effect of these changes may have been to make divided government even more popular, for the parties in government have polarized much more sharply than have party identifiers in the electorate.

The Growth of Partisan Coherence in the Electorate

The consensus explanation for the rise in party cohesion in Congress since the 1970s is party realignment in the South. The short version is that the civil rights revolution, particularly the Voting Rights Act of 1965, brought southern blacks into the electorate as Democrats, while moving conservative whites to abandon their ancestral allegiance to the Democratic Party in favor of the ideologically more compatible Republicans. The movement of jobs and people to the South also contributed to larger numbers of Republican voters, who gradually replaced conservative Democrats with conservative Republicans in southern House and Senate seats. The constituencies that elected the remaining Democrats became more like Democratic constituencies elsewhere, so the roll call voting of southern Democrats became more like the roll call voting of Democrats from other regions. The southern realignment left both congressional parties with more

Figure 3. The Rise of the Republican South, 1952–1998

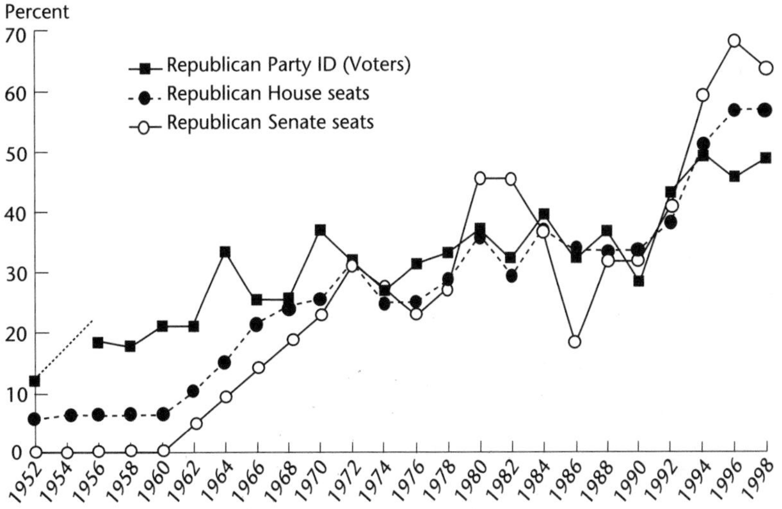

Source: National Election Studies.

politically homogeneous electoral coalitions, reducing internal disagreements and making stronger party leadership tolerable.

This analysis is certainly correct as far as it goes. The realignment of southern political loyalties and electoral habits has been thoroughly documented. Figure 3 summarizes the principal trends. As the proportion of Republicans among major party identifiers has risen, so has the share of southern House and Senate seats won by Republican candidates. Starting from almost nothing in the 1950s, Republicans now enjoy parity with the Democrats among voters and hold solid majorities of southern House and Senate seats.

Realignment in the South contributed to the increasing ideological homogeneity of the parties, but it is by no means the whole story. Other forces have also necessarily been at work, for links between ideology and party identification have grown stronger outside the South as well. Since 1972 the National Election Studies (NES) have asked respondents to place themselves on a 7-point ideological scale ranging from extremely liberal to extremely conservative. On average, nearly 80 percent of respondents who say they voted in House elections are able to locate their position on the scale. As Figure 4 shows, tau-b correlations between the voters' positions on the liberal-conservative scale and the NES's 7-point party identification scale have grown noticeably stronger since 1972 outside the South as well as within. Like other measurements of correlation, the tau-b statistic takes values from –1 (a perfect negative relationship) through 0 (no relationship) to 1 (a perfect positive relationship). In the analysis presented here

Figure 4. Correlation between Party Identification and Ideology of
House Voters, 1972–1998

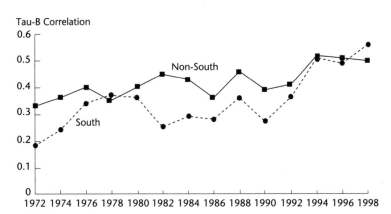

and in Figure 5, the higher the tau-b correlation, the stronger the positive relationship between party identification and the other variable of interest. The
increase was steeper for southern voters, and by 1994 they had become indistinguishable on this score from voters elsewhere.

A similar pattern of growing partisan coherence within the electorate is evident in correlations between voters' party identification and positions on several
of the NES's issue scales displayed in Figure 5. On every issue—ranging from the
government's economic role, to race, to women's role in society, to abortion policy—the overall trend is upward, with tau-b correlations reaching their highest
levels on four of the five scales in 1998. Notice that although economic issue positions are normally most strongly related to partisanship—reflecting the venera-
ble New Deal cleavage—the steepest increases have occurred on social issues.
For example, in 1980 opinions on abortion were unrelated to party identification;
now we observe a substantial correlation. In 1980 only 30 percent of voters who
opposed abortion under all circumstances identified themselves as Republicans;
by 1998, 71 percent did so.

More generally, in 1972 the voter's positions on the various scales—ideology,
jobs, aid to blacks, and women's role—predicted party identification (Republican, independent, or Democrat) with only 62 percent accuracy; in 1998 the same
four variables predicted party identification with 74 percent accuracy. Clearly, citizens now sort themselves into the appropriate party (given their ideological
leanings and positions on issues) a good deal more consistently than they did in
the 1970s, with the largest increases in consistency occurring in the 1990s. Not
surprisingly, partisan evaluations of presidential candidates, presidents, and the
parties themselves have become more divergent as well.

Figure 5. Correlation Between Party Identification and Issue Positions, House Voters, 1972–1998

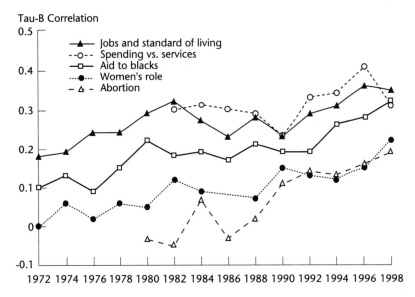

The Revival of Electoral Consistency

Both the southern realignment and growing ideological coherence of electoral coalitions have contributed to greater consistency in voting behavior. Among individual voters, party loyalty has risen and ticket splitting has diminished since the 1970s. Figures 6 and 7 display the pertinent data. Party loyalty in congressional elections declined from the 1950s through the 1970s but has subsequently rebounded, recovering about two-thirds of the decline. Party loyalty in presidential elections is trickier to measure, because some years have featured prominent independent or third party candidacies (specifically 1968, 1980, 1992, and 1996), while the rest have not. But even with Ross Perot drawing votes from both parties in 1996, 84 percent of partisans voted for their party's presidential candidate, a higher proportion than in any election from 1952 through 1980. If we consider as defectors only those who voted for the other *major* party's candidate, the rate of defection in both 1992 and 1996 was only 10 percent, the lowest of any election in the NES time series (1988 had the next lowest rate).

The trend in ticket splitting—voting for candidates of different parties on the same ballot—appears, not accidentally, as the inverse of the trend in party loyalty. Ticket splitting was relatively infrequent in the 1950s, grew more common through the 1970s, and since has declined to the levels last seen in the early 1960s.

Figure 6. Party Loyalty in Congressional Elections, 1952–1998

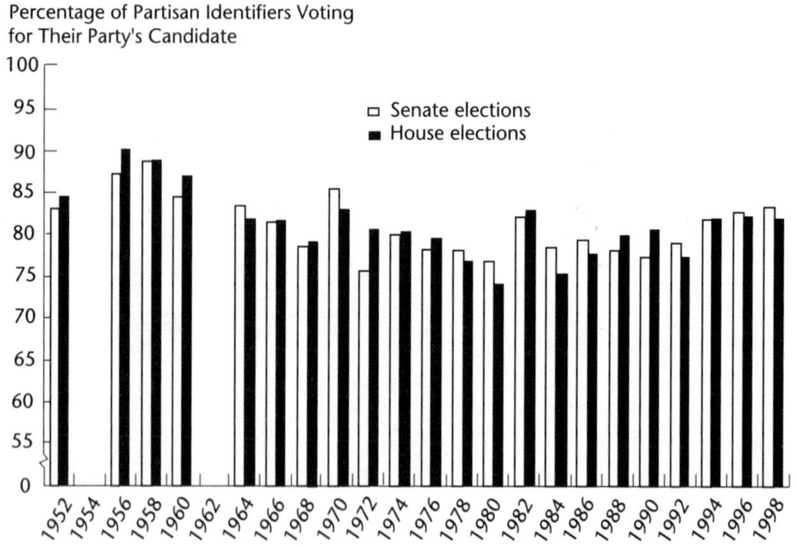

Percentage of Partisan Identifiers Voting
for Their Party's Candidate

The declines since the 1970s in partisan defections and ticket splitting are probably even greater than these NES data indicate, because both phenomena have
been artificially inflated since 1978 by changes in the wording and administration
of the vote question that produce an overreport of votes for House incumbents.

An important consequence of greater party loyalty and decreased ticket splitting is that aggregate electoral results have become more consistent across offices.
For example, the simple correlation between a party's district-level House and
presidential vote shares has risen sharply from its low point in 1972, as Figure 8
indicates. Both the decrease between 1952 and 1972 and the increase since 1972
are steepest for southern districts, but the same U-shaped trend occurs in districts
outside the South as well. By 1996 the association between House and presidential voting had rebounded to a level last seen in the 1950s (.77 in the South, .85 elsewhere, and .83 overall). Similarly, a district's presidential vote predicted which
party's candidate would win the House seat with greater accuracy in the 1990s
than at any time since the 1950s. The trend toward electoral disintegration across
offices I documented a decade ago has clearly gone into reverse since then.

Diverging Electoral Constituencies

The growth in partisan coherence, consistency, and loyalty among voters has
made the two parties' respective electoral constituencies—that is, the voters who

Figure 7. Ticket Splitting, 1952–1998

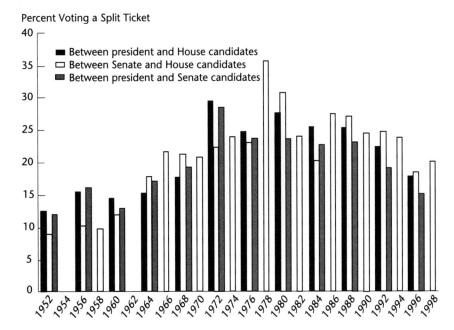

Percent Voting a Split Ticket

■ Between president and House candidates
□ Between Senate and House candidates
▨ Between president and Senate candidates

supported the party's winning candidates—politically more homogeneous and more dissimilar. It has also given the president and congressional majorities more divergent electoral constituencies when the branches are divided between the parties.

To begin with an elementary but telling example, according to NES surveys, 48 percent of the respondents who voted for members of the Democratic House majority in 1972 also voted for Richard Nixon; 36 percent of the voters supporting the Democratic House winners voted for Ronald Reagan in 1984; but only 27 percent of the voters supporting members of the Republican House majority voted for Clinton in 1996. The comparatively small proportion of shared electoral constituents was surely one source of Clinton's difficulties with the Republican congressional majority in a divided government.

More generally, the respective parties' electoral constituencies have diverged ideologically since the 1970s, with the parties' most active supporters moving the farthest apart. I measure differences in the ideological makeup of electoral constituencies by subtracting the mean ideological self-placement of NES respondents who voted for one set of winning candidates from the mean for respondents who voted for another set of winning candidates. Ideological divisions among activist constituents are gauged by repeating the analysis for respondents who reported engaging in at least two political acts in addition to voting during

Figure 8. Correlations Between District-Level House and Presidential Voting, 1952–1996

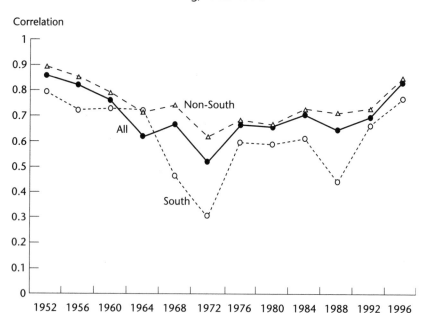

Correlation

the campaign. Figure 9 displays the changes in the ideological distinctiveness of the electoral constituencies of House Republicans and Democrats and of southern and nonsouthern Democrats since 1972.

In the 1970s the ideological differences between the two parties' electoral constituencies were modest and no wider than the gap between southern and non-southern Democrats' electoral constituencies. By the 1990s the difference between the parties' electoral constituencies had more than doubled, to about 1.2 points on the 7-point scale, and the Democrats' regional divergence had entirely disappeared. Realignment in the South again explains only part of this change, for the gap between Republican and Democratic constituencies also grew (from 0.7 to 1.1 points) outside the South. Note also that the mean ideological difference between the parties' most active electoral constituents widened even more, nearly doubling to about two points on the scale.

Figure 10 presents the equivalent data for Senate electoral constituencies, except that entries are calculated from the three surveys up to and including the year indicated on the chart, so that data from voters electing the entire Senate membership are used to calculate in each observation. The same pattern of ideological polarization between the parties' respective electoral and activist constituencies appears, although somewhat muted, reflecting the greater heterogeneity of the Senate's larger electorates.

Figure 9. Difference in Mean Ideological Self-Placement of House Activist and Electoral Constituencies, 1972–1998

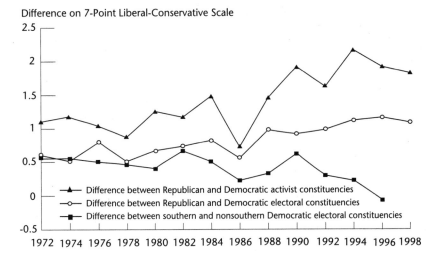

Difference on 7-Point Liberal-Conservative Scale

—▲— Difference between Republican and Democratic activist constituencies
—○— Difference between Republican and Democratic electoral constituencies
—■— Difference between southern and nonsouthern Democratic electoral constituencies

The ideological gap between the president's electoral constituency and the congressional majority's electoral constituency under conditions of divided government also has doubled. In 1972 Nixon voters were on average only 0.7 points more conservative than voters for the House Democrats elected that year. In 1996 the House Republicans' electoral constituency was 1.4 points more conservative than Bill Clinton's electoral constituency. The gap between the most active segment of each electoral constituency widened even more, from 1.3 points in 1972 to 2.2 points in 1996. An equivalent analysis of self-placement on issue positions tells the same story; on every issue dimension examined in Figure 5, the congressional parties' respective electoral coalitions are farther apart in the 1990s than they were at the beginning of the time series.

A discussion of changes in electoral coalitions would not be complete without confirming how profoundly the southern realignment has affected the demographic composition of the remaining Democratic coalition. Although it is not news, it is still worth highlighting just how dependent successful southern Democratic candidates are on African American voters. Figure 11 presents the pertinent data. For representatives, the entry is simply the proportion of all votes for the winning Democrat that were cast by black voters in each election year. For senators, it is the African American proportion of all votes for winning southern Democrats in the trio of elections culminating in the year listed. Therefore, the Senate entries indicate the proportion of African Americans in the electoral constituencies of all southern senators in the Congress following the specified election. Blacks were once a negligible part of the electoral constituencies of

Figure 10. Difference in Mean Ideological Self-Placement of Senate Activist
and Electoral Constituencies, 1976–1998

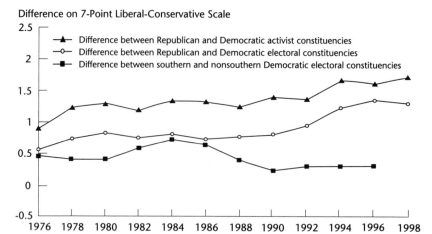

Difference on 7-Point Liberal-Conservative Scale

southern Democrats in Congress. Now they supply more than one-third of their votes. Add to this the fact that southern whites who continue to identify themselves as Democrats now share the socioeconomic profile of white Democrats elsewhere, and the nearly complete disappearance of conservative southern Democrats in Congress is no mystery at all.

Chicken or Egg?

Evidence from examination of the electorate, then, is fully consistent with the standard argument that partisan polarization in Congress reflects electoral changes that have left the parties with more homogeneous and more dissimilar electoral coalitions. When the focus of analysis is Congress, electoral change seems to be the independent variable: changes in roll call voting reflect changes in electoral coalitions. When the focus is on elections, however, it becomes apparent that causality works at least as strongly in the opposite direction: voters sort themselves out politically by responding to the alternatives represented by the two parties.

Realignment in the South *followed* the national Democratic Party's decision to champion civil rights for African Americans and the Republican Party's choice of Sen. Barry Goldwater, who voted against the Civil Rights Act of 1964, as its standard-bearer that year. Partisan divisions on the abortion issue surfaced first in Congress, then in the electorate. Electorates diverged ideologically after the parties had diverged ideologically; the divisions in Congress and among activists

Figure 11. Share of Votes for Southern Democratic Representatives and Senators Provided by African American Voters, 1956–1996

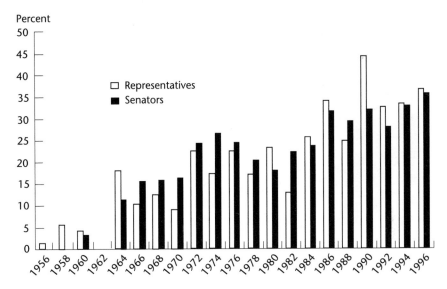

Percent

during and after the Reagan years left the two parties with more distinctive images, making it easier for voters to recognize their appropriate ideological home. Conservatives moved into the Republican ranks, while liberals remained Democrats. Notice that most of the trends among voters identified in the figures show their largest movement in the 1990s, *after* the firming up of congressional party lines in the 1980s.

This is not to say, however, that members of Congress simply follow their own ideological fancies, leaving voters no choice but to line up accordingly. As vote-seeking politicians, they naturally anticipate voters' potential responses and so are constrained by them. The Republican "southern strategy" emerged because Republican presidential candidates sensed an opportunity to win converts among conservative white southerners. Ambitious Republicans adopted conservative positions on social issues to attract voters alienated by the Democrats' tolerance of nontraditional life styles but indifferent at best to Republican economic policies. Democrats emphasized "choice" on abortion because they recognized its appeal to well-educated, affluent voters who might otherwise think of themselves as Republicans. In the budget wars of the past two decades, Democrats have vigorously defended middle class entitlements such as Social Security and Medicare, while Republicans have championed tax cuts because each position has a large popular constituency. In adopting positions, then, politicians are guided by the opportunities and constraints presented by configurations of public opinion on

Figure 12. Variance in Roll Call Ideology Explained by District Presidential
Vote and Party, 1952–1996

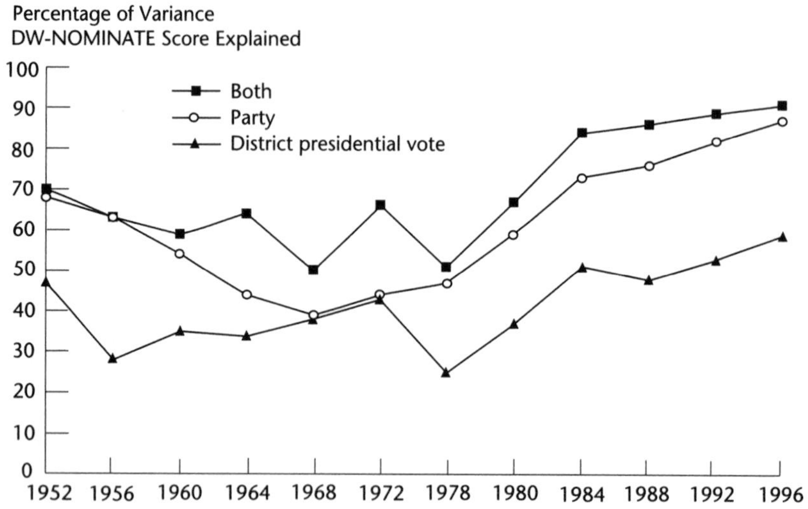

Percentage of Variance
DW-NOMINATE Score Explained

political issues. Party polarization in Congress depended on the expectation that voters would reward, or at least not punish, voting with one's party's majority.

In reality, therefore, the relationship between mass and elite partisan consistency is inherently interactive. Between the 1970s and the 1990s, changes in electoral and congressional politics reinforced one another, encouraging greater partisan consistency and cohesion in both. One important result is that the linkage between citizens' decisions on election day and the actions of the winners once they assume office has become much tighter. Indeed, election results predict congressional roll call voting on issues that fall along the primary liberal-conservative dimension accurately enough to meet one of the fundamental conditions for responsible party government. This is evident when we regress dw-nominate scores on two variables, party and the district-level presidential vote, and observe how much of the variance they explain. The presidential vote stands here as a serviceable if somewhat imprecise measure of district ideology: the higher the Republican share of the vote in any given election, the more conservative the district. The results are summarized in Figure 12, which tracks the proportion of variance in first-dimension dw-nominate scores explained by party and presidential vote, individually and in combination, in the Congresses immediately following each presidential election since 1952.

As we would expect from the information in Figures 1 and 2, the capacity of party to account for roll call voting on the liberal-conservative dimension declined from the 1950s to the 1970s but since then has risen steeply. The predictive accuracy of the district-level presidential vote remained lower than that of party through most of the period, reaching a low point in 1976 (a consequence of Jimmy Carter's initial appeal to conservative southerners), but then rising to its highest levels in the time series during the 1990s. The *relative* contribution of district ideology to explaining House members' positions on the liberal-conservative dimension tends to be greatest in the 1960s and 1970s, when party's contribution is lowest. Between 1976 and 1996, both variables become increasingly accurate predictors of congressional voting, to the point where by the 105th Congress, party and presidential vote account for a remarkable 91.5 percent of the variance in representatives' dw-nominate scores.

The voting patterns of House members, then, are increasingly predictable from elementary electoral variables: the party of the winner and the district's ideology as reflected in its presidential leanings (with these two variables themselves correlated in 1996 at the highest level since the 1950s). With this development, voters have a much clearer idea of how their collective choices in national elections will translate into congressional action on national issues. Because party labels are so much more predictive of congressional behavior, voters have good reason to use them more consistently to guide voting decisions.

The same circumstances that make the party label such an informative cue also deepen the dilemma faced by moderate voters, however. And, despite the growing divergence between the parties' respective electoral coalitions, most Americans still cluster in the middle of the ideological spectrum. In surveys from the 1990s, about 60 percent of House voters place themselves in one of the middle three positions on the 7-point liberal-conservative scale, down only modestly from about 68 percent in the 1970s. Polarization in Congress has outstripped polarization in the electorate, so the proportion of citizens placing themselves between the two parties has not diminished. Therefore, although the 1998 NES survey found party line voting to be near its highest level in thirty years, it also found that

- only 45 percent of voters preferred the continuation of the two-party system to elections without party labels (29 percent) or new parties to challenge the Republicans and Democrats (26 percent);
- 84 percent thought that the phrase "too involved in partisan politics" described Congress quite well (40 percent) or extremely well (44 percent);
- 56 percent preferred control of the presidency and Congress to be split between the parties, 24 percent preferred one party to control both institutions, and the rest did not care.

With elite polarization outstripping mass polarization, the advent of a central component of responsible party government—unified parties with distinct policy positions—may have had the paradoxical effect of strengthening support for divided government. The more divergent the parties' modal ideological positions, the more reason the remaining centrist voters have to welcome the moderating effect of divided government. But under divided government, the more divergent the parties, the more rancorous the conflict between the president and Congress, and rancorous political conflict is welcomed by almost no one.

The Clinton impeachment put the bitterest of partisan conflicts on full display, and the public did not find it a pretty sight. After the Senate acquitted Clinton, members of Congress, particularly on the Republican side, began looking for ways to soften the image of rabid partisanship that the impeachment had imparted. The trends examined here suggest that any success they achieve is destined to be temporary. Party divisions in Congress have increasingly sturdy electoral roots, particularly among activists, as well as strong institutional reinforcement from the congressional parties. Both parties' holds on their respective branches is tenuous, guaranteeing intense electoral competition across the board in 2000. The party that achieves the upper hand has an excellent chance of winning control of the whole federal government; if the Republicans can win the presidency, they are almost certain to capture undivided national power for the first time in nearly half a century. With so much at stake, no partisan political advantage is likely to be left unexploited. The only constraint on undiluted partisanship is the fear of losing ground by *looking* too partisan; if impeachment politics is any indication, it is not much of a constraint. All signs point to a new partisan era in national politics that is likely to continue for the foreseeable future.

Chapter 12

Political Parties

12-1

from *Why Parties?*

John H. Aldrich

American political parties were created by politicians and committed citizens who sought to win elections and control legislatures, executives, and even the courts. The parties exist at local, state, and national levels—wherever elections are held for coveted offices. The system of political parties that has evolved over time is fragmented and multilayered. In the following essay, John H. Aldrich describes the nature of the political problems that parties solve for candidates and voters. As much as we may dislike partisanship, modern democracies could not, Aldrich explains, function without it.

Is the Contemporary Political Party Strong or in Decline?

The Case for the Importance of Political Parties

THE PATH TO OFFICE for nearly every major politician begins today, as it has for over 150 years, with the party. Many candidates emerge initially from the ranks of party activists, all serious candidates seek their party's nomination, and they become serious candidates in the general election only because they have won

Source: John H. Aldrich, *Why Parties? The Origin and Transformation of Political Parties in America* (Chicago: University of Chicago Press, 1995), 14–27. Notes appearing in the original have been deleted.

their party's endorsement. Today most partisan nominations are decided in primary elections—that is, based on votes cast by self-designated partisans in the mass electorate. Successful nominees count on the continued support of these partisans in the general election, and for good reason. At least since surveys have provided firm evidence, all presidential nominees have won the support of no less than a majority of their party in the electorate, no matter how overwhelming their defeat may have been.

This is an age of so-called partisan dealignment in the electorate. Even so, a substantial majority today consider themselves partisans. The lowest percentage of self-professed (i.e., "strong" and "weak") partisans yet recorded in National Election Studies (NES) surveys was 61 percent in 1974, and another 22 percent expressed partisan leanings that year. Evidence from panel surveys demonstrates that partisanship has remained as stable and enduring for most adults after dealignment as it did before it, and it is often the single strongest predictor of candidate choice in the public.

If parties have declined recently, the decline has not occurred in their formal organizations. Party organizations are if anything stronger, better financed, and more professional at all levels now. Although its importance to candidates may be less than in the past, the party provides more support—more money, workers, and resources of all kinds—than any other organization for all but a very few candidates for national and state offices.

Once elected, officeholders remain partisans. Congress is organized by parties. Party-line votes elect its leadership, determine what its committees will be, assign members to them, and select their chairs. Party caucuses remain a staple of congressional life, and they and other forms of party organizations in Congress have become stronger in recent years. Party voting in committee and on the floor of both houses, though far less common in the United States than in many democracies, nonetheless remains the first and most important standard for understanding congressional voting behavior, and it too has grown stronger, in this case much stronger, in recent years.

Relationships among the elected branches of government are also heavily partisan. Conference committees to resolve discrepancies between House and Senate versions of legislation reflect partisan as well as interchamber rivalries. The president is the party's leader, and his agenda is introduced, fought for, and supported on the floor by his congressional party. His agenda becomes his party's congressional agenda, and much of it finds its way into law.

The Case for Weak and Weakening Parties

As impressive as the scenario above may be, not all agree that parties lie at the heart of American politics, at least not anymore. The literature on parties over the past two decades is replete with accounts of the decline of the political party. Even the choice of titles clearly reflects the arguments. David Broder perhaps began this stream of literature with *The Party's Over* (1972). Since then, political scientists have written extensively on this theme: for example, Crotty's *American Political Parties in Decline* (1984), Kirkpatrick's *Dismantling the Parties* (1978), Polsby's *Consequences of Party Reform* (1983) . . . , Ranney's thoughtful *Curing the Mischiefs of Faction* (1975), and Wattenberg's *The Decline of American Political Parties* (1990).

Those who see larger ills in the contemporary political scene often attribute them to the failure of parties to be stronger and more effective. In "The Decline of Collective Responsibility" (1980), Fiorina argued that such responsibility was possible only through the agency of the political party. Jacobson concluded his study of congressional elections (1992) by arguing that contemporary elections induce "responsiveness" of individual incumbents to their districts but do so "without [inducing] responsibility" in incumbents for what Congress does. As a result, the electorate can find no one to hold accountable for congressional failings. He too looked to a revitalized party for redress. These themes reflect the responsible party thesis, if not in being a call for such parties, at least in using that as the standard for measuring how short the contemporary party falls.

The literature on the presidency is not immune to this concern for decaying parties. Kernell's account of the strategy of "going public" (1986)—that is, generating power by marshaling public opinion—is that it became more common as the older strategy of striking bargains with a small set of congressional (and partisan) power brokers grew increasingly futile. The earlier use of the president's power to persuade (Neustadt 1960, 1990) failed as power centers became more diverse and fragmented and brokers could no longer deliver. Lowi argued this case even more strongly in *The Personal President* (1985). America, he claimed, has come to invest too much power in the office of the president, with the result that the promise of the presidency and the promises of individual presidents go unfulfilled. Why? Because the rest of government has become too unwieldy, complicated, and fragmented for the president to use that power effectively. His solution? Revitalize political parties.

Divided partisan control over government, once an occasional aberration, has become the ordinary course of affairs. Many of the same themes in this literature are those sounded above—fragmented, decentralized power, lack of coordination and control over what the government does, and absence of collective responsibility. Strong political parties are, among other things, those that can deliver the vote for most or all of their candidates. Thus another symptom of weakened parties is regularized divided government, in the states as well as in the nation.

If divided government is due to weakened parties, that condition must be due in turn to weakened partisan loyalties in the electorate. Here the evidence is clear. The proportions and strength of party attachments in the electorate declined in the mid-1960s. There was a resurgence in affiliation twenty years later, but to a lower level than before 1966. The behavioral consequences of these changes are if anything even clearer. Defection from party lines and split-ticket voting are far more common for all major offices at national, state, and local levels today than before the mid-1960s. Elections are more candidate centered and less party centered, and those who come to office have played a greater role in shaping their own more highly personalized electoral coalitions. Incumbents, less dependent on the party for winning office, are less disposed to vote the party line in Congress or to follow the wishes of their party's president. Power becomes decentralized toward the individual incumbent and, as Jacobson argues, individual incumbents respond to their constituents. If that means defecting from the party, so be it.

Is the Debate Genuine?

Some believe that parties have actually grown stronger over the past few decades. This position has been put most starkly by Schlesinger: "It should be clear by now that the grab bag of assumptions, inferences, and half-truths that have fed the decline-of-parties thesis is simply wrong" (1985, p. 1152). Rather, he maintains, "Thanks to increasing levels of competition between the parties, then, American political parties are stronger than before" (p. 1168). More common is the claim that parties were weakened in the 1960s but have been revitalized since then. Rohde pointed out that "in the last decade, however, the decline of partisanship in the House has been reversed. Party voting, which had been as low as 27 percent in 1972, peaked at 64 percent in 1987" (1989, p. 1). Changes in party voting in the Senate have been only slightly less dramatic, and Rohde has also demonstrated that party institutions in the House strengthened substantially in the same period (1991). If, as Rohde says, parties in the government are stronger, and if . . . others are correct that party organizations are stronger, a thesis of decline with resurgence must be taken seriously. The electorate's partisan affiliations may be a lagging rather than a leading indicator, and even they have rebounded slightly.

A Theory of Political Parties

As diverse as are the conclusions reached by these and other astute observers, all agree that the political party is—or should be—central to the American political system. Parties are—or should be—integral parts of all political life, from structuring the reasoning and choice of the electorate, through all facets of campaigns and seemingly all facets of the government, to the very possibility of effective governance in a democracy.

How is it that such astute observers of American politics and parties, writing at virtually the same time and looking at much the same evidence, come to such diametrically opposed conclusions about the strength of parties? Eldersveld . . . wrote that "political parties are complex institutions and processes, and as such they are difficult to understand and evaluate" (1982, p. 407). As proof, he went on to consider the decline of parties thesis. At one point he wrote, "The decline in our parties, therefore, is difficult to demonstrate, empirically or in terms of historical perspective" (p. 417). And yet he then turned to signs of party decline and concluded his book with the statement: "Despite their defects they continue today to be the major instruments for democratic government in this nation. With necessary reforms we can make them even more central to the governmental process and to the lives of American citizens. Eighty years ago, Lord James Bryce, after studying our party system, said, 'In America the great moving forces are the parties. The government counts for less than in Europe, the parties count for more. . . .' If our citizens and their leaders wish it, American parties will still be the 'great moving forces' of our system" (1982, pp. 432–33).

The "Fundamental Equation" of the New Institutionalism Applied to Parties

That parties are complex does not mean they are incomprehensible. Indeed complexity is, if not an intentional outcome, at least an anticipated result of those who shape the political parties. Moreover, they are so deeply woven into the fabric of American politics that they cannot be understood apart from either their own historical context and dynamics or those of the political system as a whole. Parties, that is, can be understood only in relation to the polity, to the government and its institutions, and to the historical context of the times.

The study of political parties, second, is necessarily a study of a major pair of political *institutions*. Indeed, the institutions that define the political party are unique, and as it happens they are unique in ways that make an institutional account especially useful. Their establishment and nature are fundamentally extralegal; they are nongovernmental political institutions. Instead of statute, their basis lies in the actions of ambitious politicians that created and maintain them. They are, in the parlance of the new institutionalism, *endogenous institutions*—in fact, the most highly endogenous institutions of any substantial and sustained political importance in American history.

By endogenous, I mean it was the actions of political actors that created political parties in the first place, and it is the actions of political actors that have shaped and altered them over time. And political actors have chosen to alter their parties dramatically at several times in our history, reformed them often, and tinkered with them constantly. Of all major political bodies in the United States, the political party is the most variable in its rules, regulations, and procedures—that is to say, in its formal organization—and in its informal methods and traditions. It is often the same set of actors who write the party's rules and then choose the party's outcomes, sometimes at nearly the same time and by the same method. Thus, for example, one night national party conventions debate, consider any proposed amendments, and then adopt their rules by a majority vote of credentialed delegates. The next night these same delegates debate, consider any proposed amendments, and then adopt their platform by majority vote, and they choose their presidential nominee by majority vote the following night.

Who, then, are these critical political actors? Many see the party-in-the-electorate as comprising major actors. To be sure, mobilizing the electorate to capture office is a central task of the political party. But America is a republican democracy. All power flows directly or indirectly from the great body of the people, to paraphrase Madison's definition. The public elects its political leaders, but it is that leadership that legislates, executes, and adjudicates policy. The parties are defined in relation to this republican democracy. Thus it is political leaders, those Schlesinger (1975) has called "office-seekers"—*those who seek and those who hold elective office*—who are the central actors in the party.

Ambitious office seekers and holders are thus the first and most important actors in the political party. A second set of important figures in party politics comprises those who hold, or have access to, critical resources that office seekers need to realize their ambitions. It is expensive to build and maintain the party and campaign organizations necessary to compete effectively in the electoral arena. Thomas Ferguson, for example, has made an extended argument for the "primary and constitutive role large investors play in American politics" (1983, p. 3). Much of his research emphasizes this primary and constitutive role in party politics in particular, such as in partisan realignments. The study of the role of money in congressional elections has also focused in part on concentrations of such sources of funding, such as from political action committees which political parties are coming to take advantage of. Elections are also fought over the flow of information to the public. The electoral arm of political parties in the eighteenth century was made up of "committees of correspondence," which were primarily lines of communication among political elites and between them and potential voters, and one of the first signs of organizing of the Jeffersonian Republican party was the hiring of a newspaper editor. The press was first a partisan press, and editors and publishers from Thomas Ritchie to Horace Greeley long were critical players in party politics. Today those with specialized knowledge relevant to communication, such as pollsters, media and advertising experts, and computerized fund-raising specialists, enjoy influence in party, campaign, and even government councils that greatly exceeds their mere technical expertise.

In more theoretical terms, this second set of party actors include those Schlesinger (1975) has called "benefit seekers," those for whom realization of their goals depends on the party's success in capturing office. Party activists shade from those powerful figures with concentrations of, or access to, money and information described above to the legions of volunteer campaign activists who ring doorbells and stuff envelopes and are, individually and collectively, critical to the first level of the party—its office seekers. All are critical because they command the resources, whether money, expertise, and information or merely time and labor, that office seekers need to realize their ambitions. As a result, activists' motivations shape and constrain the behavior of office seekers, as their own roles are, in turn, shaped and constrained by the office seekers. The changed incentives of party activists have played a significant role in the fundamentally altered nature of the contemporary party, but the impact of benefit seekers will be seen scattered throughout this account.

Voters, however, are neither office seekers nor benefit seekers and thus are not a part of the political party at all, even if they identify strongly with a party and consistently support its candidates. Voters are indeed critical, but they are critical as the targets of party activities. Parties "produce" candidates, platforms, and policies. Voters "consume" by exchanging their votes for the party's product (see Popkin et al. 1976). Some voters, of course, become partisans by becoming activists, whether as occasional volunteers, as sustained contributors, or even as candidates. But until they do so, they may be faithful consumers, "brand name" loyalists as it were, but they are still only the targets of partisans' efforts to sell their wares in the political marketplace.

Why, then, do politicians create and recreate the party, exploit its features, or ignore its dictates? The simple answer is that it has been in their interests to do so. That is, this is a *rational choice* account of the party, an account that presumes that rational, elective office seekers and holders use the party to achieve their ends.

I do not assume that politicians are invariably self-interested in a narrow sense. This is not a theory in which elective office seekers simply maximize their chances of election or reelection, at least not for its own sake. They may well have fundamental values and principles, and they may have preferences over policies as means to those ends. They also care about office, both for its own sake and for the opportunities to achieve other ends that election and reelection make possible. . . . Just as winning elections is a means to other ends for politicians (whether career or policy ends), so too is the political party a means to these other ends.

Why, then, do politicians turn to create or reform, to use or abuse, partisan institutions? The answer is that parties are designed as attempts to solve problems that current institutional arrangements do not solve and that politicians have come to believe they cannot solve. These problems fall into three general and recurring categories.

The Problem of Ambition and Elective Office Seeking

Elective office seekers, as that label says, want to win election to office. Parties regulate access to those offices. If elective office is indeed valuable, there will be more aspirants than offices, and the political party and the two-party system are means of regulating that competition and channeling those ambitions. Major party nomination is necessary for election, and partisan institutions have been developed—and have been reformed and re-reformed—for regulating competition. Intra-institutional leadership positions are also highly valued and therefore potentially competitive. There is, for example, a fairly well institutionalized path to the office of Speaker of the House. It is, however, a Democratic party institution. Elective politicians, of course, ordinarily desire election more than once. They are typically careerists who want a long and productive career in politics. Schlesinger's ambition theory (1966) . . . is precisely about this general problem. Underlying this theory, though typically not fully developed, is a problem. The problem is that if office is desirable, there will be more, usually many more, aspirants than there are offices to go around. When stated in rigorous form, it can be proved that in fact there is no permanent solution to this problem. And it is a problem that can adversely affect the fortunes of a party. In 1912 the Republican vote was split between William Howard Taft and Theodore Roosevelt. This split enabled Woodrow Wilson to win with 42 percent of the popular vote. Not only was Wilson the only break in Republican hegemony of the White House in this period, but in that year Democrats increased their House majority by sixty-five additional seats and captured majority control of the Senate. Thus failure to regulate intraparty competition cost Republicans dearly.

For elective office seekers, regulating conflict over who holds those offices is clearly of major concern. It is ever present. And it is not just a problem of access to government offices but is also a problem internal to each party as soon as the party becomes an important gateway to office.

The Problem of Making Decisions for the Party and for the Polity

Once in office, partisans determine outcomes for the polity. They propose alternatives, shape the agenda, pass (or reject) legislation, and implement what they enact. The policy formation and execution process, that is, is highly partisan. The parties-in-government are more than mere coalitions of like-minded individuals, however; they are enduring institutions. Very few incumbents change their partisan affiliations. Most retain their partisanship throughout their career, even though they often disagree (i.e., are not uniformly like-minded) with some of their partisan peers. When the rare incumbent does change parties, it is invariably to join the party more consonant with that switcher's policy interests. This implies that there are differences between the two parties at some fundamental and enduring level on policy positions, values, and beliefs. Thus, parties are institutions designed to promote the achievement of collective choices—choices on which the parties differ and choices reached by majority rule. As with access to office and ambition theory, there is a well-developed theory for this problem: *social choice theory.* Underlying this theory is the well-known problem that no method of choice can solve the elective officeholders' problem of combining the interests, concerns, or values of a polity that remains faithful to democratic values, as shown by the consequences flowing from Arrow's theorem (Arrow 1951). Thus, in a republican democracy politicians may turn to partisan institutions to solve the problem of collective choice. In the language of politics, parties may help achieve the goal of attaining policy majorities in the first place, as well as the often more difficult goal of maintaining such majorities.

The Problem of Collective Action

The third problem is the most pervasive and thus the furthest-ranging in substantive content. The clearest example, however, is also the most important. To win office, candidates need more than a party's nomination. Election requires persuading members of the public to support that candidacy and mobilizing as many of those supporters as possible. This is a problem of collective action. How do candidates get supporters to vote for them—at least in greater numbers than vote for the opposition—as well as get them to provide the cadre of workers and contribute the resources needed to win election? The political party has long been the solution.

As important as wooing and mobilizing supporters are, collective action problems arise in a wide range of circumstances facing elective office seekers. Party action invariably requires the concerted action of many partisans to achieve collectively desirable outcomes. Jimmy Carter was the only president in the 1970s and 1980s to enjoy unified party control of government. Democrats in Congress, it might well be argued, shared an interest in achieving policy outcomes. And yet Carter was all too often unable to get them to act in their shared collective interests. In 1980 not only he but the Democratic congressional parties paid a heavy price for failed cooperation. The theory here, of course, is the *theory of public goods* and its consequence, the *theory of collective action*.

The Elective Office Seekers' and Holders' Interests Are to Win

Why should this crucial set of actors, the elective office seekers and officeholders, care about these three classes of problems? The short answer is that these concerns become practical problems to politicians when they adversely affect their chances of winning. Put differently, politicians turn to their political party—that is, use its powers, resources, and institutional forms—when they believe doing so increases their prospects for winning desired outcomes, and they turn from it if it does not.

Ambition theory is about winning per se. The breakdown of orderly access to office risks unfettered and unregulated competition. The inability of a party to develop effective means of nomination and support for election therefore directly influences the chances of victory for the candidates and thus for their parties. The standard example of the problem of social choice theory, the "paradox of voting," is paradoxical precisely because all are voting to win desired outcomes, and yet there is no majority-preferred outcome. Even if there happens to be a majority-preferred policy, the conditions under which it is truly a stable equilibrium are extremely fragile and thus all too amenable to defeat. In other words, majorities in Congress are hard to attain and at least as hard to maintain. And the only reason to employ scarce campaign resources to mobilize supporters is that such mobilization increases the odds of victory. Its opposite, the failure to act when there are broadly shared interests—the problem of collective action—reduces the prospects of victory, whether at the ballot box or in government. Scholars may recognize these as manifestations of theoretical problems and call them "impossibility results" to emphasize their generic importance. Politicians recognize the consequences of these impossibility results by their adverse effects on their chances of winning—of securing what it is in their interests to secure.

So why have politicians so often turned to political parties for solutions to these problems? Their existence creates incentives for their use. It is, for example, incredibly difficult to win election to major office without the backing of a major party. It is only a little less certain that legislators who seek to lead a policy proposal through the congressional labyrinth will first turn to their party for assistance. But such incentives tell us only that an ongoing political institution is used when it is useful. Why form political parties in the first place? . . .

First, parties are institutions. This means, among other things, that they have some durability. They may be endogenous institutions, yet party reforms are meant not as short-term fixes but as alterations to last for years, even decades.

Thus, for example, legislators might create a party rather than a temporary majority coalition to increase their chances of winning not just today but into the future. Similarly, a long and successful political career means winning office today, but it also requires winning elections throughout that career. A standing, enduring organization makes that goal more likely.

Second, American democracy chooses by plurality or majority rule. Election to office therefore requires broad-based support wherever and from whomever it can be found. So strong are the resulting incentives for a two-party system to emerge that the effect is called Duverger's law (Duverger 1954). It is in part the need to win vast and diverse support that has led politicians to create political parties.

Third, parties may help officeholders win more, and more often, than alternatives. Consider the usual stylized model of pork barrel politics. All winners get a piece of the pork for their districts. All funded projects are paid for by tax revenues, so each district pays an equal share of the costs of each project adopted, whether or not that district receives a project. Several writers have argued that this kind of legislation leads to "universalism," that is, adoption of a "norm" that every such bill yields a project to every district and thus passes with a "universal" or unanimous coalition. Thus everyone "wins." . . . As a result, expecting to win only a bit more than half the time and lose the rest of the time, all legislators prefer consistent use of the norm of universalism. But consider an alternative. Suppose some majority agree to form a more permanent coalition, to control outcomes now and into the future, and develop institutional means to encourage fealty to this agreement. If they successfully accomplish this, they will win regularly. Members of this institutionalized coalition would prefer it to universalism, since they always win a project in either case, but they get their projects at lower cost under the institutionalized majority coalition, which passes fewer projects. Thus, even in this case with no shared substantive interests at all, there are nonetheless incentives to form an enduring voting coalition—to form a political party. And those in the excluded minority have incentives to counterorganize. United, they may be more able to woo defectors to their side. If not, they can campaign to throw those rascals in the majority party out of office.

In sum, these theoretical problems affect elective office seekers and officeholders by reducing their chances of winning. Politicians therefore may turn to political parties as institutions designed to ameliorate them. In solving these theoretical problems, however, from the politicians' perspective parties are affecting who wins and loses and what is won or lost. And it is to parties that politicians often turn, because of their durability as institutionalized solutions, because of the need to orchestrate large and diverse groups of people to form winning majorities, and because often more can be won through parties. Note that this argument rests on the implicit assumption that winning and losing hang in the balance. Politicians may be expected to give up some of their personal autonomy only when they face an imminent threat of defeat without doing so or only when doing so can block opponents' ability to build the strength necessary to win.

This is, of course, the positive case for parties, for it specifies conditions under which politicians find them useful. Not all problems are best solved, perhaps even solved at all, by political parties. Other arrangements, perhaps interest groups, issue networks, or personal electoral coalitions, may be superior at different times and under different conditions. The party may even be part of the problem. In such cases politicians turn elsewhere to seek the means to win. Thus this theory is at base a theory of ambitious politicians seeking to achieve their goals. Often they have done so through the agency of the party, but sometimes, this theory implies, they will seek to realize their goals in other ways.

The political party has regularly proved useful. Their permanence suggests that the appropriate question is not When parties? but How much parties and how much other means? That parties are endogenous implies that there is no single, consistent account of the political party—nor should we expect one. Instead, parties are but a (major) part of the institutional context in which current historical conditions—the problems—are set, and solutions are sought with permanence only by changing that web of institutional arrangements. Of these the political party is by design the most malleable, and thus it is intended to change in important ways and with relatively great frequency. But it changes in ways that have, for most of American history, retained major political parties and, indeed, retained two major parties.

REFERENCES

Arrow, Kenneth J. 1951. *Social choice and individual values.* New York: Wiley.

Broder, David S. 1972. *The party's over: The failure of politics in America.* New York: Harper and Row.

Crotty, William. 1984. *American political parties in decline.* 2d ed. Boston: Little, Brown.

Duverger, Maurice. 1954. *Political parties: Their organization and activities in the modern state.* New York: Wiley.

Eldersveld, Samuel J. 1982. *Political parties in American society.* New York: Basic Books.

Ferguson, Thomas. 1983. Party realignment and American industrial structures: The investment theory of political parties in historical perspective. In *Research in political economy,* vol. 6, ed. Paul Zarembka, pp. 1–82. Greenwich, Conn.: JAI Press.

Fiorina, Morris P. 1980. The decline of collective responsibility in American politics. *Daedalus* 109 (summer): 25–45.

Jacobson, Gary C. 1992. *The politics of congressional elections.* 3d ed. New York: Harper-Collins.

Kernell, Samuel. 1986. *Going public: New strategies of presidential leadership.* Washington, D.C.: CQ Press.

Kirkpatrick, Jeane J. 1978. *Dismantling the parties: Reflections on party reform and party decomposition*. Washington, D.C.: American Enterprise Institute of Public Policy Research.

Lowi, Theodore. 1985. *The personal president: Power invested, promise unfulfilled*. Ithaca, N.Y.: Cornell University Press.

Neustadt, Richard E. 1960. *Presidential power: The politics of leadership*. New York: Wiley.

_____. 1990. *Presidential power and the modern presidents: The politics of leadership from Roosevelt to Reagan*. New York: Free Press.

Polsby, Nelson W. 1983. *Consequences of party reform*. Oxford: Oxford University Press.

Popkin, Samuel, John W. Gorman, Charles Phillips, and Jeffrey A. Smith. 1976. Comment: What have you done for me lately? Toward an investment theory of voting. *American Political Science Review* 70 (September): 779–805.

Ranney, Austin. 1975. *Curing the mischiefs of faction: Party reform in America*. Berkeley and Los Angeles: University of California Press.

Rohde, David W. 1989. "Something's happening here: What it is ain't exactly clear": Southern Democrats in the House of Representatives. In *Home style and Washington work: Studies of congressional politics*, ed. Morris P. Fiorina and David W. Rohde, pp. 137–163. Ann Arbor: University of Michigan Press.

_____. 1991. *Parties and leaders in the postreform House*. Chicago: University of Chicago Press.

Schlesinger, Joseph A. 1966. *Ambition and politics: Political careers in the United States*. Chicago: Rand McNally.

_____. 1975. The primary goals of political parties: A clarification of positive theory. *American Political Science Review* 69 (September): 840–49.

_____. 1985. The new American political party. *American Political Science Review* 79 (December): 1152–69.

Wattenberg, Martin P. 1990. *The decline of American political parties: 1952–1988*. Cambridge: Harvard University Press.

12-2

Partisanship and Voting Behavior, 1952–1996

Larry M. Bartels

Many Americans consider themselves to be Democrats or Republicans, and a few identify with some other party. In the late 1960s and 1970s the number of Americans willing to call themselves Democrats or Republicans declined, leading political scientists to speak of a dealignment and worry about the declining importance of parties. Then partisanship appeared to rebound in the 1990s. In this essay political scientist Larry M. Bartels describes these trends and explains the importance of partisanship for the voting behavior of Americans. He argues that party identification increased in the 1980s and 1990s and that the correlation between party identification and presidential voting increased even more. He concludes by observing that changes in the behavior of elected partisans—greater partisanship among presidents and members of Congress—may have contributed to resurgent partisanship in voting in the electorate.

THE "DECLINE OF PARTIES" is one of the most familiar themes in popular and scholarly discourse about contemporary American politics. One influential journalist has asserted that "the most important phenomenon of American politics in the past quarter century has been the rise of independent voters." . . . The most persistent academic analyst of partisan decline has argued that "For over four decades the American public has been drifting away from the two major political parties," while another prominent scholar has referred to a "massive decay of partisan electoral linkages" and to "the ruins of the traditional partisan regime."

I shall argue here that this conventional wisdom regarding the "decline of parties" is both exaggerated and outdated. Partisan loyalties in the American public have rebounded significantly since the mid-1970s, especially among those who actually turn out to vote. Meanwhile, the impact of partisanship on voting behavior has increased markedly in recent years, both at the presidential level (where the overall impact of partisanship in 1996 was almost 80 percent greater

Source: Larry Bartels, "Partisanship and Voting Behavior, 1952–1996". *American Journal of Political Science* 44, no. 1 (January 2000): 35–50. Notes and bibliographic references appearing in the original have been deleted.

than in 1972) and at the congressional level (where the overall impact of partisanship in 1996 was almost 60 percent greater than in 1978). . . . My analysis suggests that "partisan loyalties had at least as much impact on voting behavior at the presidential level in the 1980s as in the 1950s"—and even more in the 1990s than in the 1980s.

The Thesis of Partisan Decline

Almost forty years ago, the authors of *The American Voter* asserted that

> Few factors are of greater importance for our national elections than the lasting attachment of tens of millions of Americans to one of the parties. These loyalties establish a basic division of electoral strength within which the competition of particular campaigns takes place. . . . Most Americans have this sense of attachment with one party or the other. And for the individual who does, the strength and direction of party identification are facts of central importance in accounting for attitude and behavior.

The so-called "Michigan model," with its emphasis on the fundamental importance of long-standing partisan loyalties, dominated the subsequent decade of academic research on voting behavior. However, over the same decade, changes in the political environment seemed to be rendering the "Michigan model" increasingly obsolete. By the early 1970s, political observers were pointing to the increasing proportion of "independents" in opinion surveys and the increasing prevalence of split-ticket voting as indications of significant partisan decline. By the mid-1970s, some political scientists were extrapolating from a decade-long trend to project a permanent demise of partisan politics. . . .

The "increase in the number of independents" in the 1960s and early '70s . . . — and the corresponding decrease in the proportion of the public who identified themselves as Democrats or Republicans—constitute the single most important piece of evidence in support of the thesis of partisan decline. These and subsequent trends are displayed in the two panels of Figure 1, which show the proportions of party identifiers (including "strong" and "weak" identifiers) and independents (including "pure" independents and "leaners"), respectively, in each of the biennial American National Election Studies from 1952 through 1996.

. . . The proportion of "strong" identifiers in the population increased from 24 percent in 1976 to 31 percent in 1996, while the proportion of "pure" independents—those who neither identified themselves as Democrats or Republicans nor "leaned" to either party in response to the traditional Michigan follow-up question—declined from 16 percent in 1976 to only 9 percent in 1996.

Figure 1. The Distribution of Party Identification, 1952–1996

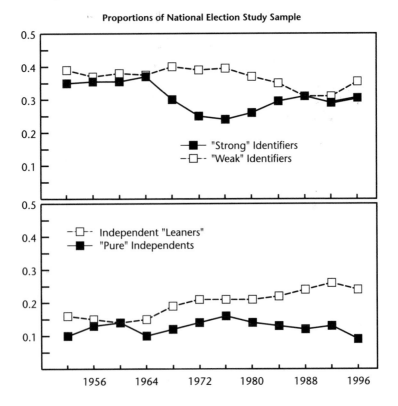

Proportions of National Election Study Sample

A Summary Measure of Partisan Voting

What significance should we attach to the shifts in the distribution of party identification documented in Figure 1? ... To the extent that our interest in partisan loyalties is motivated by an interest in voting behavior, we would seem to need (at least) two kinds of additional information to interpret the electoral implications of changing levels of partisanship. First, are the shifts documented in Figure 1 concentrated among voters or among nonvoters? Declining partisanship among nonvoters may leave the distribution of party identification in the voting booth unchanged. And second, has the electoral *impact* of a given level of partisanship declined or increased over time? Declining *levels* of partisanship might be either reinforced or counteracted by changes in the *impact* of partisanship on electoral choices.

The first of these two questions is addressed by Figure 2, which shows separate trend lines for the proportion of ("strong" or "weak") party identifiers

Figure 2. Party Identification Among Presidential Voters and Nonvoters

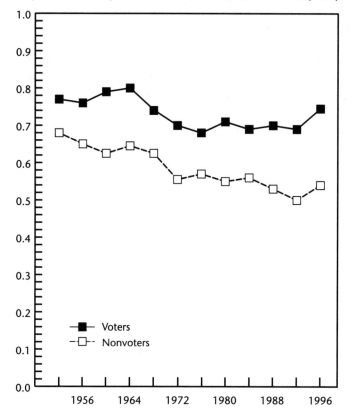

Proportions of (Strong or Weak) Identifiers in National Election Study Sample

among voters and nonvoters in presidential elections since 1952. Not surprisingly, nonvoters are less partisan than voters in every year. But what is more important to note here is that the gap in partisanship between voters and nonvoters has widened noticeably over time, from about ten percentage points in the 1950s to about twenty percentage points by the 1990s. Indeed, it appears from these results that the decline in partisanship evident in Figure 1 has been almost entirely reversed among voters: the proportion of party identifiers in the presidential electorate was 77 percent in 1952, 76 percent in 1956, and 75 percent in 1996, while the proportion among nonvoters was almost fifteen points lower in 1996 than in the 1950s. Thus, while the trend lines shown in Figure 1 suggest that the erosion of party loyalties underlying the "partisan decline" thesis has ended and probably even reversed in the last two decades, the results presented in Figure 2 suggest that these developments have been especially pronounced among actual voters.

The erosion of party loyalties among nonvoters evident in Figure 2 is of importance for any general account of the role of partisanship in contemporary American politics. It is especially important in view of evidence suggesting that declining partisanship is, at least in modest part, *responsible* for the substantial decline in turnout over the period covered by Figure 2, and that individual turnout decisions are increasingly sensitive to the strength of prospective voters' preferences for one candidate or the other, which derive in significant part from long-term partisan attachments. However, given my narrower aim here of documenting changes in the impact of partisanship *on voting behavior*, the most important implication of Figure 2 is that the distribution of partisan attachments *among those citizens who actually got to the polls* was not much different in the 1990s from what it had been in the 1950s.

Of course, the significance of partisanship in the electoral process depends not only upon the level of partisanship in the electorate, but also upon the extent to which partisanship influences voting behavior. How, if at all, has that influence changed over the four and a half decades covered by the NES data? ... [Editors: Bartels estimates the impact of party identification on voting by taking advantage of the survey from which respondents are coded as strong Republican, weak Republican, leaning Republican, independent, leaning Democrat, weak Democrat, and strong Democrat. For each category, a statistical estimate is calculated for the effect of being in that category on voting for the alternative presidential or congressional candidates. The statistical estimate, called a probit coefficient, is averaged for the partisan categories to yield an overall measure "partisan voting." Figure 3 presents the result for elections in the 1952–1996 period.]

The Revival of Partisan Voting in Presidential Elections

... Figure 3 shows noticeable declines in the level of partisan voting in the presidential elections of 1964 and, especially, 1972. These declines primarily reflect the fact that Republican identifiers in 1964 and Democratic identifiers in 1972 abandoned their parties' unpopular presidential candidates by the millions, depressing the estimated effects of partisan loyalties on the presidential vote in those years. However, an even more striking pattern in Figure 3 is the monotonic increase in partisan voting in every presidential election since 1972. By 1996, this trend had produced a level of partisan voting 77 percent higher than in 1972—an average increase of 10 percent in each election, compounded over six election cycles—and 15 to 20 percent higher than in the supposed glory days of the 1950s that spawned *The American Voter.*

Figure 3. Partisan Voting in Presidential Elections

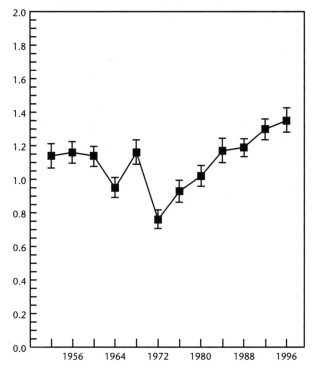

Estimated Impact of Party Identification on Presidential Vote Propensity

Note: Average probit coefficients, major-party voters only, with jackknife standard error bars.

... One possible explanation for the revival of partisan voting evident in Figure 3 is the sorting out of partisan attachments of southerners following the civil rights upheavals of the early and middle 1960s. As national party elites took increasingly distinct stands on racial issues, black voters moved overwhelmingly into the Democratic column, while white southerners defected to conservative Republican presidential candidates. What is important here is that many of these conservative white southerners only gradually shed their traditional Democratic identifications—and Democratic voting behavior at the subpresidential level— through the 1980s and '90s. Thus, it may be tempting to interpret the revival of partisan voting at the presidential level largely as a reflection of the gradual reequilibration of presidential votes and more general partisan attachments among white southerners in the wake of a regional partisan realignment.

As it happens, however, the steady and substantial increases in partisan voting over the past quarter-century evident in Figure 3 are by no means confined to the

Figure 4. Partisan Voting in Presidential Elections, White Southerners and White Non-Southerners

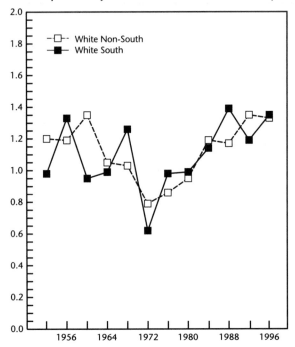

Estimated Impact of Party Identification on Presidential Vote Propensity

Note: Average probit coefficients, major-party voters only.

South. This fact is evident from Figure 4, which displays separate patterns of partisan voting for white southerners and white nonsoutherners. The trend lines are somewhat more ragged for these subgroups than for the electorate as a whole, especially in the South (where the year-by-year estimates are based on an average of fewer than 300 southern white voters in each election); nevertheless, the general pattern in Figure 3 is replicated almost identically in both subgroups in Figure 4. The absolute level of partisan voting in the 1964 and 1972 elections is only slightly lower among southern whites than among nonsouthern whites, and the substantial increase in partisan voting since 1972 appears clearly (indeed, nearly monotonically) in both subgroups.

It should be evident from Figure 4 that the revival of partisan voting in presidential elections documented in Figure 3 is a national rather than a regional phenomenon. Indeed, additional analysis along these lines suggests that the same pattern is evident in a wide variety of subgroups of the electorate, including voters under 40 and those over 50 years of age, those with college educations and those without high school diplomas, and so on. Thus, any convincing explanation of this partisan revival will presumably have to be based upon broad changes in the national political environment, rather than upon narrower demographic or generational developments.

Partisan Voting in Congressional Elections

My analysis so far has focused solely on the impact of partisan loyalties on voting behavior in presidential elections. However, there are a variety of reasons to suppose that the trends evident in presidential voting might not appear at other electoral levels. For one thing, I have already argued that the significant dips in partisanship at the presidential level evident in Figure 3 are attributable primarily to the parties' specific presidential candidates in 1964 and 1972. If that is so, there is little reason to expect those dips—or the subsequent rebounds—in levels of partisan voting to appear at other electoral levels.

In any case, analysts of congressional voting behavior since the 1970s have been more impressed by the advantages of incumbency than by any strong connections between presidential and congressional votes—except insofar as voters may go out of their way to split their tickets in order to produce divided government. Thus, it would not be surprising to find a longer, more substantial decline in the level of partisan voting in congressional elections than in the analysis of presidential voting summarized in Figure 3.

. . . Figure 5 clearly shows a substantial decline in partisan voting in congressional elections from the early 1960s through the late 1970s. Indeed, the level of partisan voting declined in seven of the eight congressional elections between 1964 and 1978; by 1978, the average impact of partisanship on congressional voting was only a bit more than half what it had been before 1964. Although the overall impact of partisanship at the presidential and congressional levels was generally similar for much of this period, the declines at the congressional level were less episodic and longer lasting than those at the presidential level.

What is more surprising is that the revival of partisanship evident in presidential voting patterns since 1972 is also evident in congressional voting patterns since 1978. While the trend is later and less regular at the congressional level than at the presidential level, the absolute increases in partisan voting since 1980 have been of quite similar magnitude in presidential and congressional elections. While partisan voting remains noticeably less powerful in recent congressional elections than it was before 1964—or than it has been in recent presidential elections—the impact of partisanship on congressional votes in 1996 was almost 60 percent greater than in 1978.

An interesting feature of the resurgence of partisan voting in congressional elections documented in Figure 5 is that it appears to be concentrated

Figure 5. Partisan Voting In Presidential and Congressional Elections

Estimated Impact of Party Identification on Presidential and Congressional Vote Propensties

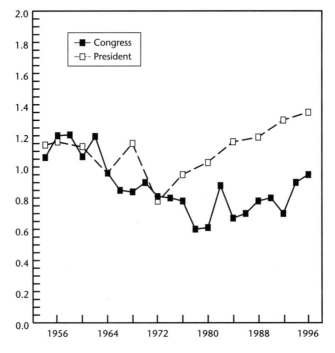

Note: Average probit coefficients, major-party voters only.

disproportionately among younger and better-educated voters. For example, voters under the age of 40 were noticeably less partisan in their voting behavior than those over the age of 50 in almost every election from 1952 through 1984, but virtually indistinguishable from the older voters in the late 1980s and 1990s. Similarly, levels of partisan voting were distinctly lower among voters with some college education than among those without high school diplomas before 1982, but not thereafter. These patterns suggest that the resurgence of partisan voting reflects some positive reaction by younger and better-educated voters to the political developments of the past two decades, rather than simply a "wearing off" of the political stimuli of the 1960s and 1970s.

Discussion

If the analysis presented here is correct, the American political system has slipped, with remarkably little fanfare, into an era of increasingly vibrant partisanship in the electorate, especially at the presidential level but also at the congressional level. How might we account for this apparent revival of partisan voting?

One plausible hypothesis is that increasing partisanship in the electorate represents a response at the mass level to increasing partisanship at the elite level. "If parties in government are weakened," [political scientist Martin] Wattenberg argued, "the public will naturally have less of a stimulus to think of themselves politically in partisan terms." But then the converse may also be true: in an era in which parties in government seem increasingly consequential, the public may increasingly come to develop and apply partisan predispositions of exactly the sort described by the authors of *The American Voter.*

Why might parties in government seem more relevant in the late 1990s than they had a quarter-century earlier? The ascensions of two highly partisan political leaders—Ronald Reagan in 1981 and Newt Gingrich in 1995—may provide part of the explanation. So too may the increasing prominence of the Religious Right in Republican party nominating politics over this period. At a more structural level, the realignment of partisan loyalties in the South in the wake of the civil rights movement of the 1960s may be important, despite the evidence presented in Figure 4 suggesting that the revival of partisan voting has been a national rather than a regional phenomenon.

Regional realignment in the South and the influence of ideological extremists in both parties' nominating politics have combined to produce a marked polarization of the national parties at the elite level. By a variety of measures . . . votes on the floor of Congress have become increasingly partisan since the 1970s. . . . These changes in the composition of the parties' congressional delegations have been "reinforced by the operation of those reform provisions that were intended to enhance collective control" by party leaders in Congress, including a strengthened Democratic caucus and whip system. The new Republican congressional majority in 1995 produced further procedural reforms "delegating more power to party leaders than any House majority since the revolt against Joe Cannon in 1910."

We know less than we should about the nature and extent of mass-level reactions to these elite-level developments. However, the plausibility of a causal link between recent increases in partisanship at the elite and mass levels is reinforced by the fact that the decline in partisan voting in the electorate in the 1960s and 1970s was itself preceded by a noticeable decline in party voting in Congress from the 1950s through the early 1970s. Moreover, some more direct evidence suggests that citizens have taken note of the increasing strength of partisan cues from Washington. For example, the proportion of NES survey respondents perceiving "important differences" between the Democratic and Republican parties increased noticeably in 1980 and again in 1984 and reached a new all-time high (for the period since 1952) in 1996.

Even more intriguingly, [political scientist John] Coleman has documented a systematic temporal relationship between the strength of partisanship in government and the strength of partisanship in the electorate. Analyzing data from 1952 through 1990, Coleman found a strong positive correlation across election years (.60) between the strength of partisanship in NES surveys and the proportion of House budget votes with opposing party majorities—and an even stronger correlation (.66) between mass partisanship and opposing party majorities on budget authorization votes. While the detailed processes underlying this aggregate relationship are by no means clear, the strength of the correlation at least suggests that students of party politics would do well to examine more closely the interrelationship of mass-level and elite-level trends. . . .

12-3

American Political Parties: Still Central to a Functioning Democracy?

L. Sandy Maisel

*In the mid-twentieth century, many political scientists argued that strong polit-
ical parties were essential to a well-functioning democracy. In their opinion,
competitive parties were motivated to offer popular policy proposals, and voters could hold elected officials closely tied to a party accountable by evaluating
the performance of the parties in office. Today party organizations, in the opinion of many observers, are weaker than they were half a century and more ago.
Now candidates run on their own, and party leaders have little influence over
the policy positions taken by candidates or elected officials. Furthermore, the
frequency of divided-party control of government makes it difficult for voters
to hold either party accountable. In this essay political scientist Sandy Maisel
asks whether parties are still important to a strong American democracy. He
concludes that they are—as they should be—but that they must move to
enhance their role in recruiting and supporting candidates for public office.*

ONE MUST BE STRUCK by certain ironies as one looks at the role of American political parties at the dawn of a new millennium. On the one hand, parties have
some evident weaknesses; no close observer can fail to recognize that certain
basic functions that parties perform in our system—for instance, the role of
mobilizing citizens to participate in politics—are not now performed as well as
would be the case in a more ideal system. On the other hand, for a democracy
such as ours to function effectively, the role of parties is still vital, and this necessary centrality, a position once clearly in evidence, is recognized by even the
critics of our current parties. In this chapter, I develop both sides of that dilemma
about the role of parties in the decades ahead.

The Role of Parties in the "Golden Age"

My first assertion in this chapter is that parties have been central to the functioning of American democracy. Of course, we are not just at the dawn of the

Source: Jeffrey E. Cohen, Richard Fleisher, and Paul Kantor, eds., *American Political Parties: Decline or Resurgence?*
(Washington, D.C.: CQ Press, 2001), 103–121. Bibliographic references in the original have been deleted.

new millennium, but, equally important to some, we are about to mark the
100th anniversary of the founding of the American Political Science Association
(APSA) and the 50th anniversary of the publication of the APSA's groundbreak-
ing committee report on political parties (American Political Science Association
1950). Those two events mark an interesting time to begin this examination.

Writing almost 100 years ago, Lord Bryce's observations of our democracy, as
a foreigner visiting our shores, were nearly as perceptive as de Tocqueville's had
been a century before that. Bryce noted that as institutions for mobilizing citizens, political parties served the role of overcoming significant impediments to
an effectively functioning participatory democracy: constraints on citizen time,
competing demands for citizen leisure time, and the complexity of political
issues.

Bryce was observing American politics during the Progressive era, as reforms
were being instituted that would undermine the strength of political parties. But
he was most struck by what American politics looked like during the time period
in which parties were central to American democracy, a period that most
observers claim extended into the 1890s. At the end of the nineteenth century,
one could claim with good reason that American political parties were viewed as
an essential, vital aspect of the functioning of our political institutions.

Why was this so? In recent years scholars have invested a good deal of time
and effort into understanding the circumstances in which political parties are
strong. John Aldrich has argued that parties are instruments that serve the needs
of politicians:

> My basic argument is that the major political party is the creature of the
> politicians, the ambitious office seeker and officeholder. They have created
> and maintained, used or abused, reformed or ignored the political party when
> doing so has furthered their goals and ambitions.

But factors other than their utility to politicians have been seen as important in
understanding party dominance as well. Among the factors to which Aldrich
points are the rules that govern the regime and the party role in it and the "historical setting," a broad phrase encompassing the competitive situation, the
issues at play, the means of political dialogue, and other factors. [Political scien-
tists] Martin Shefter and John Coleman stress the policy environment for its role
in contributing to the strength of parties. They essentially argue that parties will
dominate when issues divide the electorate in a way that is consistent and meaningful to most citizens.

What can be concluded about the so-called golden age of parties is that a combination of circumstances evolved with the result that American politics could
not be understood or appreciated without acknowledging the primary roles that
parties played. The major issue of the day—the tariff—divided the parties and

the electorate along class lines and reinforced regional and ethnic cleavages. The rules under which politics were fought gave the parties a principal role in choosing candidates, in running campaigns, and in governing. Politicians, in response to their own ambitions, found parties useful in winning office, in passing policies they favored, and in enhancing their personal power. The parties cemented citizen loyalties by providing material incentives and social benefits that were each important in the daily lives of the average American.[1] Citizens responded to these parties by giving their enthusiastic loyalty to the parties that championed their views on the most important policies of the day, a loyalty they expressed through long-term commitment and turnout at the polls.

The argument is thus that parties served a key role in the effective functioning of a participatory democracy. Citizens related to one party or the other. The parties expressed views on the issues of the day that mattered most to the citizens. Citizens knew about the party positions and turned out to vote for candidates who advocated their views.[2] Those in government attempted to implement policies that reflected the positions they had taken in campaigns. And for our purposes, parties did what Lord Bryce observed—they overcame the problems inherent in participatory democracy by making politics part of what citizens did for leisure, reducing the time politics consumed by reducing a range of choices to a rather simple one, and simplifying the task of understanding government policies by squaring off on the fundamental issues that concerned most citizens.

Abuses by Parties and the Progressive Response

What went wrong? The problem was that the golden age of partisan politics was in fact tarnished. As parties became more powerful, and as they were serving the needs of a public not consumed with politics, they were also becoming less than exemplary institutions. Corruption was widespread. Patronage was often tied to graft. The partisan press, so useful in communicating party views, frequently distorted public issues in order to increase sales. Political machines dominated city government, socializing immigrant groups to be sure but often short-circuiting the citizenship process so that newly indebted immigrants could convert their

1. Unfortunately, we do not have survey data to compare the ways in which citizens of this era felt about political parties with the ways in which today's citizens respond. Stone has pointed out the interesting converse to that data gap: We do not know how observers of politics in the golden era of politics would view partisan divisions in our time. Although these questions are interesting and in some ways troubling, we are left to deal with the best observations we can obtain for each time period.

2. Of course, in giving this very abbreviated argument, I am ignoring the fact that participation was restricted by gender and race throughout most of the nation for most of this time.

gratitude into votes. One could argue that parties began to limit political discourse, restricting alternatives that might alienate some of their voters. Party power depended on electoral victory; other goals became secondary.

The reaction to this aspect of party power was the reformist zeal of the Mugwumps and the reforms of the Progressive era. The story of these reforms is familiar and has been told in many places. From the point of view of parties, the progressive reforms instituted change after change that limited their ability to control the process: widespread adoption of the secret ballot to prevent parties from knowing for whom their supporters were casting ballots; improvement in registration systems to regularize access to the ballot; civil service reform to remove many government jobs from partisan control; corrupt practices acts to make explicitly illegal some of the actions in which parties had been involved; implementation of the direct primary to remove control of the nominating process (and thus recruitment of officeholders) from the hands of party officials; direct election of U.S. senators to transfer to the voters an important prize previously controlled by the party dominating a state's legislature; nonpartisan governments in many municipalities to handle what many felt to be routine governmental functions without partisan interference; and the institution of initiative, referendum, and recall provisions to permit citizens to retain control over policy making even after elections had been contested.

How can one evaluate the results of these reforms? That depends, of course, on the criteria one uses. First, these reforms accomplished their stated goals. The power of party bosses to control the political process abated. These reforms played a key role in the weakening of party as the central fixture in American politics. Other factors contributed to this trend as well. The expansion of the role of the federal government during the New Deal meant that government officials, not party bosses, provided jobs and welfare for those unable to manage on their own. Political communications, once carried out largely on a personal basis, moved to the realm of mass media, first to radio and then to television. Thus, during the first half of the twentieth century, parties declined for a variety of reasons. Second, the consequences of these reforms were not seen by the Progressives and their allies. Jump ahead fifty years. By the time of the APSA report (American Political Science Association 1950), scholars and activists alike were dissatisfied with the role that political parties were playing in our system of government. Parties were seen by the members of the APSA committee as an institutional vehicle that could be reformed in order to serve more fruitfully the needs of a participatory democracy. Whether the responsible party model was ever an appropriate one for American democracy is not the point. The fact that parties, once central to the system but by mid-century weakened, were seen as a vehicle for governmental reform is more relevant. Further, it can be stated without much controversy that the weakening of parties seen by mid-century continued through the last half of the century. Of course, one must acknowledge that [David] Broder's lament, *The Party's Over*, has not come to pass. Rather, as organizations parties have proven to be quite adaptive institutions. Today they provide resources, both financial and professional, that are important to candidates' campaigns. Through the use of soft money and issue ads, they help to define the issues in campaigns in certain highly competitive regions. But these roles are reactive to the new context of candidate-centered campaigning.

Thus we see an evident dilemma as we look to the future of political parties. They are moving in two apparently opposite directions. Even with the significant adaptations noted earlier in this chapter, parties and party leaders are not looked to as building blocks of the electoral process. Choose your own standard of judgment—self-reporting of party identification by voters or strength of party identification among those who do identify, ticket splitting, party switching among the political elite, control over campaigns, control over political communication, ability to discipline their own officeholders, breadth and strength of organization, centrality to the process—by these criteria or many others, parties continue to appear weak and far from central to the electoral process.

Difficulties Evident in the Electoral Process Today

How then might parties be still central to a functioning democracy? *The argument is that just as parties are weak, so too is the state of our participatory democratic system.* For a representative democracy to function effectively, citizens must be given meaningful choices at the polls. Our representative democracy rests on the consent of the governed. Citizens can give their consent to the policies passed by those in office only if they have the opportunity and take the opportunity to review the performance of those in office. Frequent elections are meaningless in the absence of competition. Thus one measure of the health of a democratic system is the extent to which citizens are given a meaningful choice. Another measure is the extent to which citizens participate in that choice.

Even with all of their flaws, political parties in their heyday contributed to these important aspects of democracy. The parties controlled access to the ballot and guaranteed that competition existed. They did so because that was viewed as the most important aspect of their role. Parties benefited when their candidates won office, controlled the spoils of victory, and implemented the policies they advocated.

But more than that, parties involved citizens in the electoral process. As I noted earlier in this chapter, party politics was relevant for most citizens, because the parties split on the key issues of the day and because they affected voters' daily lives in basic ways, serving as an important element of the community's social fabric. Parties mobilized citizens in many ways. Citizens saw the relevance of the issues raised and had a stake in the success of the party that claimed their allegiance. A deep sense of loyalty developed between voters and party leaders. In addition, involvement in party politics during campaign season was part of the leisure activities in which citizens partook—in a way that would be totally alien to even the most politically active citizens today.

The contrast between the functioning of parties in the so-called golden era and the ways in which they work today could not be more stark. One hundred years ago party leaders controlled the nominating process; their most important function—and ultimately that on which all else depended—was to contest for office. Today, throughout the nation, party nominations are determined by direct primary; in some states, party rules prohibit party officials from involvement in the nominating process. In most states, the role of parties in determining nominees is minor and informal.

One hundred years ago the parties provided a simple, coherent set of reasons for their supporters to maintain loyalty. The issues before the nation were less complex than they are today, the major parties divided on the issues of the day, and the parties connected directly with the people. Today candidates voice their own issue positions, often at odds with those of others in their parties, still more often nuanced to appeal to their particular constituents. Rather than appealing to citizens based on issue differences, the leaders of the two major parties strive to capture the middle-ground, to offend as few possible voters as possible by issue positions.

One hundred years ago parties mobilized their followers through personal contact at the precinct, ward, or, in rural areas, town level. Party workers knew all of the voters and knew their preferences. The job of the party workers was to get their supporters to the polls. Incentives were both tangible and intangible. Voters knew that the tangible incentives from their parties depended on their parties' officeholders winning elections. Social networks and peer pressure also led citizens to vote; civic participation was expected and was a clear societal norm. Today political communication is through the mass media or through computerized, impersonal mailings. Citizens do not know local party workers, often because party positions in their localities are vacant. Certainly party workers who do exist do not provide important rewards to party loyalists. Politics no longer provides the social network for many citizens; leisure time is filled by other pursuits—sports, church, family, television, movies, and the like.

Broad-based partisan mobilization has been replaced by narrowly defined issue-specific activation. Whereas once the parties tried to mobilize all of their followers to vote for their slate of candidates, now special interests, making narrower appeals to carefully selected audiences, try to convince only those who support their positions to participate. Turnout is down. Programmatic discussion has given way to narrow appeals based on specific interests or to broad appeals based on either character or capturing the middle-ground and offending as few as possible. Satisfaction with and trust in government have declined.

To cite just three indices:

1. Voter turnouts in presidential and congressional elections remain well below what they were at the beginning of the twentieth century and considerably below what they were even in the 1950s.

2. In National Election Study surveys in the 1990s, more than 70 percent of the respondents agreed with the statement, "Public officials don't care what people like me think," and 60 percent of the respondents thought, "Government is run by a few big interests looking out for themselves."

3. Competition for the right to govern has decreased drastically. In the 1998 congressional election, more than 98 percent of the incumbent representatives seeking reelection did so successfully. But more than that, ninety-four incumbents were returned to office without any major party competition whatsoever. In addition, another thirty-nine incumbents won with over 75 percent of the vote in the general election. Out of more than four hundred incumbents seeking reelection in 1998, only thirty received less than 55 percent of the vote; among those thirty were the five who lost in that election. The 1998 election was not an aberration. It merely extended a trend that has existed and has been commented on for some time. Although slightly more competition exists for more visible offices—governor and U.S. senator—there is even less competition for seats in most state legislatures and for seats in county legislatures and on city and town councils.

A number of factors are obviously at work here—and one could not argue that weakening parties are the only cause of this lack of competition. But two aspects of this phenomenon, which is a serious problem for our democracy, deserve attention.

First, candidates run on their own, frequently building their own organizations distinct from that of the party and often taking great pains to avoid association with a party. Candidate-centered organizations have been encouraged (1) by the weakening of party allegiance among the electorate and of party organization, (2) by the means through which citizens receive political communications, and (3) by campaign finance laws that require individual candidates to form their own committees, that restrict the role that party can play, and that encourage the role of special interest groups.

Second, party organization plays a limited role at best in recruiting candidates for office. The role is limited because party organization in many areas is weak or nonexistent, because parties can offer potential candidates few incentives to encourage them to run, and because national party rules have restricted what the party committees most concerned with campaigns for federal office are permitted to do.

These two developments have shifted the process through which ballot positions are filled from one of *party recruitment* to one of *candidate emergence.* However, it is difficult to pinpoint when this shift occurred. The timing of this shift varies from locality to locality and from office to office, but there is no doubt that it has occurred.

Discussions of systemic reform have gone on elsewhere. Certainly the literature on changes in political communication is more than adequate to make the point. Similarly, campaign finance reform has been an issue atop the agendas of those dissatisfied with the ways our elections have been run for decades. In fact, during the Carter administration the prestigious designation HR1 was reserved for a campaign finance reform measure in 1977. The history of the failure of campaign finance reform has been well documented.

Strengthening Parties to Address the Problems of Today's Politics

What about the weakness of party organization as a contributing factor to both the lack of competitiveness in American elections and the lack of citizen interest in those elections? Although there is widespread agreement that party organization is weak today, perhaps less agreement is found concerning what would constitute strong parties in the modern context. Certainly no one would argue that we should return to the antidemocratic, smoke-filled rooms of the past. But is it possible to strengthen party organization so that the parties can perform the important, central functions they once performed in our system (at least more effectively than today)? If so, what would constitute strong parties in that context?

The first prerequisite would be to have some influence on the selection of candidates running under their labels. Second, parties would need some additional control over the functioning of elections in order to regain strength. Third, party messages would need to be consistent (and differentiated) at least on major issues. Fourth, parties would have to be able to play an active role in implementing major parts of their programs. The argument is not that these enhanced roles for parties need to be absolute, but each needs to be altered so that parties are in a stronger position than they are now. This is not an argument for a responsible party model. Rather, it is an argument for a *relevant party model.*

The most important of these aspects—and the focus of the remainder of this chapter—is the potential impact on state and local nominations. To the extent that parties affect state and local nominations, officeholders have a stake in the party. That is, if state and local party activists are influential in an officeholder's first nomination or if they are seen as influencing an officeholder's ability to achieve renomination, then elected officials will care about what the party activists think and do. The chances of the other criteria being met increase when party becomes more relevant to officeholders.

Some years ago John Frendeis, James Gibson, and Laura Vertz demonstrated that the existence of functioning local party organizations had important consequences for electoral competition. My work with Walter Stone shows that party organization retains significant influence in encouraging strong potential candidates to run for office. In the summer of 1997, we surveyed a group of potential candidates for the U.S. House of Representatives whom we identified in a random sample of 200 congressional districts throughout the nation.[3] The Candidate Emergence Study asked potential candidates a series of questions regarding the likelihood that they would run for the House and the factors that entered into their decisions. The analysis of the data is ongoing, but some of the results to this point are suggestive of the role that political parties can play in the recruitment process.

The pool of potential candidates in the 200 congressional districts comprised individuals who were identified by one or more of the informants in their districts as someone who would be a strong candidate for Congress, regardless of whether the individual had ever expressed interest in running or been mentioned as a possible candidate. State legislators whose districts were located in the 200 congressional districts in the sample were added to this list of named potential candidates. For analytical purposes two separate datasets were created, one consisting of all potential candidates named by those in our informant pool (including potential candidates who happened to be state legislators) and one consisting of all state legislator respondents (including those who were named by our informants).

A battery of questions was asked seeking respondent assessment of the likelihood that he or she would run for the U.S. House of Representatives in 1998, in

---

3. The Candidate Emergence Project has been described in great detail elsewhere (see Maisel and Stone 1997; Stone and Maisel 1999; Stone, Maisel, and Maestas 1998; these and other papers are available on the Candidate Emergence Study web site at http:// socsci.colorado.edu/CES/home.html).

Table 1. Contact by Party Committees

	Named Potential Candidates (percent) (Largest n = 452)	State Legislators (percent) (Largest n = 875)
National Party Committees	08.2	03.2
National Congressional Campaign Committees	15.7	04.9
State Party Committees	22.2	08.8
Local Party Committees	34.7	14.4
Any Party Committee	40.7	18.7

Source: Candidate Emergence Study, Potential Candidate Survey.

the next three to four terms, or in the foreseeable future. For much of the analysis this battery of questions has constituted the dependent variable.[4] The independent variables about which respondents were questioned included contacts by various party officials. In addition to asking about the national parties, the national congressional campaign committees, state parties, and local parties, indices were created to measure multiple contacts, and a dummy variable was used to measure whether the respondent had been contacted by any party organization.

Table 1 shows the frequency with which the respondents were contacted by party organizations. Table 2 shows the numbers of organizations that contacted the respondents. Some conclusions are clear. First, as one would expect, the more local the committee, the more likely that a respondent was contacted. More than one in three of the named potential candidates and one in seven of the state legislators representing voters in the sampled congressional districts were contacted by local party officials about running for the House. By contrast, far fewer were contacted by either the national party organization or by the state party.

Second, an impressively large number of the named potential candidates (more than two in five) were contacted by some level of party organization; nearly one in five of the state legislators reported some contact. Third, although the norm was for only one organization to contact a potential candidate (if any made contact at all), nearly a quarter of the named potential candidates (and almost 10 percent of the state legislators) were contacted by more than one organization. Further analysis remains to be done, but the implication is that

4. For other aspects of the analysis, "chances of winning" has been used as the dependent variable. For still other projects, different questions have been used as appropriate.

Table 2. Total Contacts by Party Committees

	Named Potential Candidates (percent) (n = 452)	State Legislators (percent) (n = 875)
No Contacts	59.3	81.3
Contacted by One Organization	16.8	09.9
Contacted by Two Organizations	12.8	06.4
Contacted by Three Organizations	05.8	01.0

Source: Candidate Emergence Study, Potential Candidate Survey.

party organizations make a concerted effort to contact the most appealing potential candidates in order to convince them to run.

Of course the relevant question for this analysis is the extent to which these contacts were successful in convincing potential candidates to run for the House. Table 3 presents an initial answer to this inquiry, exploring the question of the relationship between a potential candidate's likelihood of running for the House in 1998 (scored on a seven-point scale) and the various measures of party contact.

Table 3 reveals a statistically significant ($p < .01$) relationship between the likelihood that a potential candidate will run for the House and that potential candidate's having been contacted by party officials in all cases except two (the national organizations contacting state legislators). The strength of the relationship varies among the types of contacts. It is strongest when named potential candidates are contacted by more than one party organization—and when the named potential candidates are contacted by the national party organization. These bivariate relationships, while highly suggestive, are just that—suggestive. Much more analysis needs to be done to understand, for example, which of the potential candidates were most likely to be contacted by which level of party organization (if at all) or to unravel the nature of the relationship between contact and likelihood of running. The nature of the contact, the expectations of the potential candidate for organizational support, the strength of the party organization, and other variables clearly enter into this relationship.

The argument then is that party organizations can have an impact on recruiting quality candidates for Congress and by extension for other offices. As the offices become more local in scope, the local organization is the likely point of contact. Clearly most local organizations—and all party organizations for most offices—do not play this role effectively. But it is there to be played, and it can be effective.

To be sure, the national parties are playing this role for some seats in Congress. Both national congressional campaign committees and those in leadership posi-

Table 3. Correlations with Likelihood of Running in 1998

Named Potential	Candidates [n]	State Legislators [n]
National Party Committees	0.2332*	0.0173*
	[299]	[762]
National Congressional Campaign Committees	0.1841*	0.0502*
	[308]	[765]
State Party Committees	0.1512*	0.941*
	[324]	[771]
Local Party Committees	0.1553*	00.1174*
	[330]	[776]
Any Party Committee	0.1800*	00.1103*
	[407]	[820]
Cumulative Party Contact	0.2449*	00.1086*
	[407]	[820]

Source: Candidate Emergence Study, Potential Candidate Survey.
* $p < .01$

tions in the House were concerned about the challengers running in 2000, because control of the House was at stake. In strategizing, both parties see congressional elections as local in nature. To determine which races they will attempt to influence, the parties use poll-derived studies of the vulnerability of incumbents. They encourage potential candidates by offering various types of campaign support, both that paid for by soft money at the party level and financial contributions or help in raising money by party leaders.[5] However, they have neither the resources nor the power to take these steps in every race throughout the nation. Thus they concentrate on only a relatively small number of seats seen to be "in play," all but guaranteeing little or no competition in the other seats.

Although stronger state legislative party organizations and state legislative leaders play active roles in recruitment in some areas, the extent of party influence in recruiting candidates below the national level seems at best to parallel the situation in recruiting candidates for Congress. That is, candidates are recruited for seats seen as likely to be hotly contested. But many seats go to one party or the other by default, because the state and local parties do not find any candidates, much less credible candidates.

The potential role that parties can play in effectively extending competition goes beyond encouraging qualified strong candidates to run for office. One of the most important tools taken away from parties by the progressive reforms was control over the nominating process. If parties cannot control nominations—or

5. I thank Paul Herrnson for suggesting how these party efforts conform with my argument.

at least strongly influence them—then party encouragement of potential candidates may be for naught. And potential candidates surely see this.

No clearer example of this can be presented than the case of the special election to fill the California congressional seat left vacant by the death of Democrat George Brown. Ten candidates filed for the special election in the fall of 1999, for a seat that was thought to be highly competitive. The Democrats feared that their party would be split between Brown's widow, Marta, and state senator Joe Baca; Baca's lukewarm position on gun control was a key issue in that race. The Democratic leadership felt that each was a strong candidate but that a united party was crucial. Republican leaders, including Rep. Thomas M. Davis III of Virginia, chair of the National Republican Congressional Committee, felt that the strongest Republican candidate was Superior Court Judge Linda M. Wilde, who had lost to Brown by fewer than 1,000 votes in 1996. But Davis and others were unsuccessful in efforts to convince the 1994 GOP nominee, Rob Guzman, and the 1998 nominee, Ella Pirozzi, who was raising money for a rematch with Brown in 2000 at the time of his death, to step aside for Wilde. As a result, Wilde stepped aside.[6]

Party efforts to derecruit can be as important as efforts to recruit. The 2000 U.S. Senate race to succeed Sen. Daniel Patrick Moynihan, D-N.Y., was characterized early on by GOP efforts to clear the nomination path for New York City's mayor Rudolph Guiliani, thought to be the Republican most likely to capture the seat against First Lady Hillary Rodham Clinton. When Guiliani dropped out of the race unexpectedly, party leaders made similar efforts on behalf of the eventual nominee, Long Island congressman Rick Lazio. In Ohio, party leaders worked hard, and successfully, to discourage controversial talk-show host Jerry Springer from seeking a seat in the U.S. Senate in 2000.

Is it possible to determine when party officials do and do not play an effective role in the nominating process? Some variables can be singled out for further testing. The most important factor is the willingness (and in some cases the ability under party rules) of party officials to be involved in the nominating process. The first step in this effort is the commitment to involvement. The second step is the recruitment of strong potential candidates to convince them to run. The third step is the effort to smooth the path to nomination for those candidates.

To achieve the first step, party organization must exist. For years there was no Republican Party organization throughout much of the South. Most seats,

---

6. The California example also points to the influence of changes in state laws that impede parties' roles in the nominating process. At the time California operated under a so-called blanket primary, in which all names appear on one ballot and voters can essentially cast ballots in the Democratic primary for some offices and the Republican primary for others. This form of ballot makes it more difficult for party activists and loyalists to exert influence over their parties' nominations.

especially those below the level of statewide office, went by default to Democratic candidates. The rejuvenation of the GOP in the South started at the top, but one clear sign of success has been the ability of southern Republicans to fill slates and win seats for lower-level offices (for example, state legislators or county officials). Where party organization does not exist, the likelihood that party will play its most basic role—contesting offices so that the citizenry has some choice—diminishes quickly.

Some party organizations are prohibited, by party rule, from intervening in primary contests. That restriction places party officials in a bind. Part of their role, almost by definition, is to guarantee that their slate is as full as possible. But they cannot even guarantee help to the candidates whom they recruit if those candidates are challenged for a nomination, much less can they guarantee them the nomination. Therein lies a serious problem for party organization at the dawn of the new millennium.

The reformist zeal to rein in parties was so strong and the image of party leaders among the electorate so tainted at the turn of the last century that party leaders today are often unable to perform what should be their most vital function in our democracy, the recruitment of candidates for office. Party leaders who are so restricted often must let the nomination process take care of itself. In so doing, they allow many seats to go uncontested, weak candidates to win nominations without serious opposition in other cases, and qualified candidates to go unrecruited and unencouraged, even if they are contemplating a contest.

What can be done to alter this situation? Some steps are already being taken. Legislative leaders are setting up their own organizations to recruit candidates for key seats. This has been seen at the national level for some time. The experience of GOPAC, a political action committee established by Rep. Newt Gingrich, R-Ga., is instructive here, but so too is the collaboration between House Minority Leader Richard Gephardt, D-Mo., and the Democratic Congressional Campaign Committee as they sought candidates for the 2000 election. It is becoming more and more true at the state level. But again, this kind of enterprise is selective; organizations concentrate only on those seats deemed winnable, not on guaranteeing competition throughout a state or region. Although these efforts are commendable, they do not allow the system to meet the minimum requirements for an effectively functioning participatory democracy.

Other steps are being taken in various parts of the country. No one would encourage reforms that would lead back to domination by party bosses or to nominations decided in secret in the proverbial smoke-filled rooms. But a number of states do permit party organizations to play a formal role in nominating contests. In many states pre-primary party conventions play some role in the process. The role may be to guarantee access to the primary ballot (as in New Mexico, Colorado, and New York) or to place the convention choice in a preferred position on the ballot (as in Rhode Island, North Dakota, and Delaware). Connecticut calls for convention (or party caucus) nominations, unless the choice is challenged by a candidate who has not prevailed at the party meeting. Party endorsements have official status in eight states and unofficial but important status in at least five more.

In addition, local party units often play key endorsing roles in other states. The states with a strong party role in the nominating process tend to be highly competitive two-party states. The party rules all but guarantee a strong party organization, because the organization has an important function to perform. In the late 1980s, Malcolm Jewell and David Olson pointed out that parties with formal roles in the nominating process were not equally successful in guaranteeing that the parties' choices won the primaries. The point is that rules of this type give the party a stake in seeking and supporting strong candidates—and that leads to improvement of the process.

Conclusion

Although American political parties appear to be weaker now than they were in their heyday, they still have important roles to play, if our political system is to function as well as it might. The dilemma about the future for political parties— that is, which of the two trends, resurgence or decline, will prevail—will be resolved according to whether parties can emerge to play a relevant role. Neither advocacy of a pure strong party model nor acceptance of an archetypal weak party model seems appropriate. Rather, what is called for is a relevant party model. Parties have taken some steps in this direction, but many more steps remain if the goal of an effectively functioning democracy is to be obtained.

First, few would argue against the proposition that American political parties appear to be weaker than they once were. The relevant question is the standard of strength one should apply. If the standard is the strong or responsible party model familiar to students of party theory (and present in many parliamentary governments), our party system falls far short. But if one adopts a more pragmatic standard, one could argue that American parties have adapted quite well to a changing political context. They behave strategically in allotting their resources, and their role is an important one for maintaining competitive elections.

One could extend that argument further. As mentioned earlier, the lack of two-party competition stands as one piece of evidence that the electoral system today fails to meet democratic ideals. Some would argue that those ideals are met throughout the nation as a whole, even if they are not met in every district. The partisan split in the House of Representatives is extremely close; congressional elections in swing districts are extremely hard fought as control of the House is at stake. Much the same can be said for the Senate. Fewer and fewer state houses are dominated by one party or the other; split state houses or divided government in the states has become more common. Presidential elections and gubernatorial elections in most states are also hotly contested, with neither party eliminated before the campaigns begin. As a result of these factors, competition for control of the national government and of most state governments is intense. Looked at in this way, citizens can use the ballot box to instruct their elected officials as to their desires.

However, this view of effective competition to ensure democratic control over the government accepts that only some citizens should have a say in the outcome. Other citizens have no direct control, though their votes offset each other. That conception of democracy fails the basic test of citizen participation, of obtaining consent of the governed. It is a view of representation that ignores the nexus between representative and constituent. It is a view that leads to increased public cynicism and disdain for politics.

Thus we return to the role of parties as these organizations might function in the twenty-first century. How can they be relevant in an evolving electoral context? How can they effectively expand their current roles to be more central to the functioning of American democracy?

Parties perform many of the functions they have traditionally performed but often do so poorly. That is to say, parties provide a framework for an overall organization. The national party conventions name the parties' nominees for president and vice president, who adopt platforms that state party positions. State and local parties try to fill ballot slates and to organize campaign activities for all of their candidates. And the parties certainly provide the structure for organizing government at the state and national levels. But these roles involve little independent input by party officials. They are carried out because they must be carried out. Little of substance is involved in the parties' roles in these functions.

Parties have adapted to a changing political context by taking on some new roles, particularly as a provider of campaign funds and a broker bringing together candidates who need financial support and interests that might provide that support and bringing together political consultants with specific expertise and candidates in need of that expertise. In so doing, they have made themselves relevant to their candidates.

But that kind of relevance is different from relevance to the democratic process. The roles parties have adopted are important for self-preservation, so that the parties do not become the dinosaurs of the political process. But can they make a positive contribution to that process?

The argument here is that they can—and that the key to their playing a central role in the current political environment lies in political recruitment. It is important to differentiate roles when noting that parties are weakening in some ways and becoming stronger in others. Recruitment is one role on which they must concentrate if they are to reassume a central position in a democracy.

In the current environment the party role in recruitment is far different from what it was in the past. In the past, parties controlled access to the ballot. They recruited candidates and guaranteed those candidates the party nomination. Today no guarantees can be given; parties have only limited power to influence nominations, and that power varies from state to state. Moreover, candidate-centered campaigns imply that candidate emergence has replaced candidate recruitment. Most candidates today are self-starters, not brought up through the ranks by party leaders.

The relevant party role in recruitment in this context takes on three aspects. The first aspect is recognition that an important party role is to guarantee, to the extent possible, that strong candidates run for all offices. As more and more districts become competitive, fewer and fewer seats are safe for either party; strength of candidacies is important in the outcome. The second aspect, following directly on the first, is the assumption that the party role is to encourage, in every possible way, good candidates who are considering running. The Candidate Emergence Study clearly shows that many strong potential candidates consider races for public office but in the end decide not to run. It also shows that party encouragement helps potential candidates tip the scales toward running but that parties are not very active in encouraging potential candidates. A clear opportunity exists for an enhanced and highly relevant role.

The third aspect is necessary to make this role possible. Parties need to increase the resources available to them to encourage potential candidates to run. Doing so would involve changes in party rules, changes that would set up mechanisms for party endorsement of potential candidates before nomination. Such mechanisms exist in some states—and those states are more successful in fielding strong slates of candidates.

It is difficult to argue for an enhanced role for political parties in an era generally viewed as anti-party. In addition, one must be concerned about who controls a party organization if one thinks it should have more strength. If party organizations are controlled by fringe elements in the party, then their domination might lead to less, not more, competition in general elections. If that were the case in both parties, the result could be increased tension in the polity. The assumption here is that an increased role for party organization would mean that traditional elements in the party would have a stake in participating. Party then could play a more central role in defining the issues of the day, in structuring campaigns, in mobilizing the electorate, and ultimately in seeing that the electoral process represents our best effort to give the consent of the governed to policies passed by our elected officials.

If citizens see the importance of electoral competition to their stake in our democracy, they should not resist efforts by state and local parties to take the steps necessary so that they can encourage strong potential candidates to run in an effective manner. By so doing, they would take a large step toward the creation of a more relevant role for parties in the politics of the twenty-first century.

Chapter 13

Interest Groups

―――――――

13-1

The Scope and Bias of the Pressure System

E. E. Schattschneider

In the mid twentieth century, many observers believed that James Madison's vision of America—as a multitude of groups or factions, none of which dominated the government—had been realized. E. E. Schattschneider provided an alternative view. In the following essay, which was originally published in 1960, Schattschneider argued that moneyed interests dominated mid-twentieth-century politics. In his view the dominance of moneyed interests limited the scope of government action and created a bias in the pressures placed on policymakers. As we enter the twenty-first century, the issues raised by Schattschneider remain relevant to debates over the influence of organized and moneyed interests in American government and politics.

THE SCOPE OF CONFLICT is an aspect of the scale of political organization and the extent of political competition. The size of the constituencies being mobilized, the inclusiveness or exclusiveness of the conflicts people expect to develop leave a bearing on all theories about how politics is or should be organized. In other words, nearly all theories about politics have something to do with the question of who can get into the fight and who is to be excluded. . . .

Source: E. E. Schattschneider, "The Scope and Bias of the Pressure System," in *The Semi-Sovereign People* (New York: Holt, Rinehart, Winston, 1960), 20–45. Some notes appearing in the original have been deleted.

If we are able . . . to distinguish between public and private interests and between organized and unorganized groups we have marked out the major boundaries of the subject; *we have given the subject shape and scope.* . . . [W]e can now appropriate the piece we want and leave the rest to someone else. For a multitude of reasons *the most likely field of study is that of the organized, special-interest groups.* The advantage of concentrating on organized groups is that they are known, identifiable, and recognizable. The advantage of concentrating on special-interest groups is that they have one important characteristic in common; they are all exclusive. This piece of the pie (the organized special-interest groups) we shall call the *pressure system.* The pressure system has boundaries we can define; we can fix its scope and make an attempt to estimate its bias.

It may be assumed at the outset that all organized special-interest groups have some kind of impact on politics. A sample survey of organizations made by the Trade Associations Division of the United States Department of Commerce in 1942 concluded that "From 70 to 100 percent (of these associations) are planning activities in the field of government relations, trade promotion, trade practices, public relations, annual conventions, cooperation with other organizations, and information services."

The subject of our analysis can be reduced to manageable proportions and brought under control if we restrict ourselves to the groups whose interests in politics are sufficient to have led them to unite in formal organizations having memberships, bylaws, and officers. A further advantage of this kind of definition is, we may assume, that the organized special-interest groups are the most self-conscious, best developed, most intense and active groups. Whatever claims can be made for a group theory of politics ought to be sustained by the evidence concerning these groups, if the claims have any validity at all.

The organized groups listed in the various directories (such as *National Associations of the United States,* published at intervals by the United States Department of Commerce) and specialty yearbooks, registers, etc. and the *Lobby Index,* published by the United States House of Representatives, probably include the bulk of the organizations in the pressure system. All compilations are incomplete, but these are extensive enough to provide us with some basis for estimating the scope of the system.

By the time a group has developed the kind of interest that leads it to organize, it may be assumed that it has also developed some kind of political bias because *organization is itself a mobilization of bias in preparation for action.* Since these groups can be identified and since they have memberships (i.e., they include and exclude people), it is possible to think of the *scope* of the system.

When lists of these organizations are examined, the fact that strikes the student most forcibly is that *the system is very small.* The range of organized, identifiable, known groups is amazingly narrow; there is nothing remotely universal about it. There is a tendency on the part of the publishers of directories of associations to place an undue emphasis on business organizations, an emphasis that is almost inevitable because the business community is by a wide margin the most highly organized segment of society. Publishers doubtless tend also to reflect public demand for information. Nevertheless, the dominance of business groups in the pressure system is so marked that it probably cannot be explained away as an accident of the publishing industry.

The business character of the pressure system is shown by almost every list available. *National Associations of the United States* lists 1,860 business associations out of a total of 4,000 in the volume, though it refers without listing to 16,000 organizations of businessmen. One cannot be certain what the total content of the unknown associational universe may be, but, taken with the evidence found in other compilations, it is obvious that business is remarkably well represented. Some evidence of the overall scope of the system is to be seen in the estimate that 15,000 national trade associations have a gross membership of about one million business firms. The data are incomplete, but even if we do not have a detailed map this is the shore dimly seen.

Much more directly related to pressure politics is the *Lobby Index, 1946–1949* (an index of organizations and individuals registering or filing quarterly reports under the Federal Lobbying Act), published as a report of the House Select Committee on Lobbying Activities. In this compilation, 825 out of a total of 1,247 entries (exclusive of individuals and Indian tribes) represented business. A selected list of the most important of the groups listed in the *Index* (the groups spending the largest sums of money on lobbying) published in the *Congressional Quarterly Log* shows 149 business organizations in a total of 265 listed.

The business or upper-class bias of the pressure system shows up everywhere. Businessmen are four or five times as likely to write to their congressmen as manual laborers are. College graduates are far more apt to write to their congressmen than people in the lowest educational category are.

The limited scope of the business pressure system is indicated by all available statistics. Among business organizations, the National Association of Manufacturers (with about 20,000 corporate members) and the Chamber of Commerce of the United States (about as large as the N.A.M.) are giants. Usually business associations are much smaller. Of 421 trade associations in the metal-products industry listed in *National Associations of the United States*, 153 have a membership of less than 20. The median membership was somewhere between 24 and 50. Approximately the same scale of memberships is to be found in the lumber, furniture, and paper industries, where 37.3 percent of the associations listed had a membership of less than 20 and the median membership was in the 25 to 50 range.

The statistics in these cases are representative of nearly all other classifications of industry.

Data drawn from other sources support this thesis. Broadly, the pressure system has an upper-class bias. There is overwhelming evidence that participation in voluntary organizations is related to upper social and economic status; the rate of participation is much higher in the upper strata than it is elsewhere. The general proposition is well stated by [political scientist Paul] Lazarsfeld:

> People on the lower SES levels are less likely to belong to any organizations than the people on high SES (Social and Economic Status) levels. (On an A and B level, we find 72 percent of these respondents who belong to one or more organizations. The proportion of respondents who are members of formal organizations decreases steadily as SES level descends until, on the D level only 35 percent of the respondents belong to any associations).[1]

The bias of the system is shown by the fact that *even non-business organizations reflect an upper-class tendency.*

Lazarsfeld's generalization seems to apply equally well to urban and rural populations. The obverse side of the coin is that large areas of the population appear to be wholly outside the system of private organization. A study made by Ira Reid of a Philadelphia area showed that in a sample of 963 persons, 85 percent belonged to no civic or charitable organization and 74 percent belonged to no occupational, business, or professional associations, while another Philadelphia study of 1,154 women showed that 55 percent belonged to no associations of any kind.[2]

A *Fortune* farm poll taken some years ago found that 70.5 percent of farmers belonged to no agricultural organizations. A similar conclusion was reached by two Gallup polls showing that perhaps no more than one third of the farmers of the country belonged to farm organizations, while another *Fortune* poll showed that 86.8 percent of the low-income farmers belonged to no farm organizations. All available data support the generalization that the farmers who do not participate in rural organizations are largely the poorer ones. . . .

The class bias of associational activity gives meaning to the limited scope of the pressure system, because *scope and bias are aspects of the same tendency.* The data raise a serious question about the validity of the proposition that special-interest groups are a universal form of political organization reflecting *all* interests. As a matter of fact, to suppose that everyone participates in pressure-group activity and that all interests get themselves organized in the pressure system is to destroy the meaning of this form of politics. The pressure system makes sense only as the political instrument of a segment of the community. It gets results by being selective and biased; *if everybody got into the act, the unique advantages of this form of organization would be destroyed, for it is possible that if all interests could be mobilized the result would be a stalemate.*

Special-interest organizations are most easily formed when they deal with small numbers of individuals who are acutely aware of their exclusive interests. To describe the conditions of pressure-group organization in this way is, however, to say that it is primarily a business phenomenon. Aside from a few very large organizations (the churches, organized labor, farm organizations, and veterans' organizations) the residue is a small segment of the population. *Pressure politics is essentially the politics of small groups.*

The vice of the groupist theory is that it conceals the most significant aspects of the system. The flaw in the pluralist heaven is that the heavenly chorus sings with a strong upper-class accent. Probably about 90 percent of the people cannot get into the pressure system.

The notion that the pressure system is automatically representative of the whole community is a myth fostered by the universalizing tendency of modern group theories. *Pressure politics is a selective process* ill designed to serve diffuse interests. The system is skewed, loaded, and unbalanced in favor of a fraction of a minority.

On the other hand, pressure tactics are not remarkably successful in mobilizing general interests. When pressure-group organizations attempt to represent the interests of large numbers of people, they are usually able to reach only a small segment of their constituencies. Only a chemical trace of the fifteen million Negroes in the United States belong to the National Association for the Advancement of Colored People. Only one five-hundredth of 1 percent of American women belong to the League of Women Voters, only one sixteen-hundredth of 1 percent of the consumers belong to the National Consumers' League, and only 6 percent of American automobile drivers belong to the American Automobile Association, while about 15 percent of the veterans belong to the American Legion.

The competing claims of pressure groups and political parties for the loyalty of the American public revolve about the difference between the results likely to be achieved by small-scale and large-scale political organization. Inevitably, the outcome of pressure politics and party politics will be vastly different. . . .

. . . Everything we know about politics suggests that a conflict is likely to change profoundly as it becomes political. It is a rare individual who can confront his antagonists without changing his opinions to some degree. Everything changes once a conflict gets into the political arena—*who* is involved, *what* the conflict is about, the resources available, etc. It is extremely difficult to predict the outcome of a fight by watching its beginning because we do not even know who else is going to get into the conflict. The logical consequence of the exclusive emphasis on the determinism of the private origins of conflict is to assign zero value to the political process.

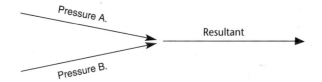

The very expression "pressure politics" invites us to misconceive the role of special-interest groups in politics. The word "pressure" implies the use of some kind of force, a form of intimidation, something other than reason and information, to induce public authorities to act against their own best judgment. [This is reflected in the famous statement by political scientist Earl Latham, in his 1952 book *The Group Basis of Politics,* that] the legislature is a "referee" who "ratifies" and "records" the "balance of power" among the contending groups.[3]

It is hard to imagine a more effective way of saying that Congress has no mind or force of its own or that Congress is unable to invoke new forces that might alter the equation.

Actually the outcome of political conflict is not like the "resultant" of opposing forces in physics. To assume that the forces in a political situation could be diagramed as a physicist might diagram the resultant of opposing physical forces is to wipe the slate clean of all remote, general, and public considerations for the protection of which civil societies have been instituted.

Moreover, the notion of "pressure" distorts the image of the power relations involved. *Private conflicts are taken into the public arena precisely because someone wants to make certain that the power ratio among the private interests most immediately involved shall not prevail.* To treat a conflict as a mere test of the strength of the private interests is to leave out the most significant factors. This is so true that it might indeed be said that the only way to preserve private power ratios is to keep conflicts out of the public arena.

The assumption that it is only the "interested" who count ought to be reexamined in view of the foregoing discussion. The tendency of the literature of pressure politics has been to neglect the low-tension force of large numbers because it *assumes that the equation of forces is fixed at the outset.*

Given the assumptions made by the group theorists, the attack on the idea of the majority is completely logical. The assumption is that conflict is monopolized narrowly by the parties immediately concerned. There is no room for a majority when conflict is defined so narrowly. It is a great deficiency of the group theory that it has found no place in the political system for the majority. The force of the majority is of an entirely different order of magnitude, something not to be measured by pressure-group standards.

Instead of attempting to exterminate all political forms, organizations, and alignments that do not qualify as pressure groups, would it not be better to attempt to make a synthesis, covering the whole political system and finding a place for all kinds of political life?

One possible synthesis of pressure politics and party politics might be produced by *describing politics as the socialization of conflict.* That is to say, the political process is a sequence: conflicts are initiated by highly motivated, high-tension groups so directly and immediately involved that it is difficult for them to see the justice of competing claims. As long as the conflicts of these groups remain *private* (carried on in terms of economic competition, reciprocal denial of goods and services, private negotiations and bargaining, struggles for corporate control or competition for membership), no political process is initiated. Conflicts become political only when an attempt is made to involve the wider public. Pressure politics might be described as a stage in the socialization of conflict. This analysis makes pressure politics an integral part of all politics, including party politics.

One of the characteristic points of origin of pressure politics is a breakdown of the discipline of the business community. The flight to government is perpetual. Something like this is likely to happen wherever there is a point of contact between competing power systems. It is the *losers in intrabusiness conflict who seek redress from public authority. The dominant business interests resist appeals to the government.* The role of the government as the patron of the defeated private interest sheds light on its function as the critic of private power relations.

Since the contestants in private conflicts are apt to be unequal in strength, it follows that *the most powerful special interests want private settlements* because they are able to dictate the outcome as long as the conflict remains private. If A is a hundred times as strong as B he does not welcome the intervention of a third party because he expects to impose his own terms on B; he wants to isolate B. He is especially opposed to the intervention of public authority, because public authority represents the most overwhelming form of outside intervention. Thus, if $A/B = 100/1$, it is obviously not to A's advantage to involve a third party a million times as strong as A and B combined. Therefore, it is the weak, not the strong, who appeal to public authority for relief. It is the weak who want to socialize conflict, i.e., to involve more and more people in the conflict until the balance of forces is changed. In the schoolyard it is not the bully but the defenseless smaller boys who "tell the teacher." When the teacher intervenes, the balance of power in the schoolyard is apt to change drastically. It is the function of public authority to *modify private power relations by enlarging the scope of conflict.*

Nothing could be more mistaken than to suppose that public authority merely registers the dominance of the strong over the weak. The mere existence of public order has already ruled out a great variety of forms of private pressure. Nothing could be more confusing than to suppose that the refugees from the business community who come to Congress for relief and protection *force* Congress to do their bidding.

Evidence of the truth of this analysis may be seen in the fact that the big private interests do not necessarily win if they are involved in public conflicts with petty interests. The image of the lobbyists as primarily the agents of big business is not easy to support on the face of the record of congressional hearings, for example. The biggest corporations in the country tend to avoid the arena in which pressure groups and lobbyists fight it out before congressional committees. To describe this process exclusively in terms of an effort of business to intimidate congressmen is to misconceive what is actually going on.

It is probably a mistake to assume that pressure politics is the typical or even the most important relation between government and business. The pressure group is by no means the perfect instrument of the business community. What does big business want? The *winners* in intrabusiness strife want (1) to be let alone (they want autonomy) and (2) to preserve the solidarity of the business community. For these purposes pressure politics is not a wholly satisfactory device. The most elementary considerations of strategy call for the business community to develop some kind of common policy more broadly based than any special-interest group is likely to be.

The political influence of business depends on the kind of solidarity that, on the one hand, leads all business to rally to the support of *any* businessman in trouble with the government and, on the other hand, keeps internal business disputes out of the public arena. In this system businessmen resist the impulse to attack each other in public and discourage the efforts of individual members of the business community to take intrabusiness conflicts into politics.

The attempt to mobilize a united front of the whole business community does not resemble the classical concept of pressure politics. The logic of business politics is to keep peace within the business community by supporting as far as possible all claims that business groups make for themselves. The tendency is to support all businessmen who have conflicts with the government and support all businessmen in conflict with labor. In this way *special-interest politics can be converted into party policy.* The search is for a broad base of political mobilization grounded on the strategic need for political organization on a wider scale than is possible in the case of the historical pressure group. Once the business community begins to think in terms of a larger scale of political organization the Republican party looms large in business politics.

It is a great achievement of American democracy that business has been forced to form a political organization designed to win elections, i.e., has been forced to compete for power in the widest arena in the political system. On the other hand, *the power of the Republican party to make terms with business rests on the fact that business cannot afford to be isolated.*

The Republican party has played a major role in *the political organization of the business community,* a far greater role than many students of politics seem to have realized. The influence of business in the Republican party is great, but it is never absolute because business is remarkably dependent on the party. The business community is too small, it arouses too much antagonism, and its aims are too narrow to win the support of a popular majority. The political education of business is a function of the Republican party that can never be done so well by anyone else.

In the management of the political relations of the business community, the Republican party is much more important than any combination of pressure groups ever could be. The success of special interests in Congress is due less to the "pressure" exerted by these groups than it is due to the fact that Republican members of Congress are committed in advance to a general probusiness attitude. The notion that business groups coerce Republican congressmen into voting for their bills underestimates the whole Republican posture in American politics.

It is not easy to manage the political interests of the business community because there is a perpetual stream of losers in intrabusiness conflicts who go to the government for relief and protection. It has not been possible therefore to maintain perfect solidarity, and when solidarity is breached the government is involved almost automatically. The fact that business has not become hopelessly divided and that it has retained great influence in American politics has been due chiefly to the overall mediating role played by the Republican party. There has never been a pressure group or a combination of pressure groups capable of performing this function.

NOTES

1. Paul F. Lazarsfeld, Bernard Berelson, and Hazel Gaudet. *The People's Choice* (New York: Columbia University Press, 1948), p. 145.

2. Reid and Ehle, "Leadership Selection in the Urban Locality Areas," *Public Opinion Quarterly* (1950), 14:262–284. See also Norman Powell, *Anatomy of Public Opinion* (New York: Prentice Hall, 1951), pp. 180–181.

3. Earl Latham, *The Group Basis of Politics* (Ithaca: Cornell University Press, 1952), pp. 35–36.

13-2

The Evolution of Interest Groups

John R. Wright

In the following essay John R. Wright provides an overview of the develop-ment of interest groups in America. Interest groups form, Wright explains, as a net result of two factors—societal disturbances and collective action prob-lems. Societal disturbances create common interests for groups of individuals, who then join forces to pursue those interests. All groups then face the collec-tive action problem known as free riding—the tendency for group members to benefit from others' contributions to the provision of a public good without contributing themselves. Interest groups must find a way to encourage people to join and contribute in order to achieve their political goals.

THE RAPID ECONOMIC and social development in the United States immediately following the Civil War created a new and uncertain political environment for members of Congress. Congress emerged as the dominant force in national pol-icy making, and members' electoral constituencies became far more heteroge-neous and complex than ever before. In this new and uncertain political envi-ronment, the informational needs of members of Congress were greater than at any previous time, and it was in this environment that the American interest group system evolved.

Although the evolution of interest groups in the United States did not begin in earnest until after the Civil War, the groundwork for their development was laid much earlier in several key provisions of the U.S. Constitution. These con-stitutional provisions have had a profound effect on the American political party system, which in turn has had a major impact on the interest group system.

Constitutional Underpinnings

The place of special interests in American politics today is largely a consequence of two competing political values expressed in the U.S. Constitution: a concern for liberty and freedom of political expression on the one hand, and the desire to

Source: John R. Wright, "The Evolution of Interest Groups," in *Interest Groups and Congress,* John R. Wright (Boston: Allyn & Bacon, 1996), 11–22. Some notes appearing in the original have been deleted.

prevent tyranny on the other. James Madison's *Federalist* No. 10 is the classic justification for the various constitutional checks and balances, which disperse
power and make it difficult for any single group of citizens to control the entire
government. Madison, whose thinking was strongly influenced by the English
philosopher David Hume, believed that it is natural for people to differ, and in
differing, to form into factions, or parties. The problem with factions, according
to Madison and his contemporaries Jefferson and Hamilton, is their potential for
subverting government and the public good. Factions, in Madison's words, are
mischievous.

Madison's primary concern in *Federalist* No. 10 was with *majority* factions—
typically, but not exclusively, political parties as we know them today—not
minority factions such as contemporary interest groups. Although he recognized
that minority factions could lead to disorder and conflict, Madison believed that
it is the possibility of tyranny by the majority that poses the greatest threat to
individual liberties. Madison did not recommend that factions be forbidden or
repressed, a practice that would conflict with the fundamental values of liberty
and freedom of expression, but instead that their negative tendencies be held in
check and controlled through explicit constitutional safeguards.

Formal mechanisms in the U.S. Constitution for controlling majority factions
include the requirements that the president be elected separately from members
of Congress and that members of Congress reside in the states from which they
are elected. These provisions disperse power horizontally—across national institutions of government—and vertically—from national to local political jurisdictions. Separation of the executive and legislative branches eased fears among the
smaller states in 1787 that large states, which presumably would control the Congress, would also control the presidency; and geographic representation ensured
that control over elected representatives would rest with local rather than
national interests, thereby lessening the influence of the national government
over state decisions.

These basic constitutional provisions have had a profound effect on the abili-
ties of modern political parties to control and manage American government.
Historically, control of the government has frequently been divided between the
two major political parties, neither of which has been capable of exerting much
discipline over its members. A single party has controlled the presidency and a
majority in the U.S. House and Senate in just 43 of the 70 Congresses—61 percent—that have convened from 1855 to 1993. Even in times of single-party control of the government, voting defections within both major parties have been
common. Since World War II, a majority of Democrats has voted against a
majority of Republicans only 44 percent of the time on average in the U.S. House
of Representatives and only 45 percent of the time on average in the U.S. Senate.

American legislators have little incentive to toe the party line for the simple reason that a cohesive majority is not required to maintain control of the government or to preclude calling new elections, as is the case in parliamentary regimes. In the absence of party discipline, American legislators look to their geographic constituencies rather than to their parties for voting cues.

Madison and his contemporaries succeeded brilliantly in designing a constitutional system to attenuate the power of majority factions, but in doing so, they also created unanticipated opportunities for minority factions to be influential. When political parties are unable to take clear responsibility for governing, and when they cannot maintain cohesion and discipline among those elected under their labels, special interests have opportunities to gain access to the key points of decision within the government. David Truman explains that when a single party succeeds regularly in electing both an executive and a majority in the legislature, channels of access "will be predominantly those within the party leadership, and the pattern will be relatively stable and orderly."[1] He notes, however, that when "the party is merely an abstract term referring to an aggregation of relatively independent factions," as in the case of the United States, then the channels of access "will be numerous, and the patterns of influence within the legislature will be diverse, constantly shifting, and more openly in conflict."[2]

One important consequence of this "diffusion of access" is that legislators will be much more accessible to interests within their local constituencies, especially *organized* interests. Simply put, interest groups will thrive in an environment in which legislators take their behavioral cues from heterogeneous constituencies rather than from cohesive political parties. E. E. Schattschneider has summed up the situation succinctly:

> If the parties exercised the power to govern effectively, *they would shut out the pressure groups.* The fact that American parties govern only spasmodically and fitfully amid a multitude of lapses of control provides the opportunity for the cheap and easy use of pressure tactics.[3]

Although the constitution makes no specific mention of interest groups, or even political parties for that matter, it has influenced the evolution of both. The weakness of the political parties in their ability to control and manage the government is an intended consequence of the efforts by the founding fathers to inhibit majority factions; the prevalence of special interests, however, is an unintended consequence of weak parties. The U.S. Constitution indirectly laid the groundwork for a strong interest group system, but that system, unlike the political party system, did not evolve right away. It took nearly 70 years from the development of the first party system in 1800 until groups began to form and proliferate at a significant rate.

Table 1. Selected Organizations and Their Founding Dates

American Medical Association	1847
National Grange	1867
National Rifle Association	1871
American Bankers Association	1875
American Federation of Labor	1886
Sierra Club	1892
National Association of Manufacturers	1895
National Audubon Society	1905
National Association for the Advancement of Colored People	1909
U.S. Chamber of Commerce	1912
American Jewish Congress	1918
American Farm Bureau Federation	1919
National League of Cities	1924

The Formation and Maintenance of Interest Groups

Although trade unions and associations have historical roots dating to the beginning of the republic, interest groups of regional or national scope as we know them today did not develop significantly until after the Civil War, and even then, pronounced growth did not really begin to take place until the late 1800s. Table 1 lists a few of the early organizations and their founding dates.

In what is known as the "disturbance theory" of interest group formation, David Truman argued that organizations will form when the interests common to unorganized groups of individuals are disturbed by economic, social, political, or technological change.[4] As society becomes increasingly complex and interconnected, Truman argued that individuals have greater difficulty resolving their differences and grievances on their own and instead must seek intervention from the government. It is at this time that political organizations will begin to take shape. Once interest groups begin to form, they will then tend to form in "wavelike" fashion, according to Truman, because policies designed to address one group's needs typically disturb the interests of other unorganized citizens, who then form groups to seek governmental intervention to protect and advance their particular interests.

The period from 1870 to 1900 was rife with disturbances favorable to the formation of interest groups in the United States. The economic, social, and political upheaval following the Civil War destabilized relationships within and between numerous groups of individuals. The completion of the railroads and the introduction of the telegraph dramatically altered communication and transportation patterns; immigration and population growth gave rise to new economic and social relationships; and commercial and territorial expansion in the

West, combined with the task of maintaining order and rebuilding the infrastructure in the South, increased demands for routine services such as post
offices, law enforcement, internal improvements, customs agents, and so forth.
The process of industrialization created further economic and political tensions
and uncertainties. The period 1870 to 1900 witnessed three economic depres-
sions: a major one from 1873 to 1879, a minor one in the mid-1880s, and the collapse of 1893. Overall, the period from 1870 to 1900 was one when conditions
were finally right for the widespread growth of organized interests in the United
States.

Margaret Susan Thompson points out that in addition to the unprecedented
economic and social upheaval at the end of the Civil War, political conditions in
the 1870s were also favorable to the formation of groups and, in particular, the
lobbying of Congress.[5] Two factors—the ascendancy of congressional power
associated with the impeachment proceedings against Andrew Johnson and the
growing heterogeneity of congressional constituencies—were instrumental in
the growth of congressional lobbying and interest group activity. Congress, by
enacting a comprehensive program on reconstruction in 1865 over the determined opposition of the president, established political preeminence over federal
policy making and, as a consequence, became the focal institution for receiving
and processing the conflicting demands of many newly recognized interests.
Then, as congressional constituencies diversified economically and socially, the
presence of multiple and competing interests began to force legislators to
develop "representational priorities."[6] Thompson notes that legislators at this
time had to determine which were their "meaningful" constituencies, and organization was the critical means by which interests achieved such designation.
Thompson refers to the nascent organization of interests during the 1870s as
"clienteles" rather than interest groups, for even though numerous subgroups of
the population began making significant demands on the government during the
1870s, there was not a great deal of formal organization then as we know it today.
Still, even these nascent groups began to provide important information to
members of Congress about the interests and priorities of their constituents.

One example of how interest groups formed in response to economic and
political disturbances during the post–Civil War period is provided by the organization of postal workers. Even before the Civil War, the volume of mail had
grown tremendously in response to the development of railroads and the resulting decrease in the costs of postage. But in 1863, another significant increase in
the volume of mail occurred when Congress lowered the long-distance postage
rates. This created additional strains for letter carriers and postal clerks who
already were greatly overworked. Then, in 1868, the Post Office Department
refused to apply the "eight-hour" law—a law enacted that same year by Congress

stipulating that eight hours constituted a day's work for laborers, workmen, and mechanics—to letter carriers on the grounds that they were government employees, not laborers, workmen, or mechanics. Finally, implementation of civil service following passage of the Pendleton Act in 1883 eliminated what little political clout the letter carriers had enjoyed. Once the patronage system was eliminated, politicians lost interest in the letter carriers and no longer intervened on their behalf.

In response to these deteriorating circumstances, the letter carriers organized into the National Association of Letter Carriers in 1889. Once organized, the letter carriers had a significant advantage over the unorganized postal clerks in the competition for wages. At the time, wages for all postal workers, letter carriers and clerks alike, were provided through a single congressional appropriation to the Post Office Department, and the letter carriers used their organizational clout to claim a disproportionate share of the annual appropriation. Thus, the postal workers came under pressure to organize as well, and so in predictable "wavelike" fashion, the National Association of Post Office Clerks was established in 1894.

Changing economic, social, and political conditions are necessary but not sufficient circumstances for the formation and development of organized interests. Even when environmental conditions are favorable to the formation of groups, there is still a natural proclivity for individuals *not* to join political interest groups. The reason is that individuals do not always have to belong to political groups in order to enjoy the benefits they provide. Wheat farmers, for example, benefit from the price supports that Congress establishes for wheat even though they do not belong to the National Association of Wheat Growers (NAWG), which lobbies for price supports. Similarly, individuals do not have to belong to environmental groups in order to reap the benefits of a cleaner environment brought about by the lobbying efforts of groups such as the Sierra Club and the National Wildlife Federation. More generally, the lobbying benefits provided by groups such as the wheat growers and the environmentalists are consumed *jointly* by all citizens affected; that is, Congress does not guarantee a higher price for wheat only to farmers who have paid dues to the National Association of Wheat Growers, and it does not and cannot restrict the benefit of a clean environment only to individuals who have paid their dues to environmental groups.

Unlike lobbying benefits, which are available even to those who do not contribute to lobbying efforts, the costs of lobbying are borne only by those who actually pay their dues to political groups or otherwise participate in lobbying activities. This creates a major organizational problem, for when it is possible to get something for nothing, many individuals will rationally choose to free ride on the efforts of others. When there are thousands of wheat farmers, for example, and the annual dues to the National Association of Wheat Growers are $100 or less, individual wheat farmers might very well conclude that their single contributions are not very important, that the NAWG will manage quite nicely without their money because there are so many other wheat farmers paying dues, and that there are much better uses for the $100 in light of the fact that the government will still provide price supports for their crop. The problem for the NAWG is that if every wheat farmer reasoned this way there would be no national association, and thus probably no price supports for wheat.

Given the natural proclivity for individuals to be free riders, all organizations must provide incentives of one sort or another to induce individuals to pay dues and otherwise contribute to the collective efforts of the organization. Generally speaking, individuals do not join interest groups because of benefits that can be consumed jointly; they join because of benefits that can by enjoyed *selectively* only by those individuals who pay dues to political groups. There are three main types of selective benefits. A selective *material* benefit includes such things as insurance and travel discounts and subscriptions to professional journals and other specialized information. A second type of selective benefit is what Peter Clark and James Q. Wilson have labelled *solidary* incentives. These, too, derive only from group membership and involve benefits such as "socializing, congeniality, the sense of group membership and identification, the status resulting from membership, fun and conviviality, the maintenance of social distinctions, and so on."[7] The third basic type of selective benefit is an *expressive* incentive. Expressive incentives are those that individuals attach to the act of expressing ideological or moral values such as free speech, civil rights, economic justice, or political equality. Individuals obtain these benefits when they pay dues or contribute money or time to an organization that espouses these values. What is important in receiving these benefits is the feeling of satisfaction that results from expressing political values, not necessarily the actual achievement of the values themselves.

Most organizations provide a mix of these various benefits, although different kinds of organizations typically rely more heavily on one type of benefit than another. Professional and trade associations, for example, are more likely to offer selective material benefits than purposive benefits, whereas environmental groups and other organizations claiming to lobby for the public interest rely more heavily on expressive benefits. Expressive benefits are also common in organizations relying heavily on mass mailings to attract and maintain members. Many direct mail approaches use negatively worded messages to instill feelings of guilt and fear in individuals, with the hope that people will contribute money to a cause as a means of expressing their support for certain values or else assuaging their guilt and fear.

That individuals are not drawn naturally to interest groups and must instead be enticed to join makes it very difficult for groups to get started. Organizations often need outside support in the form of a patron—perhaps a wealthy individual, a nonprofit foundation, or a government agency—to get over the initial hurdle of organizing collective action. In one of the leading studies on the origins and maintenance of interest groups, Jack Walker discovered that 89 percent of all citizen groups and 60 percent of all nonprofit occupational groups (e.g., the National Association of State Alcohol and Drug Abuse Directors) received financial assistance from an outside source at the time of their founding.[8] Many of these organizations continued to draw heavily from outside sources of support to maintain themselves once they were launched. Walker concluded that "the number of interest groups in operation, the mixture of group types, and the level and direction of political mobilization in the United States at any point in the country's history will be determined by the composition and accessibility of the system's major patrons of political action."[9]

In summary, the proficiency that contemporary interest groups have achieved in attracting and maintaining members has evolved from a combination of factors. Most fundamental to their evolution has been a constitutional arrangement that has not only encouraged their participation but also created unanticipated opportunities for them to exert influence. Changing economic, social, and political circumstances have also played critical roles at various times throughout American history. However, even under conditions favorable to their development, the formation and maintenance of interest groups requires leadership and creative approaches for dealing with the natural inertia that individuals exhibit toward collective activities. The number of groups continues to grow each year, however, as does the diversity of the issues and viewpoints they represent.

NOTES

1. David B. Truman, *The Governmental Process: Political Interests and Public Opinion* (New York: Knopf, 1951), p. 325.

2. Ibid., p. 325.

3. E. E. Schattschneider, *Party Government* (New York: Holt, Rinehart and Winston, 1941), p. 192.

4. David B. Truman, *The Governmental Process*, Chapters 3 and 4.

5. Margaret Susan Thompson, *The Spider Web: Congress and Lobbying in the Age of Grant* (Ithaca, NY: Cornell University Press, 1985).

6. Thompson, *The Spider Web*, pp. 130–131.

7. Peter B. Clark and James Q. Wilson, "Incentive Systems: A Theory of Organizations," *Administrative Science Quarterly* 6 (1961): 134–135.

8. Jack L. Walker, "The Origins and Maintenance of Interest Groups in America," *American Political Science Review* 77 (1983): 390–406.

9. Ibid., p. 406.

13-3

What Corporations Really Want from Government

THE PUBLIC PROVISION OF PRIVATE GOODS

R. Kenneth Godwin and Barry J. Seldon

When we think of interest groups and lobbyists, we usually have in mind efforts to influence the content of legislation—for instance, by including tax provisions that benefit an industry. In this essay, political scientist R. Kenneth Godwin and economist Barry J. Seldon observe that lobbyists representing corporations in Washington more often seek private goods—those that benefit a specific company—than collective goods—those that affect many groups or individuals. The extent of lobbying, therefore, reflects the importance of private goods—government contracts, for example—to the corporation. While corporate lobbyists may join coalitions and trade associations to pursue collective goods, they more frequently act alone in pursuit of private goods. Lobbyists target legislators of two kinds: those whose committees have jurisdiction over the private good of interest and those from the states or districts in which the corporation resides who are likely to share in its goal of acquiring government benefits for the home constituency.

A LOBBYIST FROM a major defense contractor speaking to a class on interest groups was asked, "What was the most important vote you influenced?" The lobbyist responded, "Do you mean the most important vote, or the most important thing I did for [the firm]?" She went on to explain that her most significant achievement was obtaining a 25 percent increase in the price of her firm's missile. But a recorded vote never took place. The price increase occurred during committee markup of an omnibus defense bill. Although this outcome boosted the firm's profits by $50 million over five years, no legislator voted directly on the price increase.

The Public Provision of Private Goods

Lobbying situations like the missile price increase are not rare, but they are rarely studied. Instead political scientists generally analyze highly visible issues that

Source: Allan J. Cigler and Burdett A. Loomis, eds., *Interest Group Politics,* 6th ed. (Washington, D.C.: CQ Press, 2002), 205–224.

affect numerous firms, citizen action groups, trade associations, or individuals. Political scientists then use these analyses to develop models and generalizations about what interest groups want, how they get what they want, and how public officials respond to lobbying efforts and campaign contributions. In this chapter we show that research that neglects lobbying situations like the missile price increase also neglects issues on which the largest category of lobbyists (those working for individual corporations) spend most of their time. In many ways, researchers studying interest groups are like the guy who lost his keys in the dark alley but looks for them under the streetlamp because the light is better there. It is unsurprising that interest group researchers may not find the keys to understanding lobbying behavior by studying highly visible issues that involve substantial conflict.

In this chapter we examine the hypothesis that a corporate lobbyist is less likely to ask legislators for votes on bills than for help in obtaining government contracts, regulatory waivers, and government subsidies for the lobbyist's corporation. We refer to government-provided benefits that help a single firm as *private goods*. Some examples of private goods are:

- A government contract to build a new tank for the army.
- A decision by the Environmental Protection Agency to allow a chemical company to phase out its organic-phosphate pesticide over a longer period than allowed by the original regulation.
- A decision by the U.S. Patent Office to give a pharmaceutical company a ten-year extension on a drug patent.

Collective Goods versus Private Goods

The opposite of private goods is collective goods. Collective goods are benefits that the government provides to many groups, firms, or individuals, such as a reduction in the corporate income tax rate, a change in the minimum wage, and legislation that requires all firms to provide health insurance to their workers. You can think of government benefits as lying on a continuum. At one end are purely private goods like the missile price increase, a government contract, and a regulatory waiver to a single plant. At the other end are purely collective goods such as a reduction in income taxes on all corporations or an increase in Medicare benefits to older Americans. In between are benefits with different levels of "collectiveness," such as regulations or tax changes that affect a single industry, tariffs on a single product such as computer chips, subsidies for a particular crop, and loan guarantees for first-time home buyers.

An analogy might help clarify this idea. Assume that you are a student at a state university who receives financial assistance; some of this assistance comes from working for the university. You would like the government to reduce your cost of attending college. One way to do this is for the university to give you a scholarship. This would be a private good—only you would receive the scholarship. Alternatively, the government could lower the tuition for all students at all state universities. This would be a collective good. In between these two extremes are goods that affect some, but not all, students. Your university might decide to pay higher wages to student employees who receive financial assistance, or the legislature might choose to reduce the tuition of in-state students. Figure 1 shows the private-collective continuum and some goods along it.

A strategy for obtaining these benefits would be closely related to where the benefit falls on the private-collective continuum. In the case of the scholarship, you might ask two or three professors to write letters of recommendations for you. And you would give the financial aid office information that justifies giving you the scholarship. Notice that only a few people are involved in this decision: the professors and the financial aid officer. On the other hand, lowering tuition for all university students requires action by many public officials. The members of the state board of higher education must propose a tuition cut, a majority of members of the legislature must approve the board's recommendation, and the governor must sign the bill. To gain this benefit you probably would work through the student government organization at your university, which would form a coalition with the student government organizations of other state universities. This coalition would lobby the state board of education, the legislature, and the governor.

Between these two extremes is, for example, the decision to grant student workers a wage increase. This issue might involve the university's vice president for financial affairs and the managers of campus businesses that must pay the increased wage costs. To obtain this benefit you presumably would organize the student workers on your campus, who would appeal to the university's vice president and business managers.

The number of officials needed to supply a desired benefit and the lobbying resources needed to influence those officials increase as you move from the private to the collective end of the continuum. For example, getting a regulatory waiver for a single plant could be accomplished by a single congressperson who calls an agency official and encourages him or her to grant the waiver. But reducing the corporate tax rate requires support from the Republican Party, action by several congressional committees, votes by the entire House and Senate, and the cooperation of the White House.

What difference does it make in our understanding of lobbying if political scientists concentrate on how interest groups pursue highly collective goods while corporate lobbyists pursue private goods? We would be overlooking a major portion of lobbying activity and its consequences. Collective goods such as changes

Figure 1. A Continuum of Publicly Provided Goods

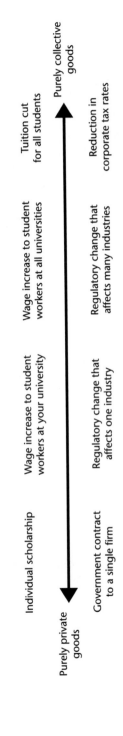

Source: Authors' example.

in the minimum wage and a decision to allow oil exploration in Arctic wilderness areas are highly visible because they involve conflicts between organized interests. And they are sources of ideological clashes between the political parties. In these conflicts both sides are organized and have extensive political resources. Because no single interest is likely to dominate collective goods issues, focusing on them alone might lead us to conclude that the American political system is so diverse and competitive that almost everyone gets represented.

But private goods are different. They involve little conflict, and often only one side (the one with a lobbyist) gets represented. Under these conditions a single interest can dominate a policy decision. In the example of the missile price increase the firm was a clear winner and the taxpayers were clear losers, but only the firm's voice was heard in committee markup. Not surprising, the side that was heard defeated the side that was not. To the extent that students of politics overlook such situations, we are likely to underestimate the impact of organized interests on public policy.

A less obvious consequence of concentrating on collective goods is that we underestimate the influence of corporate campaign contributions on policy outcomes. Congressional campaigns often cost more than $1 million, and political action committees rarely donate more than $5,000 to a particular candidate. As many disparate interests contribute to the winning candidate, it is unlikely that a single contribution will influence a legislator's decision on a collective good. If, however, most corporate lobbyists are interested in private goods, then even a $1,000 contribution may give the lobbyist the necessary access to a legislator to obtain the desired private good. When we add up the costs and benefits of all the private goods that governments supply, the total impact of these goods may be greater than the total impact of the collective goods that governments provide.

How Important Are Private Goods?

Presumably corporations don't care whether profits obtained from government actions come from a private good or a collective good. The question the firm asks is, "Where is the most efficient place on the private-collective continuum to spend lobbying resources?" If lobbying for private goods has a higher return, then corporate lobbyists will expend more resources pursuing private goods than pursuing collective goods. But if collective goods have a higher return, lobbyists will spend their time and money seeking them instead.

In the classic exchange model of lobbying and political campaigns, interests provide campaign contributions, votes, and other resources that legislators need to gain reelection. In return, legislators provide goods to the interests. Lobbyists attempt to maximize their firm's profits for the lobbying resources allotted, and legislators try to maximize their chances of reelection. We can imagine lobbyists' decision process as follows: First they identify the governmentally supplied goods that will affect their firm's profits. Then they estimate the resources needed to lobby for each good and the probability of success. The decision calculus involves weighing expected benefits against the costs involved in lobbying. The lobbyist would pursue issues where expected benefits are greater than expected costs:

$$P \times B > C$$

where P is the probability of success in obtaining the benefit, B is the value of the benefit to the firm, and C is the cost of lobbying for the good. The lobbyist would refrain from lobbying if $P \times B < C$.

Thus if the expected benefit (the value of the benefit multiplied by the probability of success) is greater than the cost of the lobbying resources, then the lobbyist will pursue the good. The lobbyist will expend resources for all goods where the expected profit return for an additional dollar spent lobbying is greater than the profit the corporation could obtain by investing that dollar in other activities such as hiring more salespeople or improving technology.

Legislators also make calculations. Legislators' actions have political benefits and costs. Legislators use the following calculation to decide which goods they will provide:

$$E = V/R$$

where E is efficiency of effort, V is the net votes gained from supplying the good, and R is the resources the legislator must expend to provide the good.

Legislators estimate the net vote gain from providing a particular good and the amount of resources needed to provide the good. By dividing the net vote gain by the required effort, legislators can determine their efficiency. Legislators then provide those goods that have the greatest efficiency. Legislators' resources include their time, influence, and expertise and the time, influence, and expertise of their staff.

An important aspect of the legislator's decision calculus is that voters will approve of some actions, be indifferent to others, and disapprove of others. If a lobbyist asks a legislator to do something that will likely cost him or her votes in the next election, then the interest must provide the legislator with enough resources to offset the lost votes and provide a net gain in votes. Thus a legislator's "price" for producing goods that constituents dislike will be higher than the price for goods that constituents are indifferent to. The legislator will charge the lowest price for goods that constituents support.

Policy researchers, such as James Wilson and Theodore Lowi, have long maintained that public officials prefer to deal with policies that have low visibility to the public, involve little conflict among competing interests, and are narrow in scope.[1] Why? Because the winners know they received the policy benefits, but the losers rarely know they have paid the costs. For example, if the senator who chairs the Environment and Public Works Committee calls the Environmental Protection Agency and encourages it to grant a regulatory waiver to a firm in the senator's district, the firm will know of this effort and will reward the senator. In contrast, those who live near the polluting firm are unlikely to be aware of the senator's effort; thus they will be unable to punish him or her.

The example of the missile price increase was a decision that had a high benefit-cost ratio for legislators. The firm knew it was $50 million richer and rewarded the legislators with electoral support. The taxpayers, who knew nothing of the action, did not punish the legislators. Even if some taxpayers had been aware of the budget change, they could not have identified the legislators responsible for the price increase because there was no recorded vote.

Compare the missile price increase with a vote on the highly publicized issue of allowing electricity producers to use more high sulfur coal. Although companies that own the coal will reward a legislator for a favorable vote, environmental groups will know of the vote and exact punishment. These groups may contribute funds and campaign workers to the legislator's opponent in the next election, and they may urge environmentally aware citizens to vote against the legislator.

So, it's safe to assume that legislators prefer policies that encourage rewards from winners and avoid retribution from losers. Those low-visibility and low-conflict policies are likely to be at the private goods end of the continuum.

Legislators also prefer policies that benefit their constituents. It is much safer politically for legislators to work on behalf of firms in their district than on behalf of firms outside their district. For example, if a legislator from North Carolina receives a large campaign contribution from a tobacco firm in the state and urges other legislators or regulatory agencies to help the tobacco firm, the public will probably deem this legitimate. The legislator simply is representing a constituent. But if a legislator from New York City receives a large contribution from a North Carolina tobacco company and lobbies on behalf of that company's interests, then the public tends to believe that the legislator has been bought.

William Browne's research on agriculture policy shows this pattern. Brown interviewed lobbyists from 130 organizations and legislators and staff from 112 congressional offices. He discovered that firms almost always approached a legislator from their home district. And 98 percent of the issues that firms named as important affected only their organization. Browne concluded that the agricultural policy process brings together legislators who need constituent support and constituents who want private goods.[2]

Legislators have good reason to prefer supplying private goods rather than collective goods—do firms also favor private goods? Yes. If the benefits a lobbyist seeks are purely private to his or her firm, then the decision to expend resources is straightforward. As the benefits move toward the collective goods end of the continuum, the lobbyist must estimate how other organizations will contribute to the lobbying effort. Mancur Olson's *The Logic of Collective Action* shows that there are substantial transaction and decision costs in the pursuit of collective goods. Olson demonstrates that firms may prefer to "free ride" on the efforts of others rather than pay a share of the lobbying costs. (Free riders are firms that reap the benefit of a collective good while paying little or none of the cost of obtaining it.) In addition, as the number of organizations pursuing a collective good grows, the difficulties involved in mobilizing for collective action increase.[3] (Think how much more difficult it would be for you to organize student workers at your university than to apply for a scholarship.)

Another reason that corporate lobbyists may prefer lobbying for private goods is that fewer public officials are needed to provide them. Sometimes a phone call from a staff member in a senator's office is enough to speed up the granting of a license or a regulatory waiver. Even in cases where large government contracts are involved, the private good can be decided by a vote in subcommittee. Decisions on highly collective goods usually involve many more decisionmakers. This greatly increases a firm's lobbying costs.

Finally, firms seek private goods because the likelihood of opposition from other firms or interest groups is low. Legislators know that when requests for goods lead to conflict between organized interests, the losers will know of their losses and may attempt to punish the legislators.[4]

In summary, the higher expected rewards to firms and legislators from private goods, the difficulties involved in collective action, and the threat of opposition from other firms and interest groups indicate that firms will concentrate on lobbying for private goods. Despite this, most political science research on lobbying and political action committee contributions investigates highly visible issues such as the confirmation of a Supreme Court nominee. But if the expected return to corporate lobbying is greater for private goods than for collective goods, then political science research is overlooking an important part of the policy process.

A Test of the Private Goods Hypothesis

If firms have an easier time obtaining private goods and public officials prefer to provide private goods, then we should be able to predict which firms will spend more on lobbying and which legislators those firms will lobby. The corporations most likely to have large lobbying expenditures are those that rely on government action to provide private goods. These will be firms that depend heavily on government contracts and firms that are heavily regulated. In contrast, firms that are not heavily regulated or whose profits do not depend on government contracts should spend little on lobbying. This will be true despite the fact that many collective goods, such as corporate income taxes, worker safety regulations, and minimum wage legislation, substantially affect all corporations.

A firm will lobby legislators who are most efficient at producing the private goods it wants. These will be legislators who sit on the committees and subcommittees that deal with the contracts or regulatory agencies critical to the firm. The legislators who will charge the lowest price for providing such goods are legislators from the firm's home district. Therefore, corporate lobbyists should concentrate on these two sets of legislators.

In addition, we predict that corporate lobbyists are more likely to lobby alone than as members of coalitions with other firms. We derive this hypothesis from Olson's arguments on the difficulties of collective action. This hypothesis is contrary to the conventional wisdom in the interest group literature. Most writers on lobbying maintain that it is better to lobby as a member of a coalition than to go it alone.[5] We believe, however, that although coalitions are appropriate for seeking some collective goods, they are inappropriate when lobbying for private goods. (Remember the different strategies involved in reducing tuition for all students and in getting a scholarship for yourself.)

To test our hypotheses we studied corporations in three industries with differing levels of government regulation: passenger airlines, rubber-resin manufacturers, and publishing.[6] We limited our analysis to firms with total assets greater than $2 billion (past research indicates that large corporations are much more likely to have lobbying offices in Washington than are smaller corporations). Five passenger airlines, seven rubber-resin companies, and seven publishing firms met our criteria for the study. Because of the small number of industries, firms, and respondents, we tested our hypotheses using a qualitative approach that maximizes the number of opportunities to falsify predictions, rather than on tests of statistical significance. Fortunately, our expectations of which firms will lobby, whom they will lobby, and the likelihood of a coalition forming generate many specific and potentially falsifiable predictions.

The Industries

Despite "deregulation," passenger airlines remain heavily regulated, and government actions strongly affect their profits. The Federal Aviation Administration (FAA) regulates airplane and airport safety and noise, allocates international routes, and decides the amount of time pilots and flight attendants may be on duty. A decision by the Treasury Department to expand customs facilities in Chicago rather than Minneapolis benefits United Airlines and harms Northwest Airlines. Fuel taxes, landing fees, and ticket excise taxes influence the production costs of all airlines. In short, numerous decisions by multiple government agencies affect an airline's profits and competitive position. Because the industry is highly regulated, we expect its firms to expend substantial resources lobbying, to direct most of their efforts toward obtaining private goods, to concentrate on home-district representatives and members of relevant committees, and to lobby alone rather than in coalitions.

Government regulation also significantly affects profits in the rubber-resin industry. But much of the regulation is at the state level because state agencies have the primary responsibility for enforcing the Resource Conservation and Recovery Act, the national legislation that contains the most important regulations affecting the industry. Therefore, we expect rubber-resin firms to divide their lobbying efforts between Washington and the state capitals. We anticipate that the lobbying patterns of rubber-resin firms will be similar to those of the airlines, but expenditures at the federal level will be smaller.[7]

Our third industry is print publishing, which we chose because its profits are relatively independent of government activity. Government regulations on newspapers, magazines, and books are minimal, and, except for postal rates and government documents, government subsidies to the industry are unimportant. Thus, of the three industries, publishing firms should expend the fewest lobbying resources.

The Lobbyists

To discover the relative importance the firms place on private and collective goods, we asked each firm's Washington lobbyists for the following information:

- Which public officials they contact regularly and how frequently they contact them.
- How much time (percentage) they spend on issues that affect only their company or their company and a competitor.[8]
- Their most important issues over the past three years.
- Their major accomplishments.
- How much time (percentage) they devoted to each issue they named during the interview and to issues we had identified before the interview.

We also collected data on which firms had a political action committee (PAC) and to whom the PAC contributed. An interviewer questioned all PAC directors from the firms in our sample, asking how they decided whom to contribute to and how much to contribute.[9] Before the interviews we gathered data on actual contributions so the interviewer could ask about contributions that didn't seem to fit the decision process.

Results

As we hypothesized, airlines spent the most resources lobbying the national government and print publishing firms spent the least. Four of five airlines had multiple lobbyists in Washington and all five had PACs. Three of the seven rubber-resin firms had a lobbyist who maintained an office in Washington, and the same number had a PAC. At the time of our interviews, only two publishing firms whose sales came mainly from publishing printed material had Washington lobbying offices. Only one had a PAC.

On Whom Do Lobbyists Expend Resources?

All airline lobbyists reported speaking almost daily with the staff of House members from districts where their airline had hubs. Each lobbying office contacts every representative from hub districts weekly and hub senators monthly. Airline lobbyists also reported that staff members of home-district legislators frequently contact them to see if the legislator could assist the firm. Subcommittees receive even greater attention from airline lobbyists. The lobbyists reported contacting members of aviation subcommittees at least weekly and subcommittee staff almost daily. Airline lobbyists rarely contact legislators not from their hub areas and not from relevant subcommittees. We also discovered that airline lobbyists spend more time with regulatory personnel than with legislators and their staff. Each airline lobbyist reported speaking daily with FAA officials.

Whereas the airlines have more than one lobbyist in each of their offices, each rubber-resin office had only one professional lobbyist. In addition, because the implementation of the Resource Conservation and Recovery Act is a state concern, the rubber-resin lobbyists reported spending a significant portion of their time in state capitals rather than in Washington. During periods of peak activity in Washington, rubber-resin lobbyists reported speaking to home district representatives and key subcommittee members about once a week and contacting the legislators' staff members three or four times a week. Rubber-resin lobbyists reported spending little time contacting federal regulatory agencies, but indicated that they spent substantial time with state regulatory officials.

The two lobbyists from the publishing firms reported less frequent contacts with legislators than did lobbyists from the other two industries. When publishing lobbyists did contact legislators, they were more likely to speak with members of relevant subcommittees than with representatives from their home district. The lobbyists reported contacting subcommittee staff members and federal agency personnel at least weekly. Though airline and rubber-resin lobbyists reported few interactions with the White House, publishing lobbyists reported working extensively with the White House staff on General Agreement on Tariffs and Trade and North American Free Trade Agreement negotiations dealing with copyright issues.

Allocating Resources between Collective and Private Goods

If we are correct about the importance of private goods, firms in highly regulated industries allocate resources to public officials based on their ability and willingness to supply those goods. Airline lobbyists reported spending 75–95 percent of their time on issues affecting only their firm or their firm and one other. Only seven of the twenty-seven priority issues listed by airline lobbyists dealt with collective goods. Among the private goods airlines sought, only three required floor votes. Every airline lobbyist we interviewed reported winning a private good as his or her most important success. Several such successes were worth hundreds of millions of dollars. For example, Southwest Airlines received a noise regulation waiver from the FAA for its entire fleet of airplanes.

The Wright Amendment is one of the best examples of how a private good can affect unorganized consumers. The amendment, which prohibited commercial airlines from flying out of Love Field in Dallas (a hub of Southwest Airlines) to any state not contiguous with Texas, was added to an aviation bill when the Dallas-Ft. Worth Airport (DFW) was built. The amendment prevented flights from Love Field from competing with flights from DFW (the home hub of American Airlines and a major hub of Delta Airlines). A Department of Transportation analysis found that the Wright Amendment caused flights from DFW to have the highest ticket costs of any major city in the United States, raising the cost of travel out of the Dallas metropolitan area by $200 million a year.[10] The Wright Amendment enormously boosts the profits of American Airlines and Delta Airlines. While Jim Wright and Newt Gingrich were Speakers of the House (Wright from 1987 to 1989, Gingrich from 1995 to 1999), they used their influence to protect American and Delta's privileged profit margins. After Wright and Gingrich resigned, Sen. Phil Gramm, R-Texas, and Rep. Dick Armey, R-Texas, have worked to preserve Love Field restrictions.

These legislators have not been alone in assisting airlines with hubs in a legislator's state or district. All airline lobbyists reported routinely seeking assistance from members of Congress. For example, when Southwest Airlines requested the noise waiver for its airplanes, more than fifty representatives wrote the FAA on Southwest's behalf. Not all the legislators were from districts where Southwest had a major hub—the chairperson and members of a key subcommittee that oversees the FAA also wrote. All airline lobbyists reported asking senators from their hub states to contact both the FAA and the White House to help their airline win international routes. The legislators then pressured the White House and the FAA for policy decisions that gave their airline an advantage over a competitor.

Private goods also dominated the agenda of the rubber-resin lobbyists. They reported spending at least 75 percent of their time on issues that dealt only with their firm, they listed private goods as priority goals twice as frequently as collective goods, and all lobbyists listed a private good as their major lobbying achievement. For example, one lobbyist listed a major military contract as her major achievement; another succeeded in obtaining a regulatory waiver for a recycling plant. As with airline lobbyists, the rubber-resin lobbyists expected their home-district legislators to provide private goods to their firms. The rubber-resin lobbyists asked their representatives to help them not only with federal regulatory agencies, but also with state legislators and state regulatory officials.

Consistent with our expectations of coalition forming, corporate lobbyists in the airline and rubber-resin industries reported little cooperative lobbying to achieve collective goods. For example, a major issue for the rubber-resin industry was the cost of disposing of scrap tires. Although this issue affected all firms in the industry, its major impact was on Goodyear. Instead of forming a coalition, the other tire firms expected Goodyear to do almost all of the lobbying.

This pattern repeated itself every time one firm had a much greater stake than other firms in a collective good.[11] For example, Delta and American airlines both benefit from the Wright Amendment. But American paid almost the entire cost of keeping these restrictions in place. When our interviewer asked a Delta lobbyist how much time he spent on the issue, he responded that the Wright Amendment was "Mr. Crandall's concern." (Robert Crandall was the chief executive officer of AMR, American Airlines' parent company.) American's full-time lobbyists made the Wright Amendment a top priority and paid several attorneys in Washington and Dallas to work on the issue. Delta's lobbyists merely alerted friends in Congress that Delta supported American's position.

Although the reports of lobbyists from the airline and rubber-resin firms supported our hypothesis that private goods dominate corporate lobbying efforts, the activities of the two publishing lobbyists did not. Both lobbyists listed a private good as their major lobbying accomplishment, but 70 percent of the priority issues they worked on concerned such collective goods as copyright provisions in foreign trade agreements and postal rates for printed materials. The publishing lobbyists did not lobby cooperatively on the collective goods issues, but divided them. Each lobbyist specialized on the collective goods that had the greatest impact on her firm. This arrangement was efficient because each issue required specialized knowledge and regular contacts with specific public officials.

In summary, the resource allocations of the lobbyists we interviewed support the hypotheses that heavily regulated firms spend more on lobbying than lightly regulated firms, that lobbyists in regulated industries concentrate on goods that are private to their firm, and that cooperative efforts by corporate lobbyists are less frequent than researchers generally suppose. The activities of the two publishing lobbyists, however, suggest that collective goods can be more important than private goods for industries that are not heavily regulated.

How Political Action Committees Allocate Their Funds

To discover if PAC contributions follow patterns similar to lobbying expenditures, we asked PAC directors to rank twenty possible reasons for giving to a candidate (Table 1). Responses were on a scale from one (not important) to four (very important). PAC directors give priority to:

- Legislators who sit on key committees and subcommittees (particularly the committee and subcommittee chairs).
- Legislators who have supported the firm in the past.
- Home-district legislators.

Federal Election Commission (FEC) data on these PACs verify the reported patterns. On average, the PACs studied gave more than three times as much to home district representatives and members of relevant committees as they gave to other legislators.

When we look at PACs within particular industries, we find that airlines contribute almost exactly as our private goods hypotheses posit. For all but one airline, PAC directors indicated that past help in obtaining a private good was the most important influence on contribution decisions.[12] For airline PACs, neither ideology nor political party was important in contribution decisions. For rubber-resin PACs, being a member of the committee with primary responsibility for the Resource Conservation and Recovery Act, past assistance to the firm in obtaining a private good, and assistance in lobbying state and federal agencies were equally important factors. The directors of rubber-resin PACs also indicated that they supported challengers against proenvironment incumbents in close races.

A factor we expected to influence the probability of a contribution was whether the PAC director expected a candidate to win. Although past research has shown that firms and trade associations give to candidates who are likely to win, PAC directors ranked this item nineteenth out of twenty possible reasons for giving. However, our analysis of FEC data showed that with the exception of rubber-resin PACs backing challengers to proenvironment incumbents in close

Table 1. Why Political Action Committees Gave to Candidates

Candidate characteristic	Average score
Sits on a committee that is important to our interests	4.00
Has been very supportive of issues important to our corporation	3.86
Is from a district or state where we have facilities	3.71
Has helped us with the executive and regulatory agencies	3.71
Leadership position places the candidate in a position of influence on issues that affect us	3.57
Has been helpful to our industry as a whole	3.43
Has a great personal interest in issues that concern us	3.43
Has helped us with other members of Congress	3.43
The opponent is definitely a threat to us	2.71
Is involved in a close race	2.71
We like his or her ideology	2.00
May be helpful to us in the future	1.43
Is a popular candidate among our contributors	1.43
A contribution would help obtain access to him or to his staff	1.43
We dislike the opponent's ideology	1.43
Has helped us with state and local governments	1.43
Was in a position to hurt us if we didn't contribute	1.43
We were asked to contribute and saw no reason not to	1.43
Was likely to win the election	1.28
Belongs to the political party most favorable to our interests	1.28

Source: Authors' data.
4 = Very important   3 = Important   2 = Somewhat important   1 = Not important

races, the PACs we studied did not give to challengers. This was the only case where the verbal responses from our interviewees differed substantially from their observed behavior.

How Corporations Obtain Collective Goods

Given the emphasis corporate lobbyists place on private goods, an obvious question is, "How do firms pursue collective goods?" A logical strategy would be to have the industry trade association lobby on issues that affect the entire industry.[13] To determine if the trade associations played a key role in lobbying for collective goods, we asked the corporate lobbyists to describe how they worked with the trade association lobbyists and how successfully the trade association lobbied on issues important to the industry. We also attempted to interview the trade association lobbyists for each of our three industries. Our interviewer successfully completed interviews with the chief lobbyists of the Air Transport Association (ATA) and the Rubber Manufacturers Association (RMA). Our interviewers were unable to interview the lobbyist for the publishing trade association, who instead

Table 2. Priority Issues for Trade Associations

Airlines	Rubber-resin	Publishing
Exise taxes on tickets	Scrap tire disposal and taxation	North American Free Trade Agreement and General Agreement on Tariffs and Trade
Modernization of air traffic control	State storm water regulations	Copyright renewal act
National fuel taxes	Superfund issues	High-performance computing act
State fuel taxes	Transportation of hazardous waste	Digital audio home recording
Noise abatement at local airports	Resource Conservation and Recovery Act reauthorization	Library of Congress fees
Trust-fund spending by Federal Aviation Authority on airports	Regulation of baby bottle nipples	Freedom of Information Act amendments
	North American Free Trade Agreement provisions for rubber-resin	Government Printing Office electronic information
	Federal funding for basic research	Postal service mailing rates
		Mail order use tax
		National film preservation
		Publisher liability for pornography and news stories

Source: Authors' data.

provided a list of the issues on which he spent either "considerable" or a "great deal of time" (but only on the condition that we not identify him or his trade association in any published material).

We asked the trade association lobbyists to list the issues they saw as most important to their industry and the time and other resources they devoted to each issue. Before the interviews we prepared a list of key issues affecting the three industries. If the trade association lobbyist did not mention an issue on our list, the interviewer asked if he or she had lobbied on the issue and, if so, how extensively. Table 2 lists the issues the trade association lobbyists identified as most important to their industries.

Our interviews with the corporate and trade association lobbyists uncovered several differences among the three industries in how the lobbyists pursued collective goods. The airline lobbyists delegated almost all responsibility to the ATA. For example, a major collective good for the airline industry is modernization of air traffic control. The ATA lobbyist developed the lobbying strategy on this issue, prepared technical information for policymakers, and coordinated the lobbying efforts. The airlines participated by contacting legislators and regulatory officials with whom they had particularly close relationships, but not until the ATA lobbyist determined the appropriate time. The airline lobbyists were uniformly supportive of the ATA's efforts.

The lobbying pattern of the rubber-resin industry was somewhat different. Each rubber-resin corporate lobbyist included a collective good as a top-three priority. Thus the corporate lobbyists were less willing to follow the RMA's lead in lobbying on the collective good issue critical to their firm. The greater independence of lobbying efforts by rubber-resin firms reflected the greater diversity of interests among RMA members. Although all the airlines produce similar services, there is substantial product diversity within the RMA. RMA members focus on such goods as tires, bushings, castings, sealants, and baby bottle nipples.

Equally important, a number of RMA members, such as Bridgestone-Firestone, are foreign corporations. This often leads to conflicts of interest among members over such issues as U.S.–regulated pollution control. Despite their different interests, our corporate respondents indicated that they generally were pleased with the RMA's lobbying efforts and left the lobbying for most collective goods to the trade association.

Because we were unable to interview the publishing trade association (the lobbyist sent in the form instead), we relied on information from the two corporate lobbyists on how their firms worked with the trade association lobbyist. The corporate lobbyists indicated that there was little cooperation or coordination between them and the trade association lobbyist. In fact, both corporate lobbyists said they devoted so much time to collective goods because their trade association was not doing enough on the collective goods issues important to their firms.

Despite the differences among the trade associations in the three industries, one lobbying pattern was clear: trade associations rarely lobbied on any issue that did not affect directly (and almost exclusively) their members. In other words, trade associations seldom lobbied for goods that were collective beyond their industry. For example, the ATA listed only airline issues, and the lobbyist for the publishing trade association listed only publishing issues as receiving lobbying attention.[14] Coupled with our information on the lobbying patterns of the corporations, this finding suggests that lobbyists concentrate their resources on goods that are at the same level of collectiveness as the lobbyist's employer. Corporate lobbyists spend their resources pursuing goods that are private to their company, and trade association lobbyists seek goods that are private to their industry.

Discussion

Although the number of industries, firms, and lobbyists interviewed for this study is small, our interviews confirm the importance of private goods to corporations in heavily regulated industries. Measures of the time lobbyists devoted to particular issues, the goods that the lobbyists named as most important to their firms, and the lobbyists' most important accomplishments showed that private goods had a higher priority than collective goods for lobbyists in the airline and rubber-resin industries. The preference of lobbyists for private goods reflects the incentive structures facing those who demand and those who supply publicly provided goods. Lobbying costs are lower for private goods because it takes fewer public officials to supply them and because lobbyists' requests for private goods often are unopposed by other organized interests.

Our interviews with the PAC directors indicated that they are influenced more by a candidate's past assistance to their firm in obtaining a private good and less by the candidate's ideology or voting record. This suggests that past researchers who concluded that corporate contributions have little influence on legislators' behavior were wrong. Although there may be little relationship between corporate PAC contributions and legislators' roll call votes, roll call votes are not the primary objectives of corporate lobbyists. To determine if an interest's contributions affect the behavior of a legislator, it is first necessary to know what the corporation wants the legislator to do.

A third aspect of corporate lobbying is the relatively small amount of coalition activity. When corporate lobbyists did participate in coalitions they were highly unequal, with the smaller stakeholders in the collective good forcing the largest stakeholder to shoulder a disproportionate share of the lobbying effort. Past interest group research detected lots of coalition activity, and the literature suggests that lobbyists almost always try to form coalitions with potential allies.[15] We believe this discrepancy in findings is the result of different methods for identifying lobbying issues.

For example, an excellent study of coalition activity by Marie Hojnacki found that two-thirds of the business group lobbying she examined took place in coalitions.[16] But Hojnacki analyzed lobbying activity by studying five highly visible collective goods issues.[17] Given that the likelihood of coalition forming is highly correlated with the level of conflict surrounding an issue and the number and strength of opposition groups, Hojnacki's issue selection made it inevitable that she would find extensive coalition behavior.[18] To see how different research methods affect findings, take the example of the family and medical leave bill, an issue Hojnacki studied. The bill affected the operating costs of all the firms in our study and was decided during the period covered by our interviews. But none of our interviewees mentioned the medical leave issue, perhaps because they viewed lobbying on the bill as an inefficient use of their resources and chose to be free riders on the efforts of others instead.

In contrast to Hojnacki's approach, our study asked two questions: "What types of publicly supplied goods attract the greatest lobbying activity by firms?" and "How do firms pursue those goods?" To answer these questions we identified industries expected to expend differing levels of resources on lobbying. We then interviewed corporate and trade association lobbyists in those industries and asked them to list the most important issues to their firm or association and the amount of time and other resources they spent on each issue. Our approach is likely to uncover lobbying on low visibility issues on which there is less conflict, but it will miss lobbying activities that require little time or effort by the lobbyist.

Conclusion

The broad implications of our research are two. First, the goods corporations seek from government and the tactics they use depend not only on the importance of the good but also on where the good lies on the private-collective continuum. If political scientists are to understand patterns of interest group influence, they must first identify where the desired benefit lies on that continuum. Only then can the political scientists identify which organizations and lobbying strategies are most appropriate to the pursuit of that benefit. Second, because past interest group research generally has neglected private goods, that research has underestimated the effects of corporate lobbying and has overestimated the amount of coalition behavior by corporate lobbyists.

NOTES

1. Theodore J. Lowi, *The End of Liberalism*, 2d ed. (New York: Norton, 1979); James Q. Wilson, *Political Organizations* (New York: Basic Books, 1973).

2. William P. Browne, "Organized Interests and Their Issue Niches: A Search for Pluralism in a Policy Domain," *Journal of Politics* 52 (May 1990): 477–509; William P. Browne, *Cultivating Congress* (Lawrence: University of Kansas, 1995).

3. Mancur Olson Jr., *The Logic of Collective Action* (Cambridge: Harvard University, 1965).

4. We offer a formal proof of our expectations for why lobbyists will prefer private goods in Barry J. Seldon and Kenneth Godwin, "Firms' Investment in Lobbying for Collective and Private Goods: Results from a Game-Theoretic Model" (paper presented at the meetings of the American Political Science Association, Washington, D.C., September 4, 1998).

5. See Marie Hojnacki, "Interest Groups' Decisions to Join Alliances or Work Alone," *American Journal of Political Science* 41 (January 1997): 61–87.

6. Using past case studies of regulation, we chose several industries as potential candidates. We then interviewed stock analysts of those industries to estimate the degree to which firms' profits depend on federal regulation and to identify public policy issues important to the industry. When dealing with conglomerates, we included a corporation only if 50 percent or more of its total sales came from the product under consideration.

7. We completed our research before the Bridgestone/Firestone tire problem on sport utility vehicles became public.

8. A private good often includes two firms because it gives one a competitive advantage over the other. For example, if one airline wins a new international route, another airline that wanted the route did not receive it.

9. To ensure that we did not inadvertently encourage lobbyists to give answers that would confirm our hypotheses, we did not share our hypotheses with the interviewer.

10. *Dallas Business Journal*, July 29, 1996. An independent economic analysis of the Wright Amendment found that it increases the average ticket price out of the Dallas-Ft. Worth Airport by between 17 percent and 20 percent. Recently the Department of Transportation reinterpreted the Wright Amendment to allow direct flights from Love Field to all states so long as the planes carry fifty-six or fewer passengers.

11. Readers familiar with *The Logic of Collective Action* will note that this pattern fits exactly Olson's expectation that in these situations smaller stakeholders will exploit larger ones.

12. The PAC directors were asked why a legislator received money. If the response was that the legislator had helped the airline achieve its goals, the interviewer asked the directors what particular goal, if any, had been most important to the decision.

13. Trade associations are institutional arrangements that firms use to reduce the cost of pursuing collective goods. If firms pursued the collective good independently there could be duplication of effort. In addition, trade associations eliminate the free rider problem that can occur when an industry pursues a collective good. Trade associations overcome the free rider problem by using funds collected from all the firms in their lobbying effort.

14. The Rubber Manufacturers Association listed federal funding for basic research as an issue where the benefits of its lobbying might seem to extend beyond the rubber-resin industry. But the lobbyists' efforts were devoted to directing research dollars toward rubber-resin research and away from alternative industries.

15. For a review of past research on coalition forming, see Hojnacki, "Interest Groups' Decisions."

16. Ibid.

17. The issues involved Energy Tax proposals, striker replacement legislation, campaign finance reform, a job training program, and family and medical leave legislation.

18. Hojnacki, "Interest Groups' Decisions," 70–73.

Chapter 14

News Media

14-1

Is Journalism Hopelessly Cynical?

Michael Schudson

The history of the news media reveals a set of institutions that are continually in flux, as professional journalists and their news organizations adapt to changes in communications technology, the business environment within which they compete, and the political setting they report to their audience. Journalistic adaptations of the past quarter-century have produced a rapid rise in negative news about politics and a growing tone of cynicism in political reporting. Michael Schudson's article below calls attention to a rarely noted irony—that the news media's coverage of politics is growing simultaneously more cynical and more comprehensive and credible, and for some of the same reasons. Schudson's explanation focuses on the growing professional autonomy of journalists and a worldwide change in political culture.

BY PROFESSION, JOURNALISTS are supposed to be great cynics. Someone else's tragedy is their scoop, someone else's private moment is their opportunity for page one. Every politician's vaporous pronouncement exists only to be skewered.

The long-standing image of the journalist as cynic is contradicted by another image that is equally well-traveled—the journalist as reformer and romantic. In this image, journalists are forever young; with red, white, and blue always in their

Source: Michael Schudson, "Social Origins of Press Cynicism in Portraying Politics," *American Behavioral Scientist* 42, no. 6 (March 1999): 998–1008.

eyes; and with their typewriters (or computers) powered by a quest to right wrongs and speak truths to power.

The latter image is alive and well, at least at J-school commencements and the occasional convention of news practitioners. But in the broader public eye, and among scholars of the media, the picture of the journalist as romantic is said to be out of date. Critics of the American press—and the world press, for that matter—have in recent years agreed on two overarching propositions:

1. political reporting is increasingly cynical and promotes cynicism in the audience;
2. the product of news institutions is increasingly "infotainment," a concoction governed by entertainment values more than news judgment.

Both of these claims are generally correct. Of course, they do not apply to all of the news media, and they do not apply equally across news institutions. Moreover, it is hard to judge if these developments are mild or severe: How much cynicism is too much? When is an interest in entertainment a legitimate effort to relate a complex situation as a compelling story? And when does the quest for sensation overtake the effort to tell a story?

My concern is not to press the issue of measuring trends toward cynicism and infotainment more precisely. Nor is it to define when enough is enough. Rather, it is to pose an uncomfortable possibility: That there's no reversing these trends. In fact, many of the most self-conscious efforts of journalists to improve their work may augment, rather than dampen, such criticism. The trends can perhaps be contained, they can be policed, but there's no going home again.

Political cynicism is a cynicism of the reporter's mind; infotainment is a cynicism of the corporate soul. As both conspire to promote in the public a cynical understanding of politics, the media have developed a character and style that corrode our civic culture. That's the last thing most journalists intend—so why is it happening?

Toward Cynicism and Entertainment

Before going on to explain the changes in journalism, I will first quickly document their direction. In *Out of Order* (1993), Thomas Patterson has made a strong case for the growth of cynicism in political reporting. He has argued that the press has developed an "antipolitics bias." Three of his points seem especially telling. First, he finds a growing trend from 1960 to 1992 in the newsweeklies of reporting bad news rather than good. In 1960, 75 percent of evaluative references to Kennedy and Nixon were positive; in 1992 only 40 percent of evaluative references were positive for Clinton or Bush.

Second, journalists leave the impression that politicians will promise anything to get elected. They neglect to mention the political science studies that show that politicians generally work hard for and often make good on their campaign pledges.

Third, journalists see political careers as more oriented to politics as a game than to politics as policy. The game schema directs attention to conflicts and to a few individuals, not to social conditions and the larger interests individuals may represent. For instance, over time journalists have shifted from reporting candidates' speeches to reporting the strategic moves behind them (and often not saying much at all about the speeches themselves). From 1960 to 1992, there has been a progressive increase in *New York Times* political stories that emphasize a "game" framework or schema rather than a "policy" one.

As for the plunge of journalism into the entertainment business, this is an old complaint, but new conditions make it more convincing. A 1998 study produced by the Committee of Concerned Journalists found a deterioration in issues coverage in television, newspaper, and news magazine journalism between 1977 and 1997, with a declining attention to policy issues and an increasing attention to scandal. In 1977, in a sample of stories from leading newspapers and news magazines, 32 percent of stories were "traditional" in their emphasis on policy or political process and 15 percent concerned personalities, scandal, lifestyle, and human interest. In 1997, "traditional" news was down to 26 percent and feature news up to 43 percent.

Political news, it appears, demeans and diminishes what citizens may hope from politics, and this has become increasingly true over the past thirty years. I have focused on America, but this is a world-wide phenomenon. Reporting styles around the world have grown more informal, more intimate, more critical, and more cynically detached or distanced in the past two generations. British television interviewing changed from a style formal and deferential toward politicians to a more aggressive and critical style that makes politicians more visibly and immediately answerable to the public. Japanese broadcasting changed in a similar direction in recent years, partly under the influence of news anchor Kume Hiroshi. As political scientist Ellis Krauss put it, Hiroshi's "alienated cynicism and critical stance toward society and government" appears to have charmed a younger, more urban, and more alienated generation. His style moved toward a type of politics "more cynical and populist" than the old bureaucratic conservatism, but one that "offers little in the way of the framing of real political alternatives" (Krauss 2000)

Meanwhile, there is a new investigative aggressiveness in Latin American journalism. In Brazil, Argentina, and Peru, revelation of government scandals emerges not from old-fashioned partisan journalism but from a new, more entertainment-oriented journalism that adopts stock narratives and a telenovela personality-focused moralizing style. The results do not contribute to a public accounting of the moral order but come from and reinforce cultural pessimism. Scandal becomes a form of entertainment, at best, and contributes to political cynicism.

In the United States, nothing better illustrates these trends than the saturation coverage of the Monica Lewinsky scandal. But Monica coverage may help us see behind the apparent cynicism of the press. Monica coverage was overdetermined. Monicagate depended on the existence of the special prosecutor's office created in Title VI of the Ethics in Government Act of 1978, the chief legislative legacy of Watergate (and one, as it happens, that was opposed by most of the chief legal figures in Watergate, including Watergate special prosecutors Archibald Cox, Leon Jaworski, and Henry Ruth). It depended also on the media's having overlearned a Watergate lesson—that where there's smoke, there's fire. This is especially true of our leading news outlets. The *New York Times* relentlessly promoted the Whitewater story for years, and both the *Washington Post* and the *New York Times* repeatedly editorialized in favor of pursuing the impeachment inquiry. Finally, it depended on the erosion of a public–private distinction once well understood. This is a result of a variety of factors—first and foremost, the successful entrance of a feminist agenda onto the political scene. Feminists took as their watchword in the early 1970s that "the personal is political." Boy, is it ever.

The Reasons Why

The Lewinsky example raises a troubling question. The conditions that made Monicagate possible included (1) the institutionalization of high standards for government ethics and new operations for pursuing government corruption; (2) aggressive investigative journalism; and (3) the recognition of the ways in which domains once considered part of private life have public dimensions and public implications. In other words, three developments one might well judge to be improvements in public life contributed centrally to one of the most sordid episodes of modern media culture.

For all of the faults of media today, Americans have more information, and more credible information, than ever. People today have unprecedented access to careful, conscientious, analytically sound, crisply presented information about national and world affairs. (Their access to local news was never very good. It is pretty bad today, but I am not sure it is any worse than before.)

Highly educated citizens have access to especially rich information. Twenty-four percent of college graduates "sometimes" listen to NPR news. There was no

NPR before 1970. Twenty-eight percent of graduates sometimes watch C-SPAN. There was no C-SPAN until 1979. Some two-thirds of college graduates sometimes watch CNN, which did not exist until 1980. Half of college graduates sometimes read the *Wall Street Journal,* the *New York Times,* or *USA Today;* the *Times* did not have a national edition with national distribution until the 1970s and *USA Today* began only in 1982 (Center for Media and Public Affairs 1997, 15–47).

How can it be that the news has grown more cynical, more infotainment-oriented, and at the same time more comprehensive and credible? Three underlying trends in journalism help account for all of these developments.

Growing Professional Interventionism

The ties between news institutions and parties began to weaken near the end of the nineteenth century. With more and more news institutions run by mega-corporations and not by egomaniacal capitalist adventurers, the straightforward use of the press to advance the political interests of an individual, faction, or party have been progressively reduced. Reporters and editors have taken on greater authority, relative to ownership. They have also taken on greater authority relative to their own sources. They are less likely to defer to official authority than they were a generation ago. Vietnam, Watergate, the adversary culture of the 1960s, the revulsion in the media toward Ronald Reagan's photo opportunities and George Bush's cynically flag-waving victory over Michael Dukakis all contributed to a self-consciousness in journalism about both its possibilities and its pitfalls.

One sign of the new interventionism is the now famous shrinking of the "soundbite" in television news. In national network coverage of elections, the average length of time a candidate spoke uninterruptedly on camera was 43 seconds in 1968; by 1988, it was 9 seconds. This has generally been understood to mean that television news has grown worse and worse, more and more trivial, but this was not the conclusion of communication scholar Daniel Hallin, who did some of the original soundbite research in the first place. His conclusion was simply that television news had become more "mediated"—that is, journalists intervene with growing frequency in order to provide a compact and dramatic story. What did this mean for the overall quality of television news? Hallin found an increase in "horse-race" coverage from 1968 to 1988, a measure of the growing "game" or "strategy" orientation others have criticized, and so confirmed everyone's worst fears. But he *also* found an increase in the coverage of "issues," showing that television news is doing exactly what the media critics think it should be doing. How can both kinds of coverage increase at the same time? The answer is that television journalists offer a more highly structured, thematic story. There is less wasted motion, less silence, more rapid-fire editing.

Meanwhile, news stories have grown longer. In a recent study of ten newspapers in 1964 and in 1999, where in the earlier paper there was typically only one A-section story that ran twenty inches or more, today there are three; in 1964 there were typically thirty-six A-section stories under six inches, today only thirteen. Local, national, and international news represents only 24 percent of the news hole in today's papers rather than 35 percent in 1964—but the news hole has doubled during this period, thus making the total amount of news in the daily papers today significantly greater than it was in the early 1960s (Stepp 1999).

Thematizing

Media critic Paul Weaver has observed that television news is more inclined to "tell a story" than newspaper news. Both television and newspaper news are "essentially melodramatic accounts of current events," Weaver wrote. But television news is "far more coherently organized and tightly unified" compared to the newspaper story that still has an inverted pyramid organization in which the news account ends with a whimper, not a bang. The newspaper story has no teleological drive to wrap things up; in fact, after the opening paragraph or "lead," which can be read as a complete capsule story in itself, the rest of the story may be presented in very loose and only semicoherent order. The newspaper story is designed not to be read in its entirety, whereas the television story is meant to achieve its significance only as a full and finished object that keeps the viewer tuned in throughout. The newspaper story may confine itself to reporting an event, uninflected by any effort to give it meaning or analysis. The television story, in contrast, "inevitably . . . goes into, beneath or beyond the ostensive event to fix upon something else—a process, mood, trend, condition, irony, relationship, or whatever else seems a suitable theme in the circumstances" (Weaver 1981).

The effort of the television news story to thematize is hard to satisfy in an age suspicious of grand narrative and in an age when the Cold War is no longer available to provide a default narrative frame. So news institutions work overtime to put what they print into some kind of coherent analytic framework. Very often, this means putting the news into historical perspective. Where we do not have master narratives, we have at least some residual faith in the coherence of chronology. There is an increase, not a decrease, in news institutions' framing of current events in historical terms.

Growing News Coherence

A century ago competing newspapers in the same city featured front-page stories that their rivals did not even carry in the back pages. There was little urgency in journalism about coming up with "the" picture of that day's reality. News institutions now monitor one another all the time. CNN is a permanent presence in the newsrooms of daily newspapers. News magazines and newspapers preview their next editions on Web sites that reporters and editors at other news institutions examine almost the moment they are available. Newspapers advertise the next day's stories on cable news stations. The result is interinstitutional news coherence. Literary or film critics have talked of intertextuality for a long time; now news intertextuality is an electronic reality, not an accidental outcome of wars that draw reporters to the same hotel or power centers that draw them to the same bars in a capital city. News is a widely distributed, seamless intertext.

This follows in part from the domination of television in the news system. As Weaver suggested, because television journalism insists on thematic coherence, it "gives credence to the idea that there exists in America a single, coherent national agenda which can be perceived as such by any reasonable and well-intentioned person." This has intensified with (1) national news distribution—the *New York Times* News Service, CNN, *USA Today*, National Public Radio, and others—and (2) the growing importance of Washington news from the time of the Kennedy administration and Vietnam War to the present. The Vietnam War created modern television news as nothing else had before it. Since Vietnam, more news comes from Washington. Various factors contribute to this—the growing role of the federal government in everyday life, the growing celebrity of national television journalists, the improved technological capacity of satellite-borne television signals, and the growing corporatization of the press. More newspapers are owned by nonlocals and run by nonlocals with incentives to rise in the national organization rather than ties to local power structures or sentimental attachment to local roots. All of this not only nationalizes news but enlarges the possibilities for cynicism. When news is local, it typically remains personal, friendly, upbeat, gossipy, homey, and it very rarely probes local power structures or the assumptions—religious, ethnic, or otherwise—of local cultures. Nationalizing news distances journalists from their audiences, for better and for worse.

Growing interinstitutional news coherence is matched by a significant increase in intrainstitutional news coherence. News reporting seeks in each news institution a new comprehensiveness and cultural inclusiveness. If you walked into a newsroom fifty years ago, you would most likely not have seen any blacks or other racial minorities, and the only women you would have encountered would have been writing on the society page. (There were black journalists, but almost all of them worked for the several hundred black newspapers in the country.) The mainstream press conscientiously, if belatedly, sought to hire and promote black Americans and to cover news and views of minorities. Not only are there now minorities and women in the newsroom, but there is an acknowledged norm that stories of special interest to these groups are legitimate general-interest news stories.

Conclusion

Amid a veritable deluge of public information, people—especially young people—exhibit a declining interest in it. According to a 1996 survey conducted for the Radio and Television News Directors Foundation, 65 percent of people over 50 think it is "very important" to keep up with the news, compared to 55 percent of those 30–49 and 40 percent of those 18–29. Not everyone lives up to their ideals, of course. Only 51 percent of those over 50 say that they follow government and public affairs "most of the time," as did 29 percent of those 30–49 and 19 percent of those 18–29. Women in every age group are significantly less likely than men to follow government and public affairs—only 12 percent of women 18–29 claim that they do so (compared to 26 percent of men in this age group).

Young people have long lagged behind older people in following the news, but there has been a decrease over time. In 1965, 67 percent of those 21–35 read a newspaper the day before being surveyed; in 1990, only 30 percent. For the 30–49 age group, the percentage who read a newspaper the prior day dropped from 73 percent to 44 percent, and for those over 50, from 74 percent to 55 percent.

Publishers are alarmed. Their newspapers still turn handsome profits, but they are losing their audience. Every newspaper faces this reality. Urging the newspaper press to higher standards isn't much use if it should lead even more people to desert the habit of reading. So the print media become even more thematizing, professionally interventionist, more coherent, more cynical, and more entertainment-oriented.

There is no reason to suppose journalists are by personality or character more cynical than in the past. Institutional and cultural changes are more than enough in themselves to explain the cynical turn. Journalists today are unwilling to rely exclusively on official statements as they once did. Their own professional culture pushes them to be analytical and judgmental—for literary (thematizing) reasons, for cultural reasons (a society-wide growing distrust of established authority), for political reasons (the decline of the Cold War metanarrative for news), and for commercial reasons (fear of losing an audience). And of course, journalists are every bit as susceptible as the next person to the powerful political moods of the day. Whether it is Reagan to Clinton or Kohl to Schröder or Thatcher to Blair, the political mood takes government's proper role to be sustaining and encouraging the forces of the market. This leads to a naturalization of antigovernment talk, especially in the government itself, and journalists cannot help but reproduce this in their own work.

It is all very well to urge that news adopt a "policy" framework rather than a "game–strategy" framework for political news, but enacting this recommendation in the face of the journalism culture's best (as well as worst) instincts is another matter. The news media represent the nation and the world well, perhaps all too well, submitting to the moods of the hour rather than scrutinizing them. It will take more than a new journalistic diction to resist today's cynical undertow.

REFERENCES

Center for Media and Public Affairs. 1997. *What the People Want from the Press* (Washington, D.C.: Center for Media and Public Affairs).

Krauss, Ellis. 2000. *Broadcasting Politics in Japan: NHK and Television News* (Ithaca: Cornell University Press).

Patterson, Thomas. 1993. *Out of Order* (New York: Knopf).

Stepp, Carl Sessions. 1999. "The State of the American Newspaper: Then and Now," *American Journalism Review*, September, 60–75.

Weaver, Paul. 1981. "TV News and Newspaper News," in *Understanding Television*, ed. Richard P. Adler (New York: Praeger), 272–293.

14-2

The People and the Press: Whose Views Shape the News?

Thomas B. Edsall

Echoes of Schudson's analysis can be heard in this essay, which examines how journalists go about characterizing public opinion and elected officials' responsiveness to that opinion. To avoid blatant bias, modern journalists rely heavily on the steady flow of public opinion surveys. Indeed, most national journalists work for employers who monthly take national readings of the public's pulse on current affairs. Whenever journalists find a disparity between an elective official's stance on an issue and the median response to their opinion survey, they are all too quick to condemn the politician as unresponsive or, worse, corrupt. In this respect, journalists adopt a more suspicious posture toward normal politics than does the general public—which is saying quite a lot. In part, Edsall argues, this posture reflects as much journalists' lack of appreciation of the views of ordinary citizens as it does the pervasive cynicism examined in the previous essay.

THE NEW KAISER *Public Perspective* survey on polling and democracy clearly suggests that journalists, especially those who make use of polling data, face substantial and potentially dangerous credibility issues. Such issues center on the public perception that the press, in terms of beliefs, ideas, and political values, stands apart from the rest of the citizenry.

First, according to the survey, journalists and others in the field tend generally to be more confident of the accuracy of poll data than either policy leaders or the public at large. Second, journalists are substantially more cynical about the motives of politicians than either the public or policy elites. Third, and perhaps most significantly, the media diverge from both the public and from the policy-making community in terms of partisanship and ideology. Only a tiny fraction of the media identifies itself as either Republican (4%), or conservative (6%). This is in direct contrast to the public, which identifies itself as 28% Republican and 35% conservative, and to policy leaders, who describe themselves as 24% Republican and 18% conservative.

Source: Thomas B. Edsall, "The People and the Press: Whose Views Shape the News?" *The Public Perspective* (July/August 2001): 29–31.

These areas of divergence between the public and the press lend themselves to conflict, both with the consumers and the makers of news, and threaten to diminish the legitimacy of American journalism.

Consider the first point: the willingness of the media to accept poll findings as accurate.

By substantial margins, members of the media hold more favorable attitudes toward polling . . . than either the general public or policy leaders. A majority, 52%, of media respondents thinks the best way public officials can learn the views of people on major issues is through polling. These respondents are doubtful as to the effectiveness of such direct-contact approaches as town hall meetings (25% said they are the best way) or talking to people under a variety of circumstances (11%). The general public, in contrast, thinks town hall meetings (43%) and talking to people (28%) are better ways to gauge public opinion than polling (25%).

While there is no doubt that in terms of statistical measurement, polling is a far better tool than random conversations with people, or town hall meetings which draw self-selected or preselected audiences, survey research does not always capture the potential impact of public opinion. The intensity of feeling on any given issue is as critical as the numbers.

For example, opponents of gun control have, over the past two decades, been more deeply convinced of their position, and more prepared to cast votes on that single issue, than supporters of gun control. In spite of majority support in any given election, gun control may be a losing issue. Any politician, including one prepared to take a principled but disadvantageous position, wants to know the likely costs. To discover these costs, home-district town meetings on the subject may be a better barometer of public opinion than a poll.

The same is true of such issues as abortion, gay rights and flag burning. Opinion surveys will quickly inform politicians in most sections of the United States that there is very little support for the view that the First Amendment confers the right to burn an American flag. Conversely, many conservative politicians now represent suburban communities where the majority of voters supports abortion rights. For the politician opposed to legislation to ban flag burning, and for the suburban pro-life politician . . . town meetings and conversations with constituents are the only ways to learn how to articulate and defend a minority stand without losing the next election. . . .

The second point, that the media are more cynical than other Americans about the motivations of politicians, is also important. The general public has doubts regarding elected officials: 59% said campaign contributors exercise a great deal of influence over the decisions of elected and government officials, and 45% said lobbyists and special interest groups have similar leverage. These numbers pale, however, in comparison to the views of journalists and other media professionals, 70% of whom said campaign contributors have a great deal of influence, and 67% of whom said lobbyists and special interests exercise similarly strong influence.

While there is no question that campaign contributions, lobbyists and special interests profoundly bear on policy decisions, the emphasis that journalists place on these sources of influence arguably distorts news coverage, discounting, for example, the occasions on which a politician may take a stand based on principle.

More importantly, this focus by journalists, on campaign contributions especially, leads to political coverage that often lacks nuance and complexity. A whole industry has emerged in recent years in Washington—exemplified by Common Cause and the Center for Responsive Politics, among others—that specializes in providing the press with the data to make simple linkages between legislative voting records and campaign contributions. Such stories have become easy to research and find sources for—a reporter can do the work entirely from his or her computer and get good, often front-page, play.

The costs of the money/vote approach, and reportorial dependence, are not trivial: the press becomes the unwitting ally of a reform politics. . . . This kind of political coverage serves to reinforce public cynicism, highlighting political motivations which stem from donor demands and shortchanging other, equally important forces working to shape political decision-making.

The tax revolt of the late 1970s and early 1980s was not, for example, driven primarily by large corporations seeking to shrink big government, but grew rather out of the combination of inflation and bracket-creep that pushed many working and lower middle class households into a steeply progressive marginal rate structure that had once applied only to the upper middle classes and the rich.

Similarly, donors often make contributions to candidates and officeholders who already share their views. Examples abound of overly narrow journalistic interpretations of complex motivations for political action. . . . [P]ress cynicism is an important contributor to ideologically constricted—and thus frequently incomplete—news coverage.

The finding that there are very few conservative and/or Republican members of the media is equally significant. The institutional structure of reporting, the culture of journalism, the kind of mindset that most easily adapts to the demands of the profession, the educational requirements for admission to the field, and so forth, combine to recruit a distinctively liberal workforce. Simply put, the media do not have good antennae to detect conservative forces at work in the electorate.

The press, in the course of the past four decades, has been blindsided by some of the most significant political developments because so few members of the media share the views of the voters who have been mobilized by these movements. Examples include the white, working class reaction in the north to the civil rights movement, starting in the late 1960s; the emergence of Richard Nixon's "silent majority" in the 1970s; the conservative upheaval of 1980 that produced Ronald Reagan and the Republican takeover of the Senate; the rise of the Christian Right; the Gingrich revolution of 1994; the popularity of welfare reform in the 1990s; and the unexpectedly conservative appointments and legislative priorities of the current Bush administration.

Whether or not members of the media agree with conservative voters on any given set of questions is not at issue. The problem is the invisibility of these men and women to the national media, and, most especially, the inability of the press to represent their views in public discourse. The failure to address the concerns of a substantial part of the American electorate has contributed markedly to the widespread perception of the media as elitist and arrogant.

Just as importantly, this blindness has prevented the media from staying abreast of developments and trends, resulting in the press playing catch-up, struggling in the aftermath, for example, to figure out what happened on Election Day 1994; who these evangelical voters are; why people would care so much about Aid to Families with Dependent Children when the costs of the program amount to less than 1% of the federal budget; and where the drive to impeach President Clinton came from.

The Kaiser/*Public Perspective* study provides useful data to the media about their own biases, loyalties, liabilities and taboos. Such data, used effectively, can direct press attention to the needs of the entire nation, encourage the press to exercise responsibly the protected position it holds at the heart of the American experiment, and restore a degree of public confidence in print, television and electronic journalism—an expanding universe in the ongoing information age.

14-3

American News Consumption during Times of National Crisis

Scott L. Althaus

In an earlier essay (Skocpol, pp. 38–46) we learned that 9/11 led less to increased participation in voluntary and patriotic activities than to more intensive television viewing. Americans turned to television—most particularly, as we learn here, to cable television—to discover what happened and why. With more than four-fifths of households subscribing to cable and satellite service, all news channels have emerged as the single most valued source for news.

HAVE 9/11 and the ensuing war on terrorism sparked a reinvigoration of civic life in the United States? Opinion surveys show dramatic changes in the political attitudes of American citizens, as detailed by other contributors to this symposium. However, it remains unclear whether these changed attitudes have resulted in higher levels of civic activity.

If Americans today are more engaged in civic life than they were a year ago, we should see evidence of this change in the amount of attention they pay to news of national and international affairs. Unlike many other civic behaviors, watching or reading the news is relatively low in opportunity costs. Because the choice between viewing a *Simpsons* rerun or a national news broadcast is made so easily, the size of the audience for national news should be fairly sensitive to shifts in the perceived importance of public affairs. And like the proverbial canary in the mine shaft, changing levels of civic-mindedness are likely to be seen first in lower-cost behaviors like paying attention to news before they are seen in higher-cost activities like volunteering or joining a group.

This article looks at changes in the size of American news audiences during the 1990–91 Persian Gulf crisis and the more recent period surrounding the 9/11 attacks. Like the current situation, the Persian Gulf crisis started suddenly, when Iraq launched a surprise invasion of Kuwait on August 2, 1990. Since there are clear starting points for both national crises, comparing the percentage of adults watching television news broadcasts before and after each precipitating event

Source: Scott L. Althaus, "American News Consumption During Times of National Crisis," *PS: Political Science and Politics* 35, no. 3 (September 2002): 517–521.

should show whether the respective crises prompted changes in levels of popular attention to the news.

Audience Trends for Network News Broadcasts

Weekly television-ratings data collected by Nielsen Media Research are available for both cases.[1] Since the television audience grows in winter months, the time of year in which a precipitating event occurs can influence the apparent impact of the crisis. For this reason, I collected weekly ratings data from each case over 16-month periods starting the first week of January in the year the crisis began and ending the last week of April in the following year. To measure the combined total audience for nightly national news programs, I combined ratings for ABC's *World News Tonight*, CBS's *Evening News,* and NBC's *Nightly News.* To ease interpretation across the two cases, I translated these ratings data into the percentage of American adults that were tuning in to the nightly news.[2]

One striking feature of these trends (Figure 1) is that the evening news audience today is only about half as large as it was a decade before. During the 1990–91 period, between 23% and 33% of American adults watched nightly network news broadcasts, depending on the time of year. Since January 2001, Nielsen data put the total size of nightly news audiences at between 11% and 16% of American adults (not counting the week of 9/11). It is unclear whether today's total audience for all forms of public-affairs content is any smaller than it was a decade before, but if it is, the falloff is likely to be slight. Instead, the once-larger broadcast news audience of 1990–91 is today spread out across a wider range of news products, with cable, the Internet, primetime news magazines, and local television news each attracting sizable portions of a national news audience that once was shared mainly by the three evening news programs.

Because news audiences have become increasingly fragmented, absolute differences in the percentage of adults watching network news during each crisis period are less telling than the relative changes in audience size within each trend. If we begin our analysis immediately before each precipitating event and follow the trends over the next several months, the two cases appear to reveal different patterns of audience response. In the Persian Gulf crisis, the Iraqi invasion of Kuwait immediately produced a four-percentage-point spike in the American news audience. The nightly news audience then grew steadily over the fall months as the American military buildup in Saudi Arabia signaled a looming confrontation with Iraq. Nearly a third of American adults were directly exposed to one of the three nightly news broadcasts in the weeks leading up to and immediately following the start of the air war, which began on January 17, as war against Iraq was vigorously debated in Congress and then witnessed live on television.

Figure 1. Weekly Percentage of American Adults Watching Nightly
Network News Broadcasts

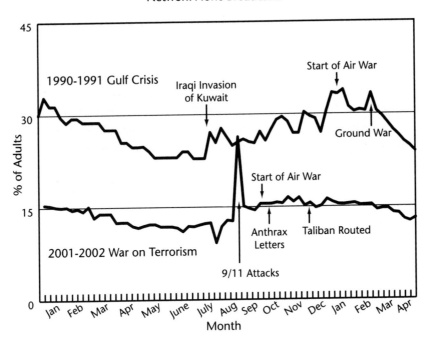

Source: Nielsen ratings data compiled from various media sources. These trends report the combined weekly audience for ABC's *World News Tonight*, CBS's *Evening News*, and NBC's *Nightly News*.

The news audience shrank somewhat in early February before experiencing a three-percentage-point jump during the week of ground combat, which began on February 23. This rapid victory over Iraqi ground forces was followed by an abrupt turn away from the news, and the nightly audience dropped nearly 10 percentage points over the eight weeks following the close of the ground campaign.

Eleven years later, the tragedies of 9/11 had the immediate effect of more than doubling the size of the evening news audience, from 13% of American adults in the week of September 3–9 to more than 26% in the week of September 10–16. Nielsen Media Research later estimated that 79.5 million viewers were tuning into any of 11 broadcast or cable networks showing news coverage on the night of 9/11. As impressive as this level of attention seems, the January 2001 Super Bowl attracted about the same number of viewers.[3] Moreover, the evening news audience just as swiftly contracted to 15% of American adults in the week of September 17–23 and never rose more than one-and-a-half percentage points above that level in the following seven months. In contrast to frequent event-driven surges in news attention throughout the Persian Gulf crisis, news attention in the post-9/11 U.S. held quite stable at about four percentage points above pre-9/11 levels for several months before declining steadily after the start of the new year in 2002. By the middle of April 2002, the size of the evening news audience had returned to the previous July's level of just 13% of adults.

When thus interpreting these postcrisis trends using the immediate precrisis period as a benchmark, it appears that the Persian Gulf crisis produced a gradual mobilization of adults into the television news audience, but that the present war on terrorism generated a smaller shock to the size of American news audiences that started decaying soon after it began. During the Persian Gulf crisis, the average size of the evening news audience grew by 13.8 million persons between the last week of July 1990, and the first week of January 1991. During the war on terrorism, the growth in the evening news audience between these two weeks was only half as large, amounting to 7.4 million more audience members in 2002.

However, this interpretation of postcrisis growth in the news audience requires us to ignore the left-hand side of Figure 1. The longer-term trends leading up to each precipitating event call into question whether either of these national crises fundamentally increased the size of the news audience. Once we take into account the cyclical shifts in the size of television news audiences, the apparent changes prompted by each crisis become harder to distinguish from normal seasonal movement. It seems impressive at first glance that 32.7% of American adults were following the evening news in a typical week during the critical month of January 1991, up from 23.2% for July 1990. However, this number loses some of its luster when we recognize that the evening news audience was nearly as large— 31.4% of adults—in the previous January. Given the seasonal variation in the size of news audiences, a more appropriate way of measuring the impact of national crises is to calculate the size of the news audience after the precipitating event compared to its size from the same period in the previous year.

This comparison paints a very different picture. During the Gulf crisis an average of approximately 2.4 million more adults per day were watching evening news broadcasts in the first four months of 1991 compared to the first four months of 1990. The same comparison for the war on terrorism produces a mean difference of just less than 900,000 more audience members per day in 2002 than in 2001. Seasonal-adjusted growth in the news audience was nearly three times as large during the Persian Gulf crisis as during the current war on terrorism, but in both cases the magnitude of growth was rather small, amounting to 0.4% of adults in 2001–2 and 1.3% in 1990–91.[4] Seen from this perspective, the clearest impact of the Iraqi invasion of Kuwait was in increasing the amount of weekly variance around the seasonal mean rather than in shifting the mean itself. Similarly, 9/11 appears to have accelerated the seasonal growth curve for the evening news audience during the fall of 2001 without producing a substantive shift in its average size.

Where Else Are Americans Getting Their News?

The preceding analysis begs the question of whether Americans are still getting their news primarily from network news broadcasts. If people are turning instead to other sources for public affairs information, then an analysis of those sources might shed a more flattering light on levels of civic engagement in post-9/11 America.

According to surveys conducted by the Pew Center for the People and the Press (Figure 2), there have been some notable changes in the mix of news media used by Americans since 9/11. The questions from which I obtained these data allowed respondents to name up to three media as primary sources of news, so these survey data capture a potentially broad range of media involvement.[5] In the first week of September 2001, newspapers were the most commonly mentioned source of information about public affairs. By the second week of January 2002, cable television news had become the most-cited news source, mentioned by over half of respondents.

All of the other pre- and post-9/11 differences are individually within the margins of sampling error for these surveys, but collectively they reveal some common patterns. First, there has been a decline in the percentage of Americans turning to print news since 9/11. Audit bureau data released by the Newspaper Association of America confirms that U.S. daily newspaper circulation in the period from September 31, 2001, through March 31, 2002, was 0.6% lower than in the prior six-month period that ended in September, 2001.[6] Second, the declining reliance on newspapers and news magazines seems to be offset by a shift toward electronic news sources. Aside from the obvious jump for cable television news, slightly higher percentages of Americans reported in January 2002 that they turn to local television news, network television news, radio, and the Internet for public affairs information. Taken together, these two changes suggest that Americans now seem to be more attentive to media that specialize in delivering the "latest" news even as they reduce their reliance on sources of news that emphasize in-depth reporting and providing context for understanding the current crisis. But how many people are actually tuning in to cable?

Audience Trends for Cable News

The Pew surveys suggest that many more people now rely on cable news outlets than before 9/11, and Nielsen ratings data confirm that the cable news audience has experienced a sizeable gain. Since cable news outlets provide continuous public affairs programming, Nielsen measures cable news audiences differently than network news audiences. Instead of estimating the average number of viewers

Figure 2. Where Have People Been Getting Most of Their News about National and International Issues?

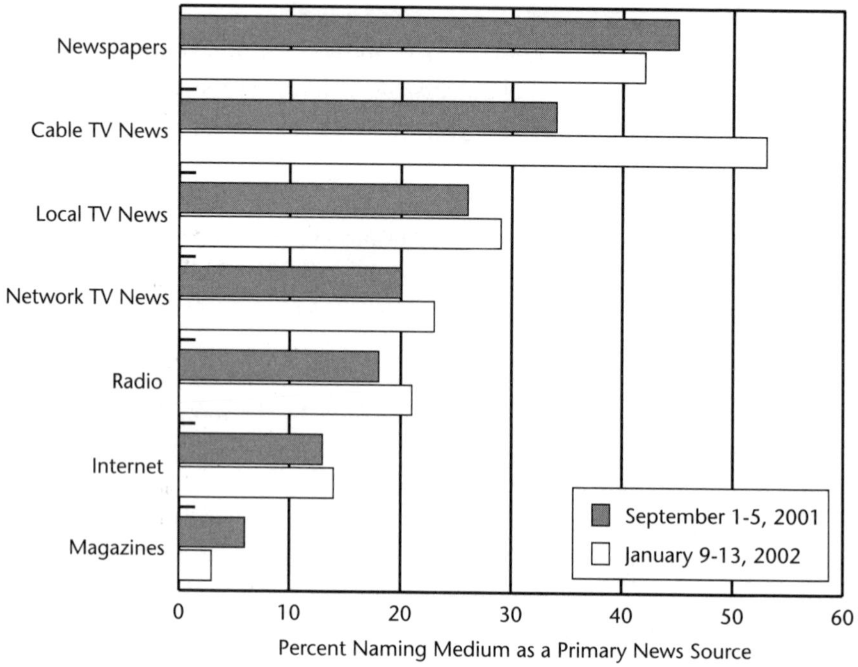

Source: Pew Center for the People and the Press surveys. Since up to three answers were accepted per respondent (see note 6), the sum for each survey adds up to well over 100 percent.

for a particular program, Nielsen estimates for each cable channel the average number of viewers per minute in an entire day. While not directly comparable to network news ratings, since these averages mask how many different people watch the cable channels across an entire day, the change in these ratings before and after 9/11 clarifies how cable audiences have responded to the terror attacks.

Figure 3 shows the combined average audience per minute for the Cable News Network, Fox News Channel, and MSNBC, which are the top three cable news channels.[7] For the six months leading up to September 2001, the combined audience for the three cable channels averaged just less than 0.4% of American adults, or about 800,000 persons. For the period from September 2001 through March 2002, the average cable audience more than doubled to nearly 1% of American adults, or approximately two million people. Figure 3 shows that the changes in the size of the cable news audience followed a similar course as that for the broadcast news audience. After a fourfold increase from 800,000 persons in August to 2.7 million in September, the average cable news audience gradually

Figure 3. Average Percentage of American Adults Watching Cable News,
March 2001 to March 2002

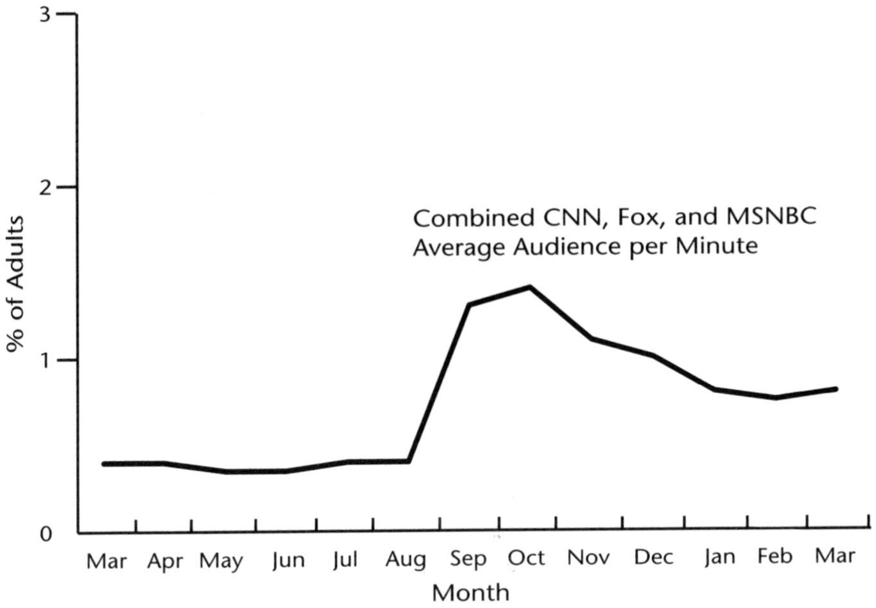

Source: Nielsen ratings data.

declined in size over the next several months. By March 2002, the combined per-minute audience for the three cable channels averaged 1.5 million viewers. While this is just half the size of the peak audience in September, it is also twice the size of the combined cable audience from a year before, indicating that cable news has indeed retained an appreciable number of new viewers.

Although Figure 3 appears to suggest that the cable audience remains far smaller than the broadcast news audience (and media reporters frequently interpret these numbers in this way), it is possible that the cumulative cable news audience—that is, the total number of unique viewers—could include a fairly large proportion of American adults on a given day. For example, the average per-minute cable news audience for November 2001 was 905,000 persons for CNN and 747,000 for Fox News. But the number of different people who watched at least 15 minutes of programming at some point during that same month was 93.4 million for CNN (or about 46% of American adults) and 58.5 million for Fox (or about 29% of American adults).[8]

However, it is unclear whether these cable viewers are getting a mix of news comparable to that received by network audiences. A recent content analysis of primetime news programming on CNN, Fox, and MSNBC during late January of this year (*News Hour* 2002) found that cable news shows focused on a small number of "headline" stories, and that much of the primetime programming took the form of personal interviews or panel discussions rather than traditional news reporting. If the past behavior of cable audiences is any guide to the present, it is also likely that these new viewers constitute an irregular audience for cable news, tuning in to catch up with developing stories or breaking news, but otherwise relying primarily on noncable sources for their daily diet of news.

Consequences of Public Disengagement from the War on Terrorism

If 9/11 has founded a new era of civic-mindedness in the U.S., it seems to have left Americans' collective appetite for news largely undisturbed. The size of the network television news audience grew only slightly, and newspaper readership continued to decline after 9/11. While the average size of the cable news audience has doubled, it remains a small fraction of American adults, and the audiences for both network and cable news have diminished with each passing month.

It is too soon to identify any long-term implications for the public's limited attention to the early stages of this war, let alone to speculate whether the trends of the last year are likely to continue into even the near future. However, two consequences of the public's disengagement are already apparent.

First, many Americans consider the war on terrorism to be a domestic issue rather than a foreign-policy issue. The Pew Research Center for the People and the Press conducted a survey in January 2002, which asked two slightly different versions of the same question (Pew 2002). The first read: "Right now, which is more important for President Bush to focus on: domestic policy or the war on terrorism?" A second version changed "the war on terrorism" to "foreign policy," but was otherwise identical. If Americans think about the war on terrorism as a foreign-policy issue, the percentages in both versions of the question should be nearly identical. Yet, the public's responses could hardly be more different. To the first version of the question, 33% of respondents answered domestic policy and 52% named the war on terrorism. These numbers were reversed in the second version, where 52% chose domestic policy and only 34% said foreign policy.

Question-wording effects of this magnitude—generating an 18-point shift in surveyed opinion—typically indicate that the mass public has insufficiently reasoned through its opinions (Yankelovich 1991). It is certainly understandable why many Americans see the war on terrorism as a domestic issue. Most paid close attention to news of the terrorist attacks in New York, Pennsylvania, and Washington, DC, but have been less attentive to the news during the Bush administration's subsequent military actions and diplomatic initiatives overseas. Further analysis of this wording effect by Pew researchers revealed that the tendency to think of the war on terrorism as a domestic policy issue was closely related to level of formal education: college graduates gave essentially the same mix of opinions in response to both versions of the question, while those with a high school education or less demonstrated the greatest sensitivity to these wording changes (Pew 2002). Since people with higher levels of education also tend to be more attentive to the news (Price and Zaller 1993), the tendency to see the war on terrorism as a matter of domestic policy may be a direct outgrowth of public disengagement from the news in the aftermath of 9/11.

A second consequence is that while opinion surveys reveal consistently high levels of support for American military action against countries and organizations suspected of sponsoring terrorism, the roots of this support may not run deep. This possibility is suggested in recent trends from Gallup polls that ask Americans to name "the most important problem facing the country today."[9] Figure 4 shows how terrorism leaped onto the public's agenda following 9/11: nearly half of Americans named terrorism as the country's most important problem in an October Gallup poll (no data are available for the month of September). However, the ensuing months saw a rapid falloff in the percentage of the public concerned about terrorism, so that by January 2002, fewer than a quarter of Americans named terrorism as the country's most important problem. In contrast, unease with the state of the economy came to rival terrorism as the top issue of public concern in the first quarter of 2002. Given the impact of a shifting public agenda on evaluations of George Bush Sr.'s job performance in the aftermath of the Persian Gulf war (Krosnick and Brannon 1993), it is notable that the declining importance of terrorism and the increasing importance of economic concerns track George W. Bush's declining job-approval rating. Although President Bush has made it clear that the allied military campaign against terrorism is just beginning, fewer people today are likely to be evaluating him on the basis of his performance as commander in chief.

The rapid decline in public concern about terrorism is a sign that American support for U.S. military involvement abroad may be less firm than it seems. If this American resolve is more closely tied to the dramatic events of 9/11 than to a new appreciation for the complexities of the post-9/11 geopolitical landscape, it becomes increasingly difficult to predict how Americans will respond to new developments or crises in the coming years of this war.

It remains to be seen whether this public disengagement has resulted from the stunning successes of the U.S. military campaign in Afghanistan, or from the secrecy in which the war on terrorism has necessarily been shrouded. But the

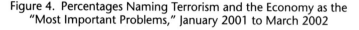

Figure 4. Percentages Naming Terrorism and the Economy as the
"Most Important Problems," January 2001 to March 2002

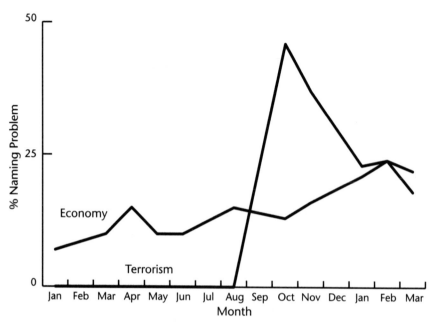

Source: Surveys by the Gallup Organization.

public's steady retreat from opportunities for news exposure should give pause to military and political leaders pondering the next step in this solemn undertaking.

NOTES

1. I compiled these data from various media sources available from the LEXIS-NEXIS database. Nielsen uses representative national samples of 5,000 television households to estimate television viewing trends for all households in the U.S. Electronic "People Meters" continuously monitor all broadcast television, satellite, cable, and VCR viewing activity for each individual in a household.

2. Nielsen currently publishes ratings in terms of millions of audience members viewing a particular program. According to the 2000 Census, there are 205.05 million persons aged 19 or older in the U.S. Since household television penetration has been nearly universal since before 1980, simply dividing the former by the latter produces a reasonable estimate of the percentage of American adults watching nightly news programs. During the 1990–91 period, Nielsen reported ratings information using its measure of rating points, in which each point represents 1% of American television households viewing a particular program. To create comparable trends for the Persian Gulf Crisis, the combined rating points for all three network news broadcasts were multiplied by the mean number of persons aged 19 or older per household in

the U.S. (1.87, according to the 1990 Census) and then by the number of households in the U.S. (91.99 million in 1990). This joint product was then divided by the total number of persons aged 19 or older (181.50 million) to estimate the percentage of adults watching nightly network news programs.

3. Lisa de Moraes, "For an Extraordinary Week, Nielsen Puts the Ratings Aside," *Washington Post*, 20 September 2001, sec. C.

4. These percentages come from the January through April averages between years for each case.

5. In these Pew surveys, respondents were first asked, "How have you been getting most of your news about national and international issues? From television, from newspapers, from radio, from magazines, or from the Internet?" Interviewers were instructed to accept two answers from each respondent, and in cases where the respondent provided only one answer, to prompt for a second. Any respondents who answered "television" were then asked "Do you get most of your news about national and international issues from network TV news, from local TV news, or from cable news networks such as CNN, MSNBC, and the Fox News Channel?" As with the first question, two answers were accepted from each respondent, and those providing only one were prompted for another. Since this question structure prompted each respondent to provide at least two and up to three answers, the sum of categories adds up to well over 100%. These data are from the January 17, 2002, report entitled "Unusually High Interest In Bush's State Of The Union" (Pew 2002).

6. Felicity Barringer, "Some Big Papers Buck Trend of Circulation Drops," *New York Times*, 7 May 2002, sec. C.

7. Cable ratings data are from Jim Rutenberg, "Audience for Cable News Grows: Programs are Holding Some Gains from Terror Coverage," *New York Times*, 25 March 2002, sec. C.

8. Reported in David Bauder, "The Different Audiences of News Networks Come into Focus," Associated Press Wire Service, 9 January 2002.

9. I obtained these data from the Roper Center for Public Opinion Research POLL database, which is available on LEXIS-NEXIS. Data from 2001 are not available for the months of February, July, September, and December.

REFERENCES

Krosnick, Jon. A., and Brannon, Laura A. 1993. "The Impact of the Gulf War on the Ingredients of Presidential Evaluations: Multidimensional Effects of Political Involvement," *American Political Science Review* 87, 963–75.

News Hour with Jim Lehrer. 2002. "Cable News Wars: Behind the Battle for Cable News Viewers—March 2002." Available from www.pbs.org/newshour/media/cablenews/index.html.

Pew Research Center for the People and the Press. 2002. "Unusually High Interest in Bush's State of the Union: Public Priorities Shifted by Recession and War." Available from people-press.org/reports/display.php3?ReportID5147.

Price, Vincent, and Zaller, John. 1993. "Who Gets the News? Alternative Measures of News Reception and Their Implications for Research." *Public Opinion Quarterly* 57, 133–64.

Yankelovich, Daniel. 1991. *Coming to Public Judgment: Making Democracy Work in a Complex World.* Syracuse, N.Y.: Syracuse University Press.

Constitution of the United States

We the People of the United States, in Order to form a more perfect Union, establish Justice, insure domestic Tranquility, provide for the common defence, promote the general Welfare, and secure the Blessings of Liberty to ourselves and our Posterity, do ordain and establish this Constitution for the United States of America.

ARTICLE I

Section 1. All legislative Powers herein granted shall be vested in a Congress of the United States, which shall consist of a Senate and House of Representatives.

Section 2. The House of Representatives shall be composed of Members chosen every second Year by the People of the several States, and the Electors in each State shall have the Qualifications requisite for Electors of the most numerous Branch of the State Legislature.

No Person shall be a Representative who shall not have attained to the age of twenty five Years, and been seven Years a Citizen of the United States, and who shall not, when elected, be an Inhabitant of that State in which he shall be chosen.

[Representatives and direct Taxes shall be apportioned among the several States which may be included within this Union, according to their respective Numbers, which shall be determined by adding to the whole Number of free Persons, including those bound to Service for a Term of Years, and excluding Indians not taxed, three fifths of all other Persons.][1] The actual Enumeration shall be made within three Years after the first Meeting of the Congress of the United States, and within every subsequent Term of ten Years, in such Manner as they shall by Law direct. The Number of Representatives shall not exceed one for every thirty Thousand, but each State shall have at Least one Representative; and until such enumeration shall be made, the State of New Hampshire shall be entitled to chuse three, Massachusetts eight, Rhode-Island and Providence Plantations one, Connecticut five, New-York six, New Jersey four, Pennsylvania eight, Delaware one, Maryland six, Virginia ten, North Carolina five, South Carolina five, and Georgia three.

Source: U.S. Congress, House, Committee on the Judiciary, *The Constitution of the United States of America, as Amended,* 100th Cong., 1st sess., 1987, H Doc 100-94.

When vacancies happen in the Representation from any State, the Executive Authority thereof shall issue Writs of Election to fill such Vacancies.

The House of Representatives shall chuse their Speaker and other Officers; and shall have the sole Power of Impeachment.

Section 3. The Senate of the United States shall be composed of two Senators from each State, [chosen by the Legislature thereof,]² for six Years; and each Senator shall have one Vote.

Immediately after they shall be assembled in Consequence of the first Election, they shall be divided as equally as may be into three Classes. The Seats of the Senators of the first Class shall be vacated at the Expiration of the second Year, of the second Class at the Expiration of the fourth Year, and of the third Class at the Expiration of the sixth Year, so that one third may be chosen every second Year; [and if Vacancies happen by Resignation, or otherwise, during the Recess of the Legislature of any State, the Executive thereof may make temporary Appointments until the next Meeting of the Legislature, which shall then fill such Vacancies.]³

No Person shall be a Senator who shall not have attained to the Age of thirty Years, and been nine Years a Citizen of the United States, and who shall not, when elected, be an Inhabitant of that State for which he shall be chosen.

The Vice President of the United States shall be President of the Senate, but shall have no Vote, unless they be equally divided.

The Senate shall chuse their other Officers, and also a President pro tempore, in the Absence of the Vice President, or when he shall exercise the Office of President of the United States.

The Senate shall have the sole Power to try all Impeachments. When sitting for that Purpose, they shall be on Oath or Affirmation. When the President of the United States is tried, the Chief Justice shall preside: And no Person shall be convicted without the Concurrence of two thirds of the Members present.

Judgment in Cases of Impeachment shall not extend further than to removal from Office, and disqualification to hold and enjoy any Office of honor, Trust or Profit under the United States: but the Party convicted shall nevertheless be liable and subject to Indictment, Trial, Judgment and Punishment, according to Law.

Section 4. The Times, Places and Manner of holding Elections for Senators and Representatives, shall be prescribed in each State by the Legislature thereof; but the Congress may at any time by Law make or alter such Regulations, except as to the Places of chusing Senators.

The Congress shall assemble at least once in every Year, and such Meeting shall [be on the first Monday in December],⁴ unless they shall by Law appoint a different Day.

Section 5. Each House shall be the Judge of the Elections, Returns and Qualifications of its own Members, and a Majority of each shall constitute a Quorum to do Business; but a smaller Number may adjourn from day to day, and may be authorized to compel the Attendance of absent Members, in such Manner, and under such Penalties as each House may provide.

Each House may determine the Rules of its Proceedings, punish its Members for disorderly Behaviour, and, with the Concurrence of two thirds, expel a Member.

Each House shall keep a Journal of its Proceedings, and from time to time publish the same, excepting such Parts as may in their Judgment require Secrecy; and the Yeas and Nays of the Members of either House on any question shall, at the Desire of one fifth of those Present, be entered on the Journal.

Neither House, during the Session of Congress, shall, without the Consent of the other, adjourn for more than three days, nor to any other Place than that in which the two Houses shall be sitting.

Section 6. The Senators and Representatives shall receive a Compensation for their Services, to be ascertained by Law, and paid out of the Treasury of the United States. They shall in all Cases, except Treason, Felony and Breach of the Peace, be privileged from Arrest during their Attendance at the Session of their respective Houses, and in going to and returning from the same; and for any Speech or Debate in either House, they shall not be questioned in any other Place.

No Senator or Representative shall, during the Time for which he was elected, be appointed to any civil Office under the Authority of the United States, which shall have been created, or the Emoluments whereof shall have been encreased during such time; and no Person holding any Office under the United States, shall be a Member of either House during his Continuance in Office.

Section 7. All Bills for raising Revenue shall originate in the House of Representatives; but the Senate may propose or concur with Amendments as on other Bills.

Every Bill which shall have passed the House of Representatives and the Senate, shall, before it become a Law, be presented to the President of the United States; If he approve he shall sign it, but if not he shall return it, with his Objections to that House in which it shall have originated, who shall enter the Objections at large on their Journal, and pro-ceed to reconsider it. If after such Reconsideration two thirds of that House shall agree to pass the Bill, it shall be sent, together with the Objections, to the other House, by which it shall likewise be reconsidered, and if approved by two thirds of that House, it shall become a Law. But in all such Cases the Votes of both Houses shall be determined by yeas and Nays, and the Names of the Persons voting for and against the Bill shall be entered on the Journal of each House respectively. If any Bill shall not be returned by the President within ten Days (Sundays excepted) after it shall have been presented to him, the Same shall be a Law, in like Manner as if he had signed it, unless the Congress by their Adjournment prevent its Return, in which Case it shall not be a Law.

Every Order, Resolution, or Vote to which the Concurrence of the Senate and House of Representatives may be necessary (except on a question of Adjournment) shall be pre-sented to the President of the United States; and before the Same shall take Effect, shall be approved by him, or being disapproved by him, shall be repassed by two thirds of the Senate and House of Representatives, according to the Rules and Limitations prescribed in the Case of a Bill.

Section 8. The Congress shall have Power To lay and collect Taxes, Duties, Imposts and Excises, to pay the Debts and provide for the common Defence and general Welfare of the United States; but all Duties, Imposts and Excises shall be uniform throughout the United States;

To borrow Money on the credit of the United States;

To regulate Commerce with foreign Nations, and among the several States, and with the Indian Tribes;

To establish an uniform Rule of Naturalization, and uniform Laws on the subject of Bankruptcies throughout the United States;

To coin Money, regulate the Value thereof, and of foreign Coin, and fix the Standard of Weights and Measures;

To provide for the Punishment of counterfeiting the Securities and current Coin of the United States;

To establish Post Offices and post Roads;

To promote the Progress of Science and useful Arts, by securing for limited Times to Authors and Inventors the exclusive Right to their respective Writings and Discoveries;

To constitute Tribunals inferior to the supreme Court;

To define and punish Piracies and Felonies committed on the high Seas, and Offences against the Law of Nations;

To declare War, grant Letters of Marque and Reprisal, and make Rules concerning Captures on Land and Water;

To raise and support Armies, but no Appropriation of Money to that Use shall be for a longer Term than two Years;

To provide and maintain a Navy;

To make Rules for the Government and Regulation of the land and naval Forces;

To provide for calling forth the Militia to execute the Laws of the Union, suppress Insurrections and repel Invasions;

To provide for organizing, arming, and disciplining, the Militia, and for governing such Part of them as may be employed in the Service of the United States, reserving to the States respectively, the Appointment of the Officers, and the Authority of training the Militia according to the discipline prescribed by Congress;

To exercise exclusive Legislation in all Cases whatsoever, over such District (not exceeding ten Miles square) as may, by Cession of particular States, and the Acceptance of Congress, become the Seat of the Government of the United States, and to exercise like Authority over all Places purchased by the Consent of the Legislature of the State in which the Same shall be, for the Erection of Forts, Magazines, Arsenals, dock-Yards, and other needful Buildings;—And

To make all Laws which shall be necessary and proper for carrying into Execution the foregoing Powers, and all other Powers vested by this Constitution in the Government of the United States, or in any Department or Officer thereof.

Section 9. The Migration or Importation of such Persons as any of the States now existing shall think proper to admit, shall not be prohibited by the Congress prior to the Year one thousand eight hundred and eight, but a Tax or duty may be imposed on such Importation, not exceeding ten dollars for each Person.

The Privilege of the Writ of Habeas Corpus shall not be suspended, unless when in Cases of Rebellion or Invasion the public Safety may require it.

No Bill of Attainder or ex post facto Law shall be passed.

No Capitation, or other direct, Tax shall be laid, unless in Proportion to the Census or Enumeration herein before directed to be taken.[5]

No Tax or Duty shall be laid on Articles exported from any State.

No Preference shall be given by any Regulation of Commerce or Revenue to the Ports of one State over those of another; nor shall Vessels bound to, or from, one State, be obliged to enter, clear, or pay Duties in another.

No Money shall be drawn from the Treasury, but in Consequence of Appropriations made by Law; and a regular Statement and Account of the Receipts and Expenditures of all public Money shall be published from time to time.

No Title of Nobility shall be granted by the United States: And no Person holding any Office of Profit or Trust under them, shall, without the Consent of the Congress, accept of any present, Emolument, Office, or Title, of any kind whatever, from any King, Prince, or foreign State.

Section 10. No State shall enter into any Treaty, Alliance, or Confederation; grant Letters of Marque and Reprisal; coin Money; emit Bills of Credit; make any Thing but gold and silver Coin a Tender in Payment of Debts; pass any Bill of Attainder, ex post facto Law, or Law impairing the Obligation of Contracts, or grant any Title of Nobility.

No State shall, without the Consent of the Congress, lay any Imposts or Duties on Imports or Exports, except what may be absolutely necessary for executing it's inspection Laws: and the net Produce of all Duties and Imposts, laid by any State on Imports or Exports, shall be for the Use of the Treasury of the United States; and all such Laws shall be subject to the Revision and Controul of the Congress.

No State shall, without the Consent of Congress, lay any Duty of Tonnage, keep Troops, or Ships of War in time of Peace, enter into any Agreement or Compact with another State, or with a foreign Power, or engage in War, unless actually invaded, or in such imminent Danger as will not admit of delay.

ARTICLE II

Section 1. The executive Power shall be vested in a President of the United States of America. He shall hold his Office during the Term of four Years, and, together with the Vice President, chosen for the same Term, be elected, as follows

Each State shall appoint, in such Manner as the Legislature thereof may direct, a Number of Electors, equal to the whole Number of Senators and Representatives to which the State may be entitled in the Congress: but no Senator or Representative, or Person holding an Office of Trust or Profit under the United States, shall be appointed an Elector.

[The Electors shall meet in their respective States, and vote by Ballot for two Persons, of whom one at least shall not be an Inhabitant of the same State with themselves. And they shall make a List of all the Persons voted for, and of the Number of Votes for each; which List they shall sign and certify, and transmit sealed to the Seat of the Government of the United States, directed to the President of the Senate. The President of the Senate shall, in the Presence of the Senate and House of Representatives, open all the Certificates, and the Votes shall then be counted. The Person having the greatest Number of Votes shall be the President, if such Number be a Majority of the whole Number of Electors appointed; and if there be more than one who have such Majority, and have an equal

Number of Votes, then the House of Representatives shall immediately chuse by Ballot one of them for President; and if no Person have a Majority, then from the five highest on the list the said House shall in like Manner chuse the President. But in chusing the President, the Votes shall be taken by States, the Representation from each State having one Vote; A quorum for this Purpose shall consist of a Member or Members from two thirds of the States, and a Majority of all the States shall be necessary to a Choice. In every Case, after the Choice of the President, the Person having the greatest Number of Votes of the Electors shall be the Vice President. But if there should remain two or more who have equal Votes, the Senate shall chuse from them by Ballot the Vice President.]⁶

The Congress may determine the Time of chusing the Electors, and the Day on which they shall give their Votes; which Day shall be the same throughout the United States.

No Person except a natural born Citizen, or a Citizen of the United States, at the time of the Adoption of this Constitution, shall be eligible to the Office of President; neither shall any Person be eligible to that Office who shall not have attained to the Age of thirty five Years, and been fourteen Years a Resident within the United States.

In Case of the Removal of the President from Office, or of his Death, Resignation, or Inability to discharge the Powers and Duties of the said Office,⁷ the Same shall devolve on the Vice President, and the Congress may by Law provide for the Case of Removal, Death, Resignation or Inability, both of the President and Vice President, declaring what Officer shall then act as President, and such Officer shall act accordingly, until the Disability be removed, or a President shall be elected.

The President shall, at stated Times, receive for his Services, a Compensation, which shall neither be encreased nor diminished during the Period for which he shall have been elected, and he shall not receive within that Period any other Emolument from the United States, or any of them.

Before he enter on the Execution of his Office, he shall take the following Oath or Affirmation:—"I do solemnly swear (or affirm) that I will faithfully execute the Office of President of the United States, and will to the best of my Ability, preserve, protect and defend the Constitution of the United States."

Section 2. The President shall be Commander in Chief of the Army and Navy of the United States, and of the Militia of the several States, when called into the actual Service of the United States; he may require the Opinion, in writing, of the principal Officer in each of the executive Departments, upon any Subject relating to the Duties of their respective Offices, and he shall have Power to grant Reprieves and Pardons for Offences against the United States, except in Cases of Impeachment.

He shall have Power, by and with the Advice and Consent of the Senate, to make Treaties, provided two thirds of the Senators present concur; and he shall nominate, and by and with the Advice and Consent of the Senate, shall appoint Ambassadors, other public Ministers and Consuls, Judges of the supreme Court, and all other Officers of the United States, whose Appointments are not herein otherwise provided for, and which shall be established by Law: but the Congress may by Law vest the Appointment of such inferior Officers, as they think proper, in the President alone, in the Courts of Law, or in the Heads of Departments.

The President shall have Power to fill up all Vacancies that may happen during the Recess of the Senate, by granting Commissions which shall expire at the End of their next Session.

Section 3. He shall from time to time give to the Congress Information of the State of the Union, and recommend to their Consideration such Measures as he shall judge necessary and expedient; he may, on extraordinary Occasions, convene both Houses, or either of them, and in Case of Disagreement between them, with Respect to the Time of Adjournment, he may adjourn them to such Time as he shall think proper; he shall receive Ambassadors and other public Ministers; he shall take Care that the Laws be faithfully executed, and shall Commission all the Officers of the United States.

Section 4. The President, Vice President and all civil Officers of the United States, shall be removed from Office on Impeachment for, and Conviction of, Treason, Bribery, or other high Crimes and Misdemeanors.

ARTICLE III

Section 1. The judicial Power of the United States, shall be vested in one supreme Court, and in such inferior Courts as the Congress may from time to time ordain and establish. The Judges, both of the supreme and inferior Courts, shall hold their Offices during good Behaviour, and shall, at stated Times, receive for their Services, a Compensation, which shall not be diminished during their Continuance in Office.

Section 2. The judicial Power shall extend to all Cases, in Law and Equity, arising under this Constitution, the Laws of the United States, and Treaties made, or which shall be made, under their Authority;—to all Cases affecting Ambassadors, other public Ministers and Consuls;—to all Cases of admiralty and maritime Jurisdiction;—to Controversies to which the United States shall be a Party;—to Controversies between two or more States;—between a State and Citizens of another State;[8]—between Citizens of different States;—between Citizens of the same State claiming Lands under Grants of different States, and between a State, or the Citizens thereof, and foreign States, Citizens or Subjects.

In all Cases affecting Ambassadors, other public Ministers and Consuls, and those in which a State shall be Party, the supreme Court shall have original Jurisdiction. In all the other Cases before mentioned, the supreme Court shall have appellate Jurisdiction, both as to Law and Fact, with such Exceptions, and under such Regulations as the Congress shall make.

The Trial of all Crimes, except in Cases of Impeachment, shall be by Jury; and such Trial shall be held in the State where the said Crimes shall have been committed; but when not committed within any State, the Trial shall be at such Place or Places as the Congress may by Law have directed.

Section 3. Treason against the United States, shall consist only in levying War against them, or in adhering to their Enemies, giving them Aid and Comfort. No Person shall be convicted of Treason unless on the Testimony of two Witnesses to the same overt Act, or on Confession in open Court.

The Congress shall have Power to declare the Punishment of Treason, but no Attainder of Treason shall work Corruption of Blood, or Forfeiture except during the Life of the Person attainted.

ARTICLE IV

Section 1. Full Faith and Credit shall be given in each State to the public Acts, Records, and judicial Proceedings of every other State. And the Congress may by general Laws prescribe the Manner in which such Acts, Records and Proceedings shall be proved, and the Effect thereof.

Section 2. The Citizens of each State shall be entitled to all Privileges and Immunities of Citizens in the several States.

A Person charged in any State with Treason, Felony, or other Crime, who shall flee from Justice, and be found in another State, shall on Demand of the executive Authority of the State from which he fled, be delivered up, to be removed to the State having Jurisdiction of the Crime.

[No Person held to Service or Labour in one State, under the Laws thereof, escaping into another, shall, in Consequence of any Law or Regulation therein, be discharged from such Service or Labour, but shall be delivered up on Claim of the Party to whom such Service or Labour may be due.]⁹

Section 3. New States may be admitted by the Congress into this Union; but no new State shall be formed or erected within the Jurisdiction of any other State; nor any State be formed by the Junction of two or more States, or Parts of States, without the Consent of the Legislatures of the States concerned as well as of the Congress.

The Congress shall have Power to dispose of and make all needful Rules and Regulations respecting the Territory or other Property belonging to the United States; and nothing in this Constitution shall be so construed as to Prejudice any Claims of the United States, or of any particular State.

Section 4. The United States shall guarantee to every State in this Union a Republican Form of Government, and shall protect each of them against Invasion; and on Application of the Legislature, or of the Executive (when the Legislature cannot be convened) against domestic Violence.

ARTICLE V

The Congress, whenever two thirds of both Houses shall deem it necessary, shall propose Amendments to this Constitution, or, on the Application of the Legislatures of two thirds of the several States, shall call a Convention for proposing Amendments, which, in either Case, shall be valid to all Intents and Purposes, as Part of this Constitution, when ratified by the Legislatures of three fourths of the several States, or by Conventions in three fourths thereof, as the one or the other Mode of Ratification may be proposed by the Congress; Provided [that no Amendment which may be made prior to the Year One thousand eight hundred and eight shall in any Manner affect the first and fourth Clauses in the Ninth Section of the first Article; and][10] that no State, without its Consent, shall be deprived of its equal Suffrage in the Senate.

ARTICLE VI

All Debts contracted and Engagements entered into, before the Adoption of this Constitution, shall be as valid against the United States under this Constitution, as under the Confederation.

This Constitution, and the Laws of the United States which shall be made in Pursuance thereof; and all Treaties made, or which shall be made, under the Authority of the United States, shall be the supreme Law of the Land; and the Judges in every State shall be bound thereby, any Thing in the Constitution or Laws of any State to the Contrary notwithstanding.

The Senators and Representatives before mentioned, and the Members of the several State Legislatures, and all executive and judicial Officers, both of the United States and of the several States, shall be bound by Oath or Affirmation, to support this Constitution; but no religious Test shall ever be required as a Qualification to any Office or public Trust under the United States.

ARTICLE VII

The Ratification of the Conventions of nine States, shall be sufficient for the Establishment of this Constitution between the States so ratifying the Same.

Done in Convention by the Unanimous Consent of the States present the Seventeenth Day of September in the Year of our Lord one thousand seven hundred and Eighty seven and of the Independence of the United States of America the Twelfth. IN WITNESS whereof We have hereunto subscribed our Names,

George Washington,
President and
deputy from Virginia.

New Hampshire:	John Langdon,
	Nicholas Gilman.
Massachusetts:	Nathaniel Gorham,
	Rufus King.
Connecticut:	William Samuel Johnson,
	Roger Sherman.

New York:	Alexander Hamilton.
New Jersey:	William Livingston,
	David Brearley,
	William Paterson,
	Jonathan Dayton.
Pennsylvania:	Benjamin Franklin,
	Thomas Mifflin,
	Robert Morris,
	George Clymer,
	Thomas FitzSimons,
	Jared Ingersoll,
	James Wilson,
	Gouverneur Morris.
Delaware:	George Read,
	Gunning Bedford Jr.,
	John Dickinson,
	Richard Bassett,
	Jacob Broom.
Maryland:	James McHenry,
	Daniel of St. Thomas Jenifer,
	Daniel Carroll.
Virginia:	John Blair,
	James Madison Jr.
North Carolina:	William Blount,
	Richard Dobbs Spaight,
	Hugh Williamson.
South Carolina:	John Rutledge,
	Charles Cotesworth Pinckney,
	Charles Pinckney,
	Pierce Butler.
Georgia:	William Few,
	Abraham Baldwin.

[The language of the original Constitution, not including the Amendments, was adopted by a convention of the states on September 17, 1787, and was subsequently ratified by the states on the following dates: Delaware, December 7, 1787; Pennsylvania, December 12, 1787; New Jersey, December 18, 1787; Georgia, January 2, 1788; Connecticut, January 9, 1788; Massachusetts, February 6, 1788; Maryland, April 28, 1788; South Carolina, May 23, 1788; New Hampshire, June 21, 1788.

Ratification was completed on June 21, 1788.

The Constitution subsequently was ratified by Virginia, June 25, 1788; New York, July 26, 1788; North Carolina, November 21, 1789; Rhode Island, May 29, 1790; and Vermont, January 10, 1791.]

Amendments

Amendment I

(First ten amendments ratified December 15, 1791.)
Congress shall make no law respecting an establishment of religion, or prohibiting the free exercise thereof; or abridging the freedom of speech, or of the press; or the right of the people peaceably to assemble, and to petition the Government for a redress of grievances.

Amendment II

A well regulated Militia, being necessary to the security of a free State, the right of the people to keep and bear Arms, shall not be infringed.

Amendment III

No Soldier shall, in time of peace be quartered in any house, without the consent of the Owner, nor in time of war, but in a manner to be prescribed by law.

Amendment IV

The right of the people to be secure in their persons, houses, papers, and effects, against unreasonable searches and seizures, shall not be violated, and no Warrants shall issue, but upon probable cause, supported by Oath or affirmation, and particularly describing the place to be searched, and the persons or things to be seized.

Amendment V

No person shall be held to answer for a capital, or otherwise infamous crime, unless on a presentment or indictment of a Grand Jury, except in cases arising in the land or naval forces, or in the Militia, when in actual service in time of War or public danger; nor shall any person be subject for the same offence to be twice put in jeopardy of life or limb; nor shall be compelled in any criminal case to be a witness against himself, nor be deprived of life, liberty, or property, without due process of law; nor shall private property be taken for public use, without just compensation.

Amendment VI

In all criminal prosecutions, the accused shall enjoy the right to a speedy and public trial, by an impartial jury of the State and district wherein the crime shall have been committed, which district shall have been previously ascertained by law, and to be informed of the nature and cause of the accusation; to be confronted with the witnesses against him; to have compulsory process for obtaining witnesses in his favor, and to have the Assistance of Counsel for his defence.

Amendment VII

In Suits at common law, where the value in controversy shall exceed twenty dollars, the right of trial by jury shall be preserved, and no fact tried by a jury, shall be otherwise re-examined in any Court of the United States, than according to the rules of the common law.

Amendment VIII

Excessive bail shall not be required, nor excessive fines imposed, nor cruel and unusual punishments inflicted.

Amendment IX

The enumeration in the Constitution, of certain rights, shall not be construed to deny or disparage others retained by the people.

Amendment X

The powers not delegated to the United States by the Constitution, nor prohibited by it to the States, are reserved to the States respectively, or to the people.

Amendment XI (Ratified February 7, 1795)

The Judicial power of the United States shall not be construed to extend to any suit in law or equity, commenced or prosecuted against one of the United States by Citizens of another State, or by Citizens or Subjects of any Foreign State.

Amendment XII (Ratified June 15, 1804)

The Electors shall meet in their respective states and vote by ballot for President and Vice-President, one of whom, at least, shall not be an inhabitant of the same state with themselves; they shall name in their ballots the person voted for as President, and in distinct ballots the person voted for as Vice-President, and they shall make distinct lists of all persons voted for as President, and of all persons voted for as Vice-President, and of the number of votes for each, which lists they shall sign and certify, and transmit sealed to the seat of the government of the United States, directed to the President of the Senate;— The President of the Senate shall, in the presence of the Senate and House of Representatives, open all the certificates and the votes shall then be counted;—The person having the greatest number of votes for President, shall be the President, if such number be a majority of the whole number of Electors appointed; and if no person have such majority, then from the persons having the highest numbers not exceeding three on the list of those voted for as President, the House of Representatives shall choose immediately, by ballot, the President. But in choosing the President, the votes shall be taken by states, the representation from each state having one vote; a quorum for this purpose shall consist of a member or members from two-thirds of the states, and a majority of all the states shall be necessary to a choice. [And if the House of Representatives shall not choose a President whenever the right of choice shall devolve upon them, before the fourth day of March next following, then the Vice-President shall act as President, as in the case of the death or other constitutional disability of the President.—][11] The person having the greatest number of votes as Vice-President, shall be the Vice-President, if such number be a majority of the whole number of Electors appointed, and if no person have a majority, then from the two highest numbers on the list, the Senate shall choose the Vice-President; a quorum for the purpose shall consist of two-thirds of the whole number of Senators, and a majority of the whole number shall be necessary to a choice. But no person constitutionally ineligible to the office of President shall be eligible to that of Vice-President of the United States.

Amendment XIII (Ratified December 6, 1865)

Section 1. Neither slavery nor involuntary servitude, except as a punishment for crime whereof the party shall have been duly convicted, shall exist within the United States, or any place subject to their jurisdiction.

Section 2. Congress shall have power to enforce this article by appropriate legislation.

Amendment XIV (Ratified July 9, 1868)

Section 1. All persons born or naturalized in the United States, and subject to the jurisdiction thereof, are citizens of the United States and of the State wherein they reside. No State shall make or enforce any law which shall abridge the privileges or immunities of citizens of the United States; nor shall any State deprive any person of life, liberty, or property, without due process of law; nor deny to any person within its jurisdiction the equal protection of the laws.

Section 2. Representatives shall be apportioned among the several States according to their respective numbers, counting the whole number of persons in each State, excluding Indians not taxed. But when the right to vote at any election for the choice of electors for President and Vice President of the United States, Representatives in Congress, the Executive and Judicial officers of a State, or the members of the Legislature thereof, is denied to any of the male inhabitants of such State, being twenty-one years of age,[12] and citizens of the United States, or in any way abridged, except for participation in rebellion, or other crime, the basis of representation therein shall be reduced in the proportion which the number of such male citizens shall bear to the whole number of male citizens twenty-one years of age in such State.

Section 3. No person shall be a Senator or Representative in Congress, or elector of President and Vice President, or hold any office, civil or military, under the United States, or under any State, who, having previously taken an oath, as a member of Congress, or as an officer of the United States, or as a member of any State legislature, or as an executive or judicial officer of any State, to support the Constitution of the United States, shall have engaged in insurrection or rebellion against the same, or given aid or comfort to the enemies thereof. But Congress may by a vote of two-thirds of each House, remove such disability.

Section 4. The validity of the public debt of the United States, authorized by law, including debts incurred for payment of pensions and bounties for services in suppressing insurrection or rebellion, shall not be questioned. But neither the United States nor any State shall assume or pay any debt or obligation incurred in aid of insurrection or rebellion against the United States, or any claim for the loss or emancipation of any slave; but all such debts, obligations and claims shall be held illegal and void.

Section 5. The Congress shall have power to enforce, by appropriate legislation, the provisions of this article.

Amendment XV (Ratified February 3, 1870)

Section 1. The right of citizens of the United States to vote shall not be denied or abridged by the United States or by any State on account of race, color, or previous condition of servitude.

Section 2. The Congress shall have power to enforce this article by appropriate legislation.

Amendment XVI (Ratified February 3, 1913)

The Congress shall have power to lay and collect taxes on incomes, from whatever source derived, without apportionment among the several States, and without regard to any census or enumeration.

Amendment XVII (Ratified April 8, 1913)

The Senate of the United States shall be composed of two Senators from each State, elected by the people thereof, for six years; and each Senator shall have one vote. The electors in each State shall have the qualifications requisite for electors of the most numerous branch of the State legislatures.

When vacancies happen in the representation of any State in the Senate, the executive authority of such State shall issue writs of election to fill such vacancies: *Provided,* That the legislature of any State may empower the executive thereof to make temporary appointments until the people fill the vacancies by election as the legislature may direct.

This amendment shall not be so construed as to affect the election or term of any Senator chosen before it becomes valid as part of the Constitution.

Amendment XVIII (Ratified January 16, 1919)[13]

Section 1. After one year from the ratification of this article the manufacture, sale, or transportation of intoxicating liquors within, the importation thereof into, or the exportation thereof from the United States and all territory subject to the jurisdiction thereof for beverage purposes is hereby prohibited.

Section 2. The Congress and the several States shall have concurrent power to enforce this article by appropriate legislation.

Section 3. This article shall be inoperative unless it shall have been ratified as an amendment to the Constitution by the legislatures of the several States, as provided in the Constitution, within seven years from the date of the submission hereof to the States by the Congress.

Amendment XIX (Ratified August 18, 1920)

The right of citizens of the United States to vote shall not be denied or abridged by the United States or by any State on account of sex.

Congress shall have power to enforce this article by appropriate legislation.

Amendment XX (Ratified January 23, 1933)

Section 1. The terms of the President and Vice President shall end at noon on the 20th day of January, and the terms of Senators and Representatives at noon on the 3d day of January, of the years in which such terms would have ended if this article had not been ratified; and the terms of their successors shall then begin.

Section 2. The Congress shall assemble at least once in every year, and such meeting shall begin at noon on the 3d day of January, unless they shall by law appoint a different day.

Section 3.[14] If, at the time fixed for the beginning of the term of the President, the President elect shall have died, the Vice President elect shall become President. If a President shall not have been chosen before the time fixed for the beginning of his term, or if the President elect shall have failed to qualify, then the Vice President elect shall act as President until a President shall have qualified; and the Congress may by law provide for the case wherein neither a President elect nor a Vice President elect shall have qualified, declaring who shall then act as President, or the manner in which one who is to act shall be selected, and such person shall act accordingly until a President or Vice President shall have qualified.

Section 4. The Congress may by law provide for the case of the death of any of the persons from whom the House of Representatives may choose a President whenever the right of choice shall have devolved upon them, and for the case of the death of any of the persons from whom the Senate may choose a Vice President whenever the right of choice shall have devolved upon them.

Section 5. Sections 1 and 2 shall take effect on the 15th day of October following the ratification of this article.

Section 6. This article shall be inoperative unless it shall have been ratified as an amendment to the Constitution by the legislatures of three-fourths of the several States within seven years from the date of its submission.

Amendment XXI (Ratified December 5, 1933)

Section 1. The eighteenth article of amendment to the Constitution of the United States is hereby repealed.

Section 2. The transportation or importation into any State, Territory, or possession of the United States for delivery or use therein of intoxicating liquors, in violation of the laws thereof, is hereby prohibited.

Section 3. This article shall be inoperative unless it shall have been ratified as an amendment to the Constitution by conventions in the several States, as provided in the Constitution, within seven years from the date of the submission hereof to the States by the Congress.

Amendment XXII (Ratified February 27, 1951)

Section 1. No person shall be elected to the office of the President more than twice, and no person who has held the office of President, or acted as President, for more than two years of a term to which some other person was elected President shall be elected to the office of the President more than once. But this Article shall not apply to any person holding the office of President when this Article was proposed by the Congress, and shall not prevent any person who may be holding the office of President, or acting as President, during the term within which this Article become operative from holding the office of President or acting as President during the remainder of such term.

Section 2. This article shall be inoperative unless it shall have been ratified as an amendment to the Constitution by the legislatures of three-fourths of the several States within seven years from the date of its submission to the States by the Congress.

Amendment XXIII (Ratified March 29, 1961)

Section 1. The District constituting the seat of Government of the United States shall appoint in such manner as the Congress may direct:

A number of electors of President and Vice President equal to the whole number of Senators and Representatives in Congress to which the District would be entitled if it were a State, but in no event more than the least populous State; they shall be in addition to those appointed by the States, but they shall be considered, for the purposes of the election of President and Vice President, to be electors appointed by a State; and they shall meet in the District and perform such duties as provided by the twelfth article of amendment.

Section 2. The Congress shall have power to enforce this article by appropriate legislation.

Amendment XXIV *(Ratified January 23, 1964)*

Section 1. The right of citizens of the United States to vote in any primary or other election for President or Vice President, for electors for President or Vice President, or for Senator or Representative in Congress, shall not be denied or abridged by the United States or any State by reason of failure to pay any poll tax or other tax.

Section 2. The Congress shall have power to enforce this article by appropriate legislation.

Amendment XXV *(Ratified February 10, 1967)*

Section 1. In case of the removal of the President from office or of his death or resignation, the Vice President shall become President.

Section 2. Whenever there is a vacancy in the office of the Vice President, the President shall nominate a Vice President who shall take office upon confirmation by a majority vote of both Houses of Congress.

Section 3. Whenever the President transmits to the President pro tempore of the Senate and the Speaker of the House of Representatives his written declaration that he is unable to discharge the powers and duties of his office, and until he transmits to them a written declaration to the contrary, such powers and duties shall be discharged by the Vice President as Acting President.

Section 4. Whenever the Vice President and a majority of either the principal officers of the executive departments or of such other body as Congress may by law provide, transmit to the President pro tempore of the Senate and the Speaker of the House of Representatives their written declaration that the President is unable to discharge the powers and duties of his office, the Vice President shall immediately assume the powers and duties of the office as Acting President.

Thereafter, when the President transmits to the President pro tempore of the Senate and the Speaker of the House of Representatives his written declaration that no inability exists, he shall resume the powers and duties of his office unless the Vice President and a majority of either the principal officers of the executive department or of such other body as Congress may by law provide, transmit within four days to the President pro tempore of the Senate and the Speaker of the House of Representatives their written declaration that the President is unable to discharge the powers and duties of his office. Thereupon Congress shall decide the issue, assembling within forty-eight hours for that purpose if not in session. If the Congress, within twenty-one days after receipt of the latter written declaration, or, if Congress is not in session, within twenty-one days after Congress is required to assemble, determines by two-thirds vote of both Houses that the

President is unable to discharge the powers and duties of his office, the Vice President shall continue to discharge the same as Acting President; otherwise, the President shall resume the powers and duties of his office.

Amendment XXVI (Ratified July 1, 1971)

Section 1. The right of citizens of the United States, who are eighteen years of age or older, to vote shall not be denied or abridged by the United States or by any State on account of age.

Section 2. The Congress shall have power to enforce this article by appropriate legislation.

Amendment XXVII (Ratified May 7, 1992)

No law varying the compensation for the services of the Senators and Representatives shall take effect, until an election of Representatives shall have intervened.

NOTES

1. The part in brackets was changed by section 2 of the Fourteenth Amendment.
2. The part in brackets was changed by the first paragraph of the Seventeenth Amendment.
3. The part in brackets was changed by the second paragraph of the Seventeenth Amendment.
4. The part in brackets was changed by section 2 of the Twentieth Amendment.
5. The Sixteenth Amendment gave Congress the power to tax incomes.
6. The material in brackets has been superseded by the Twelfth Amendment.
7. This provision has been affected by the Twenty-fifth Amendment.
8. These clauses were affected by the Eleventh Amendment.
9. This paragraph has been superseded by the Thirteenth Amendment.
10. Obsolete.
11. The part in brackets has been superseded by section 3 of the Twentieth Amendment.
12. See the Nineteenth and Twenty-sixth Amendments.
13. This Amendment was repealed by section 1 of the Twenty-first Amendment.
14. See the Twenty-fifth Amendment.

CREDITS

1. Designing Institutions

1-1: Reprinted by permission of the publisher from *The Logic of Collective Action: Public Goods and the Theory of Groups,* by Mancur Olson Jr., pp. 1–19, Cambridge, Mass.: Harvard University Press, Copyright © 1965, 1971 by the President and Fellows of Harvard College.

1-2: Excerpted with permission from *Science,* December 3, 1968, pp. 1243–1248. Copyright 1968 American Association for the Advancement of Science.

1-3: Copyright © 2002 by the New York Times Co. Reprinted by permission.

1-4: Excerpted from Robert D. Putnam, "The Prosperous Community: Social Capital and Public Life," *The American Prospect* no. 13 (spring 1993). Copyright 1993 by New Prospect, Inc.; reprinted in *Bowling Alone: The Collapse and Revival of American Community* (Simon and Schuster, 2000). Reprinted by permission. The author is the Peter and Isabel Malkin Professor of Public Policy at Harvard University.

1-5: Excerpted from the article originally appearing in *PS: Political Science & P itics 35*, no. 3 (September 2002): 537–540. Reprinted with the permission of C bridge University Press.

2. The Constitutional Framework

2-1: Excerpted from the article originally appearing in *American Politic Review 55*, no. 4 (December 1961): 799–816. Reprinted with the per Cambridge University Press. Some notes appearing in the origina deleted.

2-4: From *The Vineyard of Liberty,* by James MacGregor Burns, co by James MacGregor Burns. Used by permission of Alfred A. Kn Random House, Inc.

3. Federalism

3-1: Excerpted from *Publius: The Journal of Federalism 25* Reprinted by permission.

3-3: Copyright © 2002 by the New York Times Co. Repr

4. Civil Rights

4-1: This piece was commissioned for this volume and is based on an earlier essay, "Minorities and Direct Legislation: Evidence from California Ballot Proposition Elections," by Zoltan J. Hajnal, Elisabeth R. Gerber, and Hugh Louch, published in *Journal of Politics* February 2002, vol. 64, issue 1, pp. 154–177.

4-2: Reprinted with permission. Copyright © *The Public Interest,* no. 144, summer 2001, Washington, D.C.

4-3: Reprinted by permission of the author. Some notes appearing in the original have been deleted.

5. Civil Liberties

5-1: Excerpted from Lee Epstein, ed., *Contemplating Courts* (Washington, D.C.: CQ Press, 1995), pp. 390–419. Some notes and bibliographic references appearing in the original have been deleted.

5-2: *National Review Online,* reprinted by permission of United Feature Syndicate, Inc.

6. Congress

6-1: Reprinted with the permission of the American Enterprise Institute for Public Policy Research, Washington, D.C.

6-2: Excerpted from David R. Mayhew, *Congress: The Electoral Connection* (New Haven: Yale University Press, 1974), pp. 13–27, 49–77. Copyright 1974 Yale University Press. Reprinted by permission. Notes appearing in the original have been deleted.

7. The Presidency

7-1: Reprinted with permission of The Free Press, a division of Simon & Schuster Adult Publishing Group, from *Presidential Power and the Modern Presidents: The Politics of Leadership from Roosevelt to Reagan,* by Richard E. Neustadt. Copyright © 1990 by Richard E. Neustadt.

2: Excerpted from Samuel Kernell, *Going Public: New Strategies of Presidential Leadership,* 3d edition (Washington, D.C.: CQ Press, 1997), pp. 1–12, 17–26, 34–38, -64.

Copyright © 2003 by The New York Times Co. Reprinted with permission.

he Bureaucracy

·om *Bureaucracy: What Government Agencies Do and Why They Do It,* by James lson. Copyright © 1989 by Basic Books, Inc. Reprinted by permission of

Basic Books, a member of Perseus Books, L.L.C. Notes appearing in the original have been deleted.

8-2: Excerpted from John E. Chubb and Paul E. Peterson, eds., *Can Government Govern?* (Washington, D.C.: Brookings Institution Press, 1989), pp. 267–285. Reprinted by permission. Some notes appearing in the original have been deleted.

8-3: Excerpt originally appeared in report by Daalder et al., *Assessing the Department of Homeland Security.* Copyright © 2002 by the Brookings Institution.

9. The Judiciary

9-1: Excerpted from Lee Epstein and Jack Knight, *The Choices Justices Make* (Washington, D.C.: CQ Press, 1998), pp. 1–21.

9-2: By Simon Lazarus, from *The Atlantic Monthly,* June 2002. Simon Lazarus is a lawyer and writer who served on President Jimmy Carter's White House domestic policy staff.

9-4: Copyright © 2003 Deborah Sontag. Distributed by The New York Times Special Features Syndication Sales.

10. Public Opinion

10-1: Originally published in Herbert Asher, *Polling and the Public: What Every Citizen Should Know,* 4th edition (Washington, D.C.: CQ Press, 1998), pp. 141–169.

10-2: Excerpted from the article originally published in *American Political Science Review* 89, no. 3 (September 1995): 543–564. Reprinted with the permission of Cambridge University Press. Notes appearing in the original have been deleted.

10-3: Excerpted from Barbara Norrander and Clyde Wilcox, eds., *Understanding Public Opinion,* 2d edition (Washington, D.C.: CQ Press, 2002), pp. 301–318.

11. Voting, Campaigns, and Elections

11-1: Excerpted from Samuel L. Popkin, *The Reasoning Voter: Communication and Persuasion in Presidential Campaigns,* 2d Edition (Chicago: University of Chicago Press, 1994), pp. 212–219. Copyright © 1991, 1994 by The University of Chicago. All rights reserved. Reprinted by permission. Notes appearing in the original have been deleted.

11-2: Originally published in Candice J. Nelson, David A. Dulio, and Stephen Medvic, eds., *Shades of Gray: Perspectives on Campaign Ethics* (Washington, D.C.: Brookings Institution Press, 2002), 39–59. Notes appearing in the original have been deleted.

11-3: Excerpted from Jon R. Bond and Richard Fleisher, eds., *Polarized Politics: Congress and the President in a Partisan Era* (Washington, D.C.: CQ Press, 2000), pp. 9–30. Notes appearing in the original have been deleted.

12. Political Parties

12-1: Originally published in John H. Aldrich, *Why Parties?: The Origin and Transformation of Political Parties in America* (Chicago: University of Chicago Press, 1995), pp. 14–27. Copyright © 1995 by The University of Chicago. All rights reserved. Reprinted by permission. Notes appearing in the original have been deleted.

12-2: Excerpted from Larry Bartels, "Partisanship and Voting Behavior, 1952–1996," *American Journal of Political Science*. Published with permission from Blackwell Publishing. Notes appearing in the original have been deleted.

12-3: Excerpted from Jeffrey E. Cohen, Richard Fleisher, and Paul Kantor, eds., *American Political Parties: Decline or Resurgence?* (Washington, D.C.: CQ Press, 2001), pp. 103–121.

13. Interest Groups

13-1: From *Semi-Sovereign People Re-Issue, A Realist's View of Democracy in America* 1st edition by Schattschneider. © 1975. Reprinted with permission of Wadsworth, a division of Thomson Learning: www.thomsonrights.com. Fax: 800-730-2215. Some notes appearing in the original have been deleted.

13-2: Excerpt pp. 11–22 from *Interest Groups and Congress*, by John R. Wright. Copyright © 2003 by Pearson Education, Inc. Reprinted by permission.

13-3: Excerpted from Allan J. Cigler and Burdett A. Loomis, eds., *Interest Group Politics*, 6th edition (Washington, D.C.: CQ Press, 2002), pp. 205–224.

14. News Media

14-1: This paper is based on an earlier essay, "Social Origins of Press Cynicism in Portraying Politics," published in *American Behavioral Scientist*, volume 42, number 6 (March 1999), 998–1008. Reprinted by permission.

14-2: © *Public Perspective*, a publication of the Roper Center for Public Opinion Research, University of CT, Storrs. Reprinted by permission.

14-3: Excerpted from the article originally appearing in *PS: Political Science & Politics* 35, no. 3 (September 2002): 517–521. Reprinted with the permission of Cambridge University Press.